Stapleton's
POWERBOAT
BIBLE

Stapleton's
POWERBOAT
BIBLE

THE COMPLETE GUIDE TO
Selection, Seamanship, and Cruising

Sid Stapleton

INTERNATIONAL MARINE / McGRAW-HILL

*Camden, Maine • New York • Chicago • San Francisco • Lisbon • London • Madrid
Mexico City • Milan • New Delhi • San Juan • Seoul • Singapore • Sydney • Toronto*

For my wonderful wife Anne,
the best mate a skipper could ever hope for

International Marine
A Division of The **McGraw·Hill** Companies

2 4 6 8 10 9 7 5 3 1

Library of Congress Cataloging-in-Publication Data
Stapleton, Sid.
   [Powerboat bible]
   Stapleton's powerboat bible : the complete guide to selection, seamanship, and cruising / Sid Stapleton.
     p.   cm.
   Includes bibliographical references (p.   ) and index.
   ISBN 0-07-135634-7
   1. Motorboats—Handbooks, manuals, etc. I. Title. II. Title: Powerboat bible.
   GV835.S73 2002
   791.2´25—dc21   2001005029

Questions regarding the content of this book should be addressed to
INTERNATIONAL MARINE
P.O. Box 220
Camden, ME 04843
WWW.INTERNATIONALMARINE.COM

Questions regarding the ordering of this book should be addressed to
THE MCGRAW-HILL COMPANIES
Customer Service Department
P.O. Box 547
Blacklick, OH 43004
Retail customers: 1-800-262-4729
Bookstores: 1-800-722-4726

This book is printed on 70 lb. Citation by R. R. Donnelley, Crawfordsville, IN

Design by Irving Perkins
Production by PerfecType and Dan Kirchoff
Edited by Jonathan Eaton, Dan Fales, and Shana Harrington
All photos by the author unless otherwise noted
Illustrations by Bruce Alderson unless otherwise noted

Stapleton's Powerboat Bible is a revised, updated, and expanded edition combining *Stapleton's Powerboat Bible* (1989) and *Stapleton's Power Crusing Bible* (1992).

CONTENTS

Part 4 Navigating and Communicating

Part 5 Emergency Preparedness

Part 6   The Cruising Life

Part 7   Preparations for Voyaging

Welcome to the Dream

So you've been bitten by the cruising bug. You've heard the siren song of the waves lapping against that rocky coast in Maine or that island in the Caribbean, and your yearning has become a determination to *go!* Now you're setting out to acquire that perfect power cruiser, which will carry you in safety and comfort to distant ports and romantic anchorages. From one who has suffered from that hunger for years—and for a time, at least, satisfied it—welcome to the dream.

Whether you plan to stick close to the coast or head well offshore, as you begin your search for the vessel that best fits your lifestyle and cruising plans you'll face a bewildering array of decisions on such topics as the hull form, propulsion package, and layout best suited to the voyage you have in mind. When it comes to outfitting the boat you finally select with navigation aids, communications equipment, safety gear, and the hundreds of other accessories you'll need to turn her into a safe and comfortable home on the water, you'll encounter an even more confusing tangle of choices.

In a perfect world, you wouldn't need a book like this. Every yacht broker, marine electronics salesman, and boating accessories store clerk you dealt with would listen carefully to your description of the kind of cruising you plan to do, would have thousands of miles of cruising experience, and would sell you the exact boat and the precise equipment you really need at a fair price and fully brief you on how to use it.

Unfortunately, we don't live in a perfect world.

I'm not saying there aren't knowledgeable people with the highest levels of integrity in all three areas. But face it, the person you are about to hand thousands—maybe hundreds of thousands—of your hard-earned dollars to may never have been closer to a serious coastal or bluewater cruising powerboat than the display at the most recent boat show. Even if these salespeople are extremely experienced and knowledgeable, they are in business to sell you the boats in their line or at their dock or on their listing sheet, the radios and radars and depth-sounders on their store's shelves, the anchors and rodes and life rafts on their company's sales floor. What they are *not* in business to do is to send you down the street to buy the competition's products, even though they may be what you really need.

In buying a seaworthy power cruiser, you may well be making the largest single financial investment of your lifetime, with the possible exception of your home. At best, a significant mistake anywhere in the process of selecting and outfitting this boat could be horrendously expensive. At worst, you could find that your life and the lives of those you love depend on the choices you make. Before you even start looking for your boat or choosing a radio or a life raft, you'd better make sure you know at least enough to decide for yourself whether you're getting wise, dependable counsel or are being handed a slick sell.

Once you've bought your boat and have her rigged and ready to go, you'll still have hundreds of questions about planning your itinerary, managing your finances, getting mail forwarded, and dealing with water, fuel, and provisioning. After you've mastered those topics, you'll need to know how to handle your boat around a dock, how to make the most of the electronics you've had installed, how to anchor safely, and how to deal with emergencies and severe weather.

Suppose, before you launch yourself into the world of cruising, you could sit down and talk at length with a room full of powerboat experts —naval architects who design them, plant managers who build them, dealers and brokers who sell them, bankers who finance them, agents who insure them, and service personnel who repair them. Suppose, also, you could engage in some long, relaxed chats with a healthy contingent of robust, tanned owners who have cruised thousands of miles in just the type of boat you're considering and are happy to share with you their accumulated wisdom about the equipment and techniques they have discovered that will help make your time on the water a relaxed adventure instead of a nightmare of broken gear and anchors that drag in the night. And suppose they were willing to give you at least some idea of what all this is going to cost?

That's exactly what this book is all about.

For the past thirty years or so, in addition to owning several boats of my own, I've made a good part of my livelihood writing about boats and the people who love them. I've had the opportunity to cruise thousands of miles with a broad cross section of owners through some of the world's most beautiful cruising grounds. In the Virgin Islands, for instance, I visited with Carleton Mitchell, holder of the Cruising Club of America's prestigious Blue Water Medal and the only sailor to win the fiercely competitive Southern Ocean Racing Circuit and the prestigious Newport–Bermuda Race three times. Aboard his displacement-hull motor yacht, *Coyaba*, which was shaped by everything he had learned in a lifetime of cruising the waters of the world, we talked long into the night about what works and what doesn't work, and he showed me one of the slickest anchoring setups

I've ever seen on a pleasure yacht. As I accompanied Bob and Don Baumgartner aboard their 58-foot (17.7 m) Hatteras, *Trenora*, during portions of their transatlantic voyage from Florida to the Mediterranean, I had a chance to learn from their experience. While cruising from Sardinia to Corsica with Count Franco Antamoro, I found out much of what he learned captaining his 65-foot (19.8 m) power cruiser across the Atlantic on her own bottom. With Frank and Lee Glindmeier on segments of their 18,000-mile (29,000 km) voyage from Florida to Alaska and back or running the Mississippi River with Nat and Mary Robbins, I gained from what they had learned.

Through these experiences and hundreds of others in cruising areas ranging from the Gulf of Aqaba in the Middle East to Australia's Great Barrier Reef, from the islands of Greece and the coast of Norway to the Galápagos Islands off Ecuador, I've had the opportunity to see how owners of differing backgrounds tailored the selection of their boats to fit their distinctive lifestyles and cruising plans and to learn how they rigged and equipped their yachts to function anywhere—from the frigid zone to the tropics.

In addition to that on-the-water experience, in researching material for my columns on seamanship and boat handling in *Motor Boating and Sailing* (now *Motor Boating*) magazine and for hundreds of other boating articles, I've roamed through the factories where many of the finest cruising yachts in the world are built and have inspected them at all stages of construction and inquired about their hull layup schedules, hull-to-deck joints, electrical generation and distribution systems, and all of the other elements that go into a proper cruising vessel. I've questioned naval architects, yacht designers, marine engineers, and boat manufacturing and service personnel about the thinking that goes into a cruiser designed and built for dependability, economy of operation, seaworthiness, and comfortable accommodations under way, at anchor, and at the dock.

I first put down what I knew about selecting and commissioning a proper bluewater cruising vessel in *Stapleton's Powerboat Bible*, published in 1989. That book ended with a boat rigged and ready at the dock. I assembled what I knew about proper vessel operation and the cruising life in *Stapleton's Power Cruising Bible* (1992). Given the incredible advances made in marine electronics in the past few years, both books are now out-of-date. Now, at the invitation of Jonathan Eaton of International Marine, I've completely updated and combined both those books into this comprehensive guide for bluewater cruising under power.

This book also incorporates an experience my earlier books preceded. Following the publication of *Stapleton's Power Cruising Bible*, I put everything I knew into *Americas Odyssey*, a 49-foot (14.9 m), twin-screw, Grand Banks motor yacht that my wife, Anne, and I commissioned in Wilmington, North Carolina, and then set out on our voyage of a lifetime. We ran north to the U.S.–Canadian border in Maine, rounded West Quoddy Head light and headed south back down the entire U.S. East Coast. From Florida, we headed out to the Bahamas to cruise its azure waters, then down the entire length of the Leeward and Windward Islands as far as Granada. We cruised through the Netherlands Antilles and pressed on to Panama. After transiting the Panama Canal, we cruised the entire west coast of Central America and Mexico, then covered the coasts of California, Oregon, and Washington. From Seattle, we headed up the Inside Passage to Glacier Bay, Alaska, ran outside down to Sitka, then cut back into the Passage and returned to Seattle. In all, the voyage lasted sixteen months and covered some 16,000 miles (25,800 km).

In this book, I've tried to distill what I have learned in over thirty years of research and from the practical, hands-on experience of *Americas Odyssey*'s voyage into a volume that allows you to profit from the experience of those of us who have gone before you and to avoid unnecessary difficulties.

You'll find a wealth of advice starting with such basics as how to decide how much boat you really need. We consider together the question of whether a planing hull, a semidisplacement vessel, or a deep-bilged, full-displacement yacht would be better suited to your plans. Should your dream boat have a single engine or twin screws? Should you buy a new boat or one that has been—as one creative broker puts it—"previously loved"? Should you consider only domestic-built vessels, or do some of the imports offer better value?

If you decide to buy a new boat, I show you how to look beneath the sleek gelcoat and the varnished brightwork to choose a well-built vessel instead of a piece of glorified cardboard that will fall apart on you. If you're thinking about buying a used boat, I point out the difference between merely cosmetic shortcomings that can be repaired inexpensively and those problems that will require major outlays of cash before you can safely take the boat to sea. I tell you when a marine survey is necessary, what you can expect it to tell you, and how you might use its information to negotiate a better price.

Once I've helped you find the boat of your dreams, I give you an insider's look at the economics of the yacht-selling business to help you figure out whether you are being offered a fair deal or are putting too many dollars in the seller's pocket. I show you how to make the best financing arrangements, and I tell you about pitfalls to look out for in marine insurance. I help you decide whether state registration will be sufficient or whether you should go to the time and expense of documenting your vessel with the federal government.

I also guide you through the bewildering array of optional equipment now on the market. When it comes to navigation equipment, for instance, I make suggestions on choosing everything from an autopilot and a GPS (global positioning system) receiver to a radar and a video plotter. I also help you decide what items in this electronic cornucopia you really need and what amounts to overkill. A good VHF (very high frequency) radio may be all you need for coastal cruising, but offshore voyaging will take you well beyond its range. I explain the options in long-range communication through satellite telephones and single-sideband or ham radios. If you're preparing to strike off for foreign shores, I help you figure out whether you need an inverter, a converter, or an isolation transformer to adapt to queer dockside power supplies. If you plan to undertake extended passages or to cruise areas where the water supply may be limited or suspect, I familiarize you with water makers. I help you decide whether stabilizers are a needless expense for the type of cruising you will be doing or whether they are absolutely necessary and well worth the investment.

Once I've helped you choose the right boat and rig her properly, I cover all the things you need to know before you shove off: everything from how to plan your cruise to avoid predictable bad weather to how to prepare for medical emergencies.

The first time you look out from the helm of a diesel-engine powerboat big enough for you to live aboard for weeks or months at a time and husky enough to deal with the wide variety of situations you're likely to encounter, you'll find the view is nothing like that from the helm of the 30-footer (9 m) you may have used primarily for weekend cruising close to home. In fact, it can be a little intimidating, particularly if your decision to cast off on a cruise of months—or even years—involves a transition from sail to power, from gasoline to diesel engines, or from a single engine to twins. If you've never gotten caught offshore in heavy weather, or had to run an inlet when the weather was kicking up, or had to put your 40-footer (12 m) into a 50-foot (15 m) slot between two other vessels with a strong current and a stiff breeze setting onto the dock, you may ask yourself, "Can I really handle this thing?" You're likely to do most of your cruising with just you and your mate aboard. Are there some tricks to handling a sizable powerboat that don't require half a dozen pairs of hands?

You're going to be out on the water with freighters and tankers and all kinds of tugs—sometimes in narrow channels and sometimes at night. Are you aware how the Rules of the Road are applied—or not applied—in the real world? Do you know what a red over a white light tells

you about the vessel that is about to cross your bow? Do you know how to offset the impact of adverse tides and currents, take advantage of those that are favorable, and figure fuel consumption for a long run where fuel docks are few and far between?

If your boating to date has been limited to familiar waters, you may have become a little nonchalant with your navigating skills. In the unfamiliar waters into which you are about to venture, forgetting to allow for set and drift or not knowing how to read the bottom in tropical waters could get you into trouble in a hurry. If your lineup of navigation electronics for the first time includes a GPS receiver, do you know how to get the most out of it?

Around home, you've been able to get just about any assistance you needed with a telephone call. Now, your extended cruising adventures may well take you a long way from diesel mechanics and electronics repairmen. If your engine suddenly begins to run rough or smoke heavily, or if it quits altogether, do you know how to troubleshoot its problem and keep it running until you can get to a qualified mechanic? If your navigation receiver starts blinking uncontrollably or one of your radios goes belly up, can you troubleshoot it with some hope of restoring it to health?

Are you prepared to deal with emergencies? If an engine room fire shuts down one engine aboard your twin-screw cruiser, do you know that leaving the other one running while you check out the damage can be disastrous? If you're far offshore and have a serious medical emergency aboard, can you handle it? If not, do you know how to get in touch quickly with authoritative medical advice?

If you plan to visit other nations but have never entered a foreign port, do you know how to find out whether the buoyage systems of the countries you plan to visit are the same as that in the United States? As you enter a foreign port, do you know whether to display your quarantine flag on your bow staff or on your cruising mast? Do you know whether you should hoist the host nation's courtesy flag as you enter their waters or wait until you've cleared customs and immigration procedures? Once ashore, can you expect to find the same foods you're used to at home? Do you know how, when, and where to convert your U.S. dollars to the local currency at the best rate?

I answer these and the hundreds of other questions you'll encounter in the life of cruising under power.

One note: throughout this book, I call a spade a spade. I mention brand names of the boats and equipment commonly sold in the United States—whether built here or imported—that I and other experienced cruisers have found to perform satisfactorily and those that have failed the test of time and continuous use in the corrosive marine environment. I'm not interested in promoting or slam-ming any particular manufacturer of yachts or accessory equipment. But if a boat is lightly built or has an inefficient hull form, if an inflatable dinghy is not up to the rigors of the cruising life, or if a life raft is likely to come unglued just when your life depends on it, I think you should know it.

My purpose in writing this book is to help you select, outfit, and operate the yacht best suited to your lifestyle and cruising plans in comfort and safety. I hope—whether you are a first-time buyer of a cruising yacht or an experienced yachtsper-son who has already left thousands of miles of open water in your wake—that you will find in these pages a wealth of information, ideas, and suggestions that will help make your cruising dreams come true.

PART ONE

Choosing a Boat

Starting with the Basics

On the west coast of Florida several years ago, I met an engaging couple who were making their home aboard a boat they recently had purchased for a long-dreamed-of retirement years' cruise to the Bahamas and, if all went well, down through the Leeward and Windward Islands. The couple was bright and articulate. They had virtually no boating experience, but when they began making plans for this retirement they had been put in contact with a pleasant-sounding Gulf Coast boat dealer who had assured them he had "just the boat you need."

The husband took a quick flight down for an inspection, during which the boat's roomy interior and such amenities as reverse-cycle air conditioning, a washer-dryer, and a microwave oven easily convinced my friend it was worth the $100,000-plus asking price (all prices are in U.S. dollars). He assured his wife it was a vessel they could make into a comfortable floating home. On the checkout run, the vessel proceeded sedately across the waters of the bay opposite the dealer's dock. The deal was made, checks were passed, and

within a few weeks my friends had sold their home, stored the possessions they would not need aboard, taken delivery of the vessel, and set off to live out their dream.

The trip along the protected waters of the Gulf Intracoastal Waterway was idyllic—gulls wheeling in the bright air and the glories of a golden sunset across the marshland. At Apalachicola, with the wind out of the southeast, the Gulf of Mexico was kicking up a light chop, but my friend was certain it would present no problem to a boat the dealer had assured him was capable of carrying him and his wife in comfort and safety to the Virgin Islands and beyond. He set a course for Cedar Key, and they were off on their first open-water passage. The moment they cleared the inlet, the boat began to pound unmercifully. Even cutting the cruising speed well below what the dealer had assured them they could count on in virtually any weather helped little. By the time my bruised and battered friends reached Clearwater, they realized they had been sold a vessel that was entirely unsuited to the kind of cruising they had in mind.

What had the dealer sold them for their cruise of a lifetime through the Leewards and Windwards? A 50-foot (15 m) flat-bottomed houseboat!

This may be an extreme example of a couple with the best of intentions being sold a totally inappropriate vessel for the type of cruising they had in mind, but from Maine to Florida, from California to Washington State, it is repeated to some degree daily.

Before you plunge into the glittering world of the boat shows or head for the broker's dock to seek the cruiser of your dreams, make certain you are looking for a boat of the right size and with the hull, layout, propulsion system, and basic systems best suited to the kind of cruising you have in mind, and one you can afford to buy and operate comfortably.

HOW MUCH BOAT DO YOU NEED?

If you plan to operate your boat yourself rather than hire a crew, you need to look for a vessel large enough to deal with the seas you will encounter and to allow you to accommodate guests in comfort, yet small enough for you and your mate to operate easily.

How much boat is "too much" depends not only on the amount of money you can spend but on how energetic and mechanically inclined you are. I know several couples in their late fifties or early sixties who handle 58- to 64-footers (17.7–19.5 m) by themselves with no problems. I've also known couples who have bought elaborate 50-footers (15 m) and later sold them because they found them too complex to maintain and operate. At least one of the couples subsequently acquired a 42-footer (12.8 m) with only minimal amenities and found that what they called their "second-honeymoon cottage" was far better suited to their needs.

How much boat is "too little" is a somewhat more objective matter. For cruising protected waters, a solidly constructed boat around 35 feet (10.7 m) long might be adequate for the sea conditions you are likely to face. If you can go ashore frequently to stretch your legs and can easily find fuel, water, and provisions, you don't necessarily need a boat with spacious accommodations and voluminous storage capacities. For handling the sea conditions encountered in open-water voyaging, however, I personally feel a vessel of about 40 feet (12 m) overall is the practical minimum, and I'd really rather have a boat closer to 50 feet (15 m). People regularly venture offshore in powerboats under 40 feet, but I think they are foolishly taking their lives in their hands. It's not merely a question of the expanse of open water to be covered. It's only about 50 nautical miles (80 km) from the east coast of Florida to the Bahamas, for instance, but to get there you have to cross the Gulf Stream. I've been in the stream with 30 knots of wind opposing the stream's 4-knot current and found it a frightening experience even in a well-found boat of 50 feet or so. I shudder to think what it would be like in a lesser vessel. Further, I think it takes at least a 40-footer to provide a safe fuel reserve and adequate living space and storage capacity for at least two people and occasional guests to cruise in relative comfort for a month or more.

A good way to get a feel for how much boat you need is to add the number of people you will have aboard on a typical cruise and base your decision initially on providing comfortable sleeping accommodations for them all. If there will be just you and your significant other with only infrequent guests, a two-stateroom boat will probably be adequate. For those rare times when you have more than one other couple aboard, put a sofa in the main saloon that will fold out into a bed. On the other hand, if you often will have loads of kids and grandkids aboard, you may need three or four staterooms.

Americas Odyssey, the 49-foot (14.9 m) Grand Banks semidisplacement vessel my wife, Anne, and I cruised some 16,000 miles (25,800 km) from the U.S.–Canadian border in Maine to Glacier Bay, Alaska, was perfect for that voyage. We planned our runs with a careful eye on the weather, but when we did encounter such conditions as

30-knot headwinds between St. Martin and Antigua or 20-foot (6 m) following seas from Curaçao to the San Blas Islands of Panama, *Americas Odyssey* was big and heavy enough to handle them without putting our hearts in our throats. A lesser vessel simply would not have been up to the task. We frequently had four guests aboard for a week at a time, comfortably accommodated in the two forward staterooms. The full-beam stateroom aft was ideal for Anne and me for the full sixteen months we were aboard.

HULL AND ENGINES COME FIRST

According to the extensive marketing surveys that U.S. boat manufacturers periodically conduct, when most people begin searching for the cruiser of their dreams, the first thing they focus on is a boat's exterior styling. Does it really look like their idea of a proper cruising vessel? From styling, they progress to eyeing the interior. Does the layout offer enough space for mom, pop, and all the kids? Does it have enough heads? Is the galley big enough? After that, they spend hour after hour choosing the right color combination for the drapes and carpet in the main saloon. Only then do they take a cursory glance at the boat's deck layout and anchoring setup and wonder if there is enough space in the engine room to get around to the back side of the power plants.

I suggest that when you begin your quest for the perfect cruising boat, you work literally from the inside out rather than from the outside in. As a first step, discard for the moment all thoughts of styling, accommodation plans, galley arrangements, and deck layouts. Concentrate solely on selecting the hull form and engine package that will best suit your needs. If the hull form and power plants of the boat you eventually buy are right for the kind of cruising you have in mind, most other factors can be modified or lived with. If the hull form is wrong or the boat is seriously underpowered, no amount of cosmetic surgery or electronic gadgetry is going to make that boat do the job you

expect it to do. By concentrating on a boat's hull form and engines, I mean far more than just flipping through the builder's glossy brochure or taking a quick walk around the boat in its cradle and poking your head into the engine room. After reading this chapter, you won't be a naval architect or a marine engineer, but you should be able to analyze the configuration of a particular vessel's underbody and its propulsion system to determine whether it can be counted on to perform the way you want it to under the less-than-perfect conditions you'll encounter at sea.

In making your hull-form evaluation, it would be ideal if you could obtain station drawings of the hull you are considering, but dragging that kind of information out of most boatbuilders is difficult. In the case of a new boat, you should insist on a close inspection of the boat you are thinking of buying, or one identical to it, out of the water. In the case of a used boat already lying at a dock, try to get a good look at the underbody of a sister ship before you get into serious deliberations.

The first crossroads you come to is deciding whether to choose a boat with a planing hull, a semidisplacement hull, or a full-displacement hull, and which propulsion package is appropriate to power it (see illustration next page).

In the late 1980s, a full-displacement boat with a relatively low-horsepower engine was considered the only proper vessel for extended voyaging, and this type of boat still has strong advocates among some of the world's most experienced cruisers. Planing hull advocates scoff that the full-displacement boat's snail's-pace cruising speed and the rolling inherent in its rounded bottom should be relegated to some maritime museum. The only proper cruising vessel, they argue, is a planing hull motor yacht with a pair of husky turbocharged diesels. My California friend Rob Hixon expresses the planing hull cruiser's viewpoint clearly. Rob cruised his 60-foot (18 m) planing yacht, *Dorado*, which was equipped with General Motors 12V-71 turbocharged diesels, from New England to his home in Newport Beach, California, by way of the Caribbean and the

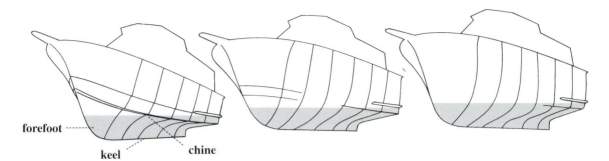

A typical planing hull (left) has relatively flat surfaces and hard, full-length chines. In a semidisplacement hull (center), the chines often disappear forward of amidships and the hull bottom is rounded in the forward sections. In a full-displacement hull (right), the chine virtually disappears and the hull sections are almost completely rounded.

Panama Canal, made a number of runs north to Alaska, and successfully voyaged 600 miles (970 km) into the Pacific to visit the Galápagos Islands. "On the long hauls," Rob told me once as we lolled stern-to at the quay of Nelson's Dockyard in English Harbor, Antigua, "we can pull her back to about 1,100 rpm to make 10 knots while burning about 20 gallons [75 L] of fuel per hour. If the weather turns sour, we can crank her up to 2,100 rpm and scoot out of its way at 20 knots."

Note: One knot is equivalent to 1 nautical mile per hour. A nautical mile equals 6,076.115 feet, while a statute mile equals 5,280 feet (nm × 1.15 = statute miles). Because knot *is used internationally, you'll see that term instead of* kilometers per hour *throughout this book. The formulas for converting nautical miles to statute miles and vice versa are in chapter 14.*

Due primarily to our national obsession with speed, in recent years the planing hull advocates have had much the better of the planing-versus-displacement argument. Planing cruisers now outsell full-displacement boats in the United States by a vast margin. Many major U.S. boatbuilders, in fact, say they can't sell a boat that isn't of the planing or semiplaning variety and doesn't cruise at about 15 to 20 knots. As a result, many companies that once offered full-displacement boats have

either gone out of the business or hardened up the lines of their boats and transformed them into semidisplacement hulls. This underbody, they claim, provides the option of either cruising at nominal displacement speeds or zipping along at planing speeds by merely advancing the throttles. We'll examine these claims in more detail than the builders provide in their sales literature.

Some people say that potential buyers of cruising boats instinctively know which type of hull will suit them best. My experience indicates otherwise. I have known a number of first-time boat buyers—particularly older people moving from sailboat to powerboat voyaging—who bought a sizable planing boat and quickly found that it pounded too much, made too much noise under way, slurped down too much fuel, and had too limited a range. When they shifted to a displacement hull boat, they found they were happy as larks. Conversely, during the oil embargo of the 1970s, when diesel fuel prices went through the roof and there were serious doubts about its long-term availability for pleasure marine use, a number of planing boat owners traded in their fuel-thirsty motor yachts for displacement boats. Some made the adjustment well. Others found they were driven close to insanity by chugging along at 8 to 10 knots. As soon as diesel fuel prices came down to around a dollar a gallon (3.785 L), they couldn't wait to get back into a planing boat and feel they were really moving again.

My point is that the choice between a planing cruiser and a semidisplacement or full-displacement cruiser should receive careful consideration. And I further suggest that the process of deciding which way you will go should not begin with the glitz and glitter of boat shows or Saturday afternoon meanderings along the used-boat broker's dock. It should begin with finding the answers to some basic questions about yourself.

How will you use this vessel? If you have the luxury of sufficient time and income to strike off for several months at a time, enjoy lazing along while drinking in the patterns of wind and sea, and feel the best part of cruising is glorying in the colors of sunset in a secluded anchorage far from the madding crowd, you probably would be quite happy with a displacement vessel. On the other hand, if family and business responsibilities will limit your cruising to shorter voyages of a few days or weeks at a time and you prefer to get the boring open-water passages behind you quickly, you probably should opt for a planing vessel.

Where will you do your cruising? If the area or route you plan to cruise allows frequent refueling and reprovisioning stops, a planing motor yacht might be practical. If you plan to seek out remote areas where fuel and provisions may well be hard to come by, you probably need a displacement boat that can carry enough fuel and provisions to allow you to stay away from fuel docks and supermarkets for weeks or even months at a time. In the following pages, I cover the basic characteristics of planing, semidisplacement, and full-displacement cruising hulls.

Planing Hull Cruisers

First, let's clarify what we're calling a *planing* hull. From the standpoint of the distinguished but late naval architect Jack Hargrave, a vessel is planing when it is lifted far enough out of the water to reduce its wetted surface to the point that the effort

needed to propel it forward equals the effort needed to overcome surface friction. "I compare planing to flying," Jack once told me. "It's easy to tell when an aircraft is flying. You can see daylight beneath the wheels." Under Jack's definition, about the only true planing hulls around are on extremely high-speed racing boats and the over-30-knot hot rods.

Although Jack's definition is doubtless technically accurate, when most cruisers refer to a planing hull, they're thinking of something a bit less dramatic. They are thinking more of a vessel that reaches a speed sufficient for it to overcome the resistance of the bow wave it creates and "climb out of the hole" to operate more or less on top of the water rather than in it (see photo next page). The technical types who subscribe to this view would say a vessel reaches that speed and is planing when its speed in knots equals twice the square root of its load waterline length (LWL). Though this may not be completely accurate, it's the definition we'll use, since that is what most people consider a planing hull.

If a planing hull is the route you want to pursue, you immediately come to a second fork in the path: should you go with some variation of a deep-V hull that carries a high degree of deadrise all the way aft (in extreme cases as much as 24 degrees), or would you be better off with a modified-V hull whose aft sections flatten out to 15 degrees of deadrise or less (see illustration and photos page 9)?

Those who favor deep-V cruising hulls argue that they pound less in a head sea and track better in a following sea. Devotees of modified-V cruising hulls counter that their boats come up on plane faster, carry a load better, and do not roll as much under way, at the dock, or at anchor.

For cruising, I have to come down on the side of the modified-V hull. It's true that deep-V hulls tend to pound less in a head sea, but that is far less important in a boat that is likely to cruise at 20 knots or less than it is in a high-performance sportfishing boat operating in the 30-knot range. To me, the key factor in a comfortable cruising boat is

SILVERTON

Planing hull cruisers like this 53-foot (14.5 m) Silverton motor yacht have sufficient power to overcome the resistance of their own bow wave and typically operate at cruising speeds of at least 17 to 20 knots.

controlling its tendency to roll. On a lengthy voyage, reducing roll by even 5 or 6 degrees, as most modified-V hulls tend to do, is an advantage that outweighs a reduction in pounding. I grant that the broad, flat stern a modified-V hull presents to a following sea can cause her to slew significantly more than the tapered stern of a deep-V hull, but I'm willing to make the trade to have a boat that stays on her feet rather than rolling drunkenly in even moderate seas, especially when they are beam on.

In searching for a good, serviceable underbody on a planing hull motor yacht, avoid extremes. Look for a hull with a fine entry forward, then lines that broaden gradually amidships and terminate with 15 degrees or less of deadrise at the stern. From just forward of amidships to her stern, the boat should have at least a moderate keel, which will materially aid tracking and help to further reduce the tendency to roll. It is unlikely you will find a keel on a true planing hull

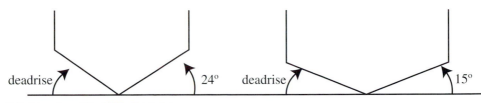

Deep-V hull (left) and modified-V hull (right).

that will offer significant protection to props, struts, and rudders in a grounding, but that is one of the compromises you have to make if you elect to go with this type of vessel. In checking over the hull of any planing boat, look out for such obstructions as excessively wide struts or water intakes forward of the props, since they will significantly interfere with the props' performance.

Aside from underbody configuration, the other major aspect you should consider in selecting a serviceable planing hull is the degree of flare at the bow. It should be deep and generous to turn back your bow wave and cut down on windblown spray. I've seen quite expensive motor yachts whose manufacturer gave way to a designer who obviously knew next to nothing about real-life conditions at sea. They have virtually no flare at the bow because a straighter line was more esthetically pleasing to the designer's eye. In any kind of a head sea, they will take heavy spray over the flying bridge.

A typical deep-V planing hull (left) carries a significant degree of deadrise well aft, whereas a modified-V hull (right) begins to flatten out amidships.

Semidisplacement Hull Cruisers

Some manufacturers advertise their boats as having semidisplacement hulls that can be operated at low engine power to achieve displacement hull fuel economy or at higher engine output for planing hull speeds (see photo). In theory, this sounds like the answer to a cruising man's dreams, and this type of boat has many satisfied adherents. There are, however, a few points to remember.

The basic difference between a semidisplacement vessel and a true planing vessel is that the semidisplacement hull will have a significantly deeper forefoot to give her a soft entry, forward sections that are slightly fuller than a planing hull but not nearly so rounded as those of a full-displacement hull, a hard chine that in most cases runs the hull's full length, and a significant keel. The aft half of most semidisplacement hulls has essentially the same flat sections found in a modified-V planing hull (see illustration page 6).

Certainly, this configuration offers some positive factors for cruising. At displacement speeds, its flatter underbody sections make it roll less than would a full-displacement hull, although the boat will tend to snap back to the vertical rather sharply when its hard chine hits the water. The semidisplacement hull's deep keel is a significant aid in

GRAND BANKS

A semidisplacement yacht such as Americas Odyssey, *a 49-foot (14.9 m) Grand Banks, normally has a maximum cruising speed of 14 to 17 knots.*

tracking and offers valuable protection to struts, props, and rudders.

Whether a semidisplacement vessel operates as a displacement hull or a planing hull depends on its engine power. As an example, let's consider a semidisplacement hull of about 40 feet (12 m) in length overall (LOA) with a waterline length of 36 feet (11 m). Suppose it has tankage for 550 usable gallons (2,080 L) of fuel (see In the Real World sidebar, page 14). If we use the definition of planing given earlier as a speed in knots equal to twice the square root of the waterline in feet, the boat in our example would begin to plane at 12 knots ($\sqrt{36} = 6$; $6 \times 2 = 12$ knots). Its most efficient hull speed is 8 knots ($\sqrt{36} \times 1.34 = 8.04$ knots).

If powered by twin diesels of 120 horsepower (hp) each and cruised at 2,000 revolutions per minute (rpm), the vessel will not plane at all but will operate essentially as a full-displacement hull at about 7.5 knots. Fuel consumption will be about 1.25 nautical miles per gallon (0.33 nm/L), and maximum range will be just under 700 miles (1,130 km).

Suppose you increase the horsepower in that same boat by replacing the 120 hp engines with naturally aspirated twins (described later in this chapter) developing 215 hp each. If the throttles are set at about 1,800 rpm, the vessel will operate essentially as a full-displacement hull at a speed of about 8 knots. With additional horsepower and increased engine weight, fuel consumption will be around 1.1 nautical miles per gallon (0.29 nm/L), and maximum range will be about 600 miles (968 km). If the engines are run up to their maximum cruise setting of about 2,150 rpm, the boat will achieve a top speed of about 12.5 knots and begin to come up on plane. At that speed, however, the boat has just barely come up onto the planing "hump" and doesn't really have the power to overcome the resistance of its own bow wave and get fully up on plane. It is operating as a planing hull but at a planing hull's least efficient attitude. The result is that its fuel consumption rate is not likely to be better than about 0.8 nautical mile per gal-

lon (0.21 nm/L), and its range will be cut to just under 450 miles (725 km).

Suppose you add turbochargers to the 215 hp engines to boost their output to 300 hp each. At 1,600 rpm, the boat will still function as a displacement hull at around 8 knots. Fuel consumption will be about 0.8 nautical mile per gallon (0.21 nm/L) with a range of about 450 miles (725 km). Run the throttles up to 2,100 rpm and the boat will come up fully on plane, but the fuel consumption rate will soar to less than 0.5 nautical mile per gallon (0.13 nm/L) and the range will drop to under 300 miles (484 km).

One tip: if you purchase a vessel that is capable of planing and plan to operate it at displacement speeds for extended periods of time, make the last half hour of each day's run at the boat's normal planing speed. This will help clean the injectors and scavenge out any oil that has slobbered into the air boxes to keep it from turning into a sticky sludge.

Semidisplacement boats are available with both single- and twin-engine configurations, and we'll discuss the pros and cons of each later in this chapter. Suffice it to say here that a semidisplacement boat equipped with a single engine will operate only in a displacement mode and will not have sufficient power to plane.

If your choice comes down to either a semidisplacement hull or a planing hull cruising boat, bear in mind that because of the deeper forefoot and keel, the semidisplacement boat operated at planing speeds will not cruise as fast for a given horsepower or be nearly as fuel efficient as the planing boat.

If you find yourself trying to choose between a semidisplacement and a full-displacement vessel, recognize that in order to get the option of both displacement and planing cruising speeds, you're going to have to put larger engines in the semidisplacement boat and pay a price in fuel economy, even if you operate the boat primarily at displacement speeds. Recognize also that because a semidisplacement boat lacks the deep bilges of the full-displacement boat, it will carry less fuel and the larger engines will consume that fuel faster. Those two factors together will cut your cruising range significantly.

Full-Displacement-Hull Cruisers

If you are leaning in the direction of buying a full-displacement vessel and are not familiar with the genre, I'd strongly recommend you spend several days aboard a friend's boat of that type or charter one for at least a week to make certain you will be happy with two aspects of this kind of cruiser: its limited speed and its tendency to roll (see photo). Going from planing to full-displacement speeds produces quite a psychological jolt, so be sure you can make the adjustment before you sign any contracts.

You'll notice that throughout the book I refer to *full-displacement vessels* rather than *trawler yachts*. Technically, a trawler is a commercial ves-

A full-displacement yacht such as this 50-foot (15 m) Nordhavn normally cruises at 10 knots or less but can carry massive amounts of fuel and provisions for extended operation away from the dock.

sel with a fully rounded bottom, most often a boat used for fishing well offshore that must incorporate every possible square foot of space to hold its catch. Rolling is not a major problem in these vessels because their trawling rigs almost invariably include outriggers that act as very effective paravane stabilizers. If you watch these boats head to sea, you will note that they drop their outriggers (booms that can be lowered to about 45 degrees off the vertical to spread their trawl nets) the minute they venture into open water, even though they may be hundreds of miles from their fishing grounds.

Builders of full-displacement vessels for pleasure use realized early that a fully rounded bottom produces more rolling action than the average yachtsperson is willing to endure. To reduce rolling to an acceptable level, they flattened the aft quarter or so of their hulls to produce the designs commonly marketed today as "full-displacement" or "trawler" yachts. You might find a fully rounded bottom on a pleasure yacht—probably one built in Scandinavia or a true commercial trawler that has been converted to pleasure use—but it will be a rarity. The term *trawler yacht* becomes even more confusing when it is applied to hard-chined semidisplacement cruising boats, whose only resemblance to a true trawler ends just aft of their deep forefoot. Even the term *full-displacement hull* is not totally accurate, but it is closer than *trawler*, so it's the one we'll use.

When considering a specific full-displacement boat, first make certain you know at what speed you actually will be voyaging. Don't rely on the manufacturer's brochure to give you that information because copywriters sometimes wax a bit creative. To determine for yourself the hull speed of a full-displacement pleasure yacht, take the square root of its LWL and multiply the result by 1.34, which is the formula marine engineers generally use to compute the maximum practical speed-to-length (S/L) ratio of this type hull. For a full-displacement vessel with an LWL of 40 feet (12 m), that computes out at just under 8.5 knots ($\sqrt{40}$ = 6.32; 6.32 × 1.34 = 8.47 knots). Up to a point, applying additional horsepower to propel a full-displacement vessel above its hull speed is simply going to create a larger bow wave, force the stern to sink deeper into its own wake, and sharply increase fuel consumption. It is possible to keep piling on the horsepower until you force a full-displacement hull to exceed its practical maximum speed, but then it ceases to be a true displacement hull and its fuel consumption rate goes off the chart.

In practice, you probably will wind up cruising a full-displacement vessel at something less than its S/L ratio of 1.34. The actual ratio is more likely to be around 1.2, which, for a vessel with a 40-foot (12 m) LWL, comes up to around 7.6 knots—better than 0.75 knot slower than its practical maximum.

Once you have worked out the numbers for a specific full-displacement boat, accept the result as the speed at which you actually will be voyaging and make certain you can live with it. If a salesperson or owner says you will cruise faster than that while still enjoying the range and fuel econ-

omy that are primary reasons for buying a vessel of the type, don't believe it. You will exceed the figures you come up with only by fractions and even then at stiff increases in fuel consumption.

As for the hull form of a full-displacement cruiser, you should look for full, well-rounded sections with no chine forward where she does her work shouldering aside the water (see photo). The lines will flatten out somewhat into a moderately hard chine in the aft quarter of the hull. The hull also should incorporate a generous keel to help her track properly and to provide protection to the props, struts, and rudders in a grounding,

My earlier comments on the desirability of a generous flare in the bow to turn back the bow wave and windblown spray applies equally to both displacement and semidisplacement cruisers. The more the better. You may notice that there are designers—especially of some boats built in Asia—who incorporate almost no flare into the bow and rely instead on exceedingly high bulwarks forward to keep the foredeck reasonably dry. Practically speaking, a bow with high bulwarks tends to

This Nordhavn exhibits a full-displacement yacht's typical deep forefoot and well-rounded bilge sections.

NORDHAVN

In the Real World

The experience of the father-son team of Bob and Don Baumgartner, who took their Hatteras 58 Long Range Cruiser Trenora across the Atlantic on her own bottom (rather than ship her), provides some hard data with regard to speed and fuel consumption in the real world of full-displacement cruising. The boat was powered by twin, naturally aspirated Detroit Diesel 4-71 engines with N55 injectors that developed 160 shaft hp each at 2,300 rpm, and she had total fuel tankage of 2,300 gallons (8,700 L) with about 2,000 gallons (7,570 L) usable. (The full capacity of a vessel's fuel tanks is never 100 percent usable. The fuel pickup tube ends a few inches short of the bottom of the tank to avoid picking up the sludge that inevitably builds up on the bottom.) To make sure they had an adequate fuel reserve for the longest leg of the voyage—the 1,779-mile (2,870 km) run from Bermuda to the Azores—the Baumgartners equipped the vessel with a 100-gallon (378.5 L) day tank graduated in 1-gallon (3.785 L) increments and did a number of carefully measured runs over a test course in calm seas at different rpm settings. With a 52-foot (16 m) waterline, the vessel's practical maximum hull speed would be 9.66 knots. During the tests, the boat was fully loaded with fuel, water, and stores, and the fuel consumption figures included the operation of a 15 kilowatt (kW) generator. They developed the numbers in the accompanying table.

THE BAUMGARTNER CALCULATIONS

RPM	Speed (in knots)	S/L Ratio	GPH (L/h)	Nautical Miles/ Gallon (nm/L)
1,400	8.3	1.15	6.6 (25)	1.25 (0.33)
1,500	8.5	1.18	8.5 (32)	1.0 (0.26)
1,800	10.7	1.48	12.0 (45)	0.89 (0.24)

Notice that even on the test runs, increasing the throttle setting from 1,400 to 1,500 rpm yielded only a 2.4 percent increase in speed but boosted fuel consumption by almost 30 percent. In going from 8.5 knots—well under the boat's practical maximum hull speed of 9.66 knots—to well over it at 10.7 knots, they achieved a 25 percent speed increase but at the heavy cost of a 41 percent increase in fuel consumption.

Contrast the test figures with those produced under the actual conditions Trenora experienced during the voyage, which included 20-foot (6 m) seas off Bermuda and 40-knot winds gusting to 60 knots on her approach to the Azores. She covered a total of 3,818 nautical miles from Ft. Lauderdale, Florida, to Vilamora, Portugal, in 460.8 hours running time at an average speed of 8.28 knots (an S/L of 1.148). According to the test run figures, at that average speed she should have burned about 6.5 gallons per hour (24.6 L/hr), or a total of just under 3,000 gallons (11,355 L) of fuel for the entire voyage. Actually, her total fuel consumption, including that used by her 15 kW generator, was more than one and a half times that—4,588.7 gallons (17,368 L), an average of 9.96 gallons (37.7 L) per hour or only 0.83 nautical mile per gallon (0.22 nm/L).

"On the run from Bermuda to the Azores," Don says, "we kept our speed just under 8 knots to stretch our fuel. But with the heavy seas we *encountered, we still got a touch less than 1 nautical mile per gallon. Toward the end of the trip, we were very tired and anxious to have the trip behind us. On the relatively short runs from the Azores to Madeira and Madeira to Vilamora, where we were not concerned about range, we ran the engines up to 1,800 rpm, which gave us about 9 knots but increased our fuel consumption to around 12 gallons [45 L] per hour. At that rate, we were only getting about three quar-* *ters of a nautical mile per gallon [0.198 nm/L]." The point here is that real-life cruising rarely produces average speed and fuel consumption figures anywhere close to those developed in test runs under controlled conditions. To get the range you may need, you will have to keep the throttles pulled back, and you should always allow yourself a 20 to 25 percent fuel reserve to deal with any adverse weather you might encounter.*

restrict the forward vision of the helmsperson, particularly from the pilothouse, and the boat is likely to take spray across the foredeck in even minimal sea conditions.

DIESEL ENGINES AND TURBOCHARGERS

I strongly recommend that for a cruising vessel, you consider boats powered only by diesel rather than gasoline. Diesels are much safer, more dependable, and have a longer service life because they operate at much lower rpm than gasoline engines, which puts less stress on their internal parts. Diesel engines long have been the power of choice for yachts over about 40 feet (12 m). Now, the newer, lighter weight models—with higher red lines of 3,600 rpms—make them practical for vessels in the 30- to 40-foot (9–12 m) range as well. Diesels typically are 25 to 30 percent more expensive than gasoline engines but are well worth the additional cost. Keep in mind that when we discuss horsepower, we'll refer to *shaft horsepower*, which is the net power a marine diesel actually delivers to a vessel's shaft and prop.

In a planing cruiser, you are unlikely to have to worry about the question of single versus twin engines. As far as I am aware, no manufacturer builds a planing hull yacht large enough to be considered a serious cruising vessel that is equipped with anything other than twin engines. A growing trend among manufacturers of boats around 30 feet (9 m) long is to combine diesel engines with outboard drives rather than conventional shafts and props. While the ability to raise an outboard drive clear of the water might be an advantage for gunkholing, over the long haul the conventional shaft-and-prop arrangement will give you more trouble-free service.

A number of manufacturers of planing-type yachts now offer their boats with a standard propulsion package and then provide buyers the opportunity to plunk down another $10,000 or $20,000 for an optional package that provides larger-horsepower engines. Some manufacturers create the option by offering the next-larger engine available from their suppliers. Others create the option by offering naturally aspirated diesels (explained later in this section) in their standard package, then boosting horsepower in the optional package by adding turbocharging. (In addition to *turbocharged*, you also may run across the terms *turbo-injected* and *turbo-assisted*. All three terms refer to the same process.) Since you are going to be buying a boat with diesel engines, if you are not already familiar with the beasts, you need to know at least the basics of how they operate. If you are considering a boat with turbocharged diesels, you should know a little about how they work as well and the different versions of cooling turbocharged engines that are available.

In order to operate, any internal-combustion

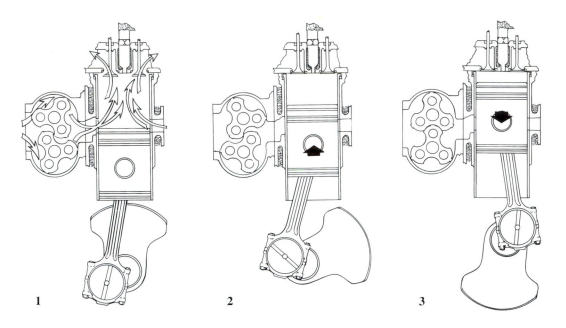

1   2   3

In a two-cycle diesel engine, the injector fires on each revolution of the crankshaft. At the lower end of its power stroke (1), the piston simultaneously exhausts burned gases and takes in air fed into the cylinder by the blower. On the up-stroke (2), it compresses the air. The cylinder is injected with fuel, which ignites under compression and forces the piston downward for its power stroke (3). Note the absence of intake valves.

engine must mix its fuel with air to create an explosive mixture inside its cylinders. A gasoline engine sucks in the air it needs through intake valves, mixes it with fuel that has been vaporized by the carburetor, compresses the air-fuel mixture on the upstroke of the piston, then ignites it by means of a spark plug.

Diesel engines are similar in certain ways to gasoline engines, but they also have several important differences. Like gasoline engines, they come in two-cycle and four-cycle versions. A two-cycle diesel (such as most of the Detroit Diesel marine engines built prior to 1998) fires on every stroke (see illustrations). Two-cycle diesels don't have intake valves to suck air into the combustion chamber. Instead, they take in outside air and feed it into the cylinder with a simple blower.

Four-cycle diesels (Caterpillar and Cummins, for instance) do have intake valves, and the injector fires on every other stroke (see illustrations). On the nonfiring stroke, the piston exhausts burned fuel and sucks fresh air through the valves to prepare for the next firing stroke.

Modern gas and diesel engines use fuel injectors to vaporize fuel. In gas engines, vaporized fuel is ignited by a spark plug. Diesel engines don't use spark plugs. Instead, they compress the air-fuel mixture with such force that the heat caused by the friction of compression causes it to ignite.

Naturally aspirated diesel engines use only intake valves or a blower to suck in outside air and feed it into the combustion chamber under atmospheric pressure.

Since compression is so important in the diesel

engine's combustion process, the engine will be able to operate more efficiently if the air that is fed into the combustion chamber is already compressed to some degree. This is what turbochargers do: compress the air and force it into the combustion chamber under twice the atmospheric pressure. Adding turbocharging to a naturally aspirated diesel engine has the effect of increasing its shaft horsepower 25 to 50 percent. (Some people refer to turbochargers as *blowers*. To differentiate between high-speed, high-pressure turbochargers and the relatively low-speed, low-pressure blower used to suck air into a naturally aspirated diesel engine, when I mean turbochargers I'll call them *turbochargers*, not *blowers*.)

As turbochargers compress the air, however, friction between the air's molecules causes the air temperature to rise. The engine will be more efficient if the air is cooled down again (and its density thus increased) after it is compressed but before it enters the combustion chamber. So, you have diesel engines that are intercooled and those that are aftercooled. In an *intercooled* turbocharged diesel engine, the air is cooled between the turbocharger and the blower or intake valves in a heat exchanger mounted on top of the engine. This external heat exchanger is cooled by circulating raw water.

In an *aftercooled* turbocharged diesel engine, the air is cooled between the blower and the combustion chamber in a heat exchanger that is an integral part of the engine itself. This internal heat exchanger is cooled by the engine's freshwater cooling system. Adding intercooling or aftercooling to a turbocharged diesel increases its horsepower 5 to 10

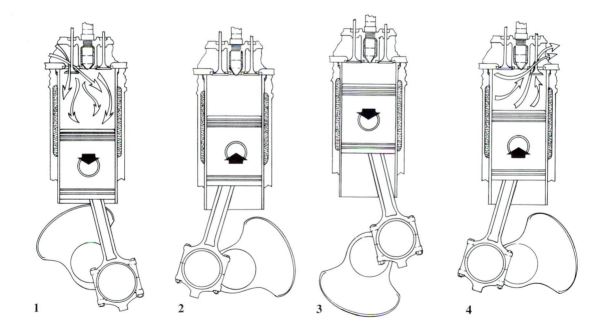

1   2   3   4

In a four-cycle diesel engine, the injector fires on every other revolution of the crankshaft. On the piston's first downstroke (1), it draws air into the cylinder through the intake valve. On its first upstroke (2), it compresses the air. Fuel is injected and ignites (3), which forces the piston down on its power stroke. On the piston's second upward stroke (4), it exhausts burned gases through the exhaust valve and is poised to repeat the sequence.

percent. (In a few cases, turbocharged diesels are both intercooled and aftercooled to wring every possible ounce of horsepower out of them. Most of these engines are used in high-performance boats and are pushed so close to their tolerances that they are not practical for use in cruising vessels.)

An aftercooled diesel engine generally is more expensive because the heat exchanger is inside the engine rather than mounted on top of it. Aftercooled diesels are also likely to be more expensive to repair because more of the engine must be stripped away to get at the heat exchanger.

Our fascination with speed has made the addition of turbochargers to cruising yachts extremely popular, and they are coming into even wider use. In the process, a couple of misconceptions have arisen about them that need to be corrected: they aren't high-maintenance items, nor do they materially affect the useful life span of a well-maintained engine. A few cautions regarding them are appropriate, however.

They operate at incredibly high speeds (75,000–100,000 rpm) and high temperatures (1,000–1,200°F, or 537–648°C). To reduce the dissipation of that heat into the engine room, some turbochargers (especially on boats built prior to about 1987) are encased in "blankets" made of heavy insulating material covered with an aluminized fabric. Because of the high temperatures and pressures at which they operate, they must be lubricated by oil, which the engine heats to about 215°F (102°C) and circulates around them at 50 to 60 pounds per square inch, or psi (4.2 kg/cm²). The fittings in this lubrication system have been known to leak and soak the blankets, which can then catch fire. If you elect to purchase a used boat whose turbochargers have insulating blankets, be certain you have the installation checked out carefully by a qualified marine surveyor or diesel mechanic before you head to sea, and keep a close eye on the integrity of their oil lines and fittings. Change them immediately at the least sign of fraying, cracking, or leaking.

Since about 1987, some manufacturers have switched to cooling their turbochargers by encasing them in cast-iron jacket manifolds through which water circulates. This is fine in quality installations that use freshwater for cooling, but some cheaper installations use raw salt water, which in contact with the cast iron is an almost certain prescription for major problems down the road. The only places raw salt water should be used for cooling is in fuel coolers, intercoolers, and heat exchangers made of copper or a copper-nickel alloy, not cast iron.

If you purchase a cruising yacht with turbocharged engines, you can do two simple things to extend the life of the engines and reduce maintenance appreciably. Because turbos are lubricated under pressure, when the engine is shut down all their lubricating oil drains away and they are dry, which leaves metal rubbing against metal. When you start the engines, run them up to 800 or 900 rpm for a couple of minutes; this assures that the turbos will be adequately lubricated before they are operated at normal cruising speeds. Merely cranking the engines and letting them idle at 500 to 600 rpm does not ensure adequate turbo lubrication. *Never* exceed 900 rpm in the first couple of minutes after starting the engines or you could burn out the turbos' shafts. Conversely, when you end a day's run, don't shut your engines down immediately; instead, allow them to idle at 500 to 600 rpm for five minutes or so to allow the oil inside the turbo housing to drain away and carry excess heat with it. Abrupt shutdown leaves the turbos spinning without oil and traps oil in the housing, which can be baked into a sludge by the high heat levels.

Another way to increase a diesel engine's shaft horsepower is to install larger injectors, which inject more fuel into the engine at a faster rate. For example, by increasing the injectors in a turbocharged Detroit Diesel 8V-92 from 115 mm to 125 mm, you increase its maximum rating at 2,300 rpm from 585 shaft hp to 625 shaft hp, a gain of 40 hp (or 6.8 percent).

Whether you elect a standard engine package or choose the next-larger engine size, whether you opt for naturally aspirated or turbocharged engines, and whether you go to larger injectors all come down to the question of how fast you want to go and how much you are willing to pay for increases in speed. The following examples may offer some guidance.

On the smaller-versus-larger-engine option: a pair of naturally aspirated Detroit Diesel 8V-71 engines equipped with 70 mm injectors will develop 325 shaft hp at 2,300 rpm. At a cruise setting of 2,100 rpm, they will propel a typical 50-foot (15 m) planing hull motor yacht at around 18 knots while consuming a total for both engines of about 30 gallons (114 L) per hour. If you increase the engine size in that same boat to naturally aspirated 8V-92 diesels with 85 mm injectors, at 2,300 rpm the engines will develop 375 shaft hp each. At a cruise setting of 2,100 rpm, they will propel the boat at about 20 knots while consuming a total for both engines of about 34.5 gallons (130 L) per hour.

On the question of natural aspiration versus turbocharging: if you add turbochargers to the 8V-71 engines in the 50-footer (15 m) mentioned above and increase the size of the injectors from 70 mm to 85 mm, the engines will develop 450 shaft hp each at 2,300 rpm. At a cruise setting of 2,100 rpm, they will increase the vessel's speed from 18 to about 22 knots, and their joint fuel consumption will increase from 30 gallons (114 L) per hour to just a shade over 42 gallons (159 L) per hour.

As for the effects of adding larger injectors: by increasing injectors in the naturally aspirated 8V-71 above from 55 to 65 mm, you will increase speed by about 1 knot and fuel consumption for two engines by about 8 gallons (30 L) per hour.

Bear in mind that as you increase fuel consumption for a particular boat by going to larger engines, adding turbochargers, or increasing injector size, you not only are increasing your operating costs but also are reducing the vessel's cruising range.

Is it true, as planing hull advocates claim, that they can throttle their engines back and get close to displacement hull economy when they want it?

It depends on what you call "close." One day I'd like to stage a test run from Ft. Lauderdale, Florida, to Bimini in moderate weather with three boats in identical condition and carrying full loads of fuel and water. Boat No. 1 would be a full-displacement cruiser with an LWL of 52 feet (15.8 m) and powered by twin, naturally aspirated 4-71 Detroit diesels equipped with 55 mm injectors and operated at its theoretical hull speed of 9.66 knots. Boat No. 2 would be a planing-hull motor yacht of the same LWL but powered by naturally aspirated 8V-71 Detroit diesels with 70 mm injectors. Boat No. 3 would be a planing hull identical to Boat No. 2 but equipped with turbochargers and 90 mm injectors. The two planing hull boats would match their speeds to that of the displacement hull boat. When the three yachts pulled into Bimini, I'll bet you a dime to a sack of doughnuts that Boat No. 1 would have consumed very close to 10 gallons (37.85 L) per hour, Boat No. 2 would have consumed close to 12 gallons (45.42 L) per hour, and Boat No. 3 would have consumed 14 gallons (53 L) per hour. Any way you slice it, at displacement speeds, the planing hull people are paying a 20 to 40 percent penalty for their reserve power to plane. If that's "close" to displacement hull economy, their claim is valid.

A few other observations need to be made about this experiment, however. The displacement hull boat is designed to operate at the speed of the crossing, and it will have handled well; the planing hulls are not, and they will have wallowed all over the place. The displacement hull boat is beamy enough to carry all the stores and provisions needed for extended cruising. The planing hull boats are not. At Bimini, the displacement boat will have enough fuel left to cruise at least another 1,500 nautical miles, while the planing boats, even if their helmspersons continue to operate them at displacement speeds, will be looking for a fuel dock after about half that distance. More likely, their operators will get bored and antsy at 10 knots and will push the throttles up to around 2,100 rpm, doing most of their cruising at 18 to 22 knots and burning about 35 to 42 gallons (132.5–159 L) an hour, and their tanks will be bone-dry after they have gone less than 600 nautical miles. My point is that for relatively short-range cruising in areas where fuel and provisions are readily available, I have no quarrel with the planing hull advocates' claim. If the plan is to do extended cruising in the boondocks, there is no way a planing vessel can touch a displacement boat's overall economy and practicality.

ENGINES: SINGLE VERSUS TWIN

The engines used on full-displacement cruisers are almost invariably naturally aspirated diesels fitted with small injectors, and you normally don't get into considerations of turbochargers. Some manufacturers of full-displacement cruisers do, however, offer their boats with either a standard engine package or optional higher-horsepower power plants. In most cases, the standard package will push the boat to its maximum efficient hull speed and is all the power you need. The option of larger engines is offered primarily as a marketing ploy to attract marginal buyers. It might provide a couple of extra knots of speed but only at a sharp increase in fuel consumption.

Several manufacturers of full-displacement boats offer both single- and twin-engine setups—sometimes in the same model. Because there are a number of single-engine, full-displacement boats on the used-boat market, this is an appropriate place to take up the single-versus-twin-engines controversy.

Whether a full-displacement boat should be powered by one engine or two is not really a matter of speed. A full-displacement-hull yacht having an LWL of 36 feet (11 m) and powered by a single 135 hp diesel engine turning at 1,800 rpm, for instance, will cruise at about 7 knots in calm seas. That same boat with twin 135 hp engines operating at the same rpm setting will cruise only about 1.5 knots faster. The reason the vessel won't achieve anything like twice the speed even though it has twice the power is that the added force will push the vessel to its maximum practical S/L ratio but will not be sufficient to overcome the resistance of its bow wave and allow it to plane. The twin-engine vessel, of course, will burn almost—but not quite—twice as much fuel.

The question of single versus twin engines really comes down to two factors: safety and maneuverability.

As for safety, the advocates of cruising on one engine point out that properly maintained diesels aboard single-engine commercial fishing and shrimping boats operate mile after mile, year after year, with no significant problems. That is true. But bear in mind that there is usually a pretty fair mechanic aboard, who constantly maintains the engine and corrects potential problems before they cause a breakdown. Even these vessels suffer situations in which an oil or a fuel pump fails or a fuel or water filtration system clogs and brings the engine to a shuddering halt. There is also the danger of a line ensnaring the prop and shaft and bringing the boat to a stop. I grant the adherents of single-engine cruising that their approach consumes less fuel for approximately equal cruising speeds and that, because a single shaft and prop can be mounted directly behind the keel, they are better protected. But I am a firm believer in Murphy's Law and its first corollary—whatever can go wrong will and at the worst possible moment. For that reason, I am a strong advocate of building in redundant systems wherever possible. The first place I would insist on redundancy in a cruiser on which my life could depend would be twin engines for its main propulsion system.

When maneuverability is brought up in the single-versus-twin-engine debate, the discussion usually revolves around docking. Some single-engine boats handle so poorly in close quarters that in adverse conditions they can only be brought to the dock with the use of a spring line or bow thruster. Certainly, there is no question that the twin-engine boat handles far more easily in tight quarters, particularly when you are trying to back into a slip with a stiff crosswind or cross-current running. But maneuverability is even more critical in inlet running, particularly in a stiff following sea. Chances are that a full-displacement boat will not be fast enough to run inside on the back of a single wave, which is the best approach with a planing hull boat. With a displacement hull boat, the best you can do is let the successive waves pass under you while keeping your vessel as nearly as possible over deep water. Since many displacement hull boats have a broad, flat stern with essentially no deadrise, their tendency in a strong following sea is to slew rather dramatically from side to side. Bear in mind that in such a circumstance, the sea will be running from the stern forward at a speed greater than your vessel's forward progress, which will make the boat's rudder essentially useless. The only way you are going to stay centered in the channel under those conditions is to have twin engines and use bursts of power first on one engine, then on the other, to overcome the boat's tendency to broach. In extreme conditions, if you get well into a broach, you may even have to put the windward engine in full forward and the leeward engine in full reverse to bring the boat back on track. If you are caught in that condition with only a single engine, about all you can do is hang on tight and pray.

Advocates of single-engine cruising bring up the question of range. My California friend Peter Fowler, for instance, argues that by sharply throttling back the single 135 hp engine in his Kady-Krogen 42, he could wring a 2,800-mile (4,516 km) range out of its 700-gallon (2,650 L) fuel capacity—enough to reach Hawaii. "I could never do that," he says, "if the fuel were being consumed by two engines." My response is that, if necessary, twin-engine vessels can be operated very effectively on only one engine. If run that way, a twin-engine boat of equal fuel capacity would have very nearly the same range but would still have the backup of a totally separate engine, transmission, shaft, and prop if they were needed.

If you select a single-engine boat, I'd suggest you create emergency "get home" power by rigging it to run off its electric generator if the main engine should fail. Most installations of this type use an electric motor, which in an emergency can be connected to the driveshaft with a cogwheel belt. A 7.5 kW generator, for example, could power about a 10 hp motor, which would propel a 42-footer (12.8 m) at around 3 knots.

Our discussion to this point has assumed that a boat with two engines would also have two props and shafts. You might come across a boat with twin engines set up to power a single shaft and prop either alternately or in tandem. That arrangement provides a backup source of power if one of the engines fails, but the vessel is still helpless if a significant problem develops with its underwater gear.

ENGINE VIBRATION DAMPENERS

In a traditional installation, a marine diesel engine must be very precisely aligned with its propeller shaft. To accomplish this, the engine is attached to stiff engine mounts, which are firmly affixed to stringers molded into the hull. This means that the engine's vibration is transmitted throughout the vessel.

Aboard *Americas Odyssey*, we installed the Aquadrive engine vibration dampening system and found that we reduced the noise and vibration levels both on deck and in the vessel's interior from 15 to 40 percent. On a voyage of over 1,600 hours of running time, that much of a reduction was very welcome.

The Aquadrive system eliminates the need for stiff, hard mounts and careful engine alignment to the propeller shaft. Instead, the propeller shaft is aligned with a rubber-mounted thrust bearing, which stabilizes the alignment and absorbs all the propeller thrust. A constant velocity joint transmits engine power to the thrust bearing and propeller shaft, which allows the engine to be installed on very soft rubber mounts. The system was so successful in dampening noise and vibration on *Americas Odyssey* that Grand Banks management later made it standard equipment on all Grand Banks over 46 feet (14 m) long.

The system's only disadvantage is its cost, which, including installation, is about $8,000 per engine.

HULL MATERIALS: WHAT'S BEST?

If the initial expense of a boat is a primary consideration, you may be attracted to the bargain-basement prices offered on used boats with wooden hulls, which often are 25 to 35 percent less than a boat of comparable size and age with a hull of a more modern material, such as aluminum or fiberglass. With proper care, wood-hull vessels can function effectively for coastal cruising in cold northern waters. For offshore voyaging or cruising in warm tropical waters, however, I would advise against their purchase. You'll find it extremely difficult, if not impossible, to obtain insurance on a wood-hull boat. If you do find someone to insure it, the premiums will be substantially higher than the cost of insuring a comparable boat with a hull constructed of more durable materials, and the insurer may well insist on a significantly higher deductible and annual surveys. In addition, many yacht financing agencies are reluctant to lend money on a cruiser with a wooden hull. In a wood-hull boat, you also may find you spend more time and money fighting dry rot and wood borers than you do cruising.

You occasionally will encounter full-displacement cruisers with steel hulls. A steel hull may be fine if you plan to venture toward the Arctic Circle and use your boat to bust through ice floes. For the more typical cruiser, however, steel's vulnerability to rust, galvanic corrosion, and electrolysis severely limits its practicality. Most insurance companies will require an audio-gauge survey on a steel-hull vessel before they will write a policy on it. Such a survey can cost upward of $1,000, and the insurer may require a new survey every couple of years. Some people who own and cruise steel-hull displacement vessels argue that the weight of their boats is an advantage. My view is that the weight differential between steel and fiberglass results in an unnecessary expenditure of power—and hence, of fuel—to push a lot of deadweight through the water. Again, I wouldn't recommend it to the average cruiser.

Aluminum is a popular material for building one-off, custom planing yachts since it does not require the construction of an expensive plug and mold before starting to build the hull. Aluminum is only rarely used in displacement cruisers, though from time to time a few custom creations using this material will pop up on the used-boat market. The basic drawback of aluminum, like steel, is its susceptibility to damage from galvanic corrosion and electrolysis. Most of the owners of aluminum-hull yachts employ professional captains well versed in fighting these underwater villains and are not bothered with the problem beyond paying the bills. Aluminum-hull cruising boats also involve insurance difficulties similar to those of steel-hull boats. Aluminum, hence, is not my first choice for the typical owner-operated cruising boat.

By far the most practical hull material for cruising yachts is fiberglass. It is inert and thus is not itself subject to damage from galvanic corrosion and electrolysis (though the shafts, struts, props, and rudders of a fiberglass yacht are). It is relatively inexpensive and easy to maintain and is incredibly tough for its weight. But even fiberglass can be subject to problems, most of which result from poor practices in the layup process.

The major potential problem with fiberglass is damage resulting from osmosis—the physical principle that a fluid will migrate from an area of higher osmotic pressure to an area of lower osmotic pressure. Osmosis causes damage in fiberglass hulls primarily because the builder fails to put down a thick enough layer of gelcoat in the mold before beginning the hull layup process. If that happens, once the boat is launched, the water outside the hull tends to be forced through the relatively porous gelcoat and forms a pocket between the gelcoat and the first layer of laminate. In time, the gelcoat will bulge up and leave the surface of the vessel's bottom pitted with blisters. Ultimately, these blisters rupture, allowing water to reach the fiberglass beneath the gelcoat. The problem can become extremely serious if the woven roving in the underlying laminate was not thoroughly saturated with resin and all the air bubbles squeezed out before the next layer and resin were added. (Builders of less-expensive boats often don't get all the air out because about the only way to do it is to use expensive labor to squeegee the air bubbles out of each layer by hand.) In that case, through a wicking action, the water will actually be sucked into the laminate by the woven roving. The result, over time, is that the water creates voids within the laminate itself, which can seriously weaken the hull's integrity.

The best way for a builder to avoid osmosis is to use a substantial layer of gelcoat (which is expensive) and plenty of resin in the layup process (which also is expensive and adds substantial weight). Another way to retard osmosis is to spray the hull (at least the bottom up to the waterline, and preferably the entire exterior) with a coat of polyurethane or epoxy paint. In addition to reducing the gelcoat's porosity below the waterline, the coating also will counter the gelcoat's tendency above the waterline to chalk and develop hairline cracks, especially under the relentless heat of a tropical sun. Coating a hull with polyurethane or epoxy paint makes a boat more expensive, but it's well worth the added cost in reduced maintenance and added resale value.

One other caution regarding boats with fiberglass hulls: make certain the hull below the waterline is solid fiberglass, not cored with balsa or some synthetic material. Some builders employ cored fiberglass below the waterline to reduce the weight of their boats and thus increase their speed. It is extremely difficult to completely bond fiberglass to coring materials. Once seawater finds a way into the coring material, it will keep coming in until it thoroughly soaks the core material. In my judgment, a boat that has a cored hull below its waterline is far more susceptible to delamination than one with a solid fiberglass hull. (Lawyers, in fact, are still trying to settle damage claims on some boats with cored hulls that delaminated, took on water, and wound up on the bottom.) A hull that is cored from the sheer down to within about 6 inches (15 cm) above the waterline is not objectionable, but I would never buy any boat that employed core material in the underbody itself. Some builders claim they have licked the problem of bonding fiberglass to coring material by curing their hulls in a vacuum. I will not be convinced this process solves the bonding problem until I have seen a number of hulls built this way hold together for at least five years under the punishment the open sea can inflict. Until then, I would not care to be part of the experiment.

ARE STABILIZERS NECESSARY?

Stabilizers are designed to reduce a vessel's tendency to roll under way. These devices come in two varieties: passive or active.

Passive stabilizers employ large booms on both sides of the vessel that can be swung out perpendicular to the vessel's centerline at about a 45-degree angle off the vertical. Adjustable cables run from the end of these booms to fins that trail behind the vessel 10 to 12 feet (3–3.6 m) beneath the water surface, helping to dampen roll. They can also be deployed as "flopper stoppers" at anchor to reduce rolling. Their leading advocate is Jim Leishman, designer of the Nordhavn line of full-displacement cruising vessels.

Active stabilizers employ large, solid fiberglass fins mounted on either side of the vessel's hull at approximately amidships, about halfway between the vessel's keel and its waterline, and project out at about a 45-degree angle. For about a 50-foot (15 m) vessel, these fins normally are 3 feet (1 m) long, 4 feet (1.2 m) high, have an airfoil shape much like an airplane wing, and are about 8 inches (20 cm) wide at their widest point. Close to their nose they have a steel rod (called a *piston*) approximately 2 inches (5 cm) in diameter, which protrudes into the hull through a watertight fitting. The ends of these rods inside the vessel are moved by a hydraulic mechanism powered off a main engine and controlled by a gyrocompass. As the gyrocompass indicates the vessel is rolling to starboard, the hydraulic system actuates the starboard fin to move back and forth, much like a fish's tail. The port fin is inactive. The lifting motion of the actuated starboard fin lifts the vessel toward a level position. As the vessel rolls to port, the reverse sequence returns the vessel to level.

Since active stabilizers depend for their function on the movement of their fins through the water and on the main engine running to power their hydraulics, they have no effect on rolling aboard a vessel at anchor.

As to whether paravane or active stabilizers are preferable, I note only that when Nordhavn sponsored an around-the-world voyage on its 40-footer (12 m), the vessel was equipped with both paravane and active stabilizer systems.

Active stabilizers are extremely expensive—on the order of $16,000 installed on a 40-footer (12 m) and up to $28,000 for a 60-footer (18 m) (see illustration). Many owners of planing hull yachts install them, which is fine if money is no object. I personally don't consider stabilizers essential for that type of vessel. Because of their hard chines and the speeds at which they normally operate, I find the degree of rolling normally experienced in them acceptable.

If you decide to purchase a nonplaning semidisplacement or full-displacement cruiser, however, stabilizers are indispensable to help counter these boats' natural rolling tendency. On *Americas Odyssey*, a semidisplacement yacht that we normally operated at about 9 knots, her Naiad stabilizers countered the effects of waves up to about 8 feet (2.4 m) high and reduced her roll by about 15 degrees either side of the vertical. Even with stabilizers, in extreme conditions you still can find your heart in your throat. On *Americas Odyssey*'s run from Aruba to Panama's San Blas Islands, we encountered following winds of 40 knots and 20-foot (6 m) seas. As long as we kept her stern perpendicular to the oncoming seas, we were fine, though it was like riding the world's largest roller coaster. But on three occasions, her stern was struck at about a 45-degree

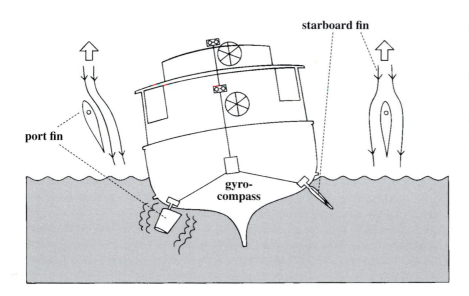

As a vessel equipped with stabilizers begins to roll to port, the system's gyrocompass activates the port fin to bring her back to a horizontal plane. The starboard fin is inactive until the vessel rolls in its direction.

angle by rogue waves. Had we turned to keep her stern squarely to the rogue wave, the prevailing wave would have gotten us. On those three occasions, we were rolled up to 40 degrees off the vertical.

If you have stabilizers installed on a full-displacement cruiser, I suggest you specify pistons and fins one size larger than the manufacturer recommends. Stabilizer manufacturers' recommendations of fin and piston sizes are based on planing hull vessels, and full-displacement vessels simply don't move water past the fins fast enough to achieve optimum efficiency.

By now, you should be getting a pretty good idea of how much boat you really need; whether you will be better off with a planing, semidisplacement, or full-displacement hull; the number and size of the boat's engines and whether they will be naturally aspirated or turbocharged; your preferred hull material; and whether the boat will require stabilizers. Next, we consider what to look for in a functional layout.

Selecting a
Functional Layout

I hope you'll have the luxury of spending weeks at a time aboard whatever cruising vessel you decide to purchase—perhaps even months or years. During that time, through fair weather and foul, this boat is going to be your floating home, complete with a patio and a swimming pool literally as big as the ocean. You're going to have to live with the choices you make for a long time, so approach the selection of the exterior and interior layout with the same degree of care you would give to selecting your home onshore.

MAIN DECK LAYOUT

The main deck of a cruising boat serves two primary functions: it provides a base for your ground tackle, windlass, docking cleats, and safety rails or lifelines; and it provides a surface for you and your crew to walk on safely when you are docking or anchoring the boat (see photos). In addition to these primary functions, it may also provide a place—either on the bow or well aft—for you and

your guests to sit or lounge when the weather is so pretty you don't want to be inside.

Make certain the foredeck of any cruising boat you consider provides a clear, unobstructed area for handling docklines and ground tackle. It should be set up to carry at least one anchor on deck, which is always attached to its rode and can be deployed instantly in an emergency and easily when it comes time to drop the hook for lunch or overnight. That means the boat should have either a bow roller or a bow pulpit. I prefer a bow pulpit because it allows the crew on the foredeck to be positioned directly over the anchor if necessary during setting and retrieval rather than behind it. The bow pulpit should be firmly affixed at the bow or molded into it, should project 3 to 4 feet (1–1.2 m) past the bow, and should accommodate at least one anchor in self-deploying chocks. It would be even better if it accommodated two—one a fluke type for anchoring in hard sand, the other a plow or Bruce style for anchoring in mud or coral (see photo page 28). The pulpit should be capable of supporting at least a 500-pound (227 kg) load in

A functional cruising boat will show such desirable aspects as (A) safety railings with through-bolted stanchions and an intermediate lifeline, (B) walk-around side decks, (C) a roomy cruising cockpit with a transom door and swim plat-form, and (D) interior access to the flying bridge.

A

B

A

C

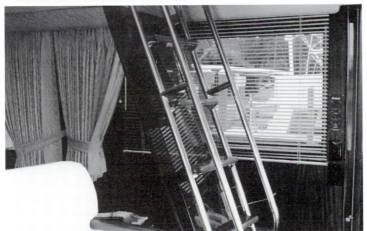

D

case you have to send a couple of crew members out on it to help free a fouled anchor, and the crew members should be securely protected in the process by a sturdy waist-high railing. (For a discussion of ground tackle and anchor-handling equipment, see chapter 10.)

The area just aft of the pulpit should have room to accommodate a hefty power winch. Directly below the mounting area for the winch, a coastal cruiser of 30 to 40 feet (9–12 m) length overall (LOA) should have a locker capable of holding 6 fathoms (36 feet, or 11 m) of ⅜-inch (9.5 mm) chain and at least 200 feet (61 m) of ⅝-inch (16 mm) nylon anchor line. An offshore cruiser should have two lockers: one for handling about 300 feet (92 m) of ⅜-inch chain and a second for holding an equal length of ¾-inch (20 mm) nylon line. The lockers should be accessible through separate deck pipes, and their bottom surface should be V-shaped rather than flat. As rope or chain is fed into a locker with a flat bottom, it tends to pile up in a pyramid. In a heavy sea, it will fall over on it-

self and be tossed about like spaghetti. The result is a god-awful tangle, and you have to crawl into the locker and straighten it out by hand.

Many yachts also incorporate some type of lounge seating on the foredeck. That may be fine on a coastal cruiser, but on an offshore boat I find such arrangements tend not to be very functional. For the offshore cruiser, a much better use of that space—seldom found on planing hull motor yachts but sometimes seen on displacement hull cruisers—is a Portuguese bridge, which allows the crew to go at least part of the way forward in foul weather without danger of being swept overboard.

Most cruising boats provide adequate line-handling space in the bow, but aft is another matter. Many motor yachts today have an aft deck that extends all the way to the stern and is enclosed by a railing, weatherboards, and side curtains or even permanent structures of molded fiberglass and fixed glass panels. The aft cleats on these boats are recessed into the lower corner of these structures and are extremely difficult to reach

A stout bow pulpit that carries a primary anchor ready for instant deployment is a must on a practical cruising powerboat. Even better is this pulpit, which also carries a secondary anchor in the same manner. Deep bulwarks also provide a welcome measure of safety.

NORDHAVN

In foul weather, a Portuguese bridge, as shown on this Nordhavn, allows crew to go on the inner portion of the foredeck in safety.

from inside the aft deck enclosure. An open aft deck that can be enclosed with side curtains in inclement weather provides a natural and valuable gathering place for the children's hour or even meals, but it should not extend all the way to the stern of the vessel. An area just forward of the transom should be reserved for an open space all the way across the width of the boat that is readily accessible from either side of the vessel and is enclosed only by a coaming or railing and a lifeline. Such an area can be on the main deck level, or, even better, it can be a water-level cockpit. This arrangement allows the person handling the docklines to get to the aft cleats on either side of the boat quickly and easily without having to reach over or around weatherboards, roll up side curtains, move furniture around, or open glass windows.

The next thing to check for is a convenient way around the outside of the boat to get between the bow and the stern quickly. That means side decks. In recent years, the manufacturers of cruising

boats have started offering designs that widen the main saloon at the expense of the side decks. I think this is a mistake. If you cruise long enough in a boat without side decks, the day is sure to come when you are trying to dock in a stiff cross-wind or you are trying to fend off a boat whose anchor has dragged and is about to slam into you amidships. You'll be stuck in the saloon powerless to do anything except cuss as you watch your beautiful boat slam into the dock or the offender bear down on you.

The manufacturers of some of these boats try to get partially around the problem by building a ledge along the sheer that is barely wide enough for a mountain goat to negotiate. Side decks don't need to be the width of a sidewalk, but they should be at least 18 inches (0.5 m) wide to allow a person of average build to walk fore and aft easily while both hands are occupied with a coil of line or a spare anchor; you shouldn't have to crab sideways while holding on to a safety rail with one hand.

On an offshore boat, the walk-around areas should also integrate significant bulwarks at the sheer—preferably 4 to 6 inches (10–15 cm) deep from stern to amidships and gradually rising to 8 inches (20 cm) or more at the bow. Many cruising boats provide only a teak toe or a caprail at the sheer. Again, if you cruise long enough, the time will come when you or a crew member has to go on deck in a stiff blow. One slip on a wet deck and that person can shoot right over such an insignificant rail and below the lower lifeline to plunge overboard. Even if the person is wearing a safety harness, the situation can be hazardous and potentially life threatening.

The deck of a cruising boat should be entirely encircled by a stout safety railing of teak, stainless steel, or aluminum, and the railing's stanchions should be through-bolted to backing plates. Stanchions that are simply screwed into the deck could well give way if a crew member is thrown against them in a heavy sea. The top of this railing should strike a person of average height at the waist or higher. If it is lower, the body's center of gravity will be above it. If the boat rolls heavily in the crew member's direction and the body is slammed into it, that person would stand a better than fair chance of being pitched over the railing into the sea.

The area between the top of the rail and the deck should be transected by a lifeline or two, most often a stainless steel cable encased in plastic that passes either through holes drilled in the stanchions or through pass-throughs welded to the inside of the stanchions. Again, anyone who must go on deck in a blow and slips on a wet deck has a much better chance of grabbing onto something if there are both a railing and a lifeline rather than a single railing. The railing port and starboard should also have boarding gates as well as lifelines. One end of the gate should be permanently affixed to one stanchion with a hinge or welded chain link, and the opening end should be secured firmly to the next stanchion with a stout bolt lock or a pelican hook.

The deck should have hefty cleats on each side to accommodate docklines at the bow and stern and spring lines amidships. Cruising boats over about 40 feet (12 m) LOA should have two spring cleats on each side that divide the hull length into about thirds. All deck cleats should be through-bolted to stainless steel backing plates, and the sheer of the boat outboard of them should be protected with a rub or chafe plate. The horns of the cleats should be at least 6 inches (15 cm) long, and there should be a minimum of 4 inches (10 cm) between the bottom of the horn and the top of the base to accommodate docklines up to ¾ inch (20 mm) in diameter. A nice touch offered by some higher-quality cruising boat manufacturers is the added fittings on a sliding track just below the sheer, which allow dockside fenders to be placed wherever they are needed. All horizontal surfaces of the deck should be covered with nonskid material to provide secure footing. Teak decks and cockpit soles are beautiful, but they are difficult to keep looking good. Over time, they tend to crack and buckle, and under a tropical sun they get hot as the devil.

CRUISING COCKPITS

To get maximum use out of every inch of space, the designers of many cruising motor yachts run an aft master stateroom right to the stern of their boats, then top it with a fully or partly enclosed aft deck. With this arrangement, access to the water at anchor for swimming, diving, or boarding the tender involves walking backward down a narrow ladder and perching on a swim platform. A much more practical arrangement is a water-level cruising cockpit incorporating a transom door that leads directly onto a platform (see photo). With this arrangement, boarding and loading and unloading the tender, especially in rough weather, is far easier. A cruising cockpit also solves the problem of adequate line-handling space aft and provides an ideal way to leave and reboard the boat for swimming and diving. If properly organized, it also can offer a handy place to store diving, snorkeling, and fishing

A roomy cockpit or aft deck close to the water, along with a transom door and swim platform, greatly simplifies boarding and exiting a vessel at anchor.

equipment without dragging it through the interior of the vessel. For safety, the cockpit of a cruising vessel should be enclosed by a coaming that is at least waist high, not the type of low coaming found on sportfishing boats, which strikes a person of average height about midthigh.

UPPER DECK LAYOUT

A good cruising boat will have a flying bridge as the primary station from which it will be helmed in fair weather (see photo). For safety in rough seas, you should be able to reach the bridge by a protected ladder from the pilothouse rather than having to go on deck. A bimini top for the flying

bridge is a virtual necessity for providing shade in the tropics (especially considering the connection between the sun and skin cancer), but you should be able to fold it down easily to secure it in high winds. On a full-displacement-hull boat, I recommend you stay away from elaborate flying bridge enclosures. They create a significant wind resistance at the worst possible point—high above the vessel's center of gravity—which contributes to the natural tendency to roll. Flying bridge enclosures are necessary only in foul weather, and under those conditions you probably will be commanding the vessel from its lower steering station anyway.

Check the flying bridge for good visibility forward and to each side. For docking, other than stepping around a companion chair next to the

The flying bridge of a cruising powerboat should provide generous space in its console for installing navigation and communications electronics and a comfortable seating arrangement for the helmsperson and at least one companion.

helm chair, you should be able to move quickly to either side and look down on your vessel's sheer without having to climb over or move anything. Also, make sure the console provides enough space to accommodate a full array of engine instruments, compass, and navigation and communications electronics. At the very least, you will need room to mount a depth-sounder repeater (or, as you will see in chapter 8, maybe even two) and a VHF (very high frequency) radio convenient to the helm. Many cruisers also like to install a radar screen and single-sideband radio or satellite telephone topside as a backup to their main units in the pilothouse. It would be nice if the flying bridge console also provided a reasonable area on which to spread a chart, but few builders plan for that amenity.

Seating for the helmsperson should be an adjustable pedestal chair rather than a bench seat, which usually will not allow adequate visibility or comfortable access to the steering wheel and controls. It's also nice if there is room to install a companion chair next to the helm chair. On long passages, you'll be grateful for a little company.

On many cruising boats, the flying bridge or the cabintop just aft of it is also used as an additional outside lounging area and tender storage area. As long as it does not interfere with the helmsperson's visibility, lounging space topside is a plus. For reasons I go into in chapter 11, I don't think the cabintop is an ideal place to store a cruising vessel's tender.

The upper deck level of a cruising yacht also should support a sturdy mast, which provides secure mounting for a radar antenna, lightning protection, and halyards for (as described in chapter 37) hoisting a courtesy flag of the nations whose waters you cruise and the quarantine flag you will be required to fly when entering a foreign port (see photo). The arch seen on some motor yachts is a good place to mount a radar antenna, but an arch alone normally won't allow the installation of a lightning rod high enough to provide an adequate zone of protection. It also doesn't give you any place to attach flag halyards.

INTERIOR LAYOUT

A current trend in the interior layouts of cruising yachts is to create a lower helm station that is little more than a bench seat in the forward part of the main saloon or in one of its forward corners. The theory behind the design is that the helmsper-

An offshore powerboat should have a stout mast for carrying its radar antenna. It also should allow the installation of halyards for hoisting a quarantine flag when entering foreign ports and a courtesy flag once clearance has been completed.

son, who usually is also the boat's owner, doesn't want to be separated from his guests while the vessel is under way. That may be fine if the boat will be used only for inshore day cruises, but it's a mistake in an offshore cruising boat. There are several reasons the offshore cruiser should have a separate pilothouse that can be closed off from the other interior areas of the boat.

First, commanding a cruising vessel at sea is a job that should have the helmsperson's primary attention. The helmsperson should be able to operate in a relatively private area, not in the main saloon subject to distraction by extraneous activities. It's fine for crew and guests to visit the pilothouse and keep the helmsperson company while the vessel is under way, but a separate pilothouse communicates that it is the vessel's command center and that the vessel's safe operation takes first priority. Second, a separate pilothouse also provides a necessary area where the charts, binoculars, compass, protractor, and parallel rules required for the vessel's navigation can be kept instantly within the helmsperson's reach, not scattered about the saloon because someone set them aside to make room for a tray of hors d'oeuvres. Finally, a separate pilothouse can be properly darkened on night runs to preserve the helmsperson's vision while the life of the vessel goes on in a fully lighted saloon. Make no mistake: in offshore cruising, night runs become a way of life.

A well-thought-out pilothouse offers good visibility to each side and forward. Visibility aft is not so important because docking normally should be done from the flying bridge. The pilothouse's console also should provide generous space for navigational and communications electronics as well as for full-sized charts to be used and stored unfolded.

The pilothouse should offer space for a comfortable helm chair directly behind the wheel, and I've seen some rather interesting approaches. In Frank and Lee Glindmeier's 48-foot (14.6 m) *Summer Wind*, for example, the dinette was immediately aft and to port of the pilothouse wheel and the passageway up from the galley was to star-

board. The space between the wheel and a cabinet directly behind it was so narrow that installing a permanent helm seat would have made it impossible for them to reach the dinette from the passageway. For most of the trip, the lack of a pilothouse helm seat was no problem, as the couple normally operated the vessel from the flying bridge. However, for the long run up and down the Inside Passage to Alaska and back, where cold, damp weather is the norm, they installed in the pilothouse sole just behind the wheel a socket to accept the pedestal-mounted helm seat on the flying bridge. In good weather, the socket was sealed with a screw-in cover to keep it flush with the sole. In bad weather, they brought the flying-bridge helm seat down to the pilothouse, installed it in the socket, and settled in to run the boat in sheltered, heated comfort.

Another cruising friend's motor yacht had not a pilothouse but simply a lower steering station at the forward end of the main saloon. For conversing with his guests at anchor or the dock, he wanted a chair at normal seating height that faced aft. His solution was to install a barber's chair behind the lower helm, which he could pivot in either direction and raise or lower with a few strokes on its hydraulic foot pump.

The pilothouse also should provide seating for people visiting the helmsperson while the vessel is under way. Some builders provide this seating by putting the dining area in the pilothouse. A number of people whose boats are arranged this way think it's fine. I find it rather cumbersome because it makes serving meals from the galley awkward and demotes the pilothouse from its function as a separate area of the vessel. To me, if space permits, a better approach is a companion chair next to the helm chair or a raised bench against the pilothouse's aft bulkhead.

You'll find it far more convenient if the pilothouse, the main saloon, and the galley are on a single level. Some cruising boat designs incorporate a pilothouse whose sole is raised above the rest of the main deck level. You'll find that after months of cruising, going up and down even three or four steps every time you enter and leave the pilothouse becomes something of a hassle.

A troubling trend among cruising yacht builders is to produce an open, airy feeling by designing saloons with expansive areas of glass on both the sides and the aft. If these boats ever take a breaking wave over the side rails or stern, those windows could easily be smashed in and the boat flooded with thousands of gallons of water. The danger is especially acute in the so-called wide-body motor yachts, whose windows are not protected by a side-deck overhang and whose saloons run all the way to the stern of the vessel. These boats may be fine for cruising protected waters, but I would not buy one for bluewater cruising. If you're considering a boat with that kind of exposure, make certain its windows are of tempered safety glass or, better still, of a Lexan-type plastic material. If you are planning to take the boat offshore, you would be wise to carry stout shutters of Lexan or plywood that could be quickly and easily secured to the outside of the windows in a blow. However, the only people I've ever known to carry them are deepwater sailors, who have an appreciation for the damage several hundred thousand gallons of seawater slamming down on a vessel at freight-train speeds can inflict.

I'd suggest you look for a boat with its galley on the main deck level rather than below decks (see photo). This arrangement allows the cook to be involved with guests during meal preparation and makes getting food to the dining area easier.

BELOW-DECKS ACCOMMODATIONS

The decisions you make regarding the number of staterooms you need will largely determine what you look for in the arrangement of sleeping accommodations. Just make certain all bunks are large enough for a grown person to stretch out in comfort and that at least one is a good sea berth, where the off watch can get a decent night's rest without being thrown on the cabin sole.

A galley equipped with all the amenities and placed reasonably close to the dining area greatly simplifies preparing and serving meals.

Check the heads carefully for sufficient operating room. In extended cruising, you'll find stall showers a great blessing. There are few more unpleasant experiences in cruising than having to pull a cold, clammy curtain around you in order to take a shower without inundating the entire head—which you usually wind up doing anyway.

To provide the owners a valuable degree of privacy, the owner's stateroom and head should be in a separate suite aft rather than forward with the guest or crew accommodations. Aboard *Americas Odyssey*, we frequently had as many as four guests aboard for a week at a time. My wife, Anne, found that our stateroom aft was her salvation. "If I got a little rattled by all the activity aboard," she said, "I could spend a couple of hours down there by myself and be ready to handle whatever happened."

In some otherwise well-thought-out, well-constructed cruising vessels, the owner's stateroom is located in the bow, which is the area of the hull most subject to motion both under way and at anchor. Think long and hard before buying a vessel with an owner's stateroom in that location. On an extended offshore passage in anything other than a flat calm, there is no way the off watch is going to get proper rest in such a berth. As the bow falls off a wave, the person will be lifted off the bunk and then slammed back down on it as the bow lifts to meet the next wave.

ENGINE ROOM LAYOUT

In chapter 3, we get into the details of the specific systems you want your engine room to house;

here, we're looking only for a good layout. Your major concern should be accessibility both to the engine room itself and to the main pieces of equipment in it.

If at all possible, select a boat whose engine space has standing headroom and is entered by a bulkhead passageway below decks rather than by a hatch in the saloon sole. This arrangement can be difficult to find in cruising boats under 50 feet (15 m), but you normally will be in and out of the engine space at least twice a day, even at anchor or at the dock, and every couple of hours or so when you are under way. After weeks or months of moving furniture aside, lifting up a hatch, and then crawling around on your hands and knees several times a day, you will be willing to sell one of your children to raise the money for a boat with an engine space that has a walk-in entrance and standing headroom.

Look for a boat with engine space that provides easy access to all sides of the power plants, generators, stuffing boxes, and batteries, especially for routine operations like checking oil and water levels, which you will be doing at least once a day. It also should be well lighted and have explosion-proof fixtures and space for any accessory equipment you might want to add. It should be sufficiently insulated for sound from the boat's living spaces. The most effective soundproofing uses a material with a lead backing.

Once you have a good idea of the type of layout that is best suited to your particular cruising needs, the next thing to figure out is what basic systems you need to make your boat a comfortable floating home.

Choosing the Right Basic Systems

As with layout, you are going to be living every day with the basic systems built into your cruising boat to handle such necessary functions as generating and distributing electricity, keeping you cool when it's hot and warm when it's not, preserving and preparing food, handling water and waste, and—most important—keeping you safe. Once you've purchased a vessel, it can be impractical and expensive—in some cases, virtually impossible—to correct deficiencies, so you want to select wisely at the outset. Here are some things to look for.

FIRE-EXTINGUISHING SYSTEMS

I would not go to sea in a cruising vessel whose engine room was not protected by an automatic fire-extinguishing system (see photos). These devices are cheap compared to the lives and property they protect, and you'll probably recoup some of their cost through lower insurance premiums. If a vessel you consider doesn't have such a system in-

stalled, you can add it later, but if one is installed, it should meet certain minimum requirements. The best systems are those that use FE-241 as a fire suppressant. The heat sensors that activate the system should be mounted just above and at the aft end of the engines and secured to a permanent bulkhead, not to a removable hatch or door that might be blown away in an explosion. The system should sound an alarm in the pilothouse and on the flying bridge and should also be equipped with remote discharge levers at both locations. Its activation should automatically shut down the vessel's electrical system and the fuel and air supplies to its engines and generators. For reasons we'll discuss in chapter 12, the engine room should also be equipped with a transparent, heat-resistant port through which you can see what is going on without having to open the door or hatch. Once you're sure a fire is out, you should be able to manually override an automatic shutdown system to restart an undamaged engine. In a tight situation, you could need power to maneuver or reach shore.

Every cruising powerboat should have a properly installed automatic fire-extinguishing system in its engine room (left) that also can be manually activated by an above-decks discharge lever (right).

ALARM SYSTEMS

At the very least, any cruising vessel you consider should have an audible alarm both at the lower steering station and on the flying bridge to alert you when the bilge pumps are working excessively, which could mean the bilge is taking on water. It also would be nice if the boat has alarms to warn of a drop in engine oil pressure or a rise in the temperature of the engine cooling water, transmission drive oil, or exhaust gases. Some yacht manufacturers offer a comprehensive monitoring system that contains these alarms and also warns if

the engine room fire extinguisher discharges or you lose AC (alternating current) power from your generator or shore lines (see photo next page).

STEERING SYSTEMS

The steering systems of most cruising vessels over about 40 feet (12 m) built since 1980 or so are powered by hydraulic systems run off a main engine. On older boats, you might find nonpowered mechanical steering systems that use either stainless steel cables or a chain-and-sprocket arrangement.

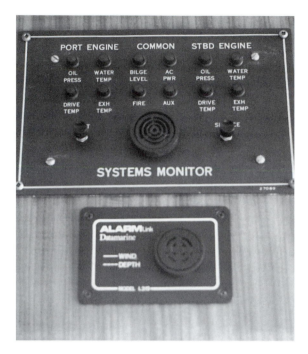

A good alarm system will not only alert the helmsperson to a problem but also quickly identify it and pinpoint its location.

If at all possible, opt for a boat with hydraulic rather than mechanical steering. When the vessel is steered manually, hydraulic steering is far less tiring. It also is easier to fit with a good autopilot.

ENGINE SYNCHRONIZER SYSTEMS

On twin-screw vessels, engines that are not in sync are not fuel efficient. The electronic rpm (revolutions per minute) gauges found on most vessels are prone to frequent interruptions and aren't particularly accurate even when they are working. The digital type are much more reliable. Mechanical rpm gauges are best, but the characteristics of their installation pretty well limit them to the engine room. Some skippers claim they can synchronize twin engines simply by their sound, but I'll wager that if you put accurate tachometers on a pair of engines set by the best of them, you'd find they still vary by 100 rpm or so. Engine synchronizers that match the rpm of the two power plants are not absolutely necessary, but they are helpful. Computerized diesel engines are self-synchronizing.

ELECTRICAL SYSTEMS

Whether or not your vessel will have a 120/240-volt AC electrical generator on board, the first thing you need is a good battery-powered DC (direct current) system. Yacht manufacturers build cruising boats with 12-, 24-, or 32-volt DC electrical systems. In understanding the differences between them, bear in mind that the higher the voltage, the more amps a DC system can push a greater distance through smaller-diameter wire with less voltage drop.

On that basis, a 32-volt system would appear to be preferable, but little of the accessory equipment found on recreational vessels is available in that rather odd voltage. The system originally entered the recreational marine industry because for years Detroit Diesel offered its larger engines only with 32-volt starting motors. Detroit Diesel now offers its larger engines with 24-volt starting motors, and most major yacht manufacturers are abandoning 32-volt systems in favor of the 24-volt alternative. The 12-volt systems are a spillover from the automotive industry. They are still used in most boats under about 50 feet (15 m) because the wiring runs on smaller vessels are not long enough to make voltage drop a serious concern.

The best choice for a DC electrical system aboard a cruising vessel over 50 feet (15 m) is 24 volts. Many of the navigation and communications electronics you will want aboard your vessel are available in that voltage. For installing equipment that is available only in 12 volts, use a small, individual 24- to 12-volt power converter for each unit rather than a single, larger unit so that a failure will not mean complete loss of your 12-volt gear.

Whatever the voltage of the DC system aboard

any vessel you consider, make certain the batteries are easy to reach and service. You'll be checking them frequently, and you don't want to have to stand on your head to top them off with water. Also, make certain they are well secured, have a meter to indicate condition (preferably as part of a DC distribution panel in the pilothouse), and are equipped with an explosion-proof switch that allows you to select the bank of batteries you want to activate.

Most yacht builders install batteries as low as possible in the engine room to help lower the vessel's center of gravity. In that location, they probably will be quickly shorted out if the vessel takes on water, and an engine room fire is likely to melt battery cables in minutes. For those reasons, I'm a strong advocate of installing an extra battery as high in the vessel as possible—under the pilothouse or flying bridge console, for instance—which in an emergency can be used to power essential communications and navigation electronics. One of the gel-cell batteries, which can't leak even if its case is ruptured, would be ideal for such an installation. It's a fairly simple matter to rig such a battery with a small voltage-regulated trickle charger to keep it up to its full-rated amps, a gauge to monitor its condition, and a switch to throw the vessel's electronics load over to it in an emergency.

Batteries-Only Cruising Systems

Like hundreds of other cruisers, Charlie and Nancy Bowen find on their cruises from Florida to Grenada and back that it's possible to cruise extensively and comfortably on a vessel that does not have a 120/240-volt AC generator but operates entirely on batteries—normally 12-volt. Under way aboard the couple's 42-footer (13 m), the batteries are kept charged by a 12-volt generator or alternator driven by a belt off the main-engine flywheel. At the dock, they can be fed by a battery charger that transforms 120-volt dockside current to 12 volts and converts AC to DC. If you go that route, carry along at least one spare generator or alternator and a couple of extra voltage regulators and know how to install and test them; be certain you have two banks of batteries so you will always have a fresh battery to start your main engine; and be very careful to keep the battery switch set in the proper position.

With a batteries-only electrical system, you will not have sufficient voltage for an electric range and oven and will need to use either liquefied petroleum gas (LPG) or compressed natural gas (CNG) for cooking. CNG is the safer of the two because it is lighter than air and, in the event of a leak, tends to rise and dissipate into the atmosphere. LPG is heavier than air and can settle in your vessel's bilge, where it could be ignited by an electrical or a static spark. CNG might be a good choice if you will be cruising well-populated areas and are willing to go searching for a source to refill your tank—which may be hard to locate. For cruising remote areas, LPG is the better way to go because in the boondocks it's almost impossible to find CNG. If you use LPG, however, you must take proper precautions. To avoid its dangers, install your LPG tank in its own well-ventilated locker on deck and equip it and any appliances it will serve with a switch that closes a valve on the tank itself when the appliance is not in use.

With battery power alone, you also will not have sufficient power for electrical refrigeration unless you run your main engine almost constantly. A better approach is to use a mechanical-holding-plate refrigeration system (addressed in more detail later in this chapter), whose compressor is driven by a belt off the main-engine flywheel rather than by DC current through the batteries.

You also won't be able to have an electric water heater on board when operating only with battery power. The units that use the heat in the main engine's cooling system through a heat exchanger work well but require rather adroit scheduling to ensure that all aboard get a hot shower.

Electrical Generator Systems

For those of us who want to take all our creature comforts with us when we go cruising, an onboard AC generator is a must. It's best to stick with the top names in the field, such as Onan, Koher, Alaska Diesel (manufacturer of the Northern Lights brand), and Westerbeke. Lesser known products may be cheaper but may also lack an adequate service network. The generators normally used on cruising vessels range in capacity from around 4 to 20 kilowatts), and you need to size the unit you select carefully. Obviously, a generator with too little capacity will not give you adequate power. But installing one with capacity well in excess of the load you will put on it is needlessly expensive and can create problems as well. Generators operate most efficiently when loaded to about 80 percent of their rated capacity. If they are run consistently with significantly less load, their windings tend to burn out quickly.

To size a generator for your vessel, add up the greatest load you are likely to put on it at any one time; then add a 20 percent margin and select a unit of appropriate kilowatt output. Wonderful as generators are, they can be the bane of the cruiser's existence. In hard cruising use, you will be lucky to get thirty days' straight running out of your generator without having some kind of problem. Most of the difficulties occur not in the generator's basic windings or engine but in its electronic controls, such as relays and printed circuit boards, which fall victim to heat and vibration. "Installing a relay on a generator," an exasperated cruiser once told me, "is like installing it on a paint-mixing machine at the hardware store." He said the best way he had found to keep relays from being vibrated out of position was to seal the screws that attach them in place with epoxy glue.

For these reasons, you'd be wise to carry not one but two generators so you will have a backup unit to maintain essential loads when your main unit is not operating well. To keep costs manageable, the backup unit can have about half the kilowatt output of your main unit. You'll have to do a little juggling to keep the loads within its limits, but that's better than being completely without a generator until you reach the next major port, where you can get your main unit back in action. Even with a backup

unit, carry extra relays and circuit boards in your spare parts inventory (see appendix 5 for a list of spares you should have on board).

A properly installed generator will be cooled by freshwater circulating inside a salt-water-cooled heat exchanger (but be sure the heat exchanger is made of copper or copper-nickel alloy, not cast iron). The saltwater intake should be equipped with a raw-water strainer, while the generator itself should have a water-lift muffler and an hour meter. Its engine also should be fitted with a fuel filter. You should be able to start and shut down the generator remotely from the main saloon or pilothouse electrical panel, which has a positive-lock switch that makes it impossible for the vessel to receive shore power and generator power—or the output from two generators—at the same time (see photo). Electric fuel-priming and oil-changing systems on a generator are nice but not essential. Optional sound boxes do help muffle the noise a generator makes, but a number of cruisers I know wind up removing them and leaving them ashore because they can make servicing the unit unduly difficult. Any vessel you consider that will carry a generator should allow you to install it where you can get to all sides of it for service easily, especially for checking its oil and water levels, which you need to do daily.

Many of us who love generators for the onboard amenities they provide also detest having their droning racket spoil the quiet of a peaceful anchorage. When I visited Carleton Mitchell aboard his 48-foot (14.6 m) *Coyaba*, he showed me how to have the best of both worlds by installing a good electric holding-plate refrigeration system and using LPG gas for cooking. "I can operate all the boat's electrical equipment and keep the batteries charged," he told me, "by running the generator only an hour each morning and night."

With such an arrangement, it also is helpful to install an inverter that, within limits, will allow you to operate small 120-volt AC appliances off 12- or 24-volt DC battery power when the generator is not running. About the only thing this setup

A well-designed electrical panel will allow all of a cruising vessel's electrical systems to operate on shore power, the vessel's own generator, or battery power, as circumstances require.

will not allow you to do is run your vessel's electrically powered heating and air conditioning system at anchor. For that, you'll still have to crank up the generator.

Shore-Power Inlet Systems

To accommodate safely the variety of docking situations you're likely to encounter in offshore cruising, the vessel you choose should have at least one adequately sized 120/140-volt shore-power inlet on both its port and its starboard side. It is even better if it has one set of inlets on either side forward and another set on either side aft, preferably in the cruising cockpit. If your vessel has only a single inlet and you must run a power cord across a foredeck or along a side deck to reach it, you could be issuing an open invitation to an accident.

Another handy device your shore-power system should include is a two-winding polarizing transformer, which eliminates any possible damage from reverse polarity of the shoreside power supply. Within limits, it also allows you to operate 240-volt onboard equipment even though only a 120-volt power supply is available at the dock. Again within limits, in situations where only 240-volt shoreside power is available, it also allows you to split it and operate 120-volt onboard equipment off either of its two hot wires and ground.

Electrical Wiring Systems

The way electrical wiring is installed in a cruising vessel is a dead giveaway to the quality of its construction (see photo next page). If you encounter a vessel whose wiring looks like a pile of multicolored spaghetti, pass it by in favor of one whose wiring looks like it belongs in a space shuttle.

Under real-life conditions on the water, even the toughest-built cruising boat is subjected to enormous straining and flexing, which can chafe through improperly installed electrical wiring and create a significant fire hazard. In a well-laid-out electrical system, all circuits will be color coded and numbered and the owner's manual will contain a detailed wiring schematic. All wiring bundles should be strapped with nonconductive bands every 18 inches (45 cm) and secured to a bulk-

One obvious hallmark of a well-built cruising vessel is a neat electrical installation in which all wiring is color coded, tightly secured to the bulkheads, and protected from chafe.

head at least every 36 inches (1 m) by a nonconductive or insulated fastener. At every point where a wiring bundle passes through a bulkhead, it should be protected by a heavy rubber collar and cushioning to prevent chafe.

To protect the vessel's electrical wiring and equipment from electrolysis, all metal masses from the engine blocks to the hull fittings should be securely bonded together by at least #8 solid copper wire or 2-inch (50 mm) copper strapping that is connected to a heavy copper groundplate installed outside the hull.

The electrical system of any vessel that has an aluminum hull or any aluminum parts below the waterline also should be equipped with an isolation transformer, which accepts power from shore through wires, then transfers it to the vessel's AC system magnetically, thus protecting those on

board from electric shock. For more information, the most comprehensive works on marine electrical systems are *Your Boat's Electrical System,* by Conrad Miller and E. S. Maloney, and *Boatowner's Mechanical and Electrical Manual,* by Nigel Calder (see resources appendix).

Through-Hull Fittings

All underwater through-hull fittings should be of such "noble" metals as brass, bronze, or stainless steel—never plastic—and should be protected by a seacock.

Heating and Air Conditioning Systems

The most practical heating and air conditioning system for cruising is a good water-source reverse-cycle unit, which extracts heat from seawater flowing through it (onshore, it's often called a *heat pump*). You can't determine if an installation aboard a vessel you're considering is adequately sized without doing a complex heat-loss calculation, so you'll have to trust the builder to provide adequate capacity. But do check that its distribution fans deliver an adequate volume of air to each area of the boat. The best of these installations will have separate compressors serving the main saloon, pilothouse, and sleeping accommodations and will provide each stateroom with its own thermostat and fan control.

Water Systems

If your cruising plans include an extensive foray into the saltwater boondocks, obtaining adequate supplies of potable water can be a major headache, especially during the dry season in such areas as the Bahamas, the Virgin Islands, and Mexico's Baja Peninsula. If you do find an adequate supply, it is likely to be expensive. In those areas, I've paid as much as a nickel a gallon (4 L) for water, then found it had all manner of little squiggly things swimming around in it. Even worse are the invisible bacteria and viruses some water contains. They can cause a disconcerting case of the yucky tummy, which can become serious if it leads to dehydration.

If you plan to rely on whatever water you can carry on board, your vessel should have a capacity of at least 300 gallons (1,135 L). Even then, if you have only two to four adults aboard and are careful with water use, you probably will be looking for a place to replenish your supply every week to ten days. If you go that route and will be cruising areas where the quality of the water can be dubious, you can avoid at least some of the potential health problems by installing a kitchen-type filter on your galley faucet, then drawing water for drinking and cooking only from there. These filters are inexpensive and are available at larger hardware stores and home improvement centers. An even better approach would be to install a larger, commercial charcoal filter in the line leading to that faucet from your water storage tank.

Another way you can help prevent illness is by sanitizing your water supply with a product called Aqua-Tabs. Use one megatab per 100 gallons (380 L) of water each time you fill your tanks. The tab effervesces and produces a slightly chlorine taste, which will disappear in a day or two. Over time, water tanks can build up scale and deposits, which are a breeding ground for coliform bacteria and protozoa that can cause dysentery and a waterborne parasite called *Giardia*. To keep your tanks clean, about once a year you should fill them, add a product called Puriclean (142 oz. per 600 gal. of water, or 3.545 kg per 2,000 L), make a brief run so it can slosh around for several hours, drain the tanks (letting part of the water run through your vessel's plumbing system and faucets), refill the tanks with clean water, and pump that water out as a rinse before you take aboard your next supply.

The best way to make sure you have plenty of germ-free potable water is to install a water maker that turns salt water into fresh. The units now on the market reduce salt and other contaminants from the 36,000 parts per million (ppm) typically found in seawater to around 500 ppm, well below the 1,500 ppm standard for drinking water established by major health organizations.

A water maker's advantages are not limited to making certain the water consumed on board won't give you and your guests a case of Montezuma's revenge. It also will free you from having to plan your cruise around stops where you can refill your tanks. By eliminating the need for carrying the tremendous weight of several hundred gallons of water, it can also increase your vessel's range and fuel efficiency. Some cruisers who install water makers aboard their vessels convert unneeded water tanks to fuel tanks, but that can be a risky practice because they aren't really designed for the purpose. Installing a water maker also allows you to consider adding such high-water-use appliances as a clothes washer (the stacked apartment-type washer-dryer units are compact and work well) and a dishwasher, which are really not practical to carry if you must rely on the freshwater your vessel can carry.

If you want to add a water maker to your boat, first consider several things. For a moderately sized cruising vessel, the most practical water makers distill water through a reverse-osmosis process, which forces seawater through a semipermeable membrane to filter out salt ions (see illustration next page). The reverse-osmosis process requires a raw-water pump that delivers a minimum of 800 psi (56 kg/cm^2) of pressure, and most units operate closer to 1,000 psi (70 kg/cm^2). In most systems, the raw-water pump is driven by the vessel's AC generator at 120 or 240 volts, with the higher voltage being the better choice. A typical 300-gallon-a-day (1,135 L) unit draws around 17 amps at 120 volts or 8.5 amps at 240 volts. There are, however, alternatives. Village Marine offers several units that operate off 12- or 24-volt battery power, while Galley Maid offers a pump driven by a separate diesel engine. An ideal water maker installation would drive the pump off the main engine while under way, then allow you to switch over to shore power when tied to a dock or to generator power when you are at anchor.

Water makers come as single-unit cabinet models or as component systems. A typical cabinet unit producing 200 gallons (750 L) a day requires

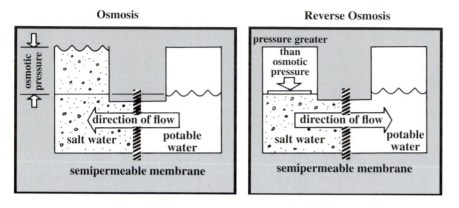

The reverse-osmosis process of making potable water works by forcing salt water through a semipermeable membrane at pressures around 1,000 psi (6,895 kPa).

about 4 cubic feet (0.11 m³) of space and weighs around 110 pounds (50 kg).

Component units allow the membrane to be located outside the engine room (see illustration). This can be a major advantage since manufacturers recommend that membranes not be subjected to 120°F (48.8°C), which can easily be exceeded in an engine room, especially when you are cruising the tropics.

Water maker prices vary widely. One company's 100-gallon-per-day (378 L) unit, for instance, lists at around $2,800, while another's is about $3,800. When comparing prices, look closely at what is included as standard and what is an extra-cost option. Most manufacturers, for example, don't include the raw-water pump, which can add $250 to $300 to your costs. Others charge extra for mounting or installation kits. Also look closely at each system's prefiltration setup. All include a basic raw-water strainer and should include an oil and water separator and a charcoal filter to remove chlorine, which the membrane will not take out. If the latter two accessories aren't part of the basic system, you should add them as extras. I carried a Standard HRO unit aboard *Americas Odyssey* that performed flawlessly, and cruising acquaintances have given me good reports on Sea Recovery and Village Marine water makers.

One necessary feature that is standard on some units but only an option on others is an automatic salinity monitor, which prevents water that has not been adequately purified from being pumped into the storage tank and contaminating freshwater already in the tank. Another worthwhile option (as a health precaution) is an ultraviolet sterilizer. Beware the salesperson who says you don't need a sterilizer because bacteria are larger than salt ions and his unit filters them out. What he says is true, as far as it goes. But you still need the sterilizer to kill viruses, which none of the membranes filters out.

Whether you choose to carry all your freshwater with you or to install a water maker, the vessel you select should have dockside water inlets both port and starboard and they should be fitted with a pressure-regulating valve. Also, check the amount of pressure the onboard pumps can actually deliver to the galley, lavatories, and heads. There also should be a freshwater outlet in the engine room for topping off the engines and generator. One nice touch you'll find useful in the cockpit is a hot and cold freshwater outlet fitted with a handheld showerhead.

Aside from a good freshwater system, it's also helpful if the vessel you buy has a pressure saltwater system with outlets on the foredeck and in the cockpit. The foredeck outlet should provide plenty of pressure to let you blast away mud from the anchor chain before it comes aboard. If mud gets into your chain locker, the microorganisms in it decay and can cause a sickening odor that takes weeks of scrubbing and gallons of disinfectant to dispel.

Waste Management Systems

The laws of most nations now prohibit the discharge of untreated waste into their coastal waters. Even though many nations—including the United States—don't adequately enforce such laws and don't provide enough dockside pump-out stations to make them practical, you should comply with them anyway in the name of protecting the environment. That means that any vessel you consider should have a sewage holding tank for use when you are in coastal waters. It should be plumbed for dockside pumpout and also should be equipped with a macerator pump for overboard discharge when you are well out to sea. Some cruisers fit their vessels' heads and galleys with Y-valves that permit them to discharge waste directly overboard. That may be all right for shower sumps, but operating marine heads that way allows the direct discharge of human solid waste overboard, which is disgusting, not to mention inconsiderate. Any such waste should empty into the holding tank and be run through a macerator before it is discharged—and then only when the vessel is well offshore.

Many cruisers simply dump their trash over the side, but I hope you will keep yours on board until you can properly dispose of it ashore. Be especially careful about properly disposing of the plastic ring holders on beverage six-packs. Seabirds and turtles get tangled in them, and the encounters are almost always fatal. The trash compactor we had aboard *Americas Odyssey* was extremely useful for reducing our solid waste to a more stowable volume.

Cruising Refrigeration Systems

For cruising well off the marina circuit, the household-type refrigerator-freezers on most production yachts are totally unsatisfactory. These units have such skimpy insulation that they require almost constant power input. The "frost-free" type have heaters to dispel frost and condensation, which draw about 2 amps even when the cooling coil's thermostat is not calling for power. Also, the units' freezer sections are too small to hold more than one or two weeks' worth of frozen provisions.

For extended cruising, the most practical approach to refrigeration is to install a holding-plate system that employs a eutectic solution of water-diluted ethylene glycol (the active ingredient in automotive antifreeze). This solution freezes solid at about 0°F (–17.7°C) and absorbs heat much more easily than the Freon gas previously used in household refrigerators. Holding-plate

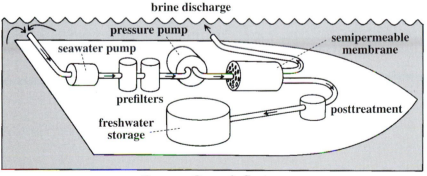

Reverse Osmosis System

A component water maker system allows its heat-sensitive membrane to be installed outside the engine room, where it won't be damaged by excessive heat.

refrigeration compressors can be powered by a variety of sources: 12- or 24-volt DC battery current; 120- or 240-volt AC current from shore power or an onboard generator; your vessel's main engine or engines through a 12-, 24-, or 120-volt alternator or a mechanical clutch; or some combination of these sources. The most desirable holding-plate system would employ two separate compressors: a mechanical unit that operates off the main engine through a clutch arrangement while your vessel is under way, and an electrical unit that operates off 120- or 240-volt shoreside power when the vessel is tied to a dock or off its AC generator when the vessel is at anchor. If a holding-plate system has two compressors, they usually must operate entirely separate eutectic circulating systems because manufacturers have not yet been able to develop a single system in which oil does not migrate between the compressors. Frigiboat, an Italian company, claims to have solved this problem, but I have not yet had an opportunity to see one of its installations in action.

A good holding-plate installation should allow you to keep food frozen solid by operating the compressor only about an hour in the morning and an hour in the evening. To operate the system that way, however, you need to incorporate a switch that allows you to force the compressor to come on when you fire up your vessel's generator. Because of the physical properties of something called the heat of fusion, the thermostat will not call for the compressor to turn on until the eutectic solution is almost entirely melted. Without an override switch, the compressor's on-off cycle would not necessarily coincide with the times you are operating the generator. A good holding-plate installation on a 50- to 60-foot (15–18 m) power yacht won't be cheap. It can easily cost from $4,000 to $6,000.

Some marine refrigeration companies will replace your boat's household-type refrigerator-freezer with an upright unit incorporating holding plates, but most will recommend that you go to a horizontal cabinet with a lid in the top. These units make it more difficult to retrieve food, but they don't spill out great quantities of cold air every time they're opened.

The key to an effective holding-plate system is thorough insulation of the freezer cabinet with at least 4 inches (10 cm) of closed-cell polyurethane foam on all sides—including the lid or door. Closed-cell polyurethane insulation is available in slabs that can be cut to fit. Some custom installers feel they get more complete coverage by purchasing polyurethane's chemical ingredients, mixing them on-site, and pouring a slurry into the insulating cavity, which, when it sets, fills all the nooks and crannies. Make certain any installer you deal with who follows this approach is experienced. If the installer gets too little slurry in the cavity, you will have gaps in your insulation coverage; if too much, you can have problems of compressed, ineffective foam and even deformation of the cabinet. If the foam is in direct contact with your vessel's hull, the installation should also include a vapor barrier of heavy plastic between the two to prevent heat absorption and condensation outside the hull. The other critical area is a tight seal on the cabinet's door or lid. If the lid or door on a holding-plate system isn't at least a little difficult to open, its seal probably isn't tight enough. At the minimum, a holding-plate system should have an easily readable thermometer on the outside of the cabinet to allow you to monitor the interior temperature without opening the unit. An even better safeguard is to install a visual or audio alarm that alerts you if the unit's temperature rises anywhere near the freezing point.

Now that you know the size and type of boat you want and what her layout and basic systems should include, you're ready to head for the boat show or the broker's dock, right?

Not quite. First, take time to get a good idea of what it's going to cost you to buy and operate the boat whose outline is beginning to take shape in your mind.

Determining What It's All Going to Cost

Once you've figured out the basic specifications of the cruiser that is best for you, you still have several key questions to answer before you actually initiate your search for the vessel that will fulfill your specifications. First, of course, you need a realistic idea of what it is going to cost you, not only to buy the boat you need and want but also to operate it. Few things can spoil your cruising fun faster than worrying how you are going to pay the bills. The answers you come up with to the money questions may well dictate your answers to two basic questions: will you look for a new or a used boat, and will you consider only vessels built in the United States or will you look at those manufactured abroad?

By this point, you've probably begun to get a pretty good idea of the size and type of boat you want and what its basic systems should incorporate. As we go along, you will develop specific ideas about the accessory equipment you need and will learn how to determine the cost of everything entailed in buying, commissioning, and operating your boat. For now, all we want to do is construct rough buying and operating budgets to help narrow your search and make certain you don't forget any major necessary items. Once you have constructed those preliminary budgets, you can refine them as you progress deeper into the buying process.

BOAT-BUYING BUDGET

Based on the ideas you have already developed about the type and size of boat you need, get an idea of your purchase range by combing through the boating magazines and getting recommendations from any cruising friends you might have. Try to come up with a list of boats that appear to meet your initial criteria.

Budgeting for a New Boat

As you come across appropriate new boats, contact their manufacturers or dealers to assemble all the literature you can, including a price list, so you can begin to construct your boat-buying budget. The prices boatbuilders normally quote for products are simply "base-boat" figures, which usually are just the beginning of what it actually will cost to buy a particular model. As you peruse the price lists, you may be surprised to find that a number of basic items—such as a flying bridge, a bow pulpit, a swim platform, an aft deck enclosure, a generator, and tender davits—that you would expect to be included in the base-boat figure are extra-cost, "factory-installed" options, which easily can increase the base-boat price by 15 to 30 percent or more. You'll have to include the costs of the essential "extras" in order to arrive at a more realistic "factory invoice price." In chapter 6, we discuss in detail how to figure the discount you can expect to negotiate off the factory invoice price, but for your preliminary figures, estimate a 6 to 7 percent markdown. Even after you arrive at that figure, you can be certain a dealer also will charge you for the cost of transporting the boat from the factory to the point of delivery and will add a commissioning fee to cover launching the boat and checking out the basic systems. And don't forget the cost of the initial fueling. Check with several dealers for any boat you are considering to get a rough idea of what those costs will run.

On top of the factory invoice price and minimum dealer charges, you generally can figure you will have another onetime expense of 25 to 35 percent of the base-boat price for outfitting the boat with everything from navigation and communications electronics to a tender with an outboard to lifesaving equipment. Throughout this book, we'll discuss in detail the specifications of the equipment you'll need for safe, comfortable operation of your vessel, but lists of the basic accessories you'll want to include for both a coastal and an offshore cruising powerboat are shown later in this chapter. In addition to these items, don't forget to include the cost of interior furnishings, entertainment gear, and the like. And, remember to take into account all of the miscellaneous items you need, from docklines and fenders to foul-weather gear. Again, check with retailers or marine catalogs for that gear to get some idea of the list prices for the equipment you need and want. At this early stage, figure you probably will be able to buy them on average for about 15 percent off list, including installation, and plug those rough numbers into your budget. By the time you get a new boat rigged and in the water, you probably will wind up actually spending on the order of 30 to 50 percent more than the base-boat price.

NEW-BOAT BUDGET

Factory Charges
    Base-boat price $_____
    Factory-installed options   +_____
    Factory invoice price $_____
Dealer Charges
    Transportation   +_____
    Commissioning   +_____
    Dealer-installed options   +_____
    Dealer list price $_____
    Less discount   −_____

Sales Price $_____
    State sales tax   +_____

Purchase Price $_____

    State registration fee   +_____
    Documentation fees   +_____
    Insurance   +_____
    Additional installed
      accessories:
        navigation and
        communications
        electronics, tender and
        outboard, water maker,
        life raft and safety
        equipment, etc.   +_____
    Miscellaneous expenses   +_____

Actual Cost $_____

Basic Accessories Lists

The following lists apply to both new boats (above) and used boats (below).

COASTAL CRUISER

For a coastal cruiser that won't venture farther than, say, the Bahamas on the East Coast or Catalina on the West, these are the minimum items you'll want.

Safety Equipment
Automatic engine room fire-extinguishing system
Portable fire extinguishers
Coastal life raft
Personal flotation devices (PFDs)
Throwable PFDs
Searchlight
Visual distress signals
Audible signaling devices
Emergency position-indicating radio beacon (EPIRB)
First-aid kit

Navigation Electronics
Global positioning system (GPS) receiver
Electronic chart plotter
Radar
Autopilot
Depth-sounder

Communications Electronics
Installed VHF marine radio and antenna
Handheld VHF marine radio and charger

Ground Tackle
Primary anchor and rode
Secondary anchor and rode
Electric anchor windlass

Miscellaneous Equipment
Tender, outboard motor, battery, and fuel tank
Tender davit system
Spare parts

OFFSHORE CRUISER

For a true bluewater cruiser that will venture far from land, these are the minimum items you'll want aboard.

Safety Equipment
Automatic engine room fire-extinguishing system

Portable fire extinguishers
Offshore life raft
Abandon-ship bag
PFDs
Throwable PFDs
Searchlight
Visual distress signals
Audible signaling devices
EPIRB
First-aid kit
Trauma kit

Navigation Electronics
GPS receiver
Electronic chart plotter
Radar
Autopilot
Depth-sounder

Communications Equipment
Installed VHF marine radio with antenna
Handheld VHF marine radio with charger
Single-sideband marine radio with coupler and antenna

Ground Tackle
Primary anchor and rode
Secondary anchor and rode
Electric anchor windlass

Miscellaneous Equipment
Tender, outboard motor, battery, and fuel tank
Tender davits
Stabilizers (full-displacement-hull or semi-displacement hull vessels only)
Holding-plate refrigeration system
Water maker
Spare parts, including spare shaft(s) and propeller(s)

Budgeting for a Used Boat

If you run across a make and model on the used-boat market that might meet your specifications, begin to construct your preliminary budget by establishing a rough value for a boat about five years old equipped with at least your basic minimum equipment. Ads for boats of that type in the boating magazines are a starting place, though their asking prices often are from 10 to 30 percent higher than what the owner will actually accept.

The most widely used reference in the marine industry on the value of used boats is the *BUC Used Boat Price Guides* (often referred to as the "BUC Books"), which gives the average whole-sale and retail prices of a wide range of used plea-sure boats (see resources appendix). Ask a dealer, broker, marine insurance agent, or banker who deals in yacht financing to let you look through a recent copy and find the average retail figure for the model and year of boat that interests you. But be aware that BUC Book figures are a starting place only, because they are six to eight months out of date by the time they appear in print. In the case of popular boat models, which have a high level of sales activity, BUC Book valuations tend to be reasonably accurate. In the case of little-known boats, for which figures may be based on only two or three sales, the figures can be off the mark.

As another resource, the National Automobile Dealers Association publishes annual editions of the *N.A.D.A. Consumer Marine Appraisal Guide,* which is available through conventional and In-ternet bookstores (see resources appendix).

The actual price of the boat in the area you are shopping can vary by 20 percent or more in either direction. To get closer to actual market values, consult several brokers where you plan to shop and find out their most recent experiences with comparable boat sales.

Once you feel you have an approximate idea of what the boat is worth, assume that you will have to either add to that figure for a newer boat or one that has major extras or subtract from it for an older boat or one that has significant deficiencies. Before buying any used boat, you should have it inspected by a good marine surveyor, and in chap-ter 6, I show you how to determine what that will cost. For now, figure $10 to $12 per foot of boat length ($33–39 per meter), which will include a haulout. For a used boat, the cost of the accessory equipment needed to bring the boat up to your specifications can run anywhere from 5 to 15 per-cent or more of the purchase price, depending on how well equipped the boat is when you take de-livery.

USED-BOAT BUDGET

Asking Price	$_____
Less discount	−_____
Negotiated sales price	$_____
State sales tax	+_____
Purchase price	$_____
Survey fee	+_____
State registration fee	+_____
Documentation fees	+_____
Insurance	+_____
Delivery expense	+_____
Additional required accessories: navigation and communications electronics, tender and outboard, water maker, life raft and safety equipment, etc.	+_____
Miscellaneous expenses	+_____
Actual Cost	$_____

Include the Unavoidables

Whether you are constructing a budget for buy-ing a new or a used boat, you will need to include a number of unavoidable expenditures. We dis-cuss them in greater detail in chapter 6, but right now we're just trying to develop a ballpark figure.

Don't forget the tax man. In some states, you will have to pay a hefty sales tax on your boat's purchase price. As we see later, there may be some situations where you can save money by buying or basing your boat in a state that levies lighter sales or use taxes (or both) on boats.

In addition to taxes, in some states you will have to figure in the cost of numbering or registering your boat. If you will be documenting it (which you do through the federal government), you'll have to add in those costs as well. (We cover the differences among those three procedures at length in chapter 6.)

Check with a couple of marine insurance agents to get a rough idea of what your first year's hull, liability, and medical insurance is going to cost. On a $200,000 boat, for example, insurance can run $2,000 to $3,000 a year or more for full coverage.

You'll also need to figure in the cost of charts, medical supplies, and spare parts, which can add up to a tidy sum.

BUDGETING FOR BOAT OPERATION

Once you have a reasonably good fix on what it is going to cost you to buy the boat you want and to rig her for extended cruising, the next step is to construct an annual operating budget to determine what it will cost to run her.

If you will be borrowing money to pay part of the cost of your boat, check typical boat loan rates and terms and carefully go over an amortization schedule for the amount you plan to borrow to be sure you can cover the payments comfortably. In many situations, loans for boats that have live-aboard amenities can be considered in the category of second-home mortgages, and the interest you pay may be deductible on your federal and state income tax returns. Check your status with a good accountant.

In some states, boats are taxed as personal property, and you could face a heavy outlay every year. You may also have to factor in the cost of annual renewal of your boat's state registration. Add in your annual insurance cost, taking into account that it may increase as you extend your policy's cruising limits.

You generally can figure from about 10 to 15 percent of the boat's purchase price as its annual operating expense for fuel, oil, filters, hauling and bottom painting, repair, routine maintenance, replacing lost or damaged gear, and the other mis-

cellaneous expenses involved in boat ownership, exclusive of insurance and taxes.

ANNUAL BOAT OPERATING BUDGET

Fixed Expenses

Loan principal and interest	$ _____
Less savings on interest deductible from federal and state income taxes	– _____
Property taxes	+ _____
Insurance	+ _____
State registration renewal	+ _____
Subtotal	$ _____

Cruising Expenses

Fuel and oil	$ _____
Hauling and bottom painting	+ _____
Routine maintenance	+ _____
Replace broken or damaged gear	+ _____
Customs fees	+ _____
Dockage	+ _____
Travel expenses	+ _____
Onboard food and beverages	+ _____
Dining out and entertainment	+ _____
Miscellaneous	+ _____
Subtotal	+$ _____

Annual Operating Expense $ _____

If you will be doing extended cruising, your expenses can vary all over the lot depending on your cruising area, your boat's fuel consumption rate, how elaborately you like to live, and whether you will spend most of your cruising nights tied to a dock or swinging on the hook. For food—including dining out—you probably should figure about 15 to 20 percent more than you normally spend at home. Unless you are extremely experienced at fishing or are practiced in the use of a speargun, forget any idea of sharply reducing your food budget by "living off the sea." If you work at it, you may pick up the occasional grouper, amberjack, or lobster, which can provide a welcome addition to the provisions you bring from home or purchase along the way, but don't count on them as staples of your cruising diet. For nonfood items, on average you'll find prices in other countries 10 to 15 percent higher than what you are used to paying in the United States for items of comparable quality—provided you can even find what you want. This is especially true in island communities, where everything must be shipped in.

Also, factor in the cost of traveling to and from your boat between cruises. Even if you will be living aboard during an extended cruise, you might want to include in your operating budget the cost of at least one trip home a year to tend to essential business.

I would say the minimum cost for a couple cruising the Bahamas and the lower Caribbean, exclusive of insurance, taxes, and any shoreside expenses, would be at least $1,500 a month, and $2,000 is probably a more realistic figure.

After you have added up all your operating numbers—plus any expenses you still have to meet at home—the total is about the nut you are going to have to crack every year. If you have the slightest hesitation about being able to handle that figure comfortably, take another look at your previous decisions to see whether you can get along with a less expensive boat.

NEW OR USED?

The figures you come up with in your boat-buying and operating budget probably will play a major role in whether you start your search for the vessel of your dreams on the new-boat or the used-boat market, but they aren't necessarily the only consideration.

Buying a new boat is something like buying a new car—it glitters and sparkles, and you have the pride of knowing you are the first owner. When buying a new boat, you also can set up the electronics and cruising accessories just the way you want. But buying a new boat has its disadvantages as well. First, of course, when buying a new boat you are likely to pay a significantly higher price than you would for the same model with comparable equipment but with a few years of age on it. You also have to go through the involved process of specifying, searching out, and purchasing all the accessory equipment needed for extended cruising and then make certain it is correctly installed. Some yacht owners love the job of detailing exactly what they want in everything from radars and radios to tenders and safety gear. Others consider the process pure drudgery and prefer to buy a boat that is already fully rigged.

In fact, one trend now among some manufacturers is to offer their boats as "sail-away" packages, which include at least what the builder considers the basic equipment and accessories most cruisers would want on board. If you consider one of these packages, even if you are satisfied that the basic boat is the one you want, go over the equipment list carefully to make certain each item meets the specifications you develop after reading this book. In some cases, builders will include the cheapest accessory equipment they can find to keep the overall price of the package low. Also, be aware that the most extensive package is probably going to lack some items—anything from sophisticated electronic equipment to proper safety gear. You will have to purchase these separately and adjust your boat-buying budget accordingly.

If you elect to buy a new boat, also take into account that all the new gear isn't going to work exactly right the moment you flip the switch. You almost certainly will have to "work the bugs out" until you get all the systems operating properly.

You can always find some excellent used boats on the market at prices substantially below what you would pay for the same models brand-new. Also, a number of the most practical cruising boats ever designed (the Hatteras Long Range Cruisers and some models designed by Art Defever and Ed Monk quickly come to mind) are no longer manufactured. To find them, you will have to turn to the used-boat market. A used boat may be a bit tired cosmetically but can still offer an excellent buy for the money. If the boat has been used for two or three years, chances are that any serious defects in her basic systems already will have come to light and have been dealt with, and if her previous owner was a knowledgeable yachtsperson, any glitches will have been worked out. In buying a used boat, you may have to put up with some things the previous owner did that you would have done differently, but you may find you get more boat for the same or less money than buying new. There are some basic things you need to look for in buying a used boat, of course, which we discuss in detail in chapter 6.

DOMESTIC OR IMPORT?

Whether you start out looking for a new boat or a used boat, another basic question is whether you will select a boat built in the United States or one built abroad and imported. If you consider comparable boats, as a general rule you will find few differences in the price and construction quality among boats built in the United States, Canada, and Western Europe.

Most significant differences in price and construction quality among boats of equal size involve vessels built in Asia. Because of the markedly lower wage rates for workers in some Asian countries compared to those in the United States, Canada, and Western Europe, boats built in Singapore, Taiwan, and Hong Kong, and more recently in South Korea, do tend to be somewhat less expensive than those of Western manufacture. Although the gap is narrowing, the prices of these boats have put the cost of buying a fair-sized cruising boat within the reach of people who might not be able to afford a vessel of comparable size built in the United States. In addition, hundreds of people have cruised boats built in Asia for years and love them.

For the most part, the well-known Asian manufacturers have long done a creditable job in fiberglass hull layup, and their interior joinery tends to equal or exceed the best the West can produce. Their propulsion systems have not been much cause for concern because they generally use the same engines and gears as Western manufacturers. But for reasons peculiar to the ways of doing business in Asia, even the most die-hard adherents of Asian-built boats will admit that the electrical and plumbing systems of some manufacturers' boats tend to have problems. For many years, the boatbuilding tradition in Asia was for the primary builder to handle hull and superstructure construction, engine installation, and joinery with its own employees. The boat's plumbing and electrical system were subcontracted to the lowest bidder. As a result, internal systems the buyer could not readily see often were built with the cheapest materials and with slipshod or nonexistent quality control. The electrical systems of some of these yachts built from the 1960s to the late 1970s often were composed of two or three sizes and colors of wire in a single circuit, with the absolute minimum of fusing and circuit protection and with nothing approaching a wiring diagram.

John Matthews, a meticulous cruising friend and electrical engineer from Atlanta, told me a story while I was cruising with him and his wife, Mary, aboard their American-built 42-footer (12.8 m), *Rigel,* from Lucaya to Great Stirrup Cay in the Bahamas. His story illustrates beautifully the potential pitfalls of buying one of these boats. "The first boat I bought was a 36-foot [11 m] displacement boat built in Asia," John said. "I felt it was a good deal as the price was considerably below the cost of an American-built boat of comparable size. The hull was built like a tank, and the propulsion system created no significant problems. But as we began to do extensive cruising, we found that the electrical system required a good deal of rework, as did the plumbing system. We also added a number of additional system components which were not included in the original boat, such as a fire-suppression system and additional bilge pumps. By the time we did all of that, we found we had about as much money tied up in the boat as we would have had in a similar boat built in the United States. Of course, much of the money spent in reworking the boat's systems was lost at the time of resale. When we decided to buy a larger boat, I made up my mind that I would buy an American-built boat, which would not have some of the problems we had previously encountered and would hold its resale value better."

Another potential problem to watch for in boats built in Asia—particularly those built prior to the early 1980s—is deterioration in the decks and superstructure. In many of these boats, the decks and superstructure were made not of solid fiberglass or even cored fiberglass but of poor-grade plywood covered with only a thin veneer of fiberglass. They are subject to extensive rot and delamination, especially in the window, door, and hatch openings, where moisture has been able to penetrate.

In the 1990s, Asian manufacturers consolidated most of their manufacturing processes and have since come a long way in bringing their electrical, plumbing, and superstructure construction standards up to those we are accustomed to in the United States. Even so, if I were to consider buying a used boat built in Asia—particularly if it were built before 1980—I would make doubly certain that it was subjected to a rigorous inspection by a well-qualified marine surveyor.

If I were considering the purchase of a brand-new Asian-built boat, I would stick with a well-known manufacturer and make certain I was working with a reputable, established dealer who would stand behind his product. The potential problems with buying one of these boats were vividly brought home to me when a yard manager showed me a 44-footer (13 m) barely a year old that he had hauled for a buyer's survey. When the boat came out of the water, he told me, the bottom looked fine. But when the surveyor began tapping the hull, he detected the dull sound that is characteristic of voids in a hull's layup. He insisted that a section of the hull be sandblasted so he could see what was underneath. The sandblasting removed the bottom paint and a thin layer of gelcoat, which had hidden the voids that covered the hull's bottom. It was obvious that in laying up the hull, the builder had not used sufficient resin to adequately penetrate the first layer of woven roving and had not rolled the layer by hand to squeeze out trapped air bubbles. The yard manager estimated it would cost a minimum of $4,000 to repair the obvious problems.

Of course, finding that kind of problem in an almost-new boat raises questions about other deficiencies that are not so readily apparent. Thanks to a competent, conscientious surveyor, the buyer was able to back out of the deal. Had he not gotten such a thorough survey, he could have wound up buying the boat and not discovering the problem until months later. The seller is not so fortunate. Unless he has a good dealer standing behind him, he is going to have to lay out a sizable chunk of cash to solve the osmosis problem and may have to spend thousands more if other difficulties are found in subsequent surveys.

Now that you have a basic fix on the type and size of boat that will fit your needs and a general idea of how much you can afford to spend for it, the next questions are where to begin your search and how to conduct it.

Finding the Cruiser of Your Dreams

The decision you make between buying a new boat and buying a used boat will pretty well determine whether you begin your search for the cruiser of your dreams at a boat show, a new-boat dealer's yard, or a used-boat broker's dock. Wherever you start your quest, the issues discussed in this chapter will help you make an informed decision.

SEARCHING FOR A NEW BOAT

If you're planning to buy a new boat, you can start by visiting dealers for the boats on your list or by scheduling a visit to one or more of the major boat shows. In either case, there are several things to consider.

Starting with a Dealer

The drawbacks to starting your search with dealers are that the dealers may be spread over a wide geographic area, they may not have at their docks the particular model you are interested in, and you

may find yourself under pressure to make a decision before you have had a chance to check out everything that is available in the type of boat you're considering. If you decide to start at the dealer level, take careful note of the physical setup as you visit each dealer's yard. If the yard, shops, and docks are busy and well maintained, chances are the dealer's business is, too. When you bring your boat back for warranty service—as you are almost certain to do—the dealer is likely to tend to the work promptly and properly without a lot of hassle.

On the other hand, if the yard shows little sign of activity or the housekeeping is sloppy, chances are the business is in the same shape. The dealer may offer you a slightly better price, but when you bring your boat back for warranty service, you may encounter frustration and delay that won't be worth enduring for the amount of money you saved. Or you may run into what's known in the industry as the "hatband" dealer. This type operates out of a small office and has no yard facilities. You'll probably be told that this dealer has an agreement with a nearby yard to handle the launching and commissioning and attend to warranty repairs. (Be aware that, unlike automobiles, there is no single warranty on the entire package. On a boat, each piece of gear, including engines, is warranted separately.) Before you get into serious negotiations with this type of dealer, ask for the names of several previous customers and check with them to see what kind of after-the-sale service they got. Unless this check comes up spotless, I'd be extremely cautious about working with this dealer.

The same warning is appropriate for boat manufacturers. In the past few years, an incredible number of new boats have been introduced to the cruising market, especially planing hull motor yachts in the 40- to 50-foot (12–15 m) range. Although some of these boats offer introductory prices substantially below those of established manufacturers of the same size of boat, you should be especially careful about checking the financial resources of the builder and the dealer. If you have serious problems with the engines or hull, you want to be sure you have a dealer and a manufacturer who are going to stand behind their product. Many of these companies will build and sell a dozen or so boats, then fold their tents and evaporate from the marketplace, often to pop up somewhere else offering the same or a slightly different boat under a new corporate name. If you are one of their unlucky victims and decide to sell your vessel, you could find that you own a boat virtually no one has ever heard of or, even worse, one that has acquired a bad reputation. In this case, selling it can prove next to impossible. If you do finally find a buyer, the boat's resale value may prove to be only a fraction of what you originally paid for it. I would hesitate to buy a boat from a manufacturer or dealer who has not been known around the industry for at least five years and couldn't give me the names of at least half a dozen customers who were pleased with their products and services.

Even if you buy a new boat built by a company that has been in business for years, be cautious about buying the first hull of a new model. Often, the first boat in a series has defects that the manufacturer discovers and corrects in subsequent production. The exception to that general rule is when the manufacturer has commissioned and outfitted hull number one for use as a sales demonstrator. If the company has a good demo captain, chances are the captain has ironed out the wrinkles and you are buying a well-proven commodity.

Starting at a Boat Show

An even better place to start comparing individual vessels is at one or more of the major boat shows. Nowhere else will you be able to examine such a wide variety of boats in such a short time. But be aware that boat shows are designed to appeal to the widest possible audience, ranging from powerboat cruisers like yourself to sailboat racers, windsurfers, and bass fishing enthusiasts. Only a fraction of the displays contain information that is really of value to you, and there is an art to getting the facts you came for.

To stay current on what's new in the boating industry, from new boat models to accessories, I visit several large boat shows a year. I have to cover a lot of territory, so I've developed a system for making sure I see what I need to see in the short time available. You may find some of the following tips helpful.

Never go to a show when it first opens to the public. That's when you get all the nonboaters with their sticky-fingered kids, who are there for the spectacle. It's far better to visit a boat show on its "trade days"—normally the Thursday and Friday before the show opens to the public. To be admitted on a trade day, you need a VIP pass from one of the exhibitors.

There are a couple of ways to go about getting on an exhibitor's VIP list. Call the sales department of the boatbuilders on your list, and ask to speak to one of their dealer sales representatives. (This individual will not be a retail salesperson but one of the people on the manufacturer's staff who handles the company's relations with its dealers.) Tell the representative of your possible interest in the company's product, and ask to have sent to you all of the available literature on the specific boat or boats in their line that interest you. Also ask what upcoming boat shows will display a representative model of the vessel you're interested in and whether it will be in or out of the water. Pick one of the shows you can fit into your schedule and ask for a trade-day or VIP pass. If the person you are talking to agrees to send you a pass, ask for the names of two or three company representatives who will be working there. Amid the show's confusion, you'll find it helpful to have a specific contact. On this initial call, some manufacturers' sales departments will try to shuffle you off to one of their dealers in your area. Tell the representative it's too early in the game for you to start talking with salespeople, and ask to get the information you requested into the mail. If the person says the company can't supply you with a VIP pass, put that down as a black mark against their product and call the next company on your list.

The other way of obtaining a VIP pass is to get one from a dealer, most of which are allotted a limited number. The only drawback to going that route is that you're likely to get more selling pressure from that dealer or dealer's representative than from a factory representative. As long as you can resist that pressure, and not feel bad if you decide to buy from another dealer, go ahead.

At a major boat show, you probably will inspect a dozen or more vessels that at first glance appear to meet your basic criteria. As you attempt later to weigh them one against another, you will find that individual features of the boats tend to run together. To help solve this problem, make a brief list of the basic elements you are looking for in underbody configuration, exterior finish, and deck and accommodations layout—see the accompanying form. Make several copies of your list, and fill out a copy for each boat you inspect. Some people even take along a video or still camera to record salient features of the boats they view. If you do that, make sure it can take clear pictures in the low light levels you sometimes find below decks. If you don't use either of these methods, at

least carry along a pad on which to make notes.

Once you have a VIP pass, arrive early on trade day before the crowds build up. On the show floor plan, circle the location of each of the exhibits you want to visit; then draw up a logical routing that will allow you to cover them in turn.

When you arrive at a particular exhibitor's display, ask the person stationed at the exhibit entrance to introduce you to one of the factory representatives who is working the show. It helps to already have one or more names from your earlier call.

Even if you get a manufacturer's representative to show you the boat, the person may try to steer you toward one of the company's dealers, who will have salespeople swarming around the display. If possible, sidestep the maneuver. If the manufacturer's representative insists that a dealer show you the boat, make clear up front that you are at a very early stage in the search for the boat you want; you may be able to avoid a lot of heavy selling pressure this way.

If you are at a dry-land show, start your evaluation of a particular boat by examining its underbody to look for the characteristics we've been discussing. For esthetic reasons—or maybe to hide defects from people like you who know what to look for—some exhibitors conceal the underbody of a boat with a decorative skirt. In some cases, you will be able to go around to the back of the display for the view you need. If not, don't hesitate to ask the factory representative to move portions of the skirt aside to give you a clear view.

If the boat is already in the water, you'll have to skip the underbody survey at this point, but see whether the factory representative can arrange for you to see the same model out of the water at a dealers' yard near the show or close to your home.

After you've looked the underbody over or made arrangements to do so later, go to the stem of the boat and—from a point about midway between the waterline and the sheer—sight down the length of the hull. At a dry-land show, you'll probably have to do this at the rear of the display since the crowd will block your view on the front side. You

BOAT-BUYING CHECKLIST

Vessel: _____ New _____   Used _____   (Year) _____
                              Domestic _____   Import _____

Engine(s): _____   Single _____   Twin _____
                                  HP _____   Turbos _____
                                  Est. Cruise Speed _____
                                  Est. Fuel Cons./Hr. _____
                                  Fuel Capacity _____
                                  Est. Cruising Range _____

Hull
Material: Fiberglass _____   Wood _____   Alum. _____   Steel _____
Type: Planing _____   Semidisplacement _____   Full-Displ. _____
Keel Protects Props/Rudders _____   Hull-Form _____
Obstructions Block Props/Rudders _____   Hull Finish _____
Hull-to-Deck Joint _____   Bow Flare _____

Main Deck
Foredeck Area _____   Side Decks _____
Bulwarks _____   Cleat Placement _____
Bow Pulpit _____   Lounge Area Forward _____
Chain/Rope Lockers _____   Lounge Area Aft _____
Stanchions _____   Cruising Cockpit _____
Safety Rails _____   Transom Door _____
Lifelines _____   Swim Platform _____
Boarding Gates _____   Fresh/Saltwater _____
Shore Power Inlets _____   Outlets _____

Flying Bridge
Access _____   Helm Seating _____
Visibility Forward _____   Companion Seating _____
Visibility Side _____   Lounge Seating _____
Console Space _____   Cruising Mast _____

Interior
Pilothouse
Separation _____   Chart Flat _____
Visibility _____   Chart Storage _____
Alarm System _____   Helm Seating _____
Instrument Space _____   Companion Seating _____

Main Saloon
Seating Space _____   Glass Expanse _____
Visibility _____   Traffic Flow _____

Galley
Appliance Placement _____
Countertop Space _____
Storage Space _____
Proximity to Dining _____

Owner's Stateroom and Head
Bed Width/Access _____
Drawer Storage _____
Hanging Lockers _____
Stall Shower _____

Guest Stateroom(s) and Head(s)
Bed Width/Access _____
Drawer Storage _____
Hanging Lockers _____
Stall Shower _____

Engine Room
Standing Entry _____
Standing Headroom _____
Fire-Ext. System _____
Engine Access _____
Generator Access _____
Battery Access _____
Accessories Space _____
Through-Hull Fittings _____
Wiring Installation _____

Notes: _____

_____

_____

_____

_____

_____

_____

_____

_____

_____

_____

_____

_____

_____

Overall Rating _____

may have to get up on a chair or ladder to put your eye at optimum viewing level. In the terrible lighting conditions at most enclosed shows, seeing what you're looking for here may be difficult, but give it your best shot. As you sight down the hull, you should see a clean, unbroken sweep without noticeable dips or bulges. If you do see dips or bulges in a fiberglass boat, this can mean any or all of the following:

- the hull layup was hurried or was not allowed to cure properly
- the layup mold was what the engineers call "tired"
- the interior bulkheads are not fitted properly, which is putting stress on the hull

In time, that boat is likely to have serious problems with hull flexing, bulkhead separation, delamination, and blistering, and you should not consider buying it—period. In the case of an aluminum or a steel hull, dips and bulges in its exterior surface don't necessarily indicate structural or material problems, just poor workmanship in its weld-up. Again, I'd pass it by.

In the case of a boat built of fiberglass, back off from the hull amidships about 4 or 5 feet (1.2–1.5 m), select a section about 1 foot square (0.093 m²), and study it from several angles. It is best if the area is painted a dark color—such as at a sheer stripe—but not covered by bottom paint. You should see a smooth surface unmarred by any discernible pattern. If you see a diagonal cross-hatching pattern, you are looking at a boat that has an extremely thin layer of gelcoat and the pattern is the first layer of woven roving showing through. At the least, that boat will be subject to excessive fading and crazing, and attempts to restore it will quickly wear through the gelcoat down to the roving. Its bottom is more likely to be subject to damage from osmosis than a boat with a thicker gelcoat. Again, I'd strike it off my list.

Ask the sales representative to give you details on how the company joins the hull to the deck in the model you are considering. Some companies will have a sample or an engineering drawing of their joining method available (see illustration). Building a boat with a proper hull-to-deck joint is expensive. Since the joint is almost impossible to inspect after the vessel is completed, this is one place where a lot of lower-quality builders cut corners.

The optimum hull-to-deck joint is composed of ⅜-inch (10 mm) or larger stainless steel bolts on 12-inch (30 cm) centers through-bolted to stainless steel backing plates inside and outside the hull with stainless steel lock washers and nuts. The hull and deck should overlap at least 1 inch (2.5 cm), and the overlap should be sealed with a waterproof urethane compound. The inside of the joint should be sealed with a continuous 6-inch-wide (15 cm) strip of fiberglass mat soaked with resin and overlayed by a second strip of fiberglass mat 8 inches (20 cm) wide, which also is soaked with resin. All air bubbles should be rolled out of both layers of resin by hand. A less desirable but acceptable method of joining the hull and deck uses 1-inch (25 mm) stainless steel screws in place of bolts. If screws are used, they should be on not less than 8-inch (20 cm) centers, and the joint should be sealed as above. If you come across a builder who doesn't come pretty close to these specifications, pass up the product and look for a boat that won't come apart on you.

If the underbody, exterior finish, and hull-to-deck joint don't measure up to these criteria, don't waste your time with the interior; just go on to the next exhibit on your list. If these factors are within acceptable limits, make whatever notes you need to remind yourself what you've seen and then you're ready to go on board. Even on trade days, you may find a long line of people waiting to get on board. That's another reason to have a contact on the manufacturer's staff before you arrive. In many cases, that person will be able to get you aboard unobtrusively through a back way reserved for serious prospects.

Begin your onboard inspection with a leisurely stroll around the deck, making appropriate notes on the layout features we've discussed. Some

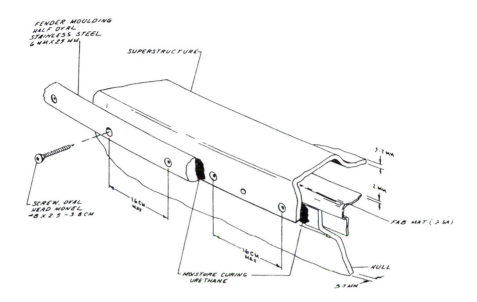

A look at an engineering drawing of a new vessel's hull-to-deck joint is the most reliable way to be sure this vital area is properly constructed.

manufacturers of boats with flying bridges block the bridges off at boat shows to reduce the possibility of someone falling off. Again, if you have the attention of a factory representative, you may be able to have an exception made in your case.

Once your deck inspection is complete, start your walk-through of the interior, again checking the key factors we've covered, especially in the engine room, and making your notes or taking your pictures.

After completing this once-over-lightly inspection of a particular boat, go ahead and assign it a rating from one to ten based simply on your overall impression, not on specific details. When you finally do an item-by-item analysis, you may be pleasantly surprised to find how well your initial reaction stands up.

Now check out the other boats on your list the same way. Once you've done that, find a quiet place where you can relax and go back over your notes. Eliminate those boats that seem to have major deficiencies, and roughly rank in order the remaining boats that might be serious possibilities. You may want to organize your list for a second, closer inspection according to the logical walk-through of the show. At this point, however, I personally find it helps to start out with the lowest-rated boat on my list and work up to the one I've rated highest.

Before embarking on this more detailed inspection, revise your checklist to zero in on those areas that are really critical and be sure you cover any significant features of a particular boat you missed the first time around or failed to note.

Now go back for your closer look and take plenty of notes or pictures. On each boat, mentally (if not physically) go through the motions of what you would actually do in each of its major areas. On the foredeck, imagine docking and anchoring the boat and note the positioning of deck cleats and hawsepipes. In the galley, mentally prepare a meal. This may be when you realize the refrigerator is positioned much too far from the sink or the sink is placed where it cannot be reached conveniently from the cooktop. In the engine room, go through the motions of checking the oil and water in the engines and generators and the acid level in the batteries. This may tip you off that the way the batteries are installed requires you to be a contortionist to top them off.

SEARCHING FOR A USED BOAT

If you are interested primarily in buying a used boat, you can start your search by checking out the trade-in inventory of new-boat dealers, perusing ads in boating magazines, or visiting brokers who deal only in used boats. I'd be hesitant to buy a vessel directly from an owner without having a competent broker involved in the transaction. As you will see in chapter 6, the legal and financial intricacies of buying a sizable cruising vessel are at least as complicated as buying a house or condominium, a transaction that most of us wouldn't attempt without the services of a qualified Realtor.

If you start your search for a used boat with a new-boat dealer, bear in mind that the dealer's first interest may be in selling you the trade-ins or the boats on consignment at the dealer's dock rather than scouring the used-boat market to help you locate the boat that best suits your needs.

The best approach is to find a good used-boat broker. Look for a broker who has been in the industry for several years, seems knowledgeable about the particular type of boat you are looking for, and shows a sincere interest in helping you find the boat you have in mind, not simply getting your money and hustling you out the door. Ask the broker to help you not only to find your boat but also to buy it on the best terms. Since the commission will be paid by the seller, the broker's services should cost you nothing. But brokers who know they're going to represent you no matter which boat you ultimately buy are more likely to

put your interests first rather than brokers who are just trying to find a buyer for a boat on their own listing sheets.

In making your selection of a broker, be extremely cautious. The best of them are highly knowledgeable, ethical people who have been in the business for years and will go to great lengths to make you happy. They want you to come back to them if you decide later to buy another boat, and they hope you will recommend them to your boat-buying friends. The worst brokers know little, if anything, about boats beyond how to talk a sharp line and are little more than skillful con artists who are in business strictly for the fast buck. Telling the difference between the two is difficult since many states have nothing in the way of licensing or qualification requirements for yacht salespeople or brokers; even those states that don't have a lot of teeth in their laws.

Under its so-called Sunshine Law passed in 1978, for instance, Florida eliminated state licensing for everything from yacht brokers to plumbers on the theory that the law cost more to administer than it produced in revenue. Ten years later, the Florida Yacht Brokers Association persuaded the state legislature to pass a law requiring yacht salespeople to post a $10,000 bond and brokers to post a $25,000 bond and to show they have at least two years' experience in yacht sales. California requires yacht salespeople to pass a written examination on the legal aspects of yacht sales transactions, then work for a broker for two years before being eligible to become a broker. Brokers in California must post a $10,000 bond. While these are steps in the right direction, most yacht brokerage contracts are so filled with disclaimers that it is difficult to collect damages for anything short of transparent fraud, and the size of the bond required provides little comfort for the cruising yachtsperson who is planning to spend $100,000—or several times that—on a vessel.

Begin your search for a qualified broker by asking boating friends, marine insurance agents, and yacht financing sources for the names of brokers they have dealt with successfully. If you find a broker who seems to meet your requirements but you have no personal recommendations, ask for the names of a couple of satisfied customers and check with them. If a broker can't give you such names, or seems hesitant to do so, move on to someone else. It would be ideal if you could locate a competent broker reasonably close to your home, but if you live well inland, you would probably do better to establish contact with a broker in one of the major boating centers, where there will be a wider range of choices to consider.

Because a good used-boat broker stays in touch with the full range of the market, he probably will know of any boat that comes close to meeting your requirements. The best of these people have an efficient network, and any one broker can sell you virtually any boat on the market, whether it is listed with that broker's own agency or with someone else.

Once you have found a broker you are comfortable with, give him a detailed list of your specifications and an accurate idea of your boat-buying budget. Within your specifications list, point out what is absolutely essential and what can be optional or negotiated. Then let him go to work. Chances are he quickly will come up with a list of boats that meet your requirements and your budget. This is when you get down to the tough job of sorting through the boats to find the one that's right for you. It's best to bring your broker with you when checking out a boat he recommends. If the inspection involves only a couple of hours and a drive of 50 miles (80 km) or so, his presence should cost you nothing. If the trip involves airfares or overnight accommodations, have a clear understanding with him up front as to whether he expects you to cover his expenses or will take them out of his commission.

Your inspection of the hull, deck, and interior and engine room layouts of the used boat should follow roughly the same procedure recommended earlier in this chapter for new boats at a boat show. You can afford to concentrate most of your attention on the suitability of layout, accommodations, and appearance since, before you buy a used boat, you are going to have it carefully inspected by a qualified marine surveyor. But even in your walk-through of a used boat, take careful note of anything that is broken, missing, badly worn, or excessively dirty. If you get to the point of serious financial negotiations, those tics against the boat may be items you can use to get the price you want. During your inspection of the engine room, watch especially for any signs of excessive oil or water leakage. This is a dead giveaway for an engine that could require an expensive overhaul.

PERFORMING THE INITIAL SEA TRIAL

At some point in your search, you will find you are looking at a particular new or used boat and saying to yourself, "This may be the one!" The next step is to arrange for a sea trial.

If you're considering a new boat at an in-the-water boat show, some manufacturers can arrange a sea trial for you on the spot. If this isn't possible, they should be able to arrange with one of their dealers or a cooperative owner for you to put one of the boat's sister ships equipped with the same power package through a sea trial's procedures. If that is the case, make clear to the dealer that you reserve the right to repeat the process with your actual boat before you finalize any deal.

It would seem logical to subject a used boat to a sea trial before you go to the trouble of making a formal offer to purchase, but often it doesn't work that way. The owner normally bears any expense involved in sea trials to cover fuel and possibly an operator. To protect themselves from wasting time and money on tire kickers and joyriders, most owners and brokers don't want to go to the trouble and expense of providing a sea trial until they have a signed offer-to-purchase contract on a boat. If you can convince the selling broker you're a genuine prospect, he or she might make an exception and arrange for you to take the boat out. If not, you will have to determine what your first offer should be (discussed in chapter 6). In any event, even if it involves significant travel, never buy a boat that you have not put through a rigorous sea trial first. If you do buy a boat without a sea trial and find it rolls too much to suit you or isn't as fast as you thought it would be, you have next to no chance of getting your money back.

In preparing to conduct a sea trial, make a checklist of things to look for and be prepared to take comprehensive notes. I find it's easier to take sea trial notes with a small handheld tape recorder than with a pad and pencil. There are a hundred things to look for in a sea trial, but something approaching the following routine will ensure that you at least cover the most critical areas.

Before the main engines are cranked, ask the person showing you the boat to crank up the generator; check its noise and vibration levels in the main saloon and the staterooms, on the flying bridge and, if the boat has one, on the aft deck. Are they levels at which you can comfortably carry on a conversation, dine, and sleep?

Make sure that the engines are completely cold at the outset of the sea trial. Beginning a sea trial with the engines already running, or restarting warm engines, is a good way for a less-than-scrupulous manufacturer, dealer, or broker to hide starting or smoking problems. Actually go into the engine room and put your hand on the block. If it is already warm, insist on the right to see the engines started when they are cold.

Before the engines are cranked, position yourself at the stern so you have a clear view of the exhaust. It's normal and acceptable for cold-started diesel engines to emit a brief belch of light gray smoke at start-up because they simply are burning off the bit of carbon residue and moisture condensation that builds up in any diesel engine after it has been idle long enough to cool off thoroughly. But if the boat emits heavy black smoke and continues to do so for more than about a minute, be alert to a potential problem. The salesperson or broker may tell you the engines "just need a bit of tweaking." My attitude is, if the seller can't keep the engines from smoking excessively when a potential buyer is aboard, how anxious is he going to be to solve the problem after I have handed over my final payment? I'd be inclined to

SEA TRIAL CHECKLIST

Vessel Sea Trialed _____
**Noise/Vibration Levels at Dock,
   Generator Only:**
Main Deck _____
Below Decks Forward _____
Below Decks Aft _____
Engine Smoking _____
      Max. No-Load RPM _____
      Max. Load RPM   – _____
      Engine Droop _____

Maneuverability:
Forward _____
Reverse _____

Roll and Pitch:

	No Stabilizers	Stabilizers
Wind/Sea Forward	____	____
Wind/Sea Aft	____	____
Wind/Sea Abeam	____	____
Wind/Sea Forward Quarter	____	____
Wind/Sea Aft Quarter	____	____

Vibration Levels Under Way:
Main Deck _____
Below Decks Forward _____
Below Decks Aft _____

Notes: _____
_____
_____
_____
_____

Overall Rating _____

believe there was a significant problem with the engines or their installation and would mark it down as a major minus against the boat.

Here's how to get a quick feel for the basic condition of the engines and propellers of a boat. After the engines have been thoroughly warmed up at the dock, with the gear in neutral, run them up to their maximum revolutions per minute (rpm). Jot that down as their "no-load" reading. Once you are in open water with the gears engaged, again run them up to their maximum rpm. They should turn up to within about 150 to 200 rpm of their no-load reading. The difference is what diesel mechanics call *droop*. If the droop from no-load to load readings in either engine is more than about 200 rpm, the engine or transmission has some internal problem or the prop it is driving is too large or has too much pitch. If the droop is less than about 150 rpm, the prop is probably too small or doesn't have enough pitch. A problem of prop size or pitch (as opposed to an internal problem with an engine or transmission) most likely will show up as too much or too little droop in both engines at the same time.

Maneuverability around the dock is the next factor you need to check out. Many manufacturers, dealers, and brokers don't want anyone but their own employees or themselves to handle their boats around a dock because of the terms of their liability insurance or for fear an inexperienced helmsman will do some damage. If you find this is the case, at least insist that you be allowed to handle the boat you are considering for a few minutes in protected water away from the dock. Swinging the boat around in a few tight circles—using only the engines if a twin-screw boat—will tell you something of how it will handle in close quarters. Back the boat down to see how it answers the helm and tracks in reverse.

Insist that your sea trial include a run in open water, not just a few minutes in protected waters. You're considering buying this boat for safe, comfortable passages at a normal cruising speed. Merely running across the calm waters of a harbor for a few minutes is hardly going to tell you how the boat will handle in open water. If you get outside and are fortunate enough to have any sea at all running, ask to take the helm and make at least brief runs with the seas head-on, astern, abeam, and on the forward and stern quarters. If the boat

has a flying bridge, make your runs from that helm station.

To determine the ideal cruising speed of a planing hull boat, bring the engines down to about 1,000 rpm; then run the throttles up slowly until the bow just falls over and the boat comes up on plane. A well-designed planing hull will nose over when the engines reach about 1,900 rpm. If you leave the throttle at that setting, the engines' governors will maintain it but will have to pump additional fuel through the injectors to do so. Also, a planing hull boat operated at a speed that barely allows the boat to plane will tend to fall away from the track when encountering the least bit of wave action. Instead of staying at that rpm setting, gently ease the throttles up until you add about 2 knots of speed, which will probably put the engines at about 2,100 rpm. You will find the boat handles better at that speed, and if you check the fuel consumption over a measured course, you should find that it is also the most efficient fuel consumption setting. With those checks out of the way, note the degree of roll and pitch with wind and waves coming from various directions. If the boat is equipped with an autopilot, activate it for a few moments on each heading to see how well it keeps the boat on course.

If you're considering a full-displacement-hull boat, it would be ideal if the one you take out for a sea trial were equipped with the same brand and size of stabilizers you plan to have, but you will probably have to make allowances. If stabilizers are installed, run the boat for a few minutes on each heading with the stabilizers off, then on, and note the degree to which they dampen rolling.

With your handling test out of the way, let someone else take the helm and go below to position yourself on the main deck directly over the engines to assess vibration and noise when they are operating at normal cruising speed. Do the same thing well aft directly over the props and below decks in each of the staterooms. Are the sound and vibration at levels you and your guests can live with comfortably for hours or perhaps days and nights on end during extended passages? If the boat is equipped with a generator, make sure it is running during this part of your inspection. While you're in the forward stateroom especially, note the degree of tossing about your crew will be subjected to in their off-watch hours.

Even after going through this orderly boat-searching process, you still may not find a boat that really measures up as the cruiser of your dreams. If so, don't be discouraged. Above all, don't let yourself be stampeded by a sales pitch into buying a boat you know deep in your heart is not the boat for you. Remember, you're probably going to be living with the boat you finally buy for a long time under a variety of circumstances. You may even wind up trusting your life and the lives of those you love to it. One cruising friend of mine who often waxes philosophical observes that buying a serious cruising boat is like choosing a wife. The blonde at the end of the bar may look great among the bright lights and glitter, but is she really the one you want to wake up to every morning for the rest of your life?

Let's suppose you have found the boat—new or used—that meets your specifications. Your next move is to negotiate a financial deal for the boat's purchase at a price you can afford.

Negotiating the Purchase

When negotiating with a salesperson of new yachts or a broker of used boats, bear in mind that, as a typical boat buyer, you might go through the boat-buying process once every three years or so. The person across the table from you makes a living selling boats all day, every day, so don't be surprised the salesperson is better at selling boats than you are at buying them. Except in rare and unusual circumstances, the chances of your getting the better of a salesperson or broker in a deal is pretty slim. Your main goal should be to make sure you're treated fairly and not taken to the cleaners. Determining which is which will be a little easier if you know some of the cards the other person is holding.

BUYING A NEW BOAT

One of the first decisions you need to make is whether you are going to allow the dealer to recommend, supply, and install the accessory equipment your vessel is going to need—everything from navigation and communications electronics to a tender and its outboard; whether you are going to handle that equipment's purchase and arrange for its installation yourself; or whether you want some combination of the two. There is no question that letting the dealer handle the details of accessorizing your vessel will mean a lot less wear and tear on you, but if the dealer does provide that service, you may well find yourself paying a handsome price for it. Some new-boat dealers recommend good accessory equipment, provide it at a fair price, and install it properly. Others don't really know what you need for extended cruising, what does and doesn't work out in the real world, or how to correctly install the equipment they sell. And some dealers charge unconscionable prices for anything they can persuade you to buy.

The key to deciding where you will buy the accessories your boat needs is making sure you know up front what you want and the fair price to pay for it. After reading this book, you should have an excellent idea of what you need in the way of accessories and an idea of what it costs to buy that equipment and have it installed. You should also have a darn good idea of what accessories you *don't* need. When you sit down to talk dollars with a dealer, compare the dealer's price for accessories with the prices you've researched. If the dealer can meet those prices within a few dollars, it's fine to go that route. If the dealer's prices are out of line, however, present your own figures. If the dealer won't come close to your prices, you're better off taking care of that part of the boat-buying process yourself.

Any number of factors can influence a deal on a particular boat, but to illustrate some of the basic economics of the boat-selling business, let's construct a hypothetical but reasonably typical example. Let's say that after going through the process described in the preceding chapters, you've decided to buy a new boat and have chosen one in the mid-40-foot (12 m) range. You find a dealer with the model in his new-boat inventory, and it has the basic factory-installed options you want, such as a flying bridge, a bow pulpit, and the like. Its base-boat price as listed in the manufacturer's literature, including the factory-installed options, is $249,500. You don't have time to chase around after the accessories you want, so you specify a list of options you will have the dealer install if you buy the boat from that dealer. The dealer's list prices for those options seem in line with other figures you have for the same equipment, and they will increase the boat's cost by roughly $48,000. Now the total list price of the boat is up to $297,500. The salesperson does a little quick figuring, huddles with the boss, and beams at you that they're willing to knock $15,000 right off the top and let you have that little jewel for only $282,500—a discount of about 5 percent off list. Is that a fair price to you, or are you funneling too much of your hard-earned money into the dealer's pocket?

To begin to answer that question, take 15 percent of the suggested list of $249,500 for the boat and its factory-installed options—that's $37,425. Most builders of sizable power yachts sell boats to their dealers at a discount of at least 15 percent off list. Some manufacturers offer dealer discounts up to about 18 percent off list, and some increase the discount even further if the dealer's annual orders pass certain volume levels. By taking 15 percent off the list price of a new boat, you can figure that if the dealer could sell the boat at list, that would be about his minimum potential gross profit on the boat alone. (If the boat you're considering is under 40 feet/12 m, figure the dealer's discount at 20 percent of the base-boat price, including factory-installed options. As a general rule, the smaller the boat, the greater the dealer markup.)

Now take 40 percent of the $48,000 in options you would ask the dealer to install, which is a typical dealer discount from the accessories manufacturers. That figure is another $19,200. Add that to the dealer's minimum potential gross profit of $37,425 on the boat itself and the dealer stands to make at least $56,625 if you buy the boat and the options at list price.

The dealer, who of course knows you aren't going to pay list, has authorized the salesperson to offer you a $15,000 discount, which brings the dealer's profit down to a minimum of $41,625. On a $282,500 deal, that is still a gross profit margin of almost 15 percent. Even after the salesperson receives the typical commission rate of 20 percent of the gross profit ($8,325), the dealer is left with $33,300—a profit after deducting the commission of almost 12 percent. Out of that, the dealer still has to pay the yard workers, the operating overhead, and such, but it's still not a bad day's work.

Now go back and work the deal your way. Take 7 percent of the manufacturer's $249,500 list price for the boat and its factory-installed options (10 percent if the boat is under 40 feet). That's $17,465, just a little less than half the dealer's minimum potential profit on the boat alone if it were sold at list. Now take 15 percent of the $48,000 in options you'd want the dealer to install. That's $7,200—again a bit less than half of the dealer's probable markup. Add the two figures together to get $24,665, and subtract that from the suggested list price of the boat and installed options of $297,500. The resulting $272,835 is about the most you ought to pay for that boat with those options installed. With hard bargaining, you should be able to buy that boat for between $265,000 and $270,000. Offer no more than $250,000 for openers; then expect to be dragged kicking and screaming up to about the $265,000 to $270,000 level before you make a deal. If you follow something approaching this scenario, eight out of ten times you'll have bought that boat on terms that are fair both to you and the dealer.

After you have worked out the numbers in a particular deal to arrive at what you feel is a realistic price, you can of course shop a number of dealers for the particular boat you want and play them one against another to get the absolute lowest price. If you do that, recognize that the dealer you finally buy the boat from has a very sharp pencil. This will have worked to your advantage in the initial purchase, but it may well work against you when the time comes for warranty work or a trade up to a larger boat. Many boat buyers find they are happier in the long run if they do all their boat-buying business with a single dealer. They may leave a few extra dollars on the table, but they build a sense of trust and rapport that pays off in quick service on warranty work and a fair deal when they buy subsequent boats.

Of the factors that can influence a particular new-boat deal, the general U.S. economy and the particular model of boat you decide to buy are among the most important. If economic times are good and the boat you pick is a popular model in short supply, the dealer may have other potential buyers on the string and may not be willing to make the concessions you want. On the other hand, if the nation is in the midst of an economic downturn, a dealer who has had in inventory for several months the boat you're considering may be getting desperate to unload it. To encourage dealers to order stock boats and thus keep their production lines busy, most yacht manufacturers agree to pay all or the lion's share of their dealers' floor financing costs for the first four to six months they have a boat in inventory. If you know of dealers who have had the boat you want for several months, the manufacturer's floor-plan support for it may be about to end. In that case, such dealers will be motivated to sell it to you at anything they can realize over cost before interest charges begin to eat them alive. (In the example above, at a 15 percent discount, a dealer's cost in the boat would be about $212,000. Once the factory's support of the floor-plan financing runs out, at a 10 percent rate that dealer would be looking at over $1,700 a month in interest charges.)

BUYING A USED BOAT

Shopping for a used cruising vessel is subject to so many variables it is difficult to make generalizations, but here are a few useful guidelines.

First, shop where the boats are. On the East Coast of the United States, that is the southeast coast of Florida. On the West Coast, it's the area from Los Angeles to San Diego. Although you may find an outstanding buy in other areas, in general you will find a much wider range of boats to choose from at lower prices in these two areas than in any other part of the country. Second, the time of year you shop can be important. The used-boat business usually slows down in the heat of the summer—July and August—and from about Thanksgiving to the end of February. If you make an offer on a boat during those slow periods, you are more likely to have a hungry broker try to argue the seller into taking it than the same broker would at the peak of the selling season in the spring and fall. In more northerly areas, an October or November offer is more likely to be accepted because the seller is looking at the cost of carrying the boat over a long winter until sales revive in the spring.

Most advertised prices for used boats listed with brokers are grossly inflated. It's human nature for owners to list their boats with the broker who claims to be able to get the highest price. Even if the owners are looking for a quick sale, most listing brokers will recommend that owners set the "asking price" at least 10 to 15 percent higher than they are willing to accept in order to leave some maneuvering room on the actual selling price and hopefully cover some of the broker's commission. If the owners aren't pressed to get their money out of their boats, some brokers will recommend that they set an asking price of 20 to 30 percent above what they'll actually accept. (Some wealthy owners, in fact, continuously keep their boats on the market just to see what kind of offers they bring. They have no real intention of selling and so set a ridiculously high price. But if some idiot comes along who is willing to buy at that price or at one that returns a 30 or 40 percent profit, they'll sell. This is why you see some bigger boats tagged in the classified section of the boating magazines as "seriously for sale.")

The discount off the asking price at which you can really buy a particular used boat, then, depends in large measure on the owner's motivation. An owner who is well fixed financially may have little reason to accept a price very much below the asking price. But an owner who has listed the boat you're considering with the broker on consignment and is making payments on a newer boat or has other personal or business situations that require immediate cash, may be willing to slash the asking price considerably.

The used-boat brokerage business works this way: brokerage contracts are either *open* or *central agency* listings. In either case, the standard commission rate is 10 percent of the price the boat actually brings. In open listings, any number of brokers can list the boat and offer it for sale, deal directly with the owner, and collect the entire selling commission. In central agency listings, the seller agrees that all offers to purchase will be channeled through a single broker. If the brokerage house holding a central agency listing sells the boat, it keeps the entire 10 percent commission. If another brokerage house sells the boat, the listing broker gets 3 percent of the selling price and the selling broker gets 7 percent.

Since any broker's income is pegged to the boat's selling price, the broker has an interest in keeping the price as high as possible. At the same time, a broker makes nothing on a boat that is priced so unrealistically high that a buyer cannot be found for it, so the broker may be inclined to persuade an owner to accept a somewhat lower price in order to close the deal and move on to the next one.

Understanding how the brokerage business works is important to you in buying a used boat because—though it doesn't happen often—in cases where you and the seller get to within about 1 or 2 percent of the boat's value and neither of you will make the concessions necessary to bridge the gap, the broker may step in and agree to make up the difference, do some minor repair, or make other concessions in order to conclude the deal. Obviously, that is more likely to happen if the broker is both listing and selling the boat, since he doesn't have to split the commission.

Once you've found a specific used boat and a careful walk-through has convinced you it is worth pursuing, figure out approximately what that boat is really worth, which may have little to do with the owner's asking price. If you've followed the advice in chapter 5 and involved a qualified broker of your own in your search for a good used boat, that broker is probably the best source of a reliable estimate of the true value of a specific used boat. If you are dealing directly with a listing broker or want to check your own broker's recommendation, repeat the process you went through when you constructed your original boat-buying budget by checking the BUC Book for its prices on boats of the make, model, and age you are considering and by querying other brokers about recent selling prices of similar boats. Once you have a pretty good fix on the value of the boat in average condition, adjust it for pluses or minuses in the particular boat you're considering.

One initial key to negotiating the purchase of a boat at a price you are satisfied with is to not be too anxious. Let the broker know you are willing to take your time and pass up several deals if necessary until you find one you feel is equitable. If you get into serious negotiation on a used boat, the broker often will suggest that you make an offer somewhat below the asking price.

If the broker is one you have retained as your buying agent, you probably are safe to accept the broker's recommendation. If you're dealing with the listing agent, the price this agent suggests you offer probably will be a bit higher than the agent is reasonably certain the owner will accept. If you're genuinely interested in the boat, you would do well to make an offer 10 to 15 percent below what the broker recommends. Make certain your offer is "subject to sea trial and survey," back it up with an earnest money deposit check made payable to the selling broker for 10 percent of your offer, and include a date a week or ten days in the future after which it will expire. The check makes yours a bona fide offer, which the listing broker is legally obligated to present to the owner.

The listing broker must hold your deposit check in escrow, and most will accept a personal check rather than insisting on certified funds. Some brokers go ahead and cash the deposit check; others simply hold it until the negotiations are concluded and return it if the deal falls through. The selling broker will want your offer-to-purchase to include a closing date and probably will try to get you to set it as early as possible, but don't let yourself be hurried. It may take a week or two to schedule a survey by a competent marine surveyor and another couple of weeks after receipt of the surveyor's written report to finalize insurance and financing. Allowing a month between your offer-to-purchase and the closing date is not excessive.

An owner in a financial bind may accept your offer, and the deal might then be closed at a price somewhat below what the broker recommended. If the owner rejects your bid and comes back with a counteroffer, at least you are getting closer to common ground. If the owner's counteroffer indicates an unwillingness to make enough of a concession below the asking price to keep you interested in the boat, you can retrieve your earnest money deposit and walk away. If the counteroffer is at least in the direction of what you're willing to pay, you can then make a new offer at somewhat less than the owner's counteroffer and go through that process as many times as necessary until you agree on a formal offer-to-purchase and offer-to-sell contract at a price that is still subject to sea trial and survey. If you make a subsequent offer-to-purchase that is higher than your original or most recent offer, you may be asked to escrow additional funds to bring your deposits up to 10 percent of your offering price.

After you have signed a contract, if you haven't had the opportunity for a sea trial, now is the proper time.

ARRANGING FOR THE MARINE SURVEY

The next step is to arrange for a qualified marine surveyor to conduct a full prepurchase condition-and-valuation marine survey. In the case of a boat only a couple of years old, your insurer and financing source may be satisfied with a less complete survey, but you should have a complete condition-and-valuation survey done anyway to make certain you know the boat's actual condition. You will be expected to bear the expenses the survey entails.

A qualified marine surveyor is a professional who inspects several hundred boats of all types every year. With that experience, the surveyor can spot a great many things the average boat buyer would miss or is simply not competent to evaluate. If a survey notes even one significant area of hull delamination, a serious electrolysis problem, or an engine in need of an extensive overhaul, it can save you many times the survey fee. At the least, the survey may uncover defects that should be corrected before you go to sea or that should properly affect the boat's selling price in your favor. Even if you wind up not buying a boat you have had surveyed, it may well be for defects the surveyor has pointed out to you, preventing you from making an expensive mistake.

The key word where marine surveyors are concerned is *qualified*. Employing a surveyor is largely a caveat emptor operation. Neither the federal government nor any state in the nation sets standards or requires any examination or other proof of qualifications for people to hang out a shingle and call themselves marine surveyors. With that lack of regulation, anyone can get in the business for nothing more than the cost of a meaningless occupational license and a few dollars for business cards and an ad in the telephone book. Also, surveyors' reports usually contain disclaimers of responsibility for "concealed deficiencies and/or latent defects," which give you little recourse in case they fail to uncover problems that later prove serious. Since in most states surveyors do not have to be bonded, even if you proved gross negligence and won a judgment, your chances of collecting probably would be minimal.

Unfortunately, membership in a professional organization is not an infallible guide to finding a qualified surveyor. The leading organization to which some surveyors belong is the National Association of Marine Surveyors (NAMS). NAMS requires applicants to have several years of practical experience and pass a rigorous examination before it certifies them, then requires them to periodically attend workshops and seminars to keep up their skills. The problem is that only a small percentage of those who call themselves marine surveyors are NAMS members, and some who are certified by NAMS survey only large commercial vessels. Also, a number of highly qualified marine surveyors for one reason or another choose not to join the organization. Membership in such organizations as the Society of Accredited Marine Surveyors, the American Boat and Yacht Council, the National Fire Protection Association, and the like is not a reliable guide in selecting a competent surveyor. These are largely advisory or informational organizations that require little if anything in the way of examinations or experience for membership, and none polices its members or punishes violations of the lofty standards it professes to uphold. Just about anyone can join any of these groups for the price of a membership fee and the payment of annual dues.

Be wary of choosing a surveyor based on the size of an ad in the telephone book. Some surveyors with the biggest ads are the most incompetent, and some of the best ones stay so busy with referrals from reputable brokers, yacht financing sources, insurance agents, and satisfied customers that they don't advertise at all.

The broker you are dealing with will almost invariably recommend a surveyor to you. The recommendation of a reliable broker may well be excellent, but check the surveyor's qualifications and reputation anyway. Some less-than-scrupulous brokers have a favorite surveyor or two whom they have found they can rely on to give the boats they are trying to sell a favorable "broker's survey" rather than performing their real job—protecting the buyer's best interest.

Check with your insurance agent to make certain your insurer will accept the report of any surveyor you plan to hire. Some companies will accept only the reports of surveyors on their approved list. If you will be financing the boat, also check the acceptability of the surveyor with your financing source. If the broker, your insurance agent, and possibly your financing source all endorse a surveyor, you probably have chosen someone who is competent. If any of these sources has doubts about a surveyor or is unfamiliar with surveyors in the area where the boat you are considering is berthed, check with several insurance agents, reputable brokers, yacht financing sources and major full-service boatyards in that area until several mention the same name. That's probably the surveyor you want.

Typical rates for a complete condition-and-valuation survey on a fiberglass-hull yacht run around $7 to $10 per foot ($23–33 per m) of boat length. Rates for surveying wood-hull boats may be slightly higher, and rates for surveying a steel- or aluminum-hull vessel may be up to twice as high if the insurer or financing source insists that the hull be tested with an audio-gauge. Some surveyors base their charges on an hourly rate, which can vary from $40 to $60 per hour. Unless I were supersatisfied with a surveyor's credentials, I'd be reluctant to enter into an hourly rate agreement because the surveyor can charge for waiting time and time spent writing the report and you would have no idea how many hours were actually invested. Most surveyors will charge less if all you need is a survey to keep your insurance in force. In that case, they will check only those factors that affect the vessel's safety and seaworthiness and won't worry about how well the stereo or the microwave oven works.

When you find an appropriate surveyor, make certain up front you are getting a full condition-and-valuation survey. A few marine surveyors limit their work to checking the hull, and you will have to hire a separate technician to check the boat's electronics and a diesel mechanic to go over the engines, each of which could cost you anywhere from $250 to $400 in addition to the surveyor's fee. A good marine surveyor should be competent to give you an informed opinion on the entire vessel. Only if the surveyor finds serious problems and recommends separate checks by a specialized electronics technician or diesel-engine mechanic should you have to go to that added expense.

Make sure you know what the surveyor's rate is and what it does and does not include. If significant driving from the surveyor's home or office to the boat's location is involved—usually more than about 50 miles (80 km)—you may be asked to pay for mileage and travel time. If air travel, overnight accommodations, and meals away from home are involved, you will be expected to pick up the tab. Have a clear agreement with the surveyor about when you will make payment. Some surveyors will allow you to pay from an invoice that accompanies their written report. Others have been stiffed so many times by prospective buyers who decided not to buy a boat after receiving an unfavorable survey that they will ask for their money as soon as they deliver their verbal report. To eliminate any possibility of confusion, settle up with your marine surveyor directly rather than paying him through a third party.

In negotiating some used-boat deals, you may be presented with a survey the seller has already had conducted. In other cases, you may be offered a copy of a survey a previous potential buyer had

done on the boat at a cost of about half or even less than what the owner paid for it. Either survey may be quite legitimate. Some conscientious sellers have a survey conducted prior to putting their boats on the market so they can go ahead and correct any significant defects. A prior prospective buyer may have forgone purchase of the boat for reasons entirely unrelated to the survey's results. That buyer paid for the survey and owns it. If the buyer wants to sell it to you to recoup some of the expense, that is the buyer's privilege, and most surveyors don't object to having their work resold. You might be safe in accepting this survey in lieu of paying for your own if, after checking the surveyor's qualifications and reputation and having a direct conversation about the boat, you are convinced of the surveyor's competence and integrity. Even in that case, the survey should be a full condition-and-valuation survey and should be less than three months old. Again, make certain your insurance company and, if necessary, your lender are willing to accept the report. Assuming the person who originally commissioned the survey agrees, for a nominal fee most surveyors will supply a new cover sheet for the survey listing you as the buyer. Before doing so, some very cautious surveyors may insist on making at least a brief recheck of the boat and will charge you a hundred dollars or so. If any of the above conditions are not met or you have the slightest question about the surveyor's competence or integrity, spend the money to have your own survey conducted.

If at all possible, you should be present when the survey is conducted. If you are there, the surveyor can give you an on-the-spot appreciation for the boat's true condition that might not come through as clearly in a written report. Give the surveyor room to work, but actually crawl down into the bilge and peer over the surveyor's shoulder. Your broker should be along as well, and it would be ideal if the seller's broker could be present, although staying in the background. If the surveyor finds a major problem area, you may be able to settle a lot of questions then and there and eliminate protracted negotiations.

Once you arrive at the boat, if your surveyor shows up for the job in work clothes and spends several hours poking and prying into anchor lockers and hatches with a flashlight, crawls all through the engine room, pulls out drawers and looks behind them, and taps the decks and superstructure all over with a plastic mallet for signs of deterioration or delamination, you're probably getting a thorough, competent survey. If the surveyor shows up in white slacks, gives a desultory glance at the boat's exterior, pokes his head into the engine room and pronounces her seaworthy, send that one packing.

Once the surveyor has completed the initial in-water inspection and announces all is well, you should give the boat a second sea trial with the surveyor aboard. By scheduling this second sea trial prior to lifting the boat out of the water, if the surveyor turns up anything that convinces you it's not the boat for you, you've saved the expense of the haulout portion of the survey. Assuming you have already satisfied yourself about the boat's handling characteristics with an initial sea trial, in this one you need not worry about getting the boat into open water. If you haven't had a chance to handle the boat in the open sea, however, now is the time to do it. Either way, make certain the engines are run up to maximum speed to allow your surveyor to check them under full load.

During the final sea trial, spend most of your time alongside your surveyor, climbing around the engine room, checking all the systems while under way, and giving the electronics a good going-over.

If everything still looks good after the in-water and sea trial portions of the survey, the surveyor should request that the boat be hauled out so he can examine the underbody. This haulout will be at your expense. Around $3 to $5 per foot ($10–16 per m) of boat length is a typical charge, which includes both lifting and returning the boat to the water. Once the boat is out of the water, the surveyor should carefully check the condition and alignment of shaft, struts, props, and rudders, go over all through-hull fittings, and tap the entire exterior of the hull with a plastic mallet for signs

of delamination, deterioration, or blistering. If you have not already done so, this is also the time for you to satisfy yourself that the boat's underbody configuration is appropriate to the kind of cruising you have in mind.

After the inspection is complete, the surveyor should be able to brief you immediately on any serious defects the survey has uncovered and give you a rough idea of what it will cost to repair them. If your broker and the seller's broker are both present, you may be able to hash out whether the seller will attend to the needed repairs or lower the price to offset the expense you will incur. You are probably better off if you can get the seller to undertake the repairs, since the boatyard may find additional problems after it gets into the job. You should reserve the right to have your surveyor check the boat again after the repairs are completed to see that they were done properly. Have a clear understanding with the surveyor as to whether the recheck of the repairs will cost you extra. If the seller is going to reduce the price and you are going to be responsible for the repairs, you should get a good boatyard to give you a quote on the work to make certain of the expense involved. Bear in mind that if you go that route and the yard finds other problems once it opens up the work, you—not the seller—are responsible for the added expense.

After completing the inspection, the surveyor should prepare a written report that details everything found, down to missing clamps and lightbulbs, and should give an estimate of the boat's present and replacement values. Most surveyors will present their written reports within about forty-eight hours of the survey itself.

With this report in hand, you're now in a position to finalize your offer.

NEGOTIATING A TRADE-IN

If you have a boat you want to trade in on a newer or larger vessel, you need to get a realistic idea of what it's worth before you get into serious negotiations. Check the BUC Book's average wholesale price for a vessel of your boat's year and model in average condition with average equipment, and check brokers for typical selling prices; then adjust the figure to fit your boat's condition. Assuming your trade-in is in average condition with average equipment, you should expect a trade-in allowance from a new boat dealer that is about 10 percent less than the current actual retail price of similar boats. If your boat is exceptionally clean or well equipped, its value should be a bit higher. If a dealer offers you a trade-in price for your boat that is substantially above what your own research has indicated it is worth, go over his offer on the new boat with a fine-tooth comb. There ain't no free lunch, and there ain't no Santa Claus.

If your trade-in is a popular model in good condition, which a dealer can turn quickly at a reasonable profit, you probably will encounter little resistance from the dealer to taking it in trade. If the boat has a wood hull, is a brand few people have heard of, has an odd layout, or has serious mechanical problems, a dealer may refuse to take it in trade but may agree to sell it for you on consignment. Most brokers would prefer to sell your boat on consignment, which ties up your money, not theirs. If you're going to sell your boat through a broker, choose one who deals in the type of vessel you want to sell. You'll probably find that giving a central agency listing will make the broker more aggressive in trying to advertise and sell it since the broker can expect a commission of at least 3 percent of the sales price even if another broker finds you a buyer. If the brokerage has slips, the broker should be willing to display your boat for a couple of months without charging you dockage. If it takes longer than that to sell the boat, you should only have to pay about half the going rate to keep your boat at the dock.

If you wind up listing your old boat on consignment, bear in mind that the dealer or broker probably is refusing to take it in trade precisely because experience teaches that it won't sell quickly. If you still owe money on your old boat, or if you will have to borrow more money for the new boat to offset the loss of the trade-in allowance, don't fool yourself into thinking a buyer will come along and bail you out in a couple of weeks. Make certain you can carry the added cost for at least six months, or you could find that you have to let your old boat go at far less than you intended just to get some of the financial load off your back.

UNDERSTANDING SALES TAXES

More and more states are beginning to realize what a financial bonanza booming boat sales represent, and they are slapping sales taxes on both new and used yachts. Florida, which is possibly the yacht sales capital of the nation, has been the trendsetter in this movement, and its approach is being implemented or at least studied by a number of states. It's a fairly safe bet that most coastal states that don't already have machinery to enforce their sales taxes on boats will have something similar to the Florida program in place in the foreseeable future.

The Florida program works like this: the sales-tax rate for both new and used boats is 6 percent of the purchase price. In the example of the boat we discussed above, at a $265,000 sale price (assuming no trade-in was involved), the sales tax would be a whopping $15,900. If a dealer or broker takes a buyer's old boat in trade, the buyer pays sales tax only on the difference between the price of the new boat and the value of the trade-in. If the dealer takes the old boat on consignment and its sale is not closed at the same time the deal on the new boat is closed, the buyer pays sales tax on the full price of the new boat. If the broker sells the buyer's old boat and the deals on both boats are closed simultaneously, the buyer of the new boat pays sales tax only on the difference in the sales prices of the two vessels.

Unfortunately, sales taxes are no longer deductible from federal income tax returns.

Individuals who purchase boats in Florida are liable for Florida's sales tax whether or not they are residents of the state. The only way to buy a boat in Florida and legally avoid paying the Florida sales tax is to remove the boat from Florida within ten days of its purchase, unless it requires repair or alteration, in which case it must be removed from the state within ten days of the completion of the repairs or alterations. In no case may it be kept in Florida more than ninety days from the date of purchase. In order to waive collection of the Florida sales tax, dealers and brokers in the state must require buyers who say they plan to remove their boat from Florida within the required time period to sign an affidavit to that effect and to send them the original of a fuel or dockage bill from another state as proof that the boat has left Florida's jurisdiction. The boat may not return to Florida within six months of its departure. Because so many East Coast owners keep their boats in the Bahamas for part of the year anyway, moving a boat there for the six-month out-of-state period will not satisfy the requirement.

Even removing a boat purchased in Florida from the state within the required period and keeping it out for the stipulated length of time may not suffice to avoid the Florida sales tax. As one Florida revenue agent told me: "Say we run across an owner who bought a boat in Florida, avoided the Florida sales tax by taking it across the state line into Georgia, then brought it back into Florida as soon as the six-month period was up. We'd look at that situation pretty carefully. If we found, for instance, that after having the boat in Georgia for a couple of months, he had made a reservation for a slip in Florida beginning as soon as the six-month waiting period was up, we'd probably rule his intent in moving it to Georgia was simply to avoid the Florida sales tax, and we'd make him pay."

The penalty for illegally avoiding Florida's sales tax is severe: the original tax, plus interest from the date it should have been paid, plus 100 percent of the tax as a penalty.

Florida and the other states that impose sales taxes on boats are getting a lot stricter in enforcing the taxes. During the early 1980s, for instance, the Florida Department of Revenue had three agents checking for boats still in the state on which

Florida's sales tax was not collected because the purchaser signed an affidavit saying the boat would be taken out of the state. Today, that section has over eighty agents. The Miami coast guard office now routinely sends information on all the vessels it documents to the Florida Department of Revenue. If the Department of Revenue does not find evidence in its files that Florida sales tax has been paid on a particular boat within its borders, it contacts the purchaser to find out why. In addition, the Florida Marine Patrol is also on the lookout for vessels purchased and operating in the state on which the state's sales tax has not been paid. The crackdown has gotten so stringent that some new-boat dealers and used-boat brokers in Florida are now requiring purchasers who say they plan to remove their boats from the state to put the sales tax in escrow; they then refund it only when they have proof from the owner that the vessel has actually been taken beyond Florida's borders.

Similar crackdowns are taking place in New York and Connecticut, where the state sales-tax rate is 6 percent. These two states compare notes on vessels that are documented with the New York office of the coast guard and check to see if sales tax has been paid in either state. If not, they go looking for the owners.

Connecticut requires all vessels berthed in its waters for longer than sixty days (rather than ninety days as in most states) to be state registered, even if they are federally documented. To register a vessel, the owner must present a bill of sale showing the date of purchase. If the boat was purchased within the preceding six months, the owner must also present proof of the price paid for the boat and proof of the sales taxes paid to any other state. If the sales tax paid to another state is less than Connecticut's 6 percent, the owner must pay the difference to Connecticut before the vessel can be registered. (Most states will give credit for sales taxes paid to other states.) An owner without proof of sales tax paid to another state must pay the entire 6 percent. The state is deadly serious about catching boatowners who try to ignore its sales-tax regulations. "The revenue agents walk the dock," one Connecticut yacht owner told me, "and take down information on the boats that are tied up. Sixty-one days later, they walk down the same dock. Any vessel that is still there and is not on their list as having had Connecticut sales taxes paid on it gets a note stuck on the windshield directing the owner to contact the state revenue department."

Any sales taxes that apply to a cruising vessel you buy also will apply to its tender.

If you buy a boat in a state with a high sales tax and want to avoid paying that tax by removing it to a state with no sales tax or a tax that is lower, where do you take it? A few buyers of really expensive yachts go to the extreme of setting up a corporation in a no- or low-tax state, listing the vessel as a corporate asset, and either basing it in that state or keeping it on the move so that it is in no one state more than sixty or ninety days, depending on that state's regulations. Listing a yacht as a corporate asset also has the advantage of limiting the owner's personal liability in case of accident. For a fee of around $1,000, a number of yacht service firms will set up such a corporation in Rhode Island, which charges no sales tax, or in North Carolina, which limits sales taxes on boats to a maximum of $300 regardless of value. For that fee, you get a legal corporation, stock certificates, a corporate seal, and the address of a registered agent in the state whom you can use as the corporation's own.

The upshot of this whole discussion of sales taxes is that you should be sure to include them in your boat-buying budget and, before you sign on the dotted line, to check with your lawyer or accountant to make sure you know what sales taxes you will be liable for.

FINANCING THE BOAT

If you plan to finance your boat, the first question is where you will go to borrow the money. The first place you should check is the bank with which you normally do your personal or business banking. Your contact there may be willing to make certain concessions in rate or terms because you are a good customer and the bank wants to keep your business. Also, your local bank is likely to retain your loan in its own portfolio. Should the time come when you need to make changes in your loan's terms and conditions, you would probably deal with someone you know who has an interest in keeping you happy.

Some banks, of course, simply don't know anything about the peculiar intricacies of yacht financing and really aren't interested in lending money on a highly mobile piece of machinery that they can't keep an eye on. If you find your local bank is not interested in giving you a boat loan, check some of the well-established banks in the primary boating markets.

In many cases, a salesperson or broker will offer to put you in touch with someone at a national finance company or a bank that offers yacht financing. Occasionally, the dealership or brokerage house may have an arrangement with the financing source, which pays them a commission or some percentage of your interest in return for steering you to them and taking care of much of the paperwork. While some would call this a kickback, there is nothing illegal about the practice. But if that is the case, you should be aware of it and take the dealer's probable "side income" from the lending transaction (typically 1.5 to 3 percent of the amount you borrow) into account when you negotiate the price of a boat.

The national financing sources frequently will offer rates a quarter to half of a percentage point lower than you will get from a local bank. Saving interest expense is always nice, but you should be aware of one potential danger. Many of these yacht financing sources make the bulk of their income originating loans or servicing them (that is, collecting and processing payments for someone else), not from tying up their own funds for fifteen to twenty years and taking their profit from the interest you pay. To keep fresh funds coming in to lend new customers, they sell the loans they originate to investors. Your loan might wind up being owned by a finance company, a bank, or even an individual halfway across the continent. If something happens down the road to make you want to modify the terms of the loan, you may find you must deal with someone you have never heard of who has no particular reason to want to accommodate your request. Again, there is nothing inherently wrong with this practice, but you should ask a potential lender about the policy on loan sales so you know all the ground rules before you sign the loan.

In any discussions about possible financing, insist on two things:

- that yours be a simple-interest loan, not an "add-on" or "Rule of 78s" loan (in which you actually wind up paying interest on interest)
- that you have the right to pay off the principal of the loan at any time without any prepayment penalty

In considering your yacht loan, a lender is going to be looking primarily for two things: where your cash flow to repay the loan will come from, and how to structure the deal so that there is always more equity in the boat than what you owe on it. In case of repossession, the lender wants to make certain the boat can be sold for enough to cover both the outstanding principal and any expenses incurred in the selling process.

To determine how large a loan you can afford, the guidelines for analyzing your cash flow vary widely by institution. One usually reliable rule of thumb is to take 75 percent of your gross annual income as theoretically disposable after taxes. Most lenders don't want to see more than 40 percent of that figure committed to fixed payments, such as your home mortgage and installment loans, or more than 60 percent committed to basic living expenses, such as food, shelter, clothing, transportation, medical care, insurance, and the like. Even if you meet these criteria, most lenders will not make you a loan whose payment will eat up more than half of 40 percent of your disposable income after meeting your basic expenses.

The primary way the lender will try to ensure that there is always adequate equity in the boat is to require a substantial down payment. In a typical case of a new cruising powerboat with a price tag of $100,000 or more, a lender will want a down payment of at least 20 percent of the purchase price and will finance the balance for up to twenty years. On a used boat, most lenders will want 25 percent down and will finance the balance over a maximum of fifteen years. There are, however, situations where a lender will take a smaller percentage for the down payment if you agree to a loan with a shorter term—say, seven to ten years rather than fifteen or twenty. In that case, you would be paying equity into the loan faster than the boat is depreciating.

It's difficult to determine the rate at which a particular yacht will depreciate. In boom times, some boats even appreciate in value. Check the BUC Book for the make and model of boat you are considering to see whether the average wholesale figures have gone up or down over several years. But remember that the figures themselves may not be all that accurate; also, they are based on past averages, which are not necessarily a reliable guide to what will happen in the future.

Having offered that caveat, however, it is possible to make a few general statements.

- *A boat built by a well-known, quality manufacturer will tend to depreciate less in bad times and appreciate more in good times than one from a manufacturer who is less well-known and offers a lower level of construction quality.* You might save a substantial sum up front by buying a lightly built boat from a little-known manufacturer, but when the time comes to trade or sell it, you probably will find that you have lost money over time.
- *New boats tend to depreciate faster than used boats in the first year or two of their operation.* The minute you take delivery of a new boat and drive it away from the dealer's dock, it becomes a used boat and is valued accordingly.

- *"Character" boats, or boats to which the owner has added highly personal or unusual features, depreciate faster than more conventional models.* That salty little cruiser with the lines of a New York Harbor tugboat may be exactly the boat you want, but be aware that if you decide to sell or trade it, you may have a tough time finding a buyer who shares your tastes and you may well take a sizable loss on your investment. Adding homemade bow pulpits, elaborate topside lounges, and the like to even a popular model may suit you perfectly but is likely to reduce the boat's value at resale or trade-in time.
- *Well-maintained boats retain a higher percentage of their values than boats that have been mistreated.* Changing engine and generator oil at recommended intervals, keeping your vessel's engine room spotless, keeping your teak handrails protected with oil or varnish, and performing all the other steps that go into proper boat maintenance may be tedious at the time, but they will pay you back in significant dollars when you resell your boat.

In financing the purchase of a boat, many people go for the lowest possible down payment and longest term they can get. That route will hold down the cost of their monthly payments, but they will pay dearly in terms of interest cost, and when the time comes to sell or trade their boat they will have little, if any, equity in it.

Most yacht financing experts recommend exactly the opposite: pay down as much as you can and structure the loan over the shortest possible time consistent with the maximum monthly payments you can afford. Consider these figures on a $100,000 loan at 10 percent: if the term is twenty years, the payments will be about $965 a month. Shorten the term to fifteen years, and the payment increases only $110 to $1,075. Shorten it to twelve years, and the payment goes up only another $120 to $1,195. But look what happens to your interest expense: assuming you pay the loan to maturity, on the twenty-year loan you will have paid $131,600 in interest; on the fifteen-year loan,

$93,500; and on the twelve-year loan, $72,080. By shortening the term from twenty to twelve years and increasing your payments by $230 per month, over the life of the loan you'll save $59,520 in interest expense—more than half of what you borrowed in the first place.

Also look what happens to your equity: after making payments for three years, on the twenty-year loan you still owe principal of $94,674; on the fifteen-year loan, the balance is $90,242; and on the twelve-year loan, it is $85,370. By reducing the term from twenty years to twelve at only slightly higher monthly payments, at the end of three years you have increased your equity in the vessel by more than $9,000. At the end of five years, the difference is almost $18,000.

In summary, shop for your yacht loan as carefully as you shop for the yacht itself. As with the boat, the right loan can make your cruising experience a joy; the wrong loan can burden you with unnecessary expense.

INSURING THE BOAT

As a yacht owner, your potential for grief from improper or inadequate insurance ranks second only to that of dealing with paid crew. The waterfront is full of horror stories from yacht owners who thought they were covered for a specific difficulty and found out they weren't, or who had their insurance company refuse to pay a claim because of some alleged failure on the part of the owner to live up to the policy's terms and conditions.

In arranging insurance on your cruising vessel, get at least three detailed quotes on the coverage you need. Premiums for exactly the same coverage can vary 25 to 30 percent from company to company. All three probably can be supplied by a single agent since most marine insurance agents are independents and deal with several companies. Insist that your yacht insurance be written only by a company that is "A-rated." Lower-rated companies may offer cheaper premiums, but a couple of multimillion-dollar liability losses could quickly leave them insolvent. Under Murphy's Law, they will suffer all those losses in the two weeks before you file your claim.

Arrange your insurance with a company that has a separate marine division that is thoroughly knowledgeable in yacht insurance. Some companies write policies on yachts the same way they do on automobiles and take depreciation on losses, which good marine policies don't. On a new yacht, depreciation could cost you 20 to 25 percent the minute you take delivery. Also, make sure the company you go with will cover you in all the navigation areas you plan to cruise, even though you may not buy coverage for all those areas initially. You want to build up a history of trust with your insurer. You don't want to wind up in the Virgin Islands with plans to head for Martinique only to find that your present insurer won't extend your navigation limits and you have to negotiate the necessary coverage with a new company over a satellite telephone or single-sideband radio.

In filing your application for insurance, be completely truthful and comprehensive. If you suffer a loss, any overstatement of your experience and qualifications or understatement of previous losses could be used by your insurer to deny payment based on the policy's "fraud and misrepresentation" clause. Before you sign anything, read the policy carefully to make certain it provides the coverage you need and says so in black and white. Verbal additions by the agent are not binding on the company.

Once you have bought a policy, read it again and make notes on what you must do to comply with its terms. Most policies, for instance, require that if your vessel has an automatic fire-suppression system in the engine room, it must be checked and recertified by an approved technician annually. If you fail to have it recertified within the required time period and have an engine room fire, you are giving the insurance company a perfect reason to deny coverage. Most policies protect against theft only if there are signs of forced entry or removal. Go ashore in your dinghy one evening, loop its rope painter over a piling, and have it disappear. When you file a claim, your insurer may deny payment by arguing that you should have used a wire painter and locked the tender securely to the dock. Good-bye to an uninsured $5,000 tender and outboard.

If you're about to embark on an extended voyage, make certain the address you list on the application is one through which you can and will be notified immediately of any changes in your policy or its cancellation. Most marine policies allow the company to cancel a policy simply by mailing a notice of cancellation to the most recent address they have for you at least ten days before the cancellation date. Some companies have been known to cancel all their marine policies arbitrarily for business reasons that have nothing to do with the policyholders themselves. Also, make certain the person responsible for your mail knows who your insurer is, opens anything from the company as soon as it arrives, and notifies you immediately of any significant changes in coverage or cancellation.

The standard yacht policy offered by all the A-rated companies has substantially the same provisions, which are divided into sections for hull insurance, liability insurance, and medical payments.

Hull insurance covers your vessel and everything on it necessary to its operation or bought specifically for use on board. The amount of hull insurance normally will be based on *agreed valuation*, which is what you and the insurance company mutually agree would be the cost of replacing the yacht in the event of its loss. There is no sense in insuring your yacht for more than its replacement cost. In the event of its loss, replacement cost is all the company will pay even though that total may not reach the limits of your policy.

From the base rate for the amount of hull insurance you buy, you will be given credits for such things as an automatic engine room fire-suppression system, separate fuel shutoffs for each fuel line and separate shutoff switches for each bank of batteries, any boating courses you may have taken, and your boating experience. You normally will be charged a penalty above the base rate if your boat is more than five years old, even more if it is older than ten years.

Before issuing a policy, the insurer will require a current survey on the boat (one not more than six months old, and in some cases not more than two months old). As mentioned earlier in this chapter, some insurers will accept only surveys conducted by marine surveyors on their approved lists. Most companies will require a new survey every couple of years or annually for boats more than five to ten years old. Some companies will refuse to issue insurance at all on wood-hull vessels. For steel- or aluminum-hull vessels, they often will require the thickness of the hull to be checked every square foot by an audio-gauge, which for a 40- to 50-footer (12–15 m) can cost $1,000 or more and must be repeated every two or three years.

Most hull insurance covers losses while the vessel is being operated by you or anyone—except paid crew—who has your permission to operate it. If you will have paid crew operating the yacht, you will have to purchase a separate endorsement to your basic policy. You should be covered for losses from any cause, even your own negligence (though repeated negligence will result in the company canceling the policy or refusing to renew it). The policy should provide for replacing "new for old" with no allowance for depreciation. The exception in some policies is that the company will pay only "actual value"—replacement less depreciation— for outboard motors and canvas items. At the time you arrange for your insurance, you should make a complete inventory of everything on your vessel that is covered by your insurance policy, gather any receipts or documents that will help establish values, and tuck the information away in a safe place onshore, not aboard the vessel.

The normal deductible on standard yacht policies is 1 percent of the agreed valuation. In the case of extremely expensive yachts, some companies will negotiate the deductible down to 0.75 or 0.5 percent. If your cruising itinerary will take you well offshore or deep into the boondocks, some companies will insist on increasing the deductible to 2 percent or more. The deductible normally will not be applied in the case of total loss of the yacht.

Hull insurance will cover your dinghy and its outboard, but the sizable deductible it carries means you probably would collect little, if anything, in the event of loss. You may want to consider covering them with a separate policy or rider that has a smaller deductible—say, $250 to $500.

Carefully check the exclusions of any insurance policy you consider buying. Most will not cover losses incurred while the vessel is being used for any kind of commercial operation or those that result from "warlike operations," which include wars declared or undeclared, insurrections, rebellions, and the like. Nor will you be covered if your yacht is confiscated for any reason, whether the confiscation is legal or illegal.

For the cruising owner, the most important exclusions concern navigation limits. The policy will specify the area in which its coverage is valid. If you exceed those limits, your coverage automatically ceases. In some cases, companies will extend your policy's navigation limits if you pay additional premiums and, perhaps, agree to a higher deductible. The additional premium to allow a yacht to cruise the Bahamas might be no more than $50; to extend its navigation limits to the Virgin Islands might cost $500. Since you will have to renew your policy each year, buy only the extended navigation coverage you need for the duration of the policy. If you decide to venture beyond your policy's navigation limits prior to renewal, contact your insurance agent as far in advance as possible—a month is not too much. In order to request the extended coverage from your insurer's underwriter, your agent will need a detailed itinerary, including your planned schedule, route, ports of call, and how far you will be venturing offshore, as well as a list of persons who will be aboard, including the boating experience of any of your guests.

Most policies also limit coverage to a certain distance offshore—10 to 50 miles (16–80 km)— so make sure the offshore limits are adequate to cover your planned route.

Before most insurance companies will insure a yacht for offshore use, they usually require that there be at least two people aboard capable of operating it. In some cases, they will require three or four. Because of that requirement, it is not unusual for a couple who dream of extensive offshore cruising but have little boating experience to find that they can get insurance for coastal cruising but are unable to obtain insurance from any source for open-water passagemaking. If you and your significant other have limited experience and ambitious plans, you may find you have to hire a professional captain acceptable to your insurer, cruise the boat under the captain's supervision for several months, and then hope to persuade the underwriter to issue you insurance based on the captain's recommendation.

Hull insurance normally will cover damage to your vessel while it is being transported on land, though some companies limit that protection to a certain number of miles from the vessel's home port. Transportation by water—shipping your yacht as deck cargo on a freighter, for instance—is not covered.

The hull insurance section of most policies specifically excludes coverage of personal property—clothing, cameras, sports equipment, and the like. Those few policies that do include personal property often have ridiculously low limits or high deductibles. Most companies will provide endorsements to their marine policies—at an additional premium, of course—to cover personal property, but even then they normally cover only actual cash value and exclude coverage of cash or jewelry. If you have a homeowner's policy, you may find it covers your personal property while cruising. As with everything else aboard your vessel, you would be wise to maintain an onshore inventory of personal property aboard along with any documents that will help establish its value.

Hull insurance also normally covers the cost of towing and assistance, but only if they are required to keep the yacht from suffering further damage. If you want coverage for towing and assistance in the event you simply run out of fuel, you will have to pay for a separate towing-and-assistance endorsement.

The liability insurance in most standard yacht policies (usually referred to as "protection and indemnity") pays for damage caused by you or your yacht while it is being operated by you or someone you have allowed to operate it, again with the exception of paid crew. Limits in the standard policy are normally $300,000 and $500,000. If you cause serious property damage, bodily injury, or death with your yacht, you can be sued for everything you own, so the best rule here is to buy enough liability insurance to cover your total personal assets.

Medical payments (including funeral expenses) under a standard yacht policy normally are limited to $5,000 or $10,000 per person per incident. With medical costs what they are today, that is likely to be totally inadequate. Buy all the extra coverage you can afford. Increments of $5,000 per person per incident usually cost only an additional $20 or so per year. Again, most standard yacht policies exclude medical payments to paid crew. To cover crew members, you must purchase a separate endorsement that meets the requirements of the Longshoremen's and Harbor Workers' Act, also called the Jones Act.

Standard yacht policies normally don't cover damages inflicted by uninsured boaters. You would be wise to add an endorsement for that coverage to your policy. There is always the possibility some yokel who has zero insurance might inadequately anchor his vessel upwind of you in a storm and sweep down on you in the dark of night.

If you have an accident, a standard yacht policy requires you to notify your insurer as soon as possible and take all reasonable actions to prevent further damage. Ideally, you will be able to reach your agent quickly and have your insurer's adjuster authorize you to have needed repairs done before the work is begun. If that proves impossible, use your best judgment. If you have to have repairs done before you get authorization from an adjuster, take pictures of the damage before it is repaired. Even better, hire a local marine surveyor, if possible, to check the damage and give you a complete report. Be certain you get good, detailed receipts for any expenses you incur. (See chapter 16 for more information on how to respond appropriately to an accident involving your boat.)

DOCUMENTING, NUMBERING, REGISTERING, AND TITLING THE BOAT

A good deal of confusion exists among cruising yacht owners as to the pros and cons, procedures, and legal distinctions involved in documentation, numbering, registration, and titling. *Documentation* is a *federal* process in which the U.S. government, acting through the coast guard, issues a Certificate of Documentation that attests to a vessel's nationality. Documentation also can establish ownership of the vessel and allow the legal recording of a first preferred ship's mortgage, which protects a lender's lien against the vessel. (Because documentation is a federal process—and only a federal process—the terms *federal documentation* and *documentation with the federal government* are redundant.) If you finance your boat, the choice of whether to document your vessel may well be made for you. Since vessels are so mobile, lenders in most cases require documentation because it allows them to legally record a first preferred ship's mortgage, which must be recognized in any state. A lender who has to repossess the vessel in a distant state can have the process executed by federal marshals rather than having to deal with individual state laws regarding repossession, which vary widely.

If you will be cruising the waters of other nations, I strongly recommend that you document your vessel even if documentation is not otherwise required. In my experience, the legal process of entering other nations is somewhat easier when you present your ship's papers to a foreign customs official in the form of a Certificate of Documentation issued by the U.S. government rather than a wallet card from some state's fish and game commission. If you should get into legal trouble in another country, the U.S. embassy or consular official you call for help may have a bit more clout with the locals if representing the owner of a U.S.-documented vessel.

The basic drawback to documentation is its cost: it runs $50 to $100 or more if you handle the process yourself and up to $500 or so (fees included) if you have a documentation service handle the paperwork for you.

Documenting a new boat is not particularly difficult. You can obtain the necessary forms from the coast guard district headquarters nearest your legal residence (or nearest the address of the corporation that owns the boat). Complete the forms and return them to the coast guard along with a bill of sale from the dealer, a builder's certificate (which the builder will supply), and a declaration (a form supplied by the coast guard) that you are a U.S. citizen. In completing the forms, however, be very careful. The coast guard is supposed to reject any documentation application that does not contain all the required information or is defaced in any way, including erasures, strikeovers, or white outs. Some district offices are not quite as strict as the law allows them to be, but many will reject an application for the most minute of reasons. If the owner of the vessel is listed on the documentation application as Joseph A. Smith, for instance, but the bill of sale shows it was sold to J. A. Smith, the coast guard may send the application back.

In the case of a vessel that is already documented or a vessel whose documentation has been allowed to lapse, you must establish a legal chain of ownership from the most recent documentation. If the vessel has never been documented, you may either establish a complete chain of ownership or present a copy of its most recent state registration and evidence that establishes the chain of ownership from that registration to you.

To be documented, a vessel must be measured (the correct technical term is *admeasured*, but it isn't used much today) to ensure that it is of at least 5 net tons (5 metric tons). For documentation purposes, net tonnage has nothing to do with a vessel's weight or displacement but refers to the interior volume of its hull. The net tonnage of a typical cruising powerboat will be 0.8 of its gross tonnage. Gross tonnage is determined by the formula

$$\tfrac{2}{3} \, (\textbf{length} \times \textbf{breadth} \times \textbf{depth} \div 100)$$

where *length* is the vessel's overall length (not including a bow pulpit or swim platform), *breadth* is the vessel's beam, and *depth* is the depth from the sheer to the keel measured on the center line amidships.

In the case of pleasure vessels, the coast guard normally will use a simplified measurement process. For a new vessel, the coast guard usually figures the vessel's net tonnage from the builder's certificate. In the case of a used vessel that has been previously documented, even though its documentation may have been allowed to lapse, the coast guard will accept the measurement from the previous documentation provided the vessel has not been subjected to major alteration. In the case of a used vessel that has never been documented, if you can supply an original builder's certificate, the coast guard will take its measurements from that document. If you cannot submit a builder's certificate, apply for a simplified measurement by accompanying your application with a letter addressed to the documentation officer giving your name and address (or the name and address of the corporation that owns the vessel) and the vessel's name, type, builder, model, length, breadth, and depth.

Documentation must be renewed annually. The coast guard will send you a renewal form when your documentation is about to expire. If there have been no changes in the status of the vessel or its ownership, no fee is required. You will have to pay additional fees of $50 to $100, however, if you change your vessel's name, home port, or ownership or allow your documentation to lapse.

A documented vessel must be marked in a fashion prescribed by the coast guard. The boat's official number—preceded by the abbreviation "No."—must be permanently inscribed in block Arabic numerals at least 3 inches (7.5 cm) high

on the interior of the vessel forward of amidships. Its name and hailing port must be inscribed together on the exterior of the hull in clearly legible letters at least 4 inches (10 cm) high. For a hailing port on a documented vessel, you may use its port of documentation or its home port, which will be the city and state of your legal residence or the legal address of the corporation in which it is held.

Numbering and *registration* are processes carried out by individual states, but the manner in which they are conducted is specified by federal law and thus is relatively uniform nationwide. The distinction between the two processes is primarily technical rather than practical, but you need to understand it so that you are aware of your options and responsibilities as a boatowner.

The Federal Boat Safety Act of 1971 requires all boats owned by U.S. residents that are used on waters subject to federal jurisdiction or on the high seas to be numbered. That same law, however, specifically exempts documented vessels from being numbered. A boat must be numbered by the state in which it is most often used on the water, not the state in which the owner resides. All states have agencies to handle vessel numbering—with the exception of Alaska, where the process is handled by the coast guard. Numbering can best be understood as a specific type of state registration in which the state issues a Certificate of Number that allows a vessel to operate in waters under that state's jurisdiction. The number assigned must be displayed on each side of the forward half of the vessel. Most states also require numbered vessels to display adjacent to their number a validation sticker that indicates the payment of current fees. Federal law prohibits a Certificate of Number from being valid for longer than three years, and many states require renewal annually. Renewal normally is evidenced by replacing the vessel's validation sticker with a new one for the current year.

Although the Federal Boat Safety Act of 1971 prohibits documented vessels from being numbered, it does allow states to require documented vessels to be "registered" if they choose to do so.

The process and the fees for registration are the same as for numbering. The only difference is that the documented vessel that is also registered will not display a number on its hull as a numbered vessel must but will instead be issued decals that must be displayed on the port and starboard side windows. Registration, like numbering, must be renewed periodically to remain valid. Renewal normally is evidenced by replacing the window decals with new ones for the current year. Fees vary widely, but as an example, the fee as of this writing for registering a class 3 vessel—40 to 65 feet (12–18 m) length overall—in Florida is $82.

Under federal law, numbering or registration by one state must be honored on a reciprocal basis in other states for at least sixty days. Some states recognize reciprocal numbering or registration for ninety days.

If you document that your vessel and your cruising plans will keep the boat outside U.S. waters or on the move so that you are not in the waters of any one state longer than sixty days, you shouldn't have to worry about state registration. If you will be operating your vessel in a state longer than sixty days at a time (ninety days in some states), you probably will be required to register it in that state as well. Some states require documented vessels to be registered, while others do not.

Titling is a state process that establishes legal ownership of a vessel and also allows for the legal recording of liens against the vessel. In most cases, however, liens will be recognized only in the state in which the title was issued. At present, only nineteen states require or allow boats to be titled.

REGISTERING A TENDER

Under federal law, states have the option of exempting from the numbering regulations tenders that are used only for direct transportation between a larger vessel *that is numbered* and the shore and are powered by motors of less than 10 horsepower. Some states provide this exemption, while others do not. In states that provide the exemption, such tenders must be identified by the number displayed by the larger vessel followed by a space or a hyphen and the numeral 1. A vessel used as a tender to a documented vessel must be numbered if it is propelled by a motor of any horsepower.

Now that you've learned how to decide what boat is best for you and how to find and buy it at a fair price, we can take a look at the accessory equipment needed to allow you to cruise in safety and comfort.

PART TWO

All the Bells and Whistles

Buying Marine Accessories

Whether the boat of your dreams is to be new or used, once you settle on the one you want, you are just beginning to create the vessel you really need. There isn't a stock new boat on the market that does not require the addition of thousands of dollars' worth of accessory equipment to turn it into a safe, comfortable cruiser—everything from navigational and communications electronics to a tender and tender-handling system, ground tackle, safety equipment, and so on. If you decide to buy a boat that a previous owner has already outfitted for cruising, you are still going to have to decide which of the gear already aboard is what you need and want, what you need to replace, and what is missing and must be added.

BUYING FROM A DEALER

In the case of a new boat, you can complete the rigging the easy way: by allowing the dealer to specify what you need, having it installed at the factory or after the boat arrives at the yard, and

paying the bill. Now I don't mean to knock competent boat dealers here. There are a number of excellent ones around, and if you are fortunate enough to work with ones who really know their stuff, you can be spared a world of time and trouble, especially if you live well inland and are having your boat commissioned at a considerable distance.

But allowing your dealer to supply all or most of your accessory gear can have its drawbacks. Bear in mind that if the dealer helps you specify all of the accessory equipment you require, makes arrangements to have it shipped in, and handles its installation, that dealer is providing you a service—and it may well cost you dearly. New-boat dealers often are not franchised dealers for the accessory equipment they sell. In many cases, they buy whatever they need through a local specialty retailer who does have a franchise. In that case, both the boatyard and the retailer have a markup in the deal. Even worse, there are boat dealers who know little about real cruising and will load you up with every piece of equipment they can persuade you to buy at the best profit margin the market will allow.

BUYING FROM A SPECIALTY RETAILER

Another option is to buy the accessories you need directly from specialty retailers: a marine electronics retailer for your navigation and communications equipment; a small-boat dealer for your tender, outboard, and davits; and a company that specializes in safety gear for your life raft, life jackets, and emergency signaling devices. Going that route requires a greater investment of time on your part, but you may find you get the advice of people who deal full-time with specific items and know more than the people at the boat dealership. Since you are one step closer to the source of the equipment you are buying, you also should be able to save a few dollars. In the case of electronics, for instance, where a new boat dealer may offer you a 12 to 15 percent discount off the manufacturer's list prices (including installation), the specialty retailer should be able to offer closer to 20 percent, again with installation included.

In the case of navigational and communications electronics in particular, if you rely on a single, competent source for your equipment—whether it's the dealer or a specialty retailer—and have that source install it, the retailer or dealer can help you work out the best placement of individual units and antennas to keep them from electrically interfering with one another as much as possible. Further, you know exactly whom to go back to if you have problems, and you may be able to negotiate a package price and have all the installation done at one time.

Even if you decide to let a dealer or specialty retailer supply most of a particular type of equipment, don't blindly accept everything offered. If the price on an item seems out of line, or if the quality is questionable, keep talking and looking until you are sure you have what you really want and can buy it at fair price. Especially in the case of marine electronics, a number of companies manufacture very broad product lines—everything from VHF and SSB radios to radar, satellite navigation equipment, and the like. A decade ago, you might have been wary of a dealer who wanted to sell you a single manufacturer's brand for everything you need. Then, one company's radar may have been the best value for the money, but its marine radios were of poor design or were overpriced. Each of those pieces of gear is important, and you should consider each on its own merits and go for the best equipment rather than opting for the convenience—or even the price advantage—of working with a single supply source or manufacturer. Today, with the advent of reliable, interconnected equipment, that picture has changed significantly. Now, most navigational gear is interdependent and integrated. A global positioning system (GPS) connects to a chart plotter, which connects to a fish-finder, which connects to a radar. Because of such sophisticated technology, single-brand buying can be an attractive proposition.

BUYING FROM A MARINE CATALOG

A third option is to buy the accessories you need through marine catalogs, which advertise prices substantially below what most new-boat dealers and specialty retailers charge. If you decide on this approach, several cautions are in order. First, when comparing prices between the catalogs and a boat dealer or specialty retailer, make sure you include all of your costs. The price a marine catalog quotes for a marine satellite telephone, for instance, may be 40 percent or more off list but probably will include only the telephone itself, not the mounting kit, coupler, antenna, and mounting brackets you also need. Make sure you're comparing apples to apples. Also, be certain to include shipping costs. The equipment normally will be shipped to you via a parcel service or motor freight. Be sure to inspect the equipment before you sign for it, especially if the outside carton shows any sign of damage.

The biggest problem with buying accessories through a catalog, especially your key electronic navigation and communications equipment, is making certain it is installed properly. As you will see in chapters 8 and 9, such installation factors as shielding from electrical interference, accurate calibration, proper grounding, and placement of antennas can be critical to the equipment's performance. In the case of SSBs, the law requires that they be installed by or under the supervision of a technician licensed by the Federal Communications Commission. Since your safety could well depend on the correct functioning of your radar, satellite navigation equipment, satellite telephones, marine radios, and depth-sounders, you should be extremely hesitant to install these items yourself. Even if you decide to handle the installation, you probably should have your handiwork checked over by a qualified technician (include what you pay him in your overall costs).

Even if you do pay a local technician to install some of the equipment you need, you will still save significant chunks of money by purchasing from catalogs—in many cases up to 30 percent or more off list and 10 to 25 percent off the dealer's or specialty retailer's prices. But you will make that savings at the expense of your own time, especially if the equipment proves to be defective and has to be returned for service or replacement.

If you buy from a marine catalog, select one that is a franchised dealer for the equipment you buy and is authorized to service it with its own factory-trained technicians. There are several good marine catalog outfits around; some I have dealt with personally or have had consistently good reports about include Consumers Marine Electronics, Landfall Navigation, West Marine, and BoatU.S.

Now that you have a basis to decide where you'll purchase your vessel's accessories, we take the next five chapters to consider the specifics of the equipment you'll need for navigating, communicating, anchoring, a tender, and safety.

Choosing a
Marine Navigation System

In the past decade or so, no aspect of recreational boating has seen more radical change than marine navigational electronics. The technological explosion in microprocessors, satellites, and digital electronics has produced an incredible array of new systems and devices to help cruisers know precisely where they are and how to get safely to their destinations. Today, we routinely employ highly sophisticated, integrated onboard navigation systems that did not exist or were in their infancy just a few years ago. As the U.S. Department of Defense's global positioning system (GPS) has come into almost universal use, we have seen vast improvements in equipment accuracy, reliability, compactness, weight reduction, and ease of operation. In the process, the cost of GPS equipment in many cases has dropped from the tens of thousands of dollars to no more than $1,000 or $2,000. Equally dramatic advances now allow us to interface our various electronic navigation systems with such devices as electronic chart plotters and autopilots to provide almost-hands-off vessel operation.

Your vessel's electronic navigation system is composed of five basic elements: a GPS or loran receiver; an electronic charting system, including its software and charts and a plotter to display information; a radar; an autopilot, with its associated heading sensor; and a depth-sounder. The rapid integration of these electronic components now makes it possible to combine several of these elements into a single piece of equipment. For this reason, we'll discuss the various elements themselves first, then consider the best way to combine them.

GPS

GPS, a system initially developed for the U.S. military forces, incorporates twenty-four active satellites and three operating spares in six orbital planes around the earth at an altitude of 10,900 nautical miles and an inclination angle to the equator of 55 degrees. Each satellite takes approximately twelve hours to complete a single orbit.

Because physical forces cause the orbits of GPS satellites to gradually change, new orbit information must be computed periodically by the master control station and fed back to the satellite to update the information it transmits. A GPS receiver determines vessel position by taking virtually instantaneous readings from at least three satellites, each of whose position becomes the radius of a sphere. The receiver then calculates the vessel's position as the point at which those three spheres intersect.

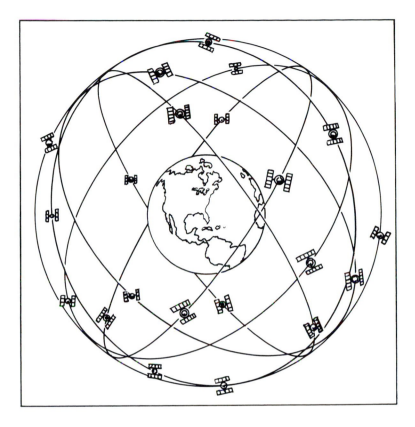

A single satellite will follow the same ground pattern on each orbit but is observable from a fixed position on earth approximately four minutes earlier each day due to the difference between its orbital speed and the speed of the earth's rotation.

This orbital precession of GPS satellites is monitored constantly, the changes are computed, and updated orbital information is fed back to them (see illustration).

Because of the altitude of the satellites and their staging pattern, at least five satellites are observable by a ground-based receiver at all times, which allows the system's "fix rate" to be continuous. Signals from any three satellites are sufficient to fix latitude and longitude. A signal from a fourth satellite is required only to better determine altitude, which is not relevant to marine navigation.

The signal transmitted from each satellite has two parts. One is a digital code unique to that particular satellite. Superimposed over that code is a navigation message (NAVmsg) that contains updated information about that satellite's orbit (technically referred to as *ephemeris data*), what time it is as far as the satellite is concerned (GPS time as calculated by the satellite's atomic clock), almanac data for all satellites in the constellation, and coefficients the receiver can plug into a computer model stored in its memory to calculate how the atmosphere is affecting the signal's transmission through the ionosphere (its propagation).

The satellite tells the receiver the instant in GPS time that it transmitted its signal, and the receiver synchronizes itself (approximately) to GPS time. By multiplying the difference between the time the satellite transmitted the signal and the time it was received by the signal's speed—186,000 miles (300,000 km) per second—the receiver is able to calculate its approximate distance (called a *pseudorange*) from the satellite. The receiver's computation of this distance could be absolutely accurate if, like the satellite, it contained an atomic clock, but that would make the receiver prohibitively expensive. Instead, a receiver uses for a time reference an affordable quartz oscillator, which synchronizes it and the satellite with near—but not total—accuracy.

Once the receiver has computed its pseudorange from three satellites, it takes the navigation process one step further. It simultaneously measures the frequency shift (Doppler effect) in the satellites' signals by comparing their frequencies against that of reference signals the receiver generates internally. From the Doppler effect, the receiver can compute its velocity relative to each of the satellites it is observing. This ability to determine its own velocity during the time it takes the receiver to read the code signals from the satellites eliminates the need for inputs of vessel speed and heading from external sources. Once the receiver has captured pseudoranges from the satellites it is observing, it uses them to solve three simultaneous equations with three unknowns and produce an estimate of position. It then recalculates those same three equations using velocity rather than pseudoranges to compute its own velocity during signal acquisition and position computation. After an allowance in the earlier estimated position for its own velocity, it produces a position fix. In essence, what the GPS receiver does is measure the distance between itself and at least three GPS satellites; use those differences as the radii of three spheres, each having one of the satellites as its center; then, with spherical geometry, determine its position as the intersection of those three spheres (see illustration). The amazing part is that a good-quality GPS receiver updates its position in this manner about every second.

Because it is continually updating its position, a GPS receiver also produces vessel speed and heading information. Because that information is derived from satellite data and has no reference to the earth's magnetic field, all GPS heading information is in true degrees rather than magnetic degrees.

The GPS receivers found in most marine applications have from eight to twelve channels to switch rapidly from one satellite to the next to collect code and NAVmsg data.

Until 2000, because of fears that GPS might be used by terrorists to inflict damage on its interests, the U.S. Department of Defense deliberately downgraded the position accuracy of GPS available to civilian users through something called Selective Availability. On May 1, 2000, Selective Availability was turned off. Since that time, properly functioning GPS receivers can be counted on 95 percent of the time to produce positions accurate to within about 98 feet (30 m).

Differential GPS

While position accuracy of 98 feet (30 m) may be acceptable for most marine navigation applications, it is not accurate enough for harbor approaches, especially for large commercial vessels. To offset that problem, the government developed differential GPS (DGPS), in which a series of stations at precisely located positions monitor GPS satellite signals, determine the atmospheric effects on their propagation in real time, and transmit corrections to GPS receivers in the area. A good DGPS receiver produces position accuracies of 3.3 to 6.6 feet (1–2 m).

GPS Integrity

One drawback to GPS that its designers have not yet been able to resolve is the "integrity issue." When the signals from a Loran-C transmitter (discussed later in this chapter) have a problem at their source, they can be transmitted in such a way that they cause the display of any equipment receiving them to blink. Such a system is not yet possible with GPS and may never be. The problem can be acute for high-velocity aircraft but is not likely to be a major problem for low-velocity marine users. But the integrity issue does reinforce the truism that prudent mariners will never rely on any single means of navigation but instead will employ and compare at least two to make certain their vessels are really where they think they are.

ELECTRONIC CHARTING SOFTWARE

Electronic charting software systems are sophisticated computer programs that display a vessel's position and course track on an electronically generated representation of the appropriate nautical chart. These electronic representations are stored on microchips, read-only-memory cards, various types of cartridges, read-only-memory compact discs (CD-ROMs), and computer floppy or hard disks.

In selecting an electronic chart system, the fundamental decision you must make is whether to go with a *raster* system or a *vector* system.

Raster Charting Software

Raster charting software, such as the programs developed by Maptech, Pin Point Navigation (under the Softchart and The Cap'n brand names) and Laser Plot, are actual National Oceanic and Atmospheric Administration (NOAA) charts that have been digitally scanned onto CD-ROMs. Maptech also scans British Admiralty charts. They most often are operated on a Windows-based personal computer, but some chart plotters will accept them as well. Raster charts contain the identical information the scanned charts contain. They are at the same scale and contain the same depth datum (feet, meters, or fathoms) as the original chart. Raster software presents data as pixels, just the way a television set does. To change scale (or "zoom in"), the system enlarges the size of the pixels. As you zoom in, the edges of the enlarged pixels become a bit fuzzy and the chart representation tends to lose a bit of its definition.

The basic advantage of using raster charting software is that you are looking at the same information you are used to seeing on NOAA or British Admiralty charts, presented in the same manner. As your course takes you from one chart to an adjacent chart, the software automatically loads the next chart. But if the scale of the second chart is different from that of the first chart, the scale of the chart representation changes as well. If the software on which you display raster charts allows you to operate in either North Up or Course Up mode, depth datum reads normally if you are in North Up mode or are in Course Up mode on a northerly heading. But if you run in Course Up mode on a southerly heading, the depth datum is upside down.

Another disadvantage of raster charts is that they require about thirty times more compact disc space than vector charts. To use raster charts, you purchase a series of CD-ROMs covering a region and physically change them in your computer or chart plotter as you move from area to area in that region, though there is some overlap.

For navigating in confined waterways, Maptech's Digital Chart Kits combine its raster charts with direct-overhead aerial photos that are georeferenced to match your chart position, coastal typographic maps, conventional aerial photos, current and tide tables, coast pilot and light list data, and information on marine facilities to put an incredible amount of information at the navigator's fingertips (see photos next page).

Maptech also produces Contour Professional, a product that allows the navigator to look at side-by-side charts, surface two-dimension charts, and three-dimensional underwater grid charts that show bottom contours and features and your vessel's position relative to them (see top photo page 97).

Vector Charting Software

Vector charting software, such as the programs developed by Nobeltec, Navionics, and C-Map, extract information from NOAA charts and other charts, then arrange it in layers of data elements

MAPTECH (4)

Maptech raster charts (top right) can be viewed in conjunction with overhead and aerial photos (bottom right and top left), tidal and current data (bottom left), and information on marine facilities to put an incredible amount of information at the helmsperson's fingertips.

that can be switched on and off. On a small-scale chart covering large areas, certain small bits of information are not displayed. As you zoom in to a larger scale, additional layers of data are switched on—either automatically or manually—to present the smaller bits of information. Since each chart is "redrawn" as you zoom in and various levels of data are switched on and off, vector chart representations tend to be sharper than raster chart representations at smaller scales. Where raster charts display the depth datum of the NOAA charts from which they were scanned, you can instruct a vector chart system to read out in your preference of feet,

meters, or fathoms. The Nobeltec and C-Map NT/PC software runs on a personal computer. Navionics and C-Map NT software are available as chips or are built into dedicated chart plotters. If the chart plotter on which you display vector charts allows you to operate in either North Up or Course Up mode, depth datum will read normally whatever your mode or course. Because vector charts are assembled in layers, they are essentially seamless and their scale remains the same as your course takes you from one area to another. To use vector charts, you purchase a single CD-ROM, cartridge, or minicartridge covering a region, then

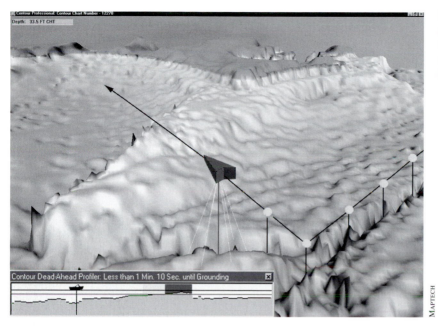

Depth: 33.5 FT CHT

Contour Dead-Ahead Profiler: Less than 1 Min. 10 Sec. until Grounding

MAPTECH

Maptech's Contour Professional provides a three-dimensional view of the bottom and its significant features.

purchase a code that allows you to access those charts you wish to use.

The basic disadvantage of vector charts is that their representations don't look exactly like NOAA or British Admiralty charts and reading them requires a bit of adjustment (see photo).

Electronic Chart Plotters

Most electronic chart plotter manufacturers base their designs on one software. Therefore, once you make the decision between using raster software and using vector software, in most cases you are limited to the manufacturers who use that software.

Navionics provides its vector charting software and charts to such plotter manufacturers as Brookes & Gatehouse, Garmin, ICOM, Koden, and Trimble.

Manufacturers who have chosen the C-Map system include Simrad, Cetrek, and Datamarine.

To thoroughly confuse matters, some chart plotter manufacturers have chosen to go with competing software in different models. Furuno, Low-

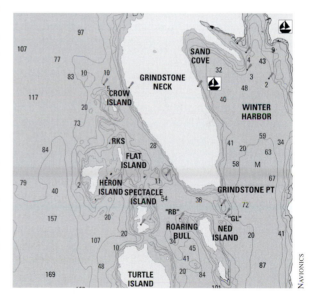

NAVIONICS

Vector charts contain information from a variety of sources in layers that can be switched on and off. They are harder to create but easier to store and more versatile in use then raster charts.

rance, Raytheon (now Raymarine), and Si-Tex produce plotters that use either the Navionics or the C-Map software and charts; Northstar Technologies produces plotters using either the Navionics vector software and charts or Maptech's raster software and charts. Leica produces a single plotter that can operate off either Maptech raster software and charts or C-Map vector software and charts.

Once you have decided to go with either raster or vector chart software, the next decision you must make in selecting a chart plotter is whether you want chart representations displayed in monochrome or full color and whether you prefer to display charts on a liquid crystal display (LCD) or on a cathode ray tube (CRT), which is much like a color television set. LCD displays come in both monochrome and color.

LCD displays are not as deep as CRTs and therefore take up less room in your helm console, and they generally are more readable in bright sunlight. CRTs offer the advantage of presenting an image much like you would see on a television screen.

RADAR

Radar is an acronym for **ra**dio **d**etection **a**nd **r**anging. The basic technology radar employs has been around since World War II, but the advent in recent years of digital signal processing and integrated circuitry has allowed a number of improvements in the way radar information is displayed. Radar may well be the most expensive piece of navigation gear you buy, but it is an indispensable piece of equipment because of its ability to detect the range and bearing of distant objects in any weather.

How Radar Works

A rotating antenna mounted as high as practical on a vessel transmits a tightly focused beam of extremely high frequency radio waves that travel at the speed of light (186,000 statute miles, or 300,000 km, per second), bounce off obstacles in their path, and return back to the antenna. By computing the time it takes the radio waves to radiate outward and bounce back, the system measures the distance between the antenna and objects in its path.

The bearing to an object is determined by the position in which the antenna is pointed when it transmits its radio-wave beam and receives a reflection (sometimes called an *echo*). The rotating motion of the antenna is not a factor in determining its position at the instant radio waves are sent and received because it makes only one revolution every two to four seconds but transmits radio waves at the rate of four hundred to six thousand pulses per second. Since it takes the radio waves only a fraction over twelve microseconds (millionths of a second) per nautical mile of range to make their round-trip, the antenna can send and receive up to thirty pulses in the time it takes to rotate just 1 degree, which means that, electronically speaking, it is standing still.

Because the radio waves radar uses bend slightly to follow the earth's curvature, the system's horizon at any particular mounting height is about 7 percent farther away than the horizon of the human eye at that same height. The maximum range at which a particular radar can detect an object depends on three factors: the strength of the signal it transmits, the height at which its antenna is mounted on the vessel, and the height of the object itself (see illustration).

As reflected radio waves are received, they are processed and displayed on a CRT or an LCD screen, which normally is mounted adjacent to the helm. The pattern of all reflected radio waves received on a single sweep of the antenna reveals the frontal outline of the objects it detects. This does not necessarily mean that the image displayed on the radar screen will match exactly what is seen with the human eye or shown on a navigation chart. Low-lying targets, such as a beach along a coast, will not show up as well as tall buildings several hundred yards inland. Radar cannot "see"

A radar's range is dependent on both the mounting height of its antenna and the height of objects that reflect the radio waves it transmits.

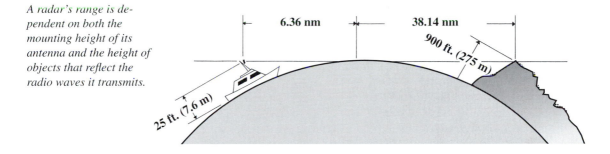

through a mountain to reveal a harbor entrance beyond, and the reflection from a large object—such as a commercial ship—can mask the reflection of a smaller object—such as another vessel—behind it.

Choosing a Radar

For the cruising yachtsperson, it's more important to be able to locate a harbor entrance between two mountains at a reasonable distance than it is to be able to detect the mountains themselves while 100 miles (160 km) at sea. Therefore, the ability of a radar to discriminate objects (that is, draw the clearest outline) is more important than its range. Discrimination is a function of the narrowness of the horizontal beam width of the radio waves the antenna transmits (see illustration page 101).

In the radars normally found on recreational vessels, horizontal beam width varies from about 1 to 6 degrees. Beam width, in turn, is determined by the length of the radar's antenna. The antennas of radar units on the recreational marine market vary in length from around 30 inches to about 8 feet (76 cm to 2.5 m). The smallest antennas often are enclosed in a fiberglass dome, which is of value principally to sailors since the dome prevents the boat's running rigging from getting tangled in the antenna. The dome itself does not affect the efficiency of the antenna's signal. The drawback to these units is that the antenna itself is not long enough to give optimum discrimination.

You will get better results with an open-array antenna. Look for a unit with the longest open-array antenna you can practically mount on your vessel, to give as narrow a beam width as possible. But bear in mind that the larger the antenna, the larger the electric motor required to turn it. For a typical cruising vessel in the 50- to 60-foot (15–18 m) range, a 4- to 6-foot (1.2–1.8 m) antenna usually strikes a good balance between adequate target discrimination and acceptable weight and power consumption.

A radar unit's range and, more importantly, its target detection performance are a function of both the height at which its antenna is mounted and the level of output or peak power at which it transmits its signal. A unit with a peak power rating of 2 to 3 kilowatts (kW) will have a range from about 24 to 36 nautical miles; with a rating of 4 to 5 kW, about 48 nautical miles; with a rating of 6 kW, about 64 nautical miles; with a rating of 10 kW, about 72 nautical miles. Bear in mind that a unit's peak power rating is a measure of signal strength, not the amount of power the unit will consume from a vessel's batteries. The unit rated at 3 kW will draw about 100 watts; the unit rated at 5 kW, about 120 watts; and the unit rated at 10 kW, about 150 to 225 watts. Pleasure-boat radars are available with maximum range of about 16 to 72 nautical miles. Many experienced cruisers find that a radar with a range of 48 nautical miles is adequate for the situations they encounter.

The display portion of radar sets on the recreational market range from 6 to 16 inches (15–25 cm) measured diagonally.

Raster-scan radar displays digitize signal information and display it on a CRT similar to the screen of a television set. The information does not fade but remains at full strength until it is replaced by updated information during the scanner's next sweep. The display also can be "frozen" to take precise bearings on a detected object.

The choice between a monochrome unit with either a green or an amber display and a unit that presents its information in color is one of cost and personal preference. Units with color displays list for about 30 percent more than monochrome units with comparable peak power output and range. Monochrome displays provide slightly sharper image resolution, while color displays tend to square off signals received from nearby objects, giving them a blocky appearance. The primary advantage of a color display is that it uses a variety of colors to represent the relative strength of returned signals: red for the strongest, yellow for those of medium strength, and blue or green for the weakest. This distinction can be an advantage when using radar to analyze weather clouds in your vessel's vicinity. Light clouds that contain little moisture will show up as blue or green signals, while those that contain heavy rain will show up in yellow or red depending on their density. Some monochrome radars differentiate between the strength of returned signals, with stronger signals appearing in the deepest green or amber and weaker signals showing up in lighter shades.

Most of the radars now on the market incorporate one or more variable range markers (VRMs) and electronic bearing lines (EBLs), both of which are useful in the real world of cruising. With either of these features, you position an adjustable circle or radial line over a target on the display and the unit will read out the target's range or bearing in a digital presentation. (Unless a radar is interfaced with some sort of external heading sensor, EBLs will be relative to your vessel's position, with the bow representing 0 degrees, not magnetic or true bearings.)

Many radars also allow you to establish a guard zone of varying dimensions around your vessel and sound an alarm if a target appears inside it. This can be useful both as an anticollision device while under way and as an anchor watch.

Radar Equipment Installation

Mount your radar's antenna as high as practical on your vessel. This location is more to provide a clear, unobstructed path for the radar's signals than to increase its range. Increasing mounting height by only a few feet will not have a noticeable effect on range. Of course, the higher you mount your antenna, the larger the blind zone around your vessel (see illustration).

The larger the display, the clearer the presentation of information, so buy a unit with the largest display you can afford and fit into the console of your primary steering station. In most power cruising applications, that will be a unit with a 7-, 10-, or 12-inch (18, 25, or 30 cm) display, with a 10- or 12-inch display being the better choice. When considering screen size and color options, you should familiarize yourself with the combination units. Today's integrated electronics can combine a radar, chart plotter, GPS, and fish-finder into one package. Here, screen size and color do become very important.

It would be ideal to have an anchor watch on both your radar and your GPS receiver. The anchor watch on your radar would alert you if another vessel drifted down to you or tried to sneak up on you while you were at anchor—assuming, of course, the intruder gave off a readable echo and was not within your radar's "blind zone," the area around your vessel that is passed over by the antenna's signals. It would at least alert you if your anchor dragged and some obstacle not in the blind zone and capable of giving off a readable echo penetrated the guard zone. The anchor watch on your GPS receiver would not alert you to physical hazards but would sound an alarm if your vessel drifted out of a preset circle, whether or not you were in danger of striking or being struck by another vessel or object.

Other radar features include the ability to inter-

Beam Widths:

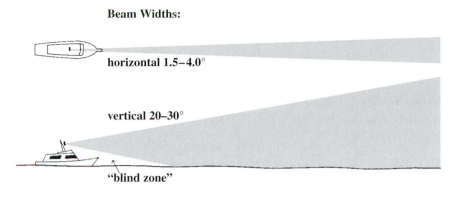

horizontal 1.5–4.0°

vertical 20–30°

"blind zone"

The narrower a radar's horizontal beam width, the more definitive will be its resolution of the targets that reflect its radio waves. Increasing the mounting height of a radar antenna affects its range only marginally but significantly extends its blind zone.

face with a heading sensor to change the orientation of the display from Course Up to North Up in order to align it with most nautical charts; the ability to offset the display by as much as 75 percent or to program in a 2x zoom on a portion of the display; and the ability to interface your radar with a chart plotter, GPS, and fish-finder.

Recently, engineers have been combining radar and computer networking technologies. Furuno's NavNet and Raymarine's High Speed Bus systems are such examples. Using broadband techniques, video images are transferred to multiple display heads with independent controls. These new displays use LCD screens, which can be housed in waterproof containers. Also available are radars without screens, which are called black box (BB) units. Such a BB radar allows owners to purchase their own display screens from an array of sunlight-viewable computer options.

Radar Equipment Recommendations

For a typical cruising powerboat in the 50-to-60-foot (15–18 m) range, the best monochrome radars on the market at the moment are Furuno's FR-7002 series. A good choice would be the

FR-7062, which has a 6 kW peak power output and a 12-inch (30 cm) CRT display (see photo). With a 4-foot or 6-foot (1.2–1.8 m) antenna, it has a range of 64 nautical miles.

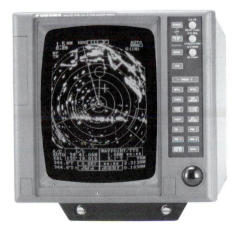

A typical bluewater cruiser's radar might be a unit such as Furuno's FR-7062. It is a 12-inch (30.5 cm) daylight CRT monochrome unit with ranges from ⅛ to 64 nautical miles. (Furuno)

Radar Licensing Requirements

If you intend to cruise only in U.S. waters and will not be contacting international shore stations, you do not need a Federal Communications Commission (FCC) Ship Station Radio License. If you plan to cruise outside U.S. waters or contact international shore stations, the radar installation aboard your vessel must be covered by a valid Ship Radio Station License. You apply by filing FCC form 605 and schedule B. No operator's permit is required.

You can install a radar on your vessel yourself, though I wouldn't recommend it. Any internal adjustments that would affect the frequency at which a radar transmits signals, however, may be done only by the holder of a General Radiotelephone Permit or a First- or Second-Class Radiotelegraph Permit, and the permit must have a ship radar endorsement.

AUTOPILOTS

At its most basic, an *autopilot* is simply a device that receives instructions from the helmsperson on the desired course, recognizes any deviations from that course, and applies to the vessel's rudder enough force to cause the vessel to return to the intended track. A good autopilot is one of the most helpful and hardworking accessories you can have on a cruising boat. Not only will it relieve you from tedious hand steering on long passages, but it also will steer a straighter course than any human helmsperson could and waste less time and fuel in the bargain. If properly interfaced with an appropriate GPS receiver, it can automatically steer your vessel through course changes. Of course, none of an autopilot's abilities relieves you of the necessity to keep an alert helm watch.

How Autopilots Work

Today's autopilots employ two sets of contact switches that open and close as the vessel deviates from its intended track to port or starboard. As long as the vessel remains on course, the autopilot is in a "dead band," where no course correction is required. Modern autopilots also make proportional-rate corrections—that is, they apply only slight pressure to the rudder to correct minor deviations from course but apply significant force to correct major deviations, just as you would if you were steering the vessel yourself.

An autopilot consists of three basic units: a control head, through which you instruct it on what course to follow; a sensor to track the intended course and your vessel's deviation from it; and a power unit to apply to the rudder the force needed to keep the vessel on track.

Control heads vary greatly in the number of functions they allow you to select. Less expensive units limit you to steering manually or engaging the autopilot and entering a course to steer. More sophisticated units allow you to determine the sensitivity with which the autopilot reacts to course deviations, to dodge around obstacles and return to your programmed heading, and to instruct the autopilot to take its course either from information you dial in or from data provided by a separate navigation receiver. In addition to course headings, the control head of more expensive units can display rudder angle and, if interfaced to a GPS receiver, position and track data. If interfaced to a wind sensor, they also can display wind direction and speed. High-tech control heads also have microprocessors that can automatically compensate for changing sea states.

The heart of a good autopilot is its fluxgate compass heading sensor, which normally is mounted separately from the control unit in a location free of electrical interference and as near the vessel's center of gravity as possible. Today's electronic gyrocompasses can also supply needed heading data.

The power unit you choose will depend on whether your vessel has mechanical or hydraulic steering. Some mechanical systems use a reversible electric motor to drive the rudder directly.

An autopilot's fluxgate heading sensor can be an integral part of the unit, or, as here, a remote unit that can be mounted in an area of minimal electronic interference. (KVH Industries)

Others work through a lead screw that exerts a push-pull motion on a tiller arm mounted to the rudder. Still others operate through a low-speed shaft coupled to the rudder with a chain-and-sprocket arrangement. For vessels with hydraulic steering, the autopilot should have a separate electric motor powering its own hydraulic pump, which controls fluid flow in the vessel's hydraulic system with electric valves.

Choosing an Autopilot

For extended cruising, I recommend you select a sophisticated autopilot that can, among other things, interface with your GPS receiver. The two units not only will work together to guide your vessel to any point you designate but will then automatically make course corrections to steer your vessel to the next point you choose. You also should select a unit that sounds an alarm if it loses input from the navigation receiver. Also, be aware that autopilots normally can handle only about a 15- to 40-degree deviation from a previous course. If your GPS receiver instructs it to make a course change beyond the maximum deviation it can

handle, it may go crazy and steer your vessel around in circles.

Select an autopilot whose control unit allows you to dial in the degree of sensitivity with which you want the autopilot to react to course deviations. In calm seas, you can crank the sensitivity up to keep your vessel on a straighter line; in rough seas, you can dampen sensitivity to keep the autopilot and your steering system from having to work so hard. The control unit also should have a dodge function, which allows you to swing the vessel to port or starboard to avoid an obstruction. The degree of deviation should depend on how long you hold down the dodge button. When you release the dodge button, the autopilot should automatically resume the course you have previously instructed it to follow.

Aside from these basic functions, there are several other autopilot features you'll find useful. The unit you select should display your deviation from a preset course either digitally or on a line or bar graph. It should also have a "manual steer" position, in which it will continue to display crosstrack error even though you are steering manually.

Autopilot Equipment Recommendation

For a new power cruising yacht, I would recommend the Simrad AP 20 coupled with the appropriate Simrad drive unit for mechanical or hydraulic steering (see photo next page). Simrad acquired Robertson, which has been in the autopilot business since the early 1940s and developed the first microprocessor-controlled autopilot, so it knows what it's doing. The design has an excellent rudder feedback system, which helps the vessel steer an extremely precise course.

DEPTH-SOUNDERS

"It's not the ocean that sinks ships," goes the old saying. "It's the hard stuff around the edges." While that statement may not be entirely accurate,

The Simrad AP 20 autopilot control head can not only steer a cruising vessel but also display its heading and crosstrack error visually. (Simrad, Inc.)

one of the cruising yachtsperson's most basic needs is a good depth-sounder that tells where the "hard stuff" is located.

How Depth-Sounders Work

At its simplest, a *depth-sounder* emits sound-wave pulses and measures the time it takes for them to be reflected back to the receiver. Since sound waves travel through water at 4,800 feet (1,464 m) per second, the device performs a simple time-to-distance conversion and displays the result. A depth-sounder has four components: a transmitter that generates an electrical signal, a transducer that converts that electrical signal into acoustic pulses, a receiver that amplifies the returning echo and performs necessary timing function, and a display that presents the computed information.

Stand-alone depth-sounders with numerical readouts only are rather rare. Most are in fact fish-finders with monochromatic or color displays. Video-recording depth-finders provide a "moving" picture of the bottom under your vessel and not only indicate depth but also can locate schools of fish and provide indications of bottom composition. The more expensive color video models also can read water surface temperature and, when interfaced to a GPS receiver, display your vessel's course and speed. Most video units come with LCD displays, and an increasing number are sunlight viewable. Some are capable of transmitting pulse signals at two frequencies: 200 kilohertz (kHz), which provides better definition in shallow water, and 50 kHz, which provides better definition at deep water depths. A few can do this simultaneously on split-screen displays.

Digital units simply read out numerical depth in feet, fathoms, or meters on an LCD screen.

Depth-Sounder Installation

The most important aspect of depth-sounder installation is correct placement of the transducer, which should be made of bronze, not nylon. It should be mounted through the hull rather than internally, though new "smart" models, able to handle 1 kW output power, can be installed inside the hull. External transducers should be positioned as nearly as possible to amidships. The face of the transducer must be exactly parallel to the surface of the water. On steel or aluminum vessels, the transducer must be insulated from the hull with a plastic washer to reduce the danger of electrolytic corrosion. On planing hull vessels, be certain it is mounted far enough back from the bow to keep its readings from being distorted by water turbulence or air bubbles. Also, position it where the flow of water is not obstructed by other through-hull fittings. Never mount a depth-sounder's transducer on the transom, since water turbulence in that location will cause inaccurate readings.

Choosing Depth-Sounders

In the name of redundancy, I suggest you install two depth-sounders on your vessel, one of the color video models at your main helm and one of the digital variety at your flying bridge helm. Both units should allow you to specify whether their readings will be in feet, fathoms, or meters, depending on how depth is indicated on the chart you are using. You should also have the ability to set the unit's "zero depth" at or 1 foot (0.3 m) below the lowest point of your vessel.

Select a unit that allows you to have it set off an alarm if minimum water depth reaches about 5 feet (1.5 m) beneath your keel or props. Some units offer multiple alarms for use as an anchor watch that sounds if water depth exceeds a maximum or a minimum you set.

The more expensive depth-sounders on the recreational marine market will read to depths of 1,000 feet (300 m), but a unit that reads to about 400 feet (120 m) or even 200 feet (60 m) is more than adequate.

Several manufacturers offer units that provide depth information in combination with such other factors as speed, total distance and trip logs, and sea temperature. These units have integral timers and are capable of being interfaced with electronic compasses or navigation receivers to provide course heading, crosstrack error, elapsed time, distance-to-go, time-to-go, estimated time of arrival, and the like. I don't see why you should spend $1,500 or so for one of these units, because all they do basically is duplicate the display functions of your GPS or DGPS receiver. You still need your navigation receiver in reasonable proximity to the helm in order to control its input function, so why duplicate information that is already close at hand?

Depth-Sounder Equipment Recommendations

My choice for a color video depth-sounder is Furuno's FCV-667 (see photo). It has a 6-inch (15 cm) display, has both 50 and 200 kHz modes, and—if interfaced to your GPS or DGPS receiver—can display course and speed information.

My recommendation for a digital depth-sounder would be the Datamarine International Offshore 3001, which has proved itself time and again in the rugged cruising environment (see

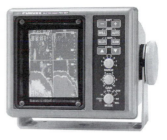

The Furuno FCV-667 is a dependable color video depth-sounder that operates at both 50 and 200 kHz. (Furuno)

The Datamarine International Offshore 3001 model is the standard in digital depth-sounders. (Datamarine)

photo). Locate the display unit so that it is easily visible from the helm and within reach. If you use a magnetic steering compass, position the depth-sounder so that it doesn't contribute to compass deviation.

INTERFACING ELECTRONIC NAVIGATION EQUIPMENT

It is virtually impossible to discuss modern electronic navigation gear without understanding a little about what is involved in interfacing various pieces of equipment. The actual mechanics are best left to a qualified electronics technician, but it would be helpful for you to understand what that technician is doing.

For two pieces of electronic equipment to exchange information, they must communicate through a structure in which a particular alphanumeric symbol or series of symbols means the same thing to both. Virtually all manufacturers of electronic navigation equipment are members of the National Marine Electronics Association (NMEA). To facilitate the interfacing of their equipment, the manufacturers have cooperated to develop several standards that specify the data formats and information protocols that two or more marine electronic devices must have in common to communicate with each other. The standards you will encounter most often in evaluating specific pieces of marine electronic navigation equipment are NMEA 0180, 0182, 0183, and 2000. Standard 0180 is an older one used exclusively in autopilots to allow them to accept crosstrack error information from an external source, such a heading sensor or a navigation receiver. The 0182 standard, an expanded variation of 0180, also is used primarily by autopilots and allows them to accept not only crosstrack error information from an external source but also such information as the bearing to the next waypoint and preset latitude and longitude position. Both 0180 and 0182 are used primarily to connect a single piece of sending equipment to a single piece of receiving equipment. Devices that use either of these standards also are limited in the rate at which they can exchange information to 1,200 baud (a baud being the smallest unit of data information). The 0183 standard is far more versatile because more types of data can be exchanged at a more rapid rate (4,800 baud) and shared between many more types of devices.

The most recent standard is NMEA 2000, in which a single cable can handle the exchange of numerical data (only data, not video) from many more devices. It's known as the "plug-and-play" standard, with open architecture so that manufacturers can have data from their electronics understood by electronics from other makers. To send video from radars, chart plotters, and fish-finders to displays only of their own making, companies like Furuno and Raymarine have developed proprietary broadband systems.

INTEGRATING ELECTRONIC NAVIGATION EQUIPMENT

Now that we've covered the basic elements of your vessel's electronic navigation system, it's appropriate to consider the choices you have when selecting equipment to provide the information you need quickly in a usable format. Given that your vessel's helm is likely to have limited space, it's also important to keep that information presentation compact without forgetting the need for redundancy.

You could, of course, purchase each element of your vessel's electronic navigation system separately:

- a stand-alone GPS receiver
- a personal computer or electronic chart plotter with its associated software, charts, and display
- a radar
- a depth-sounder
- an autopilot

You also could interface the separate units, and they would mutually support one another. But you would require a great deal of space for all that gear and would find that you are duplicating a great deal of information unnecessarily.

At the other extreme, you could go to an all-in-one unit such as the Si-Tex Genesis, which on a single 10.4-inch (26 cm) SVGA (super video graphics array) display can present GPS and DGPS position, speed and heading information, C-Map vector electronic charts, radar image overlays, weatherfax data, and video depth-finder presentations. You also can watch television and videotapes if you equip it with an optional TV sensor and VCR. You can even monitor engine room cameras or perform camera-assisted docking.

As wonderful as all this sounds, I'd be very hesitant to rely on a single display for all my navigational data. If the display itself goes out, you're blind.

It does make sense to me to combine a GPS or DGPS receiver and electronic chart display in a single unit. But I'd want my radar and video depth-finder to have their own displays. The chance of all three displays going out at once is remote, and the worst situation I'd be likely to face is having to operate on only two of my three primary navigation systems. This is the setup I installed on *Americas Odyssey*, and it served us well (see photo).

MARINE COMPASS OPTIONS

One basic decision you'll have to make regarding your navigational setup is what kind of steering compass to get. Given the recent proliferation of alternatives in steering compasses, choosing one isn't as easy as it once was. We look at various options available, discuss their pros and cons, and offer recommendations.

Standard Magnetic Compasses

For centuries, humans have navigated their way across the seas with a standard magnetic compass, a profoundly important yet simple device that uses bar magnets to align itself to the earth's magnetic north pole, then reads out bearings on a compass card that is mounted on a pivot and suspended in a clear liquid (see photo next page). It requires no external source of mechanical or electrical energy.

Wonderful as they are, however, standard magnetic compasses do pose significant problems. The first is that nearby masses of metal and strong electrical fields can cause significant deviation in the accuracy of compass readings. In a coastal-cruising powerboat, this deviation usually can be managed without a lot of fuss. But as you equip a power cruiser to head for bluewater, you probably will wind up cramming the relatively tight confines of the boat's pilothouse and flying bridge with powerful navigation and communications gear that contains a lot of metal and produces exactly the kind of strong electrical fields that

Americas Odyssey's lower helm console housed a computer monitor that displayed Maptech raster electronic charts, a 12-inch (30.5 cm) Furuno monochrome radar display, a Furuno color video depth-sounder, and a Magnavox (now Leica) GPS receiver.

The standard magnetic compass, long the key element in marine navigation, is now being supplanted by fluxgate heading sensors, gyrocompasses, and heading information from GPS and DGPS navigation sensors.

make standard magnetic compasses go haywire. As you begin to plan the installation of your electronic equipment, one of your biggest headaches will be figuring out where to install everything you want within easy reach of your helm without having it play havoc with your standard magnetic compasses.

The deviation in the compass's headings caused by metal masses and electrical fields must be compensated for by physically manipulating magnets inside or outside the compass. Even after the standard magnetic compasses on your yacht are compensated for a specific environment, their readings can be distorted because the electrical fields in the pilothouse can change as you switch various pieces of electronic gear on and off. If you add electronic equipment to the environment around a standard magnetic compass—or take it away— you may have to repeat the compensation procedure. In some cases, it is simply impossible to completely compensate a compass and you have to use deviation tables for computing the course to steer to achieve the desired heading. Under certain conditions, even after you have had your compasses compensated, you may find that the readings on your flying bridge compass differ sig-

nificantly from those on an identical unit mounted in your pilothouse.

Another problem is that the earth's magnetic north pole does not coincide with its geographic north pole. In plotting your vessel's position on a standard nautical chart that is oriented to geographic north, you have to allow for magnetic variation. To make matters worse, magnetic variation not only changes from one area of the earth to another but also increases or decreases from year to year.

As the marine electronics industry began to develop electronic navigation instruments that require some sort of heading input to perform their intended function, the problems with standard magnetic compasses multiplied. Initially, the industry simply developed ways of reading the heading information produced by a standard magnetic compass either electrically or photoelectrically and fed that information to the navigational device in the form of an electronic impulse. But as the card of a standard magnetic compass swings, it develops inertia, which can cause it to overshoot an intended heading, and the liquid in which it is suspended significantly lengthens the time it takes for the compass to settle down on a new heading.

Magnetic Fluxgate Compasses

In order to get a compass that reacts more rapidly and precisely to course changes, the industry developed the magnetic fluxgate compass. It is still a magnetic device, but rather than orienting itself to magnetic north with swinging bar magnets, it aligns itself by electronically reading the earth's magnetic flux with something called a *toroid fluxgate coil sensor*. The technical details of how a fluxgate compass works are not important here. The point is that it produces accurate magnetic heading information much more rapidly and precisely than the floating card of a standard magnetic compass. Fluxgate compasses also have other advantages. The sensing and display elements can be combined in a single unit, or they can be physically separated and the sensing element mounted in a remote location on a vessel that is relatively free of the electrical interference so often found in the pilothouse or on the flying bridge. If the remote location is selected carefully, the sensing element will not be significantly affected as electric equipment aboard the vessel is switched on or off, added, or removed. The sensing element's output then can be fed electrically to display units at one or more helm stations. Also, any compensation the sensing element requires can be accomplished electrically, which usually gives more accurate results than compensation achieved by physically moving magnets around inside or outside a standard magnetic compass.

As a result of their speed, precision, and flexibility, magnetic fluxgate compasses commonly are used as heading sensors for autopilots. A single multiport magnetic fluxgate compass such as the KVH Azimuth 1000 reads out digitally with an accuracy of ±0.5 degrees and can feed heading information to as many as fifteen different displays or navigational instruments (see photo). The use of a single sensing element eliminates the possibility of confusion due to different readings from several sensors.

Because the standard heading readouts produced by a fluxgate compass are magnetic, variation must still be taken into account when using them to plot a position on a nautical chart. However, if you manually enter local variation, they will read out in true north.

Gyrocompasses

Until the late 1990s, gyrocompasses cost upward of $20,000 and were found only on megayachts and commercial vessels. In the late 1990s, KVH began marketing its GyroTrac gyrocompass, which, at about $3,000 (including a remote sensor), puts it in reach of larger cruising powerboats whose owners have a more elaborate navigation electronics budget (see photo next page). Gyrocompasses work on a totally different principle than magnetic fluxgate compasses, and they read out in true degrees. Magnetic variation doesn't

KVH's Azimuth 1000 digital fluxgate compass is accurate to 0.5 degree and can output heading information to a variety of other navigational devices. (KVH Industries)

have to be taken into account when using their readings to plot a vessel's position on a chart.

My recommendation would be that you install a good GPS receiver and rely on its heading information as your primary steering compass. As a backup, I'd select a good gyrocompass or a fluxgate magnetic compass. As insurance in case all your electronics bite the dust, I'd install a standard magnetic compass in the most interference-free location, probably at the flying bridge helm station. As yet another backup, carry a portable standard magnetic compass or a portable electronic compass powered by batteries.

SELECTING A NAVIGATION SYSTEM: MAGNETIC OR TRUE?

Our discussion of the problems with standard magnetic compasses and the alternatives now available in electronic fluxgate compasses and gyrocompasses leads us to the question of whether you will perform your navigation chores using traditional magnetic headings or by shifting to a new system using true north headings.

The KVH GyroTrac puts the advantages of the gyrocompass at a much more affordable level than previous units. (KVH Industries)

Following the traditional approach, you would

1. install standard magnetic compasses in your pilothouse and on your flying bridge as your primary manual steering references
2. install separate fluxgate heading sensors for your autopilot and radar
3. instruct GPS receivers to produce magnetic heading information
4. allow for magnetic variation when you plotted your vessel's course or position on navigational charts.

As we discussed earlier in this chapter, the problem with this approach is that, because of the difficulties of achieving absolute and consistent compensation in standard magnetic compasses, you may get several different readings from your various instruments while your boat is on a single heading.

If you were to replace your standard magnetic steering compass with a single, remotely mounted magnetic fluxgate sensor and also interface it to your autopilot and radar, they would all produce the same heading information (but your GPS receiver might still provide a different reading). You also would eliminate the likelihood of changing deviation as you switch various pieces of electronic equipment on and off, and the arrangement would allow you greater flexibility in instrument placement. With this approach, you still would have to allow for magnetic variation in plotting your position or course on a chart.

A more radical alternative also could eliminate the problem of allowing for magnetic variation. With this option, not only would you replace your standard magnetic compasses with digital displays from the same fluxgate sensor that provides heading input to your autopilot and radar display, but you would also equip the fluxgate sensor with appropriate software to allow it to produce true rather than magnetic readings. Since your GPS receiver produces true north headings, you would base all your navigation—both manual steering and chart plotting—on true north headings. Errors in computing magnetic variation or forgetting to take it into account would never arise.

The biggest argument against replacing magnetic compasses with electronic compasses is that if you have problems with the fluxgate sensor or gyrocompass or lose electrical power, you don't even have a standard magnetic compass to help guide you to safety. There are several answers to that objection. One is to carry a spare fluxgate sensor as a backup to your installed unit. Another is to install an emergency battery as high as possible in your vessel, which at the minimum could power your electronic compass, your VHF radio, and your satellite telephone or single-sideband radio. You also could have a good handheld magnetic compass or one of the newer battery-powered handheld electronic compasses aboard in case you completely lost your electronics.

I realize the suggestion that magnetic compasses can be replaced as a primary steering reference will raise the hackles of the traditionalists, but it is a possibility worth considering.

THE LORAN-C NAVIGATION SYSTEM

Although the Loran-C navigation system has been largely displaced by GPS, I cover it briefly here on the chance you purchase a used vessel with a working loran receiver on board. The U.S. Coast Guard has committed to supporting loran through at least 2008, so it can be a useful backup to your primary GPS receiver.

Though the term *loran* is an acronym for **long-range navigation**, the system is actually a medium-range navigation system for both marine vessels and aircraft that covers only specific Coastal Confluence Zones around the world.

The Loran-C system operated by the United States in cooperation with its allies covers basically the East, West, and Gulf Coasts of North America; the Great Lakes; the Bering, Labrador, Icelandic, and Norwegian Seas; the Mediterranean; and the Pacific Ocean west of Hawaii and around Japan and Korea. Systems operated by other governments include Saudi Arabia's coverage of parts of the Red Sea, the Persian Gulf, and the Gulf of Aden; the former Soviet Union's coverage of portions of the region's east and west coasts; and the People's Republic of China's coverage of the South China Sea.

There is no Loran-C system covering such popular cruising areas as the coasts of Mexico (except for the northern tip of the Yucatán Peninsula) or Central America and the islands of the Caribbean.

How Loran-C Works

Loran-C uses a network of shore-based radio transmitters that are designed to provide extremely accurate navigational fixes within 50 nautical miles of shore or out to the 100-fathom (180 m) curve, whichever is greater.

A Loran-C "chain" consists of one master transmitter (designated M) and two, three, or four secondary transmitters (designated W, X, Y, and Z), each of which sends out pulsed radio signals on 100 kHz. To enable loran receivers to identify the source of these signals, the transmitters send out their pulses in sequence at precise intervals of an assigned number of microseconds. The interval between transmissions from the master is referred to as the group repetition interval (GRI), and each chain is assigned a distinctive GRI.

LORAN-C CHAINS

Region	GRI
United States and Canada	
Northeast U.S.	9,960
Southeast U.S.	7,980
Great Lakes	8,970
U.S. West Coast	9,940
Gulf of Alaska	7,960
Canadian East Coast	5,930
Canadian West Coast	5,990
North Atlantic	
Labrador Sea	7,930
Norwegian Sea	7,970
Iceland	9,980
Pacific Ocean	
North Pacific	9,990
Northwest Pacific	9,970
Central Pacific	4,990
Commando Lion (Korea/Japan)	5,970
Mediterranean Sea	
Mediterranean Sea	7,990
Saudi Arabia	
South Saudi Arabia	7,170
Northeast Saudi Arabia	8,990
Northwest Saudi Arabia	38,990

Once a loran receiver captures the signals from the master transmitter and one secondary transmitter in a chain whose positions are known, it measures the difference in time it took the two signals to reach it. Since speed, time, and distance are interrelated, that time difference (TD) locates the receiver on a hyperbolic line of position (LOP), a line along which that time would remain constant. The receiver then repeats the process with signals from the master and a different secondary to establish a second LOP. The point where the two LOPs intersect is the vessel's position. Using the two TDs, that position can be plotted on a chart overprinted with a grid of Loran-C LOPs.

In addition to displaying position in terms of two TDs, most Loran-C receivers are able to translate TDs into latitude and longitude.

Loran ground-wave transmissions have a maximum range of 1,000 to 1,200 miles (1,935 km) from their transmitters. Within the ground-wave coverage areas of Loran-C signals, the absolute accuracy of initial fixes normally is within 0.1 to 0.25 nautical mile. Under ideal conditions, absolute accuracy can be within 100 feet or less.

The accuracy of Loran-C's repeatability—its ability to reestablish a position it has fixed earlier—is even greater than the absolute accuracy of initial fixes. In ideal situations, it can be 50 feet (15 m) or less.

Legal Requirements

No licenses are required for either installation or operation of Loran-C receivers.

SOUND-SIGNALING EQUIPMENT

Under the U.S. Coast Guard's *Navigation Rules, International–Inland* (see resources appendix), certain vessels are required to carry sound-signaling devices with which to announce their intentions to other vessels in meeting and passing situations and to announce their presence in conditions of reduced visibility. Annex III of the Rules requires vessels 39.4 feet (12 m) or more but less than 65.6 feet (20 m) in length to carry a bell and a whistle (any sound-signaling appliance) capable of emitting a tone of 250 to 525 Hertz that is audible for at least half a mile—or "other equipment" capable of producing a tone in the required frequency band that is audible over the same distance, provided the tone can be activated manually. (Vessels under 39.4 feet or 12.0 m are not required to carry specific sound-signaling equipment, but if they do not, they must carry some other means of making an efficient sound signal, though no minimum range is defined.)

Under the "other equipment" clause in the rules, many powerboat cruisers use an electronic loud-hailer or automatic foghorn to meet the requirement for sound-signaling capability. If you choose to exercise this option, your loud-hailer or automatic foghorn should be a separate piece of equipment with a 25- to 30-watt amplifier. In my opinion, the best value for the money in such gear is Standard Communications' 20-watt LH-5 unit. With the addition of up to four speakers at around $50 each, it also can be used as a ship intercom.

Communicating while Cruising

In cruising, your marine communications equipment has one overriding purpose: to protect your own life and well-being and that of the others aboard your vessel for whom, as the boat's captain, you are legally and morally responsible. When it comes to freedom, those of us who have a passion for bashing around in the boondocks in small boats get the best of it. But there is a cost. If we get in a jam, the hospital emergency room is a little farther away than the end of the block. When trouble strikes, more often than not the only link we have with the outside world is our marine communications system and it had better work—right and the first time.

Imagine for a moment that it's a black and violent night, you are far out at sea, and you have a fire on board or your vessel strikes a submerged object and is seriously holed. Or, pretend you are in a remote anchorage on the back side of beyond and a member of your party suffers a heart attack, a broken bone, or a nasty blow to the head. Then look at the radio you are about to purchase and ask yourself: under those conditions, is this the piece of equipment I want to depend on to bring the cavalry running? This perspective will help you cut through a lot of fancy sales talk about color-coordinated front panels and remotes in the master stateroom.

In considering the marine communications gear for your cruising adventures, this chapter covers the two distinct types of marine radios you are going to need for serious cruising: a VHF set, for communicating with other vessels and coast stations within roughly 10 to 40 miles (16–65 km) of your position, and a single-sideband (SSB) unit for long-range communications. This chapter helps you equip your boat with VHF and SSB marine radios and their associated equipment—properly installed so they provide maximum communications efficiency. It also offers some hints on getting the most out of your marine radios and then reviews what you have to do to operate them legally—especially on the high seas and in the waters of other countries.

If you require or want frequent, clear, and dependable communications with family, friends, and colleagues ashore, I also discuss your options in marine satellite and cellular telephones. Some experienced long-distance cruisers also find amateur (or ham) radio useful, and I will cover it in enough detail to help you decide if it is an option you would like to explore further.

HOW MARINE RADIOS WORK

A marine radio consists of a transmitter section and a receiver section (commonly combined into a single unit called a *transceiver*). The transmitter section has an amplifier that provides power for outgoing signals, and the receiver section has a second amplifier, which increases the audio level of incoming signals to make them audible to the human ear. But the radio itself is just one part of the total system. Other critical ingredients are the radio's antenna and power supply, your boat's frequency-grounding system, and the proper installation of various components. We'll consider each of these factors in detail as we discuss each of the types of marine radios.

VHF and SSB in marine use have a number of factors in common. To understand those factors, you don't need to become a radio engineer but you do need to understand a few technical terms you're going to run into.

Radio Waves, Frequency, Wavelength, and Amplitude

All radios operate through the use of radio waves, which are described by how rapidly (how frequently) they go up and down between a high point and a low point and back to their high point again. Think of frequency as a snake: if it's just ambling along, it moves like

If it's in a hurry, it moves like

The slow-moving snake illustrates low frequency: The rate at which its ups and downs pass a given point is low. The fast-moving snake, which undulates more, illustrates high frequency.

The distance from one midpoint of a radio wave to its next midpoint is its wavelength (see illustration). The lower a radio wave's frequency, the longer its wavelength; the higher its frequency, the shorter its wavelength.

Low Frequency   *High Frequency*

Radio waves are described by their frequency—the rate at which they go up and down from a high point to a low point and back to their high point again.

The technical term for a radio wave's movement is *oscillation*. The technical term for the single movement of a radio wave from one midpoint to the next midpoint is a *Hertz*, and the frequency of radio waves is most often measured in thousands of Hertz per second, called *kilohertz* (kHz), or in millions of Hertz per second, called *megahertz* (MHz). One megahertz equals one thousand kilohertz.

The term *amplitude* refers to how high or how low a radio wave swings to either side of its midpoint.

Frequency Modulation Versus Amplitude Modulation

Marine radios transmit human speech by distinguishing the pitch and resonance of the speaker's voice in one of two ways:

VHF radios use a technique called *frequency modulation* (FM), in which the radio wave's amplitude (its high points and low points) remains the same and speech is distinguished by minute variations in the signal's frequency. Graphically, an FM signal carrying human speech would look something like

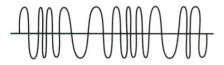

SSB marine radios use a technique called *amplitude modulation* (AM), in which the frequency remains constant and the radio distinguishes sound by minutely varying the radio wave's high points and low points. Graphically, an AM signal carrying human speech would look something like

The importance of the difference between FM and AM to the cruising yachtsperson is that FM provides a signal that is much less susceptible to interference and distortion.

The Radio Spectrum

All radio-wave transmissions—be they from commercial radio or television stations, aircraft navigation beacons, marine or aviation radios, or whatnot—operate within the same spectrum of radio-wave frequencies, which theoretically stretches from one cycle per second to infinity. To keep these various uses from overlapping and interfering with one another, most of the world's governments cooperate through the International Telecommunication Union (ITU) to allocate groupings, or *bands*, of frequencies for specific purposes: commercial broadcasting, marine communications, amateur radio, and so on. The bands reserved for marine use normally are referred to by their lower and upper limits in megahertz (often just called "megs"). We'll consider initially those bands of frequencies that are commonly used by cruising vessels (see illustration next page).

1. VHF marine radio operates in the single band between 156 and 163 MHz.
2. SSB marine radio breaks down into two subcategories that operate and are used in significantly different ways:
   - *medium-frequency* SSB operates in the 2 to 3 MHz band
   - high-frequency (HF) SSB operates in eight bands: 4 MHz, 6 MHz, 8 to 9 MHz, 12 MHz, 16 MHz, 18 MHz, 22 MHz, and 25 MHz

In SSB jargon, these bands are referred to as the 2-meg, 4-meg, 6-meg, 8-meg, 12-meg, 16-meg, 18-meg, 22-meg, and 25-meg bands. (Because the 22-meg band runs all the way up to 22.8 MHz, it is sometimes also referred to as the 23-meg band, but don't let that throw you. Both references are to the same band of frequencies.)

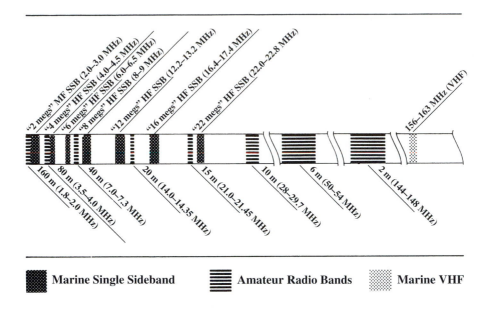

This presentation of a portion of the radio spectrum makes obvious the similarity of the frequencies used by SSB marine radio and amateur radio operators.

Channels

For two radios to establish a communications link, they must be set to operate on the same frequency or pair of frequencies. Individual frequencies or frequencies that by regulation or international treaty have been paired—one for transmitting, one for receiving—are referred to as *channels*. In some cases, channels are designated by a one- to four-digit number. In other cases, they are referred to only by their transmit and receive frequencies.

Both VHF and SSB channels come in two flavors: simplex and duplex. Simplex channels receive and transmit on a single frequency. An example would be VHF channel 16, the international distress, safety, and calling channel, over which a radio both receives and transmits on 156.8 MHz. Some simplex channels are "half" or "receive-only" channels. The VHF channel designated WX-1, for instance, allows "ship-receive-only" reception of weather broadcasts from the National Oceanic and Atmospheric Administration (NOAA) on 162.55 MHz.

Duplex channels receive on one frequency and transmit on a different one. An example would be SSB channel 403, a popular channel for ship-to-shore radiotelephone calls, through which onboard radios receive on 4363.6 MHz and transmit on 4069.2 MHz. (Note that what we refer to throughout this book as "ship-receive" frequencies are sometimes referred to elsewhere as "coast-station-transmit" frequencies. Both terms refer to the frequency at which you receive transmissions on board your vessel.) Most duplex channels used by cruisers are not true duplex channels but are *semiduplex*. The practical difference between the two is that when you are communicating over a semiduplex channel, you have to push the microphone button down to talk and then release it to hear the person to whom you're talking. On a true duplex channel, this is not necessary.

In many—but not all—cases, the transmit and receive frequencies of both VHF and SSB duplex channels are covered by international treaties and are the same worldwide.

Crystals, Diodes, and Synthesizers

Making a radio operate on a particular frequency can be accomplished in three ways: by installing *crystals*, which allow a radio to transmit or receive on a single frequency; by using *diodes*, which allow a radio to operate over a small group of perhaps a dozen frequencies; or by using a *synthesizer*, which allows the radio to transmit and receive on many different frequencies. Virtually all installed VHF and SSB marine radios in the United States now use synthesizers.

PROPAGATION

The term *propagation* refers to the manner in which radio waves of different frequencies react to the ionosphere, the naturally occurring layers of electrically charged (ionized) gas molecules around the earth.

Until a gas molecule in the earth's upper atmosphere is struck by the sun's radiation, it is electrically neutral—its positively charged nucleus is in balance with its negatively charged electrons. Ionization occurs when ultraviolet radiation released by solar storms on the surface of the sun strikes a gas molecule and knocks some of its negatively charged electrons free from its nucleus (see illustrations). What is left is a positively charged atom called an *ion*. As long as ions remain positively charged, they reflect radio waves back to earth like a mirror. As ions hurtle through the atmosphere, they in time encounter electrons that have been knocked loose from their nuclei and combine with them to become electrically balanced or neutral again. After this happens, they no longer reflect radio waves.

The ionization of the ionosphere has to be at a middle level for effective radio communication to take place. If too few ions are floating around in the ionosphere, higher-frequency radio waves pass right through the ionosphere and out into space. If the ionization level is too dense, the ionosphere can actually absorb low-frequency radio waves.

Since the ionization process depends on the sun's radiation, it is not constant. As the earth

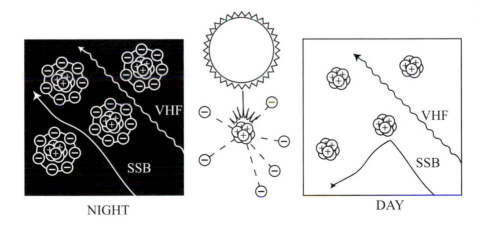

As the sun's rays strike gas molecules in the earth's atmosphere, they free negatively charged electrons from the nucleus to create positively charged ions. These ions reflect radio waves in the marine SSB frequencies back to earth.

rotates on its axis presenting various parts of its surface to the sun, ionization above the area exposed to sunlight builds to a peak shortly after local noon, then gradually decreases until it is nonexistent after dark. Also, how often the solar storms that produce the ionizing radiation occur increases and decreases in a predictable eleven-year cycle.

The ionosphere is divided into three layers (see illustration). The D layer is closest to the earth's surface—only about 30 to 50 miles (50–80 km) up. Atmospheric gases are so dense at that level that ions quickly recombine with free electrons and lose their ability to reflect radio waves. The D layer is only active about two hours before and two hours after local noon. It is so defined and turbulent that when it is active it absorbs longer waves (2 and 4 MHz), making them useless for long-distance communication during those hours.

The E layer is about 70 miles (115 km) above the earth's surface. Its ionization gradually builds during the morning hours until it peaks shortly after local noon, then gradually dissipates during the afternoon, becoming nonexistent after dark. It re-

flects relatively low frequency radio waves and is principally used for short-range communications—from a few hundred to about 1,500 miles (2,500 km).

The F layer is the highest, varying from about 180 miles to 270 miles (300–400 km) above the earth's surface. Up that high, there are very few gas molecules. When an F layer molecule has some of its electrons knocked free of its atom and becomes an ion, it tends to remain an ion for a fairly long time before it encounters free electrons, recombines with them, and loses its ability to reflect radio waves. For this reason, the F layer does not lose all its ionization when the sun goes down but tends to remain ionized, or "active," throughout the night.

The F layer actually is composed of two sublayers—F_1 and F_2—that are separate during daylight hours but combine into a single layer at night. During daylight hours, the F_1 layer is about 180 miles (300 km) above the earth's surface and is useful for reflecting higher-frequency radio waves over distances of about 2,000 miles (3,200 km). Also during daylight hours, the F_2 layer is from 225 to 270

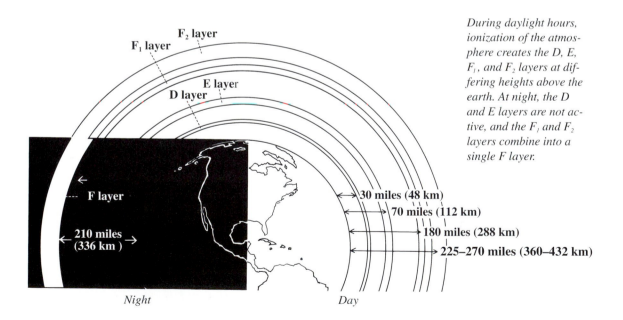

During daylight hours, ionization of the atmosphere creates the D, E, F_1, and F_2 layers at differing heights above the earth. At night, the D and E layers are not active, and the F_1 and F_2 layers combine into a single F layer.

F_2 layer

F_1 layer

E layer

D layer

F layer

210 miles (336 km)

30 miles (48 km)
70 miles (112 km)
180 miles (288 km)
225–270 miles (360–432 km)

Night

Day

miles (360–450 km) above the earth and has the greatest density of ions. It reflects higher frequencies than any of the other layers and is useful for communicating over distances of 2,500 miles (4,000 km) or more. At night the F_1 and F_2 layers combine to form the single F layer about 210 miles (350 km) above the earth, which is responsible for nighttime radio-wave propagation.

Ground Waves and Sky Waves

Depending on their frequency, radio waves have varying degrees of two components: ground waves, which for a certain distance follow the earth's curvature, and sky waves, which are radiated into the atmosphere. Radio waves in the medium-frequency (MF) SSB 2 to 3 MHz band act almost exclusively as ground waves, which allows them to be used for communications up to about 200 miles (320 km) in the daytime and about 500 miles (800 km) at night. Beyond that distance, they are absorbed by the electrical interference that occurs close to the earth's surface. Ground waves are highly susceptible to static from thunderstorms. Radio waves in the 4 MHz band also have a significant ground-wave component, although they act primarily as sky waves.

Radio waves in the high-frequency (HF) 6 to 22 MHz SSB bands and the VHF 156 to 163 MHz band act almost exclusively as sky waves. Those in the HF SSB bands bounce off one or more layers of the ionosphere, which allows them to be used for truly global communications. Radio waves in the VHF band pass right through the ionosphere, which limits their use to a "line of sight" between the antenna of the transmitting radio and that of the receiving radio.

Skip Zones and Windows

Because HF SSB radio waves reflect off the ionosphere, they pass entirely over an area between the point from which they leave the earth and the point at which they are reflected back to it (see illustration next page). In this area, called the *skip zone*, com-munication on that frequency under those conditions is impossible. The point at which the radio waves return to earth, where they can again be received, is called the *window*. Under certain conditions, HF SSB radio waves can be reflected between the earth and the ionosphere more than once. In each successive reflection, they create another skip zone, in which communication is impossible, and another window, where communication can occur.

VHF MARINE RADIO

VHF is the most common and widely used type of marine radio because—within its range limitations—it can be used for contacting lifesaving and rescue services (such as the U.S. Coast Guard), other vessels, or a host of shoreside receiving stations ranging from bridge tenders and harbormasters to marinas and restaurants. VHF frequencies also carry official NOAA marine weather reports and navigational notices, and you can use VHF to contact shore-based marine radiotelephone operators, who connect you with the land-based telephone system. These marine operators can also connect you with boats out of direct range of your VHF equipment.

As noted earlier in this chapter, because VHF radio waves have no significant ground wave and are very high frequency "fast snakes" that wiggle right through the ionosphere, they are useful only along a clear "line of sight" between the antenna of the transmitting station and that of the receiving station. Due to the curvature of the earth, the reliable range of VHF radio-wave ship-to-ship transmissions normally is limited to around 10 to 15 miles (16–25 km) because the vessels' antennas are so close to the earth's surface. Reliable VHF transmissions in ship-to-shore communications can range up to about 40 miles (65 km) because the shore-based antenna normally is several hundred feet high (see illustrations next two pages). Note the term *reliable transmissions*. Under certain atmospheric conditions, VHF radio waves can transmit considerably in excess of these approximate

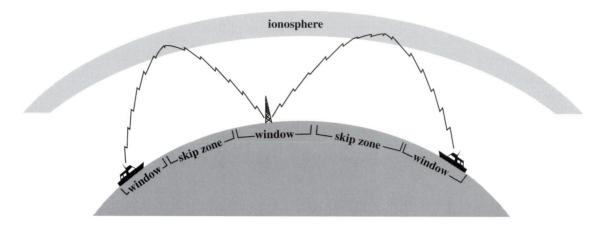

Depending on the state of the ionosphere and the characteristics of the marine SSB frequency selected, radio-wave "skip" makes communications on that frequency impossible at certain distances but allows communications through "windows," which can be thousands of miles apart.

ranges, but those anomalies should not be depended on to provide consistent communications.

Marine use of the VHF band is divided up worldwide into more than 100 working channels. In addition to the working channels, another eleven VHF channels (WX-1 through WX-9 and channels 15 and 70) are receive-only channels for weather and environmental information and other special purposes we'll discuss later. Of the world-wide total, fifty-four channels are allocated for marine use in the United States. Of these fifty-four, eleven are reserved for commercial users and five for the U.S. government.

VHF radios on board vessels are limited to a maximum 25 watts of transmitter power and are required to be able to reduce their power output to no more than 1 watt for short-range communications. Except in certain special instances, opera-

Because VHF radio waves travel in a straight line but the earth curves, vessel A can communicate with tower C but not with vessel B, whose antenna is not high enough off the water.

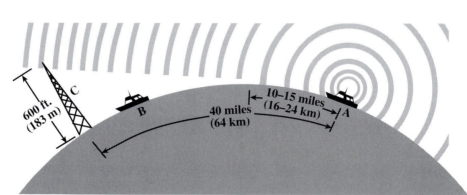

Antenna No. 1, Height in Feet	Range in Miles	Antenna No. 2, Height in Feet

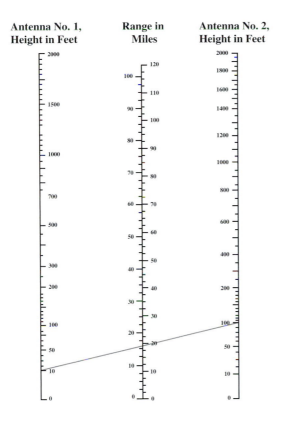

Based on the installed height of your vessel's VHF antenna and that of the vessel or coast station with which you are attempting to communicate, you can use this chart to compute your VHF radio's approximate range. (To convert to metric: feet × 0.305 = meters; miles × 1.6 = kilometers.)

tions on VHF channels 13, 17, and 67 must be conducted on this 1-watt setting, and VHF marine radios manufactured after January 21, 1987, must automatically shift to this 1-watt when transmitting on channels 13, 17, 67, and 77. They also must have a manual override to allow maximum transmitter power on channel 13 in an emergency.

Selecting a VHF Marine Radio

Depending on how elaborate you get in terms of features, options, and accessories, you can spend anywhere from a few hundred dollars for a basic installed VHF radio to more than a thousand dollars if you buy a unit with all the goodies and then add remote units and handheld equipment (see photo next page). In making your choices, you will have to wade through a lot of marketing hype. Here's a rundown of what's available and some advice from experienced cruisers on what is important and what isn't.

In deciding which particular brand and model of VHF radio to buy, the first question that comes to mind may be, "Which one will transmit the farthest?"

Wrong question.

If all other factors—including atmospheric conditions, antenna, and installation—are equal, the distance over which one VHF radio will transmit a signal compared to that of a comparable unit is basically a function of its transmitter power. Since virtually all the installed VHF units sold in the United States have the maximum 25-watt transmitter power allowed by law, that can't be your basis for comparison. Instead, the most important factor in selecting a VHF radio is its ability to *receive* signals. That ability can vary widely among units with vastly differing prices, and the most expensive unit is not always the best.

Reception ability is based primarily on two factors: selectivity and sensitivity. Probably the more important of the two is *selectivity* (also referred to as "adjacent channel rejection"), which indicates a radio receiver's ability to reject unwanted signals and accept only the signal you are trying to hear. It usually is expressed as a negative number of decibels (–dB). The higher the negative number, the better the adjacent channel rejection of the receiver. A receiver with an adjacent channel rejection of –70 dB, for instance, will perform significantly better than one with an adjacent channel rejection of –50 dB.

Sensitivity is the radio's ability to bring in weak signals over the background noise inherent in any radio transmission. It is expressed as the number of microvolts required to produce 12 dB SINAD. *SINAD* is a measure of signal strength relative to

A marine VHF radio (shown here) will be your primary unit for communicating with other vessels and coast stations within 25 to 40 miles (40–65 km). A single-sideband marine radio is a must for those who cruise offshore beyond the range of VHF marine radio. (Furuno)

background noise and distortion. The lower or smaller that signal-strength number, the better the sensitivity of receiver. For example, 0.3 microvolt for 12 dB SINAD is better than 1.0 microvolts for 12 dB SINAD.

When comparing the selectivity and sensitivity of competitive VHF radios from their manufacturers' specification sheets, bear in mind that the figures are not validated by any independent authority and should be viewed with some skepticism. Some marine radio manufacturers don't list the selectivity or sensitivity of their receivers in their consumer literature. I would insist that the dealer provide me with these figures so I could have a rough basis for comparison with those of other units I was considering.

Standard Horizon's line of marine radios use a device called a gallium arsenide field-effect transistor (GASFET), which was developed by the company's SATCOM division, a primary supplier of broadcast satellite receivers. The company's claims about its GASFET technology are not just marketing hype. In situations where an incoming signal is exceptionally weak or there is a high level of background noise, GASFET really does give the Standard Communications radios the ability to receive signals other sets can't.

Virtually all installed VHF radios now sold in the United States are synthesized sets that will operate on all the marine VHF frequencies. Most are

programmed to access all U.S. and international marine VHF channels and have a switch that aligns their transmit and receive frequencies accordingly. The number of channels most manufacturers claim is inflated; they are counting U.S. and international channels twice and boasting of "ten weather channels" when only four actually carry weather broadcasts.

Once you've found a VHF radio you are really interested in, try to get a look at that model in operation on a sunny day, preferably one that is installed on an open flying bridge with the sun shining directly on it. If you can read its display clearly then, you'll be able to read it in just about any conditions you're likely to encounter. If you can't, look for another unit. Also, make sure it provides for single-button selection of channel 16, which can be useful in an emergency.

Beyond those factors, you can buy VHF marine radios today with options to do just about everything but bring you a cold beer. You can get units that will scan all channels or scan only the channels you preprogram. Some models combine a VHF radio with a stereo receiver and compact disc player; others include a stereo and a cassette player.

One feature built into several of the VHF radios on the market that I do think is valuable is the ability to sound an alarm when it picks up the alerting signal NOAA transmits just prior to broadcasting a severe weather alert.

In addition to a basic installed VHF radio, you can also buy remote VHF units for installation aboard your vessel in locations other than your primary operating station (for instance, on the flying bridge of a vessel normally operated from a pilothouse). My preference would be to install a completely separate VHF on the bridge, along with a separate antenna, as a backup in case my pilothouse unit went on the blink or I lost an antenna.

Some VHF manufacturers advertise that their radios can be made to do double duty as a ship's loud-hailer, and some also incorporate an automatic foghorn. A VHF radio is such an important piece of equipment on a cruising boat that I feel it should be dedicated exclusively to the job of communicating with other vessels and the shore. Your loud-hailer and automatic foghorn on your boat should be a separate piece of gear.

Some VHF radios can also be made to double as a ship's intercom system. If you will be cruising shorthanded, an intercom can be valuable if, for example, you need to summon the off watch without leaving the helm. But, again, if you install one, it should be a separate system or part of a loud-hailer and not involve one of your basic links with the outside world.

HANDHELD VHF RADIOS

You need a good handheld VHF radio for communicating between your vessel and its tender, and you'll have to sort through about the same number of options on these as you do for the installed sets (see photo). Most of the units now available are about 6 inches high (15 cm) and weigh about a pound (0.4 kg). Handhelds may legally have up to 25 watts of transmitting power, but practical considerations of battery weight limit them to about 6 watts. Even with that low power, these units provide dependable communication over a 3- to 5-mile (5–8 km) radius.

Most handheld VHFs are powered by 13.2-volt rechargeable nickel cadmium battery packs with about 450 milliamp hours of capacity. With a current drain of around 1.5 amps when transmitting at

A handheld VHF marine radio is useful in a variety of cruising communications situations.

5 watts output, and around 150 milliamps when receiving at maximum audio output, you can get five to ten hours of normal operation before the battery pack needs recharging. Transmitting range drops sharply as battery power runs low. You can purchase higher-powered battery packs with up to 900 milliamps of capacity, but they weigh more.

Most handhelds come with a plug-in transformer for recharging off an onboard 120-volt generator or shore power. You will find that the optional drop-in type of charger is more convenient. The less hassle recharging is, the less likely you are to forget to do it. I would not rely on battery packs that use AA alkaline or nickel cadmium disposable batteries because they have a limited shelf life. On a lengthy cruise, the ones you brought from home may be almost dead by the time you need them, and there is no way to tell how long the ones you buy in the boondocks have been on the store's shelves.

VHF Antennas

Even the best VHF marine radio is useless without an appropriate antenna. The antenna performs its function by resonating at the same frequency at which the radio to which it is attached is sending or receiving. The frequencies that the antenna is capable of resonating are a function of its length. Within limits, its length can be modified electrically. For technical reasons we won't go into here, the higher the frequency, the shorter the antenna, and the lower the frequency, the longer the antenna. This is why a VHF antenna operating up in the 156 MHz band can be as short as 18 inches (45 cm) while an SSB antenna operating from 2 MHz to 23 MHz needs to be a minimum of 23 feet (7 m) long.

ANTENNA GAIN

You'll see VHF antennas described by their *gain*, which refers to factors in their internal construc-

tion that determine their ability to radiate and receive a signal (see illustration). In signal transmission, think of gain in terms of a lighthouse. If you put a bare lightbulb on top of a tall tower at the coast, its light would radiate with equal strength in all directions but would not reach very far. But if you put a reflector behind the bulb that focused its light in a fairly narrow beam aimed at the horizon, the light would cover a smaller area but would be much stronger and would extend much farther from the tower. In the receiving mode, think of gain as cupping your hand behind your ear. Both kinds of focusing are analogous to what gain does to a VHF antenna's ability to radiate and receive radio signals—except, of course, that the focusing occurs through 360 degrees continuously, in a kind of doughnut pattern, rather than sweeping around the horizon like a lighthouse.

The illustration below makes the point that gain affects the strength of signals the antenna can send and receive over specific distances, not simply the distance itself.

Gain is expressed in decibels and refers to the increase in the relative strength at which the

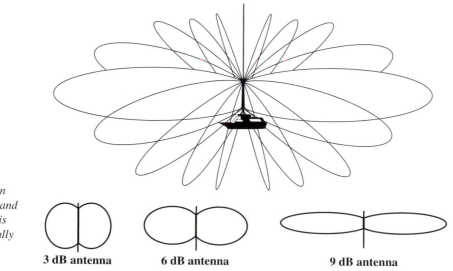

The difference in gain between 3 dB, 6 dB, and 9 dB VHF antennas is illustrated dramatically here.

3 dB antenna   **6 dB antenna**   **9 dB antenna**

antenna will radiate or accept a signal compared to a standard reference. Just what that standard reference consists of is something the engineers are still arguing about and gets too technical for us to deal with here. It will be sufficient for our purposes to say that a 0 dB–gain antenna—like the bare lightbulb at the coast—radiates its signal equally in all directions. Every time you increase an antenna's gain by 3 dB, you double its effective transmitting and receiving capability.

> 3 dB gain = 2X increase (the effect of doubling your transmitting and receiving ability)
>
> 6 dB gain = 4X increase (the effect of quadrupling your transmitting and receiving ability)
>
> 9 dB gain = 8X increase (an eightfold boosting of your transmitting and receiving ability)

Note, however, that here we are talking about "transmitting and receiving ability," which refers to signal strength and clarity and does not mean you get a one-to-one increase in actual range. For a theoretical VHF radio with a 0 dB–gain antenna, for instance, increasing its signal strength by 9 dB would approximately double the distance over which it could communicate, not increase it eightfold.

The VHF antennas commonly sold for use on power cruising yachts usually have gain ratings of 3 dB, 6 dB, 9 dB, or 10 dB. Some experts recommend either a 3 dB or a 6 dB antenna on the theory that the beam of a 9 dB or a 10 dB antenna is so narrowly focused it can overshoot or undershoot its target as the boat pitches and rolls. A substantial majority of experienced cruisers find that beam overshoot and undershoot is not normally a factor on a sizable powerboat because the angle of pitch and roll is not nearly as great as that of a sailboat and the antenna is not mounted nearly as far off the water.

I'd equip my VHF radio with the highest-gain antenna I could afford (price increases significantly as gain increases) and one that I could securely install aboard my vessel with confidence that it wouldn't be swept away in rough weather. Length and weight, like price, increase dramatically as gain increases. Whereas a 3 dB–gain VHF antenna is normally 8 feet (2.5 m) long and weighs around 5 pounds (1.9 kg), a 9 or 10 dB antenna can be up to 23 feet (7 m) long and weigh up to 12 pounds (4.5 kg).

In choosing a specific VHF antenna, look for rugged construction. Antennas that employ hollow copper or brass tubes for their radiating element hold up better than less expensive ones that use wire or coaxial cable. The unit also should incorporate a choking sleeve or stub that confines all its radiating effect to the antenna itself. Without a choking sleeve, the cable that connects the antenna to the radio may also radiate a signal and dilute the antenna's effectiveness.

Installing a VHF Radio

You may install VHF radio equipment yourself provided it has been pretested to ensure that it will operate only on its assigned frequencies. The manufacturers of all VHF radios legal for sale in the United States pretest their products before they ship them from the factory and certify that they operate only on the appropriate frequencies. Modifications that will change the operating frequencies, however, may be done only by or under the direct supervision of the holder of a General Radiotelephone Operator License.

You want a VHF transceiver within easy reach of your helm station—two if your vessel has a flying bridge. All of your cruising radios should be installed in a location that protects them from rain and salt spray and allows ample room for air to circulate around them to dissipate the heat they produce.

Marine radios can be susceptible to interference from other onboard communications and navigational electronics—and vice versa. Plan your installation carefully to keep your radios and their antennas separated as far as possible from one another and from other electronics and their antennas. In extreme cases, you may need to install electronic filters on some of your onboard units to keep them from interfering with one another. That is a job for a qualified marine electronics technician.

Some VHF radios, particularly those with all-plastic cases, can be subject to feedback from their antenna's signal, resulting in a high-pitched squeal or howl. Feedback can also play havoc with the memory of a VHF's channel programming and scanning functions. To prevent feedback, the radio and antenna should be installed so they are at least 6 feet (1.8 m) apart.

Electrical ground for the radio is provided through its negative-wire connection to the battery, but it also should be connected to your vessel's radio frequency ground (which we discuss later in this chapter). Ground for the antenna is provided by the coaxial cable connecting it to the radio. The key to assuring a good ground is to make connections only between surfaces that are scraped down to bare metal and are kept tight and clean of corrosion.

Marine radios normally operate off 12-volt DC (direct current) battery power and are extremely sensitive to inadequate voltage or amperage. The power cable should be as large in diameter as practical and should be run from your vessel's DC distribution panel to the radio as directly as possible, avoiding kinks and crimps. Leave only enough excess power cable to allow a technician to remove the radio from the bulkhead and service the set without having to disconnect it. The channel programming and scanning features offered in many VHF units can be highly susceptible to interference from main-engine and generator-engine starting loads. In extreme cases, it may be necessary to power your radios from a separate bank of batteries that is isolated from the batteries used for cranking your main engines and generators.

As discussed in chapter 3, it's a wise precaution to install a backup DC power source for your essential electronics at the highest practical point in the vessel. You also should mount your antenna as high on your vessel as you can, since the reception and transmission performance of your VHF marine radio will be directly affected. But increasing its height by only 4 or 5 feet (1.2–1.5 m) with an extension will increase its effective operating range by only about a mile (1.6 km) or so. Since your VHF antenna presents an attractive target for lightning to strike, your installation should allow you to lay it down horizontally when you are near thunderstorms.

VHF Legal Requirements

If you operate only in the United States and Canada—that is, within 12 miles (20 km) of the U.S. and Canadian coastlines, which include the coasts of Alaska, Hawaii, Puerto Rico, and all other U.S. possessions and trust territories—or international waters and do not transmit to foreign stations or visit foreign ports, you are not required to have a Ship Station Radio License (often just called a "ship station license" or a "ship license") to operate a VHF radio aboard your vessel. You may, however, apply for a license if you wish. For operation in the waters of other countries, you are required to have both a Ship Station Radio License and a Restricted Radiotelephone Operator Permit (often referred to as an "RP".)

SHIP STATION RADIO LICENSE

You apply for a ship station license on Federal Communications Commission (FCC) forms 605 and 159, which are available from most marine electronics dealers or the nearest FCC field office. Form 605 is the Ship Station License Application. Form 159 is a Remittance Advice you attach to your payment for the license fee. If you check the appropriate boxes on form 605, a single station license will cover all your electronic equipment, including VHF and SSB radios, radar, and your emergency position-indicating radio beacon (EPIRB).

When you file form 605, if your vessel has not been assigned a nine-digit Maritime Mobile Service Identity (MMSI) number, complete items 8 to 10 on form 605 schedule B to request that one be assigned. You will need it for Digital Selective Calling (DSC), which we discuss later in this chapter.

The FCC will license only marine radio equipment that it has "type-accepted." In the United States it is illegal to sell radio equipment for use on the commercial services if it has not been type-accepted. Do not buy some oddball radio on the black market or in another country that is not identified as "FCC type-accepted." The nearest FCC field office can tell you whether or not it is accepted; if it isn't, you won't be able to get it licensed. All type-accepted marine VHF and SSB radios manufactured after June 17, 1999, must contain at least minimum DSC capability.

Before you apply, your vessel must be documented or numbered. If you will be living aboard your boat for extensive cruising, you may not have a permanent home address and may wonder what to do with the "home address" line common to all FCC station and operator's license applications. You may list the address of an individual or company that will be taking care of mail for you, but you will be responsible for mail received at this address as if it were your permanent residence.

When you complete form 605, you tear off a portion and post it aboard your vessel, which gives you temporary authority to operate the radio equipment on board your vessel for ninety days from the date you mailed in the application. Until you receive your station license and call sign, on a documented vessel you use as a temporary call sign the letters "KUS" followed by your vessel's six-digit documentation number. On a numbered vessel, you use as a temporary call sign the letter "K" followed by your vessel's number.

Your station license will assign your vessel a permanent call sign of three letters and four digits in your name. Call signs may not be transferred from one boat to another or from one owner to another. If you sell a vessel that has been assigned a call sign, whether or not you leave its radios aboard, you should promptly return your station license to the secretary of the FCC and request its cancellation (see contact information for the FCC in the resources appendix). If you fail to do that and the station is improperly used, you can be held liable for any penalties involved. New owners have to file a form 605 application for a ship station license and a new call sign in their own names.

Changing your own name, your permanent address, or the name of your vessel does not invalidate a station license, but you are required to notify the FCC promptly of the change and to post a copy of the letter along with the station license (see the Pennsylvania address for this notification in the resources appendix).

Ship station licenses must be renewed every 10 years. Normally the FCC will mail the necessary renewal application to your address 120 days prior to the expiration date of the license. If you don't receive a renewal form at least 30 days before your station license expires, you should request one from the nearest FCC field office since you must complete and return it to them prior to the expiration date to stay legal. If you get it to the FCC by the renewal date, you can continue to operate until you receive your renewed license.

RESTRICTED RADIOTELEPHONE OPERATOR PERMIT

If you operate only in domestic waters, the operation of a VHF marine radio does not require a Restricted Radiotelephone Operator Permit (RP). However, because of an international treaty with Canada, an RP is required to operate VHF marine radios in the Great Lakes on pleasure vessels over 65 feet (20 m) long. If you sail out of U.S. domestic waters into international waters, you are not required to have an RP unless you transmit to foreign stations or dock in a foreign port. In all cases, you are required to have an RP if you operate a VHF marine radio in the waters of another country.

You should go ahead and get an RP so that you can operate your VHF in the waters of other countries. You will need one anyway to operate an SSB radio, even in U.S. waters. If you are eligible for employment in the United States, you apply for the permit on FCC form 753. If you are not eligible for employment in the United States, you apply on form 755. Form 753 applications normally come packaged with new radios and are available from most marine electronics dealers. Both forms are available from the nearest FCC field office. The minimum age limit is fourteen, and no fee or test is required. For temporary operating authority while your application is being processed, fill out part 3 of form 753 or 755 and keep it with you. It is valid for sixty days from the date you mailed your application. RPs normally are valid for a licensee's lifetime. In operating situations where it is required, you must have the original of your RP with you anytime you transmit.

In situations that require an RP, you may allow persons who do not have an RP to speak over the microphone of a marine radio under your supervision and to switch frequencies, but you must begin and end the transmission with the appropriate identifications and operating procedures and you are liable for any violations that occur during the transmission.

The FCC no longer requires you to maintain a radio traffic log; however, the agency does recommend that you keep a record of any emergency transmissions in which you participate. (Enter that information as a part of your normal ship's log.)

The FCC does require you to keep a log regarding your radio equipment's installation, maintenance, and service history. Forms for this purpose are available through marine electronics dealers, but you can just as easily keep the information in your regular ship's log.

The ship station license that covers your installed VHF radio also covers your handheld VHF as an "associated ship unit." However, legally (except in emergencies) you may use your handheld only to communicate with your main vessel. Unless you get a special marine utility station license, you may not operate it from shore; you may transmit at only 1 watt of output power; and you must identify transmissions using the call sign of your main vessel and the appropriate "associated unit designator" (for example, "WXY 1234, mobile one"). Every cruiser I know blithely ignores all the foregoing.

Where necessary, your operation of a handheld VHF is also covered by your RP.

VHF Equipment Recommendations

While there are a number of good VHF marine radios currently on the market, several of my cruising friends have found they get excellent service out of the ICOM IC-M502 or the SEA 156. In VHF antennas, the best units are from Shakespeare. I would go with at least a 6 dB–gain antenna in the form of Shakespeare's 8-foot model (2.4 m) 5202. In higher-gain units, you might consider Shakespeare's 9 dB, 19-foot (5.8 m) model 4018. Shakespeare's 10 dB, 21-foot (6.5 m) model 476 antenna is also an outstanding performer. In handheld VHF equipment, I'd suggest you look at the 5-watt ICOM IC-M3A.

SINGLE-SIDEBAND MARINE RADIO

Single-sideband (SSB) marine radio is completely different from VHF. Its range is much greater, and its equipment is much more expensive and complex, requiring a somewhat higher level of operator sophistication. SSB marine frequencies carry valuable official weather information and Local Notices to Mariners and can be used to contact other vessels and place distress or information calls to the U.S. Coast Guard and its counterparts in other nations. SSB radios can serve as the receiver for weather facsimile machines, and some models can be used for both voice and radiotelex transmissions.

How SSB Works

MF SSB in the 2 to 3 MHz band functions through ground waves that can follow the earth's curvature for a certain distance. They can be used to communicate as far as 200 miles (320 km) or so during the day and 500 miles (800 km) at night if conditions are good. They are, however, extremely susceptible to interference from static during thunderstorms.

HF radio waves in the 4 to 23 MHz SSB bands

can be bounced off the ionosphere to produce truly long-range communications—in some cases, virtually worldwide. As mentioned in our discussion of radio-wave propagation earlier in this chapter, because ionization of the atmosphere is affected daily by the rising and setting of the sun, the range of the various SSB bands varies greatly according to time of day. See chapter 21 for a more detailed discussion of the ranges and the best time of day to use particular SSB channels.

As with VHF, SSB has both simplex and duplex channels. Because of significant differences in their ranges and operating modes, the designations and use allocations of channels and frequencies in the MF SSB 2 to 3 MHz band and those of HF SSB in the 4 to 23 MHz bands are treated somewhat differently.

- Most frequencies in the 2 to 3 MHz MF SSB band are not covered by international treaties. The purposes for which these frequencies are used as well as the pairing of transmit and receive frequencies of duplex channels vary from country to country. Though there are exceptions (which we will cover later in this chapter), most channels in the 2 to 3 MHz band are designated by their transmit and receive frequencies rather than by channel number.
- Most frequencies in the 4 to 23 MHz HF SSB bands are covered by ITU agreements. The purposes for which these channels are used and the pairing of transmit and receive frequencies of duplex channels are essentially the same in ITU-member countries throughout the world. ITU channels are designated by three- or four-digit numbers. In three-digit channel designators, the first digit identifies the meg band in which it is located (for example, channel 401 is in the 4-meg band). In four-digit channel designators, the meg band is identified by the first two digits (for example, channel 2236 is in the 22-meg band).

Channel 2.182 MHz (almost always referred to by its kilohertz designation simply as "twenty-one eighty-two") is reserved internationally as a calling and distress frequency and is used much the same way as VHF channel 16.

SSB radios licensed in the United States are allowed a maximum transmit power of 150 watts when operating on the 2 to 3 MHz band and 1,000 watts when operating on the 4 to 23 MHz frequencies. To be type-accepted by the FCC, units with more than 150 watts of transmitter power must shift automatically to 150-watt output when they are operated on 2 to 3 MHz.

Selecting an SSB Marine Radio

Fortunately for the buyer, all the companies now marketing marine SSB radios in the United States make good equipment. Choosing among them comes down to a matter of what you want in the way of transmitter power and features—and the size of your budget.

Although SSB radios may legally have up to 1,000 watts of transmit power—which technically is referred to as *peak envelope power*—when operating in the HF SSB bands, the choices are among units with 125, 150, 300, and 400 watts of output power. (It technically is possible to boost the transmitter power of any of these units up to the maximum allowable 1,000 watts with a linear amplifier. But, to be legal, the linear amp would have to be FCC type-accepted for use on the marine SSB frequencies. The linear amps sold through ham radio shops are not type-accepted and, therefore, would be illegal if used to boost the output of a marine SSB radio.)

Except in rare instances, 125 to 150 watts of output power is quite adequate to establish worldwide SSB communications. In an experiment, Harris Corporation (using an optimally located, very tall transmission tower and waiting for just the right atmospheric conditions) established a clear communications link between Rochester, New York, and Cairo, Egypt, using only a quarter-watt of transmitter power. Higher transmitter power does not necessarily guarantee greater range, because optimum SSB performance is much more a function of antenna design, a good radio frequency (RF) ground, favorable atmospheric conditions, and proper channel selection than it is of output power. The major benefit of higher power output is that it gives users the ability to punch through electrical interference or literally overpower competing traffic on the frequency they're trying to use. Increases in transmitter power cost dearly.

All SSB marine radios sold in the United States are synthesized to transmit and receive on all assigned frequencies from 2 MHz to 23 MHz, and most receive over an even wider spectrum, so you don't have much choice regarding frequency coverage. Aside from transmitter power, the differences among SSB marine radios lie in their capacity to store transmit-and-receive frequency pairs. SSB manufacturers ship their units with the paired frequencies of anywhere from fifty to more than a hundred ITU channels already programmed into their radio's memory, then allow the user to program additional channel frequencies into a "scratch-pad memory" in the field. Field programming ability is necessary because frequency pairing in the 2 to 3 MHz band is not controlled under ITU agreements and varies from country to country. Field programming allows you to program appropriate 2 to 3 MHz transmission-and-reception frequency pairs into memory for recall as you move from country to country.

Most SSB radios house all their internal parts (except the antenna coupler) in a single case. Others have their transmitting amplifier and transceiver in a separate box, which can be mounted out of sight, requiring only the controller to be mounted in an accessible location. These split units normally can accommodate two to four remote controllers, which can be mounted in various locations around the vessel and can be used to both receive and transmit. In practice, a single controller properly located in your lower steering station will be sufficient. If you have money to burn, a second control unit on the flying bridge or next to your easy chair in the salon might be nice, but you don't really need either one.

One feature worth having that some SSB radios incorporate is an internal international alarm. In an emergency, it can be used to alternately transmit two frequency tones on 2182 kHz at the touch of a button on the front of the unit. The signal sounds something like an ambulance siren and is intended to alert receiving locations, such as the U.S. Coast Guard, that you are about to transmit an emergency message. Some receiving stations are equipped with detectors that ring a bell or sound a horn to get the attention of an operator when the international alarm signal is received. Under international agreements, you may transmit this alarm only if you follow it up with the Mayday distress or Pan-Pan urgency signal and then only for thirty seconds to one minute. (See chapter 23 for more information about using this alarm.)

Fiberglass Sticks and Antenna Couplers

To achieve optimum communications throughout the 2 to 23 MHz SSB bands, you will need a white fiberglass stick with a hollow copper tube inside it that is at least 23 feet (7 m) long. (For reasons we'll get to shortly, don't think of this stick as an "antenna"; just think of it as a white fiberglass stick with a hollow copper tube inside of it.) Larger vessels that can support the added weight can get even better performance from the same kind of fiberglass stick but that is 28 feet (8.5 m) long.

Because you will be operating your SSB marine radio on more than one band of frequencies, you also will need a coupler that automatically tunes the resonance of your antenna (here, as you'll see, it's OK to use the word *antenna*) to match the frequency on which the radio is operating. All SSB manufacturers offer their own couplers, which they suggest be used with their equipment. On the ICOM IC-700 Pro connected to the company's AT-120 coupler, you must push a button on the front of the transceiver to activate the tuning process, which takes two to three seconds. The SEA 235 connected to the SEA 1612 coupler activates tuning with the first voice syllable. The first time a frequency is used, the tuning process takes about five seconds. Once a frequency is tuned, it is contained in the 1612's memory. The next time it is needed, tuning takes only about twenty milliseconds.

All couplers require the radio and the antenna to be connected by both a coaxial cable to carry the signal itself and a control cable to handle the coupler's tuning functions.

A frequently overlooked advantage of fully automatic antenna couplers is that in an emergency they can be used to tune practically any jury-rigged wire to a frequency you can use to get help.

Installing an SSB Marine Radio

In this section, I say some things about SSB marine radios, antennas, antenna couplers, and installation that run counter to just about everything you may ever have heard on the topic. I assure you it is based on solid information from some of the best technical experts in the field.

When someone says "SSB marine antenna," you probably think of that white 23- or 28-foot-long (7–8.5 m) fiberglass stick I mentioned in the previous section. Actually, that fiberglass stick is only half of the true antenna on your boat that radiates and receives SSB radio waves. The other half is your vessel's *RF ground* (sometimes referred to as the *capacitive ground*, *ground plane*, or *counterpoise*). On a typical cruising boat, that true antenna doesn't really care where on your vessel you choose to install that fiberglass stick; it's going to start at the RF ground on your vessel, run up through the metallic strap that connects the RF ground to the fiberglass stick, and end at the top of the fiberglass stick—and there isn't really anything you can do to change that. But you can take advantage of it rather than—as most SSB marine installations do—try to fight it. (Since the fiberglass stick portion of your true SSB antenna contains a hollow copper tube, it will be an inviting target for lightning. Install it as you do your

VHF antenna in a manner that will allow you to lay it down horizontally when you are in or near thunderstorms.)

Because of this true antenna's obdurate insistence on obeying the laws of physics, its performance is not nearly as affected by how high you choose to install that white fiberglass stick as it is by how effective an RF ground you construct aboard your vessel. For effective SSB marine communications, this RF ground is absolutely, totally, and completely critical. Without it, you will never achieve optimum communications with HF SSB regardless of the quality or transmitter power of your radio or the length of your fiberglass stick.

In addition to critically affecting your SSB radio's performance, a poor RF ground—or improper connection of your SSB radio and antenna tuner to it—can make your autopilot and analog electronic instruments go crazy when you transmit over the radio, can burn out tiny integrated circuits in your electronic equipment, and can even give you a tiny RF shock when you place the microphone close to your mouth.

(Don't worry about gain in connection with SSB antennas. Because an SSB marine antenna directs its signal upward toward the ionosphere rather than toward the horizon as a VHF antenna does, the term *gain* does not properly apply.)

Creating an RF Ground

The key to creating an effective RF ground is to make a good RF connection between your vessel and the water surrounding it. Because this RF connection shares some principles and terminology with the grounding needed for the DC or AC (alternating current) electrical systems and lightning protection we discussed in chapter 3, people often get them confused. In fact, the two are quite different and must be thought of separately (and, as nearly as possible, kept physically separate). In electrical grounding, for instance, a wire conductor's ability to carry current is analogous to a water pipe's ability to carry water: the critical measurement is its diameter. In RF grounding, the critical factor is the conductor's surface area. An

SSB antenna actually works by exciting electrons. The more surface area it has, the more electrons it can excite. For this reason, a copper strap only a few mils thick will not provide much of an electrical ground but it is an ideal RF ground because of its expansive surface area. Actually, copper or brass mesh screen provides a better RF ground than strap because in equal dimensions it has greater surface area. However, it is much more susceptible to corrosion and should be used only where it can be encapsulated in fiberglass (as in a vessel's cabintop or hull). Don't use flat-braided battery cable for an RF ground because it corrodes much too rapidly.

As another example: your vessel should have a bonding system that ties its engines, generators, and all other metal masses together with round wires. That's fine and necessary for electrical grounding and lightning protection, but it does not create an effective RF ground. For effective SSB performance, your bonding system must be duplicated (not replaced) with a separate grounding system composed of metal strap. The two systems will be interconnected in that they are both tied to the same metal masses, but they should not be deliberately interconnected at other points.

For effective SSB communication, you need to have an absolute minimum of 100 square feet (9 m²) of metal surface tied into your vessel's RF grounding system. Even more is better. On nonconducting hulls, such as wood or fiberglass, you want to get as much of that metal surface as possible below your vessel's waterline. In the following section, I describe the optimum RF ground installation. While you will probably wind up doing something less expensive and time-consuming, at least you'll know what the experts recommend.

RF Grounding of Metal Hulls

Steel- or aluminum-hull vessels make an ideal RF ground. To take advantage of their RF grounding characteristics, their engines, batteries, metal through-hull fittings, metal water and fuel tanks, stainless steel or aluminum railings, and copper water, fuel, and hydraulic lines, as well as any other masses of metal, should be firmly connected directly to the hull with copper strap, not round wires. If such a vessel's engines rest on insulating rubber mounts, for instance, they should be RF grounded to the hull. The large propellers on displacement hull boats can also contribute to a good RF ground. To incorporate them, you need a metal wiper brush that rests against the shaft and is RF grounded to the hull itself.

Once you have all of the vessel's metal masses interconnected, you need to carry their grounding potential up to your electronics. To do that, drill a ⅜-inch (70 mm) hole in a stringer or other mass of metal that is below the waterline and is securely welded to the hull itself. The hole should be directly below where most of the vessel's communications and navigation electronics will be installed. Sand a 4- by 4-inch (10 by 10 cm) area around it down to bare metal. Double the end of a long 4-inch-wide copper strap over itself several times, drill a hole through the folded sections, and affix the strap securely into the stringer with a stainless steel bolt and nut. (Anywhere you attach copper strap to a metal hull, put a stainless steel washer between the two to help retard electrolysis.) Coat the area of attachment with several layers of paint to exclude water and help prevent corrosion. Run the strap up the inside of the hull to the vessel's uppermost deck. It may be painted or covered with fiberglass or interior paneling without affecting its RF grounding capability. I talk later in this chapter about tying your electronic equipment into it.

RF Grounding of Nonconducting Hulls

For vessels with nonconducting hulls, such as wood or fiberglass, RF grounding is considerably more difficult. If you should have the luxury of building your dream cruiser from scratch, you could create an ideal RF ground by having the builder laminate a minimum of 100 square feet (9 m²) of copper or brass mesh screen (remember, the more the better) inside the hull below the waterline. Again, the fact that the screen is not in direct contact with the water is no problem since RF energy passes through wood and fiberglass quite easily.

On an existing boat with a nonconducting hull, create an RF ground by running a minimum of 100 square feet (9 m²) of copper strap around the entire inside circumference of the hull below the waterline and connecting it to all metal masses inside the hull. Connect it to round through-hull fittings with stainless steel clamps, but keep it as flat as possible. Where the strap must run through a small hole, loosely roll it lengthwise, pass it through, then flatten it out on either side of the obstruction. Bring the strap to a point where you will connect it to a second strap going from the inside of the hull to your pilothouse and flying bridge electronics. If your vessel will not have metal mesh in its cabintop (as we discuss later in this chapter), you should locate that point somewhere other than in the engine space. Once you have a good RF grounding system installed inside the hull, connect it to a strap and run it up the inside of the hull in as direct a line as possible to the boat's electronics. Whether the vessel has a conducting or a nonconducting hull, when you get this grounding strap up to your pilothouse, run a separate grounding strap from it to each piece of electronics on your vessel; the straps should be like the spokes of a wheel, not strung together one after another like Christmas tree lights. Every single piece of equipment in your pilothouse and on your flying bridge should be tied into the grounding strap from the bilge.

Don't weaken your RF grounding system by using round wires to connect the ground strap from the bilge to the equipment. If the electronic equipment has a ground-post stud with a nut and washer, fold the strap back on itself, drill a hole in it, and make your connection there. If no ground stud is provided, fold the strap, drill aligning holes, and attach it to the sheet metal screws in the equipment chassis. Accordion fold enough excess into the strap to allow the equipment to be removed from the bulkhead for "live" checks of its tuning.

You also can increase the area of an RF grounding system by installing copper or bronze mesh screen in a vessel's cabintop. This screening can be installed beneath the headliner or laminated into the cabintop itself, but it also must be tied to your below-waterline RF ground with straps. It's better if that connection is made with straps at each corner of the screen rather than at a single point. Some cruising yacht manufacturers install an RF screen in their boats' superstructures at the factory. If that mesh is at least 100 square feet (9 m²) in area and is well connected to all the vessel's below-waterline metal masses, it probably will give you an adequate RF ground, and metal strapping in the bilge will not be necessary.

If installing the system described above is simply impossible, you can do what most owners do to create an RF ground—install a couple of brass or copper plates at least 1 foot square (0.09 m²) outside the hull below the waterline, and ground them firmly to all metal masses inside the boat. Use solid copper plates rather than the porous type, which, like round wires, are suitable for grounding DC and low-frequency AC electrical currents but not for RF grounding. Grounding plates won't work nearly as well as the system I've described, but they're better than no RF ground at all.

INSTALLING A COUPLER

The coupler should be installed at the base of the vessel's true antenna, not necessarily—as you have probably been led to believe—at the base of the fiberglass stick.

On properly RF grounded metal-hull vessels and vessels that have at least 100 square feet (9 m²) of properly installed metal mesh in their cabintops, the RF ground is in the uppermost deck and the true SSB antenna starts where the ground and the fiberglass stick are connected (see illustration next page). Install your antenna coupler as close as possible to that point, and ground the coupler to it with a metal strap that is as short as possible and at least 2 inches (5 cm) wide. The best location normally is in the cavity below the flying bridge console, which keeps the coupler out of the weather.

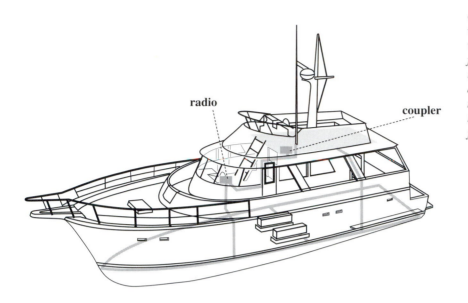

On a fiberglass- or wood-hull cruising vessel with at least 100 square feet of RF ground screen in its cabintop, the SSB antenna coupler can be mounted beneath the flybridge at the base of the fiberglass stick.

On wood- or fiberglass-hull boats that do not have at least 100 square feet (9 m²) of properly installed metal mesh in their cabintops, your true SSB antenna starts at the point where you connected the below-waterline RF ground to the strap going to the pilothouse (see illustration). Your antenna coupler should be installed as close to that point as possible, which means below decks. Avoid making the connection in the engine room, where the coupler would be subjected to high temperatures.

If you disregard this recommended location and install your coupler—as most people do—in the pilothouse overhead or beneath the flying bridge console and connect it to the fiberglass stick portion of your vessel's true antenna, you will be creating several problems for yourself. The coupler is designed to be installed at the base of the true antenna, which is below decks, but you are installing it at some unknown electrical distance up the antenna, where the impedances are significantly different than at the base and may be outside the coupler's design parameters. Further, the coupler is designed for unbalanced output, but you would be installing it somewhere in the middle of the antenna and confusing it as to whether it should provide balanced tuning (which it cannot do) or unbalanced tuning (which it also can't do if it is installed in the middle of the true antenna). You have also made the coupler, the radio, the radio's microphone, and yourself all part of your vessel's true antenna. Aside from causing all kinds of quirks in your radio when you try to transmit with it, this arrangement can also cause the microphone to give you a tiny RF shock when you key it.

INSTALLING A TRANSCEIVER

As with any piece of marine electronic equipment, an SSB transceiver should be protected from spray. Most cruisers install their SSB radios in the pilothouse. While the unit should be installed in a location handy to the helm, I don't recommend installing it in an overhead console. Selecting the proper band and switching channels to offset at-

On a fiberglass- or wood-hull cruising vessel that has no RF ground in its cabintop but only in its hull, the SSB antenna coupler should be mounted at the connection between the RF ground and the grounding strip that runs up to the fiberglass stick.

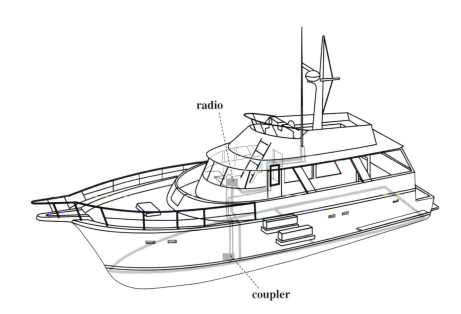

mospheric interference can take a lot of time. It's much better to install your unit where you can reach all of its controls from a comfortable sitting position.

All of the SSB units now on the market operate off 13.6-volt DC power. Current drain in voice transmission averages about 12 amps, and transmitting the international alarm uses 17 to 20 amps. You can also buy an optional power converter to operate the unit off 120-volt AC.

SSB Legal Requirements

Because SSB in the 2 MHz band overlaps that of VHF, your vessel must be equipped with a VHF marine radio before you add an SSB marine radio. The SSB radio can be installed only by or under the direction of someone who holds an FCC General Radiotelephone Operator License or a First-Class Radiotelegraph License.

The vessel on which an SSB radio is operated must have a valid Ship Station Radio License, and the operator must have a Restricted Radiotelephone Operator Permit.

SSB Equipment Recommendations

Before you make any decisions on an SSB marine radio, read through the sections on the use of amateur radio and telex in cruising and the discussion of weather-facsimile receivers and the Navigational Telex (NAVTEX) system, all of which follow later in this chapter, because the decisions you make regarding those options will affect your choice of an SSB radio.

For SSB voice communications only, most of my cruising friends who are on a budget give high marks to SEA's Model 235 and ICOM's M710, both of which are 150-watt units. My friends with more elaborate resources report excellent results from the 400-watt Furuno FS-5000. If you want to go first-class, you can spring for Radio Holland's 600-watt radio system.

As a good 23-foot (7 m) fiberglass stick for

your SSB antenna, I'd suggest Shakespeare's 390. If your choice of a VHF antenna is Shakespeare's 9 dB, 23-foot 5208 model, the company's 23-foot model 5308 stick will match it cosmetically.

Fredrick Graves's *Mariner's Guide to Single Sideband* is especially valuable for its information on worldwide SSB channels and frequencies (see resources appendix).

DIGITAL SELECTIVE CALLING

A basic problem with VHF and SSB marine communications used to be that in order for a vessel to receive a call from another vessel or from a coast station or to be made aware of critical weather and distress information, the radio on board had to be turned on, the radio had to be tuned to an appropriate channel, and someone had to be listening to it.

Digital Selective Calling (DSC) is a system developed as part of the international Global Maritime Distress and Safety System (GMDSS). Under GMDSS, appropriate authorities in each member nation are able to transmit "sel-call" messages to all vessels in any one or all of seven areas of the world. Messages to DSC-equipped vessels in A1 zones—within 40 to 50 miles (65–80 km) of each member nation's coastline—are transmitted via VHF channel 70. Messages to DSC-equipped vessels in A2 areas—within 150 miles (240 km) of each nation's coastline—are transmitted over designated MF SSB frequency 2187.5. Messages to DSC-equipped vessels in A3 zones—deep-ocean areas—are transmitted over the designated channels in each of the HF SSB bands. Under DSC, a vessel applies for a nine-digit MMSI number that is unique to that vessel. Anyone who knows that number can call that vessel, and the VHF or SSB radio on board will ring much like a telephone. When someone on board responds to the call, the radio is automatically shifted to an appropriate working channel.

DSC has two primary values:

1. coast stations can contact an individual ship, a group of ships or all ships within a given geographic area to alert them to significant weather or safety information
2. a DSC-equipped vessel can, with the push of a single button, send out a distress message

If the DSC-equipped radio is interfaced to a navigation receiver such as a GPS (global positioning system) or a loran, the distress message also can include the vessel's position. DSC-equipped radios also can automatically continue to send the distress message, even if all on board are incapacitated. Unless a choice is manually selected from a list of eight specific dangers, DSC-equipped radios send out an "undesignated distress" message. The choices that can be manually selected are

- fire or explosion
- flooding
- collision
- grounding
- listing
- danger of capsizing
- sinking
- disabled and adrift
- abandoning ship

A secondary value of DSC is that cruising buddies who know one another's MMSI can send one another alerting messages that they want to talk without having to monitor the VHF channel 16 calling frequency or the SSB 2182 calling frequency.

Member nations of the International Radio Consultive Committee have set aside VHF channel 70 (156.525 MHz) for DSC and channels in each of the SSB marine bands for the same purpose. These channels are to be used for the transmission of alerting messages only—not for normal communications.

The SSB bands designated for DSC calls are

2187.5 kHz
4207.5 kHz
6312 kHz
8414.5 kHz
12577 kHz
16804 kHz

Here's how DSC works in practice. If your vessel is equipped for DSC, you no longer need to monitor VHF channel 16 or the traffic lists of the SSB High Seas coast stations to find out if someone is trying to call you. If you have registered your vessel's DSC number with the marine operator, you will have your VHF radio monitor channel 70 and your SSB radio monitor one of the channels designated for DSC. The operator will send you a data message telling you to call back on an appropriate working channel. Likewise, cruising buddies equipped for DSC can punch in your vessel's DSC number and send you a message telling you to call them on an appropriate working channel.

Recreational vessels are not required to carry DSC-equipped VHF or SSB radios, but because you must have a DSC-equipped radio to be part of the GMDSS system, it's a wise investment. Also, make sure the DSC-equipped VHF or SSB radio you buy can be interfaced to your navigational receiver so that, in an emergency, its distress message can include your vessel's position. All marine radios manufactured since 1991 are required to have some form of DSC included.

Recreational vessels apply for an MMSI number either by requesting one on the FCC's form 506 or by contacting BoatU.S., which is authorized to issue MMSI numbers for vessels that are voluntarily equipped for DSC.

MARINE SATELLITE TELEPHONES

If you need to stay in touch with family, friends, or business associates while cruising, marine satellite telephones offer voice, fax, e-mail, and data communications worldwide.

The primary satellite service through which these communications are provided is Inmarsat, which operates four Inmarsat-3 satellites in geostationary orbit at a height of 22,000 miles (35,500 km) to provide overlapping coverage of the entire world apart

Inmarsat's mini-M satellite marine telephone service provides reliable coverage of the entire world, except for its polar regions.

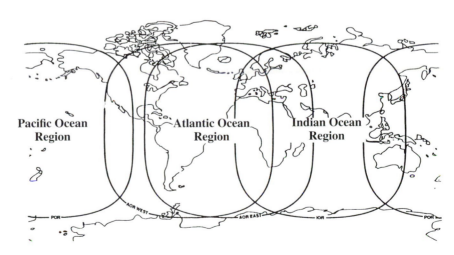

from the poles. For recreational marine applications, the most practical service is Inmarsat's mini-M service (see illustration previous page).

Equipment Recommendations

Several companies, including KVH, make Inmarsat-compatible terminals. The unit I have found most cost-effective for recreational marine use is the KVH Tracphone 25 (see photo). Its gyroscopically stabilized 9.5 dB antenna is only 11.5 inches high by 10 inches in diameter (30 by 25 cm) and weighs only 11 pounds (5 kg). It can handle voice, fax, and e-mail. Another good, though somewhat more expensive, option is Thrane & Thrane's TT-3064A Capsat Marine Telephone.

Two other systems offer satellite telephone service primarily for voice, though data, fax, and Internet features are forthcoming. Iridium, which struggled early on, is the first such system. It offers worldwide coverage. Globalstar, which covers North America and the North Atlantic as well as parts of Europe, offers cellular and satellite phone service using a single handset.

KVH INDUSTRIES

A marine satellite telephone is useful for communicating with distant stations, but it's no substitute for a single-sideband marine radio whose emergency channels are monitored by the U.S. Coast Guard and other lifesaving services.

MARINE CELLULAR TELEPHONES

Marine cellular telephones are useful for shoreside communications if you cruise in only a limited area, but billing arrangements and technical limitations make them impractical for the long-range cruiser.

WEATHER RECEIVERS

While you will be able to receive regular voice marine weather broadcasts through the VHF and SSB marine radios aboard your vessel, there are two types of equipment especially devoted to receiving more detailed marine weather information. One is a weather-facsimile recorder (usually just called a *weatherfax*), which receives actual weather maps from NOAA's National Weather Service (NWS) and its counterpart services worldwide. The other is a NAVTEX receiver, which receives, stores and prints telexed weather forecasts, warnings, and Local Notices to Mariners worldwide. While I would not say that these units are really required equipment on a cruising vessel, I would say that the more you can know about the weather the better.

Weatherfax

A weatherfax receives and prints a variety of charts on current and predicted weather conditions, which are transmitted from fifty different transmitters worldwide. While a reasonable degree of proficiency in interpreting weather data symbols is needed to get the most out of them, these charts present a more comprehensive and detailed picture of weather conditions than you can get from voice weather broadcasts. They cover such topics as the existing and forecast positions of weather highs and lows along with the speed and direction of their movement; satellite weather pictures that show cloud patterns and storm development; the direction and intensity of surface winds; wave analysis; and ocean-current analysis. The worldwide schedule of the types of charts and the time and frequencies over which they are available appears on the Internet. (See chapter 22 for details on obtaining sources and schedules of weatherfax information.)

Weatherfax units have three component parts: a signal receiver, a signal processor, and a printer. Because the majority of weather charts are transmitted over the same 2 to 22 MHz bands received by an SSB marine radio or an HF ham radio, weatherfax setups can be configured three ways: with a signal processor only, which must be connected to both an external receiver and a printer; with a combined signal processor and printer, which requires only connection to an appropriate receiver; and as a stand-alone unit, which combines all three components in a single cabinet.

With both the increase in private weather forecasting services and the instant viewing of local weather conditions available on the Internet, the number of weatherfax broadcasts and the availability of receiving equipment have decreased dramatically. Furuno is one of the few remaining companies to offer weatherfax receivers. If purchasing a receiver, I'd select from Furuno's 8-, 10-, and 14-inch (20, 25, and 35 cm) paper recorders with receivers included.

NAVTEX

With VHF and SSB marine radios, you already have access on your boat to a wide range of broadcast weather information from such agencies as the U.S. Coast Guard, the NWS, and their counterparts in other countries. The only problem is that in order to receive the information, you have to discipline yourself to note the times and frequencies of the broadcasts covering the area you will be cruising, then tune your radio to the appropriate frequency at the appropriate time. Even doing all that doesn't guarantee you will receive special unscheduled emergency warning broadcasts. Also, poor reception caused by weather or atmospheric disturbances can make voice broadcasts unintelligible. Even if the signal is clear, unless you record the broadcasts or take good notes, you can quickly forget important information, or you may simply be occupied with other chores or ashore when an important broadcast comes through.

These difficulties are some of the reasons the International Maritime Organization (IMO), the London-based United Nations agency responsible for safety at sea, has instituted its GMDSS. As part of this system, the IMO gathers weather forecasts and warnings; information regarding vessels in distress and search-and-rescue operations; Local Notices to Mariners; and signal propagation correction information for the GPS and Loran-C systems, then rebroadcasts this information at specific times for specific areas on a single frequency— 518 kHz. These transmissions are in English and are in the form of continuous wave (CW) telex, which is better able to penetrate weather and atmospheric disturbances than are voice broadcasts. The system, called NAVTEX, offers worldwide coverage, and NAVTEX signals reach approximately 200 miles (320 km) offshore.

A dedicated NAVTEX receiver is designed to operate only on 518 kHz, and you can program it to receive only the type of messages you want and only those that cover the cruising area or areas you are interested in (see photo next page). The receiver also has the ability to accept a particular message once and then reject it when it is rebroadcast. The information is then printed out on a narrow roll of thermal paper.

You can purchase a receiver devoted exclusively to NAVTEX, such as Furuno's NX300, which must be interfaced to a personal computer for printout, or its NX500, which contains its own printer.

Computer-Based Weatherfax and NAVTEX Programs

If your vessel is equipped with an SSB radio and a Windows-based personal computer, you can purchase computer software that will receive and print out weatherfax information and

A dedicated NAVTEX receiver can be programmed to automatically receive weather reports and marine safety notices applicable only to the area you're cruising. (Furuno)

NAVTEX weather broadcasts.

The best of these programs I have seen is Coretex Weather Fax for Windows. It contains an extensive database of stations and broadcast times and can be programmed to gather weather information automatically in the background, even when you are using the computer for other tasks.

HAM RADIO IN CRUISING

I won't try to qualify you here for a ham radio operator's license. All I want to do is quickly give you an idea of what ham radio equipment can and can't do for you in cruising situations and what is involved in properly using it so you can decide if it's a subject you would like to pursue.

Amateur, or ham, radio (nobody seems to know where the nickname came from) is both similar to and significantly different from the types of marine radios we have discussed so far. VHF and SSB marine operations are regarded by the FCC as commercial services. Ham is an amateur service, and there is a world of difference. In fact, ham radio is not, strictly speaking, marine radio at all. A ham radio on a cruising vessel operates over the same frequencies, uses the same equipment, and is covered by the same FCC regulations as a ham radio being operated onshore. The only difference is that when hams operate aboard ship, they are regarded as being "mobile," just as they would be if they were operating from a vehicle or a temporary location on land. The FCC has very specific rules covering a radio in mobile operation.

Ham equipment normally is less expensive than SSB gear, but it should never be considered a substitute for VHF and SSB marine radios because the coast guard does not continuously monitor ham frequencies. Many coast guard stations have ham capability and will employ it in an emergency, but you shouldn't bet your life they'll be listening when you need them most.

Cruisers who are licensed ham operators use their equipment to chat with other land-based and seagoing hams on all manner of topics. Some of the most interesting bull sessions around are the Maritime Service Nets, in which cruising ham operators all over the world "chew the rag" at agreed days, times, and frequencies about everything from where to anchor in Fiji to where to find fresh seafood in St. Thomas. Like SSB marine radios, ham radios also can be used as multiband receivers to pick up worldwide weather information and such news and entertainment services as the British Broadcasting Company on frequencies ranging from 0.1 to 30 MHz.

One reason many cruisers carry ham gear is that they can get hams ashore to patch them through to land-based telephone lines, which allows them to talk to the folks back home without paying the fairly stiff rates charged by High Seas marine coast stations. Many ham operators in the United States are quite happy to provide that service, but others strenuously object to it on the basis that their frequencies should not be tied up by a cruising yachtsperson who is only interested in using their service to save money on marine telephone calls.

In some quarters of the ham operators' fraternity, quite a bit of antagonism is directed toward the use of ham radio by cruising yachtsmen—and not without reason. A number of cruisers have put ham rigs on their boats but did not go to the trouble of getting a license. Since they don't know the proper procedures, they are easily spotted. These "bootleggers" routinely violate the law and play havoc with the operations of licensed hams. The most frequent violation they commit is using the ham bands to conduct conversations that can result in financial gain (such as establishing a phone patch to order parts), which is quite illegal. They

also transmit from the territorial waters of other countries without getting a Reciprocal Operator's Permit, and they establish phone patches from the territorial waters of countries with which the United States does not have formal traffic agreements.

As long as you get an appropriate license and conduct your operations with the proper protocol, you will be welcome to participate in ham operations from your vessel. But if you try to operate without a license and without knowledge of proper procedures, some hams will quite happily help the FCC track you down. If you decide that having a ham radio aboard is worth the effort of getting a license and you plan to transmit over the ham frequencies from the waters of other nations, request your Reciprocal Operator's Permit from the countries you plan to visit well in advance of your departure. In some instances, processing your application can take up to six months. You can get contact information for requesting Reciprocal Operator's Permits from the American Radio Relay League (see contact information in the resources appendix).

How Ham Radio Works

The most popular ham bands are 1.8 to 2 MHz, 3.5 to 4 MHz, 7 to 7.3 MHz, 14 to 14.35 MHz, 21 to 21.45 MHz, 28 to 29.7 MHz, 50 to 54 MHz, and 144 to 148 MHz. A check back at the radio spectrum shown earlier in this chapter shows that the first six of these are fairly close to the bands used by marine SSB. Since ham transmissions in those bands are "slow snakes," their radio waves can be bounced off the ionosphere just like SSB frequencies to provide truly globe-girdling communications. Notice also that the 144 to 148 MHz ham band is quite close to the 156 to 163 MHz band used by marine VHF. Just like marine VHF, transmissions on that band are essentially "line of sight," which limits their range, but they can be useful to cruisers in coastal waters.

Ham operators don't use the word *channels*. Instead, they say they are "working 40 meters" or

"20 meters" or "15 meters." Now what is all that about? Rather than learn by rote that "40 meters equals 7 to 7.3 MHz," take a moment to understand what hams are talking about and why.

Remember our slow snakes and fast snakes? Well, actually, both snakes are moving through space at the speed of light—186,000 miles per second, which translates to 300 million meters per second. The difference, as we said, is their frequency—the rate at which their ups and downs pass a given point. The guys who are into this sort of thing have figured out that if a radio wave is going up and down (oscillating) at 7 MHz (7 million cycles per second), the length of one complete undulation (high point to low point and back to high point again) would be about 40 meters. If that radio wave is oscillating at 21 MHz, the length of one oscillation would be only about 15 meters. Therefore, as we also said earlier in this chapter, the higher the frequency, the shorter the wavelength. That is why in ham jargon, there is an inverse ratio between frequency (7 MHz, 14 MHz, and so forth) and band designation (40-meter band, 20-meter band, and so forth). If that gets past you, just divide frequency in MHz into 300, which will put you close to the band designation in meters.

The relationship between megahertz and meters for each of the ham bands is shown here.

Band Frequency in MHz	Band Frequency in Meters
1.8–2.0	160
3.5–4.0	80
7.0–7.3	40
14.00–14.35	20
21.00–21.45	15
28.0–29.7	10
50.0–54.0	6
144.0–148.0	2

Radio waves in all but the 6- and 2-meter ham bands bounce off the ionosphere, so they can be used for long-distance communication. Since they do bounce off the ionosphere, their propagation—and thus their range—is affected by the rising and setting of the sun, just like those in the SSB bands.

Radio waves in the 2-meter ham band (144–148 MHz), like marine VHF, go right through the ionosphere and thus are useful only for line-of-sight communication at typical ranges of 50 to 75 miles (80–120 km). Because of their limited range, most hams who cruise primarily offshore don't even bother having 2-meter equipment on board. The 2-meter ham band is used by coastal cruisers, especially when they are within range of land-based repeaters that receive a 2-meter signal and retransmit it at a much greater power. Repeaters normally are positioned on hilltops or towers to increase their range. On 2 meters, a ham with 2-meter equipment can talk to other hams with 2-meter equipment, much of which they operate "mobile" while in their automobiles.

Ham Radio Equipment

Ham transceivers normally cover either 1.8 MHz to 30 MHz (the 160- to 6-meter bands) or 144 MHz to 148 MHz (the 2-meter band) but not both. (A single ham radio that covered all the frequencies from 160 meters to 2 meters would be like having an SSB marine radio and a VHF marine radio in a single unit.) If you want to operate on 2 meters, you will have to buy a completely separate 2-meter transceiver.

Classes for a ham radio operator's license will teach you how to set up your "shack" and give you far more information about the equipment you'll need and where to get the best deals than we can cover here, but three general comments are in order now.

1. Stick with quality gear and choose transistorized, solid-state units, which produce less heat and perform better in the tough marine environment.
2. Since ham equipment is not really designed for shipboard use, a little extra care is needed to protect it.

3. Insist on digital readout of the frequencies you are tuning (trying to tune in a ham radio without digital readout on a boat that is rocking at anchor or pitching through a head sea will make you say things not considered proper in polite society).

You will find that ham radios and their antenna tuners look very similar to and operate on almost the same frequencies as SSB marine radios, and both types of radios are made by the same companies. You may wonder why you can't buy just one radio, one antenna tuner, and one antenna that would allow you to operate on both the marine SSB bands and the ham bands.

Actually, you can. The companies that manufacture SSB marine radios don't mention it very prominently in their advertising or literature, but their radios are quite capable of receiving and transmitting on all the bands between 2 MHz and 23 MHz, which include the 80-, 40-, 20-, and 15-meter ham bands of primary interest to the cruising yachtsperson. Some SSB marine radios transmit and receive on all frequencies from 1.6 MHz to 30 MHz, which take in the 160- and 10-meter ham bands as well.

This may appear to be in violation of 47 CFR 97.101(b), the section of the FCC rules governing the amateur radio service, which states specifically that "the amateur mobile station shall be separate from and independent of all other radio equipment, if any, installed on board the same ship." This provision was written into the FCC rules to eliminate the possibility of ham radio equipment interfering with the SSB radio—which is used for emergency situations—on the same ship.

In trying to determine whether it is legal for a cruising yachtsperson with an appropriate ham license to transmit on the ham bands with such a radio, I think it must be or the FCC wouldn't let the SSB marine radio manufacturers sell such equipment in the first place. I discussed the matter with the chief of the FCC's Aviation and Marine Radio Branch, which regulates SSB marine radios. He told me there is nothing in the sections of FCC rules his branch enforces that prohibits the manufacturer of a radio that is type-accepted for use on the commercial marine frequencies from including in it the ability to operate on other frequencies. He further told me that his office has no role in enforcing 47 CFR 97.101(b), because it governs the amateur radio service, not the commercial marine or aviation services for which his office is responsible.

I then spoke to the chief of the Personal Radio Branch, which regulates the amateur radio service and is responsible for enforcing 47 CFR 97.101. He reminded me that ham radios don't have to be FCC type-accepted and said his office is concerned with regulating ham radio operators, not radio equipment manufacturers. He said it would be illegal for a seagoing ham to transmit over the ham frequencies using a radio that was not "separate from and independent of all other radio equipment, if any, installed on board the same ship." He said that Gordon West, a ham operator, yachtsperson, and writer on marine electronics, had petitioned the FCC to allow ham operators to transmit maritime mobile using an SSB marine radio, and that the FCC had rejected his petition.

The upshot of all this is that it is not illegal for the manufacturer of an SSB marine radio to build into that radio the ability to transmit over the ham bands, but it is illegal for even an appropriately licensed ham operating maritime mobile to use it for transmitting on both the ham bands and the marine bands.

While it is apparently illegal to transmit on the ham using an SSB marine radio, receiving on those bands is not illegal. To find the frequencies on which hams are operating, however, you need to know that, by mutual agreement, when working frequencies of 14 MHz and higher (that is, 20, 15, and 10 m) ham operators generally operate in the upper sideband, which is the same used by the marine SSB bands. On frequencies of 7 MHz and below (that is, 40 and 80 m), hams operate on the lower sideband. Most of the SSB marine radios on the market have a marked switch on their front panel that allows the user to select upper or lower sideband mode. On the ICOM M700 and M700TY, the lower sideband mode is not marked, but you can switch either of them to it by turning the mode selection switch to the unmarked position all the way to the left.

HAM RADIO ANTENNAS

Until the fairly recent development of sophisticated electronic antenna couplers, about the only way to operate on the lower ham frequencies was to rig an unsightly and cumbersome "long wire" antenna that needed to be at least 12 meters (39.4 ft.) long. With today's high-quality digital antenna tuners and a good RF ground, in most situations you can get excellent results with a 23-foot (7 m) whip antenna.

As of this writing, under 47 CFR 97.101, an antenna coupler used for transmitting on the ham bands has to be "separate from and independent of" similar equipment to transmit over the marine SSB bands. However, the FCC has requested comment on a proposed new rule that would allow a maritime mobile ham transceiver and an SSB marine radio installed on the same vessel to share a single antenna and a coupler.

Ham Radio Legal Requirements

Ham radio operation requires a combined station and operator license, but it has no relation to the Ship Station Radio License or the Restricted Radiotelephone Operator Permit we discussed earlier in this chapter in the sections on VHF and SSB marine radio. Unlike those licenses, the ham license requires a written examination on which the applicant must demonstrate a knowledge of basic radio theory, proper operating procedures, and the ability to receive Morse code at certain minimum speeds.

Passing the exam is relatively simple. The best approach is to enroll in a class sponsored by a local ham club or community college in your area. It probably will meet one night a week for six weeks leading up to the Novice License exam. Once

you've got your Novice ticket, another four-week class will get you ready for the General Class exam. The radio theory part of the course isn't very difficult—nor is learning Morse code if you get yourself a set of audio teaching tapes and practice about twenty minutes a night. The General Class License, which is the one you'll need to operate by voice over the frequencies most useful in cruising, requires the ability to receive Morse at five words per minute. The easiest way to find out when and where classes are held is to call the nearest electronics shop that sells amateur radio equipment. If there is no ham equipment dealer in your area, write to the American Radio Relay League to request the name of the secretary of its nearest chapter (see contact information in the resources appendix).

Don't make the mistake of trying to "bootleg"—that is, operate ham radio equipment without a license. It is illegal, and if you get caught you can have your equipment confiscated and you can be fined and barred from ever getting a ham license. The biggest drawback is that without going through the study that leads up to a license, you will never fully understand the equipment and therefore will never be able to use it to its best advantage. You also should be aware that because of the government's attempts to stem the flood of illegal drugs into this country, the FCC is much more active than it has been in tracking down all kinds of illegal radio operations aboard boats, especially those operating in the Bahamas, the Caribbean, South and Central America, and Mexico.

Ham Radio Equipment Recommendations

Until and unless the FCC starts enforcing its "separate and independent" rule, I wouldn't lose a great deal of sleep over buying an SSB marine radio capable of transmitting over the ham bands and using it for that purpose (but only with the appropriate ham license). If you decide to go that route, you'll find it best to select a radio that allows you the option of changing frequencies quickly with a thumbwheel rather than having to keypunch them into the radio's memory and then recall them. The reason is that the frequencies listed for the various maritime nets that will interest you are for contact only. To carry on a conversation, you'll need the ability to quickly shift frequencies in whatever band you are working. Given the pending rule modification regarding antenna sharing, even if I added a separate ham transceiver, I'd hook it up to my SSB marine antenna coupler and antenna with a switch to shift from one to the other.

If you want to be super cautious and buy a completely stand-alone ham rig, I suggest the ICOM M735 matched with the ICOM AH-2a antenna tuner and controller unit. In most cases, this setup will work well with any of the 23- or 28-foot (7–8.5 m) fiberglass sticks I recommended earlier in this chapter for use with your SSB marine radio. Since the AH-2a antenna tuner is not quite as electronically advanced as the antenna coupler used with most SSB marine radios, you may find you have to go to at least a 12-meter long-wire antenna to get maximum use out of the 160- and 80-meter bands (because of their low frequency) and out of the 15-meter band (because a 23-foot whip is close to that band's half-wavelength).

Now that we've covered the navigation and communications equipment you'll need aboard your vessel, we'll cover more mundane—but no less important—topics, such as your vessel's anchors, tender, and safety equipment.

Choosing Anchoring Equipment

Some people own beautiful boats that are capable of extended cruising and operate them for years without ever setting an anchor. Instead, they plan all their runs so that every night they can securely lash their vessels to the dock of some marina. In the process, of course, they severely limit their cruising options and rob themselves of one of the most rewarding aspects of cruising—luxuriating in the stillness of a beautiful anchorage with no traces of distracting civilization buzzing in their ears.

You, of course, aren't one of those people. But even if you anchor out only occasionally, you quickly will find that not all your anchorages are going to be roomy, placid, and protected. Some will be subject to heavy surge and vicious currents. Some will be so congested that you'll find the scope you can put out will be limited. The bottom into which you are trying to set an anchor is not always going to be hard sand. Sometimes it will be soft mud, with the consistency of oatmeal; other times it may be impenetrable granite. And winds will not always be gentle. Sooner or later,

you are likely to find yourself anchored out in at least half a gale—if not an actual hurricane—and the safety of your vessel and all aboard will be dependent on the holding power of one or two chunks of metal and a couple of lengths of chain or nylon line. It makes sense, then, to devote a good deal of thought to the equipment you need for anchoring your vessel securely. At a cost of $5,000 or more, good anchoring equipment can seem terribly expensive, until you realize that the entire value of your vessel—and possibly the lives or safety of everyone on it—may depend on it.

BOW PULPITS

The discussion of a cruising vessel's main deck layout in chapter 2 mentioned the advisability of selecting a boat with a good stout bow pulpit that projects about 3 feet (1 m) beyond the bow, has a sturdy railing around it, and accommodates at least your primary anchor in a self-deploying bow roller. I suggested that it would be even better if it could

This double-roller bow pulpit is equipped with a plow-type primary anchor to port, a Bruce secondary anchor, and a horizontal windlass.

accommodate your secondary anchor as well (see photo). I also mentioned the need for space just aft of the bow pulpit for mounting a hefty electric windlass; plenty of unobstructed working space on the foredeck; and roomy, V-bottomed lockers for both rope and chain in the forepeak. When we discussed water systems in chapter 3, I also mentioned that it's a good idea to have a high-pressure saltwater outlet on the foredeck to wash off any mud that might be brought up on your anchor chain.

This section's focus is on the equipment you need to put on and around that bow pulpit to ensure that anytime you drop the hook, you can be reasonably certain your vessel will stay put.

CRUISING ANCHORS

Most boating books that cover anchoring refer to three anchors: a working anchor, a storm anchor, and a lunch hook. This terminology relates most accurately to sailboats, whose anchor rodes usually are rope rather than chain and whose owners

handle their anchors manually rather than with an electric windless. In selecting anchors for a cruising powerboat that is large enough to carry the substantial weight of an all-chain rode and has the battery capacity to power an electric windlass, it's more practical to think in terms of a somewhat oversized primary anchor that combines the functions of both working and storm anchors, and a slightly smaller secondary anchor. For those situations when a stern anchor would be useful or when you lose either your primary or your secondary anchor, carry a third one: this anchor can be lighter than your secondary one but heavier than what a sailor would call a lunch hook.

While there are several different types of anchors on the market, there are three basic types for serious cruising: the plow, the fluke, and the Bruce (see photos next page).

Primary Anchors

You can get into some lively arguments with cruising people on the topic of which anchor works

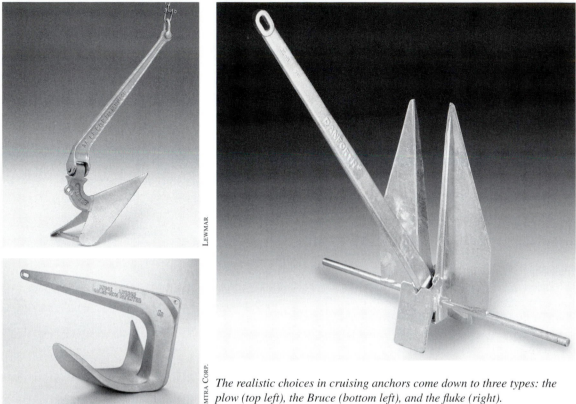

LEWMAR

IMTRA CORP.

TIE-DOWN ENGINEERING

The realistic choices in cruising anchors come down to three types: the plow (top left), the Bruce (bottom left), and the fluke (right).

best in which anchoring circumstance. The debate swirls around which has the greatest *holding power* or *drag value*. Actually, both terms are meaningless unless you also consider the type of bottom in which the anchor is set. Simpson-Lawrence's Technical and Development Department, for example, compiled and published the results of three tests of the company's 25 C.Q.R. anchor under actual anchoring situations. The tests were carried out by independent groups in three locations and were witnessed respectively by Lloyd's of France, Lloyd's of the United Kingdom, and France's Bureau Veritas. In each test, measuring instruments were used to determine the amount of load that caused the anchor to break out of the bottom, which was designated as its "maximum drag value." In sand off the beach at

Beg-Rohu, France, maximum drag value was measured at 1,102 pounds (496 kg). In sand off the beach at Studland Bay, England, it was 1,320 pounds (594 kg). At sea off Quiberon, France, in mud it measured 1,653 pounds (744 kg); in a mixture of sand and gravel, it was 2,535 pounds (1141 kg); and in compact sand, it was 3,086 pounds (1,389 kg). In other words, depending on bottom conditions, the same anchor had a maximum value that varied by almost 300 percent!

Selecting anchors for your vessel, therefore, is more a matter of matching them to the types of bottoms you are most likely to encounter in your cruising than it is to working out a technical equation. Many cruisers with experience of a wide variety of anchoring situations rely on a good heavy plow as their anchor, and they usually go with the

C.Q.R. brand, which is the original of the type. The fluke anchor has been around a long time, and some knowledgeable cruisers wouldn't use anything else. I've found it works quite well in hard sand but doesn't hold well in soft sand or mud and has a problem biting into a grassy bottom. In soft bottoms, it also tends to bring up gobs of goo. But the most serious drawback to the fluke anchor is that if a good-sized chunk of rock or coral—or even its own rode—becomes wedged between one of its flukes and its shank and the anchor rolls over on its back, its long shank prevents it from righting itself and it becomes essentially useless. If you choose a fluke anchor, go with the products of the Danforth division of Rule Industries, whose name has become synonymous with the type rather than a less expensive imitation, and buy their top-of-the-line Deepset Hi-Tensile model. It is harder to set than the standard model, but it offers a far greater tensile strength-to-weight ratio. A few cruisers prefer the Bruce, an anchor developed for holding oil rigs in place in the North Sea, on the argument that if it's deployed in an inverted position, its design forces it to roll over and bite into the bottom. I can't claim personal experience with a Bruce anchor, but its inventor, Peter Bruce, once gave me a demonstration with a scale model that convinced me the claim is valid.

Given the wide range of drag values or holding power of various types of anchors depending on the type of bottom they are set in, choosing anchors of the appropriate size for your vessel is also pretty arbitrary. My recommendations for the amount of holding power you need to anchor different sizes of moderate- to heavy-displacement cruising boats safely in winds up to about 60 knots are summarized in the accompanying table. These recommendations are based strictly on my own experience and that of other seasoned cruisers with whom I have discussed the matter rather than on any scientific evidence.

Secondary Anchors

If for some reason your primary anchor drags and fouls so that it won't reset or you lose it, your secondary anchor is your backup, so it should be a good one.

Most cruisers choose a fluke anchor as a secondary anchor because it's easy to stow. Whichever type you choose, your secondary anchor can be one size smaller than your primary anchor, but it also should be carried on the foredeck so that it can be deployed quickly in an emergency. It would be best if your vessel's bow pulpit could accommodate it in a self-deploying roller alongside your primary anchor. A poor second choice is to install a fluke anchor flat on the foredeck in chocks. You will have to walk around it and will probably stub your toe on it more than once, but

RECOMMENDED PRIMARY ANCHOR SIZES

Boat Length, ft. (m)	Minimum Required Holding Power, lb. (kg)	Recommended Primary Anchor Sizes, lb. (kg)		
		C.Q.R.	Danforth*	Bruce
40–49 (12–15)	5,500 (2,475)	45 (20)	41 (18.5)	44 (19.8)
50–59 (15–18)	6,500 (2,925)	60 (27)	60 (27)	66 (29.7)
60–69 (18–21)	7,500 (3,375)	75 (34)	90 (41)	110 (50)

* Deepset Hi-Tensile model.

at least it will be ready when you need it.

However you stow your secondary anchor, it should be attached to its rode. I see many cruisers carrying a secondary anchor on the foredeck but not attached to its rode. To me, this seems foolish. The times you are likely to need it most are also likely to be when the foredeck is pitching wildly, the wind is screeching, and the rain is pouring buckets—hardly the best of circumstances in which to be trying to thread a pin into a shackle to attach the anchor to its rode. Still worse is the practice of stowing a secondary anchor in a deck box or below, even if it is shackled to its rode. In a deck box, it invariably will work its way to the bottom of the box and burrow itself under fenders, docklines, and shoreside power cords that get tangled up with its rode. If it is stowed below decks, by the time you go down, dig it out, haul it on deck, throw it overboard, and secure its bitter end, your boat may well be on the rocks.

The third, or stern, anchor should also be a fluke—for ease of handling—but it can be one size smaller than your secondary anchor. It and its rode can be stowed in a cockpit or below decks because you are likely to be able to deploy it at your leisure after your primary anchor is well-set.

ANCHOR RODES

Your vessel's safety will rest on your primary and secondary anchor rodes, so it's important that they're properly matched to the strain your vessel will put on them.

Primary Rode

If at all possible, the rode on your primary anchor should be entirely of chain rather than rope or a chain-rope combination. The main reason for using an all-chain primary rode is that the key to the holding power of all three types of anchors is keeping the strain on them horizontal rather than vertical. In fact, to facilitate their retrieval, they are designed to break out when the angle of pull

against them reaches around 10 degrees above the horizontal. When your boat's bow is bobbing up and down wildly in a surge, the sheer weight of chain rode set out with adequate scope makes it stay on the bottom much better than rope and helps keep the strain on the anchor horizontal. Another reason to use an all-chain rode is that anchoring with rode usually requires you to put out a scope of about seven to eight times the water's depth. (Remember to add hull height from water level to bow pulpit and consider tidal range. See chapter 18.) With an all-chain rode, you get equally good holding under reasonable conditions with a scope of only three to four times the water's depth (more, of course, if the weather is unsettled). Lastly, chain can be handled efficiently by the wildcat of an electric windlass to provide essentially hands-off anchoring, and it isn't subject to chafe on rocks and coral.

Installing the massive weight of an all-chain rode in the bow of a planing hull cruiser under about 35 feet (10 m) in length may unacceptably affect its performance. In that case, the only realistic alternative is to use rope, but it should have at least 10 feet (3 m) of chain between it and the anchor to exert a horizontal pull on the anchor and resist chafe. This would be the same arrangement as the secondary rode on a larger vessel, which we discuss in detail later in this chapter.

If your vessel is capable of carrying an all-chain primary rode, it should be 300 feet (90 m) long to allow you to anchor under normal conditions in up to 100 feet (30 m) of water with the minimum safe scope of three times the water's depth.

In selecting the chain for a primary anchor rode, you want one whose "working limit" approximately equals the holding power of the anchor to which it is attached. You want to get that working limit in as light a chain as possible to reduce the amount of weight you have to carry in your vessel's forepeak. Make certain also that the chain you select is compatible with the wildcat of your windlass.

Anchor chain is made from four different grades of wire: proof coil (grade 30); BBB; high-test (grade 40); and alloy (grade 63 or 80). Grade 80 alloy chain usually is referred to as Accoloy, a branded product of American Chain and Cable Company. The four types of chain have vastly different working load limits according to their sizes and weights, as shown in the Anchor Chain Specifications table.

Proof coil has a low carbon content and should not be used as anchor chain. For years, BBB chain was the standard chain used for most recreational

ANCHOR CHAIN SPECIFICATIONS

Chain Type Trade Size, in. (mm)	Working Limit, lb. (kg)	Weight per 100 ft., lb. (kg)*	Volume per 100 ft., cu. ft. (cu. m)*
Proof Coil			
⅜	2,625	158	1.14
(9)	(1,190)	(73)	(0.03)
½	4,500	278	1.93
(12)	(2,040)	(128)	(0.05)
⅝	6,800	410	3.11
(16)	(3,085)	(189)	(0.09)
BBB			
⅜	2,750	173	1.14
(9)	(1,247)	(80)	(0.03)
½	4,750	296	1.93
(12)	(2,155)	(136)	(0.05)
⅝	7,250	447	3.11
(16)	(3,288)	(206)	(0.09)
High-Test (grade 40)			
⅜.	5,100	157	1.14
(9)	(2,313)	(72)	(0.03)
⁷⁄₁₆	6,600	213	1.93
(11)	(2,994)	(98)	(0.05)
½	8,200	274	1.93
(12)	(3,720)	(126)	(0.05)
⅝ in.	11,500	409	3.11
(16)	(5,216)	(188)	(0.09)
Accoloy (grade 80)			
⁹⁄₃₂	3,250	75	0.50
(7)	(1,475)	(36)	(0.01)
⅜	6,600	135	1.14
(9)	(2,994)	(62)	(0.03)
½	11,250	234	1.93
(12)	(5,100)	(108)	(0.05)
⅝	16,500	371	3.11
(16)	(7,485)	(171)	(0.09)

* Metric units are per 30-meter length of chain.

boating applications. It has a somewhat higher carbon content than proof coil, but pound for pound it is not as strong as the newer high-test and alloy chains. It may be fine for light-displacement powerboats, but it's not practical for those of moderate to heavy displacement. To get the minimum working load limit required to safely anchor a hefty 40- to 50-foot (12–15 m) power cruiser, you must go to the ⅝-inch (16 mm) size. The wildcat of the windlass you normally would install on that size of cruiser will not handle chain larger than ½-inch (12 mm), and 300 feet (92 m) of BBB chain would weigh over 1,300 pounds.

With the elimination of proof coil and BBB, your practical choices for anchor chain are limited to high-test or Accoloy. The advantages of Accoloy quickly becomes obvious. In order to approximately match the 6,000 to 7,000 pounds (2,700–3,150 kg) of holding power we recommend for the primary anchor of a moderate- to heavy-displacement cruising vessel of about 50 feet (15 m) in length, for example, you would need to use 300 feet (92 m) of ⁷⁄₁₆-inch (11 mm) high-test (grade 40) chain, which would have a working load limit of 6,600 pounds (3,000 kg) and would weigh 639 pounds (290 kg), or you could go down

a size smaller to ⅜-inch (9 mm) Accoloy chain and get 6,600 pounds of holding power at only 405 pounds (182 kg) of weight.

By combining the recommendations for primary anchors and all-chain rode, we can come up with a computation of the primary anchors and chain sizes needed for moderate- to heavy-displacement power cruisers in three basic size classifications (as shown in the Anchor Recommendations table).

Until fairly recently, virtually all anchor chain for use on recreational vessels was BBB chain made to standards set by the International Standards Organization (ISO), which not only established BBB chain's metallic composition but specified the dimensions of its links as well. When U.S. chain manufacturers introduced chain made of high-test and alloy wire, they shifted to a new standard created by the National Association of Chain Manufacturers that called for a slightly longer link. From the standpoint of the cruising yachtsperson, these longer links have disadvantages: they are more likely to kink, and they are more susceptible to distortion, which interferes with their proper handling by a windlass's wildcat. Further, while they fit the wildcats of windlasses

ANCHOR RECOMMENDATIONS

Boat Length, ft. (m) in./lb.	Required Holding Power, lb. (kg)	Recommended Primary Anchor, lb. (kg)			Recommended Chain Working Load Limit, in./lb. (mm/kg)	
		C.Q.R.	**Danforth***	**Bruce**	**High-Test**	**Accoloy**
40–49	5,500	45	41	44	⁷⁄₁₆/6,600	⅜/6,600
(12–15)	(2,475)	(20)	(18.5)	(19.8)	(11/3,000)	(9/3,000)
50–59	6,500	60	60	66	⁷⁄₁₆/6,600	⅜/6,600
(15–18)	(2,925)	(27)	(27)	(29.7)	(11/3,000)	(9/3,000)
60–69	7,500	75	90	110	½/8,200	½/11,250
(18–21)	(3,375)	(34)	(41)	(50)	(12/3,720)	(12/5,103)

* Deepset Hi-Tensile model.

made in the United States, they may not be compatible with the wildcats of some popular windlasses manufactured in England or its former colonies, which still employ the ISO standard. Some of the British manufacturers (for example, Simpson-Lawrence) offer optional wildcats that will handle the longer links; others (such as Maxwell-Nilsson) offer only wildcats that will handle the shorter link of the ISO standard. To further confuse the issue, some U.S. chain manufacturers now make a chain of high-test wire but with a shorter link. It does not, however, conform to the ISO's BBB standard. It is usually designated as "short-link" or "SL" chain.

The best way to make certain your windlass will efficiently handle your all-chain rode is to buy your chain from the same company that manufactures your windlass; the major U.S. windlass manufacturers have associated chain companies, whose products are specifically calibrated to fit their wildcats. If for any reason that solution is impossible or impractical (for example, if you are trying to fit new chain to an existing windlass), be certain you buy your chain from a supplier who is thoroughly familiar with the windlass model you have and can assure you the two are compatible. In some cases, you may have to remove the wildcat from your windlass and take it to your supplier to make certain the chain will fit. This is especially true if the wildcat you are trying to match is somewhat worn. It may require a larger chain than it was designed to handle when it was new. If you are trying to buy a new windlass or replace the wildcat of an existing windlass, you may have to go the other way around and send a sample of your chain to the windlass manufacturer for comparison with the new wildcat. If you do that, send a chain sample that is at least eleven links long, since that much normally is required to go all the way around a wildcat's circumference to make sure the two mesh properly.

A chain rode should be securely attached to the anchor with a screw-pin shackle that has a working load limit equal to that of the chain (see the Anchor Shackle Working Load Limits table). The

pin should be secured to the shackle with stainless steel wire to eliminate any possibility of working loose. The bitter end of a chain rode should never be affixed directly to the vessel because you would have no way to cut the vessel loose in an emergency. You should instead attach a 6-foot (1.8 m) piece of ½-inch (12 mm) nylon line to the chain's bitter end with an eye splice and a stainless steel thimble. Tie the bitter end of the line to an eyebolt securely mounted inside the chain locker. With that arrangement, you won't loose the bitter end of the chain by accident, but in an emergency you can let all the chain run out, then cut the nylon line once the chain pulls it out of the chain locker onto the deck, where you can get at it with a rigging knife. Just make sure that the eye splice and the thimble connecting the chain and the line are small enough to pass smoothly through your chain locker's deck pipe.

ANCHOR SHACKLE WORKING LOAD LIMITS

Shackle Size, in. (mm)	Working Load Limit, lb. (kg)	
	High-Test (galvanized)	Accoloy (not galvanized)
⅜ (9)	2,000 (900)	2,500 (1,135)
½ (12)	4,000 (1,800)	5,000 (2,270)
⅝ (16)	6,500 (2,950)	8,000 (3,630)
¾ (19)	10,000 (4,500)	—
⅞ (22)	13,000 (5,900)	—
1 (25)	17,000 (7,700)	—

Secondary Rode

While the weight of an all-chain rode is an advantage in getting an anchor to hold properly, it concentrates a great deal of weight in a vessel's forepeak. A stout cruising vessel of around 40 feet (12 m) should be able to handle the weight of an all-chain primary rode but not the added weight of an all-chain secondary rode as well. For that reason, rope with a length of chain between it and the anchor to resist chafe is the perfect rode for a secondary or a backup anchor and, as mentioned earlier in this chapter, for the primary rode of a planing hull cruiser under about 35 feet (10.6 m).

Rope used for a rode is properly called *line*. It should be made of nylon, which can be stowed wet and resists damage from water, oils, and sunlight better than other materials. It also should be of the hard-laid, three-strand-twist variety. Soft-laid, three-strand-twist or braided nylon line is more pleasant to handle but it does not work as well on the rope drum of a windlass. Braided nylon line also is less elastic than three-strand-twist and, therefore, does not provide as much shock absorption.

The breaking strength of three-strand-twist nylon line is a function of its diameter. Under cruising stress, rope is subject to considerable weakening. For this reason, for your secondary anchor rode you should choose new rope with a breaking strength approximately twice the holding power of the anchor to which it will be attached (see the Anchor Line Specifications table). Replace it when it shows significant fraying or exudes a chalky dust. The latter is a sign that its fibers are being broken down by the sun's ultraviolet rays.

Nylon line used as an anchor rode should have 6 fathoms (36 feet, or 11 m) of chain between it and the anchor to help keep strain on the anchor horizontal and to resist chafing on rocks or coral. The end of the line that will be attached to this chain should have an eye splice with a stainless steel thimble of sufficient size to accept the shackle used to join them, and the splice should be woven back into the line for at least 12 inches (30 cm). To prevent accidentally losing the bitter end of the rope on your secondary anchor overboard, it should be whipped and tied by a bowline or anchor hitch to an eyebolt installed inside the rope locker.

ANCHOR LINE SPECIFICATIONS

Diameter, in. (mm)	Breaking Strength, lb. (kg)	Weight per 100 ft., lb. (kg)*
5/16 (8)	2,550 (1,160)	3 (1.3)
3/8 (9)	3,700 (1,680)	5 (2.2)
7/16 (11)	5,000 (2,270)	6 (2.7)
1/2 (12)	6,400 (2,900)	8 (3.5)
9/16 (14)	8,000 (3,630)	10 (4.4)
5/8 (16)	10,400 (4,720)	12 (5.3)
3/4 (19)	14,200 (6,440)	17 (7.5)
7/8 (22)	23,000 (10,430)	21 (9.3)
1 (25)	28,500 (12,930)	25 (11.1)

* Metric units are per 30-meter length of chain.

To set the proper scope, lengths should be marked on both your primary and your secondary anchor rodes at about 25-foot (8 m) intervals. The best system I've found for marking a chain rode is to coat individual links with distinctive colors of an industrial-grade metal paint: white for 25 feet (8 m), blue for 50 feet (15 m), and red for 100 feet (30 m). Use combinations of these colors to mark the chain in 25-foot increments: white and blue for 75 feet (23 m), red and white for 125 feet (38 m), and so on. For three-strand-twist nylon line rode, you can buy kits of yellow plastic markers at 25-foot increments, which can be worked into the line's strands.

WINDLASSES

Few devices aboard your vessel will contribute more to the ease of cruising than a good electric anchor windlass (see photo). With it you can deploy and retrieve your primary anchor without any of the strain that inevitably accompanies manual anchoring.

For a moderate- to heavy-displacement cruising powerboat in the 30- to 40-foot (9–12 m) range, you will need a windlass with at least 350 pounds (158 kg) of line-pull capacity to handle its anchor and combination chain-rope primary rode. It will weigh around 50 pounds (22.5 kg). For a similar boat of 40- to 50-foot (12–15 m) length overall (LOA), you will need a windlass with at least 500 pounds (225 kg) of line-pull capacity to handle its anchor and all-chain rode, and it will weigh about 80 pounds (36 kg). For vessels 50 to 60 feet (15–18 m) LOA, you will need a windlass with about 1,000 pounds (450 kg) of line pull, which will weigh about 150 pounds (67.5 kg). For vessels of 60 to 70 feet (18–21 m) LOA, you will need a windlass with about 1,800 pounds (810 kg) of line pull, which will weigh about 200 pounds (90 kg).

The windlass you select should be capable of handling both chain and rope of the size you choose for your primary and secondary anchor rodes. Whether the wildcat and capstan operate vertically or horizontally is a matter of personal choice, but the wildcat should automatically feed the chain into its locker through a deck pipe. You

An electric anchor windlass and an all-chain primary rode can make anchoring virtually a "hands-off" maneuver.

SECONDARY ANCHOR RODE RECOMMENDATIONS

Boat Length, ft. (m)	Minimum Required Holding Power, lb. (kg)	Recommended Secondary Anchor: Danforth Deepset Hi-Tensile, lb./lb.** (kg/kg)	Recommended Rode Size* Diameter, in./lb. (mm/kg)
40–49 (12–15)	3,500 (1,590)	29/4,000** (13/1,800)	⁹⁄₁₆/8,000 (14/3,600)
50–59 (15–18)	5,000 (2,270)	41/6,000** (18/2,700)	¾/14,200 (19/6,400)
60–69 (18–21)	6,500 (2,950)	60/7,000** (27/3,150)	¾/14,200 (19/6,400)

* Based on line with a breaking strength approximately twice the holding power of the recommended anchor to offset the effects of line deterioration.

** Holding power of anchors and breaking strength of line in pounds as rated by their respective manufacturers.

should be able to operate either the wildcat or the capstan independently. You also should be able to release tension on the wildcat with a hand wrench to allow the anchor to fall away freely from its bow roller rather than having to power it down by reversing the direction of the windlass. If your vessel is being carried away from the optimum anchoring point by wind or current, powering down is too slow a process to allow you to place your anchor exactly where you want it.

The windlass should have a foot switch within easy reach of it on the foredeck and a second control station on the flybridge, but they should be rigged with an off-on switch at the flying bridge position to prevent either from being operated accidentally before you are ready to anchor. After the main power switch has been turned on, the windlass's circuitry should have an automatic cutout switch that allows only one switch to be operated at a time.

Choose a windlass that takes its power at whatever voltage you use for other accessories aboard (usually either 12 or 24 volts, and in a few cases 32 volts). Your windlass should be wired from the

ANCHORING EQUIPMENT WEIGHTS

| | Boat Length, ft. (m) | | | | | |
| | 40–49 (12–15) | | 50–59 (15–18) | | 60–65 (18–21) | |
	Type	Weight, lb. (kg)	Type	Weight, lb. (kg)	Type	Weight, lb. (kg)
Primary Anchor	Danforth	41 (18.5)	Danforth	60 (27)	C.Q.R.	75 (33.8)
Primary Rode (300 ft./92 m all-chain)	Accoloy ⅜ in. (9 mm)	405 (182.3)	Accoloy ⅜ in. (9 mm)	405 (182.3)	Accoloy ½ in. (12 mm)	702 (315.9)
Secondary Anchor (Danforth Deepset Hi-Tensile)		29 (13.1)		41 (18.5)		60 (27)
Secondary Rode Chain (6 fathoms ⅜ in./9 mm Accoloy)		52 (23.4)		52 (23.4)		52 (23.4)
Secondary Rode (three-strand-twist nylon)	⁹⁄₁₆ in. (14 mm)	30 (13.5)	¾ in. (19 mm)	51 (23)	¾ in. (19 mm)	51 (23)
Windlass Weight		100 (45)		150 (68)		200 (90)
Total		657 (298)		759 (344)		1,140 (517)

battery on its own circuit with a breaker in the line to protect its electric motor and gearbox from being burned out by an overload.

By combining the information we've assembled to this point, we can construct a chart for computing the total weight of the primary and secondary anchors, chain and rope rodes, and windlass you will be putting on the bow of your vessel (see the Anchoring Equipment Weights table).

ANCHORING ACCESSORIES

You can make your time at anchor easier, quieter, and more comfortable if you assemble a few simple accessories.

Anchoring Bridle

If you use an all-chain primary rode, you will find that when you are in an anchorage subject to heavy surge, the chain's weight will tend to cause your boat to jerk unpleasantly and the chain will grate across the bow roller with a most annoying sound. To offset these problems, you might want to rig an anchoring bridle of the type we carried aboard *Americas Odyssey*.

To construct such a bridle, eye splice the ends of two 10-foot (3 m) lengths of ¾-inch (19 mm) nylon line onto a stout stainless steel ring (see illustration). Use a stainless steel thimble inside the bight to reduce chafe, and weave the splice about 12 inches (30 cm) up into the rope. Also eye splice into the opposite end of each length of line a loop that is large enough to fit easily over the cleats on

An anchoring bridle made of nylon line can help take the shock out of an all-chain rode and prevent the chain from grating across the anchor roller.

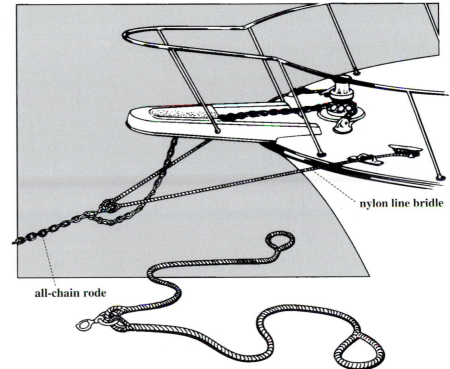

nylon line bridle

all-chain rode

each side of your bow. Again, the splice should be worked about 12 inches up into the standing part of the line. Next, attach to the ring a stout stainless steel sassor, snap shackle, or chain hook, which can hook into or over a link of your anchor chain. Stow the bridle in a foredeck box until you need it. Once you're anchored, hook the sassor to the anchor chain, secure the two ends of the bridle to the bow cleats, and loosen tension on your windlass to allow slack in the chain. The bridle will take the strain off the bow pulpit. Because the nylon line is taking the strain rather than the chain, it will act as a shock absorber and eliminate the sound of the chain grating across the roller all night. If you do not use such a bridle every time you anchor, you must install forward of the wildcat a chain stopper or devil's claw, into which you should hook your chain once you are anchored to take the strain off the windlass.

Short-Scope Snub Line

In preparing for *Summer Wind*'s voyage from Florida to Alaska and back, Frank Glindmeier came up with another useful idea for anchoring in congested harbors, where limited swinging room could prevent him from putting out as much scope of chain as he would like. Frank had a boatyard install a stout eyebolt in the boat's stem about 6 inches (15 cm) above the waterline. He then eye spliced a 15-foot (4.5 m) length of ¾-inch (19 mm) nylon line into the eye with a stainless steel thimble and eye spliced a strong snap shackle to the bitter end. Until this rig was needed, the bitter end was tied off to the bow pulpit.

When he was forced to anchor on short scope in a crowded harbor, Frank would untie the bitter end of the rig from the bow pulpit, attach the shackle to

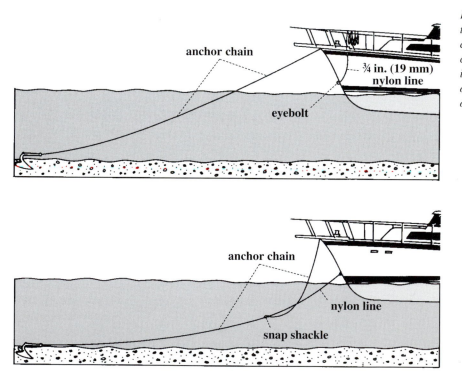

Frank Glindmeier found this rig useful for anchoring Summer Wind *in crowded harbors where it was impossible to let out a normal 3:1 scope of all-chain rode.*

his anchor chain, and then pay out sufficient chain to let the nylon line take the strain. As it did so, the snap shackle attaching the nylon line to the chain would be about 2 to 4 feet (0.6–1.2 m) underwater. "The roller in *Summer Wind*'s bow pulpit was 8 feet [2.4 m] off the water," Frank explains. "With this rig, I was able to substantially lower the anchor chain's point of attachment to the boat. If we were anchored in 8 feet of water, the rig cut the amount of scope we needed by about a fourth."

Anchor Locker Brace

Frank offers still another idea: when he and his wife, Lee, were ready to depart an anchorage, Frank would power slowly forward and control the windlass with a separate switch on the flying bridge. Lee would go below and carefully flake the chain down in the chain locker to prevent it from becoming tangled. But after runs where they encountered stiff headwinds, they would get ready to deploy the anchor only to find that the chain had become terribly tangled and would not pay out properly.

"We finally figured out that when we ran into a head sea," Frank says, "the violent up-and-down motion of the bow was tossing the chain around inside its locker like spaghetti in a bowl. I bought a truck inner tube, and the next time it looked like we were going to be pounding into a head sea, I stuffed the inner tube into the locker on top of the flaked-down chain and inflated it with a bicycle pump enough to fill the remaining space in the locker. When we got ready to anchor, we deflated the inner tube, removed it from the locker, and found the chain was still neatly flaked and ready to run out without problems."

Anchor Trip Lines

It's a good idea to rig a trip line for each of your anchors. This is a line of about 50 feet (15 m) that can be affixed to the anchor's head and has a floating buoy on its tail end. To be effective, the trip line must be stout enough to stand the force you may have to exert on it and it must be attached to the anchor's head with a stout shackle. The Bruce anchor and most plow anchors have a fitting at their heads to attach a trip line. On a fluke anchor, don't try to tie the trip line around the head or the stock because it could interfere with the anchor's holding ability. Instead, drill a hole in one of the anchor's crown plates and attach the trip line with a shackle.

Mark the trip line buoys with your vessel's name and something like "ANCHOR, DO NOT DISTURB." If you don't do that, some local youngster in a skiff may well come by and pull the trip line to see what's on the other end—and bring your anchor up in the process.

Mediterranean Moor Gangway

If your cruising itinerary calls for you to spend much time in areas where Mediterranean mooring is the norm (English Harbor, Antigua and Acapulco in North America, many harbors in the Pacific, and just about anywhere in the Mediterranean), you should include in your ship's inventory a collapsible stern gangway with a swivel fitting at the transom, rollers for the end that rests on the quay, side rails, and some kind of topping lift arrangement that allows you to raise it clear of the quay when a heavy surge is running. These gangways are available through marine catalogs. (See chapter 18 for details on how to perform a Mediterranean moor.)

Selecting and Using Tenders

While the primary job of a tender is to provide transportation between your anchored vessel and the shore, if you choose the right type of tender and put adequate outboard power on it, you can make it do additional duty as a fishing or diving boat or use it to explore shallow or inland waters you encounter in your cruising.

HARD OR SOFT?

The basic decision you have to make regarding a tender is whether you will select an inflatable model or one made of a hard material such as fiberglass or wood. Both have their devoted adherents.

Proponents of hard tenders argue that they handle better in adverse conditions, such as a stiff wind or chop; they can be rowed if the outboard quits; and they simply look the way a tender to a proper cruising yacht ought to look rather than like an elongated inner tube.

Advocates of inflatable tenders counter that their choice is lighter and easier to handle when hoisted aboard; in a comparable size will carry more load; has much more lateral stability (which is particularly valuable if you will be using your tender as a dive boat); doesn't make noise or scar up your topsides when it bumps into your vessel at anchor; and doesn't skin your shins when you are trying to board it in a rolly anchorage. They also point out that inflatables are now available with a variety of inflatable keel and rigid bottom configurations that greatly enhance their handling characteristics.

Hard Tenders

If you decide on a hard tender, your most obvious choice is a Boston Whaler, which currently dominates this particular segment of the marine market. Boston Whaler makes a fine line of boats that are especially practical for cruising because, like all small boats under 20 feet (6 m), their internal foam flotation makes them unsinkable. The Boston Whaler models most often selected for cruising tenders are the 11-foot (3.3 m) Tender (see photo), which steers from the stern, and the 13-foot (4 m) Sport or GLS, both of which have steering consoles. The Tender, with a 10-horse-power (hp) outboard and fuel, weighs about 400 pounds (180 kg) and is designed to carry three people. While the Tender is a nice little craft, in the real world of cruising its limited load-carry-ing ability can be very inconvenient. If your cruis-ing vessel can carry it, a better choice would be the Sport, which can carry five people and, with a 30 hp outboard and fuel, weighs about 750 pounds (340 kg). For extra capacity, the GLS can carry six

people and, with a 40 hp outboard and fuel, also weighs around 750 pounds.

In a hard tender, one alternative to the Boston Whaler is a rowing or sailing dinghy. With Car-leton Mitchell's extensive sailing background, it's not surprising that as a tender to *Coyaba* he selected a 9-foot (2.7 m) Dyer Dhow, which he could either take for a recreational sail or push along to the dock with a small outboard. Dyer makes four models of well-constructed fiberglass rowing and sailing dinghies ranging from 7½ to 12½ feet (2.2–3.8 m), which can be used as yacht tenders.

BOSTON WHALER

Excellent workmanship and internal flotation help make Boston Whaler's 11-foot (3.3 m) Tender among the most popu-lar of the hard cruising tenders.

Inflatable Tenders

If you decide to consider an inflatable tender, you will find a much wider choice because there are considerable differences in the materials and construction processes used by the manufacturers and even greater differences in the prices and quality of the boats they produce.

Less expensive inflatables usually are made of polyvinyl chloride (PVC). They are cheaper to assemble because their seams can be thermobonded electronically on a machine rather than cold-glued by hand. The drawbacks to PVC are that it is not very resistant to ultraviolet light, chafing, or solvents, and it can be stained easily by oil and grease. In hot weather it tends to stretch excessively, and in cold weather it becomes brittle. To make PVC pliable, it must be impregnated with plasticizing oils. Critics of PVC say that as it ages, these oils work their way to the surface and leach away, causing the material to stiffen, crack, and leak air. Some critics also believe that these plasticizers attack the glue used to attach wooden transoms to some PVC inflatables, causing them to fall off.

The more expensive inflatables are made of a compound of Hypalon—a branded chlorosulfonated polyethylene product created by DuPont—and neoprene. The neoprene is added because adhesives will not stick to pure Hypalon. Inflatables made of the compound are more expensive because the material itself is more costly and seams must be glued by hand.

PVC and Hypalon-neoprene coatings allow inflatables to hold air, but neither is very resistant to tears and punctures. The very cheapest of the PVC inflatables (all models of the Sea Eagle brand and Sevylor's Caravelle model, for example) are made of PVC only. They are fine for kids to play with in a pool but should never be considered for a cruising tender. The higher-priced PVC inflatables and all those made of Hypalon-neoprene are reinforced with a fabric backing of polyester or nylon. Reinforcing fabrics can range in density from 840 denier down to 210 denier, with the higher-denier fabrics being the more resistant to tears and punctures.

Inflatables made by France's Zodiac Group under the brand names Zodiac, Bombard, Hurricane, and Sevylor are made of PVC. Britain's Avon builds its inflatables of nylon fabric sandwiched between two layers of Hypalon-neoprene.

Manufacturers of upper-end inflatables, such as Achilles and Novurania, make their boats of some combination of Hypalon and neoprene. Achilles uses a nylon core with Hypalon-neoprene on the outside and two layers of neoprene coating on the inside. Novurania, the highest priced of the major inflatable manufacturers, uses a Trevira polyester fabric core with Hypalon outside and neoprene inside.

If you decide to purchase an inflatable as a tender, go with one of these better-known manufacturers, even though an off brand may be considerably cheaper.

Inflatables used as tenders come in four basic versions. The least expensive type has a flat bottom and an inflatable transom, and to accommodate an outboard motor, it must be outfitted with a bracket. An example would be the 9-foot, 3-inch (2.8 m) Avon Redcrest, which weighs just 40 pounds (18 kg) and is designed to carry four people or a total of 700 pounds (315 kg) (see top photo). It can also be fitted with wooden floorboards and up to a 4 hp outboard.

In the middle range are inflatables with wooden or fiberglass transoms. They usually are fitted with wooden, plastic, or aluminum flooring, and some have an inflatable keel, which aids materially in their tracking ability (see bottom photo opposite and top photo page 164). Novurania offers models in this category that employ a single wooden rib fitted between the floorboards and the fabric bottom to give the bottom a V-shape.

The third type is the rigid inflatable boat (RIB), which has a fiberglass-hull bottom and floor (see bottom photo page 164). An example would be Avon's 11-foot, 2-inch (3.4 m) Rover RIB 3.40, which, with an optional steering wheel, can be fitted with up to a 25 hp outboard. The boat with out-

An inflatable transom tender is the most economical, but its flat bottom can make it difficult to control in high winds. To be operated under power, inflatables of this type must be fitted with an outboard bracket.

board weighs just over 300 pounds (135 kg) and is designed to carry five people or a maximum load of 1,250 pounds (563 kg). This was the tender I chose for *Americas Odyssey*, and it served us well.

For cruising boats over about 50 feet (15 m), Novurania makes a line of MX center-console inflatables that range from 11 feet, 3 inches, to 21 feet, 10 inches (3.4–6.7 m) and can be powered by outboards from 30 to 90 hp (see photo page 165). Avon offers three models of its center console Seasport De luxe line ranging from 10 feet, 6 inches, to 13 feet, 4 inches (3.2–4.1 m), which can be powered by 25 to 50 hp outboards. The major drawback is their weight, which with an appropriate outboard ranges from 442 pounds to 1,054 pounds (200–474 kg).

One other version of inflatables is the type powered by integral water-jet engines, such as Avon's SE 320 Seasport Jet, which is fitted with an 83 hp

An inflatable with a hard transom can handle a larger outboard motor for better performance.

An inflatable with an inflatable bottom such as that patented by Zodiac helps it track better than an inflatable tender with a flat bottom.

ZODIAC

ZODIAC

A inflatable with a rigid bottom has much the same operating characteristics as a hard-bottomed tender.

Center-console inflata-bles make a roomy tender, but their size and weight limit them to use on cruising boats longer than about 50 feet (15 m).

NAUTICA RIBs

Yamaha. To me, its 550-pound (248 kg) weight and limited capacity make it a fun machine to play with but impractical as a cruising tender.

Most inflatables can be bought from dealers at discounts of 15 to 20 percent or through marine catalogs at discounts of 30 percent.

TENDER POWER

When shopping for an outboard for your tender, you'll find that just about all the U.S. and foreign manufacturers have essentially the same lineup of horsepower sizes. Within a particular horsepower class, they also have almost exactly the same weights. The reason is that regardless of the brand names they carry, they all are built by fewer than a dozen companies in the world. Johnson and Evinrude outboards, once built by America's OMC Corporation, are now part of Canada's Bombardier Corporation. Mercury Marine, a division of Brunswick Corporation, makes all but

one of the Mercury engines and also owns the Mariner brand. Mercury makes all the Mariners over 40 hp, but Mariner outboards below 40 hp are made in Japan by Yamaha—which also has its own brand. Tohatsu makes its own brand plus the 5 hp Mercury and all those that carry the Nissan name. Suzuki and Honda make all their own outboards. This information can be useful since parts often are interchangeable among motors made by a common manufacturer though the names are different.

Generally speaking, you can expect a dealer in U.S. and Japanese brands to offer a discount on an outboard for your tender of about 15 percent, perhaps a bit more if the same dealer is also selling you the tender.

The outboards commonly used to power cruising tenders break down into three basic categories: those under 5 hp, those from 8 to 18 hp, and those in the 25 to 40 hp range.

In the first category, all the major U.S. and foreign brands offer 2.5 and 3.5 hp models that have recoil starting, have neutral and forward gears (no reverse), and weigh around 27 pounds (12 kg). Their 5 hp motors have recoil starting; forward, neutral, and reverse gears; and a weight of around 45 pounds (20 kg). Outboards in the range of 2.5 to 5 hp have small fuel tanks built in, and some also will accept fuel from an external tank.

British Seagull used to offer a line of 2 to 5 hp outboards that had rope starting (no recoil) and were direct-forward-drive (no neutral or reverse). They were ugly as sin but tough as nails and would take just about any abuse the cruising life could dish out. Their construction was so simple that any problems that made them stop usually could be repaired by even the least mechanically minded member of the crew. Unfortunately, the company has discontinued those "classic" engines and replaced them with a line of 4 to 35 hp engines that look pretty much like every other outboard on the market.

The next category of outboards contains the 8, 9.9, 15, and 18 hp models. Again, all the U.S. and foreign manufacturers have products in these approximate sizes, and they all have forward, neutral, and reverse gearing. Outboards of 8 hp and above require an external fuel tank. An 8 hp outboard weighs about 60 pounds (27 kg) and has recoil starting. The 9.9, 15, and 18 hp models all weigh around 80 to 85 pounds (36–38 kg). They also offer electric starting (but not remote throttle control) as an option.

Above 18 hp, you get into the 25, 30, and 40 hp models. Outboards of 25 and 30 hp weigh around 100 pounds (45 kg). As an extra, in addition to electric starting, they offer remote throttle control for use on tenders with wheel steering. The typical 40 hp outboard weighs almost 130 pounds (59 kg) and offers electric starting and remote throttle control.

The best sizes of motor to use on the various types of tenders are as follows.

The outboards used on small hard tenders, such as the Dyer Dink, should be limited to no more than 5 hp.

Although Boston Whaler recommends that its 11-foot (3.5 m) standard model not be outfitted with an outboard over 10 hp, many cruisers power this model with 15 to 18 hp. With an outboard that size, you can use this model for high-speed exploring or even for pulling a single water skier if the person weighs no more than about 150 pounds (68 kg) and you put the observer in the bow to offset the weight of the operator, the engine, the fuel, and the pull of the skier. With an outboard of either size, you pay no weight penalty over a 9.9 hp outboard since all three engines weigh around 80 pounds (36 kg).

Some cruisers outfit this boat with 25 to 40 hp engines, but they are flirting with danger. Outboards of those sizes weigh between 100 and 130 pounds (45–59 kg) and also require a larger gas tank to give them a reasonable range. That weight plus the weight of an operator, when concentrated in the boat's stern without any counterbalancing weight forward, can be highly dangerous. If you hit a fair-sized wave at maximum throttle, the boat can flip over backwards. Outboards of that weight also significantly reduce the load of passengers and provisions the boat can carry safely.

Boston Whaler recommends a maximum of 25 hp for its 13-foot (4 m) Sport model, but it's common for cruisers to put 35 to 40 hp outboards that weigh about 100 pounds (45 kg) on it. They seem to have few problems because the Sport model's wheel steering places the operator's weight toward the center of the vessel rather than in the stern. Because of its weight, however, I would not recommend putting a 40 hp outboard on this model. If a youngster weighing only 80 or 90 pounds (36–41 kg) runs the boat at full throttle into a stiff chop, it can flip.

Inflatables that do not have hard transoms but must use a bracket to accommodate an outboard should not be fitted with a motor over 5 hp; a 2.5 or 3.5 hp is really better.

Hard transom inflatables usually are fitted with an outboard of up to 9.9 hp, although some cruising owners put 15 to 18 hp outboards on them. Because of the stability and load-carrying ability of an inflatable, boats of this size and type perform well with that much power.

An inflatable with a fiberglass bottom, such as the Avon Rover RIB 3.40, can safely handle an outboard of up to 18 hp, even if the operator sits in the rear and steers with the outboard's combined throttle and tiller. If an RIB is rigged with remote steering and throttle control that positions the operator's weight farther forward, it can handle up to 25 hp.

When considering higher outboard power for small boats such as tenders, always study the vessel certification label that is required by law to be affixed to every boat under 20 feet (6 m). This plate states the maximum horsepower and total weight of motor, persons, and gear that can legally be in or on the boat. Exceeding these restrictions can result in a ticket from marine patrol or coast guard officers as well as invalidate your insurance.

TENDER REGISTRATION, SALES TAXES, AND INSURANCE

A cruising tender cannot be documented because it does not meet the minimum 5-net-tons size requirement. A tender is legally subject to the same state sales and use taxes as any other vessel and may or may not be subject to state registration. You may want to cover your tender under an insurance policy of its own or under a separate schedule of the policy on your main vessel that has a smaller deductible. For details, see the discussion of state sales taxes, registration, and insurance in chapter 6.

TENDER ANCHORS AND RODES

The best anchor for a hard tender is a 4-pound (1.8 kg) fluke. However, the sharp flukes can puncture the fabric of an inflatable tender; for that use, a better choice might be a 3-pound (1.4 kg) folding anchor. For a tender anchor rode, use about 35 feet (10 m) of ⅜-inch (9 mm) three-strand-twist nylon line and add 6 feet (2 m) of ¼-inch (6 mm) chain between it and the anchor to give its small hook a bit more holding power.

TENDER SECURITY

When you are at anchor during your cruising, your tender often will be unattended and tied off to the stern of your main vessel. You also will be leaving it at all manner of places ashore with no one to watch over it. At those times, it can be a tempting target for theft, because in many parts of the world its value will represent several years' income for some passerby. In many popular cruising areas, in fact, the locals have become quite adept at the "tender scam," which works this way: at night, one fellow keeps a lookout while his friend slips up to an unwatched tender ashore or tied off to the stem of a nice-looking yacht at anchor, cuts its rope painter with the flick of a knife, and disappears with it into the night. The next morning, the pair drop by the anchored vessel, comment on the missing tender, and ask whether the owner is offering a reward. If he is, the locals will quickly "find" and return the tender. If not, the motor is taken off and sold on one island while the boat, sans its registration numbers, is sold on another.

You will, of course, have your tender identified with your main vessel's name and, if required, its registration numbers painted on its side. For your own protection, take a few additional precautions. First, rely on your rope painter only when tying up ashore where you can easily keep an eye on the tender or when you are using the tender to explore deserted islands or go snorkeling or diving. Also, equip your tender with a 10- to 12-foot (3–3.6 m) painter of high-grade, ⅛-inch (3 mm) stainless steel wire encased in plastic. Whereas a rope painter can be cut with a sharp knife, stainless steel wire can be severed only with bolt cutters, which most potential thieves aren't likely to have handy. Permanently affix one end of the painter to the tender's towing ring with a stainless steel thimble and a nicopressed fitting. Also nicopress a stainless steel thimble into the painter's bitter end and insert into it a stout, high-quality brass or bronze combination lock. Use the lock whenever you leave the tender unattended.

Second, secure your outboard to the tender

itself. With motors under 5 hp that you might be taking on and off the tender, use plastic-encased stainless steel wire, nicopressed fittings, and a bronze combination lock—as you did on the tender's painter. For larger outboards that you are unlikely to be removing from the tender, use stainless steel wire and nicopressed fittings to tie the two together so they cannot be separated without considerable effort. It's also a good idea to scratch your name or the name of your cruising vessel on the inside of the outboard's engine cowling. All of these motors look pretty much alike. If yours is missing and you find it in someone else's possession, you'll have an easy way to prove to the gendarme that you are its rightful owner.

Third, never leave any loose articles—such as fishing tackle, snorkeling gear, cameras, or your handheld VHF—in the tender when you aren't there to watch over them.

If you make it a habit to follow these simple precautions, you probably will avoid any unpleasant experiences. But if the worst happens and your tender is stolen, at least you should have no worries that your insurance company will try to claim negligence on your part.

TENDER DAVITS

Another important aspect of owning a tender is hoisting it aboard your main vessel, stowing it securely for open-water passages, and putting it back in the water the next time you want to use it—all with a minimum of fuss.

The traditional way to launch and retrieve a tender aboard a modern cruising powerboat of moderate size is to use a strongback or winch boom, both of which suspend the tender's entire weight from a single point. Unless the launching vessel is quite stable or there is someone around to steady the tender, it can easily become unbalanced and tip to one side or the other. On vessels with a motor yacht configuration, the traditional place for stowing the tender is in a cradle mounted on the aft end of the vessel's cabintop. On a 50- to 60-foot

(15–18 m) cruising vessel, this means the tender must be lowered and raised anywhere from 12 to 15 feet (3.6–4.5 m). On some boats, that distance is even greater because the tender must be lifted an additional 4 feet (1.2 m) or so to clear lifelines or safety railings. On boats like the Grand Banks Classics or the Hatteras 42 Long Range Cruiser, the tender is often stowed in a cradle mounted on top of the aft cabin. This location reduces the distance the tender has to be lowered and raised, but it also means that it must be swung across at least part of the vessel's beam.

The problem with carrying a tender in either of these locations is that if the yacht is rolling from side to side, launching and retrieving the tender can be quite difficult. In extreme cases, it can be highly dangerous or absolutely impossible.

Allow me to tell a short story here to make my point.

I was the sole guest aboard Frank and Lee Glindmeier's *Summer Wind* during one leg of the vessel's shakedown cruise to the Bahamas in preparation for a voyage to Alaska. On our run southwesterly out of Nassau toward Andros, a heavy northeaster with 30-knot winds set in on our stern, and we surfed down the face of waves that towered over *Summer Wind*'s flying bridge. When we reached Andros, Frank wisely ducked into the first reasonably protected cove he saw. We were able to hunker down behind a headland to get out of the worst of the wind, but the anchorage was still quite rolly. "No problem," said Frank with his typical élan. "We'll just take the dink down and do a bit of bonefishing in the flats."

In view of *Summer Wind*'s planned itinerary on the voyage to Alaska, Frank had decided not to carry a traditional tender but instead a larger boat that he could use for extensive side trips. For that reason, his "dink" was a 14-foot (4.2 m) runabout with a massive 70 hp outboard. Together, they weighed about 1,400 pounds (630 kg). Grabbing everything we could find to hold on to, we worked our way to the aft end of the cabintop, stripped off the dink's cover, and rigged it for launching with the strongback. As soon as we had lifted it clear of its cradle, *Summer Wind*'s rolling motion made the tender gyrate wildly from side to side. It didn't take Frank long to realize that by the time we got the tender over the side and even with the windows of the main saloon, which were directly below, *Summer Wind* was likely to lurch and the dink probably would wind up poking into the saloon. He properly suggested we secure it and wait for calmer conditions, which we did—for the next three days. At least I got caught up on my reading.

Admittedly, that's an extreme example, but it illustrates why it makes a great deal more sense to carry a powerboat's tender on davits hung off the stern (see illustration). This arrangement stows the tender much closer to the water, suspends its weight from two points rather than one, and makes

launching and retrieving it far easier and less dangerous.

We carried *Americas Odyssey*'s Avon Rover RIB 3.40 tender on a pair of manually operated Simpson Davits constructed of 316 stainless steel. I don't know of any electrically operated davits of this type, but they could be made up by a custom fabricator. If you go to an aft davit setup, you probably will find you have to reinforce your vessel's transom to bear the added weight. You also want to be sure the davits you select pull the tender up snugly against its arms and don't allow it any swinging room (see illustration). Some experienced cruisers object to carrying a tender in this fashion because it makes backing into a slip or Mediterranean mooring more difficult. I can only say that in any kind of cruising beyond marina hopping, you are far

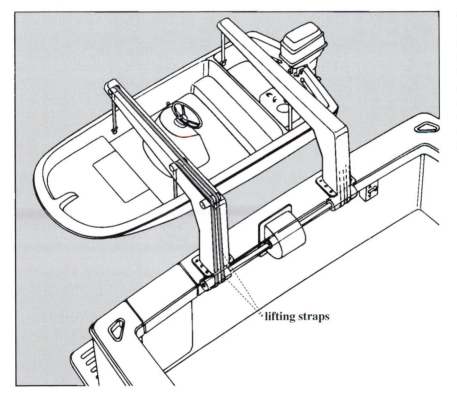

lifting straps

A pair of aft davits with lifting straps in each arm makes the tender stable as it is launched and retrieved. Starboard davit here is cut away to show lifting straps. Electric motor plus crank handle socket for manual lifting (at elbow) also shown.

more likely to find yourself anchoring out or tying up parallel to a face dock than you are to be backing into a slip or a Med moor. On *Americas Odyssey*'s voyage, we routinely pulled into transient slips bow-on because that put her aft master stateroom facing away from traffic on the dock. In the few instances where we encountered Med moor situations—such as at Nelson's Dockyard in Antigua—I simply launched the tender before I started backing in order to have the ease of launching and retrieving it with aft davits the remainder of the time.

Another alternative for carrying a tender is to use some sort of pivoting device on the main vessel's swim platform that allows the tender to be turned up on one gunwale and lashed across the boat's transom. This is the most practical arrangement on a cruiser under about 35 feet (10.7 m), which doesn't have room to mount the tender on deck. Edson International makes one such arrangement called the Flip-Out Inflatable Holder, and versions for handling small, rigid tenders the same way are made by several companies in the Northwest, where the technique is frequently employed. One is Weaver Industries of Marysville, Washington, which makes the Snap Davit. The main drawback to this approach is that the motor must be removed from the tender each time the tender is brought aboard. Thus, it is practical only if you plan to power your tender with a small, easy-to-remove outboard.

TENDER TOWING

There will be times in your cruising when you would rather tow your tender. Usually, this will be when you want to move to an anchorage not far away, and it's daylight and the weather is calm.

There is nothing wrong with towing a tender if you make proper preparations beforehand and take a few sensible precautions. First, here are the precautions.

- Don't tow a tender at night. If it breaks loose, you'll have a devil of a time trying to find it. By

daylight, it could be miles away. Even when towing a tender during the day, check it every half hour or so.
- In a displacement vessel, the speed at which you tow a tender shouldn't be a problem. With a planing or semidisplacement hull boat, you'll find your tender will tow best if your speed doesn't exceed 12 knots.
- A tender under tow is more likely to be flipped over than to be lost completely. Before you tow any tender, remove loose items, such as fishing tackle or snorkeling gear, and stow them aboard your main vessel.
- If your tender's outboard is 5 hp or less, it's best to remove it from the tender and stow it securely in your main vessel's cockpit. With a larger outboard that is too heavy to remove from the tender easily, leave it on the tender but tilt it all the way forward, lock it into that position, and lash it down so it can't slam from side to side.

Towing a Hard-Bottomed Tender

For towing a hard tender or an inflatable tender with a rigid fiberglass bottom, you'll need to make up a towing line 40 to 50 feet (12–15 m) long of at least ½-inch (12 mm) three-strand-twist nylon. If it's soft laid, it will be easier on your hands. (It's best not to use braided nylon for a tender's towing line because it isn't very elastic and therefore doesn't provide much shock absorption.) Eye splice a stainless steel sassor large enough to fit the towing eye on your tender into one end of the line, and use a stainless steel thimble to reduce chafing. Whip the bitter end.

You'll also need to rig yourself a towing bridle that will allow the tender to track as precisely as possible behind the center of your main vessel (see illustration). It should be made of at least ½-inch (12 mm) three-strand-twist nylon, and the knot in its center should be about 6 to 8 feet (1.8–2.4 m) off your cruising vessel's transom.

Once your towing line and towing bridle are made, the next step is to figure out where along the length of the towing line you should join the two

A towing bridle will help insure that your towed tender will track behind your main vessel in a straight line.

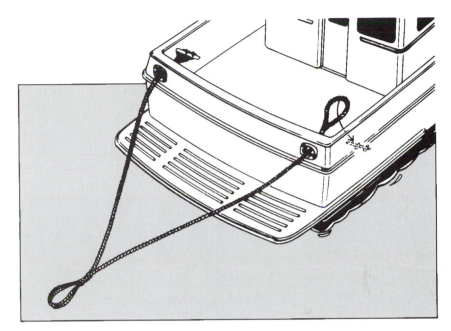

to put the tender in the best position for towing. Have someone else operate your main vessel at its normal towing speed so you can work freely in the cockpit. Slowly let the tender's towing line out until the tender's bow is riding on the back of your second stern wave (see illustration). Note where the towing line crosses the transom, subtract from that point the 6 feet (1.8 m) or so by which the loop in your towing bridle will be behind your stern when everything is in place, and tie the towing line to the center loop in the towing bridle with a bowline. If the tender slews from side to side when you let it back out, this indicates that it isn't tracking straight behind your main vessel because the knot in your towing bridle is not exactly centered. Play with the knot's location until the tender settles down and rides calmly.

Don't forget that whenever you slow down or approach your destination with this kind of towing rig, you must send someone aft to pull the tender up on short scope and fend it off. If you don't, the tender is almost certain to slam into your main

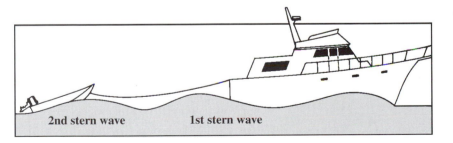

A hard tender will tow best if you allow it to ride on the back of your main vessel's second stern wave.

vessel's stern, and the towing line probably will wind up wrapped around your props.

Towing a Soft-Bottomed Inflatable Tender

Because of an inflatable tender's lightness and lack of a significant keel, the best position to tow one with a soft bottom is on the back of the first stern wave your main vessel creates, rather than the second. With the tender pulled up that short, it has less room to slew about.

To tow an inflatable with a soft bottom, you should have two towing bridles—the one for your main vessel I just described (though it may need to

be a bit longer or shorter), and a second for the tender itself (see illustration).

In making up the towing bridle for your main vessel, tie a knot in its center, but instead of making up the loop ends, for the time being just tie the ends off to your stern cleats. In towing a soft-bottomed tender, you won't use a towing line, so you must adjust the distance at which it rides behind the vessel by adjusting the length of the towing vessel's bridle.

As for the tender's towing bridle, the large handhold at the bow of an inflatable is intended primarily for pulling it out of the water and onto the shore. By itself, it isn't strong enough for towing, so you should have the dealer fit an inflatable

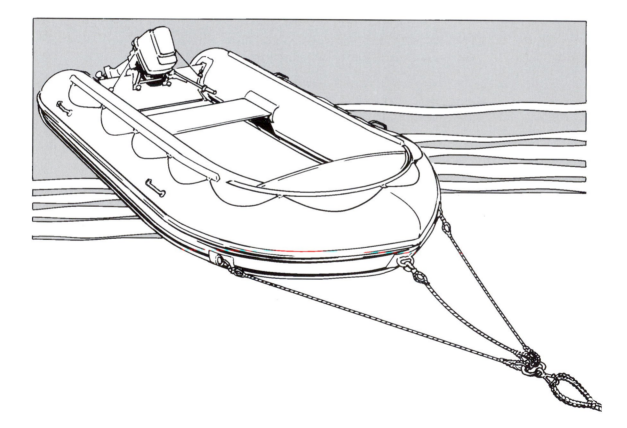

An inflatable tender should have its own bridle to distribute stress over more than one of its fittings.

An inflatable tender with a soft bottom tows best if it is pulled up short and rides on the back of your main vessel's first stern wave.

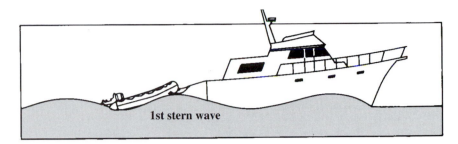

1st stern wave

with optional rings on either side of its bow just below the rubbing strake. When you make up the tender's bridle, its two side lines take the strain. The center line should have just a little slack but should take the strain if either of the fittings accommodating the outside lines separates from the tender.

To determine how long your main vessel's towing bridle should be, put everything in place and have someone operate your vessel at its normal towing speed while you're in the cockpit. Take in or let out the ends of the towing bridle on your vessel until your inflatable is tracking directly behind your main vessel and riding on the back of the first stern wave it creates (see illustration). Mark the points at which the ends of the main vessel's towing bridle go around your stern cleats, and make end loops as already suggested.

Cruising Safely

On the Ft. Lauderdale to Bermuda leg of Don Baumgartner's transatlantic voyage aboard his 58-footer (17 m), *Trenora*, he and his crew experienced seas he described as being "the size of condominiums," which rolled the vessel as much as 40 degrees off the vertical. On one roll, Don was slammed all the way across the main saloon and into a bulkhead. When I met him on the dock in St. George, one eye was swollen almost shut and ringed with deep circles of angry purple. "Even at that," he told me, "I was lucky. If I'd hit a few feet further aft, I'd have gone right through the window." As Joe Columbus cruised his 48-footer (14.6 m), *Evelyn C.*, across the Gulf of Alaska from Cape Hinchinbrook to Cape Spencer on one of his annual Anchorage to Seattle migrations, he encountered 60-knot winds and 20-foot (7 m) seas that sent green water over his flying bridge. I was in the Abacos a few years ago when one foolish crew tried to run Whale Cay Passage in the midst of a "rage" that pitchpoled their 40-foot (12 m) sailboat. Thanks to the valor of a native skipper out of Treasure Cay, no lives were

sacrificed, but one woman was seriously injured and the boat was lost. On *Americas Odyssey*'s 575-mile (930 km) offshore run from Aruba to the San Blas Islands of Panama, we encountered 40-knot winds and 25- to 30-foot (7–9 m) following seas, which put the crew in life jackets and our hearts in our throats.

My point in these brief stories is that the sea is not to be trifled with. Anytime you plan a voyage that entails an open-water passage, you must have your vessel properly rigged and equipped to withstand the worst. Making certain that you cruise in safety as well as comfort involves a great deal more than simply outfitting your vessel with the minimum emergency equipment required for its class by the U.S. Coast Guard.

RIGGING FOR A BLOW

While your vessel is still tied securely in its home slip, imagine what life aboard it would be like in 40- to 50-knot winds and 15- to 20-foot (4.5–6

m) seas, then look for areas that could present problems and figure out how you can prevent potential difficulties. Based on our discussion of a cruising vessel's layout in chapter 2, I hope you see in your vessel some very helpful features, such as stout safety railings with an intermediate lifeline; limited expanses of exposed glass; side decks; and interior access to the flying bridge. Even if all those factors are present, there probably will be several areas where you'll need to do some work.

Make certain, for instance, that your vessel has a series of readily accessible handholds that will allow you and your crew to go fore and aft safely both inside the vessel and on deck regardless of what the weather is doing. On the interior, those handholds in the overhead may be fine if you're 6 feet, 2 inches (188 cm) tall, but if your first mate is 5 feet (152 cm) even, you'll need to install handholds this person can reach also. As for the exterior, invest in a good safety harness and figure a way to rig a safety line—often referred to as a "jack" line—along the side decks when the weather turns really nasty. As nearly as possible, the safety line should be continuous to allow a crew member wearing a safety harness to clip to it and walk the length of the deck without having to unclip. If it isn't continuous, according to Murphy's Law, the few seconds a person is unattached will be the instant the rogue wave hits and the vessel is knocked on its beam ends. The safety line should run on the inboard side of your decks right up next to the house. During a severe blow, you don't want to have to work your way along your vessel's safety railings, which would put you to the extreme outside of the vessel in the perfect position to be pitched overboard in a 30- to 40-degree roll. For the same reason, figure a way to run a safety line down the centerline of the foredeck and up to the flying bridge if you must go on deck to reach it.

Bolt down the main pieces of furniture in the saloon so they can't shift. If a vessel is rolling heavily in a seaway, a weighty chair or table can be slammed across the saloon with enough force to crush a person's leg. Prepare to lash lighter furniture to a bulkhead with a stout shock cord. Find places to stow loose articles securely, or they can become deadly missiles. Check the galley carefully for positive locks on overhead locker doors, which prevent them from being knocked open and spilling their contents on someone's head. On *Trenora*'s Atlantic crossing, Don Baumgartner's bride-to-be, Donna Flaxman, rigged herself a window washer's belt clipped to stout eyebolts in the galley so she would be braced in heavy weather but would still have her hands free to prepare meals.

In chapter 3, I mentioned the need for an alarm that will alert you to high water in the bilge. It's also a good idea to attach an appropriately sized wooden plug to each of your vessel's through-hull fittings with a piece of light line or wire. If a through-hull fails, having a plug at your fingertips to ram home quickly could help save your vessel. Also have accessible in your engine room several packages of Syntho-Glass, a resin-impregnated fiberglass cloth that is activated with water and sets up in thirty minutes or less. You can use it to stop leaks in broken hoses, to wrap temporary patches around broken water, fuel, or hydraulic lines, or (balled up) to plug small holes. Since it is heat resistant to 1,100°F (593°C), it can be used to make temporary repairs to mufflers and exhaust systems.

FIRE PROTECTION

According to U.S. Coast Guard statistics, in one recent five-year period, 1,882 fires and explosions aboard recreational vessels claimed ninety-five lives, inflicted 677 personal injuries, and caused a monetary loss of over $15 million. When preparing any cruising vessel, one of your most basic safety considerations should be preventing the likelihood of a serious fire or explosion. Three key areas you should be especially concerned about are the vessel's fuel and lubricating oil systems, its electrical systems, and its fire-fighting equipment.

Fuel and Lubricating Oil Systems

A four-year study by the coast guard and Underwriters Laboratories (UL) found that the most common cause of fires in pleasure vessels was the failure of fuel-fill pipes or fuel tanks. Examine all your vessel's fuel-fill hose connections to be certain they are tightly secured at both the underside of the deck fuel fittings and at the top of all tank connections. Check for corrosion or cracking of the hoses, and make sure they are double clamped on both ends. Check fuel tank vent lines the same way.

Fuel tanks should be of UL-approved fiberglass or heavy-gauge metal with electrically welded seams—never soft soldered. Solder melts at 1,000°F (538°C), and the failure of a soldered joint could allow a small fire to become a raging inferno. Metal fuel tanks should be installed with sloping or rounded tops to encourage the runoff of condensation and to prevent puddling, which can lead to corrosion. Tanks should be installed so they can be inspected visually. Fuel tanks mounted in foam flotation should allow for adequate drainage to prevent moisture-induced corrosion.

Check flexible fuel and lube oil lines for any signs of chafing or deterioration. Check copper injector lines on diesel engines for pitting or corrosion, especially around their termination on the engine block. A high-pressure line spraying fuel or lube oil on a hot engine, turbocharger, manifold, or gearbox can create a voracious monster of a fire in seconds.

Electrical Systems

Many fires aboard recreational vessels are traced to faults in their electrical systems, and the largest single cause of those faults is chafing. Pay particular attention to wiring beneath galley counters, where it can be chafed by loose pots and pans.

Since the most effective way to snuff out an electrical fire is to deprive it of oxygen, all circuit and terminal boards should be enclosed in a box of heavy-gauge metal. Be sure all circuits are equipped with circuit breakers appropriate to the load they are designed to carry. Know where your main electrical panel shutdown is located, and be sure you can reach and deactivate it in one motion, even in the dark.

Fire-Fighting Equipment

I mentioned in chapter 3 the need to have the engine space of a cruising vessel protected with an automatic fire-extinguishing system. In addition to that system, you will need portable fire extinguishers.

U.S. Coast Guard regulations require recreational vessels 26 feet (7.9 m) to less than 40 feet (12 m) length overall (LOA) whose engine spaces are equipped with an automatic fire-extinguishing system to also carry at least one B-I type approved handheld fire extinguisher. Vessels 40 to 65 feet (12.2–19.8 m) LOA with fixed fire-extinguishing equipment installed in their engine spaces must carry at least two B-I type approved handheld portable fire extinguishers or one B-II type approved unit. (The "B" refers to the type of fire the extinguisher is designed to fight—flammable liquids—and the I and II refer to the extinguisher's size, with II being the larger.) Recreational vessels 26 feet to less than 40 feet LOA whose engine spaces are not equipped with an automatic fire-extinguishing system must carry at least two B-I type approved handheld extinguishers or at least one B-II type approved unit. Recreational vessels 40 to 65 feet LOA whose engine spaces are not equipped with an automatic fire-extinguishing system must carry at least three B-I type approved units or at least one B-I and one B-II type approved unit. These portable extinguishers must be mounted in a readily accessible location using an approved quick-release mounting bracket.

Although the coast guard requires only type B-I or B-II units (effective against flammable-liquid fires), I suggest you make all your portable fire extinguishers type A-B-C, which are effective against flammable-liquid, electrical, and combustible-material fires. My suggestion would be that you install one B-II type approved portable extinguisher in a readily accessible location just outside your engine space(s) to extinguish small engine room fires before they set off your automatic fire-extinguishing system. Also install in each of the following spaces an approved extinguisher that contains at least 5 pounds (2.2 kg) of active ingredient: pilothouse, galley, aft end of the saloon, passageway to your vessel's forward sleeping quarters, and aft owner's stateroom, if the vessel has one.

LIGHTNING PROTECTION

If you are caught in an electrical storm on the water, lightning will be attracted to the highest conductive point in the area, which well could be your boat. The best way to guard against lightning damage is to create a zone of protection around it by attracting lightning to a conductor mounted as high as possible on your vessel, then giving the lightning's current a direct, ample, and unimpeded path to run from the conductor to ground—that is, the water.

A lightning protection zone normally will include everything inside a cone-shaped area that has as its apex the highest point of your vessel. The base of the protection zone will be a circle at the water's surface that has a radius approximately twice the height of the conductor.

If your vessel has a metal cruising mast, it should be grounded to your vessel's bonding system with at least #8 copper wire. The wire should run in as straight a line as possible and avoid sharp bends. It also should be run down through your vessel inside a bulkhead to keep crew members from accidentally coming into contact with it. If your radar antenna is mounted on the mast close to the top, you should protect it by installing on the mast a solid copper rod at least ¼-inch (6 mm) in diameter that extends at least 1 foot (0.3 m) higher than the radar antenna itself.

SAFETY AND SURVIVAL EQUIPMENT

U.S. Coast Guard regulations require virtually all recreational vessels registered in the United States to carry certain safety and survival equipment on board. I concentrate here on the requirements for recreational vessels 26 to 65 feet (7.9–19.8 m) LOA. Required equipment must be "coast guard approved," which means only that the coast guard has approved that particular equipment to meet one of its specific legal requirements. The fact that a particular device is not coast guard approved does not mean that it is not good equipment, only that it will not satisfy a coast guard regulation. The coast guard's requirements are nothing more than the absolute minimum in the way of lifesaving and safety equipment that should be aboard your vessel. There are additional items that you should consider to be equally, if not more, important. In the following sections, we offer suggestions on what you should consider in personal flotation devices (PFDs), crew overboard (COB) packs, searchlights, day and nighttime visual distress signals (VDSs), emergency position-indicating radio beacons (EPIRBs), and life rafts.

The most comprehensive research into marine safety and survival being done today is that of the Safety of Life at Sea (SOLAS) Convention of the International Maritime Organization (IMO). While much of SOLAS's work is directed toward commercial shipping and fishing interests, its standards in many cases are equally applicable to cruising. While by law you must conform to the U.S. Coast Guard's regulations on safety and survival equipment, I strongly urge you wherever possible to equip your vessel to meet the more stringent—and in many cases more realistic—standards set by SOLAS. (SOLAS, incidentally, does not inspect and approve safety devices. It simply issues standards, and it's up to manufacturers who want to meet them to see that their products comply. For that reason, in referring to such equipment I use the term *SOLAS-qualified* rather than *SOLAS-approved*.)

Personal Flotation Devices

Personal flotation devices (PFDs) come in a wide range of configurations and materials, but they all have a common purpose: to save the life of anyone who accidentally winds up in the water.

WEARABLE PFDS

U.S. Coast Guard regulations require you to carry one type 1, 2, or 3 wearable PFD for each person on board.

Even if you will be venturing into open water only occasionally, all the wearable PFDs you carry should be type 1, which is intended for offshore use and is designed to turn an unconscious person from a facedown position in the water to a vertical or slightly backward face-up position and to provide at least 22 pounds (10 kg) of buoyancy (see photo). Many experienced cruisers loathe type 1 PFDs. They argue that their bulkiness makes them not only difficult to store but so uncomfortable to wear, so difficult to work in, and so unattractive that no one will use them. They

Though it is bulky and not particularly stylish, a type 1 PFD is the best choice for the offshore cruiser.

also argue—and rightly so—that type 1 PFDs are not sufficiently buoyant: the wearer does not float high enough in the water to avoid ingesting seawater. Tests have shown that type 1 PFDs will turn an unconscious person into a face-up position only about 70 percent of the time.

For several reasons, despite their limitations, I still think type 1 PFDs should be carried aboard a cruising powerboat. First, though they are not foolproof, they still offer the highest probability of turning an unconscious person over and floating that person faceup of any life jacket that satisfies coast guard requirements. Second, I think the point about their being so uncomfortable and hard to work in that no one will wear them is valid aboard a cruising sailboat where the entire crew often is on deck in bad weather and may frequently have to go forward. But on the vast majority of powerboats, most people ride out bad weather in the pilothouse or the main saloon. The only time they put on a life jacket is when they have to go on deck. Even then, they are outside only a few minutes and take it off as soon as they come back inside. Under those conditions, I don't see that the bulkiness of a type 1 is really a problem. Third, even critics of type 1 will admit that the design provides far more protection in the water than does a type 2 or type 3 substitute.

I do agree that the buoyancy of type 1 is inadequate, and I think it is wise to supplement it with a good-quality personal inflatable life ring. Several such units are on the market, but the best one I have seen is the Seacurity II unit produced by Survival Technologies Group (see photo opposite). When inflated by a manually fired CO_2 cartridge, this device deploys a horseshoe ring of polyurethane-coated nylon, which provides 26 pounds (11.7 kg) of buoyancy. It is packed in a nylon pouch designed to be worn on the belt, but I'd prefer to see it attached directly to the life jacket. The Seacurity II unit measures 7½ by 4½ by 1¾ inches (19 by 11 by 4.5 cm), weighs 10 ounces (283 g), and is available through a limited number of boating supply stores or the com-

STEARNS INC.

pany's catalog (see resources appendix). Another option is the Air Force Inflatable Pouch from Canada's Mustang Survival. Stearns and SOSpenders also have coast guard–approved, inflatable PFDs.

For years, there was a strong movement in some quarters of the PFD industry to persuade the coast guard to allow inflatable life jackets to satisfy its PFD requirements for recreational vessels. Inflatable life jackets that provide 35 pounds (15.8 kg) of buoyancy have been accepted by marine regulatory agencies in Europe for years. Recently, the coast guard has gone along with the idea and now approves type 1, 2, and 3 inflatable life jackets both of manual and of automatic-manual designs.

Whichever type of PFD you choose, make sure you carry enough of them to accommodate the largest number of people you are likely to have aboard at any one time and that they are of the appropriate sizes to accommodate the anticipated number of adults and children. (In this context, anyone who weighs over 90 pounds, or 40 kg, is considered an adult.) If the wearable PFDs you buy don't have patches of reflective tape affixed to the front of the shoulder area on each side and across the back, buy the kits available for this purpose and mark the PFDs yourself.

You are required to stow wearable PFDs so that they are "readily accessible," which doesn't mean stuffed in the bottom of a below decks hanging locker. The best place to carry them is in the seat lockers of your flying bridge. Hang them on individual hooks installed at the top of the locker's back so they don't wind up underneath whatever else you stow there.

If you will be cruising in cold-water areas above about 40 degrees North, you will need to provide immersion suits for all on board. They are expensive and you are not required by the coast guard to carry them, but in water below 60°F (15.5°C), survival time without them can be limited to an hour or less.

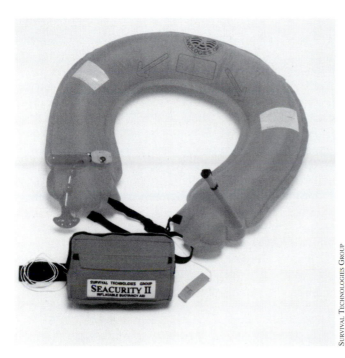

The Seacurity II from Survival Technologies Group is a wearable pouch, which when inflated by a CO_2 cartridge provides a life ring that provides 25 pounds (11.3 kg) of buoyancy. It is not coast guard approved.

Wearable PFD Accessories

You also should securely attach to each of your PFDs a signaling whistle—such as the WW-3 by ACR Electronics—and a personal rescue light. You have a choice of two basic types of personal rescue lights: xenon strobes and steady or flashing incandescents.

Xenon strobes give off a brilliant flash of 250,000 peak lumens once each second. They are especially good at penetrating rain or fog. The best unit of this type on the market is ACR's Waterbug water-activated model.

Rescue lights of the steady or flashing incandescent type were developed originally as marshaling lights for the victims of vessel sinkings or aircraft ditchings rather than as alert and locate lights for crew overboard situations. They provide only about 6 candela, which their manufacturers say makes them visible over a 3-square-mile (7.8 km²) area. That might be true on a clear, totally dark night. But in moonlight, rain, or fog, their visibility can be limited to no more than a few hundred yards—if that. On most of these units, the battery is water activated, but only after you pull a ring to remove two small sealing plugs. That seems to me to nullify the water-activated feature; the person might be unconscious or might panic and fail to pull the plugs.

Some experts in marine search and rescue object to xenon strobes by arguing that their flash is so rapid that the human eye has difficulty perceiving its exact location, which makes it difficult to vector in on. A report on xenon research issued by Great Britain's Royal Navy said that xenon strobes actually could cause short circuits in the human brain and induce seizures—even in people who aren't prone to them. In the industry, that report is still regarded with a heavy dose of skepticism.

Despite these criticisms and its greater expense, I still feel the xenon strobe is the superior choice for a personal rescue light. Its range of visibility over the widest variety of circumstances offers the best chance of enabling airborne or seaborne searchers to locate the person wearing it. I have discussed the matter with pilots and crew members on coast guard search-and-rescue helicopters. They say they use strobes themselves, they recommend them, and they have no difficulty vectoring in on them.

We discuss emergency position-indicating radio beacons (EPIRBs) in detail later in this chapter, but let me mention that you could go to the additional expense of equipping your PFDs with an ACR Personal 406 MHz Satellite EPIRB, a personal type 406 EPIRB that also transmits on the 121.5 MHz homing frequency (see photo). It weighs 18.6 ounces (527 g) and is powered by a lithium battery with an eleven-year storage life. Putting one of these units on each of your PFDs would be expensive, but if it could save a life, it would be well worth the cost.

THROWABLE PFDS

In addition to wearable PFDs, coast guard regulations also require that recreational vessels 26 to 65 feet (7.9–19.8 m) LOA carry one throwable type 4 PFD, which can be a type-approved floating cushion, ring buoy, or horseshoe buoy. Actually, regardless of the size of your vessel, you should carry one type 4 PFD on either side of the boat's forward half and one at the stern. Use ring or horseshoe buoys rather than cushions. Each should be carried in brackets for immediate use and should be fitted with a 75-foot (23 m) floating safety line. It would be ideal if all three could be horseshoe buoys because they are easier for a person who has fallen overboard to get into than a ring buoy. However, for appearance's sake, most cruisers carry ring buoys in brackets on the port and starboard sides of the pilothouse and a horseshoe buoy in the cockpit. They should have attached safety lines, but most don't.

Type 4 throwable PFDs also should be equipped with strobe lights (though few cruisers do this) that automatically activate when they are immersed in seawater. ACR produces such a light (model 566).

Ring or horseshoe buoys are hard to throw accurately for any distance. Though the heaving lines encased in a weighted bag that are available through most marine catalogs are not coast guard type-approved and will not satisfy the type 4 requirement, you might also consider carrying one or more aboard.

CREW OVERBOARD PACKS

Several companies make crew overboard (COB) packs, which contain a COB pole topped by a flag or light, a horseshoe buoy, a drogue, a whistle, a strobe light, and a dye marker (see photo). They are mounted on a vessel's stern and release their contents by gravity when someone on board yanks a lanyard or releases a shock cord. If you follow the recommendations above regarding PFDs, anyone aboard your vessel who goes overboard while wearing a life jacket will already have with the PFD everything but the COB pole and dye pack. If

A COB pack mounted on your vessel's stern is one quick way to get help to anyone unfortunate enough to fall or be swept off your vessel.

you don't care to follow the PFD suggestions, however, a COB package would be a good idea.

Searchlights

If passengers go overboard at night, you can't save them until you can see them. Many sizable cruising powerboats have one or more searchlights on the forward edge of the flying bridge that can be controlled from the pilothouse or the bridge steering station. While these units are useful for spotting navigation markers and other stationary objects ahead of your vessel, they can be somewhat slow and cumbersome to operate and their range of motion is limited. They are difficult, if not impossible, to train on a person in the water, especially since that person is likely to be aft of amidships and more likely at the stern while your crew is trying to get the person back on board. For search-and-rescue work, a more practical arrangement would be to mount three handheld, 12-volt halogen searchlights with long accordion-type cords on your vessel. Put one in the pilothouse, one on the flying bridge, and one in the cockpit. Several units with highly focused beams of up to 400,000 candlepower are available through marine retailers and catalogs. They can be mounted in brackets and can be wired to use any of the 12-volt plugs on board your vessel.

Visual Distress Signals

Coast guard regulations require all U.S.-registered recreational vessels over 26 feet (7.9 m) LOA to carry type-approved daytime and nighttime visual distress signals (VDSs). To meet the minimum requirement for a daytime VDS, you can use an orange flag (featuring a black square and a black disk), three orange smoke signals (floating canister or handheld), or three red flares (handheld, meteor, or parachute). To meet the minimum requirement for a nighttime VDS, you can carry an electric SOS light or three red flares (handheld, meteor, or parachute).

For open-water voyaging, of course, you will want to exceed those minimums considerably.

DAYTIME VDSS

The most popular daytime VDSs are handheld smoke flares that burn for about fifty seconds. A potential problem with a handheld smoke flare, however, is that you are most likely to use it in a life raft, where there is a good chance the smoke will blow right back into the raft, which may have a fixed canopy. You'll be better off with the SOLAS-qualified floating smoke canisters, which have a much greater burn time of about three minutes.

NIGHTTIME VDSS

Red handheld flares made to U.S. Coast Guard specifications burn for about two minutes and have about 500 candlepower. While they satisfy the coast guard requirement for a nighttime VDS (three required), you have to strike them like matches to ignite them, which can be impossible in a driving rain or in a life raft with seawater slopping in the sides. They also drip hot slag. A much better choice is the SOLAS-qualified type, which is fired by ramming home a mechanical plunger

and does not drip slag (see photo). It burns for only one minute rather than two, as with the coast guard–approved type but does so with thirty times the brilliance—15,000 candela. Some but not all SOLAS-qualified handheld red flares are also coast guard approved.

For offshore voyaging, you should also lay in a good supply of red aerial flares, which come in two basic varieties—meteor and parachute.

METEOR FLARES

Some meteor flares can be fired from their own casings, while others require a pistol-type launcher. The small Skyblazer is fired from its own casing, reaches an altitude of about 500 feet (152 m), and burns for about ten seconds. Because the Skyblazer is compact, waterproof, and inexpensive, it's a good idea to stick one in the pocket of your foul-weather jacket. However, because the Skyblazer's signal is limited to 500 candela, do not rely on it as your primary aerial flare.

Meteor flares are fired from their own canisters or a pistol-type, 12-gauge or 25 mm launcher. The

SOLAS-qualified flares are more dependable and safer to use than the standard type. (Pains Wessex)

12-gauge type reaches an altitude of about 250 feet (76 m) and burns at 15,000 candlepower for about six seconds. The 25 mm type is preferable to the 12-gauge type because, although it has the same six-second burn time, it goes higher (about 375 feet, or 115 m) and its 35,000 candlepower is more than twice as bright. A 25 mm launcher also can be used to fire parachute flares, whereas a 12-gauge launcher cannot.

By far the best flares available are those from Pains-Wessex that are SOLAS qualified. They are fired from their own canisters, reach an altitude of 1,000 feet (300 m)—as high as a ninety-story building—and burn for forty seconds at 30,000 candlepower.

PARACHUTE FLARES

The coast guard approves parachute flares that are fired from a pistol-type launcher, but these flares do not meet SOLAS standards. The 25 mm launcher is the most popular size. Pistol-launched parachute flares reach an altitude of about 1,000 feet (300 m), burn at 10,000 to 20,000 candlepower for about thirty seconds, and (theoretically) are visible for up to 40 miles (65 km). The best is Orion's 25 mm kit, in which the SOLAS-qualified red parachute flare is fired from its own canister. The units made by Pains-Wessex reach an altitude of 1,000 feet and burn at 30,000 candlepower for forty seconds.

I also suggest that you have on board several SOLAS-qualified white illumination parachute flares for search-and-rescue situations. Like the red parachute flares, white illumination flares also are fired from their own canisters and reach a 1,000-foot (300 m) altitude. They burn for only thirty seconds but do so at 80,000 candela, which can light up 2 square miles (5.2 km²) of ocean.

Whichever types of flares you choose to carry aboard your vessel, remember that they all will be stamped with an expiration date and must be replaced before that date passes. If the coast guard inspects your vessel and finds your VDSs are out-of-date, they will issue a citation.

Emergency Position-Indicating Radio Beacons

When activated in a distress situation either automatically or manually, emergency position-indicating radio beacons (EPIRBs) transmit signals to alert rescuers and guide them to an individual's location. Recreational vessels are not required to carry EPIRBs, but you should never venture offshore without at least one aboard. Those most practical for recreational use come in four varieties: type 406 and classes A, B, and C.

TYPE 406 EPIRBS

Two factors—a vast number of false alarms from the earlier generation of EPIRBs being inadvertently activated, and sharp cutbacks in the coast guard's budget—have made the coast guard reluctant to launch full-scale air-sea rescue efforts until it is reasonably sure an EPIRB signal indicates a genuine emergency. (It costs around $8,000 an hour to operate a coast guard C-130 rescue aircraft, and the average delay between the time an EPIRB signal is received and a full-scale search effort is launched is *twenty-six* hours.)

This situation led to the development of the type 406 EPIRB, which transmits signals on both 406 MHz and 121.5 MHz. The 406 MHz alerting component broadcasts a 121-bit serial number that is distinctive to it alone. When that serial number is received by a COSPAS/SARSAT satellite and relayed to a ground station, it is run through a computer at the National Oceanic and Atmospheric Administration (NOAA), which can identify the type and size of the vessel on which that particular EPIRB was installed. The computer file is based on information provided by the purchaser of the EPIRB through the return of a mandatory registration card. Once a search is launched in the general area indicated by the 406 MHz signal, rescuers home in by using the unit's 121.5 MHz signal and strobe light.

The latest advance in type 406 EPIRBs are units that have integral global positioning system (GPS) transmitters and can transmit their location to

Geostationary Search and Rescue (GEOSAR) satellites, which cover more than 95 percent of the earth's temperate waters. This precision allows rescuers to pinpoint the EPIRB's position within 330 feet (100 m) and reduce the search area to less than a third of a mile (530 m). The best of these units are ACR Electronic's Globalfix (see photo) and Northern Airborne Technology's GPIRB.

The type 406 EPIRB is offered in category 1 and category 2 units. Category 1 units must be in-stalled on the exterior of the vessel, must be capable of being launched by a hydrostatic release, and must be activated automatically. Category 2 units can be mounted inside the vessel and are manually launched and activated.

ACR markets its EPIRB Satellite 2 unit with strobe, which meets category I requirements. It is 17½ by 6¼ by 5½ inches (45 by 16 by 14 cm) and has a 12-inch (30 cm) antenna. With a battery (which must be replaced every five years), it weighs 4½ pounds (2 kg) and is designed to operate for at least forty-eight hours. It comes in a canister that is hydrostatically released when the vessel sinks to approximately 13 feet (4 m). There is also an ACR Satellite 2 unit that meets category 2 requirements.

Type 406 EPIRBs can be carried voluntarily aboard any vessel that is equipped with a VHF radio. Under the rules of the Federal Communications Commission, all EPIRBs must be licensed because they transmit radio signals. You can request this license when you file the form 506 application for your regular Ship Station Radio License. EPIRBs do not require any kind of operator permit, but you also must register them with NOAA.

CLASS A, B, S, AND C EPIRBS

Every offshore cruiser should carry a type 406 EPIRB, preferably with the GPS feature. On the theory that you might purchase a used vessel that has an older but functioning class A, B, or C EPIRB aboard, I cover those—as well as the class S type—briefly here.

Class A EPIRBs are designed primarily for offshore use aboard commercial vessels but can be used by recreational vessels as well. They are bracket mounted on the exterior of a vessel, float free if the vessel sinks, and activate automatically.

Class B EPIRBs are designed for offshore use aboard recreational vessels, are bracket mounted inside the vessel, and must be manually activated and deployed. Class B also includes the mini-B unit, which is designed to be attached to a life jacket or a survival raft.

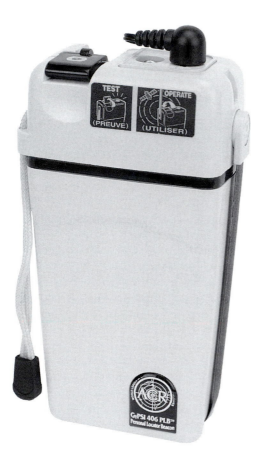

The ACR Globalfix combines the advantages of the type 406 EPIRB with an internal GPS receiver that will broadcast its position to a rescue satellite within a 100-yard (92 m) radius. (ACR Electronics)

Class S is a mini-EPIRB designed for use on the survival craft required to be carried by certain commercial vessels, but this type also may be used on life rafts aboard recreational vessels. The difference between the class B mini-EPIRB and the class S unit is that whereas the mini-B unit must be activated manually, the class S unit is attached to the raft and is activated automatically when the raft inflates.

Class A, class B (including the mini-B model), and class S EPIRBs transmit carrier signals on 121.5 and 243.0 MHz that are picked up by the joint U.S.-Russian-Canadian-French network of COSPAS/SARSAT orbiting satellites, which relay them to rescue services on the ground. Currently there are four polar-orbiting satellites in the COSPAS/SARSAT network, each of which orbits the earth every twenty-four hours. The two frequencies were chosen for EPIRB signals because 121.5 MHz is the primary emergency frequency for commercial aviation and 243.0 MHz is the primary guard frequency for military aviation. If the crews of either type of aircraft are monitoring the frequencies, they can pick up the signal as well.

Class C EPIRBs, now discontinued, were designed for use aboard recreation vessels in inland or coastal waters. They should not be used aboard bluewater cruising boats since they do not transmit on 121.5 MHz or 243.0 MHz but only on 156.75 MHz (VHF channel 15) and 156.8 MHz (VHF channel 16). Their signals cannot be picked up by overflying aircraft or satellites—only by a VHF radio. Their maximum range is advertised as 20 miles (32 km), but with their antenna at or close to water level, I doubt that would be dependable. Even if you plan to do only coastal cruising, I recommend that you carry a class B EPIRB rather than class C.

Life Rafts

Should you suffer the ultimate catastrophe and wind up in the water with your ship sunk or destroyed by fire, the most immediate danger you face is hypothermia—loss of body heat. Even 75

or 80°F (23.8–26.6°C) seawater can rob the body of dangerous amounts of heat in a few hours. For this reason, the essential lifesaving equipment of every cruising vessel must include a sturdy life raft to keep everybody out of the water until help arrives.

Life rafts come in two basic configurations: coastal and offshore. The coastal models are suitable only for vessels that will stay reasonably close to shore and in areas where help is likely to reach them within about a day. These rafts have only a single inflation ring and a single floor.

For offshore voyaging, you should carry a good ocean life raft that is large enough to accommodate at least the greatest number of people you could reasonably expect to have on board. It's really best to increase that number by two additional people. Life rafts are designed to provide only 4 square feet (0.36 m^2) of space per person. The occupants of a life raft filled to capacity would become terribly cramped in a matter of hours—not to mention days or weeks—and there would be no extra space to stow an abandon-ship bag or any other items you might be fortunate enough to salvage off your main vessel before it goes down.

Since your life could well depend on it, get a life raft with the most features you can afford. I suggest you look for the following features.

Your raft should have double flotation rings that are inflated automatically by a CO_2 cartridge within a maximum of thirty seconds after launching. It also should have a double floor to provide its occupants additional protection against hypothermia.

The major difference among the more popular life rafts sold for use on recreational vessels is the stabilization system the manufacturers employ to keep them from capsizing. For years, most life rafts offered on the recreational boating market were lightly ballasted and exhibited a dangerous tendency to ride up on the crest of a wave and tilt, which allowed wind to sweep underneath and capsize them. Once a life raft is capsized, its occupants have to get into the water to right it, exposing themselves to the effects of hypothermia. If the canopy floods during the capsize, righting the raft can be almost impossible. Several government agencies and private companies have tried to develop life raft stabilization systems to help correct this tendency.

The more expensive life rafts on the market use heavier ballasting. Switlik's six-person search-and-rescue model uses a toroidal (think of a doughnut) ballast pocket that encircles the perimeter of the raft's bottom (see photo). Switlik SAR life rafts are used aboard most U.S. Coast Guard vessels.

The life rafts made by Avon, Viking, BFA, and a number of other manufacturers are designed to meet the Icelandic Standard developed by the IMO. This stabilization system uses a series of ballast pockets in conjunction with a sea anchor. Avon's six-person Mark III model is typical of this type of raft (see photo).

Advocates of life rafts designed to the Icelandic Standard argue that since they present less resistance to wave pressure, they subject their occupants to less banging around. They say that life rafts that employ a toroidal system or a full-ballasting system present so much resistance to wave pressure that their occupants have a rougher ride. For offshore voyaging, I'll happily spend the extra money for the toroidal or fully ballasted raft and be willing to take the banging around in exchange for reducing the likelihood of capsizing.

For a life raft to be approved by the U.S. Coast Guard, its canopy must erect automatically when the raft is launched. Most life rafts inflate in that fashion. In its standard configuration, the canopy of the Switlik SAR must be erected manually. The company designs its standard rafts this way because they believe the best way to board a life raft is to jump directly into it rather than jumping into the water and then climbing aboard. Switlik argues that if the canopy is already erected, those who board it first are more likely to be injured by those who jump into it after them. To me, the argument makes sense. I also like the option of being able to lower the canopy in fair weather to air it out and give the occupants a horizon to look at, which can reduce seasickness. (Switlik makes the same raft with an automatic-erection canopy that is coast guard approved.)

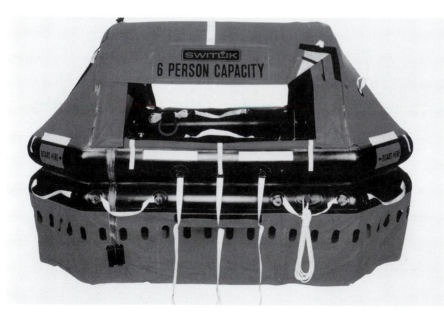

The Switlik SAR6HMKII+FL life raft features dual air chambers, a double floor, and toroidal stabilization.

SWITLIK

Avon's Ocean Life Raft is an example of a life raft built to the Icelandic Standard.

Your life raft should be mounted on deck in a canister ready for instant use (see photo next page), never in a valise stowed below decks. The most popular mounting location is the top of the aft cabin or the aft end of the upper deck. The canister should be held in its cradle by a hydrostatic release, which will automatically allow it to float free if your vessel sinks before anyone on board has time to launch the raft. Hydrostatic releases are activated by water pressure when they are submerged about 3 to 10 feet (1–3 m) below the surface.

As mentioned earlier in this chapter, you should also equip your life raft with a type 406 EPIRB, preferably with GPS included.

Even the most expensive life raft is useless if it is not in seaworthy condition and you don't know how to launch it properly. Be sure to have your raft inspected once a year by a qualified service technician, who should check its CO_2 cartridge, test the ability of its air chambers to remain inflated, and replace any supplies that are out-of-date. If at all possible, you should be present during the annual inspection (see chapter 30 for a discussion of annual life raft inspections). You also should plan exactly what you would do in the event you need to launch your raft, and you should conduct drills periodically to make certain everyone on board knows what their responsibilities would be in an abandon-ship situation.

Chances are your life raft will never do anything more than sit on deck in its canister. But if the time ever comes when you need it, you'll be glad you

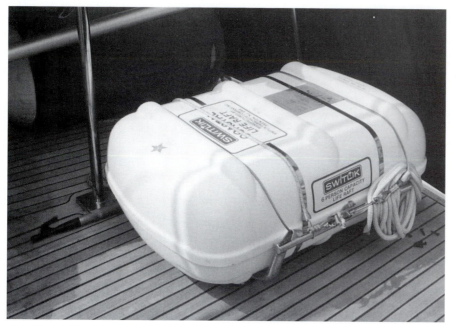

The preferred means of carrying a life raft for instant accessibility is to mount it on deck in a fiberglass canister.

took the time to buy a good one, learned how to use it, and kept it ready to save your life.

THE ABANDON-SHIP BAG

The E-pack emergency kits that come with even the most expensive life rafts are a joke. They contain no food, only minimal signaling and first-aid equipment, and only a pint (0.5 L) of water per person, which is sufficient to keep one person alive for only about five to seven days. To make matters worse, the water is packed in a can that must be opened with a can opener and can't be resealed except with a flimsy plastic lid. Since the canister most life rafts are packed in doesn't allow space for adequate additional survival supplies, you should rig a separate abandon-ship bag, stow it in a readily accessible location, and make it the first thing (along with your medical kit) that goes into your life raft after you launch it. You can buy abandon-ship bags especially designed for the purpose or use one of the large waterproof plastic bags sold for canoeing. The accompanying sidebar lists the minimum suggested contents of an offshore abandon-ship bag.

The most important thing you need in your supplemental life raft supplies is additional water. You can purchase water in sealed packets for your abandon-ship bag (eight per person) or tether plastic jugs of water to your life raft (at least half a gallon, or 2 L, per person). You also could put a solar still in your abandon-ship bag, but I've never found one that works very well. What I have found that works is the Survivor 06 hand-operated reverse-osmosis water maker (see photo). By operating its hand pump to force seawater through its reverse-osmosis membrane, you can eliminate virtually all viruses and bacteria as well as 98.4 percent of seawater's salt content. The unit can produce up to 2 pints of water per hour. The unit weighs less than 4 pounds (1.8 kg).

Most of the commercially available abandon-ship bags have built-in flotation. If you prepare your own, rig it with sufficient flotation to keep it afloat until you can get it in the life raft, and at-

Offshore Abandon-Ship Bag

Your abandon-ship bag should contain these items at the minimum.

Signaling Equipment
*1 type 406 EPIRB, preferably with GPS in-
cluded (if not packed in life raft canister)*
*3 SOLAS-qualified handheld red parachute
flares*
*3 SOLAS-qualified handheld white parachute
flares*
3 SOLAS-qualified handheld red meteor flares
2 SOLAS-qualified orange smoke canisters
12 Cyalume chemical light sticks
waterproof flashlight with spare batteries
waterproof compass

Fishing Equipment
1 fillet knife in scabbard
1 spool 30-pound (13.5 kg) test fishing line
20 feet (6 m) wire leader
3 medium fishing spoons
1 16-inch (40 cm) speargun
1 wire saw
2 propane cigarette lighters

Provisions
hand-operated water maker
1-gallon (4 L) folding plastic jug
2 packages freeze-dried food per person
*8 6-to-8 ounce (175–235 mL) packages dis-
tilled water per person*

Clothing
1 long-sleeved shirt per person
1 sun visor or billed cap per person
1 pair sunglasses per person
1 thermal blanket per person
2 rolls toilet paper in self-sealing plastic bag

Medical Supplies
1 vial seasickness pills
2 tubes sunburn cream
1 jar petroleum jelly
1 tube antiseptic ointment
1 vial Demerol pain pills
1 roll bandages
1 roll adhesive tape

tach a 50-foot (15 m) floating line to give you a better chance of grabbing it.

There will be certain items you probably won't want to put in the abandon-ship bag but would need if you had to leave your main vessel. These would include such items as any special medica-

tions you require, eyeglasses, your passport, and several dollars' worth of currency.

Now that we've considered the general topic of cruising safely, we can turn to the specifics of preparing for medical emergencies.

Preparing for Medical Emergencies

You are plowing into a stiff head sea 50 miles (80 km) offshore. One of your anchors appears to be working its way loose from its bow roller, and a crew member goes forward to secure it. She slips on the wet foredeck. Her head strikes a bow cleat, knocking her unconscious and inflicting a nasty gash on her head. Would you have the knowledge and supplies aboard to deal with such a serious medical emergency until you could get her to professional help?

Most of us in the United States suffer from the 911 syndrome; we take for granted that emergency medical assistance is always just moments away. But at sea, you are on your own. Emergency medical personnel call the first sixty minutes following a medical trauma the Golden Hour because treatment administered—or not administered—during that brief time can be literally a matter of life or death. As a skipper responsible for the well-being of your crew, you have a moral (and potentially legal) obligation to prepare and equip yourself to deal with virtually any medical emergency that might arise aboard your vessel.

EMERGENCY MEDICAL TRAINING

At the very least, you should attend a Red Cross Community First Aid and Safety course, which covers cardiopulmonary resuscitation (CPR) and basic first aid. Even better, do the First Aid: Responding to Emergencies course. An even better idea is to attend a Red Cross Emergency Response course. This course is designed primarily for "first responder" personnel, such as firefighters and law enforcement officers who might be the first to reach the scene of an accident. It covers the rudiments of handling everything from wounds and shock to broken bones and poisoning and covers the use of automated external defibrillators. It also would be wise to have a crew member attend one of these courses with you in case *you* are ever the patient. Some Red Cross chapters offer these training courses for free; others charge a nominal fee.

Even the Emergency Response course doesn't cover everything you need to know, because it is based on the assumption that in the situations its graduates are likely to encounter, professional medical help will be less than an hour away. In cruising, especially if you like to explore the back-waters, you could easily find yourself in situations where even airborne medical help is twenty-four or more hours away (in extreme cases, a lot more). One school of thought says that if amateurs try to perform more involved medical procedures than those covered in the Emergency Response course, they are likely to do more harm than good. The same school of thought also worries that people who go beyond the procedures they have been cer-tified to perform are exposing themselves to poten-tial legal liabilities. My attitude is that if the doctor is many hours (perhaps even days) away and a life is hanging in the balance, anything I can do to help save that life is better than letting the person die. On the legal side, I'd trust in a provision of the Federal Boat Safety Act of 1971 called the Good Samari-tan Act, which protects individuals who render aid to the victims of boating accidents from being held liable for civil damages as long as they acted as a reasonably prudent person might under similar cir-cumstances. One way to get much of the instruction you might find valuable is to attend the two- to three-day courses offered by Medical Advisory Systems, which I discuss later in this chapter.

EMERGENCY MEDICAL SUPPLIES AND EQUIPMENT

The medical supplies aboard your vessel should be appropriate to the type of cruising you will be doing and should be stowed in their own contain-ers, which themselves should be stowed in their own lockers with their locations clearly marked on the outside. Everyone on board should know where your vessel's medical supplies are kept, but no one should go into them without informing you so that you can keep track of their contents and re-place consumed items as soon as possible. In ap-pendix 3, you'll find a list of the medical supplies you should consider having on board for both coastal and offshore cruising.

In coastal cruising, you should at least carry a true first-aid kit to allow you to deal with medical emer-gencies until you can get the victim to professional medical assistance. You can make up your own, us-ing the list in appendix 3 as a guide, or buy one of the prepackaged versions, such as the Coastal Cruis-ing Pak by Survival Technologies Group (STG).

For offshore cruising, you also should carry a trauma kit to deal with serious injuries until you reach professional assistance or until a doctor or paramedic can reach you. Again, you can make up your own trauma kit or buy one of the prepackaged varieties. Some of the basic items required in a comprehensive trauma kit are pro-vided in STG's Trans-Ocean Medical Pak, but the prepackaged kit will require a number of ad-ditions. A less expensive trauma kit for inshore crusing is made by Practical Trauma. It doesn't contain all the first-aid supplies you need for cruising inshore, but it's a good start.

In most cases, it will be possible to carry the med-ications you should have on board without getting into controlled substances. Should you have a legit-imate need to carry controlled substances, however, you can do so quite legally provided your vessel is documented. Under the *Code of Federal Regula-tions*, part 21, section 2, a U.S.-licensed physician may legally write prescriptions for controlled sub-stances that are made out to the name of a docu-mented vessel and marked "Ship's Stores." The physician must notify the Drug Enforcement Ad-ministration (DEA) of his prescription of such sub-stances by filing DEA form 222. He also must file an annual report with the DEA on the disposition of such substances. (Physicians who regularly pre-scribe such medications file both reports as a matter of course. You would not be asking the physician to go to a great deal of trouble just for you.)

Information regarding controlled-substance medications prescribed in this manner must be en-tered in the ship's log, and the controlled sub-stances themselves must be kept under lock and key. As the vessel's captain, you may dispense those medications, but only under the control of a licensed physician (radio or satellite telephone contact has been interpreted as meeting this requirement), and you must enter into the log the date, the quantity, and the name of the individual to whom you dispensed them. Handling them in this manner conforms to the regulations of the International Maritime Organization (IMO), to which the United States is a signatory, and should help keep you from running afoul of the laws regarding such substances in any nation that is an IMO signatory. When clearing customs in some countries, you may be required to declare any controlled substances on your vessel and most certainly should do so.

EMERGENCY MEDICAL REFERENCE

Be sure to have on board a good book on handling medical emergencies. The most detailed I've seen is *International Medical Guide for Ships: Including the Ship's Medicine Chest*, published by the World Health Organization (WHO). This is a hardcover, loose-leaf book written for amateurs who are charged with medical responsibilities aboard merchant vessels and covers everything from ankle sprains to zinc deficiency. (See contact information in the resources appendix.)

If you will be cruising tropical waters, you should carry a reference to potential dangers from such marine creatures as jellyfish and stingrays and the treatment of any injuries they inflict. The best works I have seen on the subject are *A Medical Guide to Hazardous Marine Life*, by Paul S. Auerbach, M.D., and *Pisces Guide to Venomous and Toxic Marine Life of the World*, by Patricia Cunningham and Paul Goetz (see resources appendix).

SCUBA DIVING EMERGENCIES

Make certain anyone aboard your vessel who will be scuba diving is properly certified and never dives without a buddy. You also should brush up on the proper handling of a diver with a suspected air embolism (place the person on the left side so the heart is at the lowest part of the body, elevate the feet, and administer pure oxygen) and know the location of the nearest recompression chamber in the area you'll be cruising. An excellent not-for-profit organization of which any cruising diver should be a member is Divers Alert Network (DAN; see contact information in the resources appendix), which covers the United States, Canada, and the Caribbean. For a nominal annual membership fee, DAN offers a twenty-four-hour hotline through which it can provide medical advice and assistance on handling diving accidents and can coordinate the evacuation of a diving-accident victim to the nearest hyperbaric chamber. In a diving emergency, even nonmembers can use the number, and the organization will accept collect calls. DAN also offers various levels of insurance that pays up to $250,000 for any medical expenses involved in treating the effects of a diving-related accident. Since such accidents often involve air-ambulance evacuation and lengthy treatment, they can be horrendously expensive.

IMMUNIZATIONS

If you will be visiting other countries, you and your crew will require certain immunizations and may want to have others even though they aren't required. Once you have drawn up your cruising itinerary, there are a number of sources for up-to-date information regarding the immunizations required or recommended for the countries you'll be visiting. If your family physician can't supply the information, your local health department should have a current copy of *Health Information for International Travel*, published by the U.S. Public Health Service (PHS; see resources appendix), and should receive the periodic bulletins the PHS mails out to update it. You also can get current information from PHS Quarantine Stations in New York, Miami, Chicago, Los Angeles, San Francisco, Seattle, and Honolulu. If all else fails, call the Foreign Travel Division of the U.S. Public

Health Service's Centers for Disease Control and Prevention in Atlanta, Georgia (see contact information in the resources appendix).

Make certain to find out which immunizations you'll need well in advance of your planned departure since some of them could require a series of shots that must be given as much as two to six weeks apart. Immunization shots normally can be given by your family physician or county health department. Make sure you get a record of your vaccinations and the dates they were administered in the form of a validated International Certificate of Vaccination, which is approved by the World Health Organization; keep it with your passport.

MEDICAL CHECKUPS

Before embarking on any extensive cruise to areas where medical services may not be immediately available, you should be certain all crew members and guests undergo an up-to-date physical exam, inform you of any medical problems they have, and carry sufficient supplies of any special medications they require. Vital medications should be carried in sealable plastic bags next to their bunks so they can grab them rapidly should you have to abandon ship. You and your crew also should have dental checkups and attend to any sensitive teeth that might cause problems. A toothache at sea is hell.

EMERGENCY MEDICAL COMMUNICATIONS

The steps outlined above should prepare you to deal with most medical emergencies you are likely to encounter in cruising, But what if you are in the boondocks and someone on board your boat has a life-threatening emergency you really can't handle yourself—say, a heart attack or a ruptured appendix? The best thing you can do is make sure you can communicate with a doctor from wherever you might be. One way to do that is to subscribe to Medical Advisory Systems (MAS; see

contact information in the resources appendix). This is a private company that serves merchant ships and the offshore oil industry but also operates a program for recreational boaters. For a membership fee plus a charge each time you use the service, MAS maintains your medical history in its computerized files and provides you with a twenty-four-hour hotline through which you can reach its attending physicians, who are on round-the-clock standby at its headquarters, or a network of other physicians who work with them around the world. You can access the hotline through a satellite telephone or Coastal or High Seas radiotelephone operator or call the company directly over single-sideband (SSB) radio. The company continuously monitors 2182.0 and 16590.0 kHz and every five seconds automatically scans five other SSB fre- quencies: 4983.0, 7952.0, 12327.0, 16450.0, and 22722.0 kHz.

For additional fees, MAS can also provide you with a list of recommended medical supplies that should be carried on your vessel depending on its size and the number in its crew, a guide to their use, the supplies themselves, and a basic emergency medical procedures manual. You also can participate in a three-day advanced first-aid Response to Injury and Illness at Sea training course, which MAS stages quarterly in Annapolis, Maryland. I have not attended the course, but I understand it is excellent.

Another possible means of getting in contact with help in a hurry is to get yourself an amateur radio operator's license and carry a radio aboard that is capable of operating on the ham frequencies. Ham operators can be pretty fantastic friends in a crunch They have disaster networks that deal with emergencies and physicians they can get to in a hurry. Often, a ham operator will be able to connect you with medical help more quickly than any government agency.

Now that we've got your boat at the dock, properly rigged and ready to go, we can delve into the fun stuff: handling the boat in both routine and emergency situations.

PART THREE

Boat Handling

Getting Under Way

If you are concerned about your ability to handle the cruiser you've purchased and commissioned, you might want to hire a professional captain to work with you around home (or even better, accompany you on a short cruise) to get you started right. "When we decided to do some long-distance cruising," says Frank Glindmeier, who with his wife, Lee, ran their 48-foot (14.6 m) displacement vessel *Summer Wind* a total of 35,000 miles (56,450 km), which included an 18,000-mile (29,000 km) voyage from Florida to Alaska and back, "we were stepping up from a 23-footer [7 m] and were a little overwhelmed by the difference in our new boat's size and handling. We hired a delivery skipper who had a lot of experience in the same kind of boat we had bought to come aboard with us for a week or so. What little he charged was a heck of a lot cheaper than what we'd have spent if we'd seriously damaged the boat. Working with him also saved us a lot of potential embarrassment and assured us we really knew what we were doing rather than just winging it."

TAKING AN INITIAL SHAKEDOWN CRUISE

Start off easy. Instead of heading for the back of beyond on your first voyage, take a shakedown cruise in an area where you can get help if you need it but that offers a wide range of new cruising grounds and experiences. Be sure the cruise includes both offshore running and night running and is long enough to give both yourself and your boat a real test.

Before you depart on your shakedown cruise, be sure that you have all the necessary safety equipment aboard and it is working properly, that you have your compasses compensated, and that you know your boat's maximum, fully loaded draft exactly. Make certain your depth-sounder is accurately calibrated to read total water depth, and set its alarm to sound when the water's depth is within about 5 feet (1.5 m) of your vessel's draft. You also should carefully measure your vessel's structural height above water in a variety of configurations, an activity that will be critical in figuring bridge clearances. One figure should be your vessel's maximum vertical clearance with its communications and navigation antennas raised; another should be with them lowered. If conditions really get tight, you also should know how low a bridge you can sneak under by lowering your radar mast and bimini top. Also measure the height of your eye at both the pilothouse and the flying bridge steering station. (In chapter 19, I explain how to use that figure to determine approximate distance to objects in the water and to the shore.)

Before departing on your shakedown cruise, it's also a good idea to have a laboratory do an analysis of your lubricating oil and then have the process repeated at least every five hundred operating hours. Any significant changes relative to the benchmarks you've established will help alert you to potential problems inside your engine(s).

During your shakedown cruise, plan to develop some basic information about your vessel's operation and performance that you will use over and over. Make careful notes, for instance, on how much engine oil, marine gear oil, and cooling water your engines use under normal conditions and write down their operating temperatures and pressures. You might want to mark normal maximums on the gauges themselves with tiny strips of red tape to alert you if they're exceeded.

Two other basic factors you should determine accurately during your shakedown cruise are your vessel's speed over the bottom and her fuel consumption at a number of different revolutions per minute (rpm) settings in calm water. You can use the figures you establish later to determine how those factors are affected by adverse winds, currents, and heavy seas.

RPM and Speed Curve

To develop an rpm and speed curve for your cruiser, you can use a series of runs over any known distance, but the easiest way is to use your global positioning system (GPS) receiver to tell you how fast you're going at any given rpm and when you have run a mile (1.6 km). If your vessel

is not equipped with GPS, you can make your runs over one of the measured mile courses you'll find indicated on your charts.

If most of your cruising will be in coastal waters—other than the Intracoastal Waterway (ICW)—or the open ocean, set your GPS to read out in nautical miles or select a measured nautical mile course. Figure your vessel speed in knots because, in working with the charts for those areas, you normally will figure distances in nautical miles (see page 6 on converting statute to nautical miles).

If you will do most of your cruising in the ICW, the Western Rivers (the Mississippi River and its tributaries plus other designated rivers), or the Great Lakes, set your GPS to read out in statute miles (or use a measured statute mile course) and figure your speed in statute miles per hour because that is the unit of measurement used in the charts of those areas.

It's best to conduct your speed tests with full fuel and water tanks, with your vessel loaded with about the maximum stores you will have on board during a typical cruise, and with its bottom clean. If possible, conduct your test at slack water. In any event, at each throttle setting from about 900 rpm to your engine's (or engines') maximum revolutions—in about 50 rpm increments—make at least one run over the course in each direction to make sure you offset the effects of any current that might be running.

With the accuracy of GPS today, you can use this instrument to get speed figures. At any given rpm, run a steady course until the speed over ground (SOG) figure steadies. Record this figure. Then reverse course and run the reciprocal again until the speed settles down. Average the two readings.

If your cruiser has twin engines, make pairs of runs with both engines operating at the rpm settings you select, then duplicate the runs with only one engine running at each of those same rpm settings to determine the effect running on one engine will have on your vessel's speed. In the case of a diesel-powered full-displacement vessel or a semi-displacement vessel operated at displacement speeds, you may be surprised to find that at virtually any rpm setting you select, operating on one engine will give you about 80 percent of the speed you get running both engines at that same rpm. Operating on only one engine, however, will not cut your fuel consumption in half. The engine operating by itself will use about 10 percent more fuel than it will when running in tandem with the other engine, even though its rpm remains the same. This is because its governor rack will deliver more fuel to the engine to offset the increased resistance it is encountering.

If you will develop your speed curve by running a measured course, time your runs with a stopwatch and compute speed with the formula

$$s = 60\frac{d}{t}$$

where d equals distance run (1 nautical or statute mile) and t equals time. The formula is easier to work if you convert the seconds in the time part of your equation into tenths of a minute by dividing them by 60.

Once you have computed your vessel's speed at different rpm settings, create an rpm and speed curve by plotting the information on graph paper with engine rpm in hundreds across the bottom and speed in either knots or statute miles per hour up the left-hand side. Some cruisers find it more convenient to then translate the graph information into chart form.

Fuel Consumption Curve

It's best to base your fuel consumption figures on gallons per hour (GPH) at various rpm settings. If you install fuel-flow meters on the fuel lines serving your engine(s) and your AC (alternating current) generator, they will measure fuel flow and will give you GPH readouts directly during your rpm and speed tests. Another way to measure fuel consumption is to reroute your fuel supply so that all your diesel machinery temporarily runs off a single calibrated day tank. Using that method, it's best to run your vessel in calm water at each of the rpm increments you elect to chart and note fuel consumption over a one-hour period for each setting. However you measure fuel consumption, chart it on graph paper with engine rpm in hundreds across the bottom and fuel consumption in gallons per hour up the left-hand side.

Once you have speed and fuel consumption curves developed for your vessel, you can use them to compute all manner of essential information, such as your vessel's range at a particular rpm setting and an estimate of the fuel required for a particular leg of a voyage (which we'll discuss in detail later in this chapter). If you get into the habit of noting in your ship's log the length of time you run at various rpm settings during a typical day's cruise, you also can keep up with approximate fuel consumption and about how much fuel is left in your tanks. The figures you develop using that method are likely to be more accurate than relying on your vessel's fuel gauges, most of which give you only a very general idea of how much fuel you actually have on board.

If you must rely on float-type fuel gauges to keep up with the amount of fuel you have on board, you'll find that the configuration of the tank they serve can make their readings very confusing. You may well find, for instance, that it takes many hours of running for the gauge to go from full to three-quarters but only an hour or so to go from one-quarter to empty. The reason is that most tanks recessed in a vessel's keel are in the shape of a V, but the gauge reflects only the vertical distance its float travels as fuel is consumed. The float's rate of fall, then, is much slower in the top half of the V, which has greater volume, than it is in the bottom half of the V, which has less volume. Here's a technique that will help offset that inherent problem: with your tanks essentially empty, fill them in about 20-gallon (75 L) increments and note the gauge reading after each increment. You're likely to find, for example, that when the float gauge on a 200-gallon (750 L) capacity tank reads one-quarter, the tank actually contains only about 25 gallons (95 L) of fuel, not 50 gallons (190 L); when the gauge reads one-half, the tank contains only about 60 gallons (225 L) of fuel rather than 100 gallons (380 L); and at three quarters, the tank contains only about 125 gallons (475 L) of fuel rather than 150 gallons (565 L).

Computing your speed and tracking your fuel consumption on subsequent runs over known distances at consistent rpm settings when you are running against adverse winds and current will tell you how those factors are affecting your vessel's performance. Computing these factors under those conditions after your vessel's bottom becomes fouled also will show you how they are affected by accumulated growth and will convince you of the wisdom and economy of cleaning your boat's hull frequently.

After your shakedown cruise, allow yourself a reasonable length of time back at your home base to fix anything that broke along the way, replace anything that didn't work right, and learn what you determined you didn't know. Once you get all those things taken care of, you'll probably be ready to handle whatever comes your way.

PLANNING A DAILY CRUISING SCHEDULE

By this point, you've probably conceived the grand design of your first major cruise. Now comes the nitty-gritty part of planning each day's run to insure it's as pleasant as possible and to avoid any adverse factors that might lurk in your path.

An ideal daily cruising schedule might allow you to depart the dock or anchorage about nine in the morning, run until about an hour before dark, and then snug up in a quiet anchorage or tie up in a comfortable marina for the night. There will, however, be precious few times when conditions will allow you to follow an ideal cruising schedule.

The planning of any day's run begins with the basic documents you have on board that tell you what you are likely to encounter. See appendix 1 for a list of the documents you might want to con-sider including in your ship's library. With a good selection of these documents aboard, you'll be in position to take into account the basic factors you need to consider in planning a daily cruise:

Weather

If the forecast for the weather along your planned route calls for high winds, heavy seas, or fog, you may be better off to not depart at all but instead to wait for more auspicious conditions. Chapter 22 has a good deal more about interpreting the various sources of weather information available to you and how you can do some forecasting based on your own observations of local conditions.

Distance Versus Daylight

The local mean time of sunrise and sunset—which you can calculate from tables 4 and 5 of the *Tide Tables* (see resources appendix)—will determine the amount of daylight you will have to make a particular day's run. By comparing that figure to your vessel's cruising speed, you can compute the distance you can expect to cover under ideal circumstances. The hours of daylight available, however, may be only part of the story, and your run may have to be considerably shorter. In tropical areas, for instance, where patches of coral heads and unmarked channels are a primary concern, you may have to delay your departure until around 10 A.M. and plan to get into an anchorage by around 4 P.M. because only during those hours is the sun high enough in the sky to allow you to read the bottom clearly.

If the distance you plan to cover between ports or anchorages (especially if an offshore run is involved) requires you to make some of the run at night, the general rule is that you want to arrive in daylight, if at all possible.

Tidal Range and Currents

In relatively shallow cruising grounds like the Bahamas, your *Coast Pilots*, *Tide Tables*, and cruising guides will warn of areas where tidal range may force you to schedule a run at those times when there is enough water over a shoal or bank to allow you to cross it. In more northerly latitudes, your *Coast Pilots* and *Tidal Current Tables* will alert you to heavy tidal or river currents through narrow passages, which can run up to 10 knots—in some places, even more. By using your *Tide Tables*, you can construct a schedule that allows you to ride the ebb or flood going the way you want to go, avoid strong currents running in the opposite direction, or transit difficult areas during periods of slack water.

One of the most dramatic examples I've encountered of the impact of tidal current flow on a daily cruising schedule was running the Reversing Falls at St. John in the Canadian province of New Brunswick. At low water, the level of the St. John River is some 16 feet (5 m) above that of the Bay of Fundy, into which it flows. At the river's mouth, that difference creates a 1,200-foot (366 m) south-flowing waterfall, which is the equal of some of the white-water rapids on the Colorado River. At high water, the Bay of Fundy is 9 feet higher than the St. John, which creates a somewhat less chaotic waterfall flowing in the opposite direction. About two hours before high water, the level of the two bodies of water is virtually equal, making a calm and easily navigable millpond of what a few hours earlier is a raging rapid.

Bridge Clearances

If your charts show any fixed bridges along your planned route whose vertical clearance is anywhere near your vessel's maximum height above the water with your communications and navigation antennas lowered, check their clearances to determine whether (and when) you will have room to pass beneath them. (If you aren't familiar with figuring bridge clearances, you'll find the clearest discussion of the topic in the Tides and Currents chapter in *Chapman Piloting: Seamanship and Boat Handling*. See the resources appendix.) In doing your calculations, remember that the bridge clearances printed on nautical charts normally are based on heights above mean high water, which is the average of all high-water levels. Unusually high spring tides, sustained wind from certain quarters, and upland water runoff can result in predicted high water at the bridge actually being higher than mean high water, in which case the clearance would be less than is indicated on the chart. Also remember that all times listed in the *Tide Tables* are standard time, and don't forget to allow for daylight saving time if it is in effect at the time you will be passing under the bridge.

As a practical matter, once you approach a bridge about which you are concerned, you usually can call the bridge tender on VHF channel 13 to ask what its clearance is at that particular time, or you can read its clearance gauge to make certain that unusual factors have not reduced the clearance below your acceptable minimum.

Bridge and Lock Restricted Operating Hours

During certain hours (usually about 7–9 A.M. and 4–7 P.M. on weekdays), many bridges, especially along the ICW, are closed to waterborne traffic or open only on the hour or half hour. Locks use the gravitational flow of water for their operation and during dry periods in some areas limit the number of lockings each day. In a few instances, waterways pass through military reservations and may be closed for training exercises. One such area that comes to mind is the stretch of the ICW between Swansboro and Snead's Ferry, North Carolina, which passes through the Marine Corps' Camp Lejeune.

Coast pilots list standard hours of restricted bridge and lock operations and closings due to military exercises, but those times can change fairly often and vary with the seasons. Your best sources of information about such restrictions normally will be cruising guides, other cruisers who have recently passed through an area, and local marina operators. If your day's run includes a bridge or lock with restricted operating hours, you may need to depart a little early or increase your normal cruising speed to arrive at the bridge when it's open or at the lock when it's accepting traffic in the direction you want to go. It isn't usually a good idea to stick to your normal cruising routine and figure that if you arrive at the bridge or lock when it is not operating you can just anchor off until it opens. Many bridges and locks with restricted operating hours are located in narrow channels that offer little anchoring room, have poor holding ground, and are beset with troublesome currents.

Fuel Consumption

Double-check to make certain you have enough fuel on board to travel the distance involved, plus a comfortable reserve. When opportunities to take on fuel are numerous, there are two schools of thought on fueling. Some cruisers—usually the owners of semidisplacement and full-displacement boats—fill their tanks every chance they get on the theories that keeping their tanks full reduces condensation, which leads to less water in their fuel and cuts down on bacterial contamination (both of which are true); that they've always got a more than generous reserve; and that if they get into heavy weather, the added weight will give their vessel increased stability. Some planing hull owners feel that hauling around the extra weight of more fuel than they need for a particular run reduces their speed and fuel efficiency, so they take on only enough fuel to reach their destination—plus a comfortable reserve. I've no quarrel with either approach, as long as there is enough fuel aboard to deal with any conceivable contingency.

The basic figure of how much fuel you'll need for a particular run will come from the distance to be covered taken from your electronic chart system or nautical charts compared with the chart of gallons per running hour under different conditions and at different rpm settings you worked out on your shakedown cruise.

In projecting your fuel requirements for a particular run, be sure you are comparing apples to apples. If your vessel's speed figures are in knots and you happen across a chart that lists distances in both nautical and statute miles, be sure to use nautical miles in computing distances. If you must start with statute miles, multiply by 0.87 to convert them to nautical miles. If you need to convert nautical miles to statue miles, multiply by 1.15.

In addition to the miles you plan to cover, don't forget to make a generous allowance for the fuel you'll need to deal with any adverse currents, winds, or seas you're likely to encounter, and leave yourself at least a 20 percent reserve to cover difficulties you are unable to anticipate. If the amount of fuel required for a particular run gets close to the maximum capacity of your vessel's fuel tanks as listed on your vessel's specifications sheet, you should reduce that total capacity figure by about 10 percent before you begin your calculations to determine your usable fuel. This reduction is necessary because the ends of the pickup tubes in a diesel fuel system are normally kept about 2 inches (5 cm) off the bottom of a tank to avoid sucking up the water and sludge that accumulates there. As a result, you have no way to get about 10 percent of the fuel actually in each of your tanks into your engine(s).

Your vessel's rate of fuel consumption normally won't be a problem in inland cruising, where fuel is available every 50 or 60 miles (80–95 km). But in offshore cruising or voyages into the boondocks, where fuel pumps may be few and far between, it can be critical.

Course Plotting

If your day's run involves only running down clearly marked channels, all you have to do is make certain the electronic charts you'll need along the way are loaded into your chart system or that your paper charts are handy to the helm and organized in sequence. If the day's run involves an offshore passage, you should carefully plot your course on your charting system or paper charts before you leave the dock or anchorage (chapter 20 discusses this topic in detail).

With your day's run planned and plenty of fuel aboard, you're finally ready to get under way.

EVERYTHING SHIPSHAPE?

During your cruising life, you're going to be getting your vessel under way thousands of times, so develop a standard routine for doing it right and follow that routine religiously.

First, make a quick mental check to be sure you've taken care of everything ashore. Your preparations should have included filing a float plan, which includes your itinerary, with a relative or friend, making arrangements for them to send someone looking for you if you fail to check in on schedule, and leaving instructions on how to reach you in an emergency. (The procedures for contacting you via VHF or SSB radiotelephone are explained fully in chapter 21.)

Once all your shoreside preparations are complete, take a walk around the entire perimeter of your vessel to make sure anything on deck is properly secured (particularly your ground tackle) and walk through your boat's interior to make sure anything that could come loose in a significant sea is also secured.

Fire up your radios and navigation electronics to make sure they're working properly, and double-check to see that all the charts and plotting instruments, your binoculars, and any reference materials—such as cruising guides or *Coast Pilots* or *Tide Tables*—you'll need for the run are handy to the helm.

Next, go through your prestart engine room check. Check the oil and water levels in your main engines (and in your electrical generator, if you have one) and top them off if necessary. Engine oil quantity and pressure is critical to the proper operation of a diesel engine, so always make sure the oil level is right at the full level on the dipstick and not more than about ⅙ inch (4 mm) above or below it. Your engines' coolant,

however, will expand as it is heated, so leave the water level about 2 inches (5 cm) below the top of the filler tube. Check the bowl of your water and fuel separator(s) and drain off any water that has accumulated, and make a visual sweep of the entire engine room to look for frayed wiring and fuel or oil leaks. For the first few days under way, it's a good idea to make a list of all the items you need to include in your prestart check and tick off each one so you don't forget anything important. In time, the procedure will become second nature. After this initial departure check, you'll probably find it more practical to check your engine room at the end of each day's cruising so you will know that everything is ready for you to get under way the following morning.

In addition to the above routine, which you should go through daily, there are other inspections you should conduct every week or so: check all the belts on your engine for cracking, glazing and proper tension (when pressed halfway between their pulleys, they should deflect about half an inch, or 1 cm, but not more); check your batteries for proper electrolyte levels and make sure their connections are tight and free of corrosion; and check the fluid levels in your marine gears with their associated engine running at idle. Checking a gear's fluid level with its engine off can give you a false reading.

If you plan to run your generator while under way, now's the time to fire it up, shift your ship's service over to it, disconnect your dockside connections such as power, water, telephone, and cable TV lines, and store your cables and hoses properly. (Always disconnect the dockside end of your power cable before you disconnect the end that plugs into the boat; that way you are not dealing with a "hot" connection, which could fall off into the water and cause an electrical short or fire.)

Back on deck, take a look around at the wind, the state of the current or tide, and any boats fore and aft of you to see what undocking will involve and plan your departure accordingly. (We'll talk more about the specifics of undocking later in this chapter.)

ENGINE STARTING TIPS

Don't start your main engines until you are satisfied that everything aboard your vessel and in the engine room is shipshape and you are ready to cast off. In the course of your cruising, you're sure to see a lot of guys crank up their diesel engines and let them barely idle at around 500 rpm for a half hour or so before they get under way on the theory they're "warming them up." Aside from being annoying as the devil to everybody else in the marina or the anchorage, running your engines for that long at that low an idle is not good for them. The optimum operating temperature for a diesel is 170 to 185°F (76.6–85°C). At anything below about 600 rpm, its internal temperature won't get over about 100°F (37.7°C), which isn't hot enough to get its oil, coolant, or fuel systems flowing properly. Idling for prolonged periods causes incomplete fuel combustion, which can dilute the oil in the engine's crankcase, allows the formation of lacquer or gummy deposits on valves, pistons and rings, and leads to rapid accumulation of sludge in the crankcase. A five-minute warm-up while you check for adequate cooling water discharge and take a last minute look in your engine room is plenty.

Under the heavy load of starting a diesel engine, the temperature in its starter motor can quickly jump up to several hundred degrees. If you press the starter switch and your diesel doesn't fire within thirty seconds, release the start button and wait about two minutes to give the starter motor time to cool down before trying it again. If the engine fails to start after about four thirty-second tries, something is wrong and you need to find out what it is and correct it before casting off. When starting a diesel engine that has thoroughly cooled, a brief burst of white smoke from the exhaust is normal. It's simply condensation burning off. But if you get a heavy cloud of white smoke every time you start your engine and it lasts for more than about fifteen seconds, try this: as you press the start button, also hold in the stop button for about ten seconds; then release the stop button and

continue to hold the start button down until the engine cranks (but not more than thirty seconds). All you are doing is preheating your engine's cylinders, which allows them to burn off the condensation quicker. If you get a heavy cloud of black smoke when you start your engines and it lasts for more than about fifteen seconds, you've got a problem and need to have a qualified mechanic find out what it is and correct it.

Once you crank the engines, go ahead and run them up to about 750 rpm to help them get up to their optimal operating temperature quickly, and check your boat's transom to make sure a normal volume of cooling water is flowing out of your exhaust(s). After you depart from the dock, run your engines about ten to fifteen minutes at half throttle before you open them up to your normal cruising speed.

LEAVING THE DOCK

If you have plenty of room fore and aft and the wind and current are setting away from the dock, all you need to do is cast off your docklines, close your safety gates, and let the wind and current carry you clear. But it won't always be that simple.

Spring Lines

Problem: You're tied up to a dock port side–to. The stern of one boat is only 5 feet (1.5 m) off your bow, and the bow of another is only 5 feet off your stern. About a knot of current and 10 to 15 knots of wind are striking your vessel on the stern. If you simply cast off your docklines and try to pull out of the slip, the wind or current or both will carry you down on the vessel tied up ahead of you. How are you going to maneuver out of that space without damaging your boat or the ones fore and aft of you?

The best way to get out of the space without damaging the vessel ahead is to use a spring line. (Here we are concerned only with spring lines used for maneuvering your boat around a dock.

Spring lines are also used for tying your boat up to a dock or in a slip, and we discuss that use for them in chapter 17.) I see few skippers using spring lines to help them maneuver their boats, and most who do use them employ them incorrectly. In case you aren't intimately familiar with them, I'll go into a bit of detail.

Spring lines—often just called *springs*—are nothing more than your normal docklines used in a special way, but the terminology involving them can get a little confusing. They are designated, for instance, first by the direction they lead, then by the point at which they are attached to the vessel. Thus, you can have an after bow spring (which leads aft from a cleat at your vessel's bow) or a forward quarter spring (which leads forward from a cleat at your vessel's stern), and you can use either type on either side of your boat.

Preparing to Free a Spring

If you use a spring line to help you get away from the dock, it should be rigged before you get under way in such a way that your mate will be able to retrieve it without the assistance of anyone on shore. The best way to do this is to "double" it. To double a spring: secure its eye (loop) around the appropriate deck cleat on your vessel, run the standing part of the line around a piling or cleat on the dock, lead the tail back on board, and cleat it off on the same deck cleat that is securing the eye. (A released spring is less likely to foul if it's run around a piling "outside to inside," so it doesn't have to cross over itself—for example, on the starboard side, run an aft bow spring clockwise and a forward quarter spring counterclockwise; reverse the process on the port side. The tail rather than

A spring line doubled for easy release from aboard. Below: Note that the spring is rigged so it doesn't have to cross over itself to avoid the potential for fouling. Note also that the tail rather than the eye is the "running" end, again to avoid fouling.

the eye of a doubled spring should be the free or "running" end because the eye could get hung up on the dock or something on the dock.) Once you are clear of the dock, your mate can simply uncleat the tail of a doubled spring line, then quickly pull the standing part around the piling to bring the line back on board.

If you are springing off a line secured to a dock cleat, your mate can also cast it off without assistance from shore by hooking its eye over only one of the cleat's horns.

SPRING LINES AND DECK CLEATS

Some of the most common mistakes I see cruisers making in their use of spring lines is not properly securing them around deck cleats. A spring line's tail should always be led first to the horn of the cleat opposite to the direction from which the strain will be applied (see photo). This ensures that the angle between the axis of the part of the spring under tension and the axis of the cleat will always be 90 degrees or less, which takes full advantage of the cleat's strength. In many cases, the spring line will be led through a chock or hawsehole be-

tween the point at which it is secured on shore and the deck cleat, which significantly alters the direction from which the strain on the cleat will be applied. In such cases, the strain should be regarded as coming from the direction of the chock or hawsehole and the spring should be first led under the horn of the cleat opposite to it.

CONTROLLING TENSION ON A SPRING

There will be many situations where you will want your mate to be able to take in or let out a spring

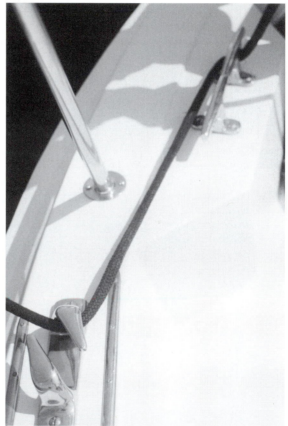

If a spring line is led through a chock or a hawsehole, the strain should be regarded as coming from the direction of the chock or hawsehole and the spring should be first led under the horn of the cleat opposite to it.

A spring hooked around only one horn of a dock cleat can be easily released by a line handler on deck.

line to control your vessel's fore and aft movement as you maneuver in tight quarters. Failure to rig the spring properly to allow the mate to safely handle the force involved can result in serious injury. The basic way of rigging the spring to control tension on it is with a half turn (see photo). Lead the spring line's tail under the horn of the deck cleat opposite to the direction from which the strain will be applied, then parallel down the side of the deck cleat, under the other horn, and back over the top of it.

A variation some cruisers use that allows the mate to handle even more force is the S-turn. Come under the horn opposite to the direction from which the strain will be applied, then go over the top of the cleat and under the other horn in the reverse direction. With either a half turn or an S-turn, even a small mate with limited physical strength can "tail" the spring and hold a boat in position or let out line as the helmsperson directs. Even a strapping mate, however, won't be able to take in on a spring line under heavy tension.

SPRINGING THE STERN OUT

In the above example, if the wind and current are setting directly onto the dock or are from astern, the best way to maneuver out of this tight spot is to force your vessel's stern away from the dock by

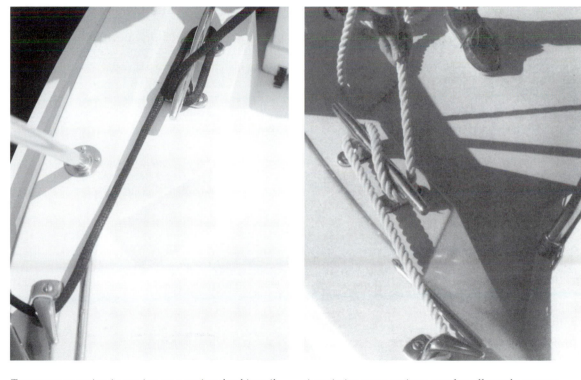

To prepare to maintain tension on a spring, lead its tail under the horn of the deck cleat opposite the direction from which the strain will be applied, then parallel down the side of the cleat, under the other horn, and back over the top of it.

A variation some cruisers use that allows the mate to handle even more strain on a spring is the S-turn, in which the line is led over the top of the cleat and under the opposite horn in the reverse direction.

going ahead against a doubled after bow spring (see illustration). To get ready to do that, double an after bow spring from your port bow cleat counterclockwise around a piling that is about one-third to halfway down the length of the vessel from the bow then back to the bow cleat, and cleat it off with no slack in it.

Springing your stern out involves making your boat pivot around a point that usually will be about a fourth of the way back from the bow. If your vessel has a stout rubrail and it is lying against a piling that is at about the pivot point and is at least 1 foot (0.3 m) above the level of your decks, pivot against that. (Be especially wary of pilings that do not extend at least a foot or so above your boat's deck because your boat's sheer could be lifted over them and cause significant damage to your hull.) If you are lying at a face dock that has no pilings, your vessel's hull will contact the edge of the dock at the pivot point. Protect the hull at that point by rigging a vertical fender on the port side about a quarter of the way back from the bow with the middle of it level with the top of the dock.

Once these preparations are complete, you're ready to spring your stern away from the dock. Man the helm from the vessel's flying bridge and have your mate cast off all docklines except the doubled after bow spring and then come aboard, shut the boarding gate, and stand by the bow cleat. Check to make certain that as you maneuver away

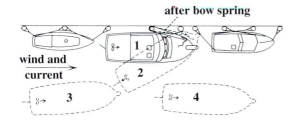

With wind and current astern, an after bow spring will prevent your vessel from striking the boat tied up ahead of you yet allow you to maneuver your stern clear of the dock.

from the dock, you won't interfere with the movement of any other vessels. Turn your helm fully toward the dock. If yours is a single-engine boat, go ahead slowly. With twin engines, slowly go ahead on the starboard engine and in reverse on the port engine. The after bow spring will keep your vessel from going forward and striking the vessel tied up in front of you, but you will still need to be careful of your bow pulpit and any anchors mounted on it. The propeller discharge against the rudder(s) will swing your stern away from the dock.

As your stern swings clear of the boat behind you, continue to pivot until your vessel's centerline is at about a 45-degree angle to the dock. Hold that position while your mate quickly uncleats the tail of the spring line from the bow cleat and casts it off, which will leave the line free to be hauled on board. The mate should bring it back aboard as quickly as possible to prevent any possibility of its falling into the water and getting fouled in your prop(s). Once the line is cast off, bring your helm amidships, continue to back until you are well clear of the vessels at the dock, and then swing your helm slightly to starboard and proceed ahead slowly. Keep your angle of departure shallow in relation to the dock. If you turn your bow too quickly to starboard and try to depart at too sharp an angle, the current could swing your stern around and force it into the vessel that was tied up ahead of you.

Springing Ahead

If wind or current or both are from dead ahead, you may find you can simply nose your bow away from the dock and the wind or current will carry you free. But if wind or current or both are penning you to the dock at an angle, you'll need to swing your bow away from the dock by backing against a forward quarter spring. This technique is neither as easy nor as effective as swinging your stern out with an after bow spring, but it's a technique worth learning and is done as follows.

Double a forward quarter spring from your vessel's port stern cleat clockwise around a dock cleat or piling that is about a third to halfway down the length of your vessel from the stern. In springing the bow out, your vessel's pivot point is going to be right at its stern. If there is a piling at your stern, you can pivot off of it using your boat's rubrail. If you're at a face dock, rig a horizontal fender at the point of your vessel's port quarter. Have your mate cast off all docklines except the doubled forward quarter spring and then come aboard, close the safety gate, and stand by the stern cleat. Check to make certain that as you maneuver away from the dock, you won't interfere with the movement of any other vessels. Turn your helm fully toward the dock. If yours is a single-engine boat, go in reverse slowly. With twin engines, go ahead slowly on the engine toward the dock and in reverse on the engine away from the dock. The forward quarter spring will keep your vessel from striking the vessel off your stern, and the propeller discharge against the rudder(s) will swing your bow away from the dock. Once your bow has swung clear of the boat in front of you and your vessel's centerline is at about a 45-degree angle to the dock, have your mate uncleat the spring line and cast it off, which will leave the line free to be hauled on board smartly to prevent its being fouled in your prop(s). As soon as the spring is cast off, you will be free to bring your helm amidships and clear the dock by going ahead.

"Walking" a Boat Sideways

If no significant wind is blowing, no strong currents are running, and yours is a twin-screw planing hull boat, another technique you may be able to use to extricate yourself from a tight spot at a face dock is to "walk" it sideways. To walk a twin-engine boat to starboard as in the undocking situation above, put the helm hard over to port and ease the port engine ahead and the starboard engine astern. The port engine going ahead will force water against its rudder to push the stern away from the dock and the bow toward it, while the starboard engine going astern will push the stern toward the dock and the bow away from it. You will probably find you need about 20 percent more

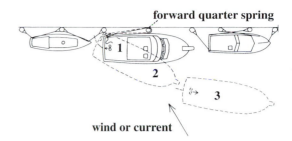

A *forward quarter spring allows you to pivot your bow into wind or current that is setting onto a dock.*

rpm on the starboard engine than on the port engine. The resulting forces will literally "walk" the boat sideways to starboard while generating only minimal forward movement.

Before you try walking your boat around a dock for the first time, it's best to practice a bit in clear water to see exactly how your boat responds. The technique generally works best with planing hull motor yachts that don't have a significant keel. The keels of semidisplacement and full-displacement twin-engine boats take such a bite on the water that it's difficult to move them sideways.

Coiling Docklines

As soon as you are clear of the dock or the slip, you or your mate should neatly coil all your docklines and stow them for the next time you need them. One good way of coiling a dockline so it

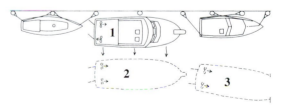

To *"walk" a vessel out of a tight spot at a dock when wind and current are not a factor, turn your helm fully toward the dock and then go forward on the engine toward the dock and in reverse on the engine away from the dock.*

won't get all tangled up is shown in the photos. By coiling your docklines this way, you keep them from getting tangled and can handle them easily. The next time you pull up to a dock, you have only to release the wrappings around the coils and shake the coils out to be ready to loop the eye over a piling or dock cleat or toss the eye end of the line to a person onshore waiting to help you tie up. (In chapter 17, we discuss why passing the eye of the line ashore rather than the tail is important.)

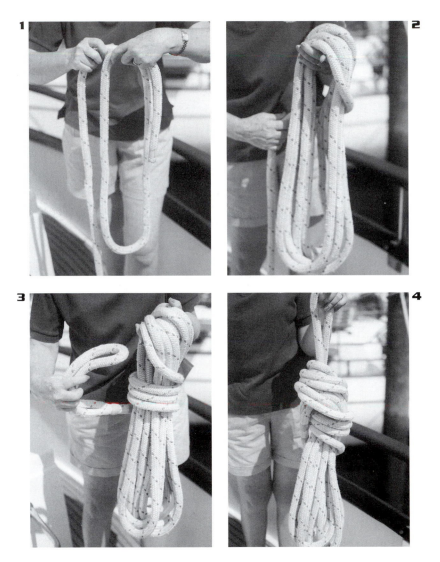

One way of coiling a dockline for stowage is to begin at the tail to form coils about 2 feet (0.6 m) in diameter (1); as you near the eye, take three or four wraps around the coils (2); then bring the eye through the loop in the top of the coils (3). You wind up with an eye by which the line can be neatly hung for stowage (4).

Handling Routine Operations Under Way

Let's assume that on this particular day's run, the weather is going to be glorious, your planned run includes no adverse tides or currents, and you don't have to schedule around bridges or locks with restricted operating hours. On even such an ideal cruising day, you are likely to encounter an incredible variety of situations with which you must be prepared to deal correctly.

THE RULES OF THE ROAD

In extended cruising, you'll be involved in thousands of situations in restricted waterways where you meet or cross courses with other boats, overtake slower boats, or are yourself overtaken by faster boats. In many of these situations, the encounters will be strictly routine and will require you to do nothing more than exercise a bit of common sense. The danger lies in those encounters when an unusual combination of circumstances or the ignorance, ineptitude, or lack of courtesy of the person running the other boat puts your vessel and those aboard it in jeopardy.

The operation of vessels in U.S. inland waters is governed by the 1983 U.S. Inland Navigation Rules (often referred to simply as the Inland Rules). The operation of vessels outside U.S. inland waters is governed by the 1992 International Regulations for Prevention of Collisions at Sea (usually referred to simply as the 92 COLREGS). The dividing lines between inland and international waters normally run from headland to headland, are as short and direct as possible, run as perpendicular as possible to vessel traffic flow, are precisely defined by physical objects that are readily visible (such as aids to navigation or prominent structures on shore), and are marked on nautical charts by dashed magenta lines, that are sometimes identified as the COLREGS Demarcation Line, and described in detail in *Coast Pilots* and the Inland Rules. In some cases, this demarcation line is much farther inland than you might expect, and entire bays, harbors, and inlets are subject to the International Rules rather than the Inland

Rules. These include most of the Down East coast of Maine and Puget Sound in the northwestern United States. At all times, you must know which navigation rules cover the waters in which you are operating as well as what your responsibilities and proper course of action are under the appropriate section of the applicable Rules of the Road.

The discussion that follows is intended not as a comprehensive explanation of the various navigation rules but only as a brief review of how they are normally applied in the real world of cruising. If you are not intimately familiar with the rules, you should get a copy of the U.S. Coast Guard publication *Navigation Rules, International–Inland*—which is required to be aboard all self-propelled vessels greater than 39.4 feet (12 m) in length—and study it thoroughly. This chapter covers only what you should know about operating under the Inland Rules. Vessel operation in international waters and the waters of other countries is covered in chapter 36.

Right-of-Way Situations

The Inland Rules are quite specific on the operation of vessels in meeting, crossing, and overtaking situations when the danger of a collision exists. In such situations, both refer to the boat that has the right-of-way and should maintain its course and speed as the "stand on" vessel and the boat that does not have the right-of-way and must alter its course or speed if necessary to avoid a collision as the "give way" vessel. In this discussion, I use more familiar and customary terminology by describing the former as the *privileged vessel* and the latter as the *burdened vessel*. Note also that in the following discussion, the term *passing* can refer to any encounter between vessels covered by the rules. For clarity's sake, it is not used here, however, to describe a situation in which one vessel overtakes another; such a situation is referred to only by the term *overtaking*.

WHISTLE SIGNALS

In the Inland Rules, you'll find numerous references to the whistle signals that are required in right-of-way situations. These whistle signals consist of short blasts, which last about one second each, and prolonged blasts, which last four to six seconds each. You will find that many—in fact most—skippers of both commercial and recreational vessels don't use whistle signals. One reason is that technically the right-of-way rules don't come into effect until the possibility of a collision between two vessels exists. A more common reason for their being omitted is simple ignorance, either of the fact that they are required or of the signals that are appropriate in a given situation. I don't recommend that you run up and down the waterways like Steamboat Willie and blast out whistle signals in every instance in which they might be used. I do, however, urge you to familiarize yourself with the signals required in right-of-way situations and be prepared to use them properly anytime the possibility of a collision between your vessel and another exists or you receive a whistle signal from another vessel that requires an appropriate response from you.

The rules allow vessels encountering each other in a right-of-way situation to agree to the manner of meeting, crossing, or overtaking by VHF radiotelephone and omit the sound signals otherwise required. That should be done by one of the vessels calling the other on channel 16. (In a meeting situation, either vessel may initiate the call. In a crossing situation, the vessel that is privileged or believes itself to be privileged normally initiates the call. In an overtaking situation, the overtaking vessel should initiate the call.) Once the vessel being called responds on channel 16, the vessel initiating the call should propose moving to channel 13, which is specifically for bridge-to-bridge communications and on which modern VHF radios automatically reduce their output power to 1 watt. Once the two vessels make contact on channel 13 (using abbreviated operating procedures that omit call signs), the vessel initiating the call should propose the side on which it intends to leave the vessel it is encountering, and the vessel being called should agree, propose another method of passing, or request the calling vessel to take some other action.

Unfortunately, it seldom works that way. In most cases where VHF is used to communicate during a right-of-way situation, the vessel operator initiating the call will simply state his request or intentions on channel 16 and the operator of the vessel being called will respond on the came channel. There are two things wrong with that. One is that it is an improper use of channel 16, which is strictly for calling, safety, and distress messages. The other is that boat operators who use channel 16 in this fashion almost never reduce their radio's output power to its 1-watt settings, and thus their communication disrupts the proper use of channel 16 for a radius of several miles around both their vessels. VHF channel 16 is already overloaded and filled with improper traffic. We'd all be better off if everyone would use whistle signals instead of VHF to communicate in right-of-way situations. In many instances, when you sound the proper whistle signal, the skipper with whom you are trying to communicate will fail to respond because he doesn't understand what you're trying to tell him. I grant that's frustrating, but I suggest you try whistle signals first. If you don't get a response, use VHF—but use it properly. I also suggest that if a skipper calls you on channel 16 and proceeds to state his request or intentions on that channel, you respond with the name of his vessel, the name of your vessel, and a polite request that he shift and answer on channel 13.

In right-of-way situations where you are contacted by VHF, you are also likely to hear a kind of shorthand, such as "Captain, I'll meet you on one," which means the calling skipper intends to leave you on his port side, or "I'd like to slide by you on two," which means he is asking to overtake you on his starboard (your port) side.

Meeting Situations

When you meet another power-driven vessel head-on or nearly head-on and your courses, if maintained, may converge and create the possibility of a collision, you are technically in a "meeting situation" and the following rules apply (see illustration). (Note that these rules do not apply in situations where two vessels will pass clear of each other if both maintain their speed and heading.)

1. Neither of you has the right-of-way.
2. Unless otherwise agreed, both of you should pass on the port side of the other.
3. Both of you must alter course to starboard, if necessary, to allow clearance for safe passage.
4. When you are within sight of another power-driven vessel and meeting at a distance of a half mile or less, both of you are required to sound one of three whistle signals. (Both of you are on an equal basis and either can signal first.)
   A. One short blast, which signals "I intend to leave you on my port side."
   B. Two short blasts, which signal "I intend to leave you on my starboard side."

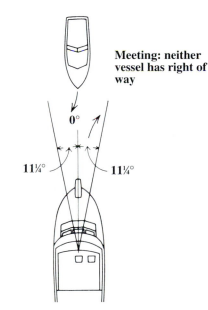

Meeting: neither vessel has right of way

In a meeting situation, neither vessel has the right-of-way and both must bear off to starboard to avoid a collision unless an alternate method of meeting is agreed to by whistle signals or VHF radio communication.

C. Three short blasts, which signal "I am operating astern."

5. If you hear the one- or two-blast signal from the other vessel and you agree with the method of passing proposed by the signal, you must give the same signal in return and make any maneuvers required to allow clearance for safe passage. If you consider the proposed method of passing unsafe or do not agree with it, you must sound five or more short blasts, which is the signal for "Danger!" and make any precautionary maneuvers necessary until a method of safe passing is mutually agreed to. You must never answer one short blast with two short blasts or two short blasts with one short blast. These are "cross signals," which are specifically prohibited by the rules.

6. If you initiate passing signals and do not receive the same signal in answer, you must immediately make any precautionary maneuvers necessary until a method of safe passing is mutually agreed to.

7. If you initiate passing signals and receive in reply three short blasts, which mean "I am operating astern," you must immediately reduce speed to the minimum required to maintain steerage and make no further attempt to pass until a safe method of passing has been agreed to by the exchange of appropriate signals.

The rules do not set mathematical limits within which the meeting situation exists, but court rulings have established it as existing when two vessels approach each other within one point (11¼ degrees) to either side of their respective bows.

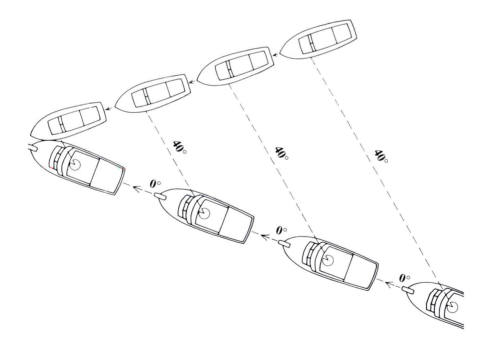

The danger of a collision exists anytime the bearing on an approaching vessel remains constant.

In daylight when visibility is good, the easiest way to determine whether you are on a collision course with another vessel is to take a series of compass bearings on the approaching vessel (see illustration). If the bearing of the other vessel relative to your own does not change appreciably, you may be on a collision course and the appropriate navigation rule or rules apply. At night, you know you are in a meeting situation if you can see both an approaching vessel's red and green sidelights or if you see two masthead lights of a vessel in line, one over the other.

In a winding channel, you may first sight an approaching vessel at an oblique angle, but the meeting situation will still apply if you will be head-on or nearly head-on and on convergent courses when you meet. In such a situation, both you and the other vessel must keep to the right of the channel and, if necessary, give way to starboard to allow clearance for safe passage.

There are a couple of exceptions to the meeting rules.

1. Vessels not under command, vessels restricted in their ability to maneuver (such as a large commercial vessel in a restricted waterway), vessels engaged in commercial (but not sport) fishing, and vessels operating under sail alone are all privileged over you as the operator of a power-driven vessel and you must give way. In a meeting situation between yourself and a vessel operating under sail alone, no whistle signals are exchanged.
2. On the Great Lakes or Western Rivers, a vessel proceeding downbound with the current has the right-of-way over an upbound vessel. If you are downbound with the current, you would propose the method of safe passing by initiating the appropriate whistle signals. If you are upbound, you must hold your course or position as necessary to permit safe passage.

Crossing Situations

When you and another vessel approach each other not head-on or nearly head-on but on a relative bearing forward of 22½ degrees abaft your respective beams and the possibility of a collision exists, you are technically in a crossing situation and the following rules apply (see illustration next page).

1. The vessel that has the other on its starboard side within an arc from dead ahead to 22½ degrees abaft its starboard beam is burdened and must make any maneuvers necessary to provide clearance for safe passage.
2. If the vessels are in sight of each other and will pass within a half mile of each other, they must sound whistle signals as discussed above for meeting situations. The rules do not state which vessel should initiate the signals, but it is customary for the vessel that is privileged—or believes itself to be privileged—to signal first.

This rule leads to the conclusion that a crossing situation exists when two power-driven vessels encounter each other within a half mile and each bears within 22½ degrees abaft their respective beams to either side. The vessel that has the other vessel within that arc on its starboard side is burdened; the vessel with the other vessel on its port side is privileged. This gives rise to the concept of this arc to starboard as a vessel's *danger zone*.

Overtaking Situations

Under the rules, you overtake another vessel any time you approach it from astern of a direction 22½ degrees abaft its beam at a speed great enough to close the distance between you (see illustration page 217). As the overtaking vessel, you are burdened and must not interfere with the progress of the vessel you are overtaking, which is privileged. The rules specifically state that once you are the burdened vessel in an overtaking situation, you

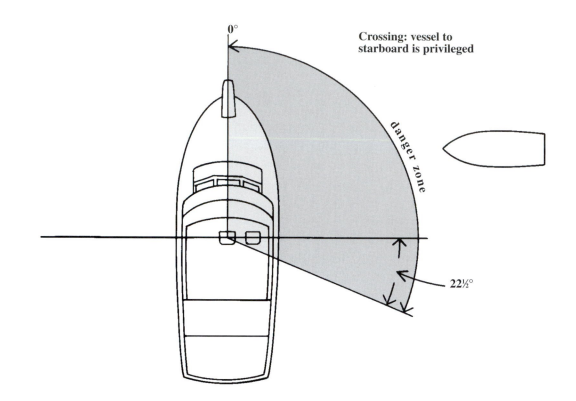

A vessel's danger zone extends from dead ahead to 22½ degrees abaft its beam on the starboard side.

remain so until you are past the vessel you are overtaking and clear of it. (This is true even if you pass a vessel on its starboard side and enter its danger zone, in which relationship you otherwise would have the right-of-way.)

Since the rules require vessels operating in a navigable channel to stay to the right of the channel and as close to its outer limit as is safe and practical, most passing is done on the port side of the vessel being overtaken. It is, however, legal to overtake in a channel on the starboard side of the vessel being overtaken if the vessel being overtaken agrees to the maneuver.

The rules require that when you overtake an-

other vessel, you give one of two sound signals. The usual signal would be two short blasts on your horn, which signal "I intend to leave you on my starboard side"; one short blast would signal "I intend to leave you on my port side."

If you are being overtaken, the rules require you to immediately answer the signal of a vessel overtaking you. An answering signal identical to the signal from the overtaking vessel signals "I agree with your passing on the side you propose." If you do not feel the overtaking vessel can pass safely on the side proposed, you must sound the danger signal of five or more short, rapid blasts. (You should also sound the danger signal if a vessel attempts to overtake you in an unsafe manner without making any signal.) If you are being overtaken, never answer one short blast with two short blasts or two short blasts with one short blast. As mentioned above, these are cross signals specifically prohibited by the rules. Though the rules don't specifically say so, if the vessel overtaking you proposes by his signal to pass in a manner you consider unsafe but you feel he could pass safely on the other side, you can give the danger signal in response to his initial signal, pause, then give the alternate

signal, which indicates "The side on which you propose to overtake is unsafe, but you may overtake safely on the alternate side." If the overtaking vessel agrees and intends to overtake on the side you propose, he should answer your signal with the identical signal.

In addition to the Rules of the Road for overtaking situations, the key to accomplishing the maneuver in narrow channels with a minimum of problems for both of the boats involved is for both to slow down (see illustration next page).

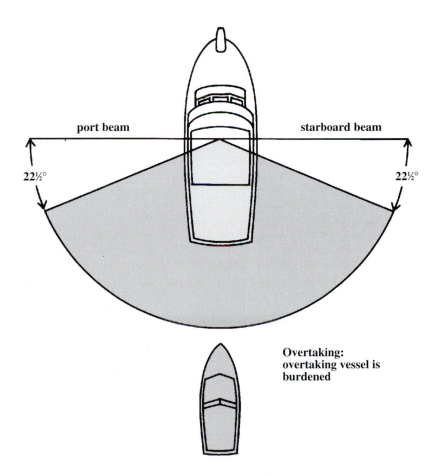

Anytime you approach a vessel from a point within an arc between 22½ degrees abaft its beam, you are burdened and must signal your request to pass by whistle or by VHF communication.

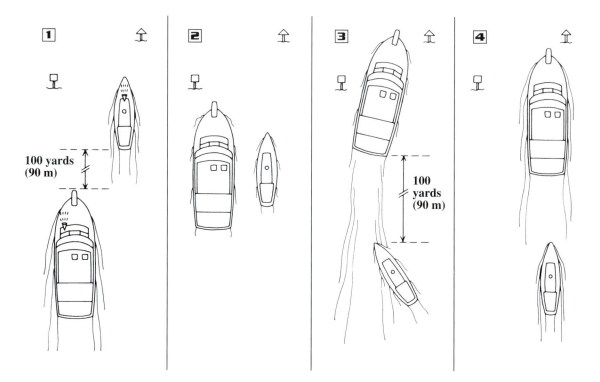

A planing hull vessel can overtake a slower vessel in a narrow channel with a minimum of delay and disruption if both vessels begin to slow down when the overtaking vessel is about 100 yards (90 m) off the stern of the vessel being overtaken (1). During the actual passing, the overtaking vessel should be fully off plane (2). Once the overtaking vessel is about 100 yards in front of the overtaken vessel, it can turn to starboard and resume normal speed while the vessel overtaken turns to port to cross its wake (3). Both vessels can then resume their normal position on the starboard side of the channel (4).

Once the appropriate sound signals have been exchanged or the side on which the overtaking vessel will leave the vessel it is overtaking has been properly agreed to via VHF, if you are at the helm of the overtaking vessel, alter course in the direction agreed to and begin to overtake. As your bow comes to within about 100 yards (90 m) of the stern of the vessel you are overtaking, you should gradually reduce power to your vessel's no-wake speed. If you are operating a planing hull vessel, by the time your vessel's bow is even with the stern of the vessel you are overtaking, your

boat's bow should be fully down and its foredeck should be parallel to the water. If you are going any faster than that, you are throwing too much of a wake. You should continue at a no-wake speed until your stern is well clear of the bow of the vessel you are overtaking, then swing across its bow to assume your proper position as far to the right of the channel as is safe. Only then should you slowly advance your throttles and resume your normal cruising speed.

If you are at the helm of a vessel being over-taken, as the bow of the overtaking vessel approaches your stern, you should reduce your vessel's speed to the minimum required to maintain steerage and pull over as far as practical to the side of the channel opposite to that on which you are being overtaken. As soon as the stern of the overtaking vessel clears your bow, turn sharply into the curl of its wake, take the plunge over it, then swing your bow in line with his stern. Doing that will put you as quickly as possible into the flattened portion at the center of his wake and lead you back into your proper position as far to the right of the channel as is safe, at which point you can resume speed.

So much for what the rules say. The fact is that in the more congested boating areas of the United States—such as the Northeast, Florida, and California—the problems associated with high-powered vessels such as planing hull motor yachts and sportfishing boats overtaking lower-powered vessels such as semidisplacement and full-displacement powerboats and sailboats have reached crisis proportions. On *Americas Odyssey*'s cruise down the Intracoastal Waterway (ICW), I was passed by faster vessels several hundred times. I can recall only two skippers of an overtaking vessel communicating their request to pass with whistle signals, and both apparently were professional captains. In about half the overtaking instances, the request to pass was communicated by VHF radio, but in every case it was done incorrectly on channel 16. In the remaining half of the instances in which I was overtaken, the overtaking vessel communicated no request to pass at all.

In about a quarter of the instances, high-powered boats roared by me at full or nearly full throttle. When their 3- to 4-foot (1–1.2 m) wakes hit my vessel's hull broadside, we took rolls of up to 20 degrees. The operators of a number of express cruisers in the 35- to 40-foot (10.7–12 m) range, and virtually all operators of boats smaller than that, seemed to feel their vessel size somehow exempted them from the Rules of the Road. Thirteen out of a group of fifteen express cruisers that were traveling together as a pack whizzed by me at speeds upward of 30 knots. The operators of some

of the planing hull boats that went by me seemed to think that if they just reduced their throttles to something below full speed, they were passing properly. Running a planing hull boat at an attitude anywhere between full planing and its no-wake speed simply digs its stern deeper into the water and causes it to throw an even larger wake. The operators of other planing hull boats seemed to think that if they passed me in a wide channel and were as much as 100 yards (90 m) or so off my beam, there was no reason for them to reduce speed. A planing hull vessel over 40 feet in length with a pair of engines generating on the order of 400 to 500 horsepower each that is operating at planing speed can easily throw a dangerous wake up to 300 yards (275 m) to either side of its course, and its operator should reduce speed accordingly.

On the other side of the coin, the operators of slower vessels must also bear some responsibility for the cavalier attitude toward passing that now prevails on the water. In several instances on the above cruise, even at my turtle-slow speed, I overtook a number of sailboats chugging along on their auxiliary engine at about 6.5 knots. In many of those situations, their operators declined to back off on their throttle at all, which meant the passing took an extremely long time. In at least two instances, oncoming traffic forced me to speed up before I should have in order to get around them.

I'm not simply being an old grouch on this subject. If someone is in the galley of a vessel that is unexpectedly rocked up to 20 degrees by an improper overtaking and has a pot of boiling water on the stove, they could easily be scalded. A small child aboard such a vessel could easily be thrown into a bulkhead and seriously injured.

The situation has become so volatile that there are threats of actual violence. In one instance, I contacted by VHF the operator of a planing hull vessel that signaled no request to pass and roared by me at full throttle and strongly criticized his performance at the helm. His reaction was to invite me to stop at the next dock and settle our differences in a fistfight. In another instance on that cruise, one of the operators I had called down stopped in the same marina where I planned to overnight and actually banged on my boat and invited me to step out on the dock for a fight.

The Rules of the Road and most state boating regulations provide penalties for both careless and reckless boat operation. Unfortunately, however, neither the coast guard nor most state or local marine patrols will ticket a vessel operator for careless or reckless operation unless their own personnel witness an incident or the improper operation results in personal injury or property damage exceeding $500. If you are the victim of an improper overtaking that does not cause personal injury but does cause property damage under $500, about the only recourse you have against the offender is to swear out a civil complaint with a local magistrate or state's attorney. Even then, you normally will have to have the vessel's state registration number and be able to definitively identify the individual who was at the helm of the vessel at the time the incident occurred. If you succeed in having a warrant issued against the individual, you will have to return to that jurisdiction to testify against the accused in court.

When the problems associated with improper overtaking have reached the level where physical violence is threatened, I suggest it's time for all of us to learn the rules for safe overtaking and obey them. If the maneuver is properly executed, it results in a minimum of delay for the overtaking vessel and a minimum of disruption for the vessel being overtaken.

No-Wake Zones

In waterway cruising through populated areas, you'll frequently encounter white rectangular signs with an orange circle, which designate no-wake zones. On the far side of the congested area, you'll see similar signs saying "Resume Normal Safe Operation." Areas marked in this fashion are legally designated as no-wake zones by the U.S. Coast Guard or another authority and must be respected. Along the waterways in many communities, the problems of damage from the wakes of

passing boats have become so serious that law enforcement agencies are strictly enforcing no-wake restrictions and handing out fines of up to $250 to vessel operators who fail to respect them.

In many other areas along waterways, you'll see homemade no-wake signs that are not legally enforceable. In those cases, your sense of consideration for others will have to determine whether you back off your throttles. You should be aware, however, that in any situation where your vessel's wake causes property damage or personal injury, you can be held responsible.

AIDS TO NAVIGATION

Extended cruising is almost certain to involve runs on some of the waterways, rivers, lakes, and canals that make up the 30,000 miles (48,000 km) of navigable inland waters in the United States. In the course of cruising those waters, you may find that some of the aids to navigation you encounter leave you scratching your head in total confusion as to which way you should go. You'll also need to employ some special techniques to keep your vessel off the bottom.

Basic Buoyage System

In 1989, the United States completed the changeover of its basic buoyage from the old lateral system to the International Association of Lighthouse Authorities' System B—Combined Cardinal and Lateral System (red to starboard). This system is now in effect on all navigable waters in the United States under federal jurisdiction except the ICW and the Western Rivers (the Mississippi River and its tributaries plus other designated rivers). It is also in effect throughout all of North and South America, the Bahamas, Korea, and Japan. The rest of the world uses System A (red to port), which we discuss in chapter 36.

As its name implies, System B combines aspects and markings of both lateral and cardinal buoyage systems. In a *lateral system,* buoys indicate the direction to a danger relative to the course that should be followed (that is, you avoid obstructions by keeping red to starboard and green to port when entering from seaward). In a *cardinal system,* buoys indicate the direction to a danger relative to the buoy itself and a buoy's color directs safe vessel movement in terms of the cardinal points of the compass (that is, you pass a red-topped white buoy to the south or west; you pass a black-topped white buoy to the north or east).

If you are familiar with the previous system of aids to navigation, you will find that the current system includes two basic changes you have to get used to:

1. green has replaced black as the color normally used to mark the port side of a channel entered from seaward
2. flashing white lights, which formerly were used wherever greater light intensity was required (including marking the sides of channels), are now used only on fairway, midchannel, and special purpose markers

Aids to navigation in the current system use four basic colors or combination of colors to indicate their function.

1. Solid red marks identify the starboard side of a channel "entered from seaward toward the head of navigation"; thus, the old "red right returning" adage still applies. In shape, they may be lighted buoys, nuns, or triangles. They normally do not bear letters but may do so in situations where an interim marker is inserted between two existing markers. Between "16" and "18," for instance, you might encounter "16A." If they bear numbers, the numbers will be even. If lighted, they will have only red lights, which can be fixed or flashing.
2. Solid green marks identify the port side of a channel entered from seaward. In shape, they may be lighted buoys, cans,

or rectangles. They only bear letters in cases where interim markers are inserted between existing markers. If they bear numbers, the numbers will be odd. If lighted, they will have only green lights, which can be fixed or flashing.

3. Combination red-and-white vertically striped marks identify safe water or midchannel and may be passed on either side. In shape, they may be lighted buoys, spheres, or octagons. They never bear numbers but may be lettered. If lighted, they will have only green lights, which will always be flashing and will flash only the Morse letter "A" (dit dah).
4. Combination red-and-green horizontally striped marks identify a junction or hazard, and you can pass them on either side if you are headed upstream. (If you are headed downstream, you must refer to the chart to determine the location of the channel or obstruction relative to the mark.) These marks indicate a preferred channel by the arrangement of their horizontal color bands. If the topmost color band is red, the preferred channel is to port of the mark and you should leave the mark to starboard when you are headed upstream. If the topmost color band is green, the preferred channel is to starboard of the mark and you should leave the mark to port when you are headed upstream. In shape, these marks may be lighted buoys, nuns, cans, triangles, or rectangles. They never bear numbers but may bear letters. If lighted, their lights will be the same color as their topmost band. Regardless of color, their lights will always be flashing and will flash in the composite group (2 + 1) of two dits, pause, dit.

In addition to these four basic colors or combinations of colors, the current system also uses yellow marks for such special purposes as marking anchorages or marking the limits of dredging areas. They may appear as lighted buoys, nuns, cans, or diamonds. If lighted, they will have only yellow lights and may flash in any rhythm not in use in the lateral system.

1. Solid yellow buoys mark special anchorage areas.
2. Yellow buoys with green tops are used to mark areas of dredging and survey operations.
3. Yellow-and-black horizontally banded buoys mark fishnet areas where fishnets and traps may be placed at or near the surface.
4. Yellow-and-black vertically striped buoys mark areas of seaplane operations.

The current system uses white buoys with international orange marks to present regulatory information, such as danger and speed limit zones. They may appear as cans or diamonds and are never lighted.

Intracoastal Waterway

The ICW has its own marking system, which is basically similar to the new system for marking aids to navigation but includes distinctive yellow bands, squares, and triangles. Channel direction on the ICW is not determined by the "entering from seaward" rule. Instead, along the East Coast, channels are assumed to run north to south. Along the Gulf Coast, channels are assumed to run first south to north (along Florida's west coast), then east to west from Apalachicola, Florida, to Brownsville, Texas. The easiest way to remember this when following ICW markings is to assume you are circling the country in a clockwise direction. The basic rule is to leave triangles (their shape resembles nuns) to starboard and to leave squares (their shape resembles cans) to port when running in the direction of the waterway.

Where the ICW crosses other channels, its yellow markings are often displayed on the aids to navigation of other systems. What do you do, then,

when you encounter a yellow square (which you should leave to port) on a red nun (which you should leave to starboard)? The answer is that when proceeding along the ICW in the above directions, always keep yellow squares on your port hand and always keep yellow triangles on your starboard hand, regardless of the color of the aid on which they appear.

This clockwise designation has in some cases led to mass confusion and even some dangerous situations. In those areas where the ICW is not continuously marked with yellow stickers, you may find a series of buoys on exactly the opposite side of the channel from what you would think is appropriate when entering from the sea. In these situations, you would presume that the red-right-return markings apply. But lo and behold, you'll suddenly discover that green-right-return is the standard. This anomaly results from the coast guard's decision to consider such a channel a north-to-south or east-to-west portion of the ICW even though—as in Maine—there is no waterway. The caution, of course, is to always check your charts.

Western Rivers

The old lateral system is still in use on the Western Rivers but includes some additional shapes and day marks not found in other areas. In some cases, however, the color green has replaced black. On these rivers, unlighted buoys are not numbered and the numbers on lighted buoys have no lateral significance. Instead, they indicate the distance upstream from a designated reference point.

State Waterways

On waterways wholly contained within the borders of a single state, you may encounter aids to navigation identified according to yet a fourth buoyage system—the Uniform State Waterway Marking System (USWMS). It is essentially a lateral system that is compatible with the basic buoyage system found in waters under federal jurisdiction, but with several major exceptions.

In the USWMS, buoys that mark the left side of a channel when headed upstream are solid black rather than green. If numbered, their numbers will be odd and will increase in the upstream direction; if lighted, their lights will be green. (Buoys that mark the right side of the channel when headed upstream are solid red. If numbered, their numbers will be even and will increase in the upstream direction; if lighted, their lights will be red.) If either a solid black or a solid red buoy is lighted, in normal situations the light will be slow flashing (not more than thirty flashes per minute); at turns, constrictions, or obstructions in the waterway, they will be quick flashing (not fewer than sixty flashes per minute). The shape of solid-colored buoys is less important than their color; in some cases, red buoys will be a can shape rather than a nun.

A red-and-white vertically striped buoy (used in the federal system to indicate safe water or midchannel) indicates that a hazard or obstruction lies between it and the nearest shore. It therefore should be passed outboard. If lighted, its light will be white and quick flashing.

The USWMS uses two aids to navigation not found in the federal system that are cardinal marks rather than lateral marks.

1. A can-shaped buoy with a red top must be passed to the south or west.
2. A similarly shaped white buoy with a black top must be passed to the north or east.

If either of these buoys is lighted, their lights will be white and quick flashing.

The USWMS also allows the use of mooring buoys, which are white with a horizontal blue band. If lighted, their light will be white and slow flashing unless they constitute an obstruction, in which case their light will be quick flashing.

Regulatory and information marks in the USWMS are white with two horizontal bands of international orange, one at the top and one just above the waterline. Between these bands will be a diamond, a circle, or a square or rectangle.

1. A diamond shape warns of danger and may contain a word or words that specify the nature of the danger, such as ROCK, SNAG, and FERRY CABLE. A diamond shape with a cross means the area marked is prohibited and may contain explanatory words below it, such as SWIM AREA, WATERFALL, and RAPIDS.
2. A circle marks a controlled area and normally contains explanatory words, such as 5 MPH, NO WAKE, and SKIN DIVERS ONLY.
3. A square or rectangle gives information and normally contains place names, distances, or availability of supplies.

Using Ranges

A *range* consists of two aids to navigation positioned so that when viewed in line you may be in safe water. The two components of a range are most often vertical rectangular panels painted in vertical stripes of contrasting colors. When encountering a range, you need to check your chart to determine the distance at which a particular range is valid. The extent of a range's limits normally are delineated by one or more buoys or day beacons. In all cases, the rear marker of a range is higher than its front marker. At a turn or bend in a channel, a single structure may support the rear marker for two ranges extending in differing directions.

Ranges on the ICW are distinguished by a yellow band at the bottom of their front markers. Many ranges are also lighted. If lighted, the front and rear lights normally will be of the same color and may be white, green, or red, but will have differing rhythms. Many ranges now show an equal interval rear light and a quick-flashing front light. In some cases, range lights will be equipped with lenses that allow you to see their full intensity only when you are directly on the range line. If you deviate to either side of the range line, the light's intensity will lessen dramatically. When running a range, remember that if the alignment of the front and rear markers diverge, you must steer your vessel in the direction of the front (lower) marker to bring yourself back on course.

In situations where it is impractical to install front and rear markers for a conventional range, the midpoint of channels is sometimes marked by a single directional light, which shows a white light in a narrow horizontal band visible only if you are centered in the channel it marks. If you enter the channel from seaward and drift to the right of the channel's centerline, you will see a red light; if you drift to the left, you will see a green light.

The compass orientation of a range is sometimes marked on nautical charts and is always given in the description of it in the Light List. You also can derive it from the chart's compass rose. In calm conditions, lining your vessel up precisely on a range line can allow you to check your standard magnetic compass's deviation. But be sure to include the variation and annual rate of increase or decrease given inside the compass rose on the chart of the area.

BRIDGES

The regulations that govern operations at opening bridges over U.S. waterways are not part of the Inland Rules but are issued by the coast guard.

Don't request that a bridge be opened if you can pass under it simply by lowering your communications and navigation antennas. The regulations, in fact, provide penalties for vessel operators who cause unnecessary bridge openings because of "any nonstructural vessel appurtenance which is not essential to navigation or which is easily lowered." Many bridges also have clearance gauges that give the clearance beneath them at the time you arrive.

The basic rule is that as you approach within about half a mile of a bridge you wish to have opened, you must signal your request with one prolonged blast (of four to six seconds' duration) followed within three seconds by one short blast (of about one second's duration).

While the whistle signal is preferred, the regulations also allow you to signal for the bridge to be opened with a bell, a shout, by any other device that can be heard clearly, or visually by raising and lowering a white flag vertically within clear view of the bridge tender. You may also request a bridge opening by calling the bridge tender on VHF radio, normally on channel 13. If you use channel 13, your radio should automatically reduce its output to 1 watt and you should use your vessel's name.

Technically, if a closed bridge will be opened immediately, the tender is supposed to answer your whistle signal with the same signal: one prolonged blast followed by one short blast. If a visual signal was used to request the openings, the tender may respond with the same visual signal. If several boats are in line and request an opening, the tender normally will respond only to the first signal.

If a closed bridge will not be opened immediately, the tender is supposed to answer a request for opening by whistle signal with five short blasts. (If the request to open was made by visual means, the tender may respond by horizontally waving a red flag in daylight or a red lantern at night.) Also, when an open bridge is to be closed immediately, the tender is supposed to sound five short blasts, which must be acknowledged with the same signal by any vessel preparing to pass through. If the vessel does not acknowledge the signal, the tender is supposed to sound the five short blasts signal until the vessel answers it with the same signal.

You are required to make the request-for-opening signal even though the bridge is already open or is opening for another vessel. If you do not receive an acknowledgment within thirty seconds, you may proceed to pass through.

If a bridge is operating on restricted operating hours, certain privileged craft, such as government vessels and tugs with tows, may request an opening with five short blasts. I've never been able to learn whether, when a bridge on restricted operating hours is opened in such a situation, a recreational vessel may fall in behind the privileged vessel and pass through on the same opening. What I have done in such situations is to position my vessel about 100 feet (30 m) astern of the privileged vessel, which declares my intention to pass through, and, as I approach the bridge, give the prolonged blast–short blast and plan to pass through unless I receive five short blasts in reply. I've always been able to pass through in such situations without incident but was never sure I was legal.

So much for what's supposed to happen. I've passed through literally thousands of bridges and cannot recall a single instance where the prescribed procedures have been followed. What usually happens is that as you approach a bridge you give the prolonged blast–short blast signal, take up station about 100 yards (90 m) off the bridge, and wait around to see what happens. Some bridge tenders could not be more considerate of vessel traffic; others seem to delight in seeing if they can get you steamed up. Lack of cooperation (let alone respect for the regulations) by bridge tenders is becoming an increasing problem for inland waterway cruisers, especially in such heavy traffic areas as the Northeast and South Florida. I think we cruisers should protest vehemently if our rights are not respected. I recognize that opening a bridge to let a lone boat through may well inconvenience dozens, even hundreds, of motorists. But technically, if a bridge is not operating on published hours of restricted operations, those of us in boats have just as much right to have it opened as motorists have for it to remain closed. I have no problem with a reasonable delay of fifteen minutes or so in opening a bridge during rush hours. What I do object to is tenders who ignore a request-to-open signal simply because they are busy eating dinner or talking to someone on the telephone.

If you request the opening of a bridge not on restricted operating hours and the tender doesn't begin to open it fairly promptly, watch the vehicle traffic going over it. During rush hours, the tender may wait fifteen minutes or so to break the traffic or may wait until several boats line up to pass through before opening the bridge. If there is no heavy vehicle traffic using the bridge and the tender doesn't open it within about ten minutes, give the request to open signal again. If another ten minutes or so goes by and nothing happens, try to raise the bridge tender on VHF channel 13 and ask what's going on. If you receive no answer, give the signal a third time. If another ten minutes or so goes by and the bridge still doesn't open, log the date, time, and specifics of the incident and complain to the appropriate coast guard district office.

Once you succeed in getting the bridge opened, pass through at no-wake speed, watch the currents that can be tricky around the base of the bridge's abutments, and watch your antennas. If vessels are passing through a single-opening bridge in both directions, vessels running with the current have the right-of-way.

LOCKS

Well before you approach a lock that you plan to pass through, check your *Coast Pilot* or cruising guide for the appropriate "request to lock through" whistle signal and any restrictions or peculiarities in its operation. The whistle signal at most locks is now the same as for bridges—one prolonged blast followed by one short blast—and should be sounded when you are about half a mile (0.8 km) away. Your signal should be answered by the lock master with the same signal but probably won't be in the United States. Answering signals are commonly used in Canada, however. Most locks are now marked with red, yellow, and green lights, much like street traffic lights. Red or flashing red lights normally mean to stay at least 300 feet (92 m) away from the lock. Yellow lights normally mean to proceed toward the lock with caution. A green light means you are free to enter the lock at no-wake speed. If you have any questions about the proper procedures at a lock, try calling the lock master on VHF channel 13. If the lock master doesn't answer, try channel 16 but manually reduce your radio's power output to 1 watt.

Well before you enter a lock, have your crew prepare to put out stout fenders fore and aft to protect your vessel's topsides. In most locks in the United States, the lock master will hand you bow and stern lines, which are affixed to the lock walls. To be on the safe side, however, be sure your crew has your vessel's own docklines ready at the bow and stern to pass to the lock master if they are not supplied. In most cases, the lock master will direct you to tie off to the side of the lock on which its lights are flashing. But there are locks where that is not the case, and other boats may have already filled all the space along the preferred side of the lock. For that reason, anytime you approach a lock you should be ready to put out fenders and bow and stern lines on either side of your vessel. In a single-engine boat, if you have a choice, tie off port side–to so your engine in reverse will walk your stern toward the lock wall rather than away from it.

Locks can be pretty nasty and will quickly soil your lines and fenders. Eventually the dirt, oil, and grease your lines and fenders collect will wind up on your vessel's decks and topsides. If your cruising plans call for you to transit locks frequently, you might want to save your good nylon docklines by investing in a set of less expensive ½-inch (12 mm) Manila lock lines (if you can find them) that you can afford to replace about once a year. You may also want to protect your fenders with covers you can remove and wash periodically or even cover them with heavy-duty plastic garbage bags.

As you approach the lock, station one line handler at the bow. If you are going to have to use your vessel's docklines rather than lines affixed to the lock, the line handler should pass the loop end of the line to the lock master then lead the standing part clear of the safety railings and secure it snugly to a bow cleat. If you are fortunate enough to have two line handlers aboard, place the second at the stern on the side of your vessel you plan to lay against the lock wall with a stern line similarly

rigged. If only you and your mate are aboard, have your mate prepare the stern line, then rig the bow line as above and stand by it. Enter the lock slowly, pull up to a bollard or ring, and have your mate secure the bow then go aft to secure the stern line while you hold position if necessary with your engines. Once your vessel is secured fore and aft, if necessary you can leave the helm to handle one line while your mate handles the other.

The systems for tying off at locks vary widely.

Most locks with a water level change of 6 feet (1.8 m) or so simply have fixed bollards on the top of their walls. In that case, both lines will have to be tended during the locking process and slack taken in or let out as your vessel is raised or lowered. To tie off in that situation using your own lines, have your crew double bow and stern lines around their respective bollards (as discussed in chapter 14): with the line's eye secured over the appropriate deck cleat, lead its standing part under the safety railing, flip the standing part over the bollard on shore, and secure it around the same deck cleat that is securing the eye with a half turn or S-turn preparatory to taking up or letting out slack. To help keep the line from fouling when it is released, it should be around the bollard "outside to inside," so it doesn't have to cross over itself—that is, on the starboard side, run the bow line around its bollard clockwise and the stern line around its bollard counterclockwise; reverse the process on the port side. In locking downstream, it's best not to cleat off a line that is secured around a fixed bollard on the lock wall; the water level could fall quickly and leave your boat dangling from the lock wall.

The locking procedure is far easier at locks with mooring rings recessed into their walls that rise and fall with the change of water level. In this type of lock, it's OK to cleat off lock lines, since your vessel can't be trapped, but have a crew member standing within reach of them anyway to let them go in case anything unusual happens.

Once the water in the lock has risen or fallen to its new level and the lock doors have begun to open, wait for the lock master's signal before releasing your lines and proceeding out of the lock at no-wake speed. In most cases, the all-clear signal will be communicated by a set of lights at the far end of the lock that will be red during the locking process and will change to green when it's safe for you to proceed.

ENGINE ROOM CHECK UNDER WAY

The best way to keep from having irritating or possibly dangerous difficulties with your boat's mechanical systems is to spot potential problems early and correct them before they become serious. The key is to check your engine room frequently while you are under way and follow a consistent routine that ensures you don't overlook anything important. Based on the layout of your particular vessel's engine compartment, make yourself a list of items to check that is arranged in a logical sequence, post it down there along with a roll of paper towels and a flashlight in their own brackets, and refer to it until your routine becomes automatic.

When you are under way, you should check your engine room every three or four hours. I know it sounds juvenile, but every time I check an engine room while under way, a phrase flits through my mind—**L**ove **v**iolets **b**ecause **t**hey are **g**ay—that I developed years ago to remind me of the five things I need to check.

The L stands for *leaks* and comes first because leaks will alert you to potential problems with your engine(s), marine gear(s), or generator quicker than anything else. Leaks around fuel, oil, and coolant lines or hoses are easiest to spot, of course, if you keep your engine(s), marine gear casing(s), and generator—and the area immediately under them—spotless.

The V in my bit of doggerel stands for *vibration*. Again, spotting a bolt or hose clamp that is vibrating loose or an electric wire chafing against metal can allow you to correct a developing problem before it affects your vessel's operation.

The B stands for *belts*. A quick glance at all the engine belts and pulleys assures me all the systems they power are working smoothly; if not, I need to take corrective action.

The TH in "they" represents the vessel's *through-hull* fittings. A quick sweep of a flashlight beam over all through-hulls that are visible in the engine room lets me spot any that might be starting to crack or pull loose.

The G reminds me to compare the readings of mechanical pressure and *temperature gauges* on the engine with the readings I have been seeing on the electrical gauges at the helm and the vacuum gauges in the fuel line to alert me if the filters are clogging up and are about to shut off my fuel supply.

Now that we've discussed the normal situations you will encounter while cruising, we'll discuss the likely "abnormal" situations, such as running aground.

Operating Smoothly in Special Running Situations

Not all of your cruising is going to be between 10:00 A.M. and 4:00 P.M. across a calm sea with a bright sun shining. Despite your best efforts in cruise planning and weather prognostication, times will come when you get caught in a storm and must either negotiate an unfamiliar inlet to reach shelter or take your lumps offshore. At other times, you'll probably find you must make an overnight run to reach your next anchorage, or fog will roll in along your course and you'll have to grope your way through the muck.

The keys to handling those special running situations in safety and as much comfort as possible are to properly rig your vessel to deal with any situation you are likely to encounter and to make sure you know what you should do as conditions change.

HEAVY-WEATHER HANDLING

If you are in open water and can see significant weather building along your intended course or if weather broadcasts are forecasting severe weather for your vicinity, don't wait for conditions to get serious before you start taking them into account. Most experienced skippers of power cruising boats in the 40- to 60-foot (12–18 m) range begin to become concerned about the weather when winds get up to around 30 knots and waves begin to approach 8 feet (2.4 m). Those are conditions that warrant a Small Craft Advisory: winds up to 33 knots. If you find conditions approaching that magnitude and weather reports indicate they are likely to worsen, go ahead and prepare your vessel and crew to handle severe weather as safely as possible. Close and dog all hatches and portlights, stow or lash down loose gear, and rig jack lines to enable you and your crew to move fore and aft on deck safely using safety harnesses. If you don't actually put on your life jacket, at least make sure it's handy and order your crew to do likewise. Also make sure your safety harnesses are accessible, and allow no crew member to go on deck without wearing one and securing it to the jack lines.

Next, you need to decide fairly quickly whether you are going to try to head for more protected waters or will continue on your course. If you are in an exposed bay or wide river and are inclined to run for cover, check your chart for the nearest landmass you can put between yourself and the oncoming storm. Unless a well-sheltered cove or harbor lies to leeward and you can reach it easily before the storm's leading edge hits, it's generally wiser to seek protection to windward, which will keep you from having to deal with a lee shore.

If you are offshore on a coastwise passage, you'll probably have to run an inlet to reach protected waters. If that's the case, major factors in your decision will be whether you can run the inlet you intend to use before the storm's leading edge arrives over it and whether the inlet can be run in adverse conditions. If the answer to both questions is yes, it's usually wise to head inshore. But bear in mind that a front's most violent weather is likely to be on its leading edge, waters are rougher inshore than offshore because shallow water compacts and magnifies wave force, and many inlets are extremely dangerous in adverse conditions, particularly at low tide.

INLET RUNNING

Running an unfamiliar inlet with the weather kicking up is quite likely to provide one of the toughest tests of your ability as a competent skipper. Before you get to the inlet itself, gather all the information about it you can to help you plan your entry. This is where you'll be glad you paid that few dollars for a *Coast Pilot*. If you don't have the applicable volume aboard, check any cruising guides for the area you do have aboard, which might give you valuable information about the inlet's buoyage or lighting system, any ranges that will help you enter on the proper course, tidal currents that can set you off course, and shoals that you'll have to avoid.

If you don't have any of these materials aboard, call the coast guard on VHF channel 16 and be prepared to switch to a working channel (usually channel 22A) to ask their advice. If for any reason you can't reach the coast guard, try the dockmaster at any marina facility near the inlet or put out a call on VHF channel 16 for "any vessel local to ——— Inlet," then switch to a working channel and ask for their suggestions. If you're lucky, you'll find a knowledgeable local captain planning to run the inlet right in front of you, and you can follow him in. Do not, however, follow just any boat into an inlet you're concerned about. Its skipper may know no more about running it than you do, and you both may wind up on the rocks.

If the information you read or hear indicates that in adverse weather you should run the inlet only with local knowledge, check your charts to see if there is an all-weather inlet farther up or down the coast you can enter in greater safety. If you're off the South Florida coast, for instance, and plan to run into either South Lake Worth or Boca Raton Inlet and aren't thoroughly familiar with either, you'd be much better off to divert north to Lake Worth Inlet or south to Port Everglades, both of which are deep, all-weather inlets used by large commercial vessels.

If you must run a dubious inlet in heavy weather, the next step is to pick your time. The best time to run deep-water inlets is on a flood tide; the best time to enter a shallow inlet is at high slack water. The worst time to enter a deep-water inlet is on the ebb when the outflowing tide is opposing incoming wind and waves; the worst time to run a shallow water inlet is low tide. If necessary, hang offshore a few hours until conditions are the least hazardous.

Let's take a worst-case scenario in which you must run a shallow, shoaling inlet without printed information or local knowledge to guide you—only your chart.

First, study your chart carefully to glean every bit of information about the inlet it provides. Make certain you understand the pattern of buoys, lights, or day marks you are about to encounter and fix their details firmly in your mind. Once you get into the inlet, you will be so busy handling your boat you may not have time to even glance at the chart, much less go over it in detail. Check the chart to see if the entry is marked by a range, which will be indicated by a dotted line through a front and rear marker installed either on shore or in the water. Under the stress of running an inlet in adverse conditions, even running a forward range can be confusing. Remember that to correct your course, you steer in the direction of the front marker.

While you're studying the chart, lay out a compass course for your entry but realize you may have to deviate from it if recent storms have caused the inlet's bottom to shift or the coast guard to relocate its aids to navigation. If the inlet is not marked by a range, extend your course ashore and see if you can pick out any landmarks you can use to judge your position relative to the channel's centerline.

Once you've gone over your chart carefully, make a couple of circles off the inlet's entrance and study its pattern of waves from your flying bridge to finalize your plan for running in. Breaking waves indicate shoaling, so plan your course to keep your vessel over the calmest water you see, even though it may not be in the exact center of the indicated channel. If waves are breaking across the full width of the channel entrance, it is blocked by a bar. If you must run the entrance anyway, make certain you do so only at high tide to give yourself the best chance of clearing the shallowest water. Also study the waves running into the inlet to note their direction and see if you can discern a pattern. Waves rarely enter an inlet exactly perpendicular to it. If they are running across it at an oblique angle right to left, for example, be aware that you are going to have to steer somewhat to the right of your planned course to keep them from setting you toward the channel's port side.

Once you've decided on your basic strategy for running the inlet, the specific tactics you adopt will depend on the type of vessel you are operating.

In a planing hull vessel that can run in at a speed at least equal to the speed of the waves, time your dash to coincide with the smallest wave in the series you've divined and run in on its back. Use power to maintain a position about a third of the way back from the wave's crest, increasing power to keep from slipping too far back, which can allow the wave coming up behind you to poop your stern, or reducing power to keep from getting ahead of the wave you are riding, which could drive your bow into the base of the wave ahead and possibly cause you to pitchpole—that is, turn end for end.

If yours is a displacement hull vessel or a semi-displacement vessel without enough power to get it up on plane, you probably won't be able to keep up with a single wave and will have to let successive waves pass under your keel while you concentrate on keeping your vessel centered over deep water and the stern squarely before the waves coming up behind you. The one thing you absolutely must avoid is a broach, which can roll you over.

If conditions are really rough and you have twin engines, you can best keep your vessel centered over deep water by alternately increasing and decreasing power on your engines. If your bow starts to veer left of your intended course, for instance, increase the power on your port engine to bring the bow back to starboard. In extreme cases where the waves catch your vessel's stern and start to slew it into a broach, you may have to increase power on the windward engine and actually throw the leeward engine in reverse to bring the stern back square to the seas.

In all this maneuvering, don't allow yourself to concentrate so single-mindedly on keeping your vessel's stern square to the approaching waves that you lose sight of your position relative to the channel itself. Keep your eye on the channel buoys, range markers, or other reference points you have picked out ashore to make certain you are not being carried out of the channel.

If you can't reach an inlet leading to safe harbor before the storm's leading edge arrives, or if the inlet is dangerous to run in adverse weather, you generally will be better off to remain in deep water until conditions moderate. The wave action in deep water is likely to be less violent than closer inshore, and you are likely to encounter big rolling waves that stay together rather than the more dangerous, short, choppy waves with breaking tops.

If you decide to ride the weather out at sea, your next decision is whether to attempt to maintain your course or bear off. In winds of about 30 to 40 knots and waves of 8 to 15 feet (2.4–4.6 m), your vessel will ride most comfortably downwind. Before running off, make certain you have plenty of room to leeward. Once you've committed to the maneuver, keep your vessel running as squarely as possible before wind and seas and be constantly alert to the possibility of a broach. In conditions of this magnitude, you generally can keep a twin-screw power cruiser dead before the wind by using a combination of the wheel and the throttles. On a single-screw vessel, streaming a long, heavy warp, a drogue, or a storm anchor from the stern will help keep the stern into the wind and the bow pointed directly downwind to help you avoid a broach.

As winds build over about 40 knots and waves pile up over about 15 feet (4.6 m), the tops of the waves will start to break and sea foam will be blown in well-defined streaks. In these conditions, the danger of a broach may make continuing downwind impossible and require you to put your vessel's head to wind. During the turn you must make to accomplish that, the beam will be exposed to the storm's full fury and the boat will be at its most vulnerable. There are several special techniques you can use to make that turn as quickly and safely as possible.

First, the longer you wait to make the turn, the worse it will be. As soon as you experience significant difficulty keeping your vessel's bow pointed dead downwind, go ahead and make plans to turn. Postponing the maneuver will only make it more difficult.

Second, keep your cool. Scuba divers have a rule: plan your dive, and dive your plan. Yachtspersons about to turn head to weather in storm conditions should have a similar rule: plan your turn, and turn your plan. Once you have your turn mapped out, follow your intentions through cleanly and smoothly. An instant's panic or hesitation could be disastrous.

Time your turn carefully. According to some oceanographers, waves tend to travel roughly in a series of seven with about every seventh wave tending to be smaller than the others and the period between it and the wave behind it tending to be longer. That rule is not absolute, but in planning your turn, observe the waves passing under your vessel and see if you can tell which in their series tends to be the smallest and has the longest period between it and the wave following. Plan to make your turn as soon as the crest of that smallest wave has passed under your vessel's keel.

You want to make as much of your turn as possible on the back of that smallest wave so that once you are into the trough behind it, your vessel is properly positioned to meet the next wave rushing toward you. Ideally, to reduce the likelihood of burying your bow in the base of that oncoming wave, it's best to meet it at an angle of about 15 degrees off the bow.

If the period between waves is so short you cannot possibly make the complete turn on the back of a single wave, bear off about 20 degrees as you are lifted on the wave's face and then complete your turn once its crest has passed beneath you.

In a single-engine vessel, about all you can do to get your vessel through the turn as quickly as possible is to put your wheel over hard to windward and increase engine revolutions per minute (rpm). With a twin-screw vessel, you can use its engines to even greater advantage. In a planing hull motor yacht, you normally can accomplish the turn quickly by leaving both engines in forward gear, increasing their power slightly, and turning the wheel sharply to windward. With a full-displacement vessel, you may find it necessary to put the windward engine in reverse (while leaving the leeward engine in forward gear) and then increase rpms on both engines to swing her bow around quickly (see illustration next page).

In any of the three types of vessels, particularly the planing hull motor yacht, just be sure you don't apply too much power. You could drive your vessel down the back of the wave you are riding so rapidly that you bury her bow in the base of the oncoming wave.

Once you are successful in getting your vessel's head to weather, it probably will ride most

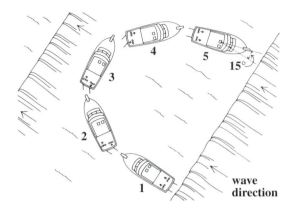

To turn a twin-engine displacement-hull vessel head to weather quickly, put the helm fully over in the direction of the turn and reverse the engine toward the inside of the turn (1, 2, 3, and 4). As the bow approaches the oncoming wave, shift the reversed engine back to forward and straighten the helm (5) to meet the wave at an angle of about 15 degrees.

comfortably if you continue to take oncoming waves at about 15 degrees off the bow rather than from dead ahead. Just be alert to the danger that an especially large wave could knock the boat so far off its track that the beam is exposed to the full force of the storm.

In extreme weather—winds over about 50 knots and waves over about 20 feet (6 m)—don't worry about making forward progress. Instead, concentrate on simply maintaining headway. Powerboats caught in extreme weather without headway eventually will lie with their beams to wind and waves. Lying in this position, they will be extremely vulnerable to structural damage because they're likely to present a significant profile against which the wind can exert its capsizing force; they probably lack a significant keel or ballast to help keep them upright; and they may have vast expanses of saloon glass, which can be caved in by the force of green water crashing into them.

In the Northern Hemisphere, if the severe weather headed your way is a tropical depression,

tropical storm, or hurricane (or, in the North Pacific, a typhoon), its counterclockwise, circular motion creates a dangerous semicircle in the half of the storm to the right of its forward track, in which the storm's forward movement intensifies its winds. You should therefore, if possible, steer your vessel toward the storm's left half, where conditions will be at least slightly less severe.

NIGHT RUNNING

Night running in rivers or inland channels like the Intracoastal Waterway or the Inside Passage to Alaska is not something you want to do if you can avoid it. Navigating at night and reading the nature and intention of other vessels you might encounter from the lights they show are tough enough, but the greatest danger is striking debris in the water that you may not be able to see regardless of how sharp a lookout you keep.

Nevertheless, in extensive cruising there simply will be times when you will not be able to cover the total distance between ports or anchorages along your planned route in daylight and will have to run at night. The best possible situation is to plan both your departure and your arrival in daylight and to confine your night running to open water. If that is not practical, it's best to plan to depart in darkness so you arrive at your destination in daylight. If your destination is a shallow-water anchorage or a poorly marked inlet in the tropics, try to plan your arrival no earlier than about 10 A.M. and no later than about 4 P.M., when the sun is high enough in the sky for you to read the bottom.

Ideally, your nighttime departure will be down a clearly marked channel and into open water. If you must negotiate a poorly marked inland channel in darkness to reach open water, try to check it out beforehand in daylight and note any obstacles you must avoid.

When preparing for an overnight run, make certain you can keep your helm station dark to protect your night vision and that you have a red light available by which to read your charts. Get your normal vessel checks out of the way by late afternoon, eat a light dinner, and get to bed early to get as much rest as possible. Before retiring, prepare whatever beverages and food the night watch will require and make sure it is easily accessible to the helm.

Most skippers find they can handle a single night's run of eight to ten hours alone with no problem, assuming they have someone to relieve them at daylight. If you are a cruising couple who normally have only the two of you aboard and your cruising itinerary calls for a run of more than one night in succession, try to invite family or friends along for that leg of the voyage to help out with the helm during daylight hours. Assuming that on the run you will be in open water and your vessel is equipped with a good autopilot, the helmsperson's main responsibility is to watch for debris in the water and for other vessels intersecting your course and to monitor the engine instruments. You should be able to set the vessel up and give even an inexperienced person enough instruction on what to do if a problem arises and under what circumstances to call you. This should allow them to run the vessel for a few hours in daylight while you get a quick nap. If you don't feel comfortable actually going below and stretching out on your bunk, sleeping in the pilothouse or the saloon will keep you almost instantly available if anything happens.

Watch Systems

For more than one overnight run in succession, you'll need to set up a watch system so you always have a rested person at the helm. The ideal length of a watch is four hours during the day and two hours at night. If you have an even number of watch standers, rotate the schedule by setting up an odd number of watches.

Depending on how many people you have aboard to whom you are comfortable trusting the helm, your watch system (using the twenty-four-hour clock) might look something like that in the table shown. Both the four- and three-person watch schedules give every crew member at least one eight-hour period in each twenty-four hours for a sound rest.

With only two qualified watch standers aboard, the ideal of four-hour daylight and two-hour night-

SAMPLE FOUR-PERSON WATCH SCHEDULE

Watch Hours	0800 1200	1200 1600	1600 2000	2000 2200	2200 2400	2400 0200	0200 0400	0400 0600	0600 0800
Watch Standers									
1st night	A	B	C	D	A	B	C	D	A
2nd night	B	C	D	A	B	C	D	A	B
3rd night	C	D	A	B	C	D	A	B	C
4th night	D	A	B	C	D	A	B	C	D

SAMPLE THREE-PERSON WATCH SCHEDULE

Watch Hours	0800 1200	1200 1600	1600 2000	2000 2400	2400 0200	0200 0400	0400 0600	0600 0800
Watch Standers								
1st night	A	B	C	A	B	C	A	B
2nd night	C	A	B	C	A	B	C	A
3rd night	B	C	A	B	C	A	B	C

time watches is impractical since it does not provide the off watch with a sufficient period of uninterrupted sleep. In that case, it works better to arrange a schedule with six-hour daylight and four-hour night watches that looks like the table below.

On *Americas Odyssey*'s voyage, Anne and I frequently made offshore overnight runs with just the two of us aboard. Because I preferred to stand the entire night watch myself, we constructed a schedule (in which I stood watch A) like the one below.

Navigation Lights Aboard Your Vessel

Check carefully to see that the navigation lights aboard your cruiser meet the requirements for a vessel of its type and size both under way and at anchor as spelled out in the 1980 U.S. Inland Navigation Rules. You should not simply assume its lights are in compliance—especially if it was built in the United States prior to the adoption of the 1980 Rules or was built abroad—because the 1980 act changed certain lighting provisions that had existed previously. Showing the proper lights in the manner required by the Rules is not simply a matter of complying with the law. It is even more important that your lights correctly indicate to other vessels you may encounter at night the type of vessel you are and how you are proceeding. Check all of your navigation lights for proper operation at least once a month and before embarking on any night runs.

You are required to show your vessel's navigation lights anytime you are under way between sunset and sunrise or in conditions of reduced visibility.

Navigation Lights on Other Vessels

Many cruising skippers pay little or no attention to the lighting regulations for other vessels with the argument that they are not operating a commercial towing service or are engaged in trawling operations and therefore don't need to understand the lighting regulations for vessels thus engaged. They do so at their own peril. If you are to conduct your vessel properly during the night runs that eventually become part of extended cruising, the lights aboard other vessels you encounter may well provide your only clue as to their type and intentions and what, if anything, you need to do with respect to them. It therefore is vital that you be able to recognize their meaning.

Lighting regulations can be confusing and, unless you make night runs frequently, are easily forgotten. My best advice is to read the section on navigation lights in the Inland Rules or in *Chapman*'s (both include illustrations in color) to make certain you understand the basics, then refresh your memory just prior to setting out on any night runs. At night, vessels can have a way of looming up in front of you quickly, and if you don't already have the light rules pretty well in mind, you may

SAMPLE TWO-PERSON WATCH SCHEDULE

Watch Hours	0800	1400	2000	2400	0400
	1400	2000	2400	0400	0800
Watch Standers					
1st night	A	B	A	B	A
2nd night	B	A	B	A	B

SAMPLE WATCH SCHEDULE WITH OVERNIGHT RUNS

Watch Hours	1000	1400	2000	0600
	1400	2000	0600	1000
Watch Standers	A	B	A	B

not have time to dig out a copy of the regulations in time to figure out whether that pattern of lights approaching you is a vessel operating under sail alone, to which you must yield the right of way, or a tug pulling a tow as long as a freight train behind it.

OPERATING IN REDUCED VISIBILITY

Fog or a heavy downpour of rain can quickly cut your visibility to next to nothing. Anytime you can't see at least half a mile ahead of your vessel's bow, the first thing to do is turn on your vessel's navigation lights. The second thing to do is slow down. Simply pulling back your throttles to about half your normal cruising speed provides an extra margin of safety by increasing the time you have to react if another vessel or an obstacle unexpectedly looms in your path. If the weather is really thick and your cruiser is not equipped with radar, you may be safer to lay-to (proceed with little or no way on) or anchor in a special anchorage area or outside normal traffic lanes until visibility improves.

The third thing to do is keep an even sharper lookout than you would when visibility is good. If your vessel has both upper and lower helm stations but no radar, in conditions of reduced visibility it's safer to operate from the flying bridge, where you can better see and hear other vessels in your vicinity, rather than from an enclosed wheelhouse or saloon, where your vision is likely to be restricted and sounds are likely to be muffled.

When visibility is restricted, your ears can become even more important than your eyes in telling you what is happening around you. This is particularly the case if visibility is limited and you must maneuver your vessel in a crowded waterway. Periodically bring your engines down to idle to quiet them, and listen carefully for at least two minutes for any vessels that might be about to cross your course. Also do this just before you make any significant course change. Be especially observant of what may be happening downwind of

your position, since even a fairly mild breeze will carry sound away from you.

In reduced visibility, it becomes even more important than usual to know exactly where you are and what lies ahead. Make certain your chart of the area you are cruising is within easy reach of the helm, and use all the means of electronic navigation at your disposal to keep your running plots of your position accurate and current. Use your GPS receiver and electronic chart plotter, for instance, to maintain a continual update of your position. If you're inshore, set your radar on its quarter- or half-mile scale to keep track of the markers along your route and check each one off on the chart as you go by it. Also, keep a sharp eye on the radar display for any other vessels that might be in your vicinity. The owner of that vessel racing through a downpour toward the inlet entrance at 20 knots might not be as careful as you are and may have no idea you're in his boat's path.

If your vessel's hull is wood or fiberglass, it presents almost no target to the radar units aboard other vessels in your vicinity. You should have a good radar reflector aboard, and in limited visibility conditions it should be rigged at your vessel's highest point.

Sound Signals

The best way to meet the sound signaling requirements of the Inland Rules is to equip your vessel with a combined loud-hailer and automatic foghorn, which will sound the appropriate signals at the touch of a switch. It also will effectively amplify many sounds within about 100 yards (90 m) of your vessel. But bear in mind that its cone-shaped horn is directional. Depending on how you have the horn (or horns) positioned, it may do little to amplify sounds coming from astern or off your beam to either side.

As in meeting, crossing, and overtaking situations, the basic sound signals for operating in reduced visibility are short and prolonged horn blasts. In conditions of restricted visibility, you are required to make sound signals appropriate to your type and size of vessel and its operational status at intervals not exceeding two minutes. Within that interval, the signals are as follow.

- If you're making way, you're required to sound one prolonged blast.
- If you're under way but stopped (not at anchor) and making no way through the water, you must sound two prolonged blasts separated by an interval of about two seconds.
- If you're towing another vessel, if your vessel for some reason is not under command, or if you are restricted in your ability to maneuver, you must sound one prolonged blast followed by two short blasts.
- If your vessel is manned and being towed, you must sound one prolonged blast and three short blasts. If possible, this signal should be sounded immediately after the signal of the towing vessel.

If you find you must maneuver through a high traffic area in reduced visibility, one way you can alert other vessels to your presence is to transmit over VHF channel 16: "Sécurité [pronounced *say-kyur-ee-tay*], Sécurité, Sécurité, channel 13," then switch to channel 13 and (at your radio's 1-watt power output) repeat "Sécurité" three times, then transmit your position in relation to the area's aids to navigation, your course, and your speed. In extremely crowded conditions—such as in a major harbor when visibility is less than about a quarter of a mile (0.4 km)—it's wise to repeat this procedure about every ten to fifteen minutes (see chapter 20).

If you're aground, you must sound the signal of a vessel at anchor and also give three separate and distinct strokes on the bell immediately before and after the rapid ringing of the bell.

You must also make appropriate sound signals if you are anchored in limited visibility conditions. These are covered in chapter 18.

RESPONDING APPROPRIATELY IF YOU HAVE AN ACCIDENT

If you have an accident with your vessel that results in personal injury or significant damage to property that you feel may involve your insurance company, you should do several things to make certain you comply with your insurance policy's terms.

One is to protect your vessel from further damage. Most standard yacht policies will pay for towing and assistance if it is necessary to keep the yacht from suffering further damage.

If other people are involved in the incident, be sure to get their full names and addresses. Also try to get the same information from anyone who witnessed the incident.

Inform your insurance agent of the problem as soon as possible. If the incident involves damage to your vessel, try to have your insurer's adjuster authorize any needed repairs before the work is begun. If that proves impossible, try to take pictures of the damage before it is repaired. Again, if possible, get estimates on repairing the damage from two or three reputable boatyards. An even better idea, if possible, is to hire a local marine surveyor to check the damage and give you a complete report. Be certain to get detailed receipts of any expenses you incur.

Arriving at a Dock

So far, so good. You've gotten away from your home dock without doing serious damage to your boat or anyone else's; you've run narrow channels without going aground; you've done everything by the book in right-of-way situations; you've correctly identified and read the intentions of other vessels at night from their lights; and you've run a couple of inlets and handled a variety of bridges and locks, a bit of fog, and some heavy weather. Now its time to put into a marina for fuel or an overnight stop. As you bring your vessel alongside or put her in a slip, you'd like to keep everyone on-shore from realizing this is your first time at this sort of thing with this particular boat and convince them you've been handling this move in tight quarters for years.

DEALING WITH DOCKMASTERS

Dockmasters come in two distinct varieties: some are eminently courteous and can't seem to do enough to help; others are surly ogres who appar-

ently neither need nor want your business and seem to take pride in developing contrariness into an art form. The kind of dockmaster you wind up dealing with at the end of a long day's run can often be determined by how you initiate the relationship.

A little common courtesy can go a long way toward making the relationship pleasant. If you are planning an overnight stay at a marina, call the dockmaster on VHF channel 16 about half an hour before your planned arrival time and be prepared to switch to a proper noncommercial, working channel. Most marinas will use channel 68 as a working channel; a few will use channels 9, 69, or 71. On this first call, simply give your vessel's length and ask whether they can accommodate you overnight. If the answer is yes, most dock-masters will ask you to call them back when you are about 1 mile (1.6 km) from their facility. It's appropriate in that initial call to mention fueling or berthing requirements and any special immediate needs you might have, but be aware that the dock-master is probably busy and don't tie up a lot of time on the working channel asking about such things as restaurants or local transportation in the area. Tend to those matters once you're ashore. If you treat dockmasters like human beings rather than servants, they can be fantastically helpful. If you are rude or overly demanding, they can make your cruising experience far more difficult than it needs to be.

On your second call just as you are approaching the marina, ask whether you'll be laying alongside a pier or entering a slip and ask on which side you should rig your fenders so your mate can prepare them in advance.

Once you're at the marina, if the dockmaster gives you docking instructions, you're probably better off trying to follow them. He should know a lot more about the effects of wind and current around his docks than you do.

Having said all that, the advice of Fred Edwards, a retired naval captain who with his wife, Alice, cruised the Mediterranean for five years, is, "Don't let dockmasters intimidate you. If you don't like the slip offered because of size or exposure, insist on a different one. If the weather starts to turn sour, move. If you are being set down on the pier because the dockmaster put you on the exposed side, don't assume a siege mentality and just start doubling up lines and adding more fenders. Move! Go to the other side of the pier, to a marina farther up the creek, or anchor out in a more sheltered area."

I heartily agree. Once you are directed to a docking space, look it over carefully to see what's going to be involved in getting your boat into it and what conditions are going to be like in it if the weather turns nasty. If you see that strong currents are running across the space, that you are going to be constantly exposed to the wakes of passing boats, or that you are going to be pinned hard against the pilings with predictable winds from a particular quarter, don't hesitate to voice your concerns and ask what else is available.

If you make a slip reservation with a marina several days in advance, find out whether there is a cutoff time beyond which they will give the space

to someone else if you haven't arrived. If you find that weather or a change in your plans prevents you from keeping a reservation, call and cancel. Nothing makes a dockmaster see red quicker than holding a slip for you then having you fail to show up. The dockmaster has not only lost the revenue from your dockage but probably has five potential customers anchored out, staring at the last empty slip in the marina you didn't take, and cussing the dockmaster for not giving it to them. Further, dockmasters have long memories. If you treat one this way and then turn up the next day or months later expecting to have a slip waiting for you, don't be surprised if you're told all the space is taken or you're stuck way out on the end of the fuel dock, where you'll take a proper bashing from the wakes of passing boats.

DOCKING ALONGSIDE A PIER

If docking involves nothing more than coming alongside a pier where you have plenty of room and no significant wind or current to worry about, one major factor in determining how best to make your approach will be the torque of your propeller(s).

If you aren't familiar with prop torque, think of a propeller as a wheel beneath your boat that actually touches the bottom. Most single-engine powerboats have a right-handed propeller, which rotates to the right and kicks the vessel's stern to starboard when going ahead and rotates to the left and kicks the vessel's stern to port when going astern. Since your boat doesn't have brakes, you know you're going to have to shift into reverse to stop it. If yours is a single-screw boat, shifting into reverse will kick your stern to port. Therefore, approach the dock port side–to whenever possible so that when you shift into reverse your propeller's torque will kick your stern in toward the dock rather than away from it.

If your boat has twin engines, you have a bit more choice. The propellers on most twin-engine boats turn outboard (that is, their tops turn toward the outside of the vessel). This means the starboard propeller normally will be right-handed and the port propeller will be left-handed. If you want to approach the dock port side–to, stop your boat by putting your port engine in neutral and shifting only your starboard engine into reverse so the torque of its propeller will pull your stern to port. (If you shift both engines into reverse, the counter forces of the propellers will cancel each other and leave your stern away from the dock.) If you want to approach starboard side–to, simply reverse the process and the left-handed prop on your port engine in reverse will help pull your stern to starboard.

Rigging Docklines

Before making your approach, alert your mate which side you plan to tie up on so that person can rig bow and stern lines at their respective cleats on that side of the vessel. To rig a dockline for instant use, the mate should uncoil it, lay its tail over the safety railings, lead the tail outboard to inboard through the chock or hawsepipe and cleat it off, and then lay the remaining line on deck with the eye on top of the coils. When the mate picks up the coils and throws the eye over a piling or passes it to someone onshore, the line won't be fouled in the safety lines and will already be in the chock or hawsepipe. Once the eye is secured ashore, the mate can uncleat the tail, take up slack in the line as necessary, and then control tension on it or cleat it off.

Rigging Fenders

If the pier you are approaching has pilings that extend at least a foot above your deck level, it's easiest to simply let your vessel's rubrail come up against them and to rig any necessary fenders when you tie up. But if you are approaching a pier that doesn't have pilings, the mate will need to rig vertical fenders at an appropriate height along the hull to protect its topsides. One fender should be rigged at the turn of the vessel's bow and a second about 1 foot (0.3 m) forward of the transom.

Getting Docklines Ashore

Under ideal conditions of no wind and no current, you can simply pull your boat up to the dock and let your mate calmly drop bow and stern lines over an appropriate piling or dock cleat and tie them off on deck. Even under adverse conditions, with a bit of practice your mate should be able to throw the eye of a dockline consistently over a piling up to about 10 feet (3 m) away by using the technique explained here.

You'll avoid a lot of confusion and potential problems if, whenever possible, your mate places the eyes of your docklines over a dock's pilings or cleats personally rather than passing them to someone on the dock. If someone on the dock offers to take your lines, instruct your mate to always give them the eye end of the line—never the tail—and indicate both verbally and by pointing exactly which piling or dock cleat around which to place the eye.

There are a host of reasons for doing this. By passing the eye ashore and controlling the tail on deck, the mate controls the line's length, which can be critical in your docking maneuvers. If the mate puts the eye over a deck cleat on the vessel and passes the tail ashore, the person on the dock controls the line's length and may tie your bow in so tight you don't have room to swing your stern in or may leave so much slack in it that your vessel strikes another vessel in front of you. Also, the helpful soul may or may not know how to tie the tail off securely. If not and you put a strain on the line to help you maneuver to the dock, it can pull loose, leaving you with no line to work against and possibly injuring someone on board your boat or on the dock.

"Walking" to a Dock

If wind and current are not a factor but you need to squeeze into a fairly narrow space at a dock, you can "walk" a twin-screw boat into it sideways the same way we discussed "walking" out of a narrow space in chapter 14.

To prepare to lasso a piling, make sure the dockline's tail is coiled loosely at your feet, extend the eye to its maximum diameter and lay the standing part of the line along the eye (1); then toss the eye toward the piling and allow the standing part to run lightly through your hand (2). Once the eye is over the piling, make sure the tail leads underneath the safety railing before wrapping it around a cleat to take up tension (3).

Unfortunately, there will be few times you can tie up to a dock under the ideal conditions of no wind, no current, and plenty of room, so let's complicate matters a bit.

Problem: you need to take on fuel for your 40-foot (12 m) cruiser, but the only space left at the fuel dock is about a 50-foot (15 m) slot between two other boats that are already tied up alongside. How are you going to get your boat into that narrow space without a lot of bumping and grinding?

The answer to this question is going to depend primarily on the strength and direction of the wind and current around the dock, so before you go charging into this kind of a tight maneuvering situation and create general havoc, lay off about 50 yards (46 m) and size up the situation.

First, glance around to see if the maneuver you intend is likely to interfere with other vessels already in your vicinity or approaching it. Next, look around to determine how wind and current are likely to act on your vessel relative to the direction you want it to go. Study the flags or pennants on your own vessel, on nearby vessels, or on shore to determine the wind's direction and approximate velocity. A 10-knot breeze, for instance, will hold a pennant or flag out from its staff, but it will not be taut nor will it snap. If pennants or flags are taut and snapping, the wind is above 15 knots. Water building up on one side of a dock's pilings will tell you the direction in which the current is flowing and its approximate strength. A good rule of thumb is that each knot of current builds up about half an inch (1 cm) of water on the side of the piling it's striking.

If both wind and current are striking your vessel from the same angle, you must add their effects together to determine their combined effect on the boat's movement. If wind and current are striking your vessel from different angles, you need to mentally compute their relative angles and strengths to figure out their net effect. Your answer to this equation will vary greatly depending on your vessel's draft and windage. Current, for instance, is likely to have greater effect on a deep-keel, full-displacement vessel than will wind, but

wind is likely to have a greater effect than current on a planing hull motor yacht with a great deal of windage, fairly shallow draft, and little if any keel.

Once you have determined the angle and velocity of wind and current, you are in a position to decide how much force you must apply—and in what direction—to counter their effects and dock your vessel with a minimum of fuss.

When planning your maneuver, make whatever combination of wind and current you find yourself facing work for you rather than against you. Since any boat handles far more effectively in forward gear than in reverse, the best way to do that is to keep wind and current on your bow rather than your stern whenever possible. This point is easily illustrated by a story.

One evening, I was placidly tied up to a face dock on a narrow stretch of the Intracoastal Waterway at Great Bridge, Virginia, enjoying the children's hour on the fantail when a 40-foot (12 m) southbound sailboat came boiling down the canal under power with a 4-knot current and about 12 knots of wind on its stern. The skipper decided to tie up in the 45-foot (14 m) space just off my stern and made his approach bow-on. As the current continued to propel him forward despite a great deal of full-astern racing of his engine and screaming at his mate to "grab something," he very nearly managed to stick his bow pulpit into my hors d'oeuvres. I fended him off and watched in horror as he made a complete circle for a second try with the same result. With a lot of frantic arm waving, I suggested he maneuver into the space against the current and wind instead of with them at his back. Once he did so, he was able to gently nose his boat to the dock without mishap.

If wind or current or both are running parallel to the dock, you don't have much of a problem. Head your bow into them and go forward with just enough way on to offset them until you are opposite the space you want to enter. With your helm, allow your bow to fall off just a bit toward the dock; then bring your wheel back to amidships. The wind and current will straighten you back up so that you are parallel to the dock but a few feet closer to it. Keep repeating this maneuver until you are close enough to the dock for your mate to get a bow line over a piling or cleat and take up the slack. Once a line is holding your bow in place, you can use your engine and helm to bring you fully alongside.

Maneuvering to a Dock with a Bow Line

Let's assume, however, that wind and current are not parallel to the dock but running at an angle to it. Suppose, for example, a 10- to 15-knot offshore breeze is blowing, and a knot or so of current is running out from the dock. Let's further suppose that the dock has pilings and you want to lie starboard side–to. With a twin-engine boat, the easiest way to come alongside is by using a simple bow line. Bear in mind that you want, if possible, to keep your boat's bow into wind and current whenever possible. To counter the forces involved, approach the open space bow-on, aiming at the left end of the slip.

While you maintain position a few feet off the dock, have your mate go forward to the bow pulpit, throw the eye of a dockline over the piling at the left end of the space you are trying to enter, secure its standing end around the starboard bow cleat with a half turn or an S-turn, and take up tension on its tail. Caution your mate not to pull the bow in too tightly to the dock because doing that will prevent you from swinging the stern in. Turn your wheel sharply to port, and shift your starboard engine into neutral and your port engine into reverse. The port engine in reverse will allow you to back against the bow line, and its propeller torque will pull your stern to starboard. If you need a bit of extra push to get your stern over toward the dock, briefly kick your starboard engine in and out of forward gear, but be careful not to get too close to the boat tied up ahead of you. As your stern swings in, instruct your mate to take in slack on the bow line to bring your bow toward the pier.

Once you are tightly alongside, hold the boat in position with its port engine in reverse while your mate cleats off the bow line then goes aft to rig a stern line.

Maneuvering to a Dock with Spring Lines

With a single-engine boat, the best way to come alongside a pier in a tight docking situation against offshore wind or current or both is to use an after bow spring. This technique can also be useful with a twin-engine boat if wind or current or both off the dock are especially strong.

To dock port side–to using an after bow spring, approach the open space bow-on but aim at its center point and have your mate throw the eye of a dockline over a piling as close to the center of the space as possible, secure its standing end around the port bow cleat with a half turn or an S-turn, and take up tension on its tail (see top illustration page 244). Again, caution your mate not to pull the boat in too tightly to the dock because doing that will prevent you from swinging the stern in. The mate should take in only enough slack to make sure your bow doesn't strike the boat tied up ahead of you.

Turn your wheel sharply to starboard and go ahead slowly. As you turn, the line off your bow becomes an after bow spring. Instruct your mate to either take in slack to keep your bow from striking the vessel ahead or let out slack to make sure your stern clears the vessel behind you. With your boat's bow held fast by the after bow spring, the discharge current of your propeller will bring your boat's stern to the dock to rest against its rubrail.

Docking with an after bow spring is even easier if your vessel is equipped with forward spring cleats (see photos page 245).

Now suppose you're faced with the same fuel-dock situation except that the 15-knot breeze is blowing onshore and the current is running toward the dock. In this instance, let's again assume you want to lie starboard side–to. If you try to approach the dock bow-on, the wind and current will slam your vessel into the dock and earn you some grimaces from the dockmaster and your fellow skip-

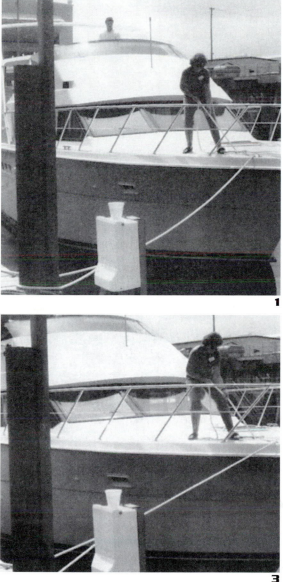

In maneuvering a twin-engine cruiser to a dock with a bow spring, have your mate maintain tension on the spring (1) while you go forward on the engine toward the dock and reverse the engine away from the dock (2). The mate should maintain sufficient tension on the spring to keep you off any vessels tied up ahead but still leave enough slack in the line to allow you to bring the stern to the dock (3).

pers. To solve the problem, have your mate rig a stout fender horizontally directly at the point of your starboard quarter (see bottom illustration next page). Pull opposite the space you wish to enter, and bring your bow into wind and current, which will point your stern toward the dock. Keep your engine(s) in forward gear and ticking over just enough to almost counter the force of the wind and the current. Steer with the helm as you allow your vessel to drift back toward the right side of the open slip until the fender on your starboard quarter touches the dock. As this happens, keep your helm to port, shift your port (outboard) engine to reverse, and maintain enough throttle to resist most of the force of the wind and tide trying to slam your bow down on the dock. If you have the right touch, your bow will be driven down on the dock with only a modest force and come to rest against a dock piling. The wind and current will keep your boat pinned against the dock while your mate rigs bow, stern, and spring lines.

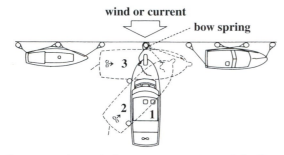

In maneuvering a single-engine cruiser into a tight slip against wind or current or both, approach a piling in the center of the slip bow-on to allow your mate to get a bow spring over it (1). While the mate maintains sufficient tension on the spring to keep you off the vessel tied up ahead, lay your helm fully over in the direction of your turn and go ahead slowly (2) until your stern rests against the dock (3).

Tying Up at a Dock

In a typical docking situation, you'll need to rig four docklines to hold your vessel securely: (1) a bow line that leads from your bow cleat to a piling or dock cleat forward of the bow; (2) an after bow spring that leads aft from your forward spring cleat to a piling or cleat about two-thirds down your vessel's length; (3) a forward quarter spring that leads forward from the quarter spring cleat to a piling or cleat about a third of the way aft from your vessel's bow; and (4) a stern line that leads aft from your stern cleat to a piling or cleat aft of the stern (see top photo page 246). Your stern line will be more effective if you run it from the outboard cleat at your stern rather than from the stern cleat closest to the dock (see bottom photo page 246).

Always tie your boat to the dock, not the dock to your boat. This is one way of saying you should always secure the eye of your docklines to a piling or dock cleat and cleat the tail off to a deck cleat on your vessel—not vice versa. If you are aboard—as you are likely to be most of the time—and anything happens to require you to move your vessel quickly, you have only to go on deck, cast your lines off, and get your vessel under way. When you cast them off, they will either fall back on the dock or fall into the water and sink to the bottom; in either case, they won't be a danger to your props. If the bights are secured aboard your vessel and the tails to the dock, you must climb down on the dock to release them, then come back aboard and get them out of the water. If you try to pull way from the dock with them trailing in the water, at least one is almost certain to get fouled in your prop(s).

Most cruisers don't like to have the tail of a dockline cleated off on deck because they don't want the extra line in their way. Some try to make a neat Flemish coil with the tail, but then they stumble over it every time they go on deck. If they stay at a dock or in a slip a few days, the coil traps all manner of dirt underneath it and discolors their deck. A better solution to the problem is simply to coil the excess line and hang it from the railings as shown in the photos on page 247.

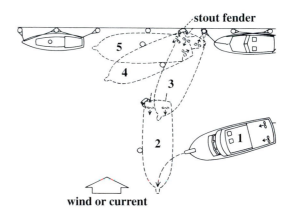

To bring a twin-engine vessel alongside starboard-to with wind or current or both setting onto the dock (1), rig a stout fender on the point of your vessel's stern that will lay against the dock, then round up just upwind, upcurrent, or both from the berth you've chosen. Keep just enough way on to allow wind and current to carry you straight toward the stern end of the space (2). As your stern contacts the dock (3), turn your helm fully into the current and shift your outboard engine into reverse to help counter the current's tendency to drive you down onto the dock (4 and 5).

Pivoting a vessel along-side a dock is even easier if the boat is equipped with spring cleats about a third of the way down its length and the eye of the spring is looped over a piling at the stern end of the slip.

Tying a vessel securely along a face dock involves a bow line and fore and aft spring lines. Note the fenders hung vertically.

In this situation, the stern line leading from the side of the transom away from the dock is much more effective than if it were attached on the side of the transom toward the dock.

Here are a few other tricks you might find helpful.

- If the eye of your dockline isn't big enough to go over an especially wide piling, reach through the eye, grab the line's standing part, and pull it through to form a slipknot.
- If you put the eye of your dockline around a piling above the dockline of another vessel already tied to it, the lower line cannot be released without first removing yours. To eliminate this problem, run the bight of your line up through the bight of the other dockline before looping it over the piling. Then, either dockline can be removed without disturbing the other.
- In areas of extreme tidal range, if the angle of a dockline from your vessel's deck to a piling is downward, a rising tide and the motion of your vessel could pull it loose. To prevent a problem, double the bight on itself to hold the bight securely in place.

When tied in a slip, you can stow the tail of a dockline neatly by coiling and wrapping it, leading the tail up through the top of the coil, and then securing it around the safety railing with two half hitches (left). An alternative is to hang the loop in a plastic loop holder (right).

Cleating Off Docklines

Over the course of your cruising life, you'll cleat off lines thousands of times, so you want to develop a quick, foolproof technique that you can execute virtually automatically. The method I've found most efficient is shown here. Cleating off a line this way has a number of advantages. By standing at the end of the cleat opposite the direction of the strain, you can quickly run the line un-

der the horn closest to you, across the top of it, and under the horn farthest from you, which puts you in the optimal position to take a strain on the line if necessary. Also, you can execute the entire maneuver without moving your feet. A line cleated off in this manner will not bind against itself no matter how much strain is put on it and will be easy to uncleat.

Unless you're preparing for a storm, there's no need to make more than two turns of line over a

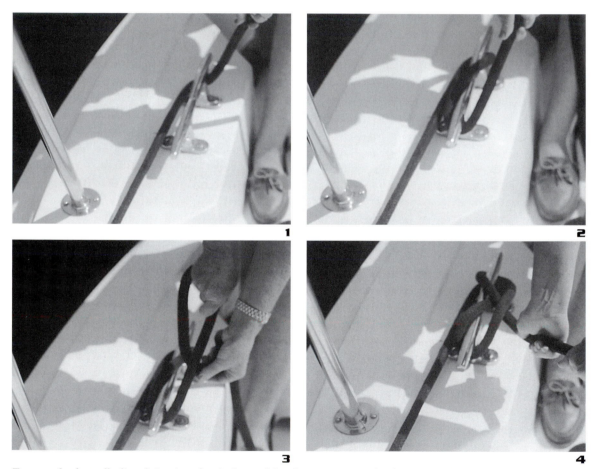

To properly cleat off a line, bring it under the horn of the cleat opposite to the direction of the strain (1); take it across the back of the cleat and under the opposite horn in the reverse direction (2). form a loop by repeating the process in reverse, (3) by flipping the line under itself, and drop the loop over the horn in the direction of the strain (4). See also captions on pages 206–7.

cleat. This will simply take more time to uncleat.

A number of cruising powerboats have hawse-holes in the transom or the cockpit covering boards, and some—particularly those built in the Far East— have hawseholes in their topsides just above deck level. Throughout the following discussion, anytime we discuss securing a dockline to a deck cleat, assume that before being cleated off, the eye or the tail of the dockline will first be lead outside to inside through the hawsehole if the vessel is equipped with hawseholes.

Using Fenders and Fender Boards

When lying alongside a face pier that does not have pilings, the most effective protection for your hull is fenders hung vertically from your deck railings (see top photo on page 246). One should be placed just aft of the turn of your vessel's bow, and the other should be 2 or 3 feet (0.6–0.9 m) forward from your stern.

For lying alongside a pier that does have pilings, the best protection is provided by fender boards between your vessel's hull and one piling just aft of the turn of your vessel's bow and a second piling 2 or 3 feet (0.6–0.9 m) forward of your stern. If you are tied up to a pier with pilings, you can use cylindrical fenders rigged horizontally to protect your topsides, but they are harder to keep properly positioned than fender boards (see photo). The keys to using these fenders successfully are to tie them just below your vessel's rubrail, to tie off the line through their center to widely spaced stanchions so its angle with the fender is shallow rather than perpendicular, and to keep your spring lines taut to limit your boat's movement fore and aft as much as possible.

ENTERING A SLIP

If an overnight stop at a marina involves putting your boat into a slip, one major factor that will help you decide whether it's best to enter it bow-on or stern first will be the direction of wind and current. Remember our dictum earlier in this chap-

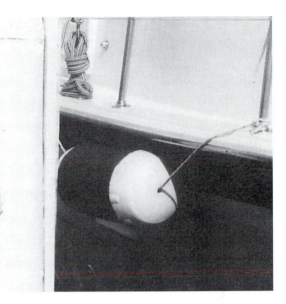

When using a round fender against a piling, tie it just below your vessel's rubrail, tie off the line through its center to widely spaced stanchions so its angle with the fender is shallow rather than perpendicular, and keep your spring lines taut to limit your boat's fore-and-aft movement as much as possible.

ter that your boat will maneuver much better going into wind and current than it will with either of them on your stern. If the wind and current are from the direction of the slip, you'll find it easier to enter the slip bow first; if they're setting toward the slip, you'll find it easier to back in.

Another consideration is how you carry your tender. If it's carried on deck, it isn't a factor. If it's mounted on davits aft, you'll probably want to enter the slip bow first regardless of the direction of wind and current. If you're towing your tender and plan to enter a slip bow first, secure the tender up snugly to your vessel's stern before you start maneuvering into the slip so its painter won't get fouled in your prop(s). If you must enter a slip stern first, stop off at the fuel dock and tie the tender off there before you enter the slip; then walk over and retrieve it.

Entering Bow First

Since entering a slip bow first is a bit less complicated than going in stern first, we'll cover that first. To keep matters simple at the outset, let's assume that the slip you want to enter faces south and the wind is either nonexistent or coming straight out of the north.

The outboard end of a slip normally is defined by two pilings in the water. As you enter the slip bow first, you need to get the bight of a dockline over each of these pilings to hold your stern. This isn't much of a problem if you have two line handlers aboard. Post both of them—each with a dockline in hand—at the bow pulpit; then ease up to the starboard piling and let one crew loop the eye of a dockline over it. While that crew member is walking the tail of the line along the starboard side deck to the cockpit (keeping it outside the railings, of course), ease your bow over to the port piling and let the second crew member loop the eye of a line over that piling and walk its tail along the port side deck to the cockpit. As the line handlers reach the cockpit, they should cross with their line to the opposite corner of the cockpit, take a quick half turn or S-turn around the stern cleat, and pull in slack as you slowly motor forward. As the stern pulls even with the pilings, they should let out the stern lines as necessary. Once your bow is about 5 feet (1.5 m) from the dock, have the crew cleat off the stern lines fully. One crew member can then step ashore to receive the bow lines and loop their eyes over dock cleats at the corners of the slip while the other crew member stands by at the bow to cleat their tails off on deck.

This maneuver gets a little more involved if you have only yourself and your mate aboard. In that event, before you attempt to enter the slip (assuming you are entering bow first), have your mate ready port and starboard bow lines on the foredeck and then ready stern lines as follows: on the starboard side, loop the eye of a dockline that is at least as long as your vessel over the starboard bow cleat; lead the tail of the dockline outside the safety railing, along the starboard side of the hull,

and across the cockpit; and then cleat it off to the port stern cleat. The line should not be pulled tight but should be cleated off with just about a foot (0.3 m) of slack in it. Repeat the process in reverse to rig the port stern line and cleat it off to the starboard stern cleat. (The tails of the stern lines are cleated off on opposite sides of the cockpit so that they will be properly crossed once they are deployed.)

With your bow lines ready and your stern lines rigged, post your mate on the bow, ease up to the slip's starboard piling, and have your mate release the eye of the starboard stern line from the bow cleat and loop it over the piling. (That line should then lead from the slip's starboard piling and across your cockpit to your vessel's port stern cleat.) Nudge your bow over to the port piling and repeat the process. Have your mate go to the cockpit and uncleat the tails of both stern lines but keep a grip on them. As you motor slowly into the slip, the mate should take up slack in both lines to keep them out of the props. Once the stern passes the pilings, the mate will need to let both lines out until you call out that the bow is about 5 feet (1.5 m) from the dock. You can then hold the boat in position while the mate cleats off both stern lines. With the stern secure, the mate should go to the bow. If someone is on shore to assist, the mate can simply throw that person the eye end of the bow lines and cleat their tails off to the bow cleats. If no one is on the dock to take your bow lines and the lines cannot be tossed over cleats on the dock, the mate will have to toss the coils ashore, go ashore to place the eyes of the lines over their respective cleats, and then come back aboard to cleat them off.

Backing Down

Since entering a slip stern first involves operating your boat in reverse, let's talk a bit about that before we get into the specifics of getting into the slip.

Many inexperienced cruising skippers attempt to back their boats just as they would back an automobile—facing forward at the helm and looking over their shoulder to see where the stern is going. Watch an experienced sportfishing charter captain put a vessel in a slip. In almost every case, the captain will face astern and operate the gears and throttles in reverse, which affords much better visibility.

If you back your vessel facing astern, don't forget that the starboard side of your vessel is still starboard and that port is still port.

Backing a twin-screw boat while facing aft can be greatly simplified by repositioning the gear and throttle levers. Most twin-screw boats come out of the factory with both gear levers paired on the starboard side of the helm and both throttles paired on the port side. Many professional captains rearrange the linkage to put port and starboard gears and throttles on their respective sides of the helm, with the throttles inboard and the gears outboard. This allows them to dock a boat facing astern with no confusion as to which levers operate which engine.

If your vessel has a single engine, anytime you operate it in reverse, don't forget to take your propeller's torque into account. Since the torque of its right-handed prop going in reverse will pull your stern to port, aim for a point slightly to starboard of where you want the stern to go and let the propeller's torque help you back in a straight line, or offset the torque with a little right rudder. Only experience will tell you how much right rudder you'll need to offset propeller torque on your particular boat. If your stern gets too far to port, you may have to kick the engine into forward gear with a quick in-and-out motion. Because of your vessel's sternward momentum, you won't actually go forward, but the propeller's right-handed torque going ahead will help swing your stern to starboard.

If your boat has twin engines, think of it as pivoting around a stake running through its center, remember that its engines are off to their respective sides of the vessel's centerline, and think of an engine in reverse as pulling the stern rather than pushing it. These ideas together may help you visualize that when you are at the helm facing aft, the starboard engine in reverse will pull the stern to port both because of its propeller's torque and because it is to starboard of the vessel's centerline. For the same reasons, the port engine in reverse will pull the stern to starboard.

Novice skippers of twin-engine boats often find the combination of a helm, two gears, and two throttles a bit intimidating when they are trying to back down. If you are fairly new to maneuvering a twin-screw boat in reverse, you will find backing down easier if you center your helm and set both throttles at about 600 rpm, then back up simply by shifting the throttles between reverse and neutral as required to bring the boat to the dock. If you want the stern to swing to starboard, for instance, leave the starboard engine in neutral and use only the port engine in reverse to bring it around. Conversely, if you want the stern to swing to port, leave the port engine in neutral and shift the starboard engine into reverse to put the boat's transom where you want it.

Entering a Slip Stern First

With wind and current either minimal or setting directly into the slip, backing into it and handling your docklines is basically the reverse of the procedures for entering bow first—but with a few minor differences. In rigging the bow lines for deployment, the mate should lead their tails outside the safety lines and cleat them off to their respective bow cleats, then lead their eyes aft and temporarily secure them to a stern cleat on their respective sides of the vessel without crossing them. As you back your stern toward the slip's outboard pilings, the mate should be in the cockpit to place the eye of each bow line over the piling on its side of the slip. If you have a second line handler aboard, this person can go forward to control tension on the bow lines as you continue to back into the slip. If only you and your mate are aboard, however, the mate need not go back to the bow to control the bow lines because they are well forward and not in danger of getting fouled in your props. As your stern approaches the dock, the mate can either toss the eyes of the stern lines to someone on shore or step onto the dock to place them over a cleat, but they should be crossed. Once the stern is secured, you can hold position in the slip with your engine(s) while the mate goes to the foredeck to take up the slack in the bow lines and tie them off to the bow cleats.

In many parts of the world you'll find the normal way of tying up is stern first to a quay with an anchor out. Known as a Mediterranean moor, this technique is a hybrid of both anchoring and tying up, and setting the anchor properly is the most critical part. I cover the technique in detail in chapter 18.

18

Anchoring

If you cruise very long, you're bound to find your-self swinging serenely on the hook in a lovely cove late one afternoon when a cruising couple will pull in and go through an anchoring routine worthy of the Keystone Kops. Papa will be on the flying bridge waving frantically and yelling orders to his frazzled and frustrated spouse, who will be scur-rying wildly around the foredeck. Their anchor will not hold on the first try—and probably not on the second. A few choice expletives will waft across the water. If they finally get an anchor to hold, it probably will be in a position where their vessel's swinging room makes it a danger to yours, and you will have to up anchor and move to a safer location. As the tide rises or the wind gets up in the night, you'll probably hear them repeat the whole rou-tine about 2:00 or 3:00 A.M. because they failed to set the anchor properly, were using the wrong kind of anchor or rode, or failed to put out sufficient scope to allow for changing conditions. Brig Pem-berton, who with his wife, Louise, has voyaged the length of the Caribbean several times in their 48-foot (14.6 m) power cruiser, *Victoire*, says, "I'm amazed that some people who have cruised for years never learn from their mistakes and go through this completely unnecessary farce every time they try to anchor their vessel."

This chapter's objective is to help you select a good anchorage and devise a technique to get the right anchor down in the right place on the first try, tie it off securely, then relax for the children's hour and enjoy a chuckle or two as you watch others in the harbor go through their anchoring antics.

SELECTING AN ANCHORAGE

When choosing an overnight anchorage, look for the optimum combination of good holding ground, protection from the wind, and water shallow enough to let you put out a safe scope of rode with a reasonable amount of chain or line yet deep enough to leave several feet of water under your keel at low water.

In the tropics, you should start deciding by midafternoon where you will anchor. Except for major harbors, aids to navigation are likely to be few and far between. To get into a suitable anchorage, you'll probably have to depend on reading the bottom (as detailed in chapter 19), and you want to do that while the sun is still high enough in the sky to give you good visibility. Even in more northerly latitudes, plan to reach your selected anchorage a couple of hours before sunset. If the spot you've selected turns out to have a bottom of solid granite or one with the consistency of oatmeal, you may need an extra hour or so of daylight to select an alternate.

The place to start looking for an anchorage in any waters is your chart, which will tell you of any areas you must avoid, such as channels or restricted areas. Your chart also will list any special anchorage areas, which will be marked on the chart with a magenta line and, in some cases, by yellow buoys in the water.

As you consider a possible bay or cove as an anchorage for the night, see what the chart says about the makeup of its bottom. Look for areas of hard sand, a mixture of mud and sand, or mixed mud and clay. Light grass is okay if your anchor's flukes can dig through it down to hard bottom, but stay away from heavy grass. Your anchor may get an initial bite in it and give you a false sense of security; with the first really heavy wind, however, the grass can pull loose at the roots and leave you adrift. If you have a choice, stay away from areas marked as soft mud or rocky. Never anchor over live coral because your anchor and rode can destroy beauty it took nature thousands of years to develop. If you carry a lead line aboard, soundings with it with a bit of hard wax or grease on the end can tell you a lot about the bottom's consistency and potential holding ability.

Cruising guides also can be a valuable source of information about anchorages in the areas they cover and usually will include sailing directions to enter the anchorages along with the location of reefs or shoals to avoid or ranges on shore you can use to make sure you keep your vessel over deep water.

In general, you want to put as much landmass as possible between your boat and the prevailing winds, but beware of snugging yourself too far up into a bay or cove without leaving yourself plenty of swinging room and making sure you won't be grounded at low tide. If the land area immediately to windward is high hills or mountains, put out plenty of scope and leave yourself plenty of room to leeward. A saddle between two hills or mountains can funnel wind into an anchorage at twice the speed of the ambient wind. If the wind increases sharply, air pressure can build up on the windward side of hills or mountains and suddenly spill over the top with incredible force. In Alaska, these winds, which can reach velocities of 100 miles (160 km) an hour or more, are called *williwaws*. Australians call them by the especially apt name of *bullets*.

In figuring the depth of water you'll have under your keel, remember that the water depths on charts list either "mean lower low water" or "mean low water," which are normal averages. At the new and full phases of the moon, spring tides can lower that figure by as much as 20 percent. Also, persistent high winds from certain quarters can drastically lower the mean water figures, so check your tide table for the area carefully and allow yourself all the leeway you can.

Once you've decided on the area in which you plan to anchor, a number of factors will influence exactly where in that general area you drop the hook. Be sure the entire 360-degree circle around your anchor through which your boat can swing as winds or currents shift is clear of obstacles. (That circle's diameter, of course, will be equal to twice the length of rode you plan to put out.) Dropping the anchor in one spot might put your boat in an ideal position as long as the wind stays out of the east, for instance, but make sure that you will still have plenty of room if the wind veers or backs to any other point of the compass.

If other boats are already anchored in the area, don't forget to allow for their swinging room as well. The two circles in which your respective vessels could swing around their anchors should be separated by at least 100 yards (90 m), and 200 yards (185 m) is even better. Don't assume that if the wind or current shifts, all the boats in a particular anchorage will swing the same way. The speed with which different boats react to a shift and the angle at which they lay to wind or current can differ dramatically depending on their draft, the configuration of their bottom, and their windage.

USING ANCHORING HAND SIGNALS

When anchoring with one person operating the boat's controls at the flying bridge helm and the other working on the bow, spoken or shouted communications can become a problem, especially if a stiff wind is blowing. To avoid confusion, work out a series of simple hand signals with your mate that allow the two of you to communicate clearly. The mate's hand held out horizontally at arm's length with its palm vertical, for instance, could indicate the direction in which the helmsperson is to steer (rather than the direction of an obstruction to avoid). A fist with the thumb pointed downward might communicate the helmsperson's instruction for the mate to release the anchor. A thumbs-up might instruct the mate to retrieve the

anchor with the windlass. A hand held palm forward like a traffic cop might mean "hold everything," and an OK sign from the mate, with the thumb and forefinger making a circle, might mean the anchor is secured and the helmsperson is clear to proceed.

USING GOOD ANCHORING TECHNIQUE

When most yacht cruisers anchor their vessels, they approach the intended point of anchoring from downwind, then cut the power and let the boat drift toward the intended anchoring point until it loses all headway. After the vessel has come to a stop, they drop the anchor and pay out chain or rode as their boat drifts back downwind. Once the anchor digs into the bottom, they finish the job off by backing down to set it firmly.

Aboard *Americas Odyssey*, Anne and I used a different technique (see illustration). Once I had picked out an anchoring spot, Anne would go to the bow and prepare the anchor for deployment by removing any tie-downs we had used to make sure it didn't break loose in a heavy sea, slack off the tension on the windlass enough to release about 1 foot (0.3 m) of chain, and kick the anchor

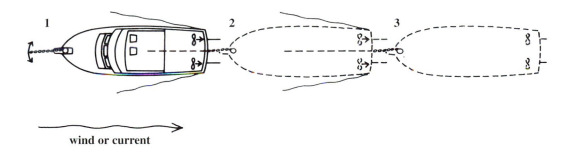

Dropping your anchor while slowly going astern (1) greatly reduces the likelihood of its fouling on its own chain. In setting an anchor with engines reversed (2), the rode should come fully taut and bearings on shoreside objects should indicate no vessel movement astern. When calculating anchor scope (3), don't forget to include the height of your bow chock above the water's surface and any increase in water depth due to tide.

out on its rollers a bit to make sure it would fall free when the tension was fully released. I'd slowly approach our intended anchoring spot in the usual manner from downwind but deliberately pass over the spot at which I wanted to drop the anchor. Once we were about 50 feet (15 m) upwind of the target, I'd drop both engines into reverse and back the boat down toward the spot with its engines just barely ticking over. As the center of the boat was about over the point where I wanted the anchor to rest, I'd give Anne a simple thumbs-down hand signal and she would release the tension on the windlass to let the anchor and chain run free.

I'd continue to back the boat down slowly as the chain paid out. When all the scope I wanted was paid out, I'd signal Anne to tighten up the tension on the windlass. Dropping the anchor while you are going slowly astern under power ensures that the chain is strung out behind the anchor rather than dumped on top of it, which would sharply increase the chances of getting anchor and chain tangled up.

When the windlass tension was down tight, I'd briefly run the engines in reverse to set the anchor. I liked to see the anchor chain bow-string tight. That way I was certain the anchor was well set and not likely to drag, no matter how the wind or current turned the boat.

As you back down to set an anchor, take a bearing on two objects ashore that create a range to make certain you are staying in the same place. Once the catenary (sag) is out of the chain, a well-set anchor should hold your boat steady as a rock. If your bearing on the range ashore indicates you are still moving backward, or if you feel any shuddering, the anchor is still skipping along the bottom and trying to find a purchase. Once you are certain your anchor is well set, periodically check the bearing on the shoreside range you've selected to make certain your anchor isn't dragging.

Anchoring Scope

Ask a cross section of yacht cruisers to define the term *scope*, and most will reply that it is "the ra-

tio of an anchor rode's length to the depth of the water." Close, but no cigar. Under that definition, to achieve a 5:1 scope, the skipper of a 48-foot (14.6 m) powerboat anchored in 8 feet (2.4 m) of water would put out 40 feet (12 m) of anchor rode. In fact, even if the water level in the anchorage doesn't rise, that is really a scope of only 2.5:1. If an incoming tide raises the water level in the anchorage, it's even less.

Here's why: the proper definition of scope is "the ratio of an anchor rode's length to the *maximum distance from a vessel's bow roller to the bottom*."

That definition takes in two important differences: the tide range and the height of the vessel's bow roller above the water. In the example above, the vessel's bow roller may well be 8 feet (2.4 m) above the water, which in an 8-foot water depth places it at least 16 (4.8 m) feet above the bottom. That being the case, a scope of 5:1 would require 80 feet (24 m) of anchor rode [(8 + 8) × 5 = 80] rather than 40 feet (12 m). If an incoming tide increases the water's depth 2 feet (0.6 m), the bow roller would be 18 feet (5.5 m) above the bottom, which would require 90 feet (27 m) of rode [(8 + 8 + 2) × 5 = 90] to achieve a 5:1 scope.

In computing scope then, always remember to include the height of your vessel's bow roller above the water plus the depth of the water at the time you anchor (taken from your depth-sounder) and any increase in the water's depth that can be caused by an incoming tide (as indicated by a tide table for the area).

The minimum scope you should allow for overnight anchoring is a function of your boat's size and type, the strength of wind you're likely to experience, and the type of rode you are using. In even the lightest conditions of wind—under 10 knots—I'd recommend that the skipper of a planing hull powerboat under 50 feet (15 m) using an all-chain rode put out a minimum scope of 3:1; for that same vessel using a combination chain-rope rode, I'd increase that to 5:1, and to 7:1 for an all-rope rode. For a heavier, semidisplacement or full-displacement vessel of that length in light winds, and for a planing hull cruiser in winds to 20 knots, I'd recommend a minimum scope of 5:1 and 7:1, respectively, depending on the type of rode they were using. If winds were expected to be over 20 knots, I'd increase scope on the planing hull boat using a chain rode to 7:1 and with a chain-rope rode to 8:1. For a semidisplacement or full-displacement vessel in winds over 20 knots with all-chain rode, I'd increase the scope to 6:1 and with a rope-chain rode to 8:1. Anytime the winds are expected to exceed 30 knots, put out all the rode of either type you have or can deploy without danger of swinging into another vessel.

Setting Two Bow Anchors

In extended cruising, you're likely to encounter a number of situations where a single anchor really won't hold your vessel securely or exactly where you want it and you will need to set two anchors off the bow.

In situations where you have adequate swinging room, it's best to set an anchor about 22½ degrees to either side of your vessel's centerline, which will leave about 45 degrees between them. That would be the case, for instance, anytime the winds in the area of your anchorage are predicted to reach over about 30 knots. Setting two anchors in this fashion can also help reduce your boat's tendency (especially if it's a planing hull motor yacht) to yaw—or "skate"—from one side of its anchor to the other in fairly high winds.

To create this kind of an anchoring setup, it's best to deploy your secondary anchor first because its rope rode will be easier to handle and make your boat easier to handle while you set your primary anchor on its all-chain rode (see illustration next page). Set your secondary anchor as suggested above, but when you drop it, note a pair of objects ashore that, when one is behind the other, establish a line perpendicular to the wind and along which your secondary anchor lies. Fall back until you have paid out about 10 percent more of your secondary rode than is necessary to establish the scope appropriate to the conditions, and set your sec-

ondary anchor well with your engine(s) in reverse.

From that point, have your mate keep the secondary rode out of your props by taking up most of its slack with the windlass's capstan while you power off at 45 degrees to the wind. Go slightly past the line along which your secondary anchor lies, then shift into reverse, go astern slowly until you cross the line, and have the mate drop your primary anchor. Have the mate let out both rodes and fall back until you have paid out about 10 percent more of your primary rode than is necessary to establish the scope appropriate to the conditions. Then have the mate leave the secondary rode slack and rig your anchor bridle or engage the devil's claw. Once the strain of the primary rode is off the windlass, set your primary anchor well with your engine(s) in reverse. Then, as you power slowly forward in the direction of your secondary anchor, have the mate take up slack in the secondary rode with the windlass's capstan until the angle of each rode to your bow is approximately equal and the tension on both rodes is approximately the same. Those relationships will indicate your vessel is lying midway between the two anchors with the proper amount of scope paid out.

This arrangement works well as long as you get both anchors well set with at least a 45-degree angle between them. There is a variation on this theme called a Bahamian moor, which involves anchors set to port and starboard off your bow at right angles to your vessel's centerline. In theory, it is useful when you must anchor in a narrow channel where you are exposed to significant current or tide reversals. The idea is that as the tide reverses, you will lie to first one anchor, then the other, with your bow merely pivoting around an essentially fixed position. The idea looks great in the neat boating magazine diagrams, but my experience has been that it seldom actually works out that way. Even if you get this rig perfectly set, what usually happens is that your boat swings around and around in small circles until the two anchor rodes are so tightly twisted together that it's almost impossible to separate them. If you should get your rodes into this kind of a tangle and

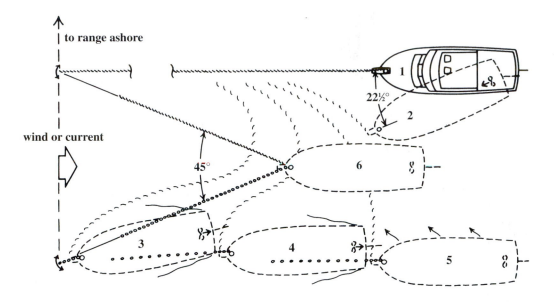

In setting out two anchors, get your secondary anchor set securely first and drop back to an appropriate scope plus 10 percent (10); then power off at about 45 degrees (2) until your secondary anchor is abeam and set your primary anchor going slowly astern (3). Set your primary anchor well with reversed engines (4), fall back to the proper scope on your primary rode plus 10 percent (5), and then take up slack on both rodes until the anchors lie off your bow at approximately a 45-degree angle (6).

have to move your vessel quickly, you would be in real trouble.

In anything short of an approaching tropical storm or hurricane whose circular motion will create up to a 180-degree wind shift, my advice is to stay away from the Bahamian moor if at all possible. First, don't anchor in a tidal channel without sufficient swinging room, if you can avoid it. If anchoring in such a place is unavoidable, bury a single good, heavy plow or Bruce anchor deeply on plenty of chain. In anything less than about 4 knots of current and 20 knots of wind, you will find that the chain dragging on even a bottom of hard-packed sand will take the strain of your vessel as it reverses direction and won't put strain on your anchor at all. Even if a heavy plow or a Bruce anchor should pull loose as the angle of pull on it is reversed, the design makes it highly likely it will re-

set itself as your vessel puts tension on it from the other direction.

Stern Anchors

You may well encounter a situation, particularly with a planing hull motor yacht, where heavy winds cause your vessel to yaw first to one side of a single anchor, then to the other. Even semidisplacement or full-displacement vessels can skate around their anchors if wind is pushing them in one direction and a strong tide or current is pushing them in another. As your vessel skates well off to one side, it can be struck nearly broadside by oncoming waves, which not only is quite uncomfortable but can be dangerous since the changing angle of tension on your anchor could pull it loose.

As already noted, setting a secondary anchor off

the bow at 45 degrees to your primary anchor can be an antidote to skating, but even that may not provide the stability you need. In such a case, set a stern anchor. If only you and your mate are aboard, set your primary anchor in the usual way but let out double the scope appropriate to the conditions, wait until your vessel is lying in line with the wind or current or both, and have your mate let a second anchor go over your stern. Slowly power straight toward your primary anchor while you take up the slack in the primary rode with your flying bridge windlass switch and your mate pays out the stern anchor rode, being careful to keep it from becoming fouled in your prop(s). Once the appropriate amount of scope is paid out astern, have your mate cleat off the stern rode and set the stern anchor by going ahead against it with a brief burst of power. With the stern anchor well set, take in most of the slack on your bow anchor rode and lie to it while tension on the stern anchor rode keeps your stern from swinging off the wind.

Anchor Signals

Vessels more than 23 feet in length but less than 65.6 feet (7–20 m) that are at anchor outside special anchorage areas from sunset to sunrise must show an all-around white light wherever it can best be seen. Such vessels at anchor outside special anchorage areas during the day must display a ball-shaped day mark at least 2 feet (0.6 m) in diameter forward where it can best be seen.

In limited visibility conditions, if your vessel is less than 65.6 feet (20 m) in length and you are anchored in a special anchorage area, you are not required to make sound signals.

If you are anchored outside a special anchorage area in limited visibility conditions, you must signal your position once each minute with your ship's bell and foghorn. If your vessel is 39.4 feet to 328.1 feet (12–100 m) in length, you must ring your bell rapidly for five seconds. If your vessel is less than 39.4 feet in length, you must make "some other efficient sound signal" at intervals not more than every two minutes. Either size vessel

may also give a three-blast signal to warn of its position and the possibility of collision with an approaching vessel: one short, one prolonged, one short.

Mediterranean Moor

In many parts of the world, the normal way of tying up is stern first to a quay with an anchor out. Known as a Mediterranean moor, this technique is a hybrid of both anchoring and tying up, but since the most critical part of the maneuver is properly placing your anchor and setting it well, I cover the topic here (see illustration next page).

Prepare for the maneuver by figuring how much anchor rode you need to pay out based on a scope of about 5:1. Also, have your mate put out vertical fenders port and starboard, lay out two stern lines for deployment in the cockpit, and get the anchor ready to fall freely.

Stand out a little farther from the quay than the length of rode you need to pay out to get the 5:1 scope, and line your vessel up in front of the spot you intend to occupy. As soon as your vessel gathers sternway, have your mate release the anchor. After you've gone astern about half the distance to the quay (and while your stern is still well clear of the bows of any boats already tied to the quay), go through your anchor setting routine. Have your mate fully tighten the tension on the windlass; then back down with your engines. With the anchor set, have your mate go to the cockpit and prepare to fend off other vessels already moored, if necessary, and rig the stern lines.

At this point, your job at the helm becomes a little like patting your head while rubbing your tummy because you must do two things simultaneously: use the flying bridge switch for your windlass to let out scope on your anchor rode (but keeping the rode taut to keep your bow from falling off); and work your gear(s) to back toward the space you're aiming for. With a single-engine boat, don't forget that in reverse your right-handed propeller will tend to set your stern to port. Aim your stern a bit to starboard of where you want it

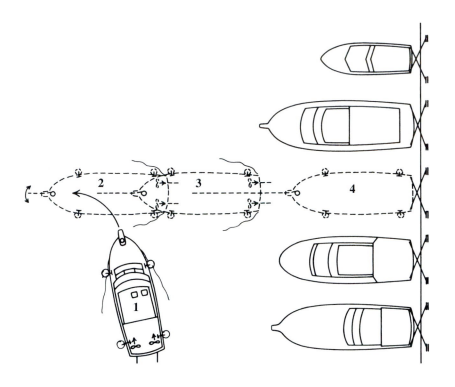

To execute a Mediterranean moor, put out fenders on both sides of your vessel fore and aft and line your stern up with the space you intend to occupy (1), drop your primary anchor while going astern (2), and then pay out rode as you continue powering astern (3) until your mate can tie off to the quay with crossed stern lines (4).

to go, or offset the prop's torque with a bit of right rudder. If a significant crosswind is blowing, your bow is likely to be set down more than your stern. If your stern gets too far to port, you may have to kick the engine ahead briefly, which will use the propeller's torque to help swing your stern to starboard.

While you're backing down, your mate at the stern should fend off the vessels to either side, if necessary. Once you are about 5 feet (1.5 m) from the dock, kick your engine(s) into neutral. If you've kept the tension on your anchor rode properly taut, it will check your sternway and hold the boat in position while your mate either passes the eye end of your stern lines to someone ashore or steps ashore to secure them. The stern lines should be crossed to help reduce the sideways motion of your stern.

Once you're safely tied up, take up the appropriate tension on your anchor rode to hold your

bow in place, set your anchor bridle, and rig your gangway over the stern.

KEEPING WATCH AT ANCHOR

If you follow the suggestions above, you should have your boat so securely anchored that under normal circumstances you won't need to wake up every few hours to check it. If the weather is turning nasty, you are unavoidably anchored off a lee shore, you are going to have a significant tide change in the middle of the night, or you are concerned about the holding quality of the bottom you're anchored in, you might want to set your alarm clock for the time of the tide change to make sure your anchor holds as your boat swings around.

Even under normal circumstances, just to be on the safe side, you might want to set an electronic anchor watch with your depth-sounder, GPS (global positioning system), or radar, or some combination of the three. (But make certain you can hear their alarms in your stateroom and that they are loud enough to wake you from a deep sleep. If not, have an electronics technician rig them to trigger a separate alarm next to your bunk.) To use your depth-sounder as an anchor watch, set its depth alarm at about 5 feet (1.5 m) less than the amount of water you should have under your keel within the circle described by your anchor rode at low tide. If your anchor drags and you drift out of that circle toward shallow water, the alarm should go off. Many modern GPS receivers allow you to describe a circle around your vessel and sound an alarm if the signals they receive indicate you have drifted out of it.

Both of these systems will alert you if your vessel moves out of the circle described by your anchor rode, but neither will warn you if something intrudes inside that circle. In a crowded anchorage with the wind getting up, you can set your radar's guard zone to cover a circle of about 100 yards (90 m) in diameter around your vessel and sound an alarm if it receives signals from anything that has intruded into it. If the radar's alarm goes off in the night, a nearby vessel has probably dragged its anchor and is bearing down on you, so you'll want to scurry topside in the hope of fending it off.

ANCHORING IN TROPICAL STORMS OR HURRICANES

If you find yourself at anchor under the threat of a tropical storm, remember that as the storm passes over you, its motion (counterclockwise in the Northern Hemisphere, clockwise in the Southern Hemisphere) will cause a 90- to 180-degree wind shift depending on whether you are at the edge of the storm or directly in its path. Because of this radical wind shift and the forces involved, about all you can do is put out anchors off your bow at appropriate angles to your vessel's centerline.

For these anchors to be effective, you need to set one in the direction from which the wind will strike your vessel as the storm approaches and the other in the direction from which the wind will strike your vessel as it recedes. Those directions will be determined by your position relative to the storm's track, which you can plot from weather broadcasts.

In the path of an approaching tropical storm or hurricane, you want to pay out the maximum scope possible on both anchors. If you set your secondary anchor by dropping back to the full extent of your primary rode and then taking up on the primary rode until you are lying roughly halfway between your two anchors, you would not get the advantage of maximum scope on your primary rode. In a storm-anchoring situation, it's better to set your primary anchor with your vessel, then set your secondary anchor with your tender at the appropriate angle from your vessel's bow and at the full extent of your secondary rode. If possible, add a sentinel or a kellet to both your primary and your secondary anchor rodes. This is simply any kind of weight of 25 pounds (11 kg) or so affixed to your rodes at about their midpoints that increase their catenary and help keep the pull on your anchors horizontal. If you rig an anchoring setup like this, you'll probably have a fine mess of tangled rodes to unscramble after the storm passes, but you may find you've saved your vessel.

In most storm-anchoring situations, the greatest danger to your vessel probably won't be from the effects of the storm itself but from other vessels seeking shelter in the anchorage where you have chosen to hole up. About all you can do to prevent damage from other vessels that are driven down on you is to put out all the fenders you have, hope you remembered to pay your boat insurance, and pray. When winds reach over about 30 knots, trying to fend off other vessels becomes an exercise in futility and could well cause you serious injury.

As a tropical storm or hurricane approaches, once you have anchored your vessel as securely as you know how, the next question you face is whether you should stay aboard and try to help her survive or seek shelter ashore and let her fend for herself. If the storm is likely to reach hurricane force by the time it reaches your position (winds of 64 knots), my advice would be to head for shore. I have ridden out winds in excess of 90 miles (145 km) an hour at anchor and have found it a truly frightening experience. Under those conditions, there is really nothing you can do to help your vessel survive and you could well be placing your own life in jeopardy. Journalistic assignments put me in St. Thomas in the U.S. Virgin Islands in the aftermath of Hurricane David; in Charleston, South Carolina, shortly after Hurricane Hugo struck; and in Wilmington, North Carolina, in the wake of Fran. I can testify that the devastation they left in their wakes was unbelievable. All three storms hurled well-constructed vessels of 60 and 70 feet (18–21 m) ashore and stacked them one atop another like cordwood. Anyone foolish enough to have tried to stay aboard them would almost certainly have been seriously injured or killed. No boat—however expensive and even if uninsured—is worth your life.

RETRIEVING AN ANCHOR

Setting an anchor can prove to be the easy part. If your anchor is really set deeply or becomes fouled, the hard part begins when you try to retrieve it.

Anytime you are bringing your anchor up, remember that it is designed to produce its maximum holding power when the force exerted on it is horizontal in the direction of its flukes and to begin to break out of the bottom when vertical force is exerted on it at an angle greater than about 10 degrees to the horizontal.

For normal anchor retrieval, post your mate on the bow and slowly motor forward while the mate directs you toward the anchor with hand signals and takes in the rode with the anchor windlass. (Never use your windlass alone to pull your boat up to an anchor because the strain could burn out its electric motor or strip its gears.) To avoid scar-

ring your topsides, be careful not to go forward faster than your mate can retrieve the rode. As your vessel's bow passes over the anchor, forward momentum should break the anchor free. Your mate can then retrieve the remaining rode, bring the anchor up tight to the bow roller, and secure it.

If the anchor doesn't break free immediately, don't force it too much by advancing your throttle(s) because all the strain is being borne by the windlass and you could strip its gears. If a little added force doesn't break the anchor free, it is either extremely well set or it is fouled and you will have to apply successive tactics to break it free. As an initial attempt to break it out, turn your rudder(s) to one side or the other, which will force your vessel to pivot around the anchor. This maneuver alone may change the angle of force on the anchor enough to break it out. If it doesn't, once you are 180 degrees to the course you were on when you originally set the anchor, shift to reverse and back slowly but steadily. If the anchor is simply well dug in, this should change the angle on its shaft enough to pull it out and let you go on your merry way.

If the anchor still refuses to budge, have your mate check to see that your bow is still directly over the anchor and the rode is hanging straight down. If it isn't, ease forward until you've gotten all the slack out of the rode and try backing again slowly but steadily. If this doesn't break the anchor out, it is clearly fouled and you will have to resort to extraordinary measures to retrieve it.

If there is any significant wave action in the anchorage, try to get all possible slack out of the rode by snubbing it tighter every time your boat's bow dips into a wave trough. Once you get virtually all the slack out of the rode, the action of the bow lifting on the waves may be sufficient to pull the anchor free.

If that doesn't help, snorkel or scuba dive down to the anchor if possible, find out what it's hung up on, and see if you can free it by hand or secure a line around its head, which you can cleat off to your vessel and use to back the head out of whatever is holding it.

If diving down to the anchor is impractical, assume that one of your problems is that the force you are exerting on the anchor rode is working on the end of the anchor's shaft, which is not the most effective angle for freeing the head. Also assume that if you apply an excessive amount of force to the rode, you're likely to part the rode or bend the anchor's shaft or break the rode off all together.

Your best option at this point is to try to get a line around the head of the anchor, which will allow you to pull it straight out in the direction opposite to that of its flukes. To do this, check again to see that your vessel is headed opposite to the direction you were going when you set the anchor; that your vessel's bow is directly over the anchor; and that you've gotten all the slack you can out of the anchor chain. In the line end of your secondary anchor rode or the heaviest, longest line you have aboard, use a bowline knot to tie a bight about 2 feet (0.6 m) across that runs around your anchor chain (that is, your anchor chain should be inside the bight). Lower this bight down around the anchor chain with a gentle shaking motion. What you're trying to do is work the bight down over the shaft of the anchor and have it settle around the anchor's head like the loop of a lasso.

Once the bight has reached the bottom, keep a little tension on its line but slack off the tension on your anchor chain. This should allow the anchor's shaft to fall into a nearly horizontal position and help hold the bight in position around the head of the anchor. While your mate pays out both the anchor chain and the line with the bight in it, slowly back your vessel until you are about 50 feet (15 m) away from the anchor and lying opposite to the direction of the point of its flukes. Have the mate leave the anchor chain fully slack but take up tension on the line with the bight and cleat it off. Once this is done, back your vessel slowly. If you've been successful in looping the bight around the head of the anchor, this should put enough tension on the anchor at the optimum angle opposite to the point of its flukes to pull it out.

If this maneuver doesn't work, about all you can do is disconnect the anchor chain from your vessel, tie a marker buoy to the end of it, and come back later with diving gear to try to retrieve your anchor and rode.

The best way to avoid getting into a mess like this in the first place is to use a trip line anytime you anchor in an area where it is likely to be severely fouled. Anytime you set a trip line, adjust its buoy so that it is as short as possible to prevent it from fouling the propeller of a passing boat.

PART FOUR

Navigating and Communicating

Understanding Coastal Piloting and Eyeball Navigation

Although you will probably rely primarily on your GPS and electronic charting system for navigation, you'll still need to plot your position on paper charts. Here are useful tips and hints for inshore navigation.

USING PAPER NAUTICAL CHARTS

Paper nautical charts are among the most valuable and essential tools we have aboard our vessels. Yet vital as they are, many of us are often careless about the way we use them, can be too trusting of what they tell us, and usually take advantage of only a fraction of the information they provide.

Many skippers who have an electronic charting system aboard their vessels no longer feel the need to carry along paper charts as a backup. This is a serious mistake. As I pointed out in chapter 8, electronic chart systems are wonderful, but they can fail. If those skippers' systems crash and they have no paper charts as backup, they can find themselves neck deep in trouble in a hurry. During

Americas Odyssey's voyage from Maine to Alaska, our Maptech electronic chart system worked beautifully, but I still carried a couple of thousand dollars' worth of paper charts, on which I constantly plotted our course.

I can't stress enough the importance of a full complement of charts of the area you plan to cruise. Without them, you are "flying blind" and have no idea of the hazards that may await you. Charts are expensive, and you may be tempted to cut corners by buying one small-scale chart covering a large area rather than investing in several large-scale charts that cover the area in greater detail. Don't do it; if conditions turn sour, you'll need all the detail you can get—and lack of it can be disastrous. Also make certain any chart you carry aboard either is the latest edition or has been completely updated from all the Local Notices to Mariners for the area it covers that have been issued since its publication. A chart even a year or two old that has not been updated can provide all manner of erroneous information. In the ensuing years, storms and erosion may have shifted channels and the entrances to inlets, the coast guard may have removed or relocated buoys, and development may have demolished some shore-side structures and erected new ones where none existed before. The result can be a significant difference between what the chart depicts and what is really there. In a tight navigation situation, particularly under adverse weather or sea conditions, that difference can be extremely dangerous.

Some cruisers try to save money by buying used charts, which are available from chart stores or from cruisers who have traversed a route and no longer need the charts they accumulated for the journey. I would buy a used chart only if I were fully comfortable that it had been completely updated from Local Notices to Mariners by someone who really knew how to do it. One indication that you're probably safe to trust a used chart is that the seller includes with it a complete file of the Local Notices to Mariners from which it has been kept current. One of the best ways to locate used charts is to join the Seven Seas Cruising Association (SSCA) as an associate member in order to receive its monthly *Commodores Bulletin* (see contact information in the resources appendix). Though the SSCA is composed primarily of people who cruise under sail, it does accept power-boaters as associates. Its active members tend to be well-qualified, knowledgeable skippers. If one of them offers a set of used charts of an area through the *Bulletin*, their updating has probably been rigorously maintained. If you use an older chart that has been updated, be especially careful to note the annual increase or decrease in magnetic variation listed inside the chart's compass rose, note its cumulative effect from the year the chart was printed to the year you are using it, and remember to apply that cumulative effect to any magnetic bearings you plot.

Even using the most recent chart published for an area or one that has been conscientiously updated by a qualified mariner doesn't necessarily guarantee its accuracy, especially if the area has been raked by severe weather. I made a run along the coast of South Carolina in the wake of Hurri-

cane Hugo and found that many inlets, channels, and markers either no longer existed or were a long way from where even the most recent charts of the area said they were. In addition to charts covering every inch of the route you plan to follow, it's also a good idea to include in your inventory charts of any inlets or harbors you don't plan to enter but might have to duck into in an emergency.

Having a complete inventory of up-to-date charts aboard doesn't do much good if you can't quickly lay your hands on the one you need or if it hasn't been properly taken care of. Develop an inventory system that tells you what charts you have aboard and where they are stowed. Ideally, your wheelhouse will include several large, shallow drawers where you can store your charts and a large area where you can work with them without having to fold them. If your wheelhouse doesn't have adequate chart stowage, the best place to stow large charts until they are needed is beneath a bunk mattress—but make sure the area isn't subject to dampness. If you must fold charts, vary the manner in which you fold them each time you store or use them to avoid developing deep creases, along which they will be likely to tear or obscure information. Anytime you take a chart to the flying bridge, encase it in a vinyl chart protector to prevent moisture damage.

Piloting Instruments

All manner of chart-plotting instruments are available, from basic dividers and parallel rules to course plotters and protractors. Which one will work best for you is largely a matter of personal preference. I find that traditional parallel rules and dividers work best. I do suggest, however, that you carry two sets of dividers aboard. For precise plotting work when you have plenty of time, one pair should have an adjustable, screw-type crossarm, which will firmly hold a separation and prevent accidental changes in the setting. For situations in which you need to work quickly and can afford to be a bit less precise, the second should be of the "one-hand" variety, which you can open by squeezing the top and close by squeezing the bottom. I've found that the simplest dividers, which have only a single pivot point, soon become so loose that you can't rely on them.

A No. 2 lead pencil is the best device to lightly draw course lines and enter information on your charts, because its markings are easily visible and can be erased without damaging the chart. Also, its relatively soft lead won't cut deeply into the chart surface. Keep your plotting pencils well sharpened so they describe a fine line, and even then hold your parallel rules or course plotter slightly off the line you are describing to allow for the thickness of the pencil lead. For erasing marks, art gum will do far less damage to the chart surface than a rubber eraser.

CHOOSING BINOCULARS

One critical piloting instrument you need is a good pair of binoculars. Good binoculars are expensive (in the $500 to $800 range through nautical catalogs), but don't cut corners. The first time you're in a nasty sea beneath gray clouds and have to depend on your binoculars to spot a tiny entrance marker to reach safety, you'll be glad you invested in the best pair you can afford. Go over the specifications of any binoculars you consider purchasing very carefully. I recommend a pair of 7 × 50 binoculars that have a relative light efficiency above 80 and individual rather than center focusing and are waterproof, armored, and reasonably lightweight. Whether you select a pair with an integral bearing compass is largely a matter of whether you are willing to pay a substantial weight penalty for the added accuracy and convenience. Let's go through these recommended specifications in more detail.

The first number in the 7 × 50 designation represents the lenses' magnification power. A 7 × glass makes an object appear seven times larger than when viewed with the naked eye and is about the highest magnification the average person can hold steady on a pitching deck. The second number is the diameter in millimeters of the objective lens (the lens farthest from your eye). The diameter of the objective lens divided by the lens's magnification equals the binoculars' exit pupil—the diameter of the sphere of light you see if you hold the binoculars at arm's length. That figure is important because the average diameter of the pupil of a human eye in bright sunlight is about 4 to 4.5 mm, but under reduced light it expands to about 7 mm. A 50 mm objective lens with a 7 × magnification has an exit pupil of 7.14, which takes maximum advantage of the eye's expanded pupil diameter in reduced visibility. Binoculars with magnification power above 7 × and objective lenses smaller that 50 mm have exit pupils as small as 5 to 6 mm, which makes them almost useless in low-light conditions.

A function of the lens's optical quality, relative light efficiency (RLE) measures the percentage of available light that a lens is able to gather and transmit through the binocular to your eye. The higher that percentage, the more expensive the binocular, but the better you'll be able to see a small marker on a gray sea under a gray sky. For use at sea, I consider an RLE of 75 an absolute minimum and feel it is well worth the extra money to buy a pair of binoculars with an RLE of at least 80.

Binoculars with center focusing must be set for the distance to an object; binoculars with individual focusing on each eyepiece are set once for your eyes and do not have to be set for distance. While individual-focusing binoculars are more expensive than the center-focus type, they are easier and quicker to use. Their construction makes it far more difficult for moisture to get inside the barrels, which means they are more resistant to fogging. In the marine environment, fogging is a major problem and can render a pair of binoculars unusable, so binoculars that have been tested not to admit moisture even when immersed in water are worth the extra cost.

Binoculars on a boat are almost certain to be dropped or knocked about. Armoring is important because it helps absorb shock and prevent the binoculars' delicate lens arrangement from being knocked out of alignment. As a further protection from shock, equip your flying bridge and wheelhouse steering stations with binocular holders and make certain you put your binoculars back in their holder every time you use them so you or a guest won't accidentally tip them over or knock them to the sole. It's also a good idea to fit your binoculars with a strap and get into the habit of flipping it over your neck every time you use them.

I find I pick up my binoculars anywhere from fifty to a hundred times during the course of a typical day's inshore cruising. Lifting a pair of binoculars to your eyes this often makes weight—which in top-quality binoculars ranges from just over 2 pounds to about 3½ pounds (0.9–1.6 kg)—important. Weight influences whether you select binoculars with an integral bearing compass or use a separate hand-bearing compass. There can be little argument that taking bearings with an integral compass in your binoculars allows you to get a more precise bearing (under ideal conditions, within a degree) simply because you can see the object more distinctly. The problem is that an integral compass significantly increases weight and you probably won't use it more than 2 to 3 percent of the time you pick up the binoculars to get a better look at a distant object. I personally prefer to forgo an integral compass to keep my binoculars as light as possible.

Choosing a Hand-Bearing Compass

If your binoculars don't have an integral magnetic bearing compass, you'll need a good hand-bearing compass. Your choice comes down to the degree of accuracy you are willing to settle for and the amount of money you are willing to spend. The simplest and least expensive type, such as the pistol-grip model offered by Davis, sells for around $30 and reads out in 5-degree increments. The Autohelm fluxgate hand-bearing compass is accurate to within about 2 degrees and sells for around $125; it has the added advantage of a timer and will remember the degrees and times of up to nine bearings. The KVH Datascope, which sells for about $350, uses a fluxgate electronic sensor that

is gimbaled up to 20 degrees, is accurate to about 2 degrees, has a timer and 5 × magnification, can remember the times and degrees of up to nine bearings, and also includes a range finder.

Because the readings of hand-bearing compasses normally are accurate only to within 2 to 5 degrees and because they normally are used away from the major sources of magnetic interference aboard a vessel, their deviation is not normally taken into account when computing bearings. You would be wise, however, to take readings with your hand-bearing compass at several locations around your vessel to find a convenient place where its readings conform most closely to the steering compasses in your pilothouse and on your flying bridge. Then you should take hand bearings only from that location.

Choosing a Night Vision Device

If you can stand the price—around $2,700—the ITT Night Mariner night vision device is handy to have aboard. It is based on light amplification technology developed for military use during the Vietnam war and lets you see objects on even the darkest night, though with a greenish glow. For an extra $89, you can equip it with a bearing compass.

Plotting Techniques

If you are running a well-defined channel, such as a stretch of the Intracoastal Waterway, in which markers are closely spaced and easily visible, it isn't really necessary to keep a running plot of your position and course. Your course will be determined by the bearings to the next mark, and all you have to do to keep up with your position is to check off each marker as you pass it. You do, of course, have to keep an eye out ahead (both on the water and on the chart) to anticipate any problems that might lie in your path. Anytime you venture out of clear sight of land, however, it is essential that you carefully and correctly plot your progress on the appropriate chart as a backup to your electronic navigation system. If your GPS receiver or chart plotter suddenly goes belly up, those marks you have made on your paper chart will be the only reference you have to where you are.

If you are not well versed in the skills and techniques of piloting, I strongly suggest you take a good course in the subject such as the one offered by the U.S. Power Squadrons. Some of the information you will learn in such a course will in time slip from your memory, so it's a good idea to occasionally review the coverage of plotting techniques in a basic boating book like *Chapman Piloting: Seamanship and Boat Handling* (see resources appendix).

Aboard *Americas Odyssey*, my practice at the start of each offshore passage was to enter my beginning point and destination into my electronic navigation system, then mark my intended course on the appropriate paper chart. Each hour, I would mark my position on the chart to make sure we were still on course.

READING THE BOTTOM

In clear tropical waters, reading the bottom visually (rather than with an electronic depth-sounder) requires at least three things: good light, a good vantage point, and a bit of experience to know whether that dark spot just off your bow is a grassy patch, a rock, or a coral head. It's also helpful if you are studying the water through a pair of sunglasses that polarize the reflection of the sun's rays off the water's surface.

Good light, preferably sunlight that is high and behind you, is essential to spotting any dangers the water in front of your vessel might hold. If at all possible, avoid trying to maneuver your vessel through shoal tropical waters before about 10:00 A.M. or after about 4:00 P.M., when the sun's rays

are slanting into the water at an oblique angle. It won't always be possible, but also try to avoid picking your way through rocks and coral heads when the sky is overcast.

The best vantage point from which to read the water ahead is a flying bridge. If your vessel doesn't have one, position a lookout right on the bow. For communications, agree on a set of clear, simple hand signals and instruct your lookout to point in the direction in which it is safe to proceed, not toward obstructions. Or, better yet, get a pair of the new Family Service radios, which are basically short-range walkie-talkies, or give your lookout the handheld VHF and reduce your installed unit to its 1-watt output setting.

As for interpreting what the various colors you see in the water indicate, a few simple rhymes may help. "Blue go through" reminds you that when the water is a rich, dark blue, it's likely to be deep enough to provide safe passage to the typical recreational powerboat with a draft of less than 6 feet (1.8 m).

"Green may be lean" reminds you that water that is deep green in color is probably 8 to 12 feet (2.4–3.7 m) deep, but a light green color indicates shallows.

"Brown go around" is a handy reminder that water appearing either brown or brownish yellow in color could well conceal a bar, a rock, or a coral outcropping. The difference in appearance between rocks and coral heads is that a coral head will often be ringed with a circle of white sand. Black or extremely dark brown spots normally indicate grassy patches.

Reading the bottom visually takes a bit of time and some practice, but it can pay big dividends in keeping your vessel off the hard stuff and over deep water where it belongs.

Using Marine Navigation Electronics

Anytime I hear a boat operator extolling the accuracy and dependability of the expansive array of electronic navigation equipment aboard his yacht, one vivid image invariably leaps into my mind: that of a beautiful 58-foot (18 m) motor yacht sitting high and dry on the rock jetty at Port Bolivar along the Texas coast. A delivery skipper was running the boat back to its home port in Galveston Bay from Cozumel, Mexico. After clearing the Yucatán Channel, he programmed the latitude and longitude coordinates of the entry to Bolivar Roads into the vessel's Loran-C receiver, engaged the autopilot interface, and settled down with his mate for a nice long snooze (assisted, I suspect, by a large bottle of Old Bilgewater). The loran's margin of error was just enough to let them hit the end of the jetty at high water and full tilt. The tide ran out and there they sat.

Modern electronic navigation devices are wonders of the age that, if properly used, can make cruising skippers' primary job of knowing where they are and where they're going a great deal easier, simpler, and safer. The key phrase in that sentence, however, is "if properly used." The great danger in relying on electronic navigation devices lies in trusting them too much. I've known more than one skipper who got into a great deal of trouble by failing to recognize that navigational electronics are mechanical gadgets that are vulnerable to a loss of power, that they all contain a degree of inaccuracy that must be allowed for, that they can be wrong either because they simply malfunctioned or because they were fed bad data, and that even accurate information they provide can be interpreted incorrectly.

The age-old adage that the prudent mariner will never rely on a single source of information to determine position or course applies in spades to the use of electronic navigation devices. All those pretty lights reading out degrees to tenths of a minute and distances to tenths of a nautical mile are great, but realize that inaccuracies not only occur but are inherent in their systems. Constantly compare what one instrument is telling you with what another is telling you to make sure they are in reasonable agreement, keep up your dead reckoning plots to alert you when something is going haywire, and at every opportunity confirm your position with visual observations and fixes.

Aside from always being a bit skeptical about the information your electronic navigation instruments are giving you, another key to using them successfully is to really master the full range of their functions. Don't content yourself with the quick run-through the electronics salesman may give you. Study the owner's manual word by word. If you don't completely understand a function and how to perform it, go over it again and again until you do. If the owner's manual doesn't tell you all you need to know on a specific topic, supplement your knowledge with research into books and magazine articles on the subject by knowledgeable experts. In the process of really getting to know your gear, get in plenty of hands-on practice, preferably in your home waters or on a shakedown cruise when conditions are favorable and a mistake is not likely to be too costly.

This chapter is not intended as a basic primer on using your radar, global positioning system (GPS) receiver, or Loran-C unit since each of these topics is well discussed in other full-length books. My intention here is to provide a few hints that might help you get the most out of this equipment and avoid some of the more common mistakes in their use.

NAVIGATING BY GPS

GPS is certainly the greatest navigational boon to the cruising skipper in the history of recreational boating. Since Selective Availability was turned off May 1, 2000, the government says a properly functioning GPS receiver can be counted on 95 percent of the time to produce positions accurate to within about 198 feet (60 m). In practice, GPS routinely provides accuracy to 16 feet (5 m) or less. The government says that differential GPS (DGPS) delivers accuracies to 33 feet (10 m), but in practice it routinely produces accuracies of 3 to 12 feet (1–3.7 m).

As marvelous and accurate a navigation system as GPS provides, there are a few things you need to know about its operation.

- In times of national emergency, Selective Availability can be turned back on, but the government has promised to give warning should that occur.

- The propagation of GPS signals can be affected by the atmosphere, and thus its accuracy levels can vary, which makes GPS alone unsuitable for precise inshore navigation. Do not rely on your GPS receiver for precise inshore navigation unless it also is equipped to receive DGPS signals and a signal is available.

- GPS signals are not subject to the additional secondary factors that affect Loran-C, and thus there is no essential difference in the system's absolute and repeatable accuracy. GPS signals are not subject to cycle slip, so there is no reason for you to have to get involved in cycle stepping.

- A GPS receiver displays position as latitude and longitude, which it derives from a computer conversion of the solution it calculates from satellite signals. Since the system provides you with no data comparable to loran time differences, you need no special charts with overlays of the type you use with loran.

- Most GPS receivers can display course and bearings in either true or magnetic degrees. If you use magnetic readouts from your GPS receiver, bear in mind that they are computer conversions of true data and are averaged over a fairly wide geographic area of 50 to 100 miles (80–160 km). They may not conform exactly to your magnetic compass, and they will not take into account strong local magnetic disturbances.

- Speed-over-ground (SOG) and course-over-ground (COG) readouts from a GPS receiver, like those from a loran receiver, are averages. But because a typical GPS receiver updates its position about once a second, changes in SOG or COG readouts are virtually instantaneous.

NAVIGATING BY LORAN-C

While GPS has largely replaced Loran-C as the navigation device of choice for the cruising yachtsperson, I cover navigating with loran for those who limit their cruising to the system's primary coverage area, which extends out to 50 nautical miles from the Atlantic, Pacific, and Gulf coastlines of the United States or to the 100-fathom curve, whichever is greater, and have a functioning loran receiver aboard and wish to use it as a check on their GPS receiver or a backup in the event GPS is unavailable. If you use Loran-C to its maximum advantage and confirm its output by other means, it also can be a useful navigation aid in its secondary coverage area, which takes in such popular cruising grounds as the Bahamas, the northern coast of South America, and the western coast of Central America and Mexico.

One key to navigating by loran effectively lies in fully understanding its limitations. Regarding loran's accuracy, think of it as a navigation system that under ideal conditions will help you find your way across a state or a city, into the right neighborhood, and even to the front yard of a particular house, but it won't lead you up to the front door. While the margin of error in Loran-C's absolute accuracy (the first time it acquires a fix on a position) is typically as little as 100 feet (30 m) and under ideal conditions can be even less, it can easily be as much as a quarter of a mile (0.4 km) and in some cases up to 2 miles (3.2 km). Its repeatable accuracy (reacquiring a fix on a location it has fixed earlier) can be as little as 50 feet (15 m) or can be up to several hundred feet. In open water, where there are no obstacles to a vessel's passage, margins of error of those magnitudes are not likely to be critical. But anytime you are relying on your loran—especially on its absolute accuracy—for inshore navigation, where an error of even 50 feet or less can be disastrous, be extremely alert to the system's potential error factor and use at least one other electronic system, such as your radar, or visual sightings to make certain you are where you think you are.

Navigating by loran is most accurate when the receiver is used in conjunction with charts printed with loran time difference (TD) overlays and plotting is based on TDs rather than on the receiver's latitude and longitude conversions. A loran receiver's latitude and longitude readouts are mathematical conversions from TDs, and the conversion process itself induces an additional margin of error.

Most skippers, however, are far more comfortable basing their navigation by loran on latitude and longitude coordinates. If you use a loran's latitude and longitude conversions as your primary navigational references, you should double-check them frequently by comparing them to known latitude and longitude positions you can confirm by laying your vessel alongside a charted aid to navigation. If there is a significant difference in the two, be sure to allow for it. Some more sophisticated loran receivers allow you to program in latitude and longitude bias, but if you use this feature, remember that the bias you input is valid only for a specific geographic area and will be wiped out of the receiver's programming if you turn the unit off.

In using magnetic bearing readouts from your loran, be aware that your receiver determines them from a computer program that can allow for magnetic variation but does not allow for local magnetic disturbances, which in some areas can induce errors of up to several miles. If you rely on this feature of your loran, also be sure that it has been programmed with the current year and periodically compare the variation it is using with the variation shown on a current chart of the area you are cruising.

If you use the SOG, COG, or steering indication functions of your loran, be aware that they are not instantaneous but are computed from a series of positions over time. In areas of weak loran signal reception, you'll find that increasing the interval of time over which your receiver averages positions to compute these readouts will make them more accurate.

Although it gets pretty technical, you'll never get the maximum use out of loran until you understand the characteristics of its signal pulse, the importance of its tracking point, the concept of cycle slip, and the uses of cycle stepping. Suffice it to say here that the optimum tracking point to which all loran receivers are set at the factory is thirty-five microseconds into the pulse, which places it at the zero crossing point of the pulse's third cycle. This point is far enough into the pulse to avoid interference from noise but not so far into the pulse that it will be contaminated by erroneous sky-wave transmissions, which first begin to arrive thirty-five microseconds after the ground-wave pulse.

In areas where loran signals are weak, your receiver can experience cycle slip, in which the point at which it tracks the signal from either a master or a secondary loran transmitter (or both) slips one or more cycles farther into the pulse or closer to its beginning. Most loran receivers flash some kind of warning when cycle slipping occurs. But since each cycle has a duration of ten microseconds, cycle slipping results in a distinctive plus-or-minus ten-microsecond error in TD readouts. You can therefore detect and identify cycle slipping yourself. If you accurately fix your position by some means other than loran on a chart with loran overlay lines and find that fix varies from the position your loran indicates, compare the two. If your position is along the line of position (LOP) described by the master transmitter in the chain you are using but is a multiple of ten microseconds off the LOP described by the secondary transmitter LOP, your receiver is experiencing cycle slip in the signal from the secondary transmitter. If your position is along the LOP described by the secondary transmitter but is a multiple of ten microseconds off the LOP described by the master transmitter, you're experiencing cycle slip in the signal from the master. If your position is a multiple of ten microseconds off the LOP described by both the master and the secondary transmitters, you're experiencing cycle slip in the signals from both.

Some loran receivers provide a "lock" or "track" mode, which allows you to manually restore the tracking point or points to their correct position. If you cannot get the receiver to hold the nominal tracking point but it will hold a consistent tracking point, you can often continue to use the signal by allowing for the ten-, twenty-, or thirty-microsecond error. If you use manual tracking to do this, particularly if you are allowing for error in the signal from both a master and a secondary transmitter, it's critical that you frequently confirm the positions your loran is giving you by other navigational means.

Some loran receivers allow you to manually force them to read a tracking point farther into a pulse where signal strength is greater. Using such manual cycle stepping is a bit tricky, but if you know how to do it properly you can get reliable readouts from your loran receiver in areas far outside its primary coverage area. In using manual cycle stepping, be sure you understand that stepping up the tracking point of a signal from a secondary transmitter by ten, twenty, or thirty microseconds causes the TD of that signal to read that number of microseconds higher and you must allow for the increase in plotting your position. Stepping up the tracking point of a signal from a master transmitter by ten, twenty, or thirty microseconds causes the TDs of the signal from both the master and the secondary transmitter to read that number of microseconds lower, and you must allow for the decreases in plotting your position. Stepping up the tracking point of a signal from all the transmitters the loran is tracking by ten, twenty, or thirty microseconds does not cause any TDs to change.

If you use cycle stepping to increase the range at which you can navigate by loran, it's critical that you remember to allow for any error you have deliberately induced and frequently confirm the positions your loran is giving you by other navigational means.

NAVIGATING BY RADAR

Radar not only is an invaluable navigating tool at night or when visibility is poor but can be equally useful in daylight when the weather is bright and sunny. Even if your boat is loaded with other electronic navigation equipment, learning to use your radar to maximum advantage can help you keep a check on the accuracy of your GPS or loran receiver and can provide a valuable backup if any of your primary navigation devices goes on the blink.

One principal value of radar as a navigation instrument is that it can see farther—and in some cases better—than you can. The distance to the horizon at sea in nautical miles is 1.17 times the square root of the height of the observer's eye in feet above sea level. Since your radar's antenna normally will be mounted higher than your eye level, its distance to the horizon will be greater. Also, because the radio waves it emits bend slightly, its view extends about 7 percent beyond the horizon.

Assume, for example, that your eye height on the flying bridge of your vessel is 12 feet (3.7 m) above sea level. The distance to the horizon will then be 4 nautical miles. If your radar's antenna is mounted 16 feet (4.9 m) above sea level and the bending of its radio waves allows it to see 7 percent past your visual horizon, it will be able to detect objects about 5 nautical miles farther away than you can, a difference of 1 nautical mile (or just over 20 percent). Your radar often can see a number of aids to navigation better than you can because many aids incorporate radar-reflecting panels that the radar can "see" electronically better and more accurately than you can visually. In coastal cruising or crossing large bodies of open water, where markers are out of your visual range but can be detected by your radar, radar's greater visual range and accuracy can be extremely useful for determining your position and the proper course to steer.

Radar can be used to determine bearings from your vessel to aids to navigation or shoreside landmarks within its range. By using this feature to determine the bearings of at least two—and preferably three—marks and then converting those bearings to bearings from the objects to your vessel and plotting them on a chart, you can create a triangle of position within which you are located. The more accurate your bearings, the smaller that triangle—and thus the more accurate your fix. The type of bearings your radar provides and the way you use this feature depend on the sophistication level of your radar.

A basic radar has a "course up" display, which indicates the boat's heading as 0 degrees, and an outer 360-degree ring. By simply lining up the center of the display's screen representing your vessel's position and any identifiable object on the display with a straight edge, you can read the bearing from your vessel to the object off the display's outer ring. But keep in mind that a bearing to an object determined in this manner is relative to your boat's heading at the time you take the bearing. It is not a magnetic or a true bearing, and before you can use it to plot your position on a chart you must convert it to one or the other.

To convert this relative bearing to a magnetic bearing, add the compass heading of the vessel at the time the bearing is taken. Then add or subtract deviation to get magnetic bearing. If the sum of those two figures is greater than 360, subtract 360 from it. The result will be the corrected magnetic bearing from your vessel to the object, and its reciprocal will be the magnetic bearing from the object to your vessel.

If you plan to do your plotting in true degrees, you must correct your vessel's heading at the time the bearing was taken by compensating for both magnetic variation and the deviation of your steering compass, which will yield your vessel's true heading at the time the bearing was taken. Add the relative bearing to this course. If the sum is greater than 360 degrees, subtract 360 degrees. The reciprocal of that figure will be the bearing from the object to your vessel in true degrees.

Virtually all radars have one or more electronic bearing lines, which will read out the bearing from your vessel to a mark either in relative or magnetic degrees. If the readout is in relative degrees, you will have to go through one of the processes above to convert that bearing to magnetic or true degrees before you can plot it on a chart. If the readout is in magnetic degrees, you need only correct your vessel's heading for compass deviation, then take the reciprocal to get the magnetic bearing from the mark to your vessel, which you can plot on a chart. Raster scan radars have the ability to "freeze" the display to determine relative or magnetic bearings even more precisely.

You also can fix your vessel's position by using your radar's range scale to compute your distance from two or more objects that are on your chart. All radar displays have concentric rings from which the distance from the vessel to an object can be roughly estimated, and most have variable range markers (VRMs), which will calculate distance down to tenths or hundredths of a nautical mile. Once you have used your radar to determine your vessel's distance from at least two—and preferably three—objects, describe the distance from each object on the chart with a pair of dividers. Where the lines cross will be your vessel's approximate position, with the accuracy of the fix dependent on the accuracy with which you measured and plotted the distances.

A third way you can fix your vessel's position with radar is to convert a relative bearing from your vessel to a single object into a true or magnetic bearing from the object to your vessel, which allows you to plot an LOP and then use the radar's range-finding ability to determine your position along that line.

Once you've mastered these position-fixing techniques, you can use your radar to determine your vessel's SOG. First, use your radar to determine your vessel's position at one point and note the time. After a convenient interval of time (such as fifteen, thirty, or sixty minutes), use your radar to again determine your vessel's position, measure the distance between the two points in nautical miles, and note the length of time it took you to travel between them. Multiply the distance by 60

and then divide the result by the time in minutes to determine your speed in knots. The speed calculation is even easier if the chart you are using has a logarithmic speed scale in the margin. In that case, put one point of a pair of dividers on distance run and the other on minutes run. Without changing the divider's spread, place its right point on 60. The left point will indicate your vessel's speed in units per hour.

You also can use your radar to detect the presence of any current that is deflecting your vessel from its course and compensate for it. That process is most simple if you are running a course between markers that are in a straight line (see illustration). Lining up your vessel's heading on the radar's display screen with a pair of markers and keeping it there will give you the course to steer. Any difference between that course and the course you plotted for the run between the two markers alerts you to the deflecting current's presence, and, if you

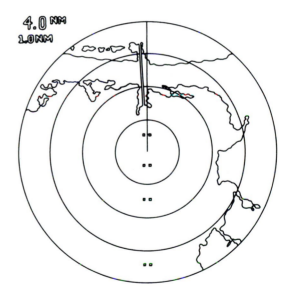

By lining your radar up on a fixed object such as a marker, you can detect the presence of any offsetting current and construct a current diagram to determine the direction that current is setting you and its strength.

wish, you can take the added step of constructing a current diagram to determine its set and drift. You can also use your radar to take aft bearings on a single mark relative to your vessel's centerline and use that information to detect the presence of a deflecting current and determine its set.

Your radar also can alert you to adverse weather you cannot see but are about to encounter. If a thunderstorm beyond your visual range shows up on your radar, you can track its progress relative to your course and decide whether you need to batten down the hatches to prepare for it or take evasive action to get out of its way.

Still another valuable use of radar is to alert you to the course and speed of other vessels in your vicinity that might pose a danger. By noting the position of a vessel within your radar's range at a series of time intervals, you can determine its speed and whether or not its course will cross your own. With that information (which some radars will even track for you), you can decide on any evasive action you need to take.

NAVIGATING BY KNOT METER–DISTANCE LOG

Should you lose all your other electronic navigation equipment, it's possible to do at least rudimentary navigation by proceeding in a certain compass direction for a certain length of time at a given speed as measured by your knot meter or for a certain distance as measured by your distance log. If you should be reduced to navigating in this manner, bear in mind that a common knot meter–distance log with a paddle-wheel-type impeller measures only speed through the water based on the speed at which its impeller turns and measures only distance through the water by the number of revolutions of its impeller at a given speed. In the presence of current, your actual speed and distance over ground can be significantly different from what your knot meter–distance log is telling you, and you will have to take that current's effects into account in your calculations.

Using Cruising Communications

The marine radios aboard your vessel are your primary links with other vessels and the world ashore, are indispensable to the operation of your vessel in such situations as passing through bridges and locks, can be critical to your vessel's safety in an emergency, and are your primary source of weather information that can materially affect your cruising plans. You need to know how to use them properly (the majority of recreational boat owners don't), how to get the most out of them, and how to fix at least minor problems if the radios go on the blink.

Chapter 9 discussed how marine radios work, recommended criteria for equipment selection, and covered proper installation. This chapter assumes you have good equipment properly installed on your vessel and emphasizes the routine use of your VHF (very high frequency) radio, which you'll use to communicate with other vessels and coast stations within roughly 40 miles (65 km) of your position, and your single-sideband (SSB) unit, which you'll need for long-range communications if you head farther than about 40 miles offshore or into foreign waters.

USING VHF MARINE RADIO

Because your VHF marine radio is such an important and useful device, you must learn how to operate it properly, both to comply with Federal Communications Commission (FCC) regulations and as a courtesy to your fellow boaters.

Selecting an Appropriate Channel

The FCC places very strict regulations on how VHF marine radios may be used. Its first requirement is that certain channels are to be used only for certain purposes.

As the operator of a noncommercial vessel, you normally will use only about nine simplex channels (which send and receive on the same frequency) plus the four receive-only channels WX-1 through WX-4, which carry weather information from the National Oceanic and Atmospheric Administration.

- Channel 16 may be used only for calling other vessels and for communicating safety and distress messages both ship to ship and ship to shore.

- Channel 6 may be used only for communicating safety messages ship to ship and is the primary channel for communicating with search-and-rescue vessels and aircraft of the U.S. Coast Guard.
- Channels 9, 68, 69, 71, 72, and 78 are the primary working channels for recreational vessels.
- Channel 13 is the primary channel for communicating navigational information with other vessels and for contacting bridge tenders and lockmasters.
- Channel 22A is the primary working channel for talking with the coast guard (after first establishing contact on channel 16) and is the primary channel over which the coast guard broadcasts messages regarding navigational safety and weather alerts. (VHF radios can be tuned to channels designated for use in the United States or to channels used in international waters. The suffix "A" following a channel number indicates its use and frequency in the United States. These frequencies are different from those in other countries. In the United States, all marine VHF channels except the public correspondence channels 24 to 28 and 84 to 88 send and receive on a single frequency. In most other countries of the world, channels send on one frequency and receive on a different frequency. In other words, you can only hear the coast guard on channel 22A if your set is tuned to the U.S. designation, not to the international designation.)

Except in certain special instances, operations on VHF channels 13, 17, 67, and 77 must be conducted at your VHF radio's minimum 1-watt power output setting rather than at its normal maximum power output of 25 watts.

In such high-traffic areas as major ports and busy commercial sea lanes, you also may find it helpful to monitor channels 12, 14, 20, 65, 66, 73, and 74 to determine the intentions of commercial and government vessels. You also may use channel 17 to communicate with state-controlled vessels, such as dredges and law enforcement officials. The remaining channels are strictly for commercial or U.S. government use, and there should be no reason for you to transmit over them with the single exception that in an emergency you may use any VHF channel to attract help and summon assistance.

Proper Use of VHF Channel 16

The improper use of VHF channel 16 for extended conversations has reached epidemic proportions, and I hope as a responsible vessel operator you'll do all you can to avoid contributing to it. Channel 16 is designated solely for calling, safety, and distress messages, and the format for using it has been carefully designed to ensure that it is kept clear as much as possible for the transmission of distress messages. Anytime it is tied up with casual conversation, it cannot be used for the purposes for which it was intended and could put someone's life or property in jeopardy.

Under normal circumstances, you should transmit on channel 16 only to establish contact with other vessels or with the coast guard. If you use channel 16 to try to contact another vessel within about half a mile of your position, manually reduce your radio's output to 1 watt, which means your transmission will occupy the channel for only about a 1-mile (1.6 km) radius around your vessel rather than the usual 15 to 20 miles (20–32 km). If you're trying to reach a shore station other than the coast guard, you should first try to contact the station on an appropriate working channel. If you're trying to reach a marina, call on channel 9. If you're trying to reach a marine operator, try one of the public correspondence channels, which in most areas are channels 24 to 28.

The correct way to call another vessel or the coast guard is to first scan the appropriate working channels (for communicating with other noncommercial vessels, those will be primarily 9, 68, 69,

71, 72 and 78; for communicating with the coast guard, it will be channel 22A) to find one that is not in use. Once you have found a clear working channel, shift your radio back to channel 16, wait for a break in any traffic that might already be in progress on the channel, and then transmit the name of the vessel you wish to contact. Unless atmospheric conditions are causing problems in communicating over VHF, you should transmit that vessel's name only once, and for goodness sake don't add such tag lines as "Come in" or "Bob, do you read me?"

Following the name of the vessel you are calling, say "This is" and transmit the name of your own vessel and your vessel's radio call sign if you have one. Call signs are no longer required in the United States. If you have had previous contact with the vessel you are calling, giving the name of your vessel once should be sufficient. If you are calling a vessel for the first time, you might want to say your vessel's name twice to make sure the person on the other end knows who to respond to. (Technically, you should end the call with the word "over," which means "I have finished my transmission, and a reply from you is required and expected," but it normally is omitted to keep things brief.)

If the vessel you are calling answers, simply say "Reply Channel ———" and give the number of the working channel you have selected. Shift your radio to the working channel and say the name of your vessel once. Once the vessel you are calling shifts to the working channel and replies with its own name, you have confirmed the contact and are free to proceed with your message.

When you have concluded your conversation on the working channel, give the name of your vessel once and say, "out," which frees the channel for others to use.

If you initiate a call on channel 16 or a working channel and receive no response, you should wait at least two minutes before repeating the call. If you initiate a call to the same vessel or a shore station three times at two-minute intervals and re-ceive no response, wait at least fifteen minutes before transmitting the call again.

If yours is the vessel called on channel 16, your proper response is to give the name of the vessel calling, say "This is," and give your vessel's name. Once the individual calling you has suggested a working channel, you should confirm that you are shifting to that channel by saying its number. If you are unable to respond on that channel, you should propose an alternate working channel. If the alternate is agreeable to the individual calling, that person should indicate agreement by repeating the number of the working channel you have proposed. Once you have completed your conversation on a working channel and the individual who initiated the call has cleared the channel with his vessel's name and the word "out," you should give your vessel's name and say, "out," which clears the channel for others to use. Don't make the mistake of saying "Over and out," which in the world of marine radio are contradictory terms. "Over" means "This is the end of my transmission, and a reply from you is required and expected." "Out" means "This is the end of my transmission to you, and no response from you is required or expected."

If you contact another vessel frequently, you can use an abbreviated format for establishing contact. To initiate such a call, transmit on channel 16 the name of the vessel you are calling, give your vessel's name, and say "Reply ———" to indicate an appropriate working channel. The operator of the responding vessel should shift to the working channel and reply with the contacted vessel's name. You then respond with your vessel's name, continue the conversation, and then end it and clear the working channel as above.

Anytime you are transmitting over marine radio, of course, you should speak slowly and distinctly. In poor atmospheric conditions, you may need to use procedure words or spell words phonetically to be sure you communicate clearly and concisely—see sidebars on the next two pages.

Radio Procedure Words

affirmative   Means "You are correct" or "What you have transmitted is correct."

break   Means "I separate the text from other portions of the message (or one message from another message that follows immediately)."

figures   Means "Figures or numbers follow." Used when numbers occur in a message such as "Layde Anne is figures four eight, repeat four eight feet in length."

I spell   Means "I shall spell the next word phonetically" (see the International Phonetic Alphabet sidebar).

Mayday   The international distress signal indicating that a vessel or a person is threatened by grave and imminent danger. The word is spoken three times. ("Mayday" is the accepted English pronunciation of the French word m'aider, which means "help me.") The Mayday distress call and message have priority over all other transmissions.

negative   Means "You are not correct" or "What you have transmitted is not correct."

out   Means "This is the end of my transmission to you, and no reply from you is required or expected."

over   Means "This is the end of my current transmission, and a reply from you is required and expected."

Pan-Pan   The international urgency signal indicating a vessel or person is in jeopardy but the danger is not life threatening. The phrase is spoken three times. Properly pronounced Pahn-Pahn, the Pan-Pan urgency signal has priority over all other transmissions except the Mayday signal.

roger   Means "I have received your transmission satisfactorily and understand your message."

Sécurité   When used as the international safety signal, spoken three times and properly pronounced say-kyur-ee-tay. The Sécurité safety signal has priority over all other transmissions except the Mayday distress message and the Pan-Pan urgency signal.

this is   Means "This transmission is from the station whose name or call sign (or both) immediately follows."

silence   When used to order the cessation of interfering transmissions over a channel or frequency being used for emergency communications, correctly pronounced see-lonce and is spoken three times.

silence fini   Used to signal the resumption of normal working on a channel or frequency previously used for distress communications. The phrase is pronounced see-lonce fee-nee.

wait   Means "I must pause for a few minutes; stand by for further transmission."

International Phonetic Alphabet

Alfa	*November*
Bravo	*Oscar*
Charlie	*Papa*
Delta	*Quebec*
Echo	*Romeo*
Foxtrot	*Sierra*
Golf	*Tango*
Hotel	*Uniform*
India	*Victor*
Juliet	*Whiskey*
Kilo	*X-ray*
Lima	*Yankee*
Mike	*Zulu*

If your VHF radio is not equipped with Digital Selective Calling (DSC) capability, FCC regulations require that if you are aboard your vessel and its VHF is turned on, you should monitor channel 16 at all times when you are not actually using your radio to transmit or receive on a working frequency. There is so much garbage on channel 16 these days that monitoring it can be both frustrating and irritating, but you need to listen in anyway. If you were in trouble and trying to use channel 16 to attract help, you'd want everyone with a VHF radio to be listening, and you owe that effort to your fellow mariners.

Digital Selective Calling

Assuming you have installed a VHF radio with DSC capability, you can receive an alerting message that another vessel or a shore station wants to talk to you without using VHF channel 16. Conversely, if you know the Maritime Mobile Service Identity (MMSI) number of another vessel or coast station, you can send an alerting message that you wish to communicate with that vessel or station.

When a vessel's MMSI number is transmitted over channel 70 as a series of electronic tones, those tones activate a receiver on board the vessel and cause the radio to ring somewhat like a telephone. When the receiving radio is answered, it is automatically shifted to a working channel the caller has selected.

In VHF, DSC will not be monitored by the U.S. Coast Guard until 2005.

Using Your Handheld VHF Radio

Technically, your installed VHF radio is your vessel's ship station. If you use a handheld VHF radio in your cruising, it is an associated ship unit and the name you should use anytime you transmit from it would be your vessel's name followed by the designation "unit 1." The proper procedure, then, for calling your main vessel would be "True Love—This is True Love unit 1—Over." (When transmitting over a handheld VHF, many cruisers use as a call sign the name of the main vessel plus the designation "mobile 1," but this is technically incorrect. That designation would be correct only if the handheld VHF were being used on board the main vessel.)

Legally (except in an emergency), you may use your handheld VHF only to communicate with your main vessel, you may not operate it from shore, and you may transmit only at 1-watt output power. Every cruiser I know blithely ignores all of the foregoing.

USING SINGLE-SIDEBAND MARINE RADIO

If your cruising plans call for you to venture more than about 25 miles (40 km) offshore, your vessel should be equipped with a single-sideband (SSB) marine radio. Its primary purpose is to enable you to call for help in an emergency. However, as you will see, it serves many other useful functions.

SSB Band Selection

Chapter 9 notes that the whole theory of SSB operation is based on the fact that high-frequency

(HF) radio waves are reflected off the layers of ionized gases in the ionosphere. Because ionization of the ionosphere is affected daily by the rising and setting of the sun, the range of the various HF SSB bands (that is, the "windows" in which communication on a particular band is possible) and the skip zone over which signals in a particular band pass and communication is impossible vary greatly by time of day. Therefore, one of the most important factors in achieving optimum SSB communications is selecting a band that will allow you to communicate over a given distance at a given time of day.

A good way to learn band selection is to listen to your SSB and make notes in a logbook on what you hear. In a loose-leaf notebook, assemble separate pages for distance groupings of less than 500 miles (800 km), 500 to 1,000 miles (800–1,600 km), 1,000 to 2,000 miles (1,600–3,200 km), and more than 2,000 miles. Down the side of each sheet, space out the hours of the twenty-four-hour clock. At their scheduled times, listen to the U.S. Coast Guard's Local Notices to Mariners broadcasts. Try each of the channels on which each broadcast is made. When you hear a station clearly, identify its location and compute its distance from you. On the sheet in your listening log for that distance, make a note of the station received and the channel under the appropriate hour heading.

Once you have twenty or thirty entries in your log and are ready to make a call, compute the distance over which you wish to communicate. On your log sheet for that distance, alongside the hour you wish to make the call will be the channels over which you are most likely to make contact over that distance at that time of day. After a month or so of this kind of practice, you'll find it becomes almost automatic to make the calculation in your head. Where your log indicates you have a choice between two or more bands, try the higher one first since it is more likely to provide the greatest signal strength and the lowest atmospheric noise. (See the sidebar for SSB range information.)

SSB Modes

All marine SSB radios on the market have a "mode" switch that allows you to select one of several modes for signal emission, but none of their manufacturers bother to explain fully how they differ or how they are used. Here's a rundown.

The bulk of SSB operation in pleasure cruising is conducted in the J3E mode on the upper sideband (USB). (On older SSB radios, this mode is referred to by its previous designation, A3J.) In addition to marine SSB, this signal emission mode is also used by amateur radio operators on their 15- and 20-meter bands. Many SSB radios allow you to also operate in the J3E mode on the lower sideband (LSB), which puts you into the 40- and 80-meter ham radio bands. You can listen to transmission on the ham bands, but transmitting over them is illegal unless you hold a valid and appropriate ham radio license. (See chapter 9 for more information about using ham radio in cruising.)

Some SSBs also operate in the R3E mode, which is used primarily for accessing marine telephone operators in parts of Europe and Canada. (In this mode, your radio's carrier signal must be reduced to 25 percent of peak envelope power [PEP]—that is, to 37.5 watts on a marine SSB radio with 150 watts PEP.)

The H3E mode is the old double sideband mode, which has been largely displaced by USB operation but is still used in some parts of the Caribbean and South America. On the mode selection switch of some marine SSB radios, it is identified as the AM or AME mode. It is a full carrier with amplitude voice modulation on the USB.

FSK stands for frequency shift keying, which is important only to those who use shipboard telex.

Placing and Receiving SSB Marine Operator Radiotelephone Calls

There are two types of marine radiotelephone services that handle SSB calls from and to your vessel—the Coastal Harbor Service and the High

SSB Band Characteristics

After you've worked with your SSB for a while, you'll find that the various SSB bands tend to have certain predictable characteristics.

- *The reliable range of frequencies in the 2 to 3 MHz band is about 200 miles (320 km) during the day and around 500 miles (800 km) at night. The band is susceptible to static from thunderstorms, but since it is ground-wave, it has no significant skip zone.*
- *Channels in the 4 MHz band can be virtually useless from sunrise to late afternoon. In early evening, range increases to around 600 miles (960 km). At night, its skip zone makes contact difficult within 100 to 200 miles (160–320 km), but maximum range stretches up to 2,000 miles (3,200 km) or more.*
- *Channels in the 6 MHz band have a range of about 500 miles (800 km) in daylight hours and stretch out to about 2,000 miles (3,200 km) at night. However, because the 6 MHz band is subject to a number of anomalies, it is the least used of the HF SSB bands.*
- *Channels in the 8 MHz band have a reliable range of around 700 miles (1,120 km) all day with minimal skip zone. At night, the skip zone is about 500 miles (800 km), but beyond that, range can be 3,000 miles (4,800 km) or more.*
- *The 12 MHz band is inactive or weak until midmorning. Around noon, its skip zone begins to stretch out to around 500 miles (800 km) and range to 2,000 to 3,500 miles (3,220–5,640 km). After sunset, the skip zone gradually widens to about 2,000 miles and the range to about 4,000 miles (6,440 km).*
- *The 16 MHz band is inactive or weak until late morning. Around noon, its skip zone widens to around 750 miles (1,200 km) and range increases to 4,000 to 6,000 miles (6,440–9,600 km). The band fades sharply about three hours after local sunset.*
- *The 22 MHz band is inactive or weak until around noon, then strengthens, with the skip zone widening to 1,500 miles (2,400 km) and range up to 7,000 miles (11,200 km). The band fades shortly after sunset.*

Bear in mind that these are averages. Any of the SSB bands can be rendered temporarily unusable by atmospheric conditions or ionospheric disturbances for periods ranging from a few hours to several days.

Seas Service. Coastal Harbor Service stations handle SSB calls only on the MF 2 to 3 MHz band and are used primarily by marine interests on the U.S. inland waterway system. Skippers who cruise offshore and elect not to invest in a marine satellite telephone can place ship-to-shore calls and receive shore-to-ship calls through coast station WLO based in Coden, Alabama, which handles calls on both the MF 2 to 3 MHz band and all of the HF bands allocated for marine use.

PLACING HIGH SEAS RADIOTELEPHONE CALLS

WLO broadcasts its "traffic lists"—the names of vessels for which they are holding calls—on specific channels at specific times. One way to place a call through WLO is to listen to its scheduled traffic list broadcasts and try to make contact as soon as the traffic list is over on the channel through which you are receiving it most clearly. The only problem with this practice is that the minute the traffic list ends, a dozen or more vessels usually try to get WLO at the same time, so you may have to wait an hour or more to get through.

To relieve congestion, WLO urges customers to place calls at times other than following the traffic list broadcasts. To do this, figure the approximate distance from your vessel to WLO. From the listening log I suggested earlier in this chapter that you create, select the highest band that is likely to provide communications at the time you want to place the call and over that distance. Tune your radio to one of the channels in that band listed for WLO, and listen to it for about three minutes. Remember that you are listening only to the channel's station transmit frequency. If someone on another vessel is talking to WLO, that person will be on the channel's ship transmit frequency and you won't be able to hear the conversation.

If after about three minutes you don't hear any traffic on the channel, go ahead and make your call. A typical call to WLO might sound like this: "Whiskey, Lima, Oscar, . . . Whiskey, Lima, Oscar, . . . Whiskey, Lima, Oscar. This is the motor yacht Mad Hatter, Whiskey, X-Ray, Yankee 1234, calling from offshore St. Lucia on channel eight three-oh." Giving the channel number you are using in your initial call helps the technician at WLO select it from among the twenty or more channels being monitored to respond to your call. Giving your vessel's position in your initial call helps the technician know where to point the station's high-gain directional antennas for the best connection. After making your initial call, wait about a minute before trying it again. If your call was heard, it probably will take the technician that long to select and tune the station's equipment. You may get a recording telling you all technicians are busy and to stand by. Stay on that channel, and the technician will get to you.

If the first channel you try is busy or after three or four calls you can't raise a technician, shift your radio to another channel in the band listed for WLO and listen there. Chances are that after two or three tries you'll find a channel that is not in use.

Once you get a technician, you will be connected to a telephone operator who will take the calling details and billing information and connect you with your party. If you want time and charges on the call, tell the telephone operator (not the technician) before the connection is made. Telephone operators will not honor time-and-charge requests after the call is completed. All High Seas calls are handled as person-to-person calls, even if you agree to speak with anyone who answers, and charges do not begin until the individual you call answers. Once you get your party on the line, if the person is not familiar with radiotelephone calls, briefly explain that you both need to say "over" after you have finished a segment of the conversation and the listener should not speak until hearing the speaker say "over." If you don't, you'll probably find you have to repeat a lot of missed conversation. If you encounter difficulties during a marine radiotelephone call, have the person you are talking to momentarily depress the switchhook on the telephone. This will stop billing time on the call and signal the operator. The telephone operator can then retry the call or, if necessary, bring in the High Seas technician to try another frequency.

When your land party hangs up, stay on the channel until the telephone operator comes back on the line. If you have other calls, go ahead and give the information and the operator will try to place them. When you are through with your last call, again wait until the telephone operator comes on the line, have the operator reconnect you with the High Seas technician, and sign off the channel.

As long as the final destination of your call is in the United States (including Alaska and Hawaii), Canada, Mexico, Puerto Rico, or the U.S. Virgin Islands, the charges will be a flat rate no matter the position of your vessel. If you are calling a country other than those listed, you will also be charged the person-to-person rate from WLO to the call's destination.

You can place calls through WLO collect or have them billed to your home or office phone. But you will save yourself a lot of time and hassle passing billing information if you register your vessel with WLO before you leave on your cruise. Once your vessel is registered, all you have to do is instruct the operator to "bill the vessel calling," and you won't have to give a string of numbers, which might become garbled in transmission. You also won't be giving out information such as your telephone credit card number, which someone else might overhear and use to charge calls without your authorization.

RECEIVING HIGH SEAS RADIOTELEPHONE CALLS

If you want your family, friends, or business associates to be able to reach you on board your vessel and you plan to use WLO as your primary radiotelephone link with shore, give these people your itinerary, your vessel's name, its radio call sign if you have one, and—if your SSB is DSC capable—its MMSI number. Instruct them to call WLO and ask for the High Seas Operator (see contact information in the resources appendix). If your vessel has DSC, the operator will send you an alerting message. When you answer, your SSB will be automatically switched to one of WLO's working frequencies. If your vessel doesn't have DSC, it's name will be listed on WLO's next traffic list and will stay on the list until you answer or the shore party cancels its call. In cases where the call is not answered and the coast station cannot contact the calling party for instructions, the vessel normally will be removed from the traffic list after twenty-four hours.

If your SSB isn't DSC capable, one way to find out if someone is trying to reach you via SSB radiotelephone is to periodically listen to the scheduled traffic list broadcast over WLO to see if your vessel's name is listed. Another is to call WLO to ask whether they are holding traffic for you. There is no charge for such an inquiry, but it's best to limit calls to other than the peak traffic hours during midmorning, late morning, and early evening.

TROUBLESHOOTING MARINE RADIOS

In an emergency, a VHF or an SSB marine radio doesn't do you any good if you can't transmit and receive over it. If you need your radio for emergency communications and it doesn't seem to be working properly, here are some things to check.

1. Is your ship's service battery system working properly?
   A. If none of the equipment aboard your vessel that is powered by your ship's service battery is working, the problem is probably with the battery itself. Check to see that it is filled with water and that the cables connected to it are tightly affixed and not corroded. If necessary, refill the battery with water and remove, clean, and reattach the battery cables securely.
   B. If some but not all of the equipment aboard your vessel powered by your ship's service battery is working, the problem is probably in your vessel's electrical distribution panel. Trace your radio's power cable to its connection at the distribution panel. Check the fuse or circuit breaker serving the terminal to which the radio's power cable is connected. If your distribution panel uses fuses, check the fuse in the circuit serving your radio. It normally will be a small, clear glass tube with metal caps on either end, each of which snap into a small pair of prongs. A thin wire or small strip of metal will run through the glass tube lengthwise.

   If either of the metal caps at the ends of the fuse shows signs of a chalky green or white substance, it is corroded. Remove the fuse from the prongs into which it snaps, and scrape both the cap and the prongs down to bright, shiny metal. (Be careful not to allow any metal such as a knife blade or a screwdriver to contact the sets of prongs that hold the two ends of the fuse at the same time. You could get an electrical shock.) Hold the fuse up to a light and shake it gently. If the wire or metal strip is broken or loose, replace the fuse with another of the same type and size.

If your distribution panel uses circuit breakers, check to make certain the breaker is not tripped and, if necessary, reset it.

If after either of these steps you still have doubts that the terminal is delivering power to your radio, disconnect the radio's power cable and attach it to another circuit serving equipment powered by your ship's service battery but that is working, such as a GPS receiver.

If your radio seems to be the only piece of equipment aboard your vessel powered by your ship's service battery that isn't working, the problem is probably with the radio's electrical power supply, its antenna system, or the radio itself.

2. Is the radio turned on?

Make certain the radio's power switch is in the on position. If the power switch is on and the radio is working, the lights on its front panel should be glowing. The fact that the lights are glowing indicates the radio is getting some electrical power, but if they aren't glowing, it does not necessarily mean the radio isn't transmitting or receiving properly. If the lights aren't glowing but you can receive any noise over the radio, even just static, the lightbulbs or the circuit board to which they are connected could be burned out, loose, or disconnected, or

their contacts corroded. If the lights aren't glowing and you can't receive even static over the radio, turn the power switch on and off several times. It may be shorted out or corroded. If so, you will have to disconnect the radio and remove it from its case to clean, tighten, or replace the switch.

3. Is the radio connected to an adequate source of power?

If the radio's front panel lights aren't glowing and you can't receive even static over it, check its fuse. The fuse can either be in the back of the radio case behind a small knob marked "fuse" or housed in a cylindrical fitting in the radio's power cable. If so, the fitting usually will be about 1 inch (2.5 cm) long and ½ inch (12 mm) in diameter and will be black. Once you've located the fuse, unscrew the knob or the fitting, remove the fuse, and check it and its contacts as suggested above for a fuse in the distribution panel. If one or both of the metal caps on the ends of the fuse are corroded, clean them and their contacts inside the fuse housing. If the wire or metal strip inside the fuse is loose or broken, replace the fuse.

4. Is the radio properly connected to a functioning antenna?

A. A marine radio will not transmit or receive adequately if it is not properly connected to a functioning antenna. Check the lead from your radio to the base of its antenna to make certain the connections at both ends are securely tightened and are not corroded. If necessary, remove, clean, and resecure them. Check along the length of the antenna lead to make certain it isn't broken.

B. Check the antenna itself to make certain it has not been damaged or swept away. In either case, connect the radio's antenna lead to an emergency replacement antenna or construct a jury rig. In the case of a VHF radio, a random length of wire will function as a jury rig antenna. It should be about 6 feet (1.8 m) long and must be oriented vertically and installed as high on your vessel as possible.

You can also jury-rig an antenna for your SSB marine radio provided you have an automatic antenna tuner installed between the jury rig and the radio. Construct the jury-rigged antenna from a length of wire about 25 feet (7.6 m) long, insulate it at both ends, and connect it to your vessel's radio frequency (RF) grounding system. Before connecting the lead from the antenna tuner to it, make certain the radio is turned off because the jury rig will carry a significant amount of electrical current. Once you have made the connection, warn your crew to stand well clear of the jury rig because they could receive a nasty electrical shock. Before you attempt to transmit with such a jury-rigged antenna, turn off all other electronic equipment aboard your vessel. The SSB's RF signals could burn them out.

5. Is the radio transmitting?
   A. If the radio appears to be receiving adequate power from your ship's service battery and to be properly connected to an undamaged or jury-rigged antenna, you may find you can receive over it but cannot transmit. When you depress the microphone's transmit button, a light on the radio's front panel marked "transmit" should glow. The fact that the "transmit" light does glow indicates you are transmitting; if it does not glow, this doesn't necessarily mean you aren't transmitting. The bulb may simply be loose, its base could be corroded, or it could be burned out. Push on the bulb and wiggle it to see if you can establish contact. If not, you will have to disconnect and disassemble the radio to clean the bulb's contacts or replace it. The best indication that you are not transmitting is that you are able to receive on a channel but when you transmit on it you receive no acknowledgment.
   B. Activate the microphone's transmit button several times to see if the transmit light comes on. The switch itself may be loose or corroded. If so, you will have to disassemble the microphone to clean, tighten, or replace it.
   C. Check any external connection between the microphone and the radio itself. Some microphones are attached to their radios by a connector, which could be loose or corroded. If your microphone has such a connector, make certain it is not corroded and is securely tightened. If necessary, clean and retighten it.

If none of the above steps convinces you that your radio is working properly, about your only recourse is to disconnect the radio, remove it from its case, and check inside for any signs of corrosion on any of its terminals or for loose or disconnected wires.

Predicting the Weather

As a cruising yachtsperson, you have few topics of more critical concern than the weather, and there are few skills you can develop that will be of more practical value than being able to predict with reasonable accuracy the weather conditions you are likely to encounter. Developing that ability involves learning something about the forces that create basic weather systems; learning how to gather information from your own observations and broadcast weather data concerning the current status and likely movement of those basic systems; and interpreting that information in terms of your own cruising plans.

You can't really make maximum use of the wealth of weather information available until you understand the fundamental processes that determine basic weather systems. Stated in their simplest terms, those processes begin with the sun's rays striking the earth and heating its surface (see illustration). Heat reflected from the earth's land masses heats the air above them, causing that air to rise. As the air rises, it leaves a center of low pressure beneath it. The heated air flows toward cooler air, becomes cooled itself, and sinks back toward earth. This downward flow of air creates a center of high pressure. The difference in pressure between the high and low thus formed creates a *pressure gradient*, which causes masses of air in the high-pressure area to flow toward the area of lower pressure, thus creating surface winds.

Since the earth is round, the sun's rays strike the earth most directly at the equator. As the earth at the equator is heated and in turn heats the air above it, that air rises. The upward rush of that heated air leaves in its wake a band of low pressure girdling the earth that meteorologists call the Intertropical Convergence Zone (ITCZ) (see illustration page 292). As this heated air rises to a height of about 12 miles (19 km), it gradually cools and becomes more dense (heavier) and a major portion of it sinks back to earth around 30 degrees North and South latitude. This air pressing down on the earth forms what meteorologists refer to as the subtropical high-pressure zones. (To put the area of the subtropical high in the Northern Hemisphere in perspective: in North America, the line

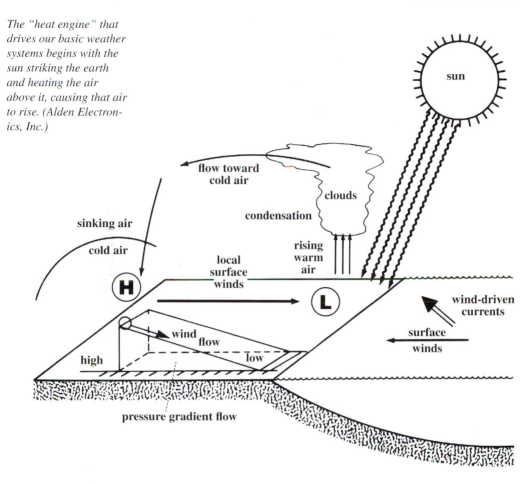

The "heat engine" that drives our basic weather systems begins with the sun striking the earth and heating the air above it, causing that air to rise. (Alden Electronics, Inc.)

of 30 degrees North latitude runs across northern Mexico; just north of San Antonio and Houston, Texas; virtually through New Orleans, Louisiana; and just to the south of Jacksonville, Florida.) The pressure gradient created by the difference in pressure between the subtropical high and low atmospheric pressure of the ITCZ causes masses of air in the subtropical high-pressure zones to flow toward the lower-pressure area of the ITCZ.

If the earth did not rotate on its axis, the high-pressure air masses from the subtropical high-pressure zone around 30 degrees North would flow directly southward toward the equator, and the air masses in the subtropical high-pressure zone around 30 degrees South would flow directly northward toward the equator. But because the earth is rotating on its axis from west to east, it creates what is known as the Coriolis force, which deflects this air flow toward the west and causes us to perceive it as coming from the east (see illustration next page).

In the Western Hemisphere, we refer to these basic air flows as the northeast trade winds, which sweep roughly across northern Africa, then

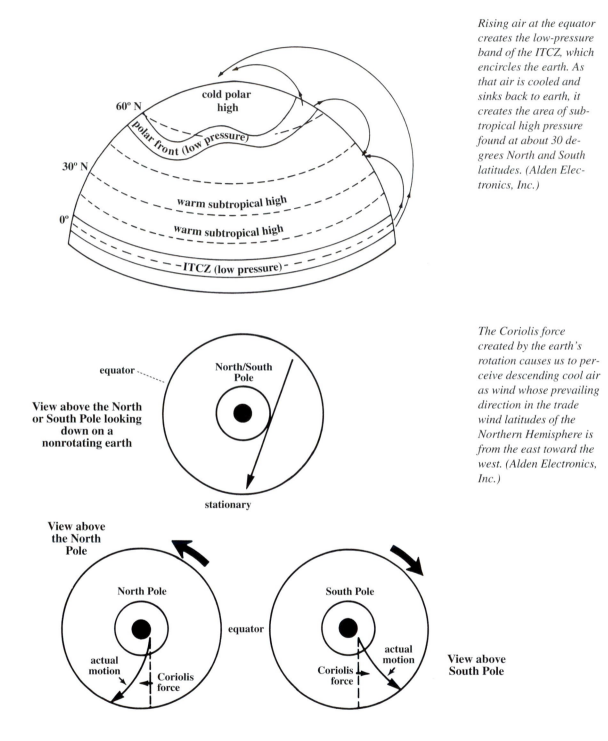

Rising air at the equator creates the low-pressure band of the ITCZ, which encircles the earth. As that air is cooled and sinks back to earth, it creates the area of sub-tropical high pressure found at about 30 degrees North and South latitudes. (Alden Electronics, Inc.)

The Coriolis force created by the earth's rotation causes us to perceive descending cool air as wind whose prevailing direction in the trade wind latitudes of the Northern Hemisphere is from the east toward the west. (Alden Electronics, Inc.)

The force of air at the equator being heated by the sun and rising, then cooling and sinking back to earth in the subtropical high, combined with the Coriolis force created by the earth's rotation, creates the northeast trade winds in the Northern Hemisphere and the southeast trade winds in the Southern Hemisphere. (Alden Electronics, Inc.)

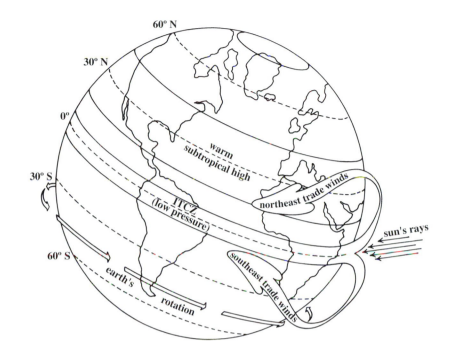

southwesterly across the North Atlantic toward the Caribbean Sea; and the southeast trade winds, which sweep roughly across southern Africa, then northwesterly across the South Atlantic toward Brazil (see illustration). In the Northern Hemisphere, as warm air rises and leaves an area of low pressure in its wake, surrounding air is drawn into the void (what meteorologists call *convergence*). The Coriolis effect, combined with centripetal force, causes the air around this area of low atmospheric pressure to circulate counterclockwise in the Northern Hemisphere (see illustrations next page). As cooled air sinks back to earth creating an area of high pressure, it is forced outward (what the meteorologists call *divergence*) and the Coriolis effect, combined with centrifugal force, causes the air around the high to circulate clockwise (see illustrations next page). In the Southern Hemisphere, both directions are reversed.

Within this basic system, of course, are subsys-

tems that create other wind patterns with which mariners are familiar (see top illustration page 295). Some of the air heated at the equator, for example, flows all the way to the poles before it sinks to earth, creating high-pressure zones around both the North and South Poles and a band of low-pressure polar fronts between the polar highs and the subtropical highs at about 60 degrees North and South latitude. In the Northern Hemisphere, air masses flowing down the pressure gradient from the polar high zone toward the lower pressure of the polar front with a clockwise rotation imparted by the Coriolis effect and centrifugal force create polar easterly winds. Pressure gradients also cause some high-pressure air masses in the subtropical high-pressure zone to flow northward toward the lower-pressure area of the polar front. Their clockwise rotation caused by the Coriolis effect and centrifugal force creates midlatitude westerlies.

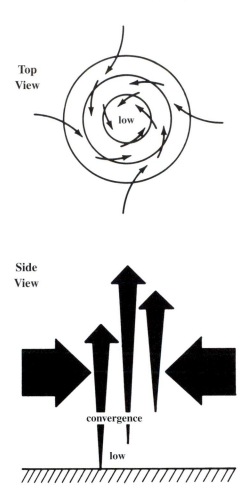

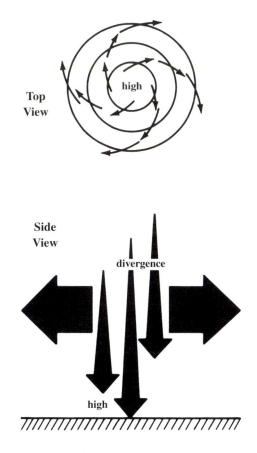

As heated air rises, it leaves an area of low pressure called convergence in its wake. The Coriolis force causes air flow around an area of low pressure to be counter-clockwise in the Northern Hemisphere (reverse in the Southern Hemisphere). (Alden Electronics, Inc.)

As air cools and sinks back to earth, it creates an area of high pressure called divergence. The Coriolis force causes air flow around an area of high pressure to be clockwise in the Northern Hemisphere (reverse in the Southern Hemisphere). (Alden Electronics, Inc.)

These factors also are primarily responsible for the basic patterns of upper air level movement that provide the steering currents for much of the surface winds with which we as mariners must deal. The same fundamental forces that create the northeast trade winds, for instance, steer hurricanes born off the west coast of Africa across the North Atlantic to landfall somewhere between the Lower Antilles and the southeast coast of the United States (see bottom illustration opposite).

The basic wind patterns created by the heating and cooling process, the Coriolis effect, and centrifugal force are in turn responsible for the basic ocean currents (see illustrations page 296). A persistent area of high pressure over the North Atlantic (often referred to as the Bermuda High), for

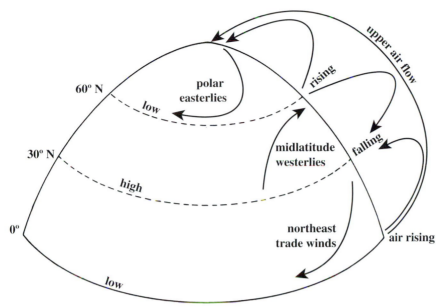

The combination of heated air rising, cooling air falling, and the Coriolis force created by the earth's rotation makes up the basic forces behind the Northern Hemisphere's northeasterly trade winds, the midlatitude westerlies, and the polar easterlies. (Alden Electronics, Inc.)

example, normally is centered roughly at about 30 degrees North latitude and creates a basically clockwise ocean current pattern in the North Atlantic (see illustration page 297). When that flow piles up against the continental shelf along the East Coast of North America, it is concentrated and creates the northeasterly flowing Gulf Stream.

All of these basic weather systems are affected by the inclination of the earth's axis of rotation at about 23½ degrees to the plane of its orbit around the sun, which means that in the summer the Northern Hemisphere is closest to the sun and thus warmer, while the reverse is true in winter. This not only accounts for the reversal of seasons in the two hemispheres but also creates winter and summer shifts in basic weather patterns. During the summer months, for instance, the Bermuda High tends to migrate to the northwest, bringing high pressures and associated fair weather to most of the East Coast of the United States. During winter, that system tends to migrate southwesterly, leaving the East Coast shrouded in the rain and fog typical of an area of low pressure.

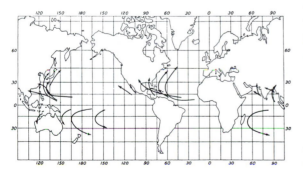

The basic forces of heated air rising, cooling air falling, and the Coriolis force create the earth's prevailing wind patterns and strongly influence the paths of tropical storms. (Alden Electronics, Inc.)

UNDERSTANDING BASIC WEATHER PATTERNS

Once you understand basic weather systems, you are in a position to predict the basic weather patterns they create in a given cruising area at a particular time of year, to take advantage of favorable conditions, and to avoid weather patterns you know will be adverse.

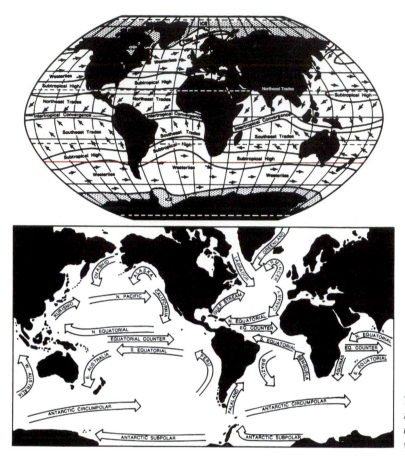

The earth's basic wind patterns give rise to the basic ocean currents that mariners encounter around the world. (Alden Electronics, Inc.)

High-Pressure Systems

The downward flow of dense, cold air that produces the subtropical and polar high-pressure zones creates four distinct types of high-pressure air masses, which are classified by the region over which they are created and by whether they are formed over land or water. While in the Northern Hemisphere all four have the characteristic clockwise air flow imparted by the Coriolis effect and centrifugal force, these high-pressure air masses vary widely in their temperature and moisture content.

1. *Maritime tropical* air masses are formed over ocean areas in the subtropical high region and tend to be warm and moist. In the northern half of the Western Hemisphere, the Bermuda High is a typical example.

2. *Continental tropical* air masses are formed over land areas in the subtropical high region and tend to be warm and dry. In the northern half of the Western Hemisphere, the fairly persistent area of high pressure centered over the desert areas of the southwest portion of the United States is a typical example.

3. *Maritime polar* air masses are formed over ocean areas in the polar high region and tend to be cold and wet. A typical

example in the North Atlantic is generally found off the northeastern coast of Canada.

4. *Continental polar* air masses are formed over land in the polar high region and tend to be cold and dry. An example is the area of persistent high pressure found generally over northwestern Canada.

As these air masses form, they are carried along by prevailing winds and atmospheric pressure gradients. The effects of unequal global warming during winter and summer cause their center in the Northern Hemisphere to move generally toward the equator during the winter months and pole-ward during the summer months. The combination of these two factors causes these high-pressure air masses to move in a more or less consistent—and therefore reasonably predictable—pattern. In North America, their pattern of movement can tell you a great deal about the basic winter and summer weather across the United States and its coastal waters.

The first of these air masses is the series of maritime tropical air masses that are spawned in the subtropical high-pressure zone off the coast of California and Mexico and flow northward toward the lower pressure of the polar front with a clockwise rotation that carries them with their heavy moisture content into the Gulf of Alaska. From there, they sweep down into North Amer-

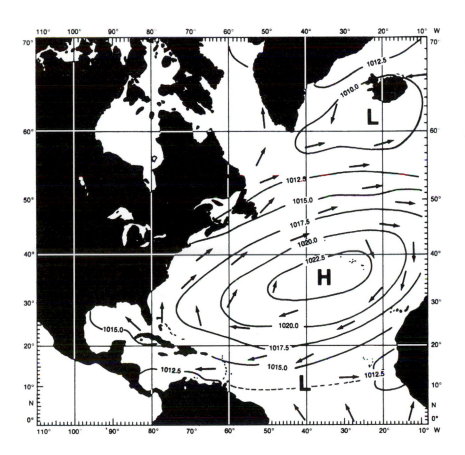

The position of the Bermuda High (shown here in summer) significantly influences weather along the Eastern Seaboard of the United States and is a primary factor in determining ocean currents in the North Atlantic. (Alden Electronics, Inc.)

ica as midlatitude westerlies and are steered eastwardly by the jet stream at a typical rate of about 400 statute miles (640 km) a day. If the jet stream is running well to the north, they come ashore about British Columbia, sweep over Canada's southern provinces and America's northern tier of states and the Great Lakes, then exit into the North Atlantic roughly between Nova Scotia and Newfoundland. If the jet stream is running approximately over the U.S.–Canadian border, these air masses tend to come ashore somewhere from Oregon to northern California, sweep eastward across the Great Plains, and cross the East Coast between roughly Washington and Boston. If the jet stream dips well southward into the central part of the United States, these air masses are driven more southeasterly across the United States and tend to exit into the North Atlantic somewhere between about Washington, D.C., and the South Carolina–Georgia border.

A second primary air mass pattern that strongly influences weather conditions in North America in winter is a strong southward shift of the subtropical high-pressure zone that leaves lower pressure in its wake and allows continental polar air masses spawned in the polar high region of western Canada to sweep down the pressure gradient and carry their icy blasts into the continental United States. The extent of the southward migration of the subtropical high combined with the location of the jet stream largely determines whether subfreezing temperatures will extend only to the midportion of the country or all the way down to the Gulf Coast. In rare instances, an extreme southern flow of the jet stream can force freezing temperatures all the way down into southern Florida and Texas.

Other primary air mass patterns that influence weather patterns in the eastern half of the United States are the maritime tropical highs that form off the west coast of Africa just above the equator, then sweep across the Atlantic and up through the eastern Caribbean at a typical rate of advance of about 250 miles (400 km) a day. A weak Bermuda High over the North Atlantic tends to allow these fronts to sweep up the East Coast of the United States. A strong Bermuda High in the North Atlantic tends to force these air masses into the Gulf of Mexico. Once in the Gulf, depending on the strength and location of the jet stream, which provides their primary steering currents, they usually head in one of three general directions. A jet stream running over northern Canada allows them to curve to the north and cross the Gulf Coast of the United States through about Mississippi and Louisiana, where they often curve again and sweep inland just to the west of the Appalachian Mountains. A jet stream running about over the U.S.–Canadian border steers them toward the Texas–Mexican border. A jet stream running even farther south forces them across the Yucatán Peninsula or into Central America.

While changing conditions can alter the speed and direction of these air masses, you can watch their ebb and flow across the United States on any daily weather map and use this basic information to make some fairly reliable predictions of boating conditions along your planned route and thus determine your schedule.

FRONTS

A *front* is simply the leading edge of one of the four types of air masses we have described and is the area along which significant weather changes are likely to take place as two—and in some cases three—air masses with differing relative temperatures encounter each other. While the basic air mass behind a front consists of high pressure, a front itself is an area of low pressure called a *trough* and is a transition zone that is likely to involve rapid change in temperature, pressure, wind, and moisture. While fronts are basically classified as cold and warm, the basic importance of those terms is not the absolute temperature of a front itself but its degree of coldness or warmth in relation to that of other air masses it encounters. The greater the temperature differential between two colliding air masses, the greater the likelihood that their collision will result in severe weather.

Cold Fronts

In the Northern Hemisphere, cold fronts such as those at the leading edge of a maritime or continental polar air mass tend to move roughly northwest to east or southeast at about 20 knots. As their leading edge encounters warmer air, the two air masses do not mix. Instead, the warm air is forced upward, where it cools and condenses into clouds and the moisture it contains often precipitates out as rain (see illustration). Because the blunt edge of an advancing cold front forces the warmer air upward at a fairly sharp angle, rain along its leading edge is likely to develop quickly and be intense but is often limited in area and clears quickly. As a cold front passes through a location, wind direction will shift from the southwesterly flow of the warm air mass in front of it to the northwest, then to the north, and possibly even into the northeast, and the temperature and humidity will drop. The atmospheric pressure will drop as the leading edge of the cold front passes, then increase as the cold air mass advances.

A cold front pushing its way beneath warm, moist air often results in a relatively narrow band of showers, which can be intense but are likely to be of only brief duration. (Alden Electronics, Inc.)

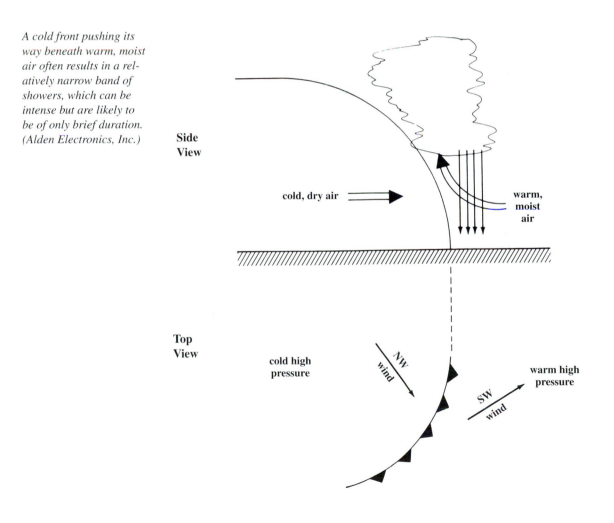

Side View

cold, dry air

warm, moist air

Top View

cold high pressure

NW wind

SW wind

warm high pressure

Warm Fronts

Warm fronts in the Northern Hemisphere—such as those at the leading edge of a maritime or continental tropical air mass—may travel in a variety of directions and even change directions but normally proceed at a somewhat slower pace than cold fronts (typically at about 15 knots). As a warm front passes a location, the wind will shift from approximately southwest to approximately west and the temperature and relative humidity will generally increase. Atmospheric pressure will decrease as the front passes, then increase as the warm air mass comes in behind it. As warm air rides up over the colder air in front of it, the warm air will be forced upward, where it will cool and condense into clouds and possibly rain (see illustration). Because the vertical slope of a warm air front normally is not as steep as that of a cold front, adverse weather where a warm front rides over colder air is likely to develop slowly; high cirrus clouds can precede the arrival of the front itself by a day or more. Adverse weather created by the arrival of a warm front is not likely to be particularly intense but is likely to cover a wide area and last for several days.

Occluded Fronts

An occluded front involves not simply cold air and warm air but air that is warm, cold, and colder. An occluded front develops this way: because

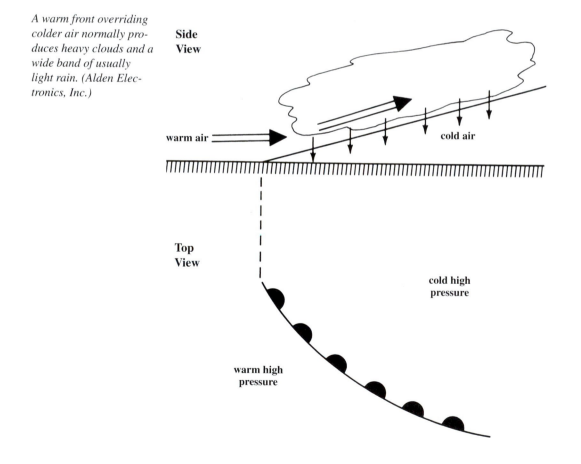

A warm front overriding colder air normally produces heavy clouds and a wide band of usually light rain. (Alden Electronics, Inc.)

cold fronts tend to travel faster than warm fronts, they overtake warm fronts fairly frequently. Remember that, by definition, the air on the front side of a warm front is cooler than the air behind it. When a cold front overrides this situation, one of two conditions occurs: if the air behind the advancing cold front is colder than the air in front of the warm front, the colder air forces the warm air upward; if the air behind the advancing cold front is not as cold as the air in front of the warm front, the advancing cold front rides up over the warm air.

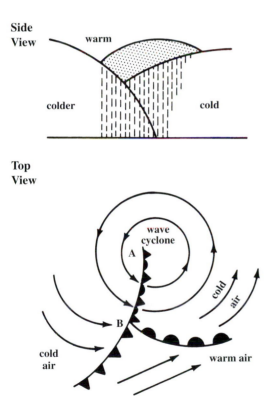

An occluded front results from cold air in the upper atmosphere overriding warmer air nearer the earth. The counter rotation of the two bodies of air can produce a wave cyclone of intense low pressure around the point where they intersect. (Alden Electronics, Inc.)

Low-Pressure Systems

While high-pressure systems are formed by fundamental weather processes, they tend to be more or less permanent and to cover vast areas, with a few exceptions, such as the more or less permanent low-pressure system in the North Atlantic over Iceland. Low-pressure systems are more transitory in nature, cover smaller areas, and tend to be formed by the collision of air masses of different temperature. The Coriolis effect, convergence, and centripetal force combine to cause air flow around them in the Northern Hemisphere to be counter-clockwise.

EXTRATROPICAL CYCLONES

The condition of a cold front overtaking a warm front resulting in an occluded front often creates an extratropical cyclone that has the counterclockwise air movement around a center of low-pressure characteristic of a tropical cyclone (called a hurricane in the North Atlantic). While the two systems are similar, they also have important differences. Extratropical cyclones have the following characteristics.

- They can occur over either land or water, whereas tropical cyclones normally are born only over water.
- They occur in the midlatitudes north or south of the ITCZ.
- They generally cover a larger area: 500 to 1,000 miles (800–1,600 km) compared to 400 to 500 miles (640–800 km) for a tropical cyclone.
- Their internal wind speeds are only about half those of a tropical cyclone.
- In the Northern Hemisphere, they tend to move from west to east where tropical cyclones tend to move from east to west.

Both systems, however, are created in the same manner (see illustration).

Because the air mass behind both a cold front and a warm front is high pressure, in the Northern Hemisphere the air flow along both fronts is clockwise, which means that where the two fronts meet, their air movement is opposed. (You may not have trouble grasping the concept that two clockwise air flows can be opposed, but I did and figured it out this way: Think of two gears side by side, both turning in a clockwise direction. If they are forced together, the right half of the gear on the left will be turning downward while the left half of the gear on the right will be turning upward; thus their movement will be opposed.)

As the cold front pushes under the warm front, the warmer air rises. The upward rush of this warm air creates a center of low pressure around which air—because of the Coriolis effect and centrifugal force—in the Northern Hemisphere begins to circulate counterclockwise. If the temperature differential between the warm front and the overtaking cold front is not extreme, then the only result of the overtaking is to create an area of bad weather that can extend outward from the center of the low pressure for several hundred miles. These are the low-pressure systems which we see on the daily weather map marching in a more or less regular rhythm across the continental United States at intervals of roughly four to ten days and spreading wind and rain along their leading edge, which can extend for several hundred miles. If tempera-

tures along the leading edge of these low-pressure systems are cold enough, the precipitation the system generates will fall as freezing rain, sleet, or snow.

If the temperature differential between the cold front and the warm front is extreme, however, the circulation around this center of low pressure can become also extreme and create the kind of storm conditions we normally associate with the word *cyclone*.

OBTAINING BASIC WEATHER PATTERN INFORMATION

The best sources of basic long-range weather pattern information for U.S. waters are the various volumes of the National Ocean Service (NOS) *Coast Pilot*s, which provide information on general weather patterns in the areas they cover and meteorological tables that list by month prevailing wind directions and percentages of observations in which winds exceed gale force (34 knots) and sea heights exceed 10 feet (3 m). Similar information for foreign waters is found in the various volumes of *Sailing Directions*, published by the National Imagery and Mapping Agency (see resources appendix).

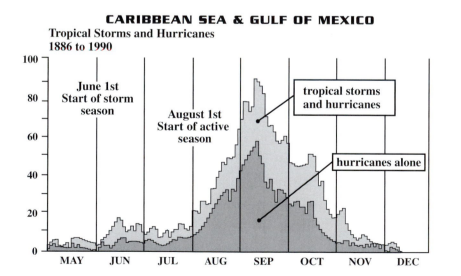

CARIBBEAN SEA & GULF OF MEXICO
Tropical Storms and Hurricanes 1886 to 1990

June 1st Start of storm season

August 1st Start of active season

tropical storms and hurricanes

hurricanes alone

This historical chart of tropical storms and hurricanes in the Caribbean Sea and the Gulf of Mexico provides ample justification for postponing the departure of a cruise to either area until late October, after the threat of storms has largely passed.

A tremendous quantity and variety of useful weather information is available from governments and private sources. Here are some suggestions on where and how to find it.

The best source of information on English-language voice marine weather broadcasts comes from a Web site—www.hffax.com—that lists the location and call signs of radio stations worldwide that broadcast marine weather information over single-sideband radiotelephone. The listings include the times, frequencies, and contents of broadcasts along with the areas they cover. It also lists the location and call signs of radio stations worldwide that broadcast radiofacsimile marine weather charts. The listings include the times, frequencies, and contents of transmissions along with the areas they cover, which makes it indispensable for programming an automated weatherfax receiver.

The Naval Atlantic Meteorology and Oceanography Center in Norfolk, Virginia, no longer broadcasts a wide variety of radiofacsimile weather charts over its high-frequency station NAM. Nor does it issue a *Facsimile Products Guide*, listing schedules. All of this information is now available over its Web site (see resources appendix).

Although the weatherfax system is in decline, both governmental and private satellite weather services are increasing in number. Direct links to the National Oceanic and Atmospheric Administration and to such computer program suppliers as Maptech, MaxSea, Nobeltec, and Raymarine are available. Through the use of satellite communication systems, weather data for practically anywhere on earth can be downloaded. Private weather forecasters also can supply real-time and future forecasts of weather along your specific cruising routes.

INTERPRETING WEATHER INFORMATION

Having access to accurate, up-to-date, comprehensive weather information does you little good if you don't know how to interpret it and apply it to both your long-range and your immediate cruising plans. Here are a few suggestions regarding what to look for.

Interpreting Basic Weather Pattern Information

Information regarding basic weather patterns is helpful primarily in long-range cruise planning.

For example, some friends once asked for my comments on a nine-month cruise they were planning that would commence in Key West, Florida, in January, take them westward across the Gulf of Mexico, through the Yucatán Channel between Cuba and Mexico, down the east coast of Belize and Central America, then along the northern coast of South America, and return them to the United States via the Windward and Leeward Islands. My response was that I didn't think much of their program. I suggested that if they were to study the available information on basic weather patterns along their planned route at the time of year they planned to be in each area, they would discover a couple of discouraging facts: that the run eastward along the northern coast of South America was certain to be a windward slog into the teeth of 15- to 20-knot easterly trade winds, and that their schedule would take them through the eastern Caribbean in August and September, which is the height of that area's hurricane season (see illustration opposite). I suggested they consider altering their schedule to depart Florida in late October, after the worst of the hurricane threat has passed, and reverse their route, which would turn their journey along the northern coast of South America into a downhill sleigh ride rather than an uphill battle against wind and current.

For a second example, when I was planning *Americas Odyssey*'s voyage from the U.S.–Canadian border, down the East Coast of the United States, through the Bahamas and the eastern Caribbean, then across the northern coast of South America, through the Panama Canal, up the west

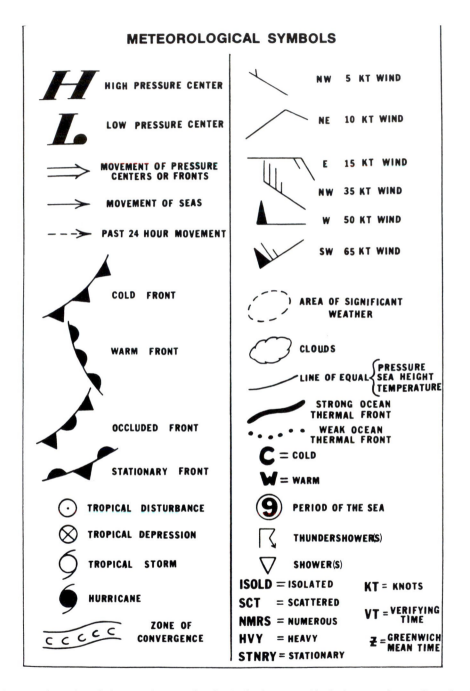

The standard meteorological symbols printed on weather facsimile charts provide the key to understanding what the charts tell you about the weather you are likely to encounter in a forthcoming leg of a cruise. (Alden Electronics, Inc.)

coast of Central America, Mexico, and the United States, then up the Inside Passage to Glacier Bay, Alaska, a study of basic weather patterns in the areas I planned to cruise revealed the following: I didn't want to depart Florida until October, after the worst of the hurricane threat has passed; I would have a beam reach across the northwest trade winds as I proceeded south down the chain of islands of the eastern Caribbean; I would have a downwind run along the northern coast of South America; and I needed to depart San Diego no earlier or later than early May to take advantage of moderate summer weather conditions for the long slog up the west coast of the United States and Canada.

Interpreting Voice Broadcast Marine Weather Information

Voice broadcast marine weather information is helpful principally for planning your cruising itinerary from one day to about a week into the future. As a typical example, suppose you are in South Florida aboard your 8-knot displacement boat planning to cross the Gulf Stream for a cruise through the Bahamas. The weather reports you are receiving over VHF indicate that winds currently are out of the southeast at 10 knots and seas are 2 to 3 feet (0.6–0.9 m). The five-day forecast predicts that a low-pressure system off the New England coast is drifting southward and is expected to arrive off South Florida in about three days. That information tells you that current conditions for crossing the Stream are close to ideal, with the winds light to moderate and out of the south, which puts them in line with the current of the Gulf Stream. It also tells you that two to three days from now, the winds will build in advance of the low-pressure system coming down from New England and will shift into the north. That will put them in opposition to the Gulf Stream current, and seas are likely to be 6 to 8 feet (1.8–2.4 m). You had better either cast off and get the Gulf Stream crossing behind you while conditions are favorable or plan to wait at least a week to depart while the low-pressure system drifting down from New

England passes through South Florida and the winds moderate and return to flow out of the south.

Interpreting Radiofacsimile Weather Charts

Radiofacsimile weather charts are useful primarily for planning your cruising itinerary from one to two weeks into the future. As an example of how this information can be used in the real world of cruising, suppose you are in English Harbor, Antigua, planning a ten-day run down through the islands to Grenada. Your preferred schedule is to depart tomorrow morning and run the first day to Guadeloupe, then run the second day to Martinique, where you will pick up friends who are flying in for a week's stay aboard. The third day will be spent touring Martinique, the fourth and fifth days visiting St. Lucia, the sixth through eighth days exploring the Tobago Keys, and the tenth day getting to Grenada, from which your friends are scheduled to fly back to the States. Is that a workable plan?

You begin to answer that question by arranging to receive by Internet links or shortwave broadcasts the following weather charts for the eastern Caribbean and the North Atlantic Ocean.

- a surface weather analysis chart, which shows current weather patterns
- three surface weather prognosis charts, which indicate predicted weather conditions over the coming twenty-four, thirty-six, and forty-eight hours
- several extended surface weather prognosis charts, which indicate predicted weather conditions over the coming two to five days
- a wave analysis chart, which depicts current wave heights and directions
- a wave prognosis chart, which forecasts wave heights and directions for the coming twenty-four hours
- a satellite weather photo, which shows cloud cover and indicates positions of disturbances and tropical cyclones

- a radar chart, which shows areas of storm development, including local thunderstorms

In order to take maximum advantage of these charts, you must first understand the symbols they employ and what they represent (see page 304). The meanings of most of these symbols, such as H for the center of an area of high pressure and L for the center of an area of low pressure, are self-explanatory. The symbols used to represent cold, warm, occluded, and stationary fronts are a bit more difficult to keep straight but are extremely important since most significant weather occurs along these fronts. (I find it helps me remember which symbol depicts which type of front by thinking of the triangles that represent a cold front as icicles and the semicircles that represent a warm front as small suns.)

Among the most valuable symbols on the charts are the following.

- wind arrows, whose shafts show the direction of winds and whose feathers and pennants show the strength of winds: a half feather indicates 5 knots; a full feather, 10 knots; and a solid triangular pennant, 50 knots
- wave symbols, which indicate dominant wave direction, dominant wave period, and dominant wave height

Once you have received the charts you have selected, you find that the surface weather analysis and wave analysis charts for the eastern Caribbean indicate current conditions for your planned voyage are close to ideal: winds are 15 to 20 knots out of the east-northeast, the wave period is fourteen seconds, and the dominant wave height is 6 feet (1.8 m). The surface weather prognosis and wave prognosis charts indicate these conditions are likely to remain unchanged for the next twelve, twenty-four, and thirty-six hours. The radar chart shows no significant area of storm development in the eastern Caribbean.

The extended surface weather prognosis chart, however, indicates that trouble may be on the way.

It shows that on the fourth day of your trip, wind velocities in the eastern Caribbean are predicted to increase to 30 knots, the wave period will decrease to nine seconds, and dominant wave heights will increase to 14 feet (4.3 m). On the fifth day, winds are expected to build to 40 knots, the wave period will further decrease to six seconds, and dominant wave heights will build to 20 feet (6.1 m).

A check of the satellite weather photo for the North Atlantic identifies the source of your difficulties: a significant system of low pressure that is building off the western coast of North Africa and that over the next ten days will drift inexorably toward the eastern Caribbean.

On the basis of the information you have drawn from your radiofacsimile weather charts, you probably will be able to meet your friends in Martinique with no problem. Your planned crossing of the St. Lucia Channel on day four in 30-knot winds and 14-foot (4.3 m) seas, however, would be a bit adventurous. You might be well advised to step up your schedule and make that crossing on day three, before conditions build. It's obvious your cruise through the Tobago Keys will have to be postponed because that low-lying area is no place to be in predicted 40-knot winds and 20-foot (6 m) seas. You decide to call your friends and tell them to plan to reschedule their departure from the international airport at Vieux Fort, St. Lucia, because it is unlikely the coming weather will allow you to get them to Grenada in time for their scheduled departure.

For further information on interpreting radiofacsimile weather charts, I suggest you obtain a copy of *A Mariner's Guide to Radiofacsimile Weather Charts*, written by Dr. Joseph Bishop (see resources appendix).

READING LOCAL WEATHER SIGNS

Late one summer evening early in my boating career, I was at anchor with my family in the Intracoastal Waterway just north of Belhaven, North

Carolina, when one of my daughters pointed skyward and asked, "What does that pretty halo around the moon mean, Daddy?" "Oh," I replied sagely, "that means we're going to have beautiful weather tomorrow."

The hurricane struck about four o'clock the following afternoon.

Since that rather humbling experience, I have developed a more than casual interest in being able to read the signs of coming weather that Mother Nature offers us in abundance if we will but take the time to read and understand them. If you will do likewise and devote a little time to observing such factors as changing patterns of cloud formation, changing wind directions, and halos around the sun and moon, you will find you can develop the ability to predict weather approaching your vicinity with an amazing degree of accuracy.

If I were asked that question about the halo around the moon today, for instance, I would quote the rhyme of the ancient mariners: "When a halo rings the moon or sun, the rain will come upon the run." Since that night north of Belhaven, I've learned that the rhyme's accuracy is based not on mystic superstition but on scientific fact. A halo around the sun or moon is caused by light passing through ice crystals in the high, thin layer of cirrostratus clouds that form well in advance of the low-pressure systems that bring wet weather.

Close observation of halos around the sun or moon will even tell you something about the severity of the approaching weather and the quarter from which it will come. The halo will begin to form on the side of the sun or moon from which the low pressure is approaching. A light, broken halo indicates only scattered cirrostratus in advance of a weak low-pressure system whose effects will not be severe. A bright, well-defined halo and even double and triple halos indicate the thick cirrostratus associated with deep low-pressure systems and their accompanying heavy rain and high winds. As the storm approaches, the dark altostratus clouds on its leading edge will obscure a portion of the halo and the wet weather will

come from the obscured quarter. Observations by the National Weather Service have established that a halo around the sun accurately predicts wet weather about 75 percent of the time and that a halo around the moon accurately predicts wet weather about 65 percent of the time.

The formation of rainbows also can tell you whether the coming weather is to be fair or foul. If a rainbow forms to windward of your position, you can expect the curtain of moisture in which it forms to be headed in your direction. If a rainbow is to leeward of you, the moisture with which it is associated is receding from you. If you see a rainbow in the morning, it is likely to be in the west and you probably are in for a wet day. If you see a rainbow in the late afternoon or early evening, it is likely to be toward the east. The storm has probably passed your position, and the sky behind it will be clearing.

One of the best ways to detect the approach of foul weather is to observe cloud formations in your vicinity. Thin, wispy cirrus clouds, often called "mare's tails," normally portend fair weather. But if they lower and thicken into the cirrocumulus clouds of a "mackerel sky," wet weather probably is on the way. The mackerel sky is likely to broaden into cirrostratus clouds, which form their characteristic halo around the sun or moon, then thicken to an almost uniform layer of altostratus and then to dark nimbostratus clouds, which will bring heavy rain.

By the same token, white, puffy cumulus clouds normally mean fair weather. But on hot summer afternoons, if they build up and rise high into the sky and their tops begin to be sheared off by the jet stream, they are transformed into cumulonimbus—with their characteristic flat anvil top and dark, boiling layer of nimbostratus underneath—which spawn violent thunderstorms. The direction in which the horn of their anvil shape points will be the direction in which they are being carried by winds aloft. Because the prevailing wind currents across the United States tend to be northwest to southeast, if you note the development of these thunderstorm clouds to the west or northwest of you, they are likely to come in your direction. They normally set off bright flashes of lightning and deep rolls of thunder. Because the lightning travels to you at the speed of light and the sound of the thunder reaches you at the slower speed of sound, you can estimate the thunderstorm's proximity by timing the interval between lightning and thunder in seconds and dividing by five. The result will be the storm's approximate distance from you in statute miles. If you sense a distinct drop in air temperature, the storm has probably approached to within about 3 miles (4.8 km) of you and will be on top of you shortly.

If cumulonimbus clouds form to the south or southeast of you, the rain and high winds they contain are likely to be carried away from you by the prevailing winds.

Still another interesting way you can detect the onset of wet weather is by listening. In fair weather, sound tends to dissipate quickly. If sounds become unusually bright and clear and seem to carry a longer way than normal, sound waves are being held close to the earth by a lowering, thickening atmosphere. A low-pressure center, with its characteristic rain, is probably on the way.

Interpreting Barometer Readings

If you carry a barometer aboard your vessel, you can combine its readings with observations of wind direction to determine the direction from which the approaching bad weather will come and how winds will shift in the storm's wake. If the barometer begins to fall and the wind is from points between south and southeast, the storm is approaching from west or northwest and will pass near you or to your north within twelve to twenty-four hours. As it passes, winds will veer (swing clockwise) into the northwest. If the wind is from points between east and northeast, the storm is approaching from the south or southwest and will pass near or to the south of you within twelve to twenty-four hours.

As it passes, winds will back (swing counterclockwise) into the northwest. You can determine approximately how rapidly the low-pressure system is approaching and its likely severity by the speed with which the barometer is falling. A rate of fall of 0.02 to 0.03 inch (0.5–0.76 mm) of mercury per hour indicates a weak, slow-moving storm; a rate of fall of 0.05 to 0.06 inch (1.27–1.52 mm) per hour indicates that the low-pressure system is a deep one and it is approaching rapidly.

Understanding the Law of Storms

If an approaching storm is an extratropical cyclone, with its characteristic counterclockwise wind pattern, you can determine its approximate position relative to your own by the law of storms. As you face the wind, the storm's center will be in the direction of your outstretched right hand. If you take a series of bearings on the storm's center in this fashion over a period of hours, you can predict its course. If the position of your right hand moves clockwise or counterclockwise, the storm's center will pass you to the appropriate side. If the position of your right hand does not change appreciably, the storm's center is headed right toward you. If you are at sea in such a situation, you should remember that in the right half of an extratropical storm, relative to its centerline, winds and seas are highest because they are augmented by the storm's forward movement. You would therefore want to set your vessel's course to carry it toward the storm's left, or navigable, semicircle.

Employing the techniques recommended here to make certain you have access to comprehensive weather information, interpret it correctly, and observe the signs of weather all around you won't guarantee that you'll never have to deal with howling winds and angry seas, but it can help you be aware of any adverse weather coming your way and help you prepare to deal with it.

PART FIVE

Emergency Preparedness

Using a Marine Radio during Emergencies

In any emergency on the water, your short-range VHF (very high frequency) and long-range single-sideband (SSB) marine radios are likely to be your primary means of summoning help. If you find it necessary to use them in an emergency, whether to deal with a problem aboard your own boat or aboard another vessel you are trying to assist, you need to know how to use them properly. The procedures presented here are not simply the way the Federal Communication Commission's (FCC's) rules and international treaties require you to handle emergency radio traffic, nor are they arcane formats left over from the blue-blazer-and-white-bucks school of yachting etiquette. Their primary value is that they are internationally agreed-to ways of handling distress radio traffic that compress essential information into practical and efficient formats which clearly communicate critical details in the shortest possible time.

Before we go any further, it's important to understand the three levels of priority communications over both VHF and SSB frequencies. Mayday, of course, takes precedence over all else.

This is the "distress" message signal. Pan-Pan (pronounced *pahn-pahn*) is an "urgent" message alert and takes priority over all communications except Mayday. And finally, there is Sécurité (pronounced *say-kyur-ee-tay*). This announces an upcoming "safety" message.

KEEP CALM

Emergencies on the water seldom seem to happen at midday in calm seas when communication conditions are ideal. Under Murphy's Law that whatever can go wrong will—and at the worst possible moment—marine emergencies seem far more likely to occur in the dead of night when the wind is howling, the sea is heaving, rain is pouring in buckets, your engine has quit, you're off a lee shore, and every communications channel you try is jammed with traffic you can't break through or is crackling with static. Anytime you're involved in distress radio traffic, the last thing you want to do is confuse the situation with inaccurate, incomplete, or incomprehensible transmissions. Remain calm, and take extra care to speak slowly, clearly, and distinctly. Use radio transmission procedure words properly, and be careful to pronounce them correctly. If you feel there is any doubt that you will be understood, use phonetic spelling (see the International Phonetic Alphabet sidebar in chapter 21).

INTERNATIONAL RADIOTELEPHONE ALARM SIGNAL

Some older VHF and SSB marine radios are equipped with an automatic international radiotelephone alarm generator, which is activated by pressing a clearly marked button on the front of the radio's panel. If your radio is so equipped, you should activate the alarm signal before every transmission of the Mayday distress call and message. The signal consists of two audio frequency tones transmitted alternately for a duration of a quarter second each. One tone has a frequency of 2200 Hertz (Hz) and the other a frequency of 1300 Hz. Transmitted together, they sound something like the wail of an ambulance siren. The signal alerts radio officers on watch at coast stations and aboard a number of commercial vessels that a Mayday distress call and message is about to be transmitted and activates automatic equipment to record it. Once you punch the button on your set, it will generate the alarm for the required interval of at least thirty but not more than sixty seconds, over any transmit frequency to which the radio is tuned.

With one exception, the radiotelephone alarm may be transmitted from a vessel only to announce that a Mayday distress call and message will follow. The single exception to that rule is that it also may be used to precede a Pan-Pan urgency call and message involving a man overboard where assistance is required that cannot be satisfactorily obtained by the use of the urgency call and message without preceding it with the radiotelephone alarm signal.

AUTOMATIC DISTRESS CALLS

The latest wrinkle in marine communications is Digital Selective Calling (DSC). This mandated technology requires that every radio manufactured after 1999 have in it an automated calling device. Every new VHF and SSB transceiver is now equipped with an additional automatic feature that can actually place a call, like a telephone, to other DSC receivers. When a position locator such as a global positioning system (GPS) is plugged into the back of this type of radio, the radio's position is broadcast as well as the name of the vessel and the reason for the call. In an emergency, simply push the red button on the face of the unit to broadcast a distress signal. (See the discussion of DSC in chapter 9.)

To be effective, a DSC radio needs two important things. First is a number (like a telephone number) to identify your particular radio. Second, another similarly equipped radio must be available to receive your distress call. For recreational boaters, getting a number has been difficult. Only recently has BoatU.S. stepped forward to issue such numbers free of charge (see contact information in the resources appendix).

The other problem has been a budget shortfall in the U.S. Coast Guard that has restricted the installation of DSC to SSB radios only— not on VHF radios. In other words, the coast guard can't hear a DSC distress message over its VHF transceivers. By 2005, however, this deficiency should be corrected.

MAKE AN URGENCY OR DISTRESS CALL IMMEDIATELY

If you get into a life-threatening situation at sea without a DSC radio, the first thing you must do is get off a Pan-Pan urgency call or a Mayday distress call and its associated message.

The importance of getting off an urgency or distress call and message the instant a serious emergency strikes is best illustrated by the experience of my friend Sumner Pingree when a turbocharger fire erupted aboard his 53-foot (16 m) sportfishing boat, *Roulette*, off the coast of Puerto Rico. He opened the engine room door, and the fire reignited with a whoosh. He raced back up to the flying bridge to call the coast guard again, but the fire had already burned through the battery cables and the radio was dead. Ten minutes after he first realized he had a fire aboard, he and his crew were in the water.

Mayday Distress Call and Message

The Mayday distress call and message has absolute priority over all other radio traffic.

Transmit a Mayday using the format given in here. Don't omit any items or use any other format. The first distress call and message you transmit may be the only one you are able to send, and the format provides the essential information potential rescuers will need quickly, clearly, and concisely.

Technically, the Mayday distress call and message procedure consists of three elements.

1. The international radiotelephone alarm signal
2. The distress call, consisting of
   a. the distress signal "Mayday" spoken three times
   b. the words "This is"
   c. the name of the vessel in distress spoken three times
   d. if you have one, the radio call sign of the vessel in distress spoken once
3. The distress message, consisting of
   a. the distress signal "Mayday" spoken once
   b. the name of the vessel in distress spoken once
   c. the position of the vessel in distress expressed
      —as degrees and minutes of latitude north or south and longitude east or west, or

—by bearing (specify whether true or magnetic) and distance to a well-known reference point, such as an aid to navigation or a shoreside landmark
   d. the nature of the distress
   e. the type of assistance required
   f. any other information that might facilitate rescue, such as
      —the length of the vessel
      —the type of the vessel
      —the color of the vessel's hull, superstructure, and trim
      —the number of adults and children on board

FORMAT FOR TRANSMITTING
Mayday DISTRESS CALL AND MESSAGE

Fill this form out for your vessel. Speak SLOWLY—CLEARLY—CALMLY.

1. Activate international radiotelephone alarm signal.
2. "MAYDAY—MAYDAY—MAYDAY."
3. "THIS IS _____ , _____
     (your boat name)   (your boat name)
   _____ , _____ ."
     (your boat name)   (your call sign,
                              if appropriate)
4. "MAYDAY: _____ ."
              (your boat name)
5. "POSITION IS: _____ ."
   (your vessel's position in degrees and minutes of latitude NORTH or SOUTH and longitude EAST or WEST; or as distance and bearing [magnetic or true] to well-known navigation landmark)
6. "WE _____ ."
        (state nature of your emergency)
7. "WE REQUIRE _____ ."
               (state type of assistance required)
8. "ABOARD ARE _____ ."
   (give number of adults and children on board and conditions of any injured)
9. "_____ IS A _____ -FOOT
   (your boat name)   (length of your boat in feet)
   _____ WITH A _____
   (type: sloop, motor yacht, etc.)   (hull color)
   HULL AND _____ TRIM."
              (color of trim)
10. "I WILL BE LISTENING ON CHANNEL 16/2182."
    (cross out channel or frequency that does not apply)
11. "THIS IS _____ , _____ ."
              (your boat name)   (your call sign,
12. "OVER."   if appropriate)

—the injuries suffered by anyone on board and the medical assistance they require.

The word "Over" indicates the end of your Mayday transmission and requests a response.

If your Mayday is acknowledged and you are uncertain of the extent of your emergency, ask the vessel or station you have contacted to stand by. If, as in Sumner's case, the emergency escalates rapidly and knocks out your radio, you will at least know that someone is aware you are in trouble and knows your position, knows the nature of your distress and the number of people on board, and has a description of your vessel. Even if you do not receive an acknowledgment, you have the hope that someone heard your message but was unable to acknowledge it before you lost the ability to receive.

The Mayday distress call and message should never be transmitted in any but extreme emergencies that pose genuine and serious dangers to your vessel or threaten the lives of your crew. Such situations as being lost, having someone aboard suffer a serious but not life-threatening illness or injury, having mechanical difficulties, or running out of fuel are not sufficient justification for transmitting a Mayday unless those factors place your vessel or crew in grave and immediate danger.

Anyone foolish enough to transmit a Mayday for frivolous or nonexistent reasons is subject to significant criminal and civil penalties. Using your radiotelephone to transmit a false Mayday can subject you to a fine of up to $10,000 or up to a year in jail or both. In addition, the coast guard has prosecuted individuals who transmitted false Maydays and has won judgments against them to recover the costs of search-and-rescue efforts running into thousands of dollars.

Don't transmit the Mayday distress call and message in a crew overboard situation, even if you require the assistance of other vessels. Instead, transmit the Pan-Pan urgency call and message, the proper procedure for which is briefly recounted later in this chapter.

VHF Distress Calls

In an emergency serious enough to require you to transmit the Mayday distress call and message, you may use any VHF channel to attract attention. Your first choice, however, should be channel 16 (156.8 MHz), which is the international distress, safety, and calling channel both ship to coast and intership and is continuously monitored by the coast guard.

Since VHF radio waves travel only in a line of sight, 20 miles (32 km) is about the maximum distance over which you can reliably expect to communicate from your installed VHF radiotelephone. Its range may be considerably greater if you are within line of sight of a tall receiving antenna onshore. If your VHF antenna is 10 to 15 feet (3–4.5 m) off the water, for instance, and is in the line of sight of a 2,000-foot-high (610 m) receiving antenna onshore, your radio's range under optimum conditions could be as much as 75 miles (120 km), but you don't want to bet your life on it.

If you encounter a serious emergency well offshore and do not have an SSB marine radio aboard, you should of course transmit your Mayday distress call and message on your VHF radiotelephone because there is always the possibility that your transmission could be received by another vessel within a 20-mile (32 km) radius of your position. But, again, you don't want to trust your vessel or your life to that kind of a gamble.

After transmitting the distress call and message on VHF channel 16, wait thirty seconds for any vessel receiving it to respond. If no answer is received, retransmit the distress call and message a second time over that same channel. If no answer is received following that transmission, try channel 6 (156.3 MHz, the intership safety channel). If you still receive no response, retransmit the distress call and message on any VHF channel frequently used in the area. One technique is to scan the VHF channels until you hear traffic, then break into the traffic with your Mayday distress call and message. If you do not hear traffic on any

VHF channel, try transmitting your Mayday on channel 22A (157.1 MHz), the primary coast guard liaison channel, or channel 72 (156.625 MHz), which at sea is used as an international ship-to-ship channel. If you still receive no acknowledgment and have time, try one or more of the public correspondence channels, which are monitored by marine operators. The public correspondence channels (24, 25, 26, 28, 84, 85, 86, and 87) vary from area to area, but the primary ones are channel 26 (ship's transmit, 157.3 MHz; ship's receive, 161.9 MHz) and channel 28 (ship's transmit, 157.4 MHz; ship's transmit, 162.0 MHz).

SSB Distress Calls

In an emergency serious enough to require you to transmit the Mayday distress call and message, you may use any SSB channel or frequency to attract attention. Your first choice, however, should be frequency 2182 kHz, which is the SSB international distress, safety, and calling frequency both ship to coast and intership and is continuously monitored by the coast guard.

After transmitting the distress call and message on 2182 kHz, wait thirty seconds for any vessel receiving it to respond. If no answer is received, retransmit the distress call and message a second time over that same frequency. If no answer is received following that transmission, retransmit the distress call and message on any SSB frequency used in the area. Good second choices would be 2670 kHz, a primary coast guard working channel, or one of the following International Telecommunication Union (ITU) channels, which have been designated for radiotelephone safety and distress traffic as part of the Global Maritime Distress and Safety System (GMDSS).

If you still receive no acknowledgment, scan the ITU channels used by the High Seas Stations and break into any traffic you hear with your Mayday. You will have a better chance of being heard if you break in when you think the person on land is speaking. If you hear no traffic, you can try trans-

EMERGENCY CARRIER FREQUENCIES

ITU Channel	Ship Transmit, kHz	Ship Receive, kHz
421	4125.0	4417.0
606	6215.0	6516.0
821	8255.0	8779.0
1221	12290.0	13137.0
1621	16420.0	17302.0
1806	18795.0	19770.0
2221	22060.0	22756.0
2510	25097.0	26172.0

mitting your Mayday over one or more of the channels used by the High Seas Stations, but to have a reasonable chance of being heard you will have to select an appropriate megahertz band based on your distance from the station and the time of day.

Canceling a Mayday

If, after you transmit a Mayday, you find that you're able to handle the emergency in such a way that you do not require assistance and you have not yet delegated control of the distress traffic to another vessel or coast station, you must cancel your distress call and message whether or not it was acknowledged. If your Mayday was acknowledged by the coast guard or other appropriate authority, contact them in the normal, nonemergency way and inform them of the cancellation. They then normally will transmit a "notification of resumption of normal working." If your Mayday was not acknowledged by the coast guard or other appropriate authority, or you cannot contact the authority that acknowledged your Mayday, you are required to cancel it using the format described on the next page.

Pan-Pan Urgency Signal and Message

The Pan-Pan urgency signal and the message that follows it have priority over all other transmissions except the Mayday distress call and message. The

---

FORMAT FOR CANCELLING A Mayday DISTRESS CALL AND MESSAGE BY A VESSEL

To cancel a Mayday distress call and message that you, as a vessel in distress, previously transmitted when the cancellation cannot be accomplished through a coast station:

1. "MAYDAY"
2. "HELLO ALL STATIONS, HELLO ALL STATIONS, HELLO ALL STATIONS."
3. "THIS IS_____, _____."
   (your boat name) (your call sign, if appropriate)
4. "THE TIME IS:_____."
   (state time of transmission by 24-hour clock)
5. "_____, _____."
   (your boat name) (your call sign, if appropriate)
6. "SEELONCE FEENEE."
7. "_____, _____."
   (your boat name) (your call sign, if appropriate)
8. "OUT."

To cancel a Mayday distress call and message you have previously transmitted on behalf of a vessel in distress, although you were not in distress yourself.

1. "MAYDAY"
2. "HELLO ALL STATIONS, HELLO ALL STATIONS, HELLO ALL STATIONS."
3. "THIS IS_____, _____."
   (your boat name) (your call sign, if appropriate)
4. "THE TIME IS:_____."
   (state time of transmission by 24-hour clock)
5. "_____, _____."
   (the name of the vessel and call sign of the vessel in distress)
6. "SEELONCE FEENEE."
7. "_____, _____."
   (your boat name) (your call sign, if appropriate)
8. "OUT."

A typical situation in which you would address the Pan-Pan urgency signal to a specific vessel would be one in which you observed a person fall overboard from that vessel and no one aboard that vessel appeared to be aware of the accident.

Another proper use of the urgency call and message would be situations in which you face a serious but not life-threatening medical emergency on board or your vessel has struck a submerged object and is taking on water but is not in imminent danger of sinking. If you feel the situation might become serious enough to require assistance, transmit the Pan-Pan urgency call and message to alert rescue services or other vessels in your vicinity that you may need their help. Still another example would be a situation in which your vessel has lost power or steering in a busy traffic area and could pose a hazard to other vessels.

If you transmit the Pan-Pan urgency signal addressed to "all stations," you must cancel it once the emergency is over by transmitting the cancellation on that same frequency using the accompanying format. If you addressed the urgency signal to a specific vessel, its cancellation is not required.

urgency signal may be transmitted to a specific vessel or to "all stations." The proper format for transmitting the Pan-Pan urgency signal and message is given here.

A typical situation in which you would transmit the Pan-Pan urgency signal to "all stations" would be one in which a person fell overboard from your own vessel and you required the assistance of other vessels to retrieve the person. That is the only emergency in which the Pan-Pan urgency call and message may be preceded by the radiotelephone alarm, and even then, the alarm should be used only if you feel you cannot satisfactorily obtain the assistance you require through the urgency signal alone without the use of the radiotelephone alarm.

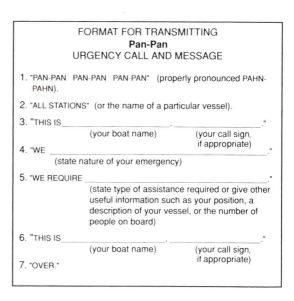

FORMAT FOR TRANSMITTING Pan-Pan URGENCY CALL AND MESSAGE

1. "PAN-PAN PAN-PAN PAN-PAN" (properly pronounced PAHN-PAHN).
2. "ALL STATIONS" (or the name of a particular vessel).
3. "THIS IS_____, _____."
   (your boat name) (your call sign, if appropriate)
4. "WE _____."
   (state nature of your emergency)
5. "WE REQUIRE _____."
   (state type of assistance required or give other useful information such as your position, a description of your vessel, or the number of people on board)
6. "THIS IS_____, _____."
   (your boat name) (your call sign, if appropriate)
7. "OVER."

Sécurité Safety Signal

The Sécurité safety signal and message are transmitted to alert others to information concerning navigation safety or important meteorological warnings. They are most often transmitted by coast stations, to warn of hazards to navigation or severe weather systems, and by commercial traffic such as ships and tugs, to announce their positions, routes, and destinations. However, they also may be transmitted by vessels. The safety signal is broadcast on a distress channel and includes instructions for receiving stations to switch to a working channel, such as channel 13, the bridge-to-bridge channel. The safety message is then transmitted over the working channel specified in the safety signal.

A typical situation in which you might transmit a safety signal and message would be if you spot a large, submerged object that could pose a serious danger to other vessels. You should first attempt to contact the coast guard to alert them to the danger, and they would then probably transmit a Sécurité signal on VHF channel 16 instructing vessels to switch to VHF channel 13 or channel 22A to receive the message. If you are unable to reach the coast guard and feel the object poses sufficient danger to require notifying other vessels in the area, find a working channel that is not in use.

```
FORMAT FOR TRANSMITTING
         Securite
SAFETY CALL AND MESSAGE

To transmit the SECURITE safety signal:
Transmit on VHF Channel 16 or SSB frequency 2182 kHz:

1. "Say-curiTAY—Say-curiTAY—Say-curiTAY—ALL STATIONS."
2. "THIS IS _____, _____."
               (your boat name)        (your call sign,
                                         if appropriate)
3. "LISTEN:_____."
           (state working VHF channel or SSB frequency)
4. "_____OUT."
           (your call sign, if appropriate)

To transmit the SECURITE safety signal:
Transmit on working VHF channel or SSB frequency designated
above:

1. "Say-curiTAY—Say-curiTAY—Say-curiTAY—ALL STATIONS."
2. "THIS IS _____, _____."
               (your boat name)        (your call sign,
                                         if appropriate)
3. "_____."
           (state securite message)
4. "_____OUT."
           (your call sign, if appropriate)
```

Good working channels on VHF would be channels 6, 68, or 72; on SSB, channels 2635 kHz and 2638 kHz (and in U.S. waters, 2738 kHz). Then transmit a Sécurité signal over a distress channel (inshore you normally would transmit on VHF channel 16; offshore, on SSB 2182 kHz) and instruct receiving stations to switch to the working channel you have selected to receive the message. Switch to the working channel you specified in the Sécurité signal, and transmit the safety message, which should include a description of the object, its location, its approximate depth below the surface, and the direction it is drifting, if any. The proper format for transmitting the Sécurité safety signal and message is given here.

IF YOU RECEIVE A MAYDAY DISTRESS CALL AND MESSAGE

Under federal law (Public Law 98-89, Duty to Provide Assistance at Sea, 46 U.S. Code

```
FORMAT FOR CANCELLING A
        Pan-Pan
URGENCY CALL AND MESSAGE
      BY A VESSEL

1. "PAN-PAN  PAN-PAN  PAN-PAN."
2. "HELLO ALL STATIONS, HELLO ALL STATIONS, HELLO ALL
    STATIONS."
3. "THIS IS_____, _____."
             (your boat name)     (your call sign,
                                    if appropriate)
4. "THE TIME IS:_____."
           (state time of transmission by 24-hour clock)
5. "_____."
        (your boat name)        (your call sign, if appropriate)
6. "SEELONCE FEENEE."
7. "_____."
        (your boat name)        (your call sign, if appropriate)
8. "OUT."
```

2301–2304), as the individual in charge of a vessel in waters subject to U.S. jurisdiction or of an American-flag vessel operating on the high seas, you are legally required to render assistance to any individual found at sea "in danger of being lost" so far as you can do so without serious danger to your own vessel or crew. If you fail to render such assistance, you are liable to a fine of up to $1,000 or two years' imprisonment or both.

Acknowledging Mayday Distress Calls

The FCC rules state that if you receive a Mayday distress call and message from a vessel that beyond any possible doubt is in your vicinity, you must immediately acknowledge it. The lone exception to the rule is that if you are in an area where reliable communication between the vessel in distress and a coast station is "practicable," you may defer your acknowledgment for a "short interval" so that a coast station may acknowledge receipt. The regulations adopted by the World Administrative Radio Conference governing radio communications in the GMDSS contain similar wording, but neither set of regulations precisely defines the length of a "short interval."

The language of the regulations can put a responsible cruising skipper who receives a distress call and message in a bit of a quandary. On the one hand, he would want to respond as quickly as possible to let the vessel in distress know someone had heard the signal. On the other, he would not want to interfere with communication between the vessel in distress and a coast station that had also received the call. Given the sophistication of maritime radio services today, there's really nowhere in the world in which reliable communication between a vessel in distress (assuming it has a functioning SSB radio) and a coast station is not "practicable." (The exception, I suppose, would be a situation in which you were more than about 50 miles, or 80 km, offshore and received a distress signal on VHF that might indicate the vessel in distress either didn't have SSB or its SSB wasn't working.)

The conventional wisdom on this topic says that if you receive a Mayday, you should do nothing, just listen. I have written elsewhere that I strongly disagree and that if I were in an area where there was the least doubt about the ability of a vessel in distress to reach a coast station and I received a Mayday call from a vessel anywhere near me, I would acknowledge it as quickly as the distress message was concluded and I could get to my radio's microphone. After discussing the matter with the experts at the Radio Technical Commission for Maritime Services (RTC), I have modified my position. The RTC staffers point out that after receiving a distress signal, it may take land stations up to a minute to swing their antennas around to the direction from which the distress signal was received in order to respond effectively. Their primary concern is that a number of vessels don't jump onto the frequency immediately and make it impossible for them to get through. On that basis, then, if I heard a distress signal I would wait about a minute before acknowledging to give land stations time to respond. But if no land station responded within about a minute, I would acknowledge the call so the hapless soul in deep enough trouble to be transmitting the Mayday would know someone had heard the call.

If you are called on to acknowledge a Mayday distress call and message, do so using the accompanying format.

If you acknowledge receipt of a Mayday distress call and message and a legitimate authority such as the coast guard later comes on the channel, you should state your vessel's name and call sign

---

FORMAT FOR ACKNOWLEDGING
Mayday DISTRESS CALL AND MESSAGE

On channel or frequency over which you received the MAYDAY:

1. "_____, _____, _____."
   (name of vessel in distress, spoken three times)

2. "THIS IS_____, _____, _____, _____."
   (your boat name, spoken three times) (your call sign, if appropriate)

3. "RECEIVED MAYDAY."

4. "OVER."

(if you have one) and ask if they wish you to continue to attempt to provide assistance to the vessel in distress or simply stand by on that frequency in case your assistance is required.

If you receive a Mayday distress call and message from a vessel that beyond any possible doubt is not in your vicinity, the FCC rules say you must allow a "short interval of time" to elapse before acknowledging receipt of the call and message to allow stations nearer the vessel in distress to acknowledge the vessel without interference. Again, the FCC doesn't define "short interval." The World Administrative Radio Conference regulations governing radio communications under the GMDSS specifically state that a ship receiving a distress alert on the SSB radiotelephone frequencies shall not acknowledge it at all but, if it is not acknowledged within three minutes, relay it to a coast station. The bureaucrats can make all the rules they want to, but if I heard a Mayday from a vessel I knew was far away from me and no one else acknowledged it within about a minute, I would let the poor fellow know someone had heard and was relaying the message.

Cease Transmitting and Listen

The FCC rules state that anyone who hears a Mayday must immediately cease any transmission capable of interfering with the distress traffic and continue to listen on the frequency over which it was transmitted. The FCC rules prohibit any vessel not involved in the distress from transmitting on the frequency being used until the station controlling the traffic broadcasts a "resumption of normal working" with the French *silence fine* (pronounced *see-lonce feenee*) or *prudence* (*prudonce*). If the vessel in distress were in my vicinity, its distress call had been acknowledged by a coast station, and I apparently were the vessel best positioned to render possible assistance, I would alter my course in the direction of the vessel in distress and attempt to contact the controlling coast station through normal, nonemergency means. If I were able to contact the coast station,

I would inform the personnel there of my position, ask if I could help, and follow their instructions. If I were unable to contact the controlling authority by nonemergency means, I would get back on the frequency carrying the distress traffic, wait for a break, quickly inform the controlling authority of my position, ask if my assistance was required, then follow their instructions.

If another vessel apparently in a better position to assist were involved in the distress, my actions would be determined by the situation. If I felt there were any reasonable chance my assistance might be required, I'd steam toward the vessel in distress and inform the controlling authority of my availability to assist if needed. If there appeared to be little likelihood my assistance would be required, I'd continue on my course but monitor the frequency until I heard the message announcing resumption of normal working. If I clearly were not in a position to assist, I'd probably continue to monitor the distress traffic as a matter of personal interest and make certain I did nothing to interfere with it but otherwise go about my normal business.

The FCC rules do state that if you hear a Pan-Pan urgency signal, you must continue to listen on the frequency over which it was broadcast for three minutes. If no message follows the urgency signal, you should relay to the nearest coast station that you heard an urgency signal but no message followed it. If a message follows the urgency signal but is not addressed "to all ships," after three minutes you may resume normal working. Beyond that, the FCC rules get a little murky. They say if the urgency message was addressed "to all ships," the vessel that transmitted it must cancel it as soon as it knows action is no longer required. The rules are silent, however, on what those who have heard the urgency signal and message are supposed to do. If the emergency were in my vicinity, I'd monitor the channel over which the urgency message was transmitted until I heard the cancellation or was pretty certain no action on my part was required. If the emergency were clearly well away from me, I'd probably go back to normal working.

Offer of Assistance

Once you acknowledge receipt of a Mayday distress call and message, you not only are required by federal law to respond but are also required by FCC rules to transmit an offer-of-assistance message to the vessel in distress as soon as possible. (Wait long enough to allow coast stations or other vessels to respond to the Mayday and to work out your own position relative to the vessel in distress and formulate your intentions.) The format for your offer of assistance message is given here.

If, after you transmit your offer of assistance and are under way to provide assistance, a legitimate authority such as the coast guard enters the search-and-rescue effort, state your vessel's name and call sign (if you have one) and ask the authority whether you should proceed or simply stand by to render assistance if it should be required.

Relay of Mayday Distress Messages

Under certain circumstances, if you learn a vessel is in distress, you must relay a Mayday distress call and message, even if you are not in a position to assist. Under FCC rules, you must relay a Mayday distress call and message in the following circumstances.

- If the vessel in distress cannot transmit the distress call and message
- If you believe that further assistance is required
- When you hear a distress message that has not been acknowledged, even if you are not in a position to assist. In this case, you must also attempt to notify a proper authority, such as the coast guard, of the distress message you have received.

The proper format for relaying a Mayday distress call and message is given here. Note that it should be preceded, if possible, by the radio telephone alarm.

Control of Distress Radio Traffic

If you transmit a Mayday and it is acknowledged by the coast guard or other appropriate authority, that authority normally will assume control of any radio traffic related to the distress. If your Mayday is not acknowledged by the coast guard or other appropriate authority, you are the controller of the distress traffic. You may retain that control yourself or you may delegate it to another vessel.

Being the controller of distress traffic imposes on you certain responsibilities. The station controlling the distress traffic has the authority to impose silence on the frequency being used for distress traffic on all vessels or coast stations that interfere with the distress traffic. Such imposition of silence on the frequency being used for the distress traffic may be addressed to "all stations" or to an individual vessel or coast station, followed by the words Seelonce Mayday. No further instructions or identification of the controlling station is required, and the Seelonce Mayday order must be respected.

If essential, any other vessel in the vicinity of

FORMAT FOR OFFER OF ASSISTANCE MESSAGE
IN RESPONSE TO A
Mayday DISTRESS CALL AND MESSAGE

On channel or frequency over which you acknowledged receipt of the MAYDAY distress call and message:

1. "_____"
   (the name of the vessel in distress, spoken once)
2. "THIS IS _____"
   (your boat name)
3. "OVER."

On hearing the word "OVER" from the vessel in distress, continue:

4. "I AM _____"
   (state your intentions: i.e., "PROCEEDING TOWARD YOU FROM TEN MILES. EXPECT TO ARRIVE IN ONE HOUR")
5. "_____"
   (state other useful information: i.e., " COAST GUARD HAS BEEN NOTIFIED, INCLUDING YOUR NEED FOR DOCTOR")
6. "_____ , _____"
   (your boat name)   (your call sign, if appropriate)
7. "OVER."

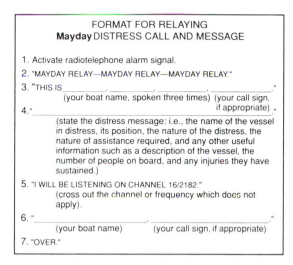

the vessel in distress—even though it has not been delegated as the station controlling the distress traffic—may also impose radio silence on the frequency with the words: "Seelonce Distress" fol-

lowed by that vessel's own vessel name and call sign (if it has one).

EMERGENCY MEDICAL COMMUNICATIONS

If you encounter a medical emergency at sea that you do not feel qualified to handle without professional advice, you usually can make contact with a doctor through the coast guard on VHF channel 16 or SSB frequency 2182 kHz. The coast guard has access to military and U.S. Public Health physicians and, through its AMVER (Automated Mutual-Assistance Vessel Rescue) system, keeps track of ships at sea that have medical staff aboard.

If you can't contact the coast guard in a serious medical emergency on board, you can call Medical Advisory Systems (MAS). See chapter 13 for more information about the services offered by MAS.

Reacting to Loss of Power or Steering

If you have a mechanical problem with your vessel around home, it's a fairly simple matter to call a mechanic to come fix it. But once you launch into extended cruising, at some point you're almost certain to find yourself with a balky engine or transmission a long way from the nearest engine shop and will have to solve the problem yourself. To do that, you need to have at least a basic understanding of how a diesel engine and its associated marine transmission and underwater gear work.

Reduced to its essentials, even the most elaborate diesel marine engine is a fairly basic device that must have only three things to start and continue to operate: a source of motive power to get it started; a dependable source of clean, combustible fuel; and some means of dissipating the exhaust gases and excess heat it generates.

Diesel marine engines employ four elements for initiating their operation: the engine's battery, the ignition key or starter switch, a starter solenoid, and a starter motor. The starter solenoid and starter motor normally will be the two cylindrical units bolted to the side of the engine. The starter solenoid will be the smaller of the two and will be connected directly to the battery by the battery's positive (red) cable. In some cases, the starter solenoid is an integral part of the starter motor.

COMMON PROBLEMS AND SOLUTIONS

There are a number of difficulties you're almost certain to encounter at some point in your cruising. To keep matters simple, I cover them using a problem-solution format.

PROBLEM: You turn the ignition key or depress the engine start button, and nothing happens.

SOLUTION: First, check the battery. If your vessel is equipped with a battery paralleling switch, make certain it is set to the battery of the engine you are trying to start. Also, make certain the vessel's transmission is in neutral. Most modern marine engines have a neutral safety switch, which

322

prevents the engine from being started if the transmission is in gear. Make certain the ignition key is switched to the on position. If you have a voltmeter on board, check the voltage across the battery's positive and negative terminals. If you detect no—or almost no—voltage, the battery is dead and must be recharged from an external electrical source before it will develop sufficient voltage to start the engine.

If you don't have a voltmeter aboard, check the battery's acid level; if the battery's plates are exposed in one or more cells and the battery made no attempt to turn the engine's starter motor, it is probably fully discharged and cannot generate enough voltage to start the engine without being recharged from an external electrical source.

On a vessel that has more than one battery, set the battery paralleling switch to "all" and attempt to start the engine with another of the ship's batteries. (If the engine starts, don't forget to reset the battery switch to the engine's battery to recharge it.) If the vessel is fitted with an AC electrical generator, attempt to recharge the battery through the vessel's battery charger. If you have neither a charged battery nor an AC generator aboard and cannot start the engine by hand cranking it, you have no chance of starting the engine. If you are inshore, you might try reaching safety by using your tender for auxiliary power, as discussed later in this chapter. If you are offshore, about your only alternative is to call for assistance.

On a 12-volt system, if your check of the battery's voltage with a voltmeter shows it is charged to at least 7 volts and the level of battery acid is close to the fill ring, make certain the cables connected to the battery's positive and negative terminals are tight and clean of corrosion. If not, clean and tighten them. Also, make certain the cable connected to the battery's negative terminal is clean and tight where it is connected to ground. Make certain the cable connected to the battery's positive terminal is tight and free of corrosion where it is connected to the starter solenoid.

If you find no problem with the battery, its controls, or its cables, check the starter switch. First, make certain the wires connecting it to the battery and to the starter solenoid are clean and tight. If the starter switch is connected to a separate key switch, also check the connections between them. If you have a voltmeter aboard, close the ignition switch (that is, turn it to the on position) and check the voltage across its terminals. If you detect no voltage, the switch itself could be bad. Check it with the key in the on position by shorting across its terminals with a screwdriver. If the starter motor attempts to turn, the switch itself is malfunctioning and you will have to temporarily bypass it to start the engine. If nothing happens, the switch is probably all right and the problem is either in the battery, the starter solenoid, or the electrical connections in the engine's starting circuit.

Next, check the starter solenoid. The starter solenoid serves two important functions: it delivers electrical current to the starter motor, and it mechanically engages the starter motor and the engine until the engine starts, then disengages them.

If you have a voltmeter aboard, close the ignition switch and check the voltage between the battery side of the starter solenoid and ground. On a 12-volt system, the starter solenoid should be receiving a minimum of 7 volts of starting current from the battery. Check the voltage between the starter solenoid terminal serving the starter motor and ground. Also check the voltage between the starter motor terminal and ground. If you have lost voltage at any of those points, you will have isolated your problem and may be able to correct it by cleaning the appropriate terminal connections. If cleaning the terminals does no good, the electrical windings inside the starter solenoid are probably corroded and there is little you can do if you don't have a spare aboard. Call for assistance.

PROBLEM: You turn the ignition key or depress the engine start button and hear a clicking sound.

SOLUTION: The problem is either low voltage in the battery or a mechanical problem inside the starter solenoid.

First, check the condition of the battery. If you have less than 7 volts across the battery's terminals, the battery will have to be recharged before it will start the engine or you will have to use another of the vessel's batteries. If you have at least 7 volts across the battery terminals, check all the connections between the battery, the ignition switch, and the starter solenoid. Corrosion at any of those connections could reduce voltage to the point that the starter solenoid will not turn the starter motor, which in turn will not crank the engine.

Two other problems are possible. One is that rust or corrosion has frozen the starter solenoid's helical spring or plunger, which engages the starter motor and the engine. Try rapping the starter solenoid sharply on its case with a hammer two or three times to see if you can free the spring or the plunger. The other possible problem is that the starter motor is not firmly secured to the engine. It is that mechanical connection that provides the starter solenoid's ground. If the bolts securing the starter motor to the engine block are loose, clean off any corrosion and tighten them.

PROBLEM: You turn the ignition key or depress the engine start button, and the starter motor struggles but will not crank the engine.

SOLUTION: Check the voltage across the battery terminals and at all connections. On a 12-volt system, if you have at least 7 volts at the starter motor terminal, either the starter is defective or one or more engine cylinders or the engine's fuel line is locked with water, air, or fuel vapor. If the blockage is in one or more engine cylinders, removing the injectors from a diesel engine and trying to crank the engine will clear it. Clearing an air lock on a diesel engine is covered later in this chapter.

PROBLEM: You turn the ignition key or depress the engine start button, and the engine starts but then stops as soon as you release pressure on the start button.

SOLUTION: The ignition switch or start button probably is rigged with an auxiliary starting shunt whose ballast is defective. You will have to bypass the ignition switch to start the engine and keep it running.

PROBLEM: You can start the engine, and it runs for a few minutes but quickly overheats.

SOLUTION: Shut the engine down immediately, and troubleshoot its lubrication-cooling system. Inspect the engine's dipstick to make certain it has sufficient oil in the sump to keep it lubricated. If the oil in the engine sump is below the full mark on the dipstick, add oil but be careful not to overfill the engine. Also, check the oil on the dipstick for the presence of water. If water is detected, you may have a hole in the engine's water jacket. If this is the case, you probably also will notice an abnormally high reading on the engine's oil pressure gauge. There is nothing you can do to keep an engine with a ruptured water jacket from overheating, and you will have to call for assistance.

Check the engine's freshwater cooling reservoir. This is just like checking the coolant in an automobile engine. Allow the engine to cool down before removing the reservoir's pressurized cap because it could release steam or scalding water. If the reservoir is low, fill it to within about 2 inches (5 cm) of the neck. If the reservoir was low simply because you forgot to refill it before you left the dock, topping it off will probably solve the overheating problem. If the engine runs for a few minutes but overheats again, either the engine's freshwater pump is malfunctioning or its raw water cooling system is not operating properly.

To check the freshwater pump, remove the plug on the side of its housing and make certain it is full of water. If it is not, fill it and replace the plug. If the engine continues to overheat, the pump's impeller may be defective. If you have a spare impeller on board, install it. If you do not have a spare impeller on board, you will probably have to call for assistance.

To check the vessel's raw water cooling system, look at the engine's exhaust outlet at the vessel's transom. When the engine is running, the outlet should be discharging a significant stream of water. If it is, the raw water cooling system is functioning properly. If it isn't, the problem is most likely a clogged or malfunctioning through-hull fitting on the raw water inlet or a failed impeller in the engine's raw water pump. To check the raw water pump, loosen the clamps on the raw water hose where it enters the engine's raw water pump. If water begins to seep out of the junction, you probably have adequate raw water reaching the pump but its impeller has failed. If you have a spare impeller on board, install it. If you do not have a spare impeller on board, you will not be able to repair the pump and will need to call for assistance.

If water does not seep from the junction, carefully loosen the hose from the inlet of the raw water pump. If no water gushes from the hose, the problem is most likely a clogged or malfunctioning raw water inlet. Reattach the raw water inlet hose to the raw water pump and tighten its clamps. Make certain the seacock or gate valve serving the raw water inlet is open. If it is open, the raw water inlet is probably clogged and you will have to go beneath the vessel to remove the obstruction.

PROBLEM: You turn the ignition key or depress the engine start button, and the engine turns over but will not fire.

SOLUTION: If a vessel's engine doesn't start after turning over for thirty seconds, don't just keep cranking it because you will simply run down the battery. Find out why it isn't starting, and try to eliminate or solve the problem.

Since the engine turns over, the problem is not in its electrical starting circuit but in its ignition or fuel system, which consists of a primary filter-separator, which removes large particles and water from the fuel; a fuel pump; a secondary filter, which removes small particles from the fuel; and the injectors themselves, which inject the fuel into the engine's cylinders. Most marine diesel engines use unit injectors that do the entire job of pressurizing the fuel. Some marine diesel engines, however, have a separate high-pressure pump that delivers fuel to the injectors at about 20,000 pounds per square inch (137,900 kPa). A diesel engine does not burn all the fuel that is fed to its injectors. For this reason, in addition to its fuel supply line, it also has a fuel return line, through which unburned fuel is returned to the tank.

If the vessel is equipped with a manual shutdown system, which stops the engine by shutting off its air supply, make certain its controls are set in the open position (that is, the plungers are pushed all the way into their seats). Some marine engines are equipped with mechanical or hydraulic governors. If the engine is equipped with such a device, make certain the stop lever on the cover of a mechanical governor is in the run position; on a hydraulic governor, make certain the stop knob is pushed all the way in. If the engine is equipped with an air filter or breather, make certain it is not clogged.

Visually check the bowls housing the engine's primary and secondary fuel filters; both should be full of fuel, and the fuel should be clear. If you see excess water in the bowl of the primary filter, drain it off. If the primary filter bowl is full but the secondary filter bowl is empty, your problem may be a clogged primary filter; try replacing it. If both bowls are full, the fuel in the primary filter bowl is clear, and the fuel in the secondary filter bowl is dark, your problem may be a clogged secondary filter. Try replacing it. Some secondary filters are not housed in a bowl but are simply a screen-type filter in the fuel line itself. To find out whether fuel is flowing through an in-line filter, loosen the connection on its outlet side and attempt to crank the engine. If fuel flows from the fitting, the filter is probably clean. If fuel does not flow from the outlet fitting, retighten it, loosen the fitting on the filter's inlet side, and try to crank the engine. If fuel flows out of the fitting, the filter is clogged. Remove and clean it. If no fuel flows from the fitting, your problem is a lack of fuel in the tank, a clogged primary fuel filter, or a malfunctioning fuel pump.

If the bowl of the primary filter is empty, the engine has lost prime and you must reprime it. Make certain you have at least enough fuel in the tank serving the engine to reach the fuel pickup tube and that any valves in the fuel system serving the engine are in the open position. If necessary, shift the fuel manifold to serve the engine from a tank that contains sufficient fuel to reach its pickup tube. Some vessels are fitted with automatic fuel priming pumps, which are handy gadgets. If your engines aren't equipped with priming pumps, experiment to see if one of your tanks is installed high enough in the boat to be above the dry engine's fuel inlet. If it is, you may well find that by setting your fuel manifold to fuel the engine from that tank, gravity will force fuel through the primary filter to the fuel pump and you can crank the engine. As you reprime the engine, you will have to clear the air from the fuel system by opening the bleed screws on the primary and secondary filters and possibly the fuel pump, a process that is covered later in this chapter.

If both the primary and secondary filter bowls are empty, your problem is probably a malfunctioning fuel pump. If you have a spare fuel pump on board, install it. If you don't have a spare fuel pump on board, you will probably have to call for assistance.

If both filter bowls are full and the fuel is clear, your problem is probably an air lock in the fuel supply line. The housings for both the primary and the secondary filters should have bleed screws. Remove the bleed screw on the primary filter housing, and attempt to start the engine. If air rather than fuel flows out the bleed screw opening, let all the air escape before replacing the screw, then try to start the engine again. If that doesn't clear the lock, repeat the process with the bleed screw on the secondary filter housing. If you clear an air lock but it recurs, make certain all fittings along the fuel supply line are tight, check the seating of O-rings, and check valves in both the primary and the secondary fuel filters.

If fuel flows from both bleed screw openings when you remove the bleed screw but the engine still will not start, remove the fuel line from one of the injectors and try to start the engine. If fuel does not flow from the fuel line, your problem is probably a malfunctioning injector pump. If you

have a spare injector pump aboard, install it. If you don't have a spare injector pump on board, you will not be able to get the engine to run and will have to call for assistance.

PROBLEM: The engine runs, but when you shift to forward gear, the vessel doesn't make headway.

SOLUTION: Shut down the engine immediately, and troubleshoot the vessel's transmission, shafts, and propellers to identify the problem and attempt to remedy it.

In the engine room, check the coupling between the transmission and the propeller shaft. If it has come loose, tighten it. If it is broken and you have a spare coupling aboard, install it. If the coupling is broken and you don't have a spare coupling aboard, you will have to call for assistance.

If the coupling is not the problem and you can go over the side, check the vessel's underwater gear. If the prop is fouled, clear it. With the engine off but the transmission in gear, attempt to rotate the propeller. If the propeller rotates while the shaft does not, you have sheered off the key that joins the two together. Replacing the key involves removing and replacing the propeller, which is virtually impossible at sea. You will have to call for assistance. If both the shaft and the propeller rotate while the transmission is in gear, your problem is probably that the transmission itself is not engaging. If neither the shaft nor the propeller turns, have a crew member shift the transmission to neutral and again try to rotate the propeller. If neither the propeller nor the shaft will turn, you probably have a frozen cutlass bearing. Replacing it at sea is virtually impossible, and you will have to call for assistance.

If your troubleshooting to this point indicates that your problem lies in the transmission, return to the engine room and have a crew member start the engine and shift to forward gear while you check to see if the shaft exiting from the transmission is turning. If it is not, have a crew member shift the transmission from neutral to forward several times. If this does not engage the transmission, check the linkage between the helm control and the transmission itself. If it is mechanical, tighten it as necessary. If it is hydraulic, check the fluid level in the hydraulic pump and its fluid supply lines. Also check the fluid level inside the transmission and top it off if it's low—but be sure not to overfill.

If you find no problem with the transmission's linkage or fluid level, your problem is inside the transmission itself. Some marine transmissions are equipped with "come home bolts," which, when engaged, lock the transmission to the engine's flywheel. If you have to engage these bolts, be aware that whenever the engine is operating, the transmission will be in gear. Once you near a dock, you will probably need to shut down your engine and get someone else to tow you to it or use your tender as auxiliary power to come alongside. If your transmission is the problem and it does not have "come home bolts," there is little you can do to repair it. You will have to call for assistance.

PROBLEM: The engine runs and when you engage the gears, the vessel will go forward or backward but will not answer its helm.

SOLUTION: First, check to see whether your rudder has been carried away or severely damaged. If your rudder is still attached and will pivot, troubleshoot the vessel's steering mechanism.

On vessels with hydraulic steering, make certain the hydraulic fluid reservoir is full. If it is not, you probably have a leak in a hose, a fitting, or an O-ring somewhere in the system and will have to locate and repair it before you top off the reservoir. Even after you have stopped the leak and refilled the reservoir, you still may not have full steering control because of air trapped in the hydraulic lines. The hydraulic system should have an air bleed valve in the fluid reservoir, the pump, or the lines. Locate it and bleed the air out of the system; then add enough fluid to the reservoir to replace the air you have expelled.

On vessels with mechanical steering, trace out the system to locate the problem, which most likely will be a broken cable, chain, clamp, or sprocket wheel. Once you identify the problem, replace the broken part if you have a spare on board or attempt to rig a temporary repair that will hold together long enough to get you to shore.

The loss of rudders on a twin-screw vessel can be temporarily offset by steering with the engines. But if the rudder of a single engine vessel has been carried away entirely or its post is so badly bent that it will not pivot, you probably will have to jury-rig a replacement. The easiest replacement to construct will be a sweep made from a hatch cover and a boat hook lashed to a vertical stanchion on the stern. A more difficult alternative is to rig a replacement out of lines and blocks.

PROBLEM: You are fairly close inshore, but your vessel's engine(s) will not run and all your efforts to repair it have failed.

SOLUTION: If you have a tender with an outboard motor, you may be able to use it to reach safety. Rather than trying to tow your vessel with the tender, lash it alongside (see illustration next page). If your vessel's steering system is operative, the operation can be conducted in greater safety by lashing the tender's engine down in its fore-and-aft position and steering with your main vessel's controls. If your main vessel's steering is not operative, you will have to steer with the tender engine. If the weather is unsettled, be sure you wear a life jacket.

If you are unable to restore sufficient propulsion to reach safety and cannot get to shore using your tender as emergency power, use your marine radios or audible or visual distress signals to summon assistance.

You normally will be able to summon assistance from the coast guard or a commercial towing service by calling them on VHF channel 16 or SSB frequency 2182 kHz, then switching to a working channel. If you are unable to reach either the coast guard or a commercial towing service, broadcast a Pan-Pan urgency signal on VHF channel 16 or SSB frequency 2182 kHz. If other boaters who might be able to render assistance are nearby, employ visual and audible distress signals to attract their assistance.

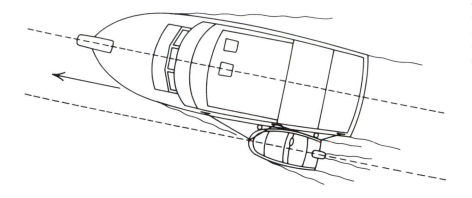

A tender lashed along-side may provide "get-home" power and emergency steering for a disabled power cruiser.

TIPS ON TOWING AND BEING TOWED

Unless towing operations are conducted carefully and with proper procedures, they can be dangerous to both of the vessels involved and to their crews. Here's the right way to do it.

1. If possible, use braided nylon for the towing line. For a given diameter, it is stronger than three-strand-twist nylon line. When three-strand-twist nylon breaks under a heavy load, it snaps back like a whip and can inflict serious injury on crew members aboard either vessel.

2. Using a bridle aboard the towing vessel will distribute the strain and help the vessel being towed track in a straighter line. The bridle should not, however, be rigged to the towing vessel's stern because it will severely restrict the towing vessel's maneuverability. Instead, rig the ends of the bridle as far forward on the towing vessel as possible to leave the stern free to turn as needed. Wrap the line where it comes in contact with the towing vessel's house to keep it from marring the surface. Rig the bitter end of the towing line to both forward cleats on the vessel being towed, and lead it as nearly as possible directly over the vessel's bow rather than off to either side.

3. Post lookouts on both vessels to watch the towline, but be certain they are positioned well clear of the line to avoid injury if it breaks and whips back. The lookout on the towing vessel should be especially alert to keep the line from fouling the towing vessel's propeller.

4. The vessel to be towed will track straighter if it is trimmed slightly by the stern (that is, shift weight aft) to keep its bow light. The vessel being towed should keep an anchor ready for instant deployment in case the towline breaks.

5. The towing vessel should take up slack on the towline slowly and begin the tow with just enough power to overcome the two vessels' inertia. Once under way, it should maintain a moderate speed to keep the vessel being towed from yawing.

6. If any sea is running, adjust the length of the towline to keep both vessels synchronized on the crests or in the troughs of successive waves. If the two vessels are not properly spaced, the towing vessel will run down the face of one wave while the vessel being towed is struggling up the back of the next wave, creating maximum resistance. Conversely, while the towing vessel is struggling up the back of one wave, the vessel being towed will

run down the face of the wave behind, possibly resulting in a collision.

7. If the towing operations must be conducted at night, the towing vessel should shine a searchlight on the vessel being towed to warn other vessels in the vicinity of the relationship between the two vessels.

8. If the towing operation must be conducted in fog, the towing vessel should sound one prolonged blast and two short blasts of its horn every two minutes. If the vessel being towed is manned, it should sound one prolonged blast and three short blasts on its horn immediately following the signal of the towing vessel.

9. If the towing vessel's intention is to bring the vessel being towed to a dock, come to a gradual stop a good distance off and pull the vessel up to the towing vessel with the towline. Never attempt to fend off either vessel with hands or feet, which could become trapped between the two hulls and broken or crushed. Lash the two vessels together so they will both respond to the towing vessel's steering. This will allow the towing vessel to bring the vessel being towed to the dock under control rather than out of control at the end of a long towline.

Knowing What to Do
If You Go Aground

Running aground can be a traumatic experience, particularly if the grounding is unexpected and your vessel has significant way on when it strikes the bottom. Regardless of the drama of the situation, you need to keep your wits about you. In some cases, doing the right thing quickly can free your vessel in moments; doing the wrong thing—or waiting too long to do the right thing—can leave your vessel exposed to serious damage and your crew exposed to possible injury. Panic reactions are only likely to get you in a worse predicament.

Anytime your vessel goes aground, check first for crew injuries. When a sizable vessel strikes the bottom at even 3 or 4 knots, your crew can suffer significant personal injuries as inertia slams them into bulkheads or tosses them from their bunks. Quickly assess any injuries to your crew to determine whether they are serious enough to require you to immediately call for assistance.

Next, check for damage to your vessel's hull, steering, and propulsion system. In a hard grounding, rudders, struts, and drive shafts can be torn away, leaving gaping holes that can allow hundreds of gallons of water to gush into your hull in seconds. If your vessel has suffered any severe threat to the integrity of its hull and you require assistance, get off a distress or urgency call immediately because your batteries could quickly be shorted out by rising water and leave you with no means of radio communication. The correct procedure for transmitting either call is covered fully in chapter 23. If your hull's integrity has been breached in the grounding, you're probably better off allowing your vessel to remain grounded until you can make temporary repairs.

If no crew have been injured and your vessel does not appear to have been seriously damaged, quickly determine which way deep water lies. In warm tropical waters, go over the side to assess the situation firsthand. In cold or murky water, take soundings around your vessel with a boat hook or lead line to figure out which way you need to move your vessel to get back to water in which it can float.

In tidal areas, the state of the tide at the time of

a grounding is critical. If the tide is rising and your vessel is not actually banging on the bottom, you can afford to relax and let the tide come in and lift it free. Even on a rising tide, if wind and current are in the direction of the obstruction, you should immediately set an anchor toward deep water to keep your vessel from going harder aground. If the tide is falling, you must work quickly and purposefully if you are to free your vessel as the tide ebbs.

After the state of the tide, wind and current normally will be the two most critical elements in deciding whether you can free your vessel quickly or whether you will be left high and dry for hours. In either case, try to make the situation work for you rather than against you. If wind and current are pushing your vessel toward deeper water, attempt to turn your stern toward the wind and current to give them additional area to work against.

If your vessel doesn't seem to be hard aground, your prop(s) and rudder(s) are clear of the bottom, and you are certain deeper water lies astern, try backing down with your engine(s). But don't try that maneuver more than a couple of times and

then only for about a minute each time. You could easily clog your engine's raw water intake with sand or mud and cause it to overheat, which is only going to compound your woes. Unless you're certain deep water lies ahead, it isn't a good idea to try to go forward since that's probably what got you in trouble in the first place.

If you're unable to get your vessel off the bottom quickly and wind or current or both are setting you harder aground, the first thing you must do is set a kedge anchor toward deep water as quickly as possible and keep its rode taut so you don't drift up farther on whatever your vessel's keel is resting against (see illustration). In order to get the kedge out far enough from your vessel and in the correct position to do some good, you normally will have to launch your tender. In warm waters and calm weather, you can deploy the kedge more rapidly by resting it on a boat cushion or other floating platform and swimming it out to where you want to set it.

If you're going to try to refloat the vessel yourself, first lessen its draft any way you can. Shift as

A kedge anchor set 45 degrees to wind or current or both with its rode led to your anchor windlass can help you pivot your bow off a grounding.

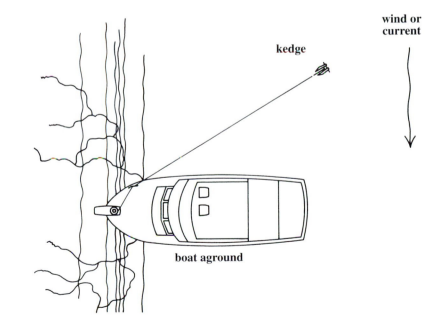

kedge

wind or current

boat aground

much weight as possible, including the crew, to the shallow-water side, which may help force the boat toward deeper water. Before you try backing off whatever you've run up on, check your raw-water strainers and, if they have gotten clogged, clean them out. Have a crew member maintain tension on the kedge with a half turn or an S-turn around a stern cleat while you back down slowly and steadily.

If going astern doesn't work, the next step is to try to pivot your vessel to get the bow pointed back toward deep water. If you have a dinghy with a sizable engine, use it to try to pull the bow around. If your vessel is only lightly aground, you might try leading the rode of the kedge anchor forward and using your anchor windlass to crank the bow around. If your vessel is hard aground, however, most electric anchor windlasses won't stand up to the strain this maneuver will put on them.

If it becomes obvious you can't get your vessel off the bottom until the tide floods, about all you can do is protect the hull as best you can until the rising tide refloats the boat. Set out boat hooks, dinghy oars, or anything else you can lay your hands on against the sheer as braces (but pad them well). If the vessel is about to lay on her chine or the turn of her bilge, pad it with any type of cushioning material you have on board.

EXTRICATING A GROUNDED VESSEL WITH AN ASSISTING VESSEL

Here are some helpful tips for situations when a second vessel is involved in freeing a grounded vessel.

1. Before approaching a grounded vessel, the captain of the assisting vessel must make certain that assistance can be provided without allowing the assisting vessel to become grounded.

2. If yours is the vessel aground, to help avoid potential disputes over salvage rights, it's best to pass your towline to the assisting vessel rather than accepting a line from the vessel offering assistance (see the section on legal issues of assistance later in this chapter). To avoid the possibility of the towline fouling the prop of the assisting vessel, bend a floating messenger line—such as polypropylene ski rope—onto your towline, weight its bitter end, and heave the messenger line rather than the towline. If the distance between your grounded vessel and the assisting vessel is too great to heave a messenger line, attach the towline to your own vessel and ferry it over to the assisting vessel in your tender, allowing it to pay out as you go. In warm waters, you can swim the line over. Wear a life jacket, attach the towline to your own vessel first, and support its coils on a float, allowing it to pay out as you go. If the assisting vessel lies downwind and downcurrent from you, attach a float to the towline or to a messenger line and allow it to float down to the vessel offering assistance.

3. If yours is the assisting vessel and you must pass your towline to the grounded vessel, make certain you can approach the grounded vessel close enough to heave the towline or a messenger line without endangering your own vessel. If yours is a single-screw vessel, it will be more maneuverable and its prop exposed to less danger if you approach the grounded vessel bow-on. If yours is a twin-screw vessel that you are adept at handling in reverse and the bottom poses no threat to your props, backing down on the grounded vessel will leave your bow pointed toward open water and put you in the proper position for making the tow. If you cannot approach the grounded vessel close enough to heave a messenger line, row or swim the line over as above or attach a float to its bit-

ter end, launch it upwind and upcurrent of the grounded vessel, and allow it to float down to the vessel in distress.

4. Once a towline has been passed, the captains of both the grounded vessel and the assisting vessel should see that it is attached to the strongest point of their respective vessels. On many modern boats, that point of attachment should not be a deck cleat because these cleats often are not strong enough to withstand the severe stresses involved in freeing a vessel that is hard aground. It normally is best to pass a line entirely around the house, padding it heavily at the points of greatest stress.

5. The propellers of all boats produce far more power going ahead than they do in reverse; therefore, the bow of the assisting vessel should be pointed toward open water. While the assisting vessel is attempting to pull the grounded vessel free, the maneuverability of the assisting vessel will be severely restricted and provision must be made to keep it from

being swept aground itself. If wind and current are striking the assisting vessel from other than abeam, the towline should be rigged to the assisting vessel's stern and the pull made in a straight line. If wind and current are striking the assisting vessel on its beam, the towline should be attached just aft of abeam on the upwind or upcurrent side to allow its bow to be headed into—or at least quarter to—wind and current.

In conditions of strong beam wind or current, the captain of the assisting vessel may need to set the assisting vessel's kedge 45 degrees to windward and have a crew member maintain a strain on the anchor line to help keep the assisting vessel's bow from falling off and possibly allowing the vessel to be swept aground (see illustration). The anchor winch, however, should be used only to help keep the bow of the assisting vessel into or quarter to wind and current. It should not be used to help exert pulling force itself because

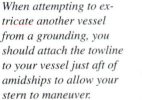

When attempting to extricate another vessel from a grounding, you should attach the towline to your vessel just aft of amidships to allow your stern to maneuver.

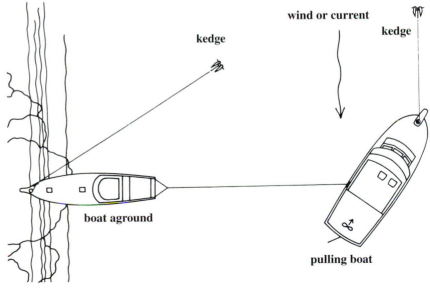

it most likely will not be strong enough to stand the strain involved.

6. Before the attempt to free the grounded vessel begins, the captains of both the grounded vessel and the assisting vessel should have a clear channel for communicating with each other. That preferably will be over a working VHF radio channel, such as channel 13, 6, or 68. If one or both vessels do not have a working VHF radio aboard, they should agree on a set of hand signals with which they can communicate.

7. Before the towing operation commences, the crew of both vessels should stand well clear of the towline. Under the pressure of towing, it can snap and lash back toward either vessel, causing severe injuries.

8. Before the attempt to free the grounded vessel begins, the grounded vessel's captain should make certain that a kedge is out and a crew member is taking up slack in its line to keep the vessel from being swept back aground once it's freed. If the grounded vessel is without power, it's also a good idea to have a crew member ready to set a second anchor, if necessary, once his vessel is freed.

9. During the towing maneuver itself, the captain of the assisting vessel should exert slow, steady pressure on the towline and avoid sudden accelerations, which can break the towline or cause severe damage to one or both vessels.

UNDERSTANDING THE LEGAL ASPECTS OF ACCEPTING AND PROVIDING ASSISTANCE

In most cases where your vessel is aground, you can accept assistance from a fellow recreational boater without concern that the assisting party might lay claim to your vessel under maritime law

pertaining to salvage rights. Maritime law on salvage rights is extremely ill defined and in most cases relates primarily to vessels that have been physically abandoned. In most cases, in order to claim salvage rights, the captain of a salvaging vessel must show that the vessel had been abandoned by its owner, who was making no attempt to salvage the vessel himself. The fact that you are aboard the vessel and making an attempt to extricate it from danger is what the lawyers call "proof on its face" that you have not abandoned your vessel; therefore, the laws on rights of salvage would not apply.

In the absence of a contract, you also can accept assistance from a fellow recreational boater without undue concern that the assisting party will attempt to charge you an exorbitant fee for his services. Unless this person states a price for the services before the attempt to free your vessel commences and you agree to pay the stated fee in front of witnesses, any subsequent attempts made to charge you would fall under the "just and reasonable" concept. If the person took you to court, you might have to pay something for the efforts, but these charges would have to be "just and reasonable" for the service performed. You could find you are liable for any damages to the assisting vessel that resulted from the attempt to assist you, but they would probably be covered by the liability clause of your boat owner's insurance.

Even if the assisting party does state an unreasonable fee and you verbally agree to pay it in front of witnesses, most of the lawyers I've discussed the matter with say you could argue that the contract was made under duress and a court would probably order you to pay only a fee that was "just and reasonable" for the service performed.

If you're dealing with a commercial towing service, however, the situation can be significantly different. Their representative, either the captain of the vessel they send to assist you or someone in their office you talk with over the radio, will clearly state a price and require that you agree to pay it before assistance commences. The price some of these services charge is outrageous, but if you agree to it, you probably will have no choice but to pay it.

The hull insurance of a good yacht policy normally covers the cost of towing and assistance if it is required to keep the yacht from suffering further damage. Under recent changes in the laws, commercial towing services can often claim salvage even with you aboard. This is especially true if they come aboard with pumps. Such salvage claims can result in charges amounting to significant percentages of the boat's total value. If you have an agreement with a national tow assistance company, see what constitutes salvage and what its cost is before your next cruise. (See chapter 6 for more information on marine insurance.)

Handling Crew Overboard Situations

Crew overboard (COB) emergencies are not nearly as common on powerboats as they are on sailboats, where crew members are often scrambling around the deck. However, they do occur—most often in bad weather.

ADVANCE COB PREPARATION

Before you head out on a cruise, you should instruct your crew on their responsibilities should anyone fall overboard. Make sure they stay current on the procedure by conducting periodic COB drills.

You also should make certain your vessel is equipped to keep a COB situation from turning into a disaster. As we discussed in chapter 12, all the personal flotation devices (PFDs) aboard your cruiser should be type 1 when running far offshore, where rescue is likely to be delayed. Each should be fitted at least with reflective patches and a whistle. A number of experienced cruisers also add a personal rescue light and possibly a class mini-B emergency position-indicating radio beacon to each PFD aboard. You also should have one of the commercially available COB rigs mounted on your vessel's transom and have several type 4 throwable PFDs mounted at strategic points around your vessel fore and aft. Other valuable equipment in a COB situation includes a water-activated COB strobe light; at least one, and preferably two, handheld searchlights; and a good supply of white parachute flares and their associated launcher.

BASIC COB PROCEDURE

Your basic procedure in a crew overboard situation should go like this: Any person on board who sees someone go overboard should immediately and loudly shout, "Crew overboard!" then continually keep constant eye contact on the COB, point emphatically toward the person in the water, and not assume, accept, or be given any other duties. This reaction must be instantaneous, and the eye contact must be constant without any distractions in gaze. Under the best of conditions, a human being in the sea can be difficult to spot. In heavy seas or conditions of poor visibility, spotting a person can be virtually impossible. Once visual contact is lost, it can be extremely difficult—if not impossible—to re-establish. If you are at the helm and see someone fall overboard, order someone else on board to locate and keep the person in the water in sight before you return your attention to running the boat.

The crew member keeping visual contact on the COB will provide your primary reference for returning to the COB. By emphatically pointing toward the COB with a fully extended arm, this "spotter" will give you vital information as to how to maneuver to return to the pickup point. Ideally, the spotter will be able to remain in your full view while performing this vital task, but keeping the COB in sight is the primary—indeed the only—responsibility. If necessary, another crew member must relay the spotter's directions to you.

If several people on board spot the COB, they also should keep their eyes fixed firmly on the COB and point emphatically in the COB's direction until you order them to assist in handling the vessel or getting the person back on board. One crew member, however, must be clearly assigned as a spotter to keep the COB in sight and continuously point to him.

Jettison your COB rig the moment you hear the "Crew overboard!" cry. If you don't have a COB rig aboard, throw a life jacket, life ring, or floating cushion overboard. Your purpose is not only to give the COB something to cling to but to provide yourself a visual reference to return to the person's vicinity. If the person goes overboard at night, in rain, or in fog, throw your COB light overboard as well. Unless the weather is calm, visibility is excellent, and you have the COB clearly in sight, it's also a good idea to have a crew member jettison anything that floats and is easily visible at about one-minute intervals throughout the rescue process. If you have difficulty immediately locating the COB, this trail of floating objects will give

you information about wind and current conditions and will be invaluable in helping you determine how to conduct your search most effectively. It's a good idea, in fact, to keep a large magazine or catalog close to the helm for just this purpose and have a crew member tear out a page, ball it up, and throw it overboard at one-minute intervals.

If you have a GPS receiver or a chart plotter or both aboard, immediately press its "COB" or "MOB" (man overboard) button to record your position. Note your compass heading, the wind speed, the wind direction, and the time. If you lose sight of the COB and must conduct a search, you will find yourself calculating current vectors over time to estimate the direction in which the COB is likely to have drifted and the distance the COB is likely to have been carried. The baseline of that search will be the reciprocal of the course you were running when you first realized the person had gone over the side. There is no way you can establish that baseline if you do not know your original course, so note it before you make your turn. The time the person went overboard is equally critical. In the tension of a search, time can become compressed and you could easily be mistaken as to how long the COB has been in the water and thus miscalculate the person's most likely position. If at all possible, write these factors down. If that's impractical, tell them to another crew member with orders to help you remember them in case they slip your own mind in the excitement.

Reduce throttle and reverse your course in as tight a turn as possible. If the wind is from other than dead astern, make your turn to leeward. The objective of this maneuver is to get your vessel turned around and headed back toward the COB as quickly as possible and, starting from a position as closely as possible to the point at which the alarm was sounded, to travel back toward the COB on as close as possible to a reciprocal of your original heading.

If you don't reduce speed before making your turn, it can describe an arc of up to several hundred yards, depending on how fast you are going, which will alter your starting point on the reciprocal by the diameter of the turn's arc.

As nearly as possible, you want to spin your vessel on its keel so you begin the reciprocal course as close as possible to the point at which you began to make the turn. If yours is a single-engine boat, reduce throttle, shift to neutral, shift briefly to reverse, give a brief burst of throttle to lose as much headway as possible, reduce throttle, shift back to forward gear, then make your turn tightly. In a twin-screw boat, do the same, but leave your windward engine in forward and put your leeward engine in reverse to pivot your vessel in the tightest possible turn.

The reason for turning to leeward if the wind is other than dead downwind is that from the moment the COB went over the side, the person has been floating downwind. By turning your vessel to leeward, you increase your chances of putting yourself on a reciprocal that will intercept the COB. If you turn to windward, you are increasing your vessel's divergence from the person's likely course. Reaccelerate toward the person in the water, following directions of the crew member pointing, and approach from downwind to within about 10 feet (3 m). By approaching the COB from downwind, you reduce the likelihood of your vessel being driven down on the person by wind and current. You also increase your ability to maneuver with less danger of striking the COB with the vessel or its propeller(s). To further reduce the danger of injuring the COB with the vessel, approach only to within about 10 feet rather than bringing the vessel right up to the person.

As you approach the person in the water, shift your engine to neutral to reduce the danger of striking him or her with a rotating propeller, but leave it running in case you require it for additional maneuvering, and have a crew member on board throw a line to the person in the water. Use a floating line, if possible, to reduce the danger of fouling the line in your vessel's prop just when it is most needed for maneuvering. Assuming the COB is conscious and able to function, throwing a line to bring the person to the vessel is safer than bringing the vessel right up to the person or having another crew member enter the water.

In settled weather, bring the COB aboard over your vessel's transom (but only after double-checking to make certain your engine is in neutral). In unsettled weather, amidships will be the most stable part of the vessel and is therefore the safest place to hoist a COB aboard. If you attempt to bring the COB aboard at the stern in heavy weather, the stern could be lifted on a wave and the COB could be struck by it or trapped beneath it.

If the person in the water is injured or unconscious, approach to within about 10 feet (3 m); then send your strongest crew member into the water to retrieve him. Entering the water to rescue an injured or unconscious person can be dangerous and arduous, and the assignment should be given to your strongest crew member. Allow no one to enter the water without being attached to the vessel by a safety line because they could be swept away from the vessel by wind and current, compounding your problems. The rescuer should remove shoes and wear a life jacket, both for the rescuer's own protection and to provide additional buoyancy during the recovery procedure.

If you require the assistance of other vessels in locating or recovering a COB, the proper signal to transmit is the Pan-Pan urgency signal rather than the Mayday distress signal. The format for transmitting this signal is shown in chapter 23. You may precede the Pan-Pan urgency signal with the radiotelephone alarm signal only in a COB situation and only if you feel you cannot obtain the required assistance without it.

In crowded conditions, if you will be able to retrieve the COB yourself but may have to violate the normal rules of the road to do so, use the Pan-Pan urgency signal to alert other vessels in your vicinity to your intentions and instruct them to stand clear.

The Pan-Pan signal can be directed toward one or more specific vessels or to "all ships." Once the emergency has passed, you are not required to cancel a Pan-Pan urgency signal addressed to one or more specific vessels. If you broadcast a Pan-Pan urgency signal "to all ships," however, once the emergency has ended you must cancel the signal using the format noted in chapter 23.

TIPS FOR CONDUCTING A COB SEARCH

If one of your crew sees a fellow crew member go overboard during daylight hours and the visibility is good, recovering the person using the above procedure is relatively simple.

But if no one sees the COB go over the side or you lose sight of the person, here are some tips for conducting a search that should improve your chances of a successful recovery (see illustration).

1. As soon as the COB alarm is sounded, hit the emergency button on any electronics, such as a GPS. Note the time and your present speed and heading; then stop your vessel.
2. If no one saw the COB go over the side, attempt to establish the amount of time

that has elapsed since the person was last seen on board.

3. Plot your vessel's present position on your chart and label it "Fix." If your vessel's track is not already charted, plot it as a reciprocal of your present heading. (To compute a reciprocal course from a present course of greater than 180 degrees, subtract 180 degrees. If your present course is less than 180 degrees, add 180 degrees.)
4. From the time elapsed since the last sighting of the COB and your vessel's speed during that time, plot the most remote point along your vessel's track at which the COB is likely to have gone over the side. Label that point "COB 0."
5. A person in the water presents so little surface to the wind that wind speed and direction can be virtually discounted as factors in determining the COB's likely speed and direction of drift. Because virtually all of the COB's bulk is in the

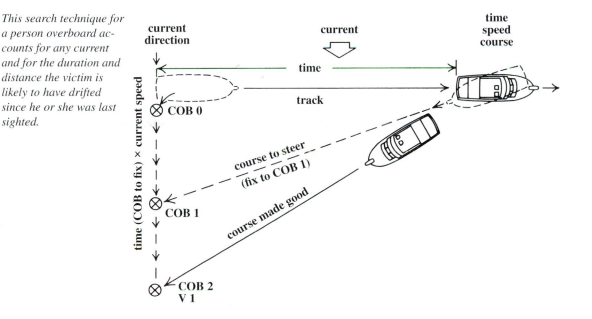

This search technique for a person overboard accounts for any current and for the duration and distance the victim is likely to have drifted since he or she was last sighted.

water, the person will be affected far more by current. Determine the speed of any current that is running, and establish the direction in which it is setting. You should always be aware of the speed and direction of set of any current that is affecting your vessel. If you are not already aware of those factors when the "Crew overboard!" alarm is sounded and cannot determine them from your navigational instruments (such as a GPS unit), here's how to get a basic estimate quickly. Lay your vessel directly head to wind, and reduce power to the minimum required to maintain steerage. Note the position of your watch's second hand and, at your mark, have a crew member at the point of your bow toss overboard a half-full gallon milk jug or other similar container that can be sealed. Note the number of seconds (T) it takes the jug to float from bow to stern. Divide your vessel's length overall by T and multiply the result by 0.6, which will give you the current's approximate speed in knots.

To determine the approximate direction of the current's set, observe the angle at which the jug floats away from your vessel with a hand-bearing compass. If the jug drifts dead downwind, you can use the wind's angle as the current's direction of set. If the angle of the jug's drift differs significantly from the angle of the wind, you know that a strong current is running whose direction of set is not coincident with the wind angle. In that case, disregard wind angle and use the current's direction of set in your calculations.

Plot the direction of set as a line through the point you have labeled "COB 0," and note the current's estimated speed.

6. Based on the elapsed time since the COB was last seen and the speed of the current, plot the COB's estimated present position along the line of the current's set and label it "COB 1."

7. Plot a course from "Fix" to "COB 1" as the course you will steer with lookouts posted at your vessel's highest point. Measure the distance from "Fix" to "COB 1," and calculate the time it will take you to get there based on your vessel's speed alone. Remember that during this run, your vessel will be affected by the same current set and drift that is affecting the COB. Factor the current's effects into your vessel's speed and heading, and label the resulting position "V 1."

8. If your reaction was instantaneous and your figures are precisely correct, "V 1" and "COB 2" will coincide. Regardless of the point along your vessel's track the COB actually went over the side, the person overboard theoretically will have drifted right onto your course. Since it is unlikely your reaction was instantaneous or that your figures were exactly precise, the person could be to either side of your course, but at least you will have determined a line of position along which to conduct your search.

9. Once you have worked out the COB's estimated present position and the direction and speed the person is likely to drift, use the Pan-Pan urgency signal to enlist the aid of any other vessels that might be in that vicinity or along the line of drift.

Assessing and Reacting to Severe Hull Damage

A significant quantity of water coming into your vessel's hull can quickly become a dangerous and even life-threatening emergency. At the first sign there has been a serious breach of your hull's integrity, do whatever you must to quickly identify where the water is coming in and the nature of the leak with which you are dealing. Speed here is of the essence. If a dangerous amount of water is gushing into your vessel from an inaccessible location beneath a berth or below the galley sole, for instance, don't be delicate about stripping away whatever is blocking your view of the problem. You can repair a few hundred dollars of damage much more cheaply than you can replace your entire boat, and you can't replace human lives, period.

FINDING THE SOURCE

Other than hull damage that results from a collision, the most common sources of significant leaks are the failure of through-hull fittings, hoses, underwater exhausts, rudder posts and stuffing boxes. Check those locations first.

ASSESSING THE DAMAGE AND TAKING ACTION

If your vessel has suffered hull damage as the result of a collision, be alert to the possibility that the collision might also have damaged the vessel's electrical system. Water is an excellent, and potentially deadly, conductor of electricity. If a live electrical wire has been knocked loose and is discharging current into bilge water, anyone stepping or reaching into the bilge water could receive a serious (possibly fatal) shock. If any electrical wires have been pulled loose and come into contact with bilge water or if you notice any electrical sparking, shut down the main breakers in your vessel's AC and DC electrical panels before exposing yourself to water in the bilge.

The action you take to try to stem the flood of water coming into your vessel will depend on the nature of the leak itself.

If the problem is a ruptured raw water intake hose, simply closing the seacock or gate valve that serves it should solve the immediate problem. If the hose is one that delivers cooling water to your main engine(s) or your generator(s), shut the engine or generator down until you effect repairs to avoid the danger of burning it out.

Stuffing boxes are designed to weep a minimal amount of water as a lubricant to ensure they are not too tight, but vibration can cause the packing nuts to work loose and allow a significant amount of water to enter the hull in a short time. Make certain you always have on board a pair of large pliers, a wrench, or a special packing nut tool big enough to retighten the nuts if they work loose while under way.

All through-hull fittings serving raw water intakes should be fitted with a seacock or a gate valve, but if you come across one that isn't, you can at least slow the flood of incoming water by wrapping the hose with waterproof tape or rags or both. Every vessel's engine room should be equipped with several rolls of a resin-impregnated tape called Syntho-Glass. The resin sets up within thirty minutes of being saturated with water and forms a strong, temporary repair. Since it is heat resistant to 500°F (260°C), it can even be used on exhaust systems and mufflers. It can be wrapped around a broken hose or balled up and used to plug small openings, such as a failed through-hull fitting.

Every through-hull fitting should have a conical wood plug of appropriate diameter attached to it with a piece of light line. If a through-hull fails and its seacock or gate valve cannot be closed, simply ram the plug home to stem the flow of water. Shaft glands also should be fitted with wooden plugs. (In 1989, a sailing vessel went down off Bermuda because its prop became entangled in a fishing net and the entire shaft was literally wrenched out of the boat. One life was lost in the incident.) Plugs also should be fitted to any rudder post glands that open into the hull.

If the problem is a breach in the hull itself as a result of a collision, stuff the opening from inside the hull with any soft materials you can lay your hands on, such as berth cushions, pillows, or blankets (but never life jackets—you might need them). As quickly as possible, reinforce these soft materials with something flat and solid, such as a hatch cover or dinette table top, and wedge it into place with whatever bracing material you have at hand, such as a dinette table support, a boat hook, or tender oars. You also can reduce the flow of water by covering the hole on the outside of the hull with a collision mat or awning material held in place by ropes. Water pressure outside the hull will help hold it in position. If you are going to try to reach shore with such a rig in place, make certain its top edge is well above your vessel's waterline.

As soon as you have the source of the incoming water under a reasonable degree of control, make sure your vessel's automatic electric bilge pumps are working properly by placing your hand near their water inlets to check for suction. If you don't feel water being sucked into a pump, make certain its inlet is not clogged with debris, that its float valve is not stuck in the off position, and that it is receiving proper electrical power. The best electric bilge pump—or even two or three of them—probably can't handle a serious breach of hull integrity. The electric bilge pumps typically found on vessels under 50 feet (15 m) are rated at about 1,500 to 2,000 gallons (5,675–7,500 L) per hour, which translates to only 25 to 33 gallons (100–125 L) per minute. Those on vessels over 50 feet may go up to about 3,500 gallons (13,250 L) per hour, but that works out to less than 60 gallons (225 L) per minute. A 4-inch (10 cm) hole in your hull well below the waterline could easily admit as much as 200 gallons (750 L) per minute.

You can supplement your vessel's electric bilge pumps with manual bilge pumps, the largest of which can move up to a gallon (4 L) a stroke. The problem, of course, is that you have to have the crew to handle them, and operating them is strenuous work. Most people will not be able to operate a good-sized manual bilge pump at thirty to forty strokes per minute for more than about ten minutes, so you'll have to set up a rotating schedule.

In a serious emergency, you can remove a significant quantity of water from your vessel by using your main engine or the engine powering your electrical generator as an emergency bilge pump. The raw water pump on a typical six-cylinder diesel engine, for instance, has a flow rate of about 75 gallons (280 L) per minute, and one on a twelve-cylinder engine pumps up to 140 gallons (530 L) per minute. I had *Americas Odyssey*'s engines fitted with Y-valves with which I could divert their raw water intake from the normal through-hull fittings to a hose deep in the bilge with the flip of a lever. I'd suggest you rig your engine(s) the same way. If you don't, here's the procedure for turning an engine into a high-volume bilge pump. If the engine is running, turn it off. Close the seacock or gate valve of the through-hull fitting serving the engine's raw water intake, disconnect the hose clamps, remove the hose from the through-hull, cover its end with some kind of screening to keep out debris (if nothing else, cut the screen out of a portlight), lay the end of the inlet hose in the bilge, and restart the engine. The end of the inlet hose must be completely covered by bilge water to ensure the engine gets an adequate supply of cooling water. You also should post a crew member at the end of the inlet hose to make certain it does not become clogged and to alert you when the engine pumps out enough water to the point it is no longer receiving an adequate supply of cooling water.

WHEN TO CALL FOR HELP

The instant you doubt your ability to control the flow of water coming into your vessel's hull or at least to pump the water overboard faster than it is coming in, broadcast a Pan-Pan urgency message over VHF channel 16 or SSB frequency 2182 kHz using the format shown in chapter 23. Do not omit any items. If you reach the coast guard and are within range of one of their helicopters or C-130s, they may be able to air drop an emergency, gasoline-powered bilge pump to you. The instructions for operating it will be on the canister. Don't put off making at least an alerting call because your batteries could quickly be shorted out by the incoming water.

The moment you become convinced you are not going to be able to keep your vessel from foundering, broadcast a Mayday distress message using the format shown in chapter 23. If you don't get a satisfactory reply to your Mayday, set off visual and possibly audible distress signals. Even if you cannot see any other vessels in your immediate vicinity, fire a red parachute or meteor flare. It might be spotted by a vessel out of sight over the horizon, which will come to investigate. If other vessels are nearby, sound repeated short blasts on your horn, raise and lower your fully extended arms, and display your orange distress flag with square and circle, or fire an orange smoke flare.

These steps, of course, assume you are far from shore when your hull's integrity is seriously breached. If you are inshore and can reach shoal water, simply run your vessel aground. You may do some damage to your hull and underwater gear, but at least you will keep her from going under. If all else fails, launch your life raft and go through your abandon-ship drill, which is covered in chapter 30. If your vessel doesn't sink completely but is simply awash, stay near it if at all possible so you will have a better chance of being spotted by rescuers.

Fighting Fires Afloat

The potentially disastrous effects of a fire at sea and what you should—and should not—do if one erupts are best illustrated by the experience of a friend of mine, Sumner Pingree, when a turbocharger caught fire in the engine room of his immaculate sportfisher, *Roulette*, off the coast of Puerto Rico (see page 313).

"We were running with the engine room door open to get more air to the engines," Sumner told me later. "The mate was in the cockpit when he spotted the fire and slammed the engine room door shut. By the time my son Richard was halfway up the flying bridge ladder to tell me about the fire, smoke was everywhere. We had already lost power on the starboard engine and the generator. I yanked the port engine back to idle and immediately got off a Mayday call to the coast guard. I said I was not declaring an emergency at that moment but had a fire on board and asked them to stand by. We opened the engine room door to see what was going on. Our automatic engine room fire extinguishing system had already gone off and extinguished the fire. As best we

could tell, the high-pressure fuel line on the starboard engine had ruptured and saturated the insulating blanket around the turbocharger, and it had been ignited by the hot exhaust gases which power the turbocharger.

"Since the fire was out, we thought we were okay. But while we were trying to figure out exactly what had happened, the fire reignited with a whoosh. I raced back up to the bridge to call the coast guard again, but the fire had already burned through the battery cables and the radio was dead. Within two or three minutes, the entire cockpit and main saloon were engulfed in flames. Flames were all around me. I yelled to everybody to abandon ship. We launched the life raft and leaped into the sea. Ten minutes after we first realized we had a fire aboard, we were swimming. I was amazed how quickly she burned."

In the situation they faced aboard *Roulette*, Sumner and his crew did some things that were very right and a couple of things that proved disastrous. We'll examine their actions in detail in this chapter and see which was which.

TIPS ON FIRE DEFENSE

Your first line of defense against a fire on board is preventing it from occurring in the first place. Doing that involves a lot of plain common sense. Make certain, for instance, that all your vessel's electrical wiring is properly installed and protected by appropriately sized fuses on all circuits; then check periodically for corrosion and chafe. Regularly check your vessel's fuel-fill system to make certain all its connections are tight, and always ground the fuel-fill nozzle to your fuel-fill deck plate before you pump fuel aboard. Also, keep a close eye on the fuel and lubrication lines on your engine(s) and generator(s), and replace them at the first sign of fraying or leaking. Never store flammable materials near a heat source or allow oily rags to accumulate in an enclosed space, and be extremely careful with open flames, such as those around a shipboard barbecue grill.

Your second line of defense against the potentially disastrous effects of a fire on board is to protect your engine spaces with an automatic engine room fire extinguishing system and to mount appropriately sized portable fire extinguishers of the proper class in strategic areas throughout your vessel: just outside the engine space door or hatch; on the flying bridge; in the pilothouse, saloon, and below decks accommodations; and in the galley. The law doesn't require you to carry a portable fire extinguisher in your tender, but it's a wise precaution.

If you take these precautions and still have the misfortune of a fire aboard your vessel, here are some suggestions for handling it.

ENGINE ROOM FIRE

When Sumner pulled his port engine back to idle rather than shutting it down altogether, what he didn't realize was that it was sucking the fire suppressant chemical out of his engine room and at the same time sucking fresh oxygen into the engine room to refuel the fire.

Diesel-powered vessels fitted with an automatic engine room fire extinguishing system should also be fitted with an automatic engine shutdown system that operates anytime the fire extinguisher goes off. If your vessel doesn't have such a shutdown system or it malfunctions and a fire erupts in your vessel's engine room, the first thing you should do is shut down all engines and generators that share the engine space involved with the fire. This also will help close off any supplies of fuel or lubricating oils that might be fueling the flames.

A fire cannot continue to burn without oxygen. Shutting any open engine room doors or hatches will help starve the fire of oxygen and snuff it out.

If your vessel's engine room fire extinguisher system has not discharged automatically, activate it manually. Automatic engine room fire extinguishers normally are quite dependable and discharge as soon as a fire raises the temperature in the engine room to their activation point. But like anything else mechanical, particularly in the corrosive marine environment, they can malfunction. Your vessel should have manual activation levers at both its flying bridge and its pilothouse steering stations, in the saloon, and in its below decks accommodations.

The best thing Sumner did was to transmit a Mayday distress call immediately. As his experience proved, had he waited to make his call until after he assessed the damage the fire had caused, it would have been too late.

Anytime you have fire break out in the engine room, go ahead and transmit at least a Pan-Pan urgency call and message to alert potential rescuers that you may need their help. If the situation seems serious, you are fully justified in transmitting the Mayday distress call and message. Use the format detailed in chapter 23, and do not omit any items. If, by the time you get in contact with someone, you are not certain you will require assistance, have the person stand by while you assess the situation. If, while you are doing that, your radio is disabled, at least someone will be alerted to your problem and your position.

The minute you realize you have an engine room fire aboard your vessel, take the precautions of ordering a crew member to stand by the life raft and prepare to launch it, and ordering your crew into their life jackets. If you are able to quickly bring the fire under control, you can order a stand-down and will have lost nothing. If the fire gets out of hand and you must abandon ship, you at least will be that much further along in your preparations.

When you've got smoke boiling out of your engine room and your automatic fire extinguishing system has discharged, there naturally is a great temptation to yank the engine room door or hatch open immediately to see what's going on. But don't do it! Wait at least fifteen minutes to be certain the engine and any flammable material in the engine room have cooled below the reflash point. If you open the door before everything in the engine room has cooled below the flash points, you will admit oxygen to fuel the fire.

If your engine space is protected by an older CO_2 fire extinguishing system, once you are certain the fire is out and any metals and flammable liquids in it have cooled below the flash point, open the engine space and allow it to ventilate for fifteen minutes before you enter it. In concentrations sufficient to choke off a fire, CO_2 is deadly. If you must enter an engine space where a CO_2 system has discharged before the space has had time to ventilate (for example, to rescue a person trapped in the space when the system discharged), cover your mouth with a piece of fabric as a filter, hold your breath, and do not crouch down any lower than is absolutely necessary. CO_2 is heavier than air and will tend to sink toward the vessel's bilges.

Halon and FE-241 are also heavier than air and will sink into the vessel's bilges, but they are safe to breathe in the 7 to 8.5 percent concentration normally used in automatic engine-room fire extinguishing systems.

Before opening any door or hatch that may have fire behind it, feel its exterior first. If it's too hot for you to hold your hand against, the fire probably is still burning. Even if the door or hatch is cool enough for you to hold your hand against, have a portable fire extinguisher ready for action and open the door cautiously. The door or hatch may be heavily insulated. Even if it is relatively cool, fire could be raging on the other side of it or you could experience a reflash.

If your vessel is not equipped with an automatic fire extinguishing system and you plan to try to put the fire out with a portable extinguisher, open the door cautiously, stay as low as possible since heat and flames tend to rise, and keep the door between yourself and the possible fire (see illustration).

Directing the stream of a portable fire extinguisher at the flames of a fire does little good. You must direct the stream at the base of the fire to rob it of heat and oxygen at its source. Hold the stream as steady as possible. Once you get the stream focused on the base of the fire, keep it there until you are sure the fire is out. Do not use short bursts of fire suppressant because that can give the fire time to reignite between bursts.

GALLEY FIRE

Galley fires are most likely to be fueled by flammable liquids, such as grease, propane, or alcohol, or by combustible solid materials, such as paper, wood, or fabric. A good type A-B-C extinguisher will be effective against both types.

If no fire extinguisher is available, for a small fire use materials you have on hand, such as baking soda or a water-soaked towel. Water will put out an alcohol fire but may spread the flames. Baking soda is a good dry chemical suppressant because it robs the fire of oxygen. Rather than just dumping baking soda on the fire right out of the box, dump some in your hand and then broadcast it at the base of the flames. Do not use water on grease fires. The grease will float on top of the water and can carry flames to other parts of the vessel, such as wood cabinets and drapes.

Make certain any fuel supplying the fire is turned off at the source. Most galleys that use

In fighting an engine room fire, keep a hatch between yourself and the fire and aim the fire extinguisher's stream at the base of the fire rather than at the flames (Ralph Futrell).

propane for cooking are equipped with an electronic control allowing you to turn off the propane at the tank. (The propane tank itself should be housed in its own well-ventilated compartment on the vessel's exterior.) Unburned propane is heavier than air and will sink to the vessel's lowest point, where it could explode. If you extinguish a propane fire, be certain the propane is turned off at the tank so unburned propane does not build up.

ELECTRICAL FIRE

A primary concern in fighting an electrical fire is that you use a suppressant that is not a conductor of electricity. Type A-B-C fire extinguishers use chemicals that are not electrical conductors. The suppressant used in foam-type extinguishers will corrode electronics; the suppressant used in FE-241, Halon, and CO_2 extinguishers will not.

If possible, restrict an electrical fire's access to oxygen. In most electrical fires, the initial combustible material is the insulation around the wiring itself. Fires in electrical wiring insulation

cannot be sustained without a great deal of oxygen. In many cases, simply encasing circuit panels in a heavy metal box and closing up the box if a fire breaks out will be sufficient to extinguish it.

Never use water to extinguish an electrical fire. Water is an excellent conductor of electricity. If you throw water on an electrical fire and are standing in water yourself, the electrical power could be conducted through the water and electrocute you.

ACCOMMODATIONS FIRE

Fires in a vessel's accommodations most often will be fueled by such combustible materials as wood, paper, or fabric. You should have a type A-B-C extinguisher mounted in your accommodations where you and your crew can get to it easily, even in the dark. If no type A fire extinguisher is available, flood the base of the fire with water, which is an effective suppressant for type A fires.

If possible, restrict the fire's access to oxygen. Type A fires cannot continue to burn without a generous supply of oxygen. Robbing a fire of oxygen simply by closing a door or hatch often can snuff it out.

DECK FIRE

A common source of deck fires aboard yachts is the gasoline used to fuel the tender's outboard motor. Although coast guard regulations do not require that a fire extinguisher be carried in most tenders, you should keep a type A-B-C extinguisher aboard and make certain it is handy anytime you are handling gasoline.

If an on-deck fire is fueled by such combustible materials as wood, paper, or fabric, extinguish it with a type A-B-C extinguisher or water. Water is an excellent suppressant for extinguishing type A fires. You should always keep handy on deck a stout bucket with a rope tied to its handle that is long enough to allow you to scoop up water from over your vessel's side rails.

If possible, jettison the burning material overboard. The closest water to extinguish a deck fire normally will be the water in which your vessel is floating. If possible, use a tender oar, whisker pole, or other long object to push the burning material over the side.

Handling Medical Emergencies

This chapter focuses on the steps you should take if a medical emergency strikes a member of your crew or a guest aboard your boat when qualified medical assistance is not immediately available.

Except where specifically noted, the recommendations in this chapter assume the victim is an adult or a well-developed child at least eight years old. For infants and children younger than eight, the procedures are essentially the same, but the frequency at which procedures are executed and the force exerted by the rescuer may vary considerably. If you are likely to have infants or children under age eight aboard your vessel frequently, you should secure specialized training in dealing with any medical emergencies they might experience.

ASSESSING THE VICTIM

If a crew member or guest suffers an accident or becomes ill aboard your boat, your first step should be to conduct a rapid assessment of the individual's condition to identify the primary medical emergency and determine whether your intervention is required. The injury or difficulty you notice first is not necessarily the victim's most serious nor the one with which you should attempt to deal first. For example: a crew member slips on your vessel's foredeck. You rush to the person and note an obvious broken arm and a severe gash on his forearm. Before you attempt to treat the broken arm or the wound, check to make certain no far more serious difficulty exists, such as an injury to the spinal column. In this situation, hasty action on your part before you determine the primary medical emergency could result in an even more serious injury or possibly even death.

If the victim is conscious, ask, "Are you OK?" As detailed later in this chapter, the response or lack of a response will tell you much about the person's condition. Ask next, "What happened?" Again, the response will help direct your attention toward the primary emergency.

If the victim does not respond to your questions or is unconscious, do the following.

Check Respiration

Within seconds after being deprived of oxygen, the heart begins to develop dangerous irregular beats. If the brain is deprived of oxygen for as little as four to six minutes, irreversible damage is possible; after six minutes, irreversible damage is highly likely; after ten minutes, it is virtually certain unless the victim's core body temperature has been drastically reduced. For this reason, checking the victim for adequate respiration is your first responsibility.

If the victim is not obviously inhaling and exhaling on his own, put your ear to his lips to listen for the passage of air into and out of his lungs. Try to feel his breath on your cheek. Look for chest movement. If he is heavily clothed in a sweater or a foul-weather suit, rest your hand lightly on his upper abdomen to feel for movement. A conscious victim grabbing his throat or struggling for breath or the presence of a wheezing noise in the breathing of an unconscious victim indicates an obstruction in his airway. The absence of breathing may indicate an airway obstruction, respiratory failure, or a heart attack. A conscious victim who complains of severe chest pain may be suffering angina or be in the early stage of a heart attack.

Check Circulation

Feel for the presence of a pulse, preferably at one of the carotid arteries in the victim's neck, which are more pronounced than a pulse in the wrist. To locate a carotid artery, place an index and middle finger on the victim's Adam's apple and then slide them to one side into the groove between the Adam's apple and the neck muscle. Check for the presence of a pulse in only one carotid artery at a time, and exert only light pressure; heavy pressure could restrict the flow of blood to the victim's brain.

In checking the victim's circulation, you are primarily concerned with the presence or absence of a pulse. Count the pulse for fifteen seconds by your watch. In a normal, healthy adult, you should count between fifteen and twenty beats. Fewer than twelve beats in fifteen seconds could indicate the victim is going into shock. The absence of a pulse indicates the victim has already gone into serious shock or cardiac arrest.

Check Skin Temperature and Moisture

Cool, clammy skin indicates shock, heat exhaustion, or insulin shock. Hot, dry skin indicates heatstroke or diabetic coma. Flushed skin, swollen welts over large areas of the body, or swelling of the face and lips indicate anaphylaxis (allergic reaction).

Check Skin Color

Reddened skin indicates heatstroke. Pale, white skin indicates shock or insulin shock. Bluish skin indicates an airway obstruction, respiratory failure, or cardiac arrest.

Check Eye Pupils

Significant differences in the size of the two pupils can indicate head injury. Significant dilation of both pupils indicates cardiac arrest.

Check Mental Alertness

Significant disorientation indicates a head injury. A victim who is knocked unconscious in an accident, rouses to near-normal alertness, and then later lapses into unconsciousness again could be suffering from internal bleeding in the head.

Check Mobility

In a conscious victim, total inability to move indicates a spinal injury in the vicinity of the neck. The ability of a conscious victim to move the arms but not the legs indicates a spinal injury below the neck.

WHEN TO PROVIDE ASSISTANCE

After you have determined the victim's primary medical emergency but before you do anything, make certain your intervention is truly necessary and warranted. The human body is a remarkable mechanism that often has the capacity to care for itself if simply left alone. Deciding whether and when to intervene is one of the toughest areas of providing emergency medical assistance, especially when professional medical care is a long way off.

Your immediate intervention is appropriate in three medical emergencies: the victim is not breathing at all; the victim has no pulse; or the victim is bleeding profusely from an open wound. No immediate action on your part other than preventing further injury is appropriate if you suspect the victim has suffered a spinal injury, if a conscious victim is choking on a foreign body in his throat (he may well expel it through his own exertions), or if the victim is suffering a convulsion or seizure.

"Wait and see" is the appropriate attitude if a victim is conscious but breathing weakly or gasping for breath, if the victim has a weak or racing pulse, or if the victim is unconscious but breathing on her own and has a pulse. In these situations, avoid the "hero syndrome" of rushing to provide assistance that may not be necessary and could actually do more harm than good. Instead, watch the victim carefully and see if a condition develops that warrants your intervention.

THE ABCS OF EMERGENCY MEDICAL CARE

Attend to the ABCs of emergency medical care first: **A**irway, **B**reathing, and **C**irculation.

Airway and Foreign Object Obstruction

The victim's airway can be blocked by a foreign object or, especially if she is unconscious and lying on her back, by the soft tissues of her own throat and tongue.

If a conscious victim is choking and you suspect his airway is blocked by a foreign object, do not immediately attempt to assist him if he is passing any air in and out of his lungs. Give him time to dislodge the obstruction on his own. Only if he ceases to pass any air in and out of his lungs should you attempt to help him expel the obstruction by employing the Heimlich maneuver. Ask first to be sure the victim actually wants your help.

If the victim is standing, get behind him and wrap your arms around his torso just above his waist (see illustration next page). Grasp one fist with the other hand, and place the thumb side of your fist halfway between the victim's belly button and the arch of his ribs where they divide at the lower end of the breastbone. Thrust your fist into his abdomen with a sharp, decisive upward squeeze. If the maneuver does not immediately dislodge the object, repeat it until the object is expelled or the victim loses consciousness.

Choking often causes the muscles in the victim's throat to spasm, thereby trapping the object and preventing the passage of air in and out of the lungs. Once the victim loses consciousness, the spasm often ceases, the object is released, and the victim resumes breathing normally. If a choking victim lapses into unconsciousness, assist him gently to the sole or deck, lay him flat on his back, and clear his airway. Never attempt to clear a victim's airway by lifting up on his neck. If he has suffered a spinal injury in the vicinity of the neck, exerting pressure in that area could inflict severe damage or death. Instead, use the chin-lift-and-head-tilt method (see illustration next page).

Place one hand on the victim's forehead. Place two fingers of the other hand under the front edge of the victim's jaw. Simultaneously tilt the victim's head backward by pressing on his forehead with one hand while you lift the jaw upward with the fingers of the other. This maneuver will bring the tongue forward and clear it from the airway. Check the victim's respiration. Often simply clearing the victim's airway will allow him to pass air in and out of his lungs and expel the foreign object.

If the victim is still not breathing and his mouth

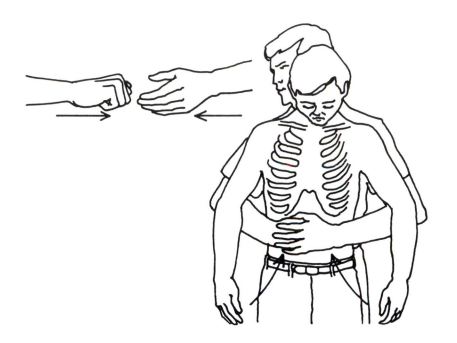

To perform the Heimlich maneuver on a standing victim, get behind the person and wrap your arms around his torso just above the waist. Grasp one fist with the other hand, and place the thumb side of your fist halfway between the victim's belly button and the arch of the ribs. Thrust your fist into the abdomen with a sharp, decisive upward squeeze (Ralph Futrell).

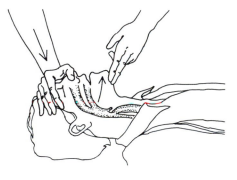

To use the chin-lift-and-head-tilt method to clear a victim's airway, place one hand on the victim's forehead, place two fingers of the other hand under the front edge of the victim's jaw, and then simultaneously tilt the victim's head back by pressing the forehead backward with one hand while lifting the jaw upward with the fingers of the other (Ralph Futrell).

is not already open, open it using the cross-finger technique: cross your index finger over your thumb. Place the tip of your thumb on the bottom of the victim's upper teeth and the tip of your index finger on the top of his lower teeth, then force them apart. Holding the mouth open in this fashion, use the forefinger of the other hand to sweep the inside of the victim's mouth and attempt to locate the foreign body and remove it.

If you are unable to locate the foreign body, straddle the victim's hips. Place the heel of one hand against his abdomen halfway between his belly button and the arch of his ribs where they divide at the lower end of the breastbone. Point the fingers of that hand toward the victim's head. Place your second hand on top of the first. Thrust inward and upward toward the victim's head with a sharp, decisive motion (see illustration). If the maneuver does not immediately dislodge the object, repeat it six to ten times. Employing the Heimlich maneuver on an unconscious victim who is lying on his back may dislodge the foreign body from his airway but not expel it from his mouth. If the object is not expelled from the mouth, it may fall to the back of the victim's throat and continue to obstruct his breathing. Open his airway as described above; then see if you can locate the obstruction with a finger sweep and remove it.

Breathing

If an unconscious victim is not breathing after you open her airway, administer artificial ventilation using mouth-to-mouth ventilation (see illustration next page).

Use the head-tilt-and-chin-lift method to clear the victim's airway. Keep her head tilted back by continuing to exert pressure on her forehead with the heel of one hand. Use the thumb and forefinger of that same hand to pinch the fleshy tips of her nostrils together. Use the thumb of the other hand to pull down on the victim's chin to keep her mouth open. Open your mouth wide, as if you were preparing to take a big bite out of an apple. Take a deep breath, place your mouth completely over the victim's mouth, and exhale deeply. Out of the corner of your eye, if you exhale hard enough, you should be able to see the victim's chest rise. After exhaling, remove your mouth to allow the chest to fall. Keep your ear near the victim's mouth to listen for her breathing, try to feel her breath on your cheek, and watch her chest for signs of movement. If necessary, release the hand holding her chin and place it on her upper abdomen to feel for movement. If the victim is not breathing on her own, put your mouth completely over her and exhale into it a second time hard enough to make her chest expand. You should complete these two breaths in three to five seconds.

If the victim is not breathing on her own after your second exhalation, release the hand holding her chin and use it to check the pulse in her carotid artery as discussed earlier in this chapter. If you detect a pulse, continue mouth-to-mouth ventilation at the rate of one exhalation about every five seconds, with each exhalation lasting approximately one and one-half seconds, until the victim is breathing on her own.

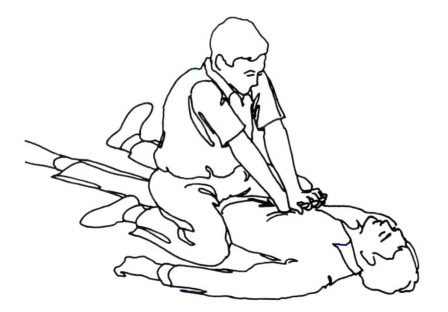

To execute the Heimlich maneuver on a prone victim, straddle the victim's hips, place the heel of one hand against the victim's abdomen halfway between the belly button and the arch of the ribs, point the fingers of that hand toward the victim's head, place your second hand on top of the first, and then thrust inward and upward with a sharp, decisive motion (Ralph Futrell).

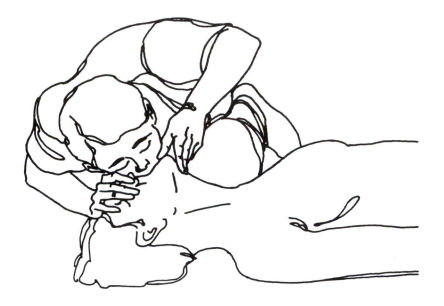

To perform mouth-to-mouth ventilation, tilt the victim's head back by exerting pressure on the forehead with the heel of one hand. Use the thumb and forefinger of that same hand to pinch the fleshy tips of the victim's nostrils together. Use the thumb of your other hand to pull down on the victim's chin to keep the mouth open. Open your mouth wide, as if you were preparing to take a big bite out of an apple. Take a deep breath, place your mouth completely over the victim's mouth, and exhale deeply (Ralph Futrell).

Circulation

If you do not detect a pulse in the carotid artery, the victim may be suffering cardiac arrest and you must immediately begin to administer chest compressions.

If the victim is not already lying on his back on a hard, flat surface, move him to such a position as quickly as possible. Kneel next to his chest with your knees slightly apart. One of the most important phases of administering chest compressions is placing your hands in the proper position. Improper hand placement can result in ineffective compressions, broken ribs, or damage to the victim's internal organs.

To locate the proper hand position, place the middle finger of your hand that is nearer the victim's feet as high as possible into the arch where his ribs divide at his breastbone. Lay the forefinger of that hand immediately adjacent to the middle finger. Place the heel of your other hand on the victim's breastbone immediately adjacent to your forefinger. Release your hand nearest the victim's feet, place it exactly on top of your other hand, interlock your fingers, and raise them slightly so that you are exerting pressure on the victim's breastbone with the heel of your lower hand only (see illustration opposite).

To execute chest compressions, lock your elbows and lean forward, rising slightly so that your shoulders are directly over the victim's chest and you are exerting pressure directly downward. After depressing the victim's chest 1½ to 2 inches (4–5 cm), release your pressure on the victim's chest just enough to allow it to return to its original position. Your hands should not bounce off the victim's chest. Repeat this process until you have delivered fifteen chest compressions evenly and rhythmically. The process should take about ten seconds.

After fifteen chest compressions, quickly shift back to the mouth-to-mouth ventilation position described above and check the victim's breathing. If he is not breathing on his own, deliver two full exhalations into the victim's lungs, with each exhalation lasting approximately one and one-half seconds.

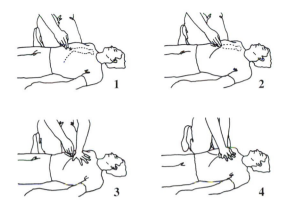

To locate the proper hand position for chest compressions, place the middle finger of your hand that is nearest the victim's feet as high as possible into the arch of the victim's ribs (1); lay the forefinger of that hand immediately adjacent to the middle finger (2); place the heel of your other hand immediately adjacent to your forefinger (3); and release your hand nearest the victim's feet, place it exactly on top of your other hand, and interlock your fingers and raise them slightly so that you are exerting pressure on the victim's breastbone with the heel of your lower hand only (4) (Ralph Futrell).

Allow the victim's chest to fall between breaths.

After two exhalations, return to your chest-compression position, place your hands properly as described above, and deliver another fifteen chest compressions evenly and rhythmically over the next ten to eleven seconds. This combination of mouth-to-mouth ventilation and chest compressions is generally referred to as cardiopulmonary resuscitation (CPR). You should always begin and end CPR with mouth-to-mouth ventilation. Maintain this ratio of fifteen chest compressions to two mouth-to-mouth ventilations until the victim is breathing on his own, until you are relieved by professional medical assistance or another rescuer, or until you are exhausted.

If, in addition to administering CPR, you are the only person aboard your vessel who can call for help, the best time to do so is after you have performed four cycles of fifteen compressions and two mouth-to-mouth ventilations each. By that time, you should have forced enough air into the victim's lungs and circulated enough oxygenated blood through his vital organs with chest compressions to give you a minute and a half to two minutes to try

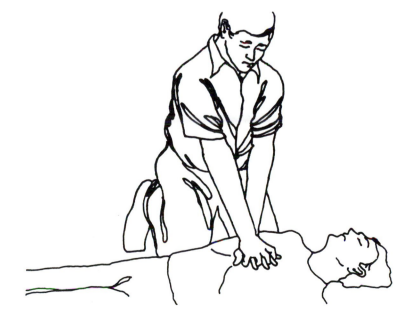

To perform chest compressions, put your hands in position, lock your elbows, and lean forward, rising slightly so that your shoulders are directly over the victim's chest and you are exerting pressure directly downward. After depressing the victim's chest 1½ to 2 inches (3.8–5 cm), release pressure just enough to allow the victim's chest to return to its original position (Ralph Futrell).

to summon help. Broadcast a Mayday call on VHF channel 16 or SSB frequency 2182. If you do not get an immediate response, return to the victim and resume CPR, beginning with two exhalations of mouth-to-mouth ventilation.

CPR conducted by two rescuers, with one performing the mouth-to-mouth ventilation and the other performing the chest compressions, requires precise coordination and should not be attempted unless both rescuers are well trained in the procedure. If you have initiated CPR and another individual offers to help, continue CPR by yourself and send the other person to summon help.

UNDERSTANDING THE TYPES OF MEDICAL EMERGENCIES

Once the victim's airway, breathing, and circulation are stable, attend to other medical emergencies as recommended here.

Severe Bleeding

If uncontrolled, severe bleeding, either externally or internally, can quickly cause the victim to lapse into unconsciousness and then death. Once the victim's airway and heart beat have been restored, controlling severe bleeding should therefore be your next concern.

EXTERNAL BLEEDING

Apply direct pressure to an open wound by putting your hand over it and pressing steadily. As soon as possible, put a sterile dressing between your hand and the wound. Once the bleeding stops or slows significantly, apply a compression bandage to the wound. To do so, leave the sterile dressing in place and position the center of a long strip of cloth over it. Maintain a steady pull on the cloth strip as you wrap both ends of it around the extremity; then tie a knot directly over the sterile dressing.

If possible, elevate the wound above the level of the victim's heart to further retard the flow of blood. If the wound continues to bleed profusely, restrict the blood flow at the primary artery serving the affected area by pressing the artery against a bone at a pressure point (see illustration).

Apply a tourniquet only if you cannot control severe bleeding with direct pressure. If applied, a tourniquet should not be so tight that it completely cuts off the blood supply from the remainder of the extremity. If the remainder of the extremity beyond the wound begins to turn blue, the tourniquet is too tight. Ease its pressure slowly and gradually. Once you have a tourniquet properly applied, do not loosen or remove it. The sudden loss of blood from the heart could throw the victim into severe shock.

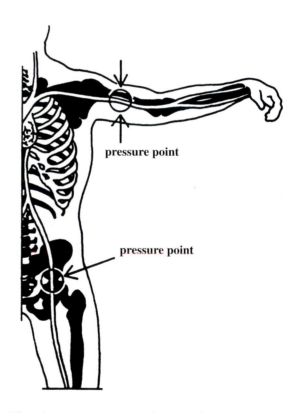

The primary pressure points for controlling severe bleeding in an arm or a leg are located on the inside of the upper arm and on the inside of the groin (Ralph Futrell).

Where blood loss is substantial, treat the victim for shock as detailed in the section on shock later in this chapter.

INTERNAL BLEEDING

An individual who suffers a major blow to the abdomen that injures the spleen or a blow to the head that ruptures an artery; a victim who suffers a simple fracture of the ribs or of a large bone; or a person who suffers from the eruption of a bleeding ulcer can lose a life-threatening amount of blood with few or no external, observable signs of the bleeding.

Bleeding, however slight, from the rectum; nonmenstrual bleeding from the vagina; blood in the victim's urine or stool; or the coughing or spitting up of blood should lead you to suspect serious internal bleeding. Bleeding from the nose, mouth, or ears can also indicate internal bleeding, especially if it is not obviously the result of a cut inside the mouth or of recent scuba diving activity.

If the victim is suffering from severe internal bleeding, these signs often will be accompanied by such other indications as a weak, rapid pulse; cold, moist skin; dull eyes with pupils that are slow to respond to light; excessive thirst; nausea; vomiting; anxiousness; and a marked feeling of depression. The stomach of a person suffering from a lacerated spleen will become tender and swollen.

If the internal bleeding is the result of a large broken bone in the arm or leg, applying a splint will help slow the bleeding. Aside from applying a splint and treating the victim for shock, there is virtually nothing you can do to treat severe internal bleeding without advanced medical training and sophisticated equipment. The victim's condition may well be life-threatening. You should call for help and, if you cannot transport the victim to professional medical assistance within half an hour, request helicopter evacuation.

Shock

Shock is a collapse of the cardiovascular system in which the flow of blood that carries oxygenated

blood to the body's vital organs slows and eventually ceases. After even a few minutes without an adequate flow of oxygenated blood, the cells of certain organs, primarily the brain and the heart, die and cannot be regenerated.

Shock can be brought on by many causes, including severe blood or fluid loss caused by a large open wound or burn or internal bleeding; damage to the spinal cord that disrupts its control of the nervous system; the dilation of blood vessels in reaction to excessive heat; panic reactions; and failure of the heart to pump effectively. Respiratory shock is caused by a failure of the respiratory system.

The signs of shock include cold, clammy skin; profuse sweating; a pale skin color and, in the advance stages of shock, a bluish color to the lips; shallow, labored, gasping, or rapid breathing; a weak, rapid pulse; extreme thirst; and nausea or vomiting.

To treat for shock, clear and maintain the victim's airway. Lay the victim on her back and keep her warm with blankets or clothing, but do not employ artificial sources of heat, such as heating pads, electric blankets, or hot water bottles, and do not allow her to become overheated. Administer oxygen, if available. If the victim exhibits no signs of head, neck, or back injury; is not experiencing convulsions, seizures, or respiratory distress; and is not bleeding severely, elevate her feet 8 to 12 inches (2–30 cm) higher than her head. Elevating the feet places the weight of the internal organs on the diaphragm, which could cause breathing problems, so watch the victim carefully for signs of labored breathing and lower her feet if these occur.

A victim of shock is likely to complain of intense thirst. If medical help is less than two hours away, do not give her fluids but do allow her to suck on a piece of moistened gauze or cloth. If medical assistance is more than two hours away, give her fluids only if she is conscious, is not convulsing, and shows no signs of brain, abdominal, or respiratory injury. The best fluid to administer is a mixture of 1 level teaspoon of salt and ½ level teaspoon of baking soda dissolved in a quart of tepid water. For adults, give not more than one ounce every fifteen minutes in small sips; for children age one to twelve, give half that amount; for infants younger than one year, give one-quarter that amount. Never give a victim of shock any type of alcohol.

Anaphylaxis, a type of shock that can be caused by severe allergic reaction to certain types of ingested poisons and by stings from insects and hazardous marine life, is discussed in the section on poisoning later in this chapter.

Open Wounds

If a wound is bleeding severely, attempt to staunch the flow of blood as discussed earlier in this chapter; then treat the victim for shock. If a severe wound is in one of the victim's extremities, apply a splint, which will help control the bleeding, prevent bleeding from resuming if the victim must be moved or transported, and relieve the victim's pain.

If an open wound involves a flap of skin that has been torn from the body, attempt to maintain blood circulation in the flap by realigning it to its original position, making certain the portion that remains attached is not twisted or kinked. Apply a saline-dampened sterile dressing and a compression bandage. If the injury involves a flap of skin or a portion of an extremity that has been entirely torn from the victim's body, wrap it in saline-dampened sterile gauze, place it in a plastic bag, and keep it in a cool place until you can transport it and the victim to professional medical assistance. Do not allow the flap or portion of the extremity to freeze.

An open wound that exposes internal organs in the abdomen must be kept moist. Cover or wrap the wound with a moistened sterile dressing, cover the dressing with material that is impermeable to air (such as plastic food wrap or aluminum foil), and then secure the impermeable material with a bandage.

In the case of a sucking chest wound through which air is escaping from the victim's lung, cover the wound with a sterile dressing, shut off the escaping air by wrapping the victim's chest with plastic food wrap or another air-impervious dressing, and then secure the impermeable material with tape on three sides only.

If an open wound is not bleeding profusely, remove foreign particles with gauze, cleanse the wound with soap and water, and blot it dry. If professional medical attention will be available within six hours, apply a dry, sterile dressing and a bandage. If medical attention will not be available within six hours, saturate the wound with an antiseptic solution before applying the sterile bandage. One exception to this rule is cuts from coral, which should be cleaned as above but left open to the air. Open cuts should not be reimmersed in salt water until they are well healed.

Puncture Wounds

Do not remove an object protruding from a puncture wound if its removal is likely to induce severe bleeding. Leave the object in place, saturate the entry and (if necessary) the exit wound with antiseptic solution, cover the wound(s) with a dry, sterile dressing, and bandage the object securely in place. If the injury is severe, treat the victim for shock.

If you remove the object, cleanse the entry and (if necessary) the exit wound with soap and water, saturate the wound(s) with antiseptic solution, and then apply a dry dressing and bandage. If the injury is severe, treat the victim for shock.

A fishhook that has penetrated the skin far enough to bury its barb is best left in place if medical assistance will be available within approximately eight hours. If it will be much longer than eight hours before the victim can reach medical assistance, the possibility of a serious infection in the bloodstream dictates that the hook should be removed. First, determine how far the barb has penetrated below the skin surface. If it is less than a quarter of an inch, clean the area around the hook's entry into the skin, saturate it with antiseptic solution, and make a small incision with a razor blade or sharp knife that has been sterilized by dipping in alcohol or holding over a flame and then allowing to cool. Make a small incision behind the barb to expose its tip, grasp the shank of the hook with a pair of needle-nose pliers, and back the hook out. If the barb has penetrated much more than a quarter of an inch beneath the surface of the skin, the best course is to force the point of the hook on through the flesh until the barb emerges, clip it off with wire cutters, then grasp the shank of the hook with a pair of needle-nose pliers and back the remainder of the hook out. In either case, soak the area liberally with antiseptic solution and massage the area to encourage the solution to penetrate into the wound as deeply as possible. Blot the wound dry, and cover it with a sterile dressing and bandage. If available, administer a general antibiotic such as penicillin. As soon as possible, consult a doctor to see whether the victim needs a tetanus booster shot.

Fractures and Dislocations

Do not attempt to set a fracture or force a dislocated bone back into its socket. Immobilize the affected area with a splint constructed of any suitable material on hand, such as a tender oar, a rolled newspaper or magazine, or even a pillow. If the skin in the vicinity of the fracture is broken, treat it as an open wound, control any severe bleeding, and treat the victim for shock.

If you suspect a spinal injury, do not move the victim. Immobilize him, especially his head and neck, using materials on hand, such as pillows, settee cushions, or boat cushions placed on each side of the head. Call for professional medical assistance immediately.

Chest Pain

A victim who complains of a tightness or a severe pain in his chest may be suffering from a lack of oxygen to his heart muscle. If the tightness or pain follows a period of exertion, emotional stress, or even a big meal, it may be angina, which is caused by a constriction of the vessels that deliver blood to the heart. The pain of angina most commonly begins beneath the breastbone and may spread to the left arm, the jaw, and the upper region of the abdomen. An attack of angina in itself is not life-threatening and does not result in permanent damage to the heart. If it is the result of exertion or stress, it often is relieved simply by allowing the victim to rest in a cool, calm location, during which the supply of oxygen gradually equals the heart muscle's oxygen requirement. Many individuals who suffer occasional attacks of angina carry with them a small bottle of nitroglycerin tablets, which rapidly dilate blood vessels, thus dramatically increasing the flow of oxygenated blood. If nitroglycerin is available, place one tablet beneath the victim's tongue and allow it to dissolve. If the pain persists, administer additional nitroglycerin tablets at the rate of about one every three to five minutes. If the pain is indeed angina, it should subside within six to eight minutes. Due to nitroglycerin's rapid dilation of blood vessels, the victim may be left with a mild or even a severe headache, which should ease after a half hour or so of quiet rest.

If an individual experiences tightness or severe pain in the chest that does not follow a period of exertion or stress, is not relieved by nitroglycerin, or lasts more than ten to fifteen minutes, it may be the result of a far more serious situation—a blood clot blocking the main artery that delivers blood to the heart muscle. If the blockage is complete, the heart can immediately develop an irregular beat or cease to beat at all and death can be virtually instantaneous. If the blockage is not complete but is substantial, death or serious damage to the heart muscle may result within four minutes of the onset of the attack.

If an individual aboard your vessel complains of tightness in his chest or severe chest pain that meets the above description, your response can be literally the difference between his life and his death.

First, remain calm and deal with the victim in a reassuring manner. Agitating or alarming him can cause the situation to deteriorate quickly. Have the victim sit in a cool, quiet location, and observe him to see whether the pain passes. Make certain he is breathing easily and regularly. If nitroglycerin is available, place one tablet under his tongue about every three to five minutes. If the pain increases rather than decreases and persists for more than about fifteen minutes, call for help. If you will not be able to transport the victim to professional medical assistance within thirty minutes, request emergency helicopter evacuation.

If the victim experiences difficulty breathing or breaks out in a profuse sweat, his skin pales, and his eyes lose their focus or roll back in his head, he may well be experiencing serious and life-threatening cardiac arrest.

As quickly as possible, lay him on his back on a hard surface, make certain his airway is clear, assist his breathing with two slow, full mouth-to-mouth ventilations, and check his pulse. If you do not detect a pulse, assist his circulations with chest compressions as detailed earlier in this chapter. Call for help as soon as possible to request emergency evacuation.

(There is some anecdotal evidence that ingesting an aspirin tablet immediately after an attack can help minimize permanent damage, but this presupposes professional medical attention within minutes, which is rarely possible on a boat.)

Drowning Accidents

Enter the water to rescue a drowning victim only as a last resort because you risk becoming a drowning victim yourself. The rule is "Throw, tow, row" and only then "Go." First, throw the victim a floating object, such as a life jacket, a life ring, or a buoyant cushion. If that is impractical, throw or push an object such as a rope or a tender oar out to the victim and tow her to safety. If the distance is too great, attempt to row out to the victim in a tender or even on a surfboard, a wind surfer, or any other object that will float. Only if all these methods are impractical, should you enter the water and attempt a rescue yourself. Even then, be alert to the probability that the person will be panicky and

may well attempt to grab hold of you and could pull you down with her. If at all possible, approach her from behind and try to calm her; then wrap your arm over her shoulder, grabbing her with your hand below her armpit to tow her to safety on her back.

Remove the victim from the water, and immediately check her airway. In a drowning incident, the victim's larynx often involuntarily constricts in a spasm in an attempt to keep water from entering the lungs. The spasm normally will relax as soon as the victim is removed from the water. Attempt to restore the victim's breathing by administering two slow, full exhalations of mouth-to-mouth ventilation. Check her circulation by taking her pulse at the carotid artery. If no pulse is felt, execute chest compressions. Alternate fifteen chest compressions with two mouth-to-mouth ventilations until the victim is breathing on her own, until you are relieved by trained medical assistance or another rescuer, or until you are exhausted.

Scuba Diving Accidents

The most serious scuba diving accidents are those related to ascending from a dive to the surface too rapidly or failing to breathe normally during an ascent.

As a scuba diver descends into the water, the pressure on his body, and thus on the air in his lungs and on the oxygen and nitrogen dissolved in his bloodstream, is greatly increased. If, following a dive, he ascends to the surface slowly, the differing pressures inside and outside his body are gradually equalized without injury. If he breathes normally during such an assent, the nitrogen dissolved in his bloodstream is also released gradually and is expelled by the normal action of his lungs.

If, however, a scuba diver ascends to the surface too rapidly, the air pressure in his lungs remains at a high level while the external pressure on his body decreases rapidly. As a result, the air in his lungs expands rapidly and ruptures tiny vessels in his lungs. The air thus released can enter the space in his chest that contains his lungs, the space in his chest that contains his heart, or his bloodstream and create a plug that blocks the normal flow of blood to his brain, his heart, and other vital organs. An air bubble trapped in the bloodstream will often lodge in a joint where blood vessels are smallest. Because of the differences in air pressure involved, air bubbles in the bloodstream can occur in dives as shallow as 6 feet (1.8 m).

A scuba diver suffering the effects of ascending too rapidly will experience difficulty breathing or pain in his chest, pain in his joints or abdomen, dizziness, nausea, or vomiting, and he may have a mottled coloration to his skin and exude a pink or bloody froth from his mouth and nose. He normally will experience these difficulties immediately upon returning to the surface.

If a scuba diver fails to breathe normally during an ascent from a single or repetitive dives to a depth exceeding 60 feet (18 m) for a total bottom time greater than sixty minutes, the nitrogen dissolved in his bloodstream is not expelled by the normal action of his lungs and can create bubbles in his bloodstream that also block the normal flow of blood to his brain, his heart, and other vital organs. A diver suffering from nitrogen bubbles in his bloodstream will exhibit the same signs as the diver suffering the effects of an air bubble but with two important differences. First, pain in his abdomen and joints will be so severe that he will actually double over (a condition known as the bends). Second, he may not suffer difficulties until several hours after he has returned to the surface.

The emergency treatment for both types of scuba diving injuries is the same.

If necessary, clear and maintain the victim's airway, restore his breathing with mouth-to-mouth ventilation, and restore his circulation with chest compressions. Once the victim's ABCs are restored, lay him on his left side to help keep the air or nitrogen bubbles in his bloodstream from migrating to his heart, elevate his feet 8 to 12 inches (20–30 cm) to help keep the bubbles from migrating to his brain, keep him warm and, if possible, give him pure oxygen. Call for help immediately,

and arrange to evacuate him to the nearest recompression chamber. You normally can obtain information on the nearest recompression chamber's location and arrange evacuation through the coast guard. An excellent resource for advice and assistance in handling any diving accident victim is the Divers Alert Network (DAN), a nonprofit organization staffed twenty-four hours a day (see contact information in resources appendix). You can reach DAN through a VHF or High Seas marine radiotelephone operator or by satellite telephone. If evacuation is to be made by air, make certain the pilot understands you suspect the victim has air or gas bubbles in his bloodstream. The air pressure inside the aircraft should not exceed that experienced at 500 feet (150 m) above sea level.

Burns

First- and second-degree burns, whether from heat or chemicals, are painful but not normally life threatening. Third-degree burns over a significant portion of the victim's body can be deadly and must be treated quickly.

HEAT BURNS

If the victim's skin is red but not blistered or weeping, the injury is a first-degree burn, which has injured only the top one or two layers of the skin. Immerse the affected area in cold (not ice) water or cover it with a cloth soaked in cold water. Apply an anesthetic spray or ointment to relieve the pain. If necessary, apply a dry dressing, cover it with a bandage, and administer an oral pain medication such as aspirin.

If the victim's skin is blistered or weeping, she has a second-degree burn. Immerse the affected area in cold (not ice) water or cover it with a cloth soaked in cold water. Do not break any blisters that are present, do not attempt to remove burned tissue, and do not apply any kind of antiseptic sprays, ointments, or grease. Apply only a dry dressing and a bandage. If possible, keep the affected area above the level of the victim's heart. If the affected area is extensive, treat the victim for shock.

If the victim's skin exhibits a whitish charring, she is suffering from a third-degree burn. Do not attempt to remove any burned tissue or adhered clothing. If the affected area is extensive, do not immerse the victim in cold water or apply cold compresses because cold could intensify her reaction to the shock that invariably accompanies a sizable third-degree burn. If the affected area is small, cold compresses can be applied. Do not apply any sprays or ointments. Apply only a dry, sterile dressing and a bandage. If the affected area is the victim's head or an extremity, elevate it above the level of her heart. Administer oral pain medication. If the burned area is large or deep, treat the victim for shock. Administer fluids as recommended in the section on shock earlier in this chapter only if the victim is conscious and not vomiting and medical help is more than an hour away.

CHEMICAL BURNS

If necessary, remove the victim's clothing from the area of the burn and flush the affected area with water for five minutes. Depending on the severity of the burn, treat the affected area according to the previous section on heat burns.

Poisoning

Poisoning, whether by ingesting a poisonous substance or by coming into contact with toxic marine life, snakes, or insects, can be deadly. Here are some ways to deal with poisonings of both types.

POISONING BY MOUTH

First, if the victim is conscious, give him water or milk to dilute the poison. If medicinal charcoal is available, give him that. Next, attempt to determine the source of the poisoning. If the container is found and indicates a specific antidote, give the antidote to the victim if it is available. Do not attempt to administer fluids if the victim is unconscious.

If the source of the poisoning is unknown but an acid, alkali, or a petroleum product is possible, do not induce vomiting. If a substance other than acid, alkali, or a petroleum product is known to be the source of poisoning, induce vomiting by administering an emetic solution or poking your finger down the victim's throat.

Poisoning by Seafood

One of the joys of the cruising life is the opportunity to harvest the bounty of the sea, but there are dangers of which you should be aware.

Ciguatera. Larger specimens of carnivorous reef feeders—such as grouper, snapper, jack, and barracuda—can become infected with ciguatera toxin, which can be extremely poisonous and, in extreme cases, fatal.

Individual reactions to ciguatera vary widely. Where two individuals eat the same amount of a contaminated fish at the same time, one may experience no or very mild effects while the other may become extremely ill. Symptoms normally appear within about six hours. A distinctive symptom of ciguatera poisoning is the victim's reversed reactions to hot and cold. Other telltales signs include numbness or a tingling sensation, especially around the mouth; severe stomach cramps; often violent vomiting; diarrhea; excessive sweating; and a pale complexion. Some victims may become disoriented or hallucinate, and some may exhibit varying degrees of paralysis. A suspected victim of severe ciguatera poisoning must be transported to professional medical assistance as quickly as possible.

Many physicians are not familiar with treating ciguatera poisoning. If you encounter such a situation, you might inform the physician of the procedures suggested by Dr. Richard J. Lewis of Santa Monica, California, an avid cruiser who has extensively researched treatment of ciguatera poisoning. His recommendations, as published in the *Commodore's Bulletin* of the Seven Seas Cruising Association (see contact information in the resources appendix), are as follows. For severe cases, establish a 30 mL/hour flow of intravenous saline or Ringer's solution; then piggyback 20 percent Mannitol at 500 mL/hour until symptoms disappear or to a maximum dosage of 5 mL per kilogram of the victim's body weight. The infusion of Mannitol should be interrupted if blood pressure drops more than 15 mm Hg. Symptoms usually respond to this treatment within ten minutes. For mild cases of ciguatera poisoning, Dr. Lewis recommends prescribing one 25 milligram (mg) tablet of amitriptyline twice daily for two to three weeks.

Paralytic Shellfish Poisoning. Bivalves such as oysters, scallops, clams, and mussels can become infected with a toxin associated with the so-called red tides, which is very similar to that responsible for ciguatera. It can cause paralysis and, in extreme cases, can be fatal. It is not destroyed by cooking or steaming.

Incidents of paralytic shellfish poisoning most often occur during the summer months and are most common along the coasts of New England and the Pacific Northwest.

Symptoms normally occur within thirty minutes. Victims may experience a tingling or numbness of the facial muscles (especially around the mouth), labored breathing, headache, nausea, vomiting, diarrhea, abdominal cramps, a floating sensation, muscle weakness, increased salivation, increased thirst, and difficulty in speaking, which may indicate the onset of muscular paralysis.

A suspected victim of paralytic shellfish poisoning should be transported to professional medical assistance as rapidly as possible. Antihistamines such as epinephrine can help relieve respiratory distress, if present.

Neurotoxic Shellfish Poisoning. Bivalves harvested along the coasts of Florida during the summer months can become infected with a poisonous waterborne organism related to—but not the same as—the organism that causes paralytic shellfish poisoning. Neurotoxic shellfish poisoning is not fatal, and the symptoms normally will disappear within a few days.

The signs of neurotoxic shellfish poisoning are similar to those of paralytic shellfish poisoning except that victims of the former do not exhibit respiratory distress or muscular paralysis.

Tetrodotoxin. This toxin, a chemical relative to the toxin that causes paralytic shellfish poisoning, is principally associated with the puffer fish—the Japanese delicacy fugu—but is also found in porcupine fish, ocean sunfish, and blue-ringed octopus. It concentrates primarily in the liver, intestines, gonads, and skin of the fish and can be eliminated only by cutting away the toxic parts, a task that in Japan can be performed only by a licensed chef who has received special training.

Fugu devotees consider a mild toxic reaction from eating the dish—a tingling of the lips and tongue, flushing of the skin, and mood elevation—part of its appeal. Of the three thousand cases of fugu poisoning reported in Japan over a twenty-year period, 51 percent were fatal.

Scombroid Poisoning. Fish with dark meat—such as tuna, wahoo, bluefish, amberjack, bonito, mackerel, skipjack, and mahimahi—are susceptible to scombroid poisoning, which is most often caused by inadequate refrigeration of the fish after it is caught. Lack of prompt refrigeration can cause bacteria on the surface of the fish to penetrate the flesh and contaminate it. This bacteria is not eliminated by cooking. Occasionally, it may impart a sharp or peppery taste to the meat.

Symptoms of scombroid poisoning may appear within minutes after contaminated fish is eaten or up to several hours later. They can include labored respiration, dizziness, nausea, vomiting, diarrhea, and a flushed or burning sensation. The victim's skin may become reddened to the point that it appears sunburned. Scombroid poisoning is not fatal, and symptoms normally will disappear within twelve to twenty-four hours. Antihistamines such as epinephrine can help relieve respiratory distress, if present.

POISONING BY INSECT

For reactions to poisoning from insect bites or stings, such as severe swelling, apply a mildly constricting band between the site of the bite and the heart and keep the affected area below the level of the victim's heart. Apply ice or cold cloths to the infection site, and administer a mild pain reliever such as aspirin.

In the case of a sting from a wasp or hornet or bees other than the honeybee, scrub the site of the bite with soap and water; then attempt to remove the stinger and venom sac with tweezers sterilized by immersing in alcohol or heating over a flame and allowing to cool.

The barbed stinger of a honeybee can continue to inject poison into the victim for up to twenty minutes after the initial attack. Do not use tweezers to remove the stinger because their squeezing action can inject more poison. Instead, remove the stinger by scraping it from the skin.

POISONING BY MARINE LIFE

The world's waters are full of strange and wonderful marine life, some of which are dangerous if humans come in contact with them.

Tentacle Stings

Contact with jellyfish, Portuguese man-of-war, anemones, and certain types of coral can deposit toxic cells on the victim's skin that can cause significant skin irritation, pain, nausea, vomiting, and muscle cramps.

First, flood the affected area with rubbing alcohol, ammonia, or household vinegar, which will help to neutralize the toxin. If available, cover the affected area with meat tenderizer, which contains an enzyme that will destroy the toxin. Lastly, if available, cover the affected area with talcum powder, which will dry the skin and cause the toxic cells to stick together so they can be scraped from the skin.

Puncture Wounds by Marine Life

Puncture wounds from such marine life as stingrays, sea urchins, cone shells, catfish, and stone, toad, weever, oyster, scorpion, zebra, and surgeon fish contain a toxin that is susceptible to heat. Immerse the affected area in water as hot as the victim can stand for 30 to 60 minutes, but be careful not to scald her because her reaction to the toxin may temporarily negate her normal reaction to the pain of excess heat.

Once the pain has subsided, flood the puncture wound with rubbing alcohol, ammonia, or household vinegar to deactivate the toxin. If medical help is more than six hours away, wrap the extremity between the wound and the heart with a mildly constrictive elastic bandage (not a tourniquet) to retard the flow of the toxin to the victim's vital organs.

Appropriate treatments for poisoning by marine life are summarized in the sidebar.

POISONING BY PLANTS

Remove any of the victim's clothing that may have become contaminated by the plant's poisonous oils. Generously flush the affected area with water; then wash it with soap and water. If possible, follow this scrubbing with rubbing alcohol, ammonia, or household bleach diluted 50 percent with water. If the skin rash is mild, apply calamine or aloe lotion.

POISONING BY VENOMOUS SNAKE

Encourage the victim to sit or lie down and calm him to slow the spread of the toxin through his system. If the affected area is an arm or leg, wrap constricting bands (not a tourniquet) both above and below the bite to contain as much as possible of the toxin in the bite area. A pulse should still be detectable beyond the band farthest from the heart. Immobilize the arm or leg with a splint. Do not give the victim any fluids.

If possible, have your crew kill or capture the snake. Knowing what kind of snake caused the bite will be important to professional medical personnel in determining which antivenin to administer.

If the victim can be transported to professional medical personnel within thirty minutes, keep him lying down and calm and transport him as quickly as possible. If possible, contact professional medical assistance and let them know you are on the way and what kind of snake was involved. In many locations, snake antivenin must be ordered from central supplies and your call will help speed the process.

If professional medical assistance is more than

Emergency Treatment of Injuries Inflicted by Marine Animals

Type of Injury	Marine Animal Involved	Emergency Treatment	Possible Complications
Major bite or laceration	Shark Barracuda Alligator gar	Control bleeding. Cleanse wound. Treat for shock. Administer CPR. Splint injury.	Shock. Infections.
Minor bite or laceration	Moral eel Turtle Corals	Cleanse wound. Splint injury.	Infections.
Sting	Jellyfish Portuguese man-of-war Anemones Corals Hydra	Inactivate toxin with alcohol or meat tenderizer. Apply talcum powder, and scrape nematocysts from skin.	Allergic reactions. Respiratory arrest.
Puncture	Urchins Cone shells Stingrays Spiny fish	Soak in hot water.	Allergic reactions. Respiratory and circulatory collapse. Infections. Tetanus.
Poisoning	Puffer fish Scombroids (tuna species) Ciguatera Shellfish	Induce vomiting. Give victim water or milk. Administer CPR. Prevent self-injury from convulsions.	Allergic reactions. Asthmatic reactions. Numbness. Temperature reversal. Respiratory and circulatory collapse.

thirty minutes away, attempt to assess whether the snake actually injected a significant quantity of venom into the victim. If the bite area exhibits two distinct puncture wounds about 1 inch (2.5 cm) apart, the bite is likely from a pit viper, such as a rattlesnake, a copperhead, or a cottonmouth. If within five to ten minutes of the attack, the victim does not experience a burning sensation at the site of the bite, it is unlikely that a significant quantity of venom was injected. Keep the victim calm, and transport him to professional medical assistance as quickly as possible.

If the bite area exhibits two distinct punctures and the victim experiences a burning sensation at the site of the bite, a significant quantity of venom has probably been injected, which could be life threatening. If medical assistance is more than thirty minutes away, you will have to suction as much of the venom out of the wound as possible. With a razor blade or sharp knife that has been sterilized in alcohol or by being heated over a flame and allowed to cool, make a ½-inch incision ¼ inch (1 by 0.5 cm) deep over each puncture wound. The cut should run along the long axis of the victim's arm or leg to avoid cutting across muscle tissue. If a snakebite kit is available, use its suction cup to suction out the venom. If no snakebite kit is available and you have no open cuts or sores in your mouth, suck and spit out as much of the venom as possible. Snake venom works through the bloodstream and is not harmful in the digestive track. Transport the victim to professional medical assistance as rapidly as possible.

ANAPHYLAXIS

Many victims of certain types of ingested poisons and of stings and bites from insects and hazardous marine life suffer a severe allergic reaction called anaphylaxis, which is a type of shock.

Anaphylaxis is often marked by a flushing, itching, or burning of the victim's skin, especially in the face and upper chest; swollen welts spreading over the body; swelling of the face, tongue, and lips; and a bluish coloring to the lips. The victim may also experience a tightness or constriction in the chest, wheezing or coughing, and difficulty exhaling.

Many individuals who are subject to such severe allergic reactions carry with them a small kit containing injectable epinephrine and an oral antihistamine. If such a kit is available, inject the epinephrine into a muscle in the victim's upper arm or hip. If the victim is conscious, administer the kit's oral antihistamine. Watch the victim closely. The injection of epinephrine may relieve symptoms momentarily, but they may recur and she may require additional injections of epinephrine or oral administrations of antihistamines.

If epinephrine and antihistamines are not available, the victim of anaphylaxis may well experience severe difficulties breathing and may

experience cardiac arrest. If the victim stops breathing, open and maintain her airway and administer mouth-to-mouth ventilation. If she does not have a pulse, execute chest compressions. (See the earlier sections of this chapter on how to perform these procedures.)

Insulin Shock and Diabetic Coma

Glucose (sugar) is as vital to the functioning of the brain as oxygen. Brain cells deprived of glucose can suffer severe and permanent damage. Glucose enters the body in the foods we eat, but it cannot enter the body's cells without the presence of insulin, a natural hormone normally produced by the body itself.

Diabetics are individuals whose bodies produce either no insulin or insufficient levels of insulin. Diabetics whose bodies produce no natural insulin must inject insulin daily. Diabetics whose bodies produce insufficient levels of insulin often can control their condition by balancing their intake of glucose in the foods they eat.

Diabetics can suffer medical emergencies from either of two situations: insulin shock, in which the level of glucose in their blood is too low; or diabetic coma, in which the level of glucose in their blood is too high.

The signs of both conditions are similar and make distinguishing between and treating them appropriately very difficult (see the accompanying table). The primary difference, which will be readily apparent, is that the symptoms of insulin shock often appear in a matter of minutes while the symptoms of diabetic coma normally appear over several hours. Diabetics normally are quite familiar with their disease and, if they are conscious, can tell you which condition they are suffering from and what you should do to help them.

INSULIN SHOCK

Of the two conditions, insulin shock is by far the more serious. If it is not treated promptly, severe brain damage can result. Insulin shock can be brought on by the victim taking too much insulin,

SIGNS OF INSULIN SHOCK AND DIABETIC COMA

Observation	Insulin Shock	Diabetic Coma
Skin	Pale and moist	Warm and dry
Pulse	Normal, or rapid and full	Rapid and weak
Breathing	Normal or rapid	Gasping
Breath odor	Normal	Sweet or fruity
Thirst	Absent	Intense
Hunger	Intense	Absent
Vomiting	Unlikely	Likely
Headache	Present	Absent
Mood	Irritable	Restless
Food intake	Insufficient	Excessive
Insulin dosage	Excessive	Insufficient
Possible complications	Seizure or coma	Coma
Response to treatment	Immediate—after sugar is administered	Gradual—within six to eight hours following medication

taking a regular dose of insulin but not eating enough food, or exercising excessively and using up his body's available store of glucose. The victim of insulin shock usually will have pale, moist skin, sweat profusely, experience dizziness or headache or both, and may appear to be drunk before suffering a convulsion or seizure or lapsing into unconsciousness or both.

The appropriate treatment for insulin shock is to give the victim sugar. Fortunately, administering sugar to the victim of insulin shock is likely to correct his condition in a few minutes and prevent serious brain damage or death, which can result from diabetic coma.

For that reason, if you suspect either insulin shock or diabetic coma and the victim is conscious, give him sugar. The best way to administer sugar is in fruit juice (sweetened with sugar, if possible), a candy bar, or even cake decorating gel.

If the victim is not conscious, check and maintain his airway. If he suffers a convulsion or seizure, treat him as detailed in the section on

convulsions and seizures later in this chapter. Attempting to administer sugar in a liquid form (such as fruit juice) to an unconscious victim of insulin shock risks choking him. However, if it will be more than thirty minutes before you can get the victim to professional medical assistance, you must get sugar in some form into his bloodstream. Place a glucose-laden substance—such as refined sugar, syrup, or cake decorating gel—beneath his tongue, allow it to dissolve, and replenish the supply often. Since the victim will not be able to swallow, not much of the glucose will enter his stomach and then his bloodstream, but you will have done all you can. Transport him to professional medical assistance as quickly as possible.

DIABETIC COMA

The breathing of a victim of diabetic coma often will be rapid and consist of deep sighs, her skin will be warm and dry, and her breath will smell sweet or fruity. The victim may suffer a convulsion or seizure or lapse into unconsciousness or both. If either of these conditions is evident, treat the victim as detailed in the following section on convulsions and seizures.

Most diabetics who are dependent on insulin carry injectable insulin with them. If the victim shows signs of diabetic coma and insulin is available, inject a dose into the muscle of the victim's arm or thigh. If insulin is not available, the victim should be transported to professional medical assistance. Since the serious effects of diabetic coma develop over a period of several hours, that transportation should be carried out as quickly as practical but does not need to be conducted as an emergency evacuation.

Convulsions and Seizures

Prevent the victim from injuring herself, but do not attempt to restrain her. Loosen her clothing. If the victim's jaw is clinched, do not attempt to thrust an object between her teeth. If her mouth is open, insert a soft object—such as a rolled handkerchief—between her back teeth.

Most convulsions and seizures last only a few moments, and your best course of action is to prevent the victim from injuring herself and to observe her closely. Some victims will experience respiration difficulties immediately after the attack. If this occurs, maintain an open airway by placing the victim in a reclining position on her side or stomach. If she stops breathing, ventilate using a mouth-to-nose technique.

Once the convulsion or seizure has passed, the victim is likely to be exhausted and may be dazed or semiconscious. Allow her to rest quietly, and do not attempt to give her any fluids until she is fully conscious.

If the victim has suffered convulsions or seizures in the past, the incident probably is not serious and requires no further intervention on your part. If the victim has never suffered a convulsion or seizure before, the incident may well be extremely serious. If the victim shows any of the other signs related to stroke (described in the following section), transport her to professional medical assistance as quickly as possible.

Stroke

Stroke is the result of an insufficient supply of oxygenated blood to the brain. If the flow of oxygenated blood to the brain is interrupted for more than six minutes, irreversible damage can occur in that portion of the brain that has lost its supply of oxygen.

Stroke can be caused by a gradual narrowing of the arteries that supply blood to the brain, by the blockage of these arteries by a blood clot that forms elsewhere in the body (such as in the heart), or by the rupture of an artery. The first two causes of stroke normally are associated with elderly people or those who suffer from heart disease. The rupture of an artery serving the brain, however, can be the result of an inherent weakness in the artery and can occur in young and otherwise healthy people.

The signs of stroke include partial or complete paralysis of the face muscles or the extremities or both on one side of the body (both sides of the body are rarely affected at the same time); varying levels of consciousness ranging from confusion or dizziness to a total loss of consciousness; difficulties with speech, vision, or swallowing; convulsions; and headache.

Stroke victims often suffer paralysis of the airway following the incident. If you suspect stroke, immediately check and, if necessary, open and maintain the victim's airway. A stroke victim is likely to be extremely frightened because of his inability to communicate. Calm and reassure him as much as possible. If he suffers paralysis, lay him with the paralyzed side down and pad his extremities carefully to avoid further injury.

There is nothing you can do aboard ship to relieve the symptoms of stroke or determine its likely consequences, which can range from mild and temporary disability to severe disability and death. Any victim whom you suspect has suffered stroke should be transported to professional medical care as quickly as possible.

Eye Injuries

Small foreign bodies, such as sand or grit, lying in the lower half of the eye usually can be flushed away with clean water or a mild saline solution.

Foreign bodies that have adhered to the eyeball or are lodged under the upper eyelid usually must be removed manually. While the victim is looking down, grasp the eyelashes of the injured eye with your thumb and index finger. Lay a matchstick or cotton-tipped applicator on top of the eyelid and fold the eyelid back over it. Carefully remove the object from the eyeball with a cotton-tipped applicator or a small piece of gauze folded into a point.

The victim of a blow to the eye from a blunt object may complain of difficulty seeing or of double vision. The eye may bleed inside the covering of the iris. Have the victim lie down and close his eye; then cover the injured eye with a sterile dressing loosely taped in place. Since both eyes move together, also loosely tape a dressing over the uninjured eye to prevent unnecessary movement. Transport the victim to professional medical assistance as rapidly as practical. The victim should remain lying down and stay as still as possible during transportation to avoid further potential injury.

If the eyeball has been penetrated by an object, make no attempt to remove it. Have the victim lie down. Do not apply any pressure to the eye, even if severe bleeding is present. If possible, place a paper cup or other protective covering over both the eye and the penetrating object and tape it in place. Loosely tape a dressing over the uninjured eye to prevent unnecessary movement. Have the victim lie as still as possible on his back, and transport him to professional medical assistance as quickly as practical.

If the victim has suffered a chemical burn to his eyes, flush them with clean water continuously and thoroughly for ten to fifteen minutes. If only one eye is affected, turn the victim's head so that the injured eye is lower than the uninjured eye, to avoid flushing the caustic solution into the uninjured eye. If pain or instinctive reaction prohibits the victim from opening an injured eye wide enough to ensure thorough and complete flushing, place your thumb as close as possible beneath his lower eyelid and your index finger at the top of his upper eyelid and force the eyelid to remain open during the flushing process. Once you have thoroughly flushed out the injured eye, cover both eyes with a loosely taped dressing and transport the victim to professional medical assistance as quickly as practical.

Heatstroke and Heat Exhaustion

Move the victim to the coolest possible area, and use fans or air conditioning, if available. Remove her clothing and immerse her in cold (not ice) water, cover her with towels soaked in cold water, or sponge off her skin with cold water until her body temperature returns to normal. If the victim is conscious and not vomiting, administer liquids. Do not administer alcohol.

Hypothermia

Symptoms of hypothermia appear when the body's core temperature—normally 98.6°F (37°C)—falls below 95°F (35°C). As the body's core temperature drops, hypothermia progresses through five general stages.

1. When core temperature falls to between 90 and 95° F (32.3–35°C), the victim is likely to shiver, stamp his feet, and jump up and down in an effort to create additional internal heat. When the core temperature drops below about 90°F, shivering stops.
2. With a core temperature from 90°F down to about 86°F (30°C), the victim will exhibit a loss of small muscle activity, such as a lack of coordinated finger motion.
3. As core temperature drops below about

85°F (29.4°C), the hypothermia victim will become lethargic and sleepy and lose interest in battling his condition.

4. At a core temperature of around 80°F (26.6°C), the victim's pulse and respiration slow and become weaker. The victim may become irrational and then lapse into unconsciousness and finally into a coma.

5. When the core temperature reaches 78°F (25.5°C), death can occur.

Recent incidents and studies have shown that when core temperature is reduced rapidly (such as when an individual falls into icy water and becomes trapped), the body's metabolism can slow to remarkably low levels. Hypothermia victims revived after being deprived of oxygen for several hours have suffered no apparent damage to their brain, heart, or other vital organs. For this reason, rescuers attempting to revive a hypothermia victim should continue resuscitation efforts until the victim's body temperature has risen to near-normal levels and he still does not exhibit such vital signs as a heartbeat, a pulse, or breathing. Emergency medical technicians assume no hypothermia victim is dead until he is "warm dead."

Treat hypothermia as follows.

1. Immediately remove a suspected victim of hypothermia from the cold environment.

2. If the victim is unconscious, check his respiration and pulse. If either is weak or absent, begin basic life support immediately by clearing an airway, administering mouth-to-mouth ventilation and, if necessary, performing chest compressions.

3. As soon as respiration and a pulse are restored, move the victim to a warm area, strip away any wet clothing, and wrap the victim completely in warm blankets. Hypothermia victims whose core temperature has fallen low enough to weaken their respiration or pulse or trigger irrational behavior or unconsciousness can experience severe cardiac arrhythmias as their core body temperature returns to normal, and they must be transported as rapidly as possible to professional medical assistance. If medical help is more than fifteen minutes away, attempt to arrange helicopter evacuation.

If a victim of mild hypothermia has not lost consciousness, has strong respiration and pulse, and is alert and well oriented, he is unlikely to require hospitalization. Make the victim rest, keep him warm and dry, and administer small sips of warm liquids until the victim's external body temperature returns to normal.

Frostbite

Transport the victim suffering from frostbite to shelter. If possible, warm the affected area by immersing it in tepid water, then gradually adding warm water until the water temperature is between 102 and 105°F (38.8–40.5°C). If warm water is not available, warm the affected area by wrapping it in clothing or blankets. Do not rub the affected area, do not apply excessive heat, and do not allow the victim to expose the affected area to excessive heat. Discontinue warming efforts as soon as normal skin color returns to the affected area. If normal color does not return to the affected area and it still appears whitish, transport the victim to professional medical assistance as quickly as possible.

Seasickness

Seasickness results from a disruption of the balance mechanism in the inner ear, which can be triggered by the motion of the vessel on the sea or by such visual signals as a tossing foredeck or rolling waves. While seasickness itself is hardly a life-threatening emergency, extreme cases can lead to severe dehydration, which can have severe consequences.

The best approach for individuals who are prone

to seasickness is to prevent its onset. Many individuals find the most effective preventative is a patch affixed to the mastoid bone just behind the ear that slowly releases a 0.5 mg dose of scopolamine every twenty-four hours. Such patches normally contain a total of 1.5 mg of the drug and are designed to be effective for seventy-two hours. If prevention for longer periods is required, additional patches may be affixed over the mastoid bone on alternate sides every seventy-two hours. Other people find they are best helped by such oral motion sickness compounds as Dramamine or Bonine. Either type of preventative should be employed at least four hours prior to embarking on any trip to sea, and either can cause extreme drowsiness and a dry mouth. Still other people have reported success from wristbands that purport to work through exerting force on an acupressure point, but these results may be more psychological than physical because there is little scientific evidence to support the claim.

Once at sea, anyone who begins to feel queasy should refrain from eating heavy foods or drinking alcoholic beverages. Some people do, however, find that nibbling on soda crackers and sipping carbonated beverages helps settle their stomachs. Individuals who feel a bout of seasickness coming on should stay on deck rather than going below. Confinement in a closed space often makes the malady worse and can trigger vomiting, whereas fresh air often dissipates symptoms. It's best if such individuals station themselves at the vessel's most stable point, such as in the cockpit rather than on the flying bridge. Focusing their eyes on the horizon rather than on the vessel or the sea tossing around them may also help restore a sense of equilibrium to the balance mechanism in their inner ears and cause the symptoms of seasickness to subside.

Individuals who experience severe seasickness to the point of actually vomiting often react in one of two ways: after the initial attack, some people "get their sea legs" and have no further problems; others find themselves completely unable to keep anything on their stomachs and become caught up in a cycle of violent vomiting. If this goes on for more than about twelve hours, it can lead to serious consequences from dehydration. The most dependable treatment is simply to return the individuals to shore. After a few hours on dry land, they normally will be able to take liquid nourishment and will recover without medical attention.

If returning to land is impossible (such as on a long open-water voyage) or does not relieve the symptoms, the most effective treatment is administration of Dramamine or Compazine suppositories. After the administration of two or three suppositories about four to six hours apart, seasick individuals normally will be able to take enough liquids to avoid dehydration until they can reach land. Once onshore, they should seek professional medical assistance.

WHEN TO CALL FOR EMERGENCY EVACUATION

Evacuating a victim from your vessel to another vessel or a helicopter can be an extremely hazardous undertaking for the victim, for those aboard your own vessel, and possibly for the crew of the rescue unit to which the victim is to be transferred, especially if the weather is rough.

Your decision whether to attempt emergency evacuation should be guided by your answers to five critical questions.

1. Does the victim require professional medical assistance you cannot provide aboard your vessel in order to survive?
2. How quickly must she get to that professional medical care in order to live?
3. How quickly can you transport her there aboard your own vessel?
4. How quickly can she be transported there by another vessel or a helicopter?
5. Is the difference between the time you can get her to professional medical care and the time she can be transported to

that care by another vessel or a helicopter sufficient to justify exposing the victim, your crew, and the crew of the rescue vessel or aircraft to the potential hazards of emergency evacuation?

Your answers to the first two questions depend on the victim's emergency and your estimation of the seriousness of her condition. Emergencies that put life in critical danger and about which you can do virtually nothing without advanced medical training and life-support equipment include heart attack, stroke, severe airway obstructions you cannot relieve, serious head injury, severe internal bleeding, severe external bleeding you cannot control, significant open chest or abdominal wounds, significant third-degree burns, and severe poisoning. Transporting victims of these medical emergencies to professional medical care as quickly as possible and by any means possible is absolutely critical if they are to survive.

Your answers to the last three questions depend on circumstances. How far are you away from professional medical care? What is your vessel's maximum speed, and how long will it take you to transport the victim there? How soon can an emergency vessel or helicopter reach you? How severe is the weather, and what hazards will it impose on the evacuation procedure?

CONDUCTING EMERGENCY EVACUATION

If your answers to the above questions convince you that emergency evacuation is necessary, contact the coast guard on VHF channel 16 or SSB frequency 2182 kHz to arrange for the dispatch of a rescue unit. Once you reach the coast guard, they usually will instruct you to shift to a working channel, which most likely will be VHF channel 22A or SSB channel 2670 kHz. Be prepared to tell them why emergency evacuation is necessary and give them detailed information about your vessel's position and wind and sea conditions. Once evacuation is agreed on, it's imperative that you or a crew member to whom you assign the task monitors the working frequency until the evacuation is complete.

While the rescue unit is en route, prepare the victim for evacuation. Tag her with a brief but specific description of the injury or illness she has sustained or the symptoms she has exhibited, list any medications you have administered or procedures you have performed, and include any other information that might be pertinent (for example, the victim has previously suffered heart problems or epileptic attacks or is allergic to certain medications). If the victim is unconscious, include her name and age, name and telephone contact information for her next of kin, and her blood type, if you know it.

In cold weather, the victim should be dressed warmly if the injuries permit, but avoid loose-fitting clothing or headgear, which could become entangled in hoisting equipment. If the injuries permit, the victim should be fitted with a life jacket.

Clear an evacuation path aboard your vessel. To avoid exposing the victim to the weather, it's best if you can keep her inside the vessel until the rescue unit arrives, but clear a wide, unobstructed path between the holding area inside the vessel and the area on deck from which the victim will be offloaded. If a litter is required to transport the victim to the rescue unit, the coast guard will provide one. If the nature of the victim's illness or injuries requires you to bring the litter inside your vessel to load the victim, you will need to clear an unobstructed path that will admit a rigid litter approximately 7 feet long by 2½ feet wide (2 by 0.8 m).

You and all members of your crew should put on life jackets before the rescue unit arrives, even those who are assigned to stay inside the vessel, because their presence might be required on deck. Make certain your flare kit, spotlight, and any other signal devices you have on board are accessible and ready for service in case they're required to pinpoint your location, but don't fire a flare unless requested to do so by the rescue unit or the coast station.

If the rescue unit the coast guard dispatches is to be a ship, break out your fenders and docklines in preparation for rafting alongside it.

Evacuation by Helicopter

If the rescue unit the coast guard dispatches is a helicopter, it will be an H-3, which can fly a maximum of 300 nautical miles seaward from the closest refueling point, loiter over a vessel for a maximum of twenty minutes, then return to land. Coast guard rescue helicopters normally do not conduct rescue operations in conjunction with the U.S. Navy.

For helicopter evacuation, you will need to clear a hoist area aboard your vessel. On a large powerboat, the preferred hoist area normally will be its highest and aftmost deck, which in most cases will be the cabintop.

If your dinghy is stowed on the cabintop, launch it, if possible, to get it out of the way and tow it astern on a long painter. Also, lower and secure any bimini tops on the upper deck and any masts or antennas that will not be needed to communicate with the coast station or the helicopter.

If the evacuation must be conducted at night, arrange to light the hoist area and any obstructions with mast lights or handheld flashlights or both. Handheld flashlights must, however, always be focused on the hoist area or any obstructions and not pointed toward the helicopter because they could temporarily blind the pilot.

Assign each member of the crew specific duties, such as manning the helm and the radio, lighting the hoist area and any obstructions, receiving the litter on deck, getting the patient to the hoist area, and steadying the litter as it is hoisted into the helicopter. Once the helicopter arrives overhead, the noise from its rotors will be deafening and normal spoken communications will be impossible. Agree on a simple set of hand signals for such commands as "wait," "go back," "come on," and "OK." The universal signal for the helicopter to lower the litter is to hold both arms horizontal with fists clinched and thumbs pointed downward. The universal signal for the helicopter to hoist the litter is to hold both arms above the horizontal with fists clinched and thumbs pointed upward.

As the helicopter approaches your position, the pilot normally will contact you by radio and ask for particulars of wind and sea conditions and your vessel's hoist area.

Helicopter pilots normally fly from the starboard seat, the chopper's hoist is mounted on the starboard side, and due to the counterclockwise rotation of the helicopter's rotor, the helicopter is most maneuverable if the wind strikes it from ahead or on the starboard forward quarter. For maximum visibility, therefore, the helicopter pilot normally will want to put the starboard forward quarter of his craft toward your vessel.

Once the helicopter arrives, reduce your vessel's speed to the minimum required to maintain steerage. If the pickup is to be made from your vessel's stern, put the wind 30 degrees on the port bow. If the pickup is to be made from your vessel's bow, put the wind 30 degrees on the starboard bow.

In many cases, the helicopter's hoist man will first lower a trail line, which will be attached to the bottom of the litter and will allow your crew to guide the litter to the hoist area. This line will be nonstatic and can be handled safely (see illustration next page).

When the litter approaches your vessel, allow it to touch the deck and discharge any static electricity before handling it.

At no point in the evacuation should the helicopter be attached to your vessel by either the trail line or the hoist line. Make certain neither becomes entangled with any part of your vessel, and warn your crew to stand clear of both. In severe weather, the helicopter pilot may instruct you to detach the litter from the hoist cable to give him more maneuverability while you load the patient. In other cases, you may have to move the litter from the hoist area to the inside of your vessel to load the patient. The litter must never be moved from the hoist area without first detaching it from the hoist cable.

Put the victim in the litter, making sure her arms

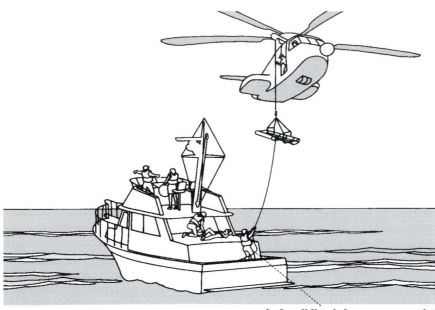

When evacuating a victim by helicopter, guide the litter to your vessel's deck by using the trail line. Never tie it off, but make sure it doesn't become entangled.

end of trail line is loose, unentangled

and legs are well inside. If the litter has straps, use them to strap the victim in the litter securely. It normally is not a good idea to cover the victim with a blanket because it could become entangled in the hoist mechanism.

Do not give the helicopter the hoist signal until you are certain the patient is well secured in the litter and all crew members are clear of the litter, the hoist cable, and the trail line. Once you are sure everything is ready, signal the helicopter with the thumbs-up signal to hoist the litter.

During hoisting, use the trail line to steady the litter until it is clear of your vessel. Hoisting the litter with a victim in it is potentially the most dan-

gerous part of the evacuation process, particularly in heavy winds or seas. Use all available crew to help steady the litter, but caution them to watch themselves as well. The last thing you need in this situation is to have one of your healthy crew members fall overboard.

During the hoisting operation, the pilot will attempt to hold the helicopter as steady as possible and allow the hoist operator to bring the litter aboard with an electric winch. Once the litter is clear of your vessel, throw any remaining part of the trail line overboard to leeward, making certain it does not become entangled with any part of your vessel or any of your crew.

Understanding Abandon-Ship Procedures

Abandoning ship is a procedure filled with potential hazards and should be undertaken only if your vessel is fully involved with a fire or is in imminent danger of sinking. In many cases, even vessels that have been seriously holed will remain afloat for hours or even days due to their natural buoyancy or to air trapped inside their hulls or superstructure.

At the first inkling that a fire or a breach of your hull's integrity may become serious enough to require you to abandon ship, mentally run through the steps the procedure requires and alert your crew that you are considering that extreme course of action. But don't give the actual abandon-ship order until you are certain there is no way you can contain the fire or the hull damage to allow you and your crew to remain on board until help arrives. (Recommended procedures for fighting a fire on board are covered fully in chapter 28. Recommended procedures for dealing with severe hull damage are found in chapter 27.)

If the situation aboard your vessel is serious enough for you to consider abandoning ship, you and your crew may already be dressed in warm clothes and wearing life jackets. But if a serious emergency arises suddenly (a fire or severe hull damage resulting from striking a submerged object in the middle of the night), as soon as you even wonder if you might have to abandon ship, put on warm clothes and your own life jacket and order your crew to do likewise. If you have to order your crew into the raft, they could very well wind up in the water, and warm clothing and a life jacket could prove to be, literally, the margin between life and death.

Exposure to hypothermia (extreme loss of body heat) is one of the greatest dangers you and your crew face in an abandon-ship situation. Long pants, long-sleeved shirts, jackets, and sweaters can help preserve valuable body heat, even if they are soaked.

Instruct a trained crew member to stand by the life raft and prepare to launch it. As a part of the routine safety training aboard your vessel, you should have thoroughly familiarized at least one crew member with your life raft and its proper deployment. That crew member should, for instance, know how to make certain the raft is tethered to the main vessel before it is launched. Ideally, you stow your life raft on deck in its own canister, and it is equipped with a CO_2 automatic inflation device. If you carry your life raft below decks or it must be manually inflated, the crew member should know where it is located and how to inflate it quickly.

While your crew is preparing to launch the life raft, transmit the Mayday distress call and message the moment the situation aboard your vessel becomes serious enough for you to decide to abandon the boat. If you delay transmitting the distress call and message, rising water or fire could disable the batteries that power your radio in a matter of minutes. The circumstances under which you should transmit both the Pan-Pan urgency call and message and the Mayday distress call and message and the correct procedure for doing so are covered fully in chapter 23.

If your boating takes you off the beaten path, you should have assembled an abandon-ship bag, which you can grab quickly on your way to the life raft. It should be fitted with flotation and a 50-foot (15 m) floating lanyard, which ideally you will have time to attach to your life raft before you depart your vessel. Its most important contents will be at least half a gallon (2 L) of freshwater per person or a hand-operated reverse-osmosis water maker or solar still (or both).

One item you should be certain gets into the life raft is your vessel's emergency position-indicating radio beacon (EPIRB). Other items that normally will not be part of your abandon-ship bag but you should try to grab if you have time include your handheld VHF radio (preferably one classified as "submersible" or one housed in a waterproof container), your medical kit, any special medications or eyeglasses you require, your passport, and a few dollars in American currency. It's a good idea, in fact, for each member of the crew to keep special medications, eyeglasses, their passports, and a little cash close by their bunk in a waterproof container, which they can grab quickly on their way out.

If you have time, also grab any additional flares or other signaling devices, water, provisions, and clothing you can get to quickly.

Make certain the life raft is tethered to your vessel, and launch it. Ideally, your life raft will already be tethered to your vessel in its canister. If it isn't and you fail to tether it, there is a good chance it can be swept away by the sea.

In calm seas, launch the life raft at your vessel's stern, where the freeboard is likely to be lowest, to make loading and boarding the raft easiest. In heavy seas, launch the life raft to leeward amidships, which will position it opposite the most stable part of the vessel, make it easier to board, and provide a bit of protection from the weather in the lee of the vessel's superstructure. Another reason for launching the raft to leeward is that the inflation lanyard on most CO_2-equipped life rafts is 25 to 40 feet (7.5–12 m) long and must be pulled out entirely before the life raft will inflate. Launching the life raft to leeward will carry it away from your vessel and speed the inflation process. A life raft launched to windward is likely to be blown up onto the vessel, making boarding it difficult. As heavy seas lift the stern of your vessel, a life raft launched to windward can become trapped under the stern and could be punctured by the rudder or propeller. In a heavy sea, launching a life raft to leeward does create the possibility that the vessel could be driven down on it. To avoid this, do not pull the life raft's tether line up tightly to your vessel, but leave 2 to 3 feet (0.5–1 m) of slack in it.

Once you launch the raft, one crew member should steady it while a second crew member boards. If you have time, the crew member in the life raft should release the heaving line attached to the side of the raft and throw it back to a crew member on deck. The tether line should then be slackened and the life raft lashed alongside the vessel using its tether and heaving line. Attach these to your vessel at angles of approximately 45 degrees to make the life raft more stable and easier to board and load. Again, leave enough slack in the lines to allow the life raft to ride 2 to 3 feet (0.5–1 m) to leeward of your vessel's hull.

Load your crew and emergency supplies into the life raft, and have them fend it off from your vessel while you load your emergency gear to avoid snagging the life raft on anything that might puncture it. If at all possible, the crew should step or lower themselves directly from your vessel into the life raft rather than jumping into the water and then trying to crawl up into the raft. If you can accomplish this maneuver, you lessen the danger of crew members being swept away from the raft. In cold waters, you also reduce the danger of hypothermia.

A class A EPIRB and a type 406 category 1 EPIRB are automatically activated by immersion in water. A class S EPIRB packed inside a life raft is automatically activated when the life raft inflates. Class B and mini-B EPIRBs and type 406 category 2 EPIRBs must be manually activated. Make certain your EPIRB is securely attached to your life raft, and activate it as soon as you enter the raft.

It makes sense to fire a red meteor or parachute flare as soon as you depart your vessel. In heavily traveled areas, there is a reasonable possibility it will be sighted by a nearby vessel. Even in remote areas, there is always the possibility that it will be spotted by a vessel out of your line of sight over the horizon or obscured by darkness or weather and that the vessel will come into your vicinity to investigate its source. Do not fire any other flares until rescuers are within sight or hearing.

Keep the life raft tethered to your vessel as long as possible. Obviously, if your vessel is afire or about to sink, you will have to cut the lines. But if your vessel is merely awash, keep the life raft tethered to it as long as possible. (In heavy seas, free the heaving line and pay out the full length of the life raft's tether to keep the raft away from your main vessel and avoid its being trapped beneath the vessel or punctured by any protrusions.) You may be able to go back aboard for other supplies or provisions you failed to get into the life raft when you abandoned ship, and even an awash vessel provides a larger target for potential rescuers to spot than a lone life raft.

TIPS ON LIFE RAFT SURVIVAL

If you ever have the misfortune to find yourself adrift at sea in a life raft for an extended period of time, here are the tough realities of some of the problems you would face and several hints that might ensure your chances of surviving the ordeal.

Do Not Leave the Life Raft

No matter how tantalizingly close land may seem, *never* leave the life raft and attempt to swim for shore. Distances over water are deceptive, and your goal almost inevitably will be much farther away than you think it is. You may well be in a severely weakened state physically—and perhaps mentally—and find you are unable to swim even a short distance that you could handle easily under more normal circumstances. You also expose yourself to hypothermia and attack by sharks.

Assume That Rescue, If It Comes at All, Will Arrive Later Rather Than Sooner

Don't delude yourself into thinking that just because you activated an EPIRB, help is on the way. Even if your signal reaches the coast guard, there are several reasons they are not likely to launch a full air-sea rescue search for you immediately. One is that more than 90 percent of the distress signals the coast guard receives from both marine EPIRBs and their close cousins, the emergency location transmitters carried aboard aircraft, turn out to be false alarms due to the unit being activated accidentally. (Of the 7,700 alerts the coast guard receives over 121.5 MHz in a typical quarter, it ultimately determines the source of only about 220—less than 3 percent. In those cases where it is able to identify the source of the alert, only about fourteen turn out to be genuine distress situations.) Another is that the coast guard's expanded responsibilities for illegal drug interdiction have strained its resources, and it may not have men or equipment available to deploy immediately. A third reason is that the coast guard is under tremendous pressures to hold down its expenses (it now costs some $8,000 an hour to operate a C-130 air-sea rescue aircraft).

For these reasons, the coast guard has an extensive—and time-consuming—list of procedures it goes through to try to confirm that a signal from a class A, B, mini-B, or S EPIRB represents a genuine emergency. Even if the coast guard receives a 121.5 MHz distress alert, which was relayed from a satellite, in the absence of other corroborating evidence of an actual distress such as receipt of a distress call over VHF or SSB radio or receipt of the EPIRB signal by an overflying aircraft, it normally will wait for verification by a second satellite pass before it launches a search (which can take up to two hours). For these reasons, the average time between the receipt of a distress signal from one of these EPIRBs and the commencement of full-scale air-sea rescue effort is twenty-six hours!

Once a full air-sea search is initiated, the rescuers still have to find you. If your class A, B, mini-B, or S EPIRB's signal is picked up by a satellite, it provides a fix that is accurate only within 10 to 20 nautical miles. If its signal is picked up by a lone aircraft flying overhead at 35,000 feet (10,575 m)—a typical altitude for over-water flights—that single fix narrows the area potential rescuers must search only to some 600 square miles (1,560 km²), which is still a lot of ocean.

The coast guard responds much more rapidly to distress alerts received from type 406 EPIRBs because the 406 MHz component of its signal transmits a 121-bit serial number that is distinctive to a particular unit. For type 406 EPIRBs registered in the United States, the coast guard can use that serial number to access a computer that stores information about the vessel aboard which that EPIRB is carried. With that information, they can check with the vessel's owner or the owner's representative who has a float plan to confirm that the vessel is in fact in the vicinity from which the signal was received.

A type 406 signal received by a COSPAS/ SARSAT satellite significantly narrows the search area because it provides a fix accurate to within 1½ to 3 nautical miles (2.5–5 km). Newer EPIRBs with GPS included narrow the reported location to within feet.

Ration Your Water and Provisions for an Extended Stay at Sea

Those who have spent long periods adrift at sea on a life raft say that for the first few days it's fairly easy to ration food and water. After about a week, however, it's easy to convince yourself you might as well go ahead and eat and drink everything you have on board because if you save it, you won't live long enough to benefit from it. Half a cup of freshwater or other liquid per person each twenty-four hours is about the minimum required to sustain life over an extended period. On that basis, half a gallon (2 L) of water per person would be sufficient only for a little over two weeks, after which a handheld reverse osmosis water maker or solar still becomes an indispensable necessity. *Never* drink unpurified seawater. The salt it contains leads only to faster dehydration and eventual death.

Depression Will Be Your Most Deadly Enemy

No matter how long your ordeal lasts, you must keep your spirits up at all cost. Think of home, family, and friends. If you are religious, think of your God. When hopelessness tries to close in, exert all your strength to shove it out of your mind. One of the earliest signs of depression will be a disinterest in food. If you encounter that in any of your crew, you must force the person to eat. Failure to do so will only hasten the person's spiral into death.

In Cold Water, Hypothermia Will Be Your Second Most Dangerous Enemy

In a survival situation in cold waters, do everything you can to conserve body heat. Remain as much as possible in a fetal position, and use available clothing to cover your head and your crotch area, which are the two greatest areas for loss of body heat.

In Tropical Waters, Your Second-Worst Enemy Will Be Sharks

Bill and Simone Butler survived sixty-six days in a life raft after their sailboat was rammed by whales and sank 1,200 miles (1,935 km) off the coast of Central America. "We were attacked by thirty to forty sharks a day," Bill told me after they were rescued. "They didn't attack the raft with their teeth but butted it with their heads. They came at us day and night so that it was almost impossible for us to get any rest, and each one would ram us ten to fifteen times. They would slam into us at bullet speed, then flip over on their backs and spray the raft with urine. They could spray urine up to 15 feet [4.5 m] into the air. To finish off the attack, they'd give the raft a great slap with their tails."

Fish and Turtles Are Your Most Likely Source of Life-Sustaining Protein

In the open ocean, sea creatures tend to congregate in the shadow of any bit of flotsam they happen across—such as your life raft. Bill and Simone Butler survived their ordeal largely because of the 400 to 500 pounds (180–225 kg) of fish—mostly trigger fish—Bill was able to catch. In one instance, Bill was able to catch a small turtle and wrestle it into the raft. Another time, a marauding undersea predator drove a school of flying fish to the surface near the raft and he was able to catch four of them by hand. The fishing supplies you include in your abandon-ship bag, including artificial and preserved baits, can well provide the critical margin between life and death.

Seabirds Can Be Your Second Most Valuable Resource

Seabirds frequently alight on life rafts and can be caught if you move quickly. Their flesh provides both edible protein and a valuable source of bait to catch other sea creatures.

TIPS ON AIR-SEA RESCUE

Only twelve hours after Bill and Simone Butler's boat sank out from under them, a commercial vessel came within a quarter of a mile (0.4 km) of their life raft but never spotted them. Commercial vessels are required to keep a lookout posted at all times but are notorious for failing to do so.

If you are adrift in a raft and spot a vessel or low-flying aircraft in your vicinity during the day or hear its engines at night, fire off a red meteor or parachute flare. If it's during the day, wave your arms at your sides, preferably holding some bright article of clothing in each hand. If the sun is shining, use a signal mirror. In the case of an aircraft that isn't actually searching for you, you'll probably get only one brief chance to attract the attention of its crew. In the case of a vessel, if you managed to get your VHF radio aboard the raft, transmit a Mayday call over channel 16. (Do not point the radio's antenna at the ship but hold it straight up; radio waves radiate from an antenna in concentric circles.)

If you spot a ship and signal to it but after about fifteen minutes it does not alter course in your direction, fire one more flare, transmit one more Mayday if possible, and continue to wave or flash your signal mirror. If you get no response after that, it's likely they have no lookout or radio watch posted and further effort on your part is probably useless. In either case, don't make the mistake of draining your handheld VHF radio's battery or firing all your flares in a single encounter. You may need both desperately if you happen upon another low-flying aircraft or a commercial vessel that is maintaining a lookout.

As soon as you see a coast guard vessel, fixed-wing aircraft, or helicopter or hear its engines, fire off a red or white meteor or parachute flare, if you have one. In the case of an aircraft, aim the meteor in front of it; aircraft are virtually blind to the rear. As a second choice, in daylight fire a handheld red flare or orange smoke canister, use a signal mirror if the sun is shining, and wave your arms at your sides; at night fire a handheld flare or activate your personal rescue or crew overboard light. If you managed to get a handheld VHF radio aboard your raft, turn it on and broadcast a Mayday distress message on channel 16, remembering to hold the radio straight up.

If the coast guard spots you, what happens from that point on will depend primarily on the type of search-and-rescue craft that has located you and the current weather conditions.

If you are located by a coast guard ship and the sea is calm, it will probably just come alongside your life raft and take you aboard. If a heavy sea is running, the cutter is more likely to launch a rescue team in one of its small boats (probably a rigid-bottom inflatable) to come get you.

If you are located by a helicopter and it approaches you, stay as nearly as possible in the center of your life raft and hang on to it tightly because the helicopter rotors' strong downdraft can flip the raft over. If the weather conditions are at all manageable, the helicopter's crew probably will lower a rescue sling, basket, net, or seat. If you aren't able to communicate with them via a handheld VHF radio, use the hand signals discussed in the previous chapter. If those aboard the life raft are able to get into or onto the conveyance, do so one at a time. If anyone on board the raft is not physically able to manage the transfer, one of the helicopter crew will likely enter the water to assist you. If anyone on the raft is seriously injured, the crew probably will lower a rescue litter to hoist the person aboard.

If you are located by a C-130, it will circle you and wiggle its wings to let you know you have been spotted. If you do not have an operable handheld VHF radio aboard, it will probably drop you a package containing one along with other survival supplies. If that becomes necessary, the aircraft normally will approach your raft from downwind at an altitude of about 300 feet (90 m), drop the package about 100 feet (30 m) from you, then continue to pay out a 200- to 300-foot (60–90 m) lanyard attached to the package, which it will attempt to drop alongside or to windward of you so that it will drift down across your raft. A C-130 cannot effect a pickup at sea but will radio your position to the nearest coast guard ship or helicopter in your vicinity. The C-130 can stay aloft for up to fourteen hours and normally will circle your position as long as its fuel supply will allow it to. As its fuel begins to run low, it may be replaced on station by a second aircraft. If it must leave you, don't panic. It has relayed your position to a helicopter or ship that can pick you up. Help is definitely on the way, but it may take it a while to arrive. If you are out of range of a helicopter and have to wait for a ship to pick you up, it will be steaming toward you at only about 15 knots, so be patient and hang on.

LIFE RAFT INSPECTIONS

As you can see from this chapter, the condition of a life raft and the equipment in it can ultimately affect your survival. Unfortunately, recent cases uncovered by the coast guard have found some life rafts to be totally inadequate for the job. These rafts were packed by unscrupulous or untrained personnel. In some extreme cases, life rafts were actually missing from their canisters, while in other cases inappropriate substitutes were made or rafts were improperly packed.

A life raft should be inspected annually. Such inspection requires certified people who are factory trained by the manufacturer of your particular brand of life raft.

Obviously, it's to your advantage to be present during the annual repacking process. During this time, you can personally check the condition and suitability of the equipment on board. You can add gear or make sure outdated accessories, such as flares and water rations, are upgraded. But, above all, you can make sure the repacking job is done properly. Remember, life rafts are like parachutes. You don't know whether they will work properly until you need them.

PART SIX

The Cruising Life

Handling Money and Mail

If you're planning an extended cruise that will leave you out of touch with home for extended periods of time, there are some basics concerning mail, money, and legal matters you'll want to attend to before you leave.

COVERING THE HOME FRONT

First, update your will and leave a witnessed, notarized copy with your attorney or a trusted relative or friend. Don't make the mistake of leaving the only copy of your will in a safe deposit box. If something happens to you, the authorities normally will seal the box and your survivors will have to go to court to get it opened. It usually can be opened only when federal and state revenue agents are present to list its contents for possible estate taxes.

It's also a good idea to leave your power of attorney with your lawyer or a trusted relative or friend. Ideally, the person won't need to exercise it, but if something serious at home requires your legal authorization, it is most likely to be at a time when it is difficult or impossible for you to get home to sign on the dotted line.

If you expect to have regular income—such as dividend, social security, or pension checks—coming in while you're gone, arrange to have the checks deposited directly to your bank account. You also may need to make provisions for regular payment of such expenses as insurance premiums, home mortgage payments, and estimated taxes. You can have these payments drafted from your checking or savings account, the trust department of most banks will make such payments for you, or you can ask your CPA or a trusted friend or relative to handle them for you. Whoever you ask to handle financial matters for you at home, put your instructions in writing. If something goes wrong, you both will have at least a base of reference as to what you agreed to.

If you have stock options that need to be exercised, bond coupons that need to be clipped, certificates of deposit that need to be rolled over, or investment decisions that need to be executed in your absence, don't forget to set up an arrangement with your banker, accountant, stock broker, or that trusted friend or relative. Again, put your instructions in writing.

KEEPING A CRUISING KITTY

I was visiting aboard the boat of some cruising friends several years ago, and the husband withdrew a small square of paper from his wallet, handed it to me, and said, "If you can figure that out, it's worth about $25,000 to you." On the paper were ten lines of undecipherable letters and numbers. After I had puzzled over it for a few minutes, he took it back and said with a laugh, "We're carrying about $25,000 aboard, which is broken up into packages of $3,000 to $5,000 each, wrapped in plastic, and hidden in various places around the boat. This piece of paper is to remind me where I've hidden it."

I suppose that's one way to handle the matter of cruising funds, but I'd suggest you handle your cruising kitty somewhat differently.

Certainly, it's a good idea to have some ready cash aboard in both U.S. funds and the currencies of the countries you'll be visiting. You can't very well give a check to a customs official who wants his *mordita*—bribe, literally a "little bite"—and you might need fuel, provisions, or repair services in some out-of-the-way place where cash is the only acceptable means of exchange. I suggest you keep a cushion of at least $2,500 available at all times in case you encounter a major expense that can be handled only with cash on the barrelhead, but I wouldn't carry much more than about $5,000 in cash aboard at any one time. If your vessel is robbed or sinks, most marine insurance policies won't cover the loss of cash. Carry your cruising cash in bills no larger than $20 because breaking larger denominations can be a problem in many foreign countries. For the rest of your cash, go to a large regional or national bank and get $100 or so in small denomi-

nations of the currencies of each country you plan to visit. You may have to pay customs and duty fees before you are cleared to go ashore and make a currency exchange. Like my friend, divide your cash into several packages, stash them in various locations around your boat, and make yourself a cue card to help you remember where you hid them. If your vessel is broken into (as *Americas Odyssey* was in St. Anne's Martinique; see chapter 33), at least maybe the robbers won't find all of them.

Carry the bulk of your cruising kitty in traveler's checks so you can get it back if they are lost or stolen, but be sure to keep the receipt apart from the checks themselves.

You generally will find that banks are the best place to convert currency to another currency or to cash traveler's checks. In many countries abroad, banks have limited hours of operation, and catching them when they are open can call for a bit of extra planning, but their exchange rate usually will be better than you'll get in currency-exchange houses, which are open longer hours. When changing money or cashing traveler's checks at a bank, shop for the best rates, since even bank rates can vary a percentage point or two.

Carry a wide variety of credit cards, and use them whenever possible to pay major expenses such as fuel bills, repair services, and shoreside costs. In my travels to some thirty-five countries around the world, I have found MasterCard and Visa the most widely accepted. American Express is also widely recognized, but some smaller merchants refuse to honor it because it carries a higher discount rate. When you pay a bill rendered in a foreign country with a credit card, and then pay the credit card bill in your nation's currency, the rate of exchange will be the one in effect on the day the charge is posted to your account. I've done this a number of times and never felt I was treated unfairly on the exchange rate.

The best arrangement for replenishing your cruising funds during an extended voyage is to maintain an account in a large international bank that has branches in the countries you plan to visit. With today's sophisticated banking computers, you often can get cash within hours, even though you are thousands of miles from home, and pay little or nothing for the service.

In areas where these banks do not have offices of their own, they usually maintain correspondent relationships with local banks. Get a list of your bank's correspondents, and try to work through one of them when you need a fresh infusion of cash or have an emergency. You are likely to get quicker service than you will at a noncorrespondent bank and probably will save money in the bargain. With this kind of setup, your home bank can send you money by wire transfer to its correspondent bank in about two days and the transaction usually will cost you only about $10 U.S.

In my experience, the U.S. bank with the most foreign branches is Citibank. Another international bank with widespread branches is Barclays.

FORWARDING MAIL

If you have a fairly firm itinerary, give a relative or friend the addresses of marinas, yacht clubs, and resorts you plan to visit along the way and your approximate arrival dates at each. Have the person bundle only the important items from a month's or so worth of mail, put it in a sturdy envelope, and mail it to your destination marked with your name, the name of your vessel, and "Hold for Arrival." Caution the person, however, that it can take as much as a week for mail to arrive at its destination and that it's unwise to include checks, cash, or other valuable items.

If you prefer not to ask a relative or friend to handle mail forwarding for you, several companies will do it for you—for a fee, of course. Look for their ads in the major boating magazines.

Don't forget to tell key contacts at home how to reach you via your satellite telephone, VHF, e-mail, or High Seas operators, as we outlined in chapter 9.

Maintaining the Essentials

During a cruise, you probably won't be able to maintain your vessel as immaculately as if it were tied to your home dock, but if you don't keep up with essential maintenance on a consistent basis, the penalty is likely to be at least a significant loss in your vessel's value, which could cost you hundreds or thousands of dollars to restore. Even worse, lack of essential maintenance could result in the failure of a critical part or system just when you need it most. On the plus side, a consistent program of maintenance will help protect your investment in your boat and alert you to potential problems so you can correct them before they cause a serious difficulty.

ALL SYSTEMS

Begin your maintenance program before you ever depart on a cruise. Start by assembling a complete collection of owner's manuals for every basic system and important piece of equipment on your vessel, and organize them alphabetically or in some other logical grouping in a set of loose-leaf notebooks. Extract from the manuals the manufacturer's maintenance recommendations, and compile that information into a maintenance calendar for your particular boat, which tells you what maintenance tasks you need to perform daily, weekly, monthly, semiannually, annually, and after a certain number of operating hours.

Most manufacturers' literature also includes a list of spare parts, supplies, and tools you need to perform recommended maintenance; make sure you get all of them aboard. It's a good idea to develop an inventory system that tells you where spare parts and supplies are stowed aboard your vessel and helps you keep track of their use so you can replace depleted supplies at the earliest opportunity. Also, make a list of manufacturers' hotline telephone numbers and e-mail addresses you can contact to ask questions or order parts if the need arises. For offshore cruisers, some manufacturers will list a single-sideband radio channel they monitor. You also can purchase Vessel Information Management, a computer software program that stores data and tells you when you need to perform particular maintenance functions, keeps up with your inventory of spares, and alerts you when particular items in your spare parts inventory approach minimums and need to be replenished. (See appendix 5 and chapter 34 for more information on the spare parts you should have aboard and how to keep track of them.)

ENGINE MAINTENANCE

Your most critical maintenance tasks will be to keep your main engine(s) and the engine that powers your AC (alternating current) electrical generator humming smoothly.

If you are not intimately familiar with the care and feeding of a diesel engine, I strongly recommend that you attend one of the owner maintenance courses offered by diesel engine distributors. Find out where and when these courses are held by contacting the distributors in your area of the make of engines aboard your vessel or contacting the manufacturer's home office. Owner maintenance courses normally are held over two days, during which you learn the basics of a diesel engine's four flow systems—fuel, oil, coolant, and air—and the specifics of how those systems are handled in your vessel's particular make of engines. If at all possible, attend a course that covers the make of engines with which your vessel is equipped because there are significant differences between the flow systems of two-cycle diesels manufactured by companies like Detroit Diesel and four-cycle diesels made by companies like Caterpillar and Cummins. It's also best to attend a course that is tailored to the specific concerns of the owners of marine diesels rather than of engines used in trucks or industrial equipment, even if it involves a bit of travel and some additional expense on your part.

The best of these courses not only will cover the theory of diesel engine operation but also give you some hands-on instruction in such matters as tim-

ing, disabling, and changing an injector. If you can't find such a course in your area, you can get at least a general overview of diesel engine maintenance by auditing a diesel-engine mechanic's course at a local community college. If attending any kind of diesel engine course is out of the question, at least get a good diesel mechanic to walk you through a diesel's basic operation and show you how to change fuel and oil filters, replace a water pump impeller, prime a dry engine, and clear an air lock.

Fuel Flow Maintenance

Maintaining a dependable flow of clean fuel to the engines on board your vessel begins with the fuel itself and the tanks in which it is stored.

The diesel fuel you take on board your vessel is likely to be full of all manner of contaminants, such as rust from storage tanks, sludge, and plain old dirt. But the most troublesome contaminants are algae, fungi, and other microorganisms that live off nutrients in the fuel itself. If their growth is not prevented or checked, they can congregate in large strings, clumps, or mats of black, brown, or green slime, which can clog your primary and secondary fuel filters and damage metal fuel tanks and rubber gaskets. At best, this buildup will require you to change your fuel filters much more frequently than if you were working with clean fuel; at worst, it can actually shut off your engine's fuel supply, which—under Murphy's Law—invariably will happen when you are trying to navigate a twisting, poorly marked channel at night during a raging storm.

There isn't much you can do to improve the quality of the fuel you buy. You can, however, maintain good fuel-handling procedures and treat your fuel with biocides to inhibit microorganism growth. If your vessel has dark globules in its fuel filters or the engine room has a faint odor of rotten eggs, it probably has slime buildup in its tanks. You also can check for the presence of microorganisms in diesel fuel with test kits available from your fuel dealer.

If your vessel shows signs of significant microbial buildup, you would be wise to thoroughly clean its tanks before embarking on an extended voyage. The best way to do this is to drain and properly dispose of all the fuel on board and have the tanks thoroughly cleaned with pressurized steam. If your vessel's tanks don't have clean-out ports or are otherwise inaccessible, fill them with fresh fuel. (If necessary, drain off enough fuel to allow you to add at least one-third of their capacity in fresh fuel to allow proper mixing and dilution of the biocide you are going to add.)

As the fuel is flowing in, add to it a biocide in the proportions directed by its manufacturer. Good biocides include Kathon FP 1.5 from Rohm and Haas, Bio Kleen, and Cal-5. Follow the manufacturer's recommended concentrations both for a cleanup dose and for continual maintenance of your fuel supply.

Allow the cleanup dose of biocide to work at least twenty-four hours (preferably forty-eight hours) before operating your vessel. As you burn the fuel, the biocide will circulate through your vessel's entire fuel system to clean it. As you burn this load of treated fuel, the microorganisms destroyed by the biocide will migrate to your fuel filters. If you suspect you have a severe case of microbial buildup, this could shut down your fuel system entirely. Restrict your first several hours of operation to fair weather and areas where you can deal with a shutdown, if it occurs, until you can clear it. Carry at least a case of fresh primary filter elements and half a case of secondary filter elements on board, check your fuel filters at least every half hour, and change them if they begin to clog.

Even with clean tanks, your battle against microorganisms isn't over. They can still get into your tanks in fuel you take on and even condense into your fuel from the air that flows into your tanks through their vents.

Although these bedeviling little critters subsist on nutrients in the fuel itself, they cannot exist without water. Therefore, your first line of defense is keeping water out of your fuel. Since diesel fuel is the lighter of the two fluids, most of the water it contains—or that evaporates out of the air in the tank and mixes with it—eventually will settle to the bottom of the tanks of a vessel at rest. Of course, you will prevent the water in your fuel from reaching your engine by trapping most of it in the fuel-water separators on your engine(s), but that doesn't do anything to prevent water getting into your tanks in the first place.

One way to keep the water out of your tanks would be to install fuel-water filters in your fuel inlet hoses to separate as much water (and other contaminants) as possible out of the fuel before it ever gets into your tanks. I know few cruisers who do this, but it's an idea that could pay big dividends—particularly for the long-distance cruiser, who must take on fuel in remote ports that contains God-only-knows what. Some cruisers add isopropyl alcohol to their fuel as a water precipitant. This is not a good idea, particularly in vessels with fiberglass fuel tanks built prior to about 1980, as it can deteriorate the resins used up until then. Isopropyl alcohol in concentrations of 1 pint per 124 gallons (0.4 L per 400 L) of fuel is appropriate only to prevent diesel fuel from freezing during the winter in northern climates.

Your second line of defense is to keep your fuel treated with a biocide to inhibit the growth of any bugs that get into it. For this, you can use a lower level of concentration than is needed for a cleanup. If you operate your boat only about twenty-five hours a month, you should add biocide at a maintenance level to every load of fuel you take on. If you run your engine(s) more than about twenty-five hours a month and thus consume fuel rapidly, you need to add biocide at a maintenance level to only about every third or fourth load of fuel you take aboard.

A biocide is about the only additive you should put in your fuel on a regular basis. In particular, stay away from any additives that contain heavy concentrations of isopropyl alcohol or metallic substances such as barium. If you are getting heavy carbon buildup on your diesel engine's injectors, which causes it to run rough or emit heavy smoke, the first step is to have a good mechanic check the fuel-flow adjustment. If this doesn't solve the problem, ask about using a detergent dispersant, which eases the surface tension of the molecules in fuel and helps prevent particulate matter from conglomerating. Some cruisers favor STP's Concentrated Injector Cleaner for this purpose, but I would not add it to my fuel without the advice of a diesel mechanic I trusted.

Follow your engine manufacturer's recommendations regarding fuel filters exactly. Most diesel engine makers specify a 30-micron element for the primary filter and a 10- to 12-micron element for the secondary filter. Some skippers try to use a 2-micron element in the secondary filter on the theory that because it is finer it will trap more contaminants, but unless your engine manufacturer specifies such an element, don't use it. A 2-micron element is so fine that the fuel pump has to work harder to force fuel through it. The reduced fuel flow can prevent adequate fuel from reaching the injectors and curtail the engine's performance. Change your fuel filters religiously according to the manufacturer's suggested schedule. Under normal operation, that will be at least every three hundred operating hours.

Another good idea is to install mechanical fuel pressure gauges on the outlet side of each engine's secondary fuel filter. If the fuel is flowing properly, these gauges should show about 60 to 70 pounds per square inch (psi) (414–483 kPa) when the engine is running at 1,800 revolutions per minute (rpm). A drop in their normal readings will alert you that either your primary or secondary fuel filters—or both—are clogging up and need to be changed. Without these pressure gauges, you won't know that clogged filters have shut off the fuel supply to the engine until the engine stops. If the needle on a fuel pressure gauge flutters, this indicates that air is leaking into the fuel system.

If a diesel engine begins to run rough, suddenly sounds louder, begins to misfire, or will not produce as many no-load rpm at full throttle as it did formerly, the problem may be air leaking into its fuel system. You can check for air in a diesel engine's fuel system by performing a "spillback test": loosen the fuel return line where it enters the tank, put the end of the line in the bottom of a gallon bucket, and run the engine at about 1,200 rpm. If the fuel is cloudy or air bubbles to the surface, you have an air leak and the air is probably getting into the system somewhere between the fuel tank and the fuel pump. (If a leak is after the fuel pump in the fuel-flow system, it will not suck air into the system but will spray fuel out of the engine's fuel line or one of its fittings.) If the fuel in the primary filter bowl is cloudy, the air leak is between the tank and the primary filter. If you cannot find any leaks between the fuel tank and the fuel pump but the engine is still running rough, disconnect the fuel line on the inlet side of the fuel pump, connect a flexible hose to it, and run the other end of the hose to a fuel tank. If the engine continues to run rough, your problem may well be a leak in the fuel pump itself.

Another cause for a diesel engine to run rough is a clogged, blown, or mistimed injector. To check the injectors, remove the engine's valve cover and run the engine in neutral at around 1,200 rpm. Use a screwdriver to disable each injector in turn by holding down its follower. If an injector is functioning properly, you should notice a significant decrease in rpm as you temporarily disable it. If you notice no difference in rpm, the injector is not functioning properly.

To retime an injector, make certain both exhaust valves are open and the injector is all the way up; then loosen the rocker arm linkage and insert the injector timing tool between the rocker arm linkage and the injector follower. Adjust the rocker arm linkage so that the timing tool just clears the top of the injector follower.

If a diesel engine suddenly begins to emit heavy black smoke, the problem may be a "blown" injector, which most often results from a miniscule amount of water in the fuel getting into the sac at the tip of the injector below the needle valve. The heat of compression inside the cylinder—which normally reaches about 1,000°F (537°C)—boils the water, which loosens carbon inside the tip.

That loosened carbon plugs up most or all of the tiny holes in the injector tip, which measure only five- to ten-thousands of an inch (0.1–0.25 mm) in diameter. On the next compression stroke, the pressure inside the injector tip goes from its normal 20,000 psi of pressure to over 50,000 psi (137,900–344,750 kPa), which literally blows off the tip of the injector. The tip itself will be blown out through the exhaust. The heavy black smoke is the result of unatomized fuel being sprayed into the cylinder. The only remedies for a blown injector are to replace it with a spare or to disable it. Before changing or disabling an injector, be certain to close the valves in both the fuel supply and the fuel return lines. If you don't have a spare injector aboard, disable a blown injector by diverting fuel from it: remove the spring screw, disengage the rack, and then install your shortest fuel jumper from the blown injector's fuel inlet to its fuel return as a fuel bypass.

Anytime you work on your engine's injector, you should retighten all critical bolts with a torque wrench to the manufacturer's recommendations listed in your owner's manual. If the owner's manual doesn't list the torque, use 90 foot-pounds (122 Nm) of pressure on the rocker arm bracket bolts; 25 foot-pounds (34 Nm) on the injector hold-down bolts; and 12 to 14 foot-pounds (16–19 Nm) on the fuel jumper line nuts. Be sure you don't overtighten the fuel jumper line nuts because you could crack the line's flaring and create a leak. To check for leaks after retightening a fuel jumper line nut, replace the valve cover, run the engine a few minutes, shut the engine down, and then remove the valve cover. You should see a small pool of lubricating oil around the joint where the fuel jumper line joins its nut. If you do not see a puddle of oil there, the fuel jumper is leaking and must be replaced. Also check for any clean streaks on the cylinder head, which indicate fuel leakage. If fuel leaks around the cylinder head are not corrected, the fuel could catch fire. At the least, it will go directly into the lubricating oil sump and be recirculated back through the engine, which could destroy the engine.

Oil Flow Maintenance

The primary mission of a diesel engine's oil flow system is to lubricate all its moving parts to prevent metal-to-metal contact and thus excessive wear. The key to doing this is to maintain the oil's pressure at normal operating speeds at the manufacturer's recommended levels, which usually will be between 50 and 70 psi (345–480 kPa). If an engine's oil pressure does not rise to at least 50 psi within about ten seconds of starting it, or at the engine's normal operating speed its oil pressure drops below 50 psi or rises above 70 psi, shut the engine down immediately, determine the cause of the incorrect pressure, and correct it before restarting the engine. Operating a diesel engine with inadequate oil pressure can destroy it in a matter of minutes. Low oil pressure can result from an inadequate supply of oil in the crankcase sump, a leak in the oil supply line, or a malfunctioning oil pump. Excessively high oil pressure can result from coolant or fuel getting into the oil flow system.

The oil flow system's secondary mission is to help extract excess heat generated by the engine's operation. Some high-horsepower marine diesels generate so much excess heat that they use oil coolers to help extract it. Check your engine manufacturer's specification for oil temperature in normal operation, which usually will be around 200 to 235°F (93.3–112.7°C) or about 20°F (11°C) higher than the engine's coolant temperature. If an engine's oil temperature falls below that figure or rises above it, shut the engine down immediately, locate the problem, and correct it before restarting the engine.

Diesel engines are designed to consume a little oil during normal operation, with a typical rate of 1 quart (1 L) every ten to twelve operating hours. You should check your engine's oil at the end of every day's run. After shutting down an engine that has been run long enough to get up to its normal operating temperature, wait at least fifteen minutes before checking its oil level, to give all the oil time to drain down into the sump and show up on the dipstick. If you will be running for longer than twelve hours, shut the engine down at the end of that period and check its oil level. Keep the level of oil in the sump within no more than $\frac{1}{16}$ inch (1.5 mm) of the full mark on the dipstick, and be sure never to overfill the sump. Be especially cautious if an engine appears to suddenly quit using oil or appears to have more oil in the sump after a period of operation than it did at the start. Either could be an indication that fuel or coolant is leaking into the lubricating oil system, and the results could be disastrous.

Be sure to use lubricating oil that meets the engine manufacturer's specifications. For normal operation, that will be straight (not multigrade), heavy-duty oil with an SAE viscosity grade of 40 and an API classification of CD 1 or CD 2. Its total base number (TBN)—which measures the oil's ability to neutralize acids—should be between 7 and 10, and its sulfated ash content should be below 1 percent. Be sure to use a detergent oil. (Each time a diesel cylinder fires, some of the exhaust gas blows by the piston's compression rings and gets into the crankcase, where it mixes with the engine's lubricating oil. Detergent oil helps keep those contaminants in suspension in the oil until it is removed at the next oil change.)

For extended operations in such areas as South and Central America and Mexico, where diesel fuel normally contains higher levels of sulfur (above 0.5 percent) than is found in fuel available in the United States, you should use an oil with a TBN higher than 10, even though it contains more than 1 percent sulfated ash. You also will need to decrease the interval between oil changes, which is discussed later in this chapter.

As long as an oil meets the engine manufacturer's specifications, brand name means nothing and you can safely use the brand on which you can get the best price. Never use oil additives.

Be sure to use only oil filters that meet the engine manufacturer's specifications. In most cases, those specifications will call for a 12-micron element. Change oil filters every time you change the oil. If you don't and an oil filter becomes clogged, you won't know it because the oil will simply by-pass the clogged filter and recirculate potentially damaging contaminants through the engine. (Marine diesel engines are designed to have lubricating oil bypass the oil filter when the engine is started cold, so that the oil be heated to operating temperature more rapidly.)

Make sure you understand and rigorously follow the engine manufacturer's recommendations on oil-change intervals. For normal cruising, most marine diesel engine manufacturers recommend changing lubricating oil after every 150 hours of operation. If you cruise extensively in the waters of South or Central America or Mexico (again, where diesel fuel contains high levels of sulfur), once you begin burning diesel taken aboard in those areas you should use a lubricating oil with a TBN above 10 to help neutralize the acids that high-sulfur fuel contains and shorten the interval between oil changes to get that sulfur out of your engine. If you don't, the sulfur will eat up the cylinder liners and cause damage that will be extremely expensive to repair. To be on the safe side, I recommend that if you use an oil with a TBN of 20 to 30, reduce your oil-changing interval to one hundred hours. If you are using an oil with a TBN of 10 to 19, change oil every fifty hours. An even more scientific answer to the problem would be to send a sample of your engine oil into a laboratory for analysis after about every five hundred hours of operating in those areas and follow the recommendations on oil-change intervals that will be contained with the lab's test report.

Coolant Flow Maintenance

The whole purpose of the cooling system on a marine diesel engine is to get rid of the excess heat the engine's operation generates. Most marine diesel cooling systems consist of two parts:

1. a sealed freshwater system, which circulates coolant through the engine to absorb excess heat, then through one side of a heat exchanger, where the heat is dissipated

2. a raw water system, which picks up seawater, circulates it through the other side of the heat exchanger to extract the heat from the freshwater, then dumps the water with its captured heat overboard

A few marine diesels don't have a raw water system but instead circulate freshwater through a keel cooler to dissipate its captured heat directly into the sea. If a marine diesel's cooling system is working properly, the temperature of its coolant will remain between roughly 170 and 190°F (76.6–87.7°C).

Check the level of coolant in your engine's reservoir after every run, and keep it about 2 inches (5 cm) below the fill cap to allow for expansion. If possible, use distilled water or the purified water from a reverse-osmosis water maker. Undistilled or unpurified water contains large amounts of minerals. When it is heated, those minerals precipitate out of the water and adhere as a whitish scale to the hottest part of the engine, normally the cylinder head (also called the *fire deck*). As that scale builds up, it acts as a very effective insulator, which can destroy your cooling system's efficiency. One-sixteenth of an inch (1.5 mm) of scale, in fact, equals the insulation of about 4 inches (10 cm) of cast iron and can reduce heat transfer by up to 40 percent.

If your cooling system cannot efficiently dissipate the excess heat your engine generates, the metal overheats and raises the temperature of your lubricating oil. As the temperature of the lubricating oil exceeds about 250°F (121°C), it breaks down. The result is metal-to-metal wear, which further increases the temperature inside the engine until the engine fails, most often with a cracked cylinder head. If you encounter an engine with heavy scale buildup, the best product I have found for cleaning it out is the 2015 Twin Pac Cooling System Cleaner and Conditioner produced by Nalco Chemical Company.

If you operate your vessel in freezing temperatures, you should, of course, use the recommended concentration of antifreeze. Be sure you use only a low-phosphate, low-silicate permanent type of antifreeze, such as that produced by Nalco. If your cruising is only in tropical areas where freezing is not a danger, I don't recommend using antifreeze at all because it is less efficient in dissipating heat than is water alone.

Another problem with cooling water is the rust it can cause, and you must add a good rust inhibitor to your coolant and keep it up to the correct concentration. Don't count on antifreeze alone to protect your engine against rust. Even the best antifreeze contains only minute amounts of rust inhibitor, and you need additional additives. Use a nonchromate inhibitor such as Nalco Chemical's Nalcool 3000. Properly inhibited coolant can also help protect an engine against cavitation pitting and keep its pH level between 7.5 and 11, the level needed to avoid lead phosphate corrosion (also called *solder bloom*). You can buy a test kit from Nalco that will tell you when the concentration of inhibitor in your cooling system is at its correct level.

If you find you must add water to your cooling system frequently, be aware that in the process you are also diluting your rust inhibitor. If this is the case, test your coolant every month or so and, if necessary, bring the concentration of inhibitor back up to the recommended level. Don't use chromate inhibitors. Chromate is highly destructive to some engine seals, and doesn't get along with the ethylene glycol in antifreeze. The two in combination will turn your coolant into a dark green gel or slime, which will plug up your coolant system and fry your engine. If you encounter an engine whose coolant has been turned to gel, the best product for cleaning up its coolant system is Nalco's Nalprep 2001.

The flow of coolant through your engine and its heat exchanger is controlled by a thermostat, which normally is located in a housing on the top of the engine at its front end and reads the coolant's temperature through a sensor mounted in or near the heat exchanger. (Engines with in-line cylinders normally have one thermostat and one sensor; V-block engines normally have a separate thermostat and a sensor on each bank of cylinders.) When you start a cold engine, the thermostat normally remains closed to circulate the water only through the engine (rather than through the heat exchanger as well), which brings the engine up to its operating temperature more quickly. When the engine reaches operating temperature, the thermostat opens to circulate water through the heat exchanger. If a thermostat fails, it normally will do so in the open position. The first sign of thermostat failure in the open position will be that the engine is slow to reach its operating temperature. If a thermostat fails in the closed position, you'll know soon enough because the engine will quickly overheat because its coolant is not being circulated through the heat exchanger. You should, of course, include several thermostats and thermostat sensors, along with their associated seals and gaskets, in your spare parts inventory and replace a failed thermostat or sensor immediately.

One other problem you may experience with a coolant thermostat is the buildup of scale on its sensor or on the thermostat itself, which—because of the scale's insulating qualities—will result in false readings. If you notice your temperature gauge reading lower than normal, check the sensor and the thermostat. If either exhibits a white scale, it's a sign of problems in the coolant itself. Scraping off the scale will provide only a temporary fix because the scale is likely to reform quickly. The best way to solve the problem is to clean the engine up with Nalco's 2015 Twin-Pac product, then flush the system and refill it with water and Nalcool 3000 in the recommended concentration.

Most diesel engines have pumps on both their freshwater and raw water cooling systems. Keep an eye on the housings of both pumps for any signs of leaking, which indicate the seal is deteriorating and should be replaced. Anytime you have your boat hauled out of the water, be sure to close the seacocks on your raw water inlets in the hull to keep from draining it and having to reprime it. Put your engine's ignition keys over the seacock to make certain you don't return the boat to the water and start the engines without reopening the seacocks.

Air Flow Maintenance

A proper amount of air flowing into a diesel engine, where it is mixed with fuel, is essential to the engine's proper operation. Once the air-fuel mixture is burned by the engine's heat of compression, the air must be properly exhausted from the engine to help carry away excess heat and contaminants.

The key to maintaining a proper flow of air into the engine is to keep its air filters (sometimes called *air silencers*) clean. Some marine diesel manufacturers install replaceable paper filters on their engines' air inlets. Others use permanent air filters, which must be cleaned periodically. Check your owner's manual to determine the type of air filters with which your engine is equipped, and follow the manufacturer's recommendations for replacement or cleaning.

The first sign that an engine is getting an insufficient supply of air is black smoke from its exhaust, which is the result of incomplete fuel combustion caused by a lack of air in the air-fuel mixture.

Some marine diesel engines require so much air for proper combustion that they are equipped with turbochargers to force additional air into the combustion process. A turbocharger is powered by the engine's exhaust gasses flowing over its turbine wheel, which turns at up to 100,000 rpm and spins its compressor wheel at the same speed. The shaft connecting the turbine wheel and the compressor wheel lies in an aluminum or bronze bushing, which reaches temperatures of up to 900°F (481.7°C) and must be continuously lubricated by an external oil line running from the engine's cylinder block to the top of the turbocharger housing. Turbocharger maintenance therefore begins with keeping the engine's lubricating oil clean by changing the oil and oil filters and replacing or cleaning the engine's air filters at appropriate intervals.

You can extend the life of turbochargers by starting and stopping your engine correctly. If a turbocharged engine has not been run for more than about two months, before cranking it remove the oil supply line from the top of the turbocharger housing, pour about 1 pint (0.5 L) of clean engine oil into the housing, and rotate the compressor wheel by hand to lubricate the shaft. Add enough oil to fill the housing; then replace the oil supply line securely. After starting a turbocharged engine, allow it to idle for two to three minutes before applying a load, to ensure that the turbocharger shaft is properly lubricated. Never shut down a turbocharged engine that has reached normal operating temperatures without running it at idle speed for three to five minutes, which gives the turbocharger time to cool. If you shut it down without allowing proper cooling, the 900°F (481.7°C) heat inside the turbocharger can cook the lubricating oil around its shaft and lead to shaft failure.

With the engine turned off, you also should periodically remove the air inlet housing and check the turbocharger's compressor wheel and its housing for excessive dust or dirt buildup. If they are dirty, clean them and replace or clean the air filter. Also, make sure that the compressor wheel isn't making contact with its housing and that its shaft turns easily but does not have any play in it. If the shaft does have play in it, the bearings may soon fail. If the bearings fail while the turbocharger is operating, you will hear a high whining noise and may notice excessive vibration. Rebuilding a failed turbocharger is not a job most cruising boat owners are equipped or knowledgeable enough to undertake. Unless you have a spare turbocharger aboard and can install it, do not operate the engine until you can get it to a qualified diesel mechanic who has the parts and know-how to rebuild the turbocharger.

Cruising Securely

On our *Americas Odyssey* voyage, Anne and I reached St. Anne's, Martinique, late one afternoon and anchored well away from several cruising sailboats in the harbor. Hearing music coming from onshore, we decided to take a quick run into the village to see what was going on. Since we only planned to be gone for a few minutes, we didn't lock the boat. Onshore, we found an African dance festival in full swing, complete with food stalls selling all kinds of savory delicacies. We decided to stay awhile to enjoy both the dancing and the food. When we returned to the boat about three hours later, we noticed nothing amiss.

The next morning, we made the run to St. Lucia and anchored up in Marigot Bay. I reached into our cruising kitty—which at that time came to around $7,000—for some cash to pay our entry fees. It was empty! Anne quickly checked her jewelry drawer and found all her costume jewelry was there still neatly arranged, but the only two expensive items she had aboard—her diamond engagement ring and a lovely diamond and emerald ring she had bought on a trip to Greece—were gone. We knew both the cash and the jewelry were aboard when we left Fort de France, Martinique, and the only interim stop we had made was in St. Anne's, so that's where the theft had to have occurred.

As we reconstructed events, we decided that while we were ashore, someone had slipped aboard *Americas Odyssey* and taken only our cash and jewelry. They must have been professional thieves, as they ignored anything that could be traced through serial numbers, such as a video camera and an underwater camera that had been lying in plain sight.

With that experience in mind, the question arises as to the steps you should take to protect yourself, your property, your crew, and your guests, especially if you are planning to venture far off the beaten path.

The topic of cruising security need not be of particular concern. In most cruising situations, you will find you are safer than if you were walking down a dark street in many major American cities. There are, however, a few things simple common sense indicates you should do.

SECURING YOUR VESSEL

For security at anchor, round-the-world sailor Joshua Slocum spread tacks on the decks of his sloop, *Spray,* to discourage natives from creeping aboard in the dark of night. I knew one experienced sail-cruising couple who, before retiring in a lonely cove at night, would crisscross open hatches with black thread attached to a tin pie plate and a large spoon separated by about 4 inches (10 cm). The separation was enough to compensate for normal roll and surge, but the presence of anyone trying to slip aboard was announced soon enough to allow the couple to get out the rolling pin. You'll want to be a bit more elaborate, however, in making sure your vessel is protected from uninvited guests when you are away from it or asleep on board.

First, protect all saloon or pilothouse doors with a stout deadbolt lock. On sliding doors, install the lock at a top corner and place it vertically rather than horizontally, with its deadbolt going into the overhead plate. You could go to the extreme of installing one of the commercially available marine alarm systems that set off a loud horn if anyone tries to enter your vessel without disarming it (though most cruisers I know don't use one).

If you're planning to cruise remote areas and intend to leave deck hatches open at night for ventilation, you might be wise to cover them with stout stainless steel grates that you can secure from the inside.

FILING A FLOAT PLAN

We yacht cruisers treasure our independence, but it is only common sense to file at least a general float plan with a relative or friend at home whom you talk to regularly over your satellite telephone or radiotelephone or with cruising friends you meet along the way. As you prepare to depart a port, if you've met some fellow cruisers you feel you can trust, make certain they can give an accurate description of your vessel, tell them where you plan to make your next stop, and set a deadline by which you will contact them to say you've arrived safely.

AVOIDING TROUBLE SPOTS AND PIRATES

The most obvious precaution you can take is to stay away from potential trouble spots. On *Americas Odyssey*'s voyage, Anne and I stayed about 50 miles (80 km) offshore Colombia, Nicaragua, Guatemala, and El Salvador. Likewise, you need have no undue concern about cruising most of the Bahamas, but plan your itinerary to avoid anchoring off the west coast of Andros Island, which is a favorite base of those running drugs into South Florida.

At an unfamiliar dock, be suspicious of anyone who expresses excessive interest in your immediate cruising plans, especially if those plans involve a night run off a deserted coast. If you'll be leaving shortly, tell this person you intend to stay for several days; then slip out to sea at first light. When paying shoreside expenses, don't flash large rolls of cash—an open invitation for the wrong people to pay unwanted attention to you and your plans.

Before any long-range cruising into foreign waters, including the Bahamas, the Caribbean, and the Pacific side of Central America, check for reports of pirates. This can easily be done on the Internet by going to the home page of NIMA's Maritime Safety Information Center (see contact information in the resources appendix). The site contains reports of all known pirate activity, such as the following one from subregion #28.

CARIBBEAN SEA
The son of the owner of the Dutch yacht HAYAT was shot and wounded 28 Mar. Assailants, who appeared to be fishermen boarded the craft by invitation while it was anchored at Half Moon Cay, about fifty miles east of the Nicaraguan-Honduras border which is in dispute along its seaward ex-

tension. After boarding, the wife of the owner was assaulted and her son shot by an attacker with an AK-47, who fled with the other assailants in their 18-foot wooden boat. The shooting is not believed to be directly linked to the border dispute. However cutbacks in patrols by rival militaries to avoid confrontation undoubtedly contribute(s) to an atmosphere in which smuggling and piracy can flourish.

REFUSING TO BOARD A STRANGER

Do not under any circumstances allow anyone aboard your vessel whose bona fides you cannot check thoroughly, even if the person is only 4 feet (120 cm) tall and blind and says he is only trying to reach the bedside of his dying mother on the next island.

At anchor in remote areas, be cautious about inviting natives aboard. Some of them are fascinated by the glittering toys of modern society, and they might possibly walk off with one or two of them. If you do invite natives aboard, first stow away everything small and easily portable, invite them in small groups you can keep an eye on, limit their time aboard, and be wary of spreading around too much hospitality (soft drinks are better than anything alcoholic). One easy way to make friends in truly primitive areas is to carry along a large supply of inexpensive ballpoint pens (the kind that go "click") and an instant developing camera with plenty of film.

CHOOSING WHETHER TO CARRY WEAPONS

The topic of cruising security always raises the debate as to whether or not you should carry firearms aboard. My rule of thumb is if you are comfortable around guns ashore, know how to use them, and believe you would actually shoot at another human being to protect your own life or the lives of your crew and guests, carry a gun. If not, you probably will shoot yourself in the foot while getting it out of its case and should leave it at home. If you are uncomfortable having firearms aboard your vessel, bear in mind that a pistol-fired or canister-launched aerial flare dropped into the cockpit or onto the foredeck of a threatening vessel might well keep its crew occupied while you figure out your best avenue of escape.

If you do decide to carry weapons aboard, you will need to consider rifles, shotguns, and handguns. Their exterior surfaces should be stainless steel or hard-chrome plated to protect them from the corrosive marine environment, and you should clean and oil them regularly. Keep them loaded with appropriate ammunition, but be sure their safety is engaged, make certain all adults cruising with you know where they are stowed, and keep them well out of the reach of any curious children who might come on board.

An important question regarding firearms on board a cruising vessel is what you do about declaring them when you enter other countries. In most cases I would declare them, especially in Venezuela and Guadeloupe. In those countries, detailed searches are common, and if you are found to be carrying undeclared weapons, you will be arrested and your entire vessel confiscated. You may carry rifles and shotguns into Canada if you declare that they are to be used for hunting. If you declare a handgun, Canadian authorities will either seal it in a pouch that must be presented—unopened—when you exit the country, or they will impound it and you can pick it up on your way back across their border. I learned the hard way about the Canadians' lack of tolerance for visitors who fail to declare handguns. I tried it once and for my trouble had the gun confiscated, was hit with a heavy fine, and now have a framed document on my wall that officially declares me a smuggler.

In most of the countries you visit, the customs official will simply take note of the presence of any weapons you declare and tell you not to carry them on deck or ashore. In a few countries—Cuba and the Netherlands Antilles islands of Aruba, Bonaire, and Curaçao being prime examples—the customs officials will impound your weapons during your visit and hand them back to you—along with your docklines—when you depart. In entering a few countries, I would not declare any weapons on board my vessel but would bury them deep—really deep. In countries like Mexico and Jamaica, any weapons you declare will be confiscated and you will not get them back. You also may be arrested, and your entire vessel can be confiscated. If you're carrying weapons aboard your vessel and decide not to declare them, remember also to keep their ammunition and any descriptive literature or cleaning apparatus well out of sight. The best up-to-date advice regarding the declaration of weapons in the various countries you will visit will come from other cruisers who have visited those countries recently.

BEHAVING APPROPRIATELY
IF YOU ARE BOARDED

The escalating war on drugs makes it increasingly likely that if you cruise extensively, sooner or later you will be boarded and your vessel subjected to a search for illegal drugs.

American cruisers returning to the United States from areas such as the Bahamas and Mexico are experiencing a sharp increase in random boardings by the U.S. Coast Guard and U.S. Customs in search of drugs. In addition, you can expect blockades like Operation Glass Eye, in which, during one summer weekend, fifteen coast guard boats, two customs boats, and four boats from the New York Harbor Police stopped every recreational vessel transiting the Verrazano Narrows on the way into New York Harbor.

Like most law-abiding Americans, I'm all for stemming the flood of illegal drugs being smuggled into our country, but with the increase in boardings we need to be aware of our position under the law and the possible penalties we face should we transgress that law, even without meaning to do so.

On land, as American citizens we have all manner of Fourth Amendment rights against unreasonable search and seizure. In most cases, law enforcement personnel must have probable cause to suspect we are breaking the law before they stop and search us. It would not be unreasonable to think we carry those same rights when we go to sea.

Not so. When it comes to our legal rights in a boarding situation, the blunt truth is we don't have any. Under 14 U.S. 89, the U.S. Coast Guard has the right to stop and search any U.S. flag vessel anywhere (even outside U.S. territorial waters) anytime, whether or not it has reason to believe any U.S. law is being violated. The same goes for U.S. Customs if the vessel (whether of U.S. or foreign registry) is within our nation's 12-mile (20 km) customs zone.

If you are shown a blue light by either of these agencies, you must stop. You cannot refuse to allow their personnel to board your vessel, nor can you stop them from searching every nook and cranny of your vessel (including ripping out bulkheads and the like) or even searching your person and that of everyone else aboard.

"So what?" you say. "I'm not breaking any law. Being stopped may be a nuisance and may delay my trip by a few minutes, but that would be my only concern."

That's exactly what one friend of mine thought as he was bringing his sportfishing yacht back to Florida from a trip to the Bahamas. Upon entering U.S. waters, he was stopped by the coast guard and his vessel searched. Beneath a forward bunk, the boarding party found 3 pounds (1.4 kg) of marijuana a crew member had bought in the islands, intending to sell it to his friends back home. My friend didn't know the substance was aboard, but as the master of the vessel he was held legally responsible. He was arrested on the spot and handcuffed, as was everyone else aboard. The coast guard boarding party assumed control of his boat and took it into the nearest U.S. port, where it was turned over to U.S. Customs and seized.

Once the case reached the courts and the crew member testified that the owner knew nothing about the marijuana being aboard, the criminal charges against my friend were dropped. He went down to reclaim his boat, which had been in the customs impound lot for over two months. He was certain that since the charges had been dropped, customs would return his boat without a hassle.

Again, not so. Customs had seized his boat under an administrative procedure that does not involve any court review. My friend finally got his boat back, but it cost him over $8,000 in legal fees and repair bills for damage done to the boat while it was in the impound lot.

Under the coast guard's Zero Tolerance policy, the same thing can happen even if the quantity of illegal drugs found aboard your vessel is minuscule. The moral of the story is that you need to be extremely careful about what you allow anyone to bring on board your vessel, particularly if you are reentering the United States from another country.

So much for being boarded by U.S. authorities. What if you are stopped by authorities of another country? Frank and Lee Glindmeier were aboard their 48-foot (14.6 m) full-displacement cruiser, *Summer Wind,* off the coast of Nicaragua one night when a blip appeared on their radar and started to close in on them. The vessel refused to answer Frank's VHF call, and he had to change course twice to avoid a collision. The vessel turned out to be a Nicaraguan gunboat with a soldier manning a 50 mm machine gun on its bow. Frank finally was able to yell across the water in broken Spanish that he was a peaceful American yachtsman. The gunboat backed off but escorted them until 10:00 the next morning, when they reached the Honduran border.

Since hearing Frank's harrowing tale, I've done a bit of thinking on how I would handle such a situation. You'll have your own ideas, but these are mine.

Most nations of the world claim a territorial limit of 3 miles (4.8 km) off their shores and a customs zone of 12 miles (20 km). Some nations claim up to a 200-mile (320 km) territorial limit. The military of governments that are threatened by armed insurrection frequently patrol 100 miles (160 km) or more off their shores and stop any vessel they encounter. If my cruise plan called for a run off the coast of a nation I knew was in political turmoil, I would inform the U.S. Coast Guard of my schedule and set a deadline by which, if I didn't contact them with an "all-clear," they would at least know I was missing. I would make my run at night, stay as far offshore as possible, and know at all times exactly how far I was off the coast in case the matter came into dispute later. I'd also make the run without lights and would remove my radar reflector.

If, in the course of the run, I was approached by an official vessel, I would try to raise it on VHF. If I got no response, I would carefully note my position and contact the coast guard or anyone else I could reach to tell them what was going on. If the vessel kept coming toward me and it was at night, I'd turn on my running lights and shine a light on my American ensign. I would maintain speed and course until ordered to stop or until the approaching vessel blocked my course. If they called me on the radio or hailed me over a loudspeaker, I would appear on deck but show no firearms.

If ordered to, I would stop, but I would make every attempt to argue them out of boarding my vessel. If they insisted on boarding, I would have little choice but to allow it but would be coolly indignant while arguing my right to cruise in international waters without interference. I'd drag out my U.S. passport and my vessel's documentation papers. If asked if I was armed, I'd declare any weapons on board. Hopefully, once they had checked me out and found I wasn't trying to smuggle M-16s to the guerrillas, they would let me go on my way. If they insisted that I put into the nearest port, I'd go into my indignant act again. If they continued to insist, I'd try to talk them out of placing any of their personnel on my boat, arguing that in light of their superior speed and firepower, I would have little choice but to follow them.

If all argument failed, I would do as ordered but only under the severest protest, liberally invoking the name of my brother the senator, my uncle the president, and any other fiction I could dream up on the spot. I'd also keep trying to contact the coast guard until ordered away from my radio at the point of a gun.

If I were forced into port, either under tow or under my own power, the minute I touched land I'd raise hell to see the nearest U.S. consul, rousting him out of bed if necessary. If that were refused, I'd demand to see the superior of the individual I was dealing with and start my indignation routine all over again.

As a last resort, I'd steal a spoon and try to dig my way out of jail.

If I were convinced the vessel approaching mine was unofficial and might really be carrying sea pirates, I'd handle the situation entirely differently. I would not turn on my running lights. I'd try to reach the coast guard and, failing that, broadcast a Mayday. I'd try to determine the approaching vessel's size, speed, manpower, and firepower. If it tried to impede my progress and I couldn't outrun it, I'd take every evasive action possible, up to and including ramming it, but in no case would I stop or peacefully submit to its crew boarding my vessel. Instead, I'd make as much of a show of force of my own as possible, letting the intruders see all men on board, hopefully armed, but keeping the women out of sight. If it looked like there was no way to avoid a fight, I wouldn't start shooting until they did. But after the first shot was fired, even though I'm not Catholic, I'd cross myself, say three Hail Marys, and throw everything at them but the kitchen sink. I've never met any real sea pirates face-to-face, but I like to think they basically are cowards who, if opposed strongly, would break off the engagement and go looking for easier prey.

PART SEVEN

Preparations for Voyaging

Assembling Spares and Preparing for Repairs

The night is dark and violent. You have been warned that the entrance lights marking the unfamiliar channel you are trying to negotiate are unreliable, so you are picking your way through carefully on the compass course given in your cruising guide. Suddenly, your compass goes dark. All it needs is a fifty-cent lightbulb. Did you remember to put spares aboard? If so, where are they? In your toolbox? In that catch-all drawer in the galley? And where's that tiny screwdriver you need to get inside the compass in the first place? In this situation, having the spare part you need and the tools to fix it aboard and being able to lay your hands on them quickly can mean the difference between arriving inside the harbor or arriving on the rocks.

ASSEMBLING A CRUISING TOOL KIT

Put together a first-rate tool kit that includes a good ½-inch (12 mm) drive socket-wrench set and open-end and box wrenches that will handle bolt heads up to about 1 inch (25 mm) in diameter.

Your socket-wrench set should have at least a 12-inch (30 cm) extender. Aside from a good assortment of screwdrivers and the other tools you'd normally carry, you need some specialized tools, such as two pairs of large Channellock pliers whose jaws open up to about 3 inches (75 mm) to keep your stuffing box nuts tight, a pair of Vise-Grip pliers, and a good volt-ohm meter to run down electrical problems. Another handy gadget to include is a small mirror with an angled handle, which will let you look into all manner of hard-to-get-to places, such as the underside of your main engine(s) and generator.

GATHERING SPARES

For coastal cruising, you need at the minimum to carry backups for those items whose failure would completely disable your vessel, its key navigation and communications equipment, or its tender. On a twin-engine vessel, the thing most likely to disable both engines at the same time would be contaminated fuel that clogged the primary and secondary filters on both engines. Carry a generous supply of replacements. On a single-engine vessel, you would be wise to carry a spare engine generator or alternator and its drive belt, a thermostat and gasket, an impeller for the raw-water pump, a couple of injectors and the tools you need to install them, a valve cover gasket, and a spare ignition switch. I also would have aboard a spare starter motor and be sure I knew how to install it. Also carry backup fuses for at least your VHF radio, depth-sounder, and radar, and a spark plug and ignition kit for your tender's outboard.

For voyaging into the boondocks, your spare parts inventory needs to be much more extensive and should include such items as a spare shaft, prop, strut, and rudder (on a vessel with twin engines, two of each is even better), along with a wheel puller and all the nuts, bolts, washers, cotter pins, and lubricants you need to install them. Also, be certain you take along an extra-generous supply of the replacement items you're likely to need, such as oil, fuel, and water filters (three times the number you think you could possibly need usually works out about right), hoses and clamps of appropriate diameters, gaskets, belts, pump impellers, lightbulbs, fuses, and the like.

Many owner's manuals for marine equipment include a recommended list of spare parts you should carry with you. Make certain all those are aboard along with a complete spare bilge pump, fuel pump, alternator, and a couple of spare injectors. See appendix 5 for a more complete list of spares you should have aboard.

A Spares Inventory System

The most elaborate inventory of spare parts aboard a vessel is useless unless you can lay your hands on the part you need quickly. If you don't use a computerized inventory system, the best system I've seen for doing this is one Frank Glindmeier developed for *Summer Wind*. He emptied the vessel of everything—and I mean everything—and identified every locker, bin, nook, and cranny aboard where he might be able to stow spares. He assigned each space a designator of three or four letters and numbers (PHD3, for instance, referred to "pilothouse drawer, third from the top") and listed them in a notebook. As he put an item into each stowage space, he dutifully noted a description of it and the quantity. He then cross-referenced that information alphabetically by item. Each time he used an item, he reduced its quantity in the inventory system appropriately.

This system gave Frank several advantages. If he needed a particular spare part, a quick check of the notebook told him exactly where it was stowed and how many he had on board. When he reached a major port, he could quickly tell exactly what diaphragm he used in Venezuela or which Allen wrench fell overboard in Ketchikan.

You also can purchase Vessel Information Management, a computer software program that will store data and tell you when you need to perform particular maintenance functions, keep up with your inventory of spares, and tell you when particular items in your spare parts inventory approach minimums and need to be replenished.

PERFORMING ROUTINE MAINTENANCE

Before departing on a major cruise aboard a used vessel, have a qualified mechanic tune up your main engines and generator and check any systems you may have doubts about. Perform all routine maintenance, even that which might not be quite due, and pay extra attention to replacing any doubtful pump impellers, slightly frayed alternator belts, rusted clamps, suspicious fuel and water hoses, and the like. Put new bulbs in all your running lights.

Also, be sure to check all the electrical connections you can get at and clean and tighten any that appear to be corroded or loose. Thoroughly scrape down your battery terminals, make certain they are tight, and coat them with petroleum jelly to help prevent corrosion. Check and lubricate all the seacocks on your vessel's through-hull fittings and make sure the raw-water strainers are clean.

TAKING A SHAKEDOWN CRUISE

Before you depart on an extensive cruise with either a new or a used vessel, I'd strongly advise you to take a shakedown cruise of at least a week before you head to the boondocks. Operate all of the vessel's systems, make careful notes, and attend to any problems before you head out on your main voyage. (See chapter 14 for more details about shakedown cruises.)

If you are not sufficiently experienced in night cruising, plan to include at least one overnight passage in familiar waters. Everything is different at night, and the overnight run will help you work out a watch system (see chapter 16). Before you go, update yourself on the lighting regulations. It's nice to know whether that object out there with the funny lights on it headed your way is a freighter bearing down on you at 20 knots or a slow-moving tug towing a barge behind it on half a mile (0.8 km) of steel cable.

ANALYZING ENGINE OIL

Prior to departing on an extended cruise, send a sample of your engine oil to a good testing company and have them perform an engine oil analysis; this can be a valuable benchmark for monitoring your engine's condition. If you submit follow-up samples after every 3,000 miles (4,800 km) or so of cruising and compare the results, the lab might alert you to developing problems, which you can correct before they get too serious. This precaution is especially important if your cruising will take you to the lower Caribbean, South America, or Mexico, where diesel fuel often is not as highly refined as the fuel available in the United States. It often contains high levels of sulfur, which can eat away at your engines' valves and piston rings and damage the interior cylinder walls. The first time you take on fuels in these areas, reduce your interval between engine oil and oil filter changes by one-third. The first time you change lubricating oil that was used with that load of fuel, submit a sample to your testing laboratory. The results may well indicate that you should further reduce your interval between oil and oil filter changes by another third.

Some newer diesel engines, such as Detroit Diesel's DEDC models, can be diagnosed by a module that will report anomalies in any of its systems. In some cases, that information can be electronically transmitted back to a service center and its technicians can tell the owner how to correct the problem.

Planning Cruises

During one September, some friends of mine arrived in Road Town, Tortola, eagerly anticipating a dream cruise through the British Virgin Islands aboard a charter vessel. They had scheduled their trip during the off-season because the charter rates were significantly lower than during the other months of the year.

The only problem was that the charter service had failed to point out to them that September is the height of the hurricane season in the Caribbean. As my friends waited for a checkout of their boat, they learned that a severe tropical storm was building up 350 miles (560 km) southeast of Grenada and was headed their way. Their boat was almost ready and they could go aboard in a couple of hours, they were told, but their checkout would be delayed. All of the company's personnel were busy ferrying its remaining yachts to safe harbor to avoid the storm's possible onslaught!

There is no doubt that the charter company was irresponsible in not informing my friends of the weather conditions they were likely to encounter in the Caribbean at that time of the year and in allowing them to depart with a storm brewing. But my friends were also unwittingly guilty of poor cruise planning.

A few years ago in Fort-de-France, Martinique, I made a similar sort of cruise-planning mistake—but in reverse. At the end of a beautiful week's run down the Windwards from Antigua, I got up before dawn to pack for an early-morning flight home. As the sun peeked over the mountains, I began to hear the strains of a steel band drifting in through the porthole. I stuck my head out to find the wharf jammed with dancing natives. When I asked one of the revelers what was going on, he beamed and said, "Why, Mon, it's the first day of Carnival!" After a couple of frantic calls back stateside to persuade a somewhat irritated editor to revise a deadline, I was able to extend my stay for long enough to join in at least part of the festivities. With a little better planning, I would have scheduled my cruise for a week later or a week longer to participate fully in the celebration, and the last-minute schedule change would not have been necessary.

As you plan your next voyage, dig out the pilot charts and a calendar early to make certain you don't miss something special or run into conditions you'd just as soon avoid.

CONSIDERING THE WEATHER

The first consideration in cruise planning, of course, is the weather. You wouldn't strike out across the Atlantic in November, nor would you attempt to cross the Pacific at the height of the cyclone season, but what is the best time to go? You may be like a farmer friend of mine who says the best time to plant his garden is "when I got time, and it ain't too wet to plow." But if you have a little leeway in your schedule, here are a few suggestions.

First, consult the pilot charts for the area you plan to visit to find out about typical temperatures, wind strengths, and sea states month by month. That information would suggest, for instance, that you should plan to cruise the Bahamas, the Gulf of Mexico, and the Caribbean sometime other than August and September, since that is the worst of their hurricane season. From mid-December to mid-January, the Windwards and Leewards normally experience "Christmas winds," which can blow 40 knots or better for days on end. The best time to cruise those areas is February through April, before the heat really begins to bear down in May, or in November, after the likelihood of tropical storms has passed.

If you dream of cruising the South Pacific, try to avoid January and February, which is the heart of their cyclone seasons. For areas below the equator, such as Australia, remember that their seasons are the reverse of those in the Northern Hemisphere: in summer—roughly November through March—the rains can be drenching. The best time for cruising an area like the Great Barrier Reef is May through August—the Australian winter—when the climate is drier.

For cruising the east or west coasts of the United States and Canada above 40 degrees North (roughly anything above New York and San Francisco), plan on May through September or pack your warm woollies. The same goes for any place in Europe north of the English Channel.

CHECKING OUT CELEBRATIONS

Once you've figured out the best time of year to cruise the area you have in mind, check with the national, state, and local tourist boards for the dates of any special events that you can tie into your schedule. Many foreign nations have offices in New York, and their staffs tend to be competent and helpful. To enjoy Carnival, for example, try to wind up in heavily Catholic countries just before Lent.

I'm a great one for clipping and filing magazine articles on other folks' cruises and picking up local handouts wherever I go. A quick check of the files tells me when to plan a visit to Chesapeake Bay to coincide with the greatest number of crab festivals or when to visit the Gulf Coast for Jambalaya or Jamaica for Goombay.

COLLECTING CHARTS AND CRUISING GUIDES

Once you know the approximate route your cruise will follow, start assembling a complete collection of up-to-date charts, coast pilots, and cruising guides to the areas you will be visiting.

Between the National Oceanic and Atmospheric Administration (NOAA) and the National Imagery and Mapping Agency (NIMA) in the United States, the British Admiralty, and the French and Canadian hydrographic services, there is hardly a spot on earth that hasn't been charted, though the information on some of the more remote areas may not have been updated since the days of the whaling ships. Choose the largest-scale charts you can find because they will show more detail. (Remember, small-scale charts cover large areas, whereas large-scale charts cover small areas.) Pay particular attention to harbor charts, even for places a bit off your route that you don't actually plan to visit. In severe weather, you might have to duck into some unintended harbors or anchorages, and you don't want to be running an entrance channel blind.

*Coast Pilot*s, usually hardbound volumes published by the same government agencies that produce maritime charts, provide valuable information about the weather you can expect to encounter in an area at various times of the year and also include elaborately detailed sailing directions for entering various harbors and anchorages. Their prose is usually dry and bureaucratic, but when you are feeling your way through unfamiliar waters, they can be worth their weight in gold.

Cruising guides can be marvelous storehouses of information about the areas you'll be visiting and often will bring to your attention a bit of history or an out-of-the-way sight worth visiting. Some are big and filled with glossy photographs, and others may be thin, printed on cheap paper, and crudely illustrated, but having them is far better than visiting an area with no guide at all.

Today, computer software databases are also available that have thousands of possibly useful aerial photos of inlets and harbors. There are, of course, now electronic charts for virtually the entire world.

ACQUIRING AND UPDATING PASSPORTS AND VISAS

If your cruising plans will take you outside the United States, make certain your passport and those of your crew are up-to-date or make plans to renew them.

More and more countries now require advance applications for visas rather than simply granting them at their border. Once you have figured out which countries you will be visiting, check with a good travel agency or the U.S. State Department to find out whether any of them require advance visa applications. If they do, file early,

since processing through normal channels can take up to two months. If you get in a time bind, there are companies in Washington, D.C., that for a fee will hand-carry visa applications through the bureaucratic maze for you and can cut the time to a week or less. Ask your travel agent to recommend a good one, based on the countries you plan to visit.

If you plan to rent automobiles for shoreside sightseeing during your cruise, get an international driving permit, which is honored in countries ranging from Argentina to Zimbabwe. In the United States, they are issued by the American Automobile Association. You will need a passport photo to go along with your application. The permit is valid only if you also have a valid U.S. driver's license, and you must carry both documents with you.

SCHEDULING GUESTS

Once you have a cruising plan in mind, it's a good idea to go ahead and make out at least a rough itinerary with major stopover points penciled in. Be sure to include plenty of time along your route to account for weather and mechanical delays.

With such an itinerary, you can begin working out a schedule with family members or friends you might ask to join you along the way. Early planning is necessary to give them time to look into work and school vacations and arrange their own passports, visas, and travel schedules. Guests who are not familiar with visiting aboard cruising vessels will find it helpful if you write out for them step-by-step instructions covering what they need to do in advance, how to pack (lightly and in soft luggage, which is easier to stow on board), and the clothes they should bring, including boating shoes with nonslip soles. (Either in that memo or as soon as they arrive on board, make certain to tell them exactly what they can and cannot dispose of in your marine head.)

The earlier you get your schedule of guest visits worked out, the earlier you can start your own planning for provisioning your vessel to make sure you have everything you need on board when they arrive.

PROVISIONING

When Anne and I provisioned *Americas Odyssey* for her voyage, we knew that we would have a number of guests aboard—usually two couples for a week at a time. We also knew that throughout the Caribbean and in South and Central America, re-provisioning with good-quality meats at reasonable prices would be difficult, if not impossible. Because of that, we wanted to leave Florida carrying all the meat we would need for the leg from Florida to San Diego. In San Diego, we would re-provision for the San Diego–Glacier Bay–Seattle leg. In order to preserve that much meat, we had a deck freezer installed on the flying bridge.

Anne purchased all the meat we would need for the first leg in bulk in Ft. Lauderdale and had it cut, wrapped, and labeled to her specifications. She started with the final week of the leg and worked backward. All the meat for that week went into its own freezer bag, labeled by contents and quantity, and that bag went into the bottom of the freezer. Similar bags for prior weeks went into the freezer in successive order. Each Sunday evening, I would transfer the meat for the coming week from the flying bridge freezer to the galley freezer. This meant not only that the meat for each week was convenient in the galley but also that the freezer was opened only once a week, which helped reduce its energy consumption.

SETTING A DAILY CRUISING SCHEDULE

Ideally, each day that you'll be under way you'll be able to depart the dock or anchorage around 10:00 A.M. and get the hook set in the next beautiful spot by around 4:30 P.M. (not much later in tropical areas since coral heads and reefs can be almost impossible to spot when the sun is low in the sky).

There will, of course, be times when your vessel's speed and the distance to be traveled won't allow you to cover all of a run in daylight hours. In those instances, time your departure in the dark if necessary, but plan to arrive at your destination during daylight hours, preferably between mid-morning and midafternoon. Trying to feel your way into an unfamiliar harbor or anchorage in the dark is no way to ensure a trouble-free cruise. (See chapter 14 for more about planning a daily cruising schedule.)

With some careful advance planning, you can make certain your cruising will be enjoyed under sunny skies with the wind at your back and timed to allow you to take part in the best your cruising area has to offer. Without careful cruise planning, like my friends in Tortola, you may find yourself setting out into a gale or hearing the line I encounter every time I go fishing: "You shoulda been here last week!"

Understanding International Buoyage, Lighting, and Chart Systems

Once you have become familiar with the buoyage, aids to navigation lighting, and chart systems used in U.S. waters, you will have little difficulty translating that knowledge to the waters of other nations—provided you recognize a few basic facts and understand a couple of fundamental differences.

BUOYAGE SYSTEMS

In chapter 15, I explained the basic buoyage system now in use in U.S. territorial waters—the International Association of Lighthouse Authorities' (IALA's) System B, Combined Cardinal and Lateral System (red to starboard)—and pointed out that that same system is in effect in North and South America, the Bahamas, Korea, and Japan. Navigation using the buoyage systems of Canada and Mexico, and along the northern coast of South America, therefore, is little different technically from navigating in U.S. waters.

Nations on the continents of Europe, Africa,

Asia (excluding Korea and Japan), and Australia employ the IALA System A, Combined Cardinal and Lateral System (red to port), in which red marks are to port when entering a channel from seaward.

Having made that basic distinction, however, I must note that some confusion can arise in the Caribbean, where areas that physically are in IALA Region B and therefore might be expected to use the System B of buoyage do not, due principally to their political status. The Windward Islands of Guadeloupe and Martinique, for instance, are departments of the government of France and employ the IALA System A buoyage used by their home countries. The islands of Aruba, Bonaire, and Curaçao off the northern coast of Venezuela are dependencies of the Netherlands and also employ System A buoyage.

One other fact that should be noted is that among the favored cruising grounds of American yacht cruisers, Canada has developed a buoyage system whose completeness, accuracy, and maintenance equals that in the United States. The

Bahamas, Mexico, South America, and many of the islands of the Caribbean, however, have not had the resources to develop and maintain so extensive a system. In many of those areas—particularly outside major commercial roadsteads—aids to navigation are inaccurate or nonexistent, and the cruisers are very much on their own. In those areas, proper navigation by alert coastal piloting and all the electronic means at the helmsperson's disposal is an absolute must.

AIDS TO NAVIGATION LIGHTING SYSTEMS

One major advantage of the IALA Systems A and B to the cruising yachtsperson is that light patterns and their meanings are now essentially standard throughout the world—with the important difference that in System A red is to port entering from seaward and in System B red is to starboard entering from seaward.

In the varied cruising grounds the world has to offer, there may be some minor differences in buoy shapes, but the meaning of their lights—where they exist—is the same.

CHARTING SYSTEMS

In the past fifty years the symbols used in nautical charts have become highly standardized and are often in English. Virtually any of the international charts available through the sources listed in appendix 6 use symbols that are readily recognizable to a knowledgeable American cruiser.

Most charts published by foreign nations do present depth and height in meters rather than the feet-and-fathoms system employed on most charts published in the United States. (To determine feet, multiply meters by 3.28.) Most foreign charts, however, include an easy-to-use scale for converting meters to both feet and fathoms. Should you encounter a foreign chart that uses kilometers, convert distances to nautical miles by multiplying kilometers by 0.54.

Keeping Legal
in Foreign Ports

In most cases, the legal aspects of cruising the waters of foreign nations involve little more than a bit of bureaucratic red tape and the payment of a few dollars' worth of fees. You can, however, save yourself a good deal of grief and money if you know what to expect and make proper preparations. Here's what to look for.

LEAVING U.S. WATERS

Prior to departing on a voyage outside U.S. waters, you should, of course, make certain your ship's papers (documentation papers issued by the federal government or registration papers issued by the state in which the vessel is principally used) are up-to-date. Also, be sure you have proof of insurance covering the waters you intend to cruise and know how to contact your insurer quickly in case you have a problem. Each person on board should have a U.S. passport that will remain valid for the duration of the voyage and contains any visas that are required in ad-

vance. Each person aboard also should have a current International Certificate of Vaccination, which records any immunizations required by the countries you will be visiting. If you plan to do any driving in other countries, you also should have a valid international driving permit, which can be obtained in the United States through the American Automobile Association. You also should have a good supply of crew lists, which give the name, age, nationality, and home address of all on board, or a computer and printer or typewriter and plenty of carbon paper to make up the list en route.

If you have on board expensive new items manufactured abroad, such as still and video cameras or portable electronics, you might want to register them with the U.S. Customs Service before you leave to avoid any possibility of being charged import duty on them when you return to the United States.

Most private yachts don't do it, but you can have your vessel inspected by the U.S. Public Health Service and receive a bill of health, which can make the entering process to other countries somewhat easier.

Some countries prohibit certain items (particularly firearms and, in some cases, fruits and meats) or limit the amount of certain merchandise (such as cigarettes and alcoholic beverages) you may bring into their nations. Some countries ignore their own regulations, while others levy stiff import duties on quantities you declare in excess of their limits and impose stiff civil or criminal penalties for failure to declare excess merchandise or prohibited items. Prior to leaving the United States, you should determine any prohibitions or limits imposed by the countries you plan to visit by contacting their embassy or consulate in this country or talking to other cruisers who have visited those countries recently and then decide before you cast off what you are going to declare. If you plan not to declare anything, make provision for keeping it well out of sight.

Prior to departure and at points along your route, you should check the internal political situation in the countries you plan to visit as well as their political relations with other nations that might be included in your itinerary. You could encounter situations in which a country is in political turmoil or refuses to grant entry to vessels that have previously entered the waters of a nation with which it is having problems. The best sources of information on potential difficulties are the U.S. State Department, its embassies in foreign countries, and other cruisers who have recently visited the areas you plan to cruise.

Private yachts documented or registered in the name of a U.S. citizen and not engaged in commerce are not required to "clear" (that is, secure permission to sail) before departing U.S. waters for a foreign port.

ENTERING FOREIGN COUNTRIES

If you have never before cleared a boat through customs in another country, you're in for an interesting experience.

It's a sad fact of the cruising life, particularly in poorer third world nations, that customs and immigration officials are paid less than a living wage precisely because their bosses know they will make up any shortfall by hitting up visitors for either cash or a "gift" of goods that are hard to come by in their own countries. Yacht cruisers often are favorite targets for these rip-off artists, so you need to know the ropes.

When you enter a foreign country for the first time, make certain your initial landfall is a legal point of entry. In many countries, the smaller fishing villages closest to the border don't have customs or immigration offices. If you go ashore looking for one, technically you have entered the country illegally and might have some rather complicated explaining to do when you finally locate a customs official farther down the coast. Your best source of information on where to clear is a good cruising guide or other cruising folks who have been there before you.

Try to time your arrival so you enter a legal port between 9:00 A.M. and about 3:00 P.M. Monday through Friday, except on religious or political holidays or the president's birthday or during the siesta hours of noon to 2:00 P.M. The point is that if you try to clear on weekends or after normal business hours, you probably will be hit with fairly stiff overtime charges. "Normal business hours," of course, are whatever the guy with the badge on his chest and the gun on his hip jolly well says they are.

Prior to entering a port of entry, you should hoist your plain yellow quarantine flag prominently and as high as practical on a flag halyard or radio antenna on the starboard side of your vessel. In the International Flag system, this is the Q-flag, which signals you are formally requesting pratique (that is, permission to enter from that nation's health service). Anchor up in the harbor or tie to the dock, and just relax for an hour or so. Chances are the dockmaster, the harbormaster, or a helpful fellow yachtsperson will come along to tell you what to do next. If no one turns up in a reasonable length of time, the captain or owner should go ashore alone, taking along the ship's papers, some local currency, the crew's passports and vaccination records, and a crew list.

Entering a foreign port often involves dealing with at least four agencies: a customs service, which checks for any prohibited or limited items and collects any applicable duties; an immigration service, which is concerned with the legal status of individuals on your vessel; a health service, which is concerned with the presence of any infectious diseases among those on board; and, in some countries, an agricultural service, which inspects vessels for any prohibited plants or animals. Some countries also require clearance by some type of federal or state militia and possibly a maritime authority of the port you have entered.

In most countries, customs and immigration are handled by a single agency, and you may find one official will handle work for all four groups. In some countries, however, you may have to deal with four or more separate individuals in as many offices.

The entry process normally must be completed each time you enter the waters of one country from the waters of another country. In one special exception, U.S. cruisers who wish to cruise in Canada can obtain at the initial port of call a permit that allows free and repeated entry into Canadian waters from May 1 to October 1. Once this cruising permit is secured, the yacht to which it is granted may cruise throughout Canadian waters, but reports of arrival must be made at any Canadian port visited where a customs officer is located and the permit must be surrendered on the yacht's final departure from Canadian waters at the end of the season.

You normally will be issued some type of document that permits your vessel to cruise the waters of the foreign nation for a specified period of time. If you plan to visit other ports in that country, be sure to ask whether you are required to present your cruising permit or whatever the document is called each time you go ashore and, if so, to whom. Also ask whether you are required to formally clear before you depart that nation's waters.

Once the formalities are completed, haul down your quarantine flag and hoist in its place the courtesy flag of the nation you are visiting. If your vessel does not have a flag halyard, the courtesy flag should be flown from your bow staff.

If the clearance process is conducted in the customs office ashore, chances are it will be crisp, efficient, and over quickly. If the customs officer wants to come aboard your boat, tell your crew to make themselves scarce below decks until the bogeyman is gone, then spread out your documents on the saloon table. Be polite and friendly, but not overly so, and try to keep things on a businesslike basis and get the procedure over with quickly. If the official seems inclined to chat, offer a seat. If the official seems impressed by your boat, say something like, "Yes, she is nice," but don't offer a tour unless one is requested. That's an open invitation for the official to start opening drawers and poking into lockers.

To this point, keep the booze out of sight. If the official seems in no hurry to get down to business, then offer some "refreshment," not "a drink." If the offer is accepted, rattle off the list of options, from soft drinks to beer and whiskey, and let the official make the choice. If the person has a couple of shifty-eyed corporals along, don't offer them anything unless the commandant suggests it, then provide soft drinks rather than beer or liquor.

As early as possible, nudge your papers forward a bit and hope the official will take the hint and get on with the business at hand. If the move is ignored, be on guard. Chances are the official will eventually take a cursory glance at your papers and start talking about "problems," most likely that you are trying to enter after normal business hours—even though it's 11:00 on an otherwise unremarkable Thursday morning. Try to get the difficulty stated clearly. If there is a real problem, try to get it cleared up quickly. An official who continues to be vague is probably just looking for *mordita* or *baksheesh* or whatever they call it where you happen to be, so give a deep but silent sigh and say something like, "If there is anything I can do to get this problem straightened out . . ."

That gives the official the opening to hit you up for a few bucks without directly asking you for a payoff. The average hit will run around $5 to $25, disguised as a "fee" of some sort. As soon as you fork over the dough, all "problems" will magically disappear. Don't expect a receipt.

Once your papers are stamped, the official may continue the chat and admire the quality of your scotch, which is your cue to offer another drink. If the person persists in hanging about after that, offer the rest of the bottle and try to work the official toward the door. Some experienced cruising people carry along a case of rotgut for just such occasions and keep the good stuff hidden. After the official is gone, relax, get the good stuff out of the bottom galley locker, forget the rip-off, and enjoy your visit.

OPERATING MARINE RADIOTELEPHONE AND AMATEUR RADIO ABROAD

To transmit legally over your vessel's single-sideband (SSB) marine radio while in foreign waters, you must have a valid Ship Station Radio License and a Restricted Radiotelephone Operator Permit. Your U.S. license and permit will be honored by all but a tiny handful of foreign nations, and you are not required to have any special license or permit from the host country.

Except for those channels used for public correspondence, the VHF channels used most frequently in U.S. waters are simplex (that is, they transmit and receive on the same frequency). With the exception of channel 16, the international distress, safety, and calling channel, the VHF channels most frequently in countries outside the United States are semiduplex (that is, they transmit on one frequency and receive on a different frequency). Modern synthesized VHF marine radios are programmed for both U.S. and international channels and automatically set the appropriate transmit and receive frequency or pair of frequencies when a channel is dialed in to the unit. See chapter 21 for a list of the international

channels normally built into modern VHF marine radios along with their assigned use. As quickly becomes obvious from that list, the most important VHF channels for cruisers in foreign waters are likely to be channel 22, for communicating with other nations' equivalent of the U.S. Coast Guard, and channel 78, for communicating with other noncommercial vessels. (Remember, in the United States, it's channel 22A; in international zones, it's channel 22.)

In SSB operation, the transmit and receive frequencies of channels in the high-frequency 4 to 24 MHz bands are the same worldwide. The transmit and receive frequencies of channels in the medium-frequency 2 to 3 MHz band vary from country to country and must be manually programmed into an SSB radio's memory.

In order to transmit legally over the amateur radio frequencies from your vessel while it is in the territorial waters of foreign nations with which the United States has third-party traffic agreements, you must have an appropriate class station or operator license and a Reciprocal Operator's Permit issued by the nation from whose waters you wish to transmit. You should apply for a Reciprocal Operator's Permit from each nation you plan to visit well in advance of departing the United States because processing your application can take up to six months. You can find out where to apply for Reciprocal Operator Permits from the American Radio Relay League (see appendix 6).

UNDERSTANDING VESSEL LIGHTING REGULATIONS

If your vessel is registered or documented in the United States and its lights comply with the U.S. Inland Rules appropriate to its type and size, you may legally operate in international waters.

Although as the skipper of a U.S. registered or documented vessel, you are not subject to differing international requirements regarding the positioning of your vessel's navigation lighting, you are required to comply with international regulations regarding the use of these lights anytime you are in waters the regulations cover. The only significant difference you'll encounter is that the international regulations make no provisions for the "special anchorage areas" found in the U.S. Inland Rules, in which anchor lights are not required for vessels less than 65.6 feet (20 m) in length. The only exception regarding anchor lights contained in the international regulations is for vessels less than 23 feet (7 m) in length anchored in areas free of waterborne traffic.

DEPARTING FOREIGN COUNTRIES

Some countries require you to clear with their customs officials prior to departing their waters, which basically ensures that you have paid all fees due and their police aren't looking for you. If required, the clearing process usually involves nothing more than returning any cruising permits you received for cancellation. In a few cases, you may be required again to produce all the documents you presented in the initial entering process. Some

nations require payment of a departure tax before you are granted clearance to sail.

If clearance is required, be sure to respect its provisions and keep any clearance documents you are issued as a part of your ship's papers. The next country on your itinerary may require you to produce a clearance document from your last port of call before they will grant entry to their nation.

RETURNING TO U.S. WATERS

The procedures for a private vessel reentering the territorial waters of the United States after landing in a foreign country are substantially the same as those detailed earlier in this chapter for entering a foreign port. When you return to the United States, be sure your initial port of call is a legal port of entry. Hoist your quarantine flag, and go ashore alone with your ship's papers, crew passports, crew list, and some U.S. currency to contact the nearest office of customs and immigration and request entry. In some harbors, this may be done by phone; in others, an official will visit your boat.

EPILOGUE
Just Do It!

In the course of this book, we've considered hundreds of the questions you'll face in selecting, outfitting, and operating a powerboat appropriate to the type of voyage on which you plan to embark. If I've done my job well, you're a lot better prepared now to take on the challenges and excitements of the cruising life than you were when we started.

I have only one final bit of advice: do it!

Many of us put off launching our cruising dreams until we can afford exactly the boat we want, outfit it down to the last luxury we possibly could want aboard, and have all the money we could conceivably need tucked away in the bank. Prudence is fine—to a point. But carried too far, it can mean "someday" never comes.

Let the sound of the waves lapping against that rocky coast in Maine or that beach in the Caribbean makc you a little crazy. Set yourself a timetable and proclaim, "By then, by God, we will go!" and do whatever you must to meet it. Find a boat you can afford in the realizable future. Within the limits of safety and reasonable comfort we've discussed, rig her with only the basics if you have to. But make your plans and take off. Some of the happiest cruisers—in fact, the happiest people —I've ever met were aboard minimal boats and had no ice for their drinks. But they were on the water and living their dreams—not just planning for them.

When you pull into Casco Bay up in Maine, or English Harbor down in Antigua, or Elfin Cove in Alaska, if you spot a nifty little cruiser named *Layde Anne* quietly tucked away in a corner, that'll be me and Anne. Drop by and say hello.

Until then, bon voyage!

Appendix 1
Powerboat Hull Forms

DISPLACEMENT-TO-LENGTH RATIO

One of the best rules of thumb for determining how much heft the builder of a particular boat you are considering has built into it is to determine the boat's displacement-to-length ratio with the formula:

$$D/L = \frac{\text{displacement (in long tons)}}{(\text{LWL} \div 100)^3}$$

(To convert displacement in pounds into long tons, divide by 2,240.)

The smaller a boat's load waterline length, the larger its D/L ratio should be.

In a displacement-hull boat with an LWL of around 50 feet (15 m) intended for extensive bluewater cruising, look for a D/L ratio of at least 250. A boat of that type with an LWL of around 40 feet (12 m) should have a D/L ratio of 320 or better.

In semidisplacement or planing hulls, the D/L ratio for cruisers with an LWL of around 50 feet (15 m) should be not less than 180, and 200 is even better. Those type boats with LWLs of around 40 feet (12 m) should have a D/L ratio of 220 or higher.

We are now seeing on the market a number of planing-hull boats in the 40-foot (12 m) range which their builders advertise as "high performance family cruisers." In order to keep down weight and thus increase speed, these boats are constructed with cored hulls and all manner of lightweight materials, which in many cases result in D/L ratios of 160 or less. They may be acceptable for family outings close to home in fair weather, but they are far too lightly built to stand up to the conditions you sooner or later are certain to encounter in serious cruising.

SPEED-TO-LENGTH RATIO

One of the basic facts of life in yacht design is that at a speed in knots equal to 1.34 times the square root of its LWL, the hull of a vessel moving through water produces a wave equal in length to its own LWL. If the vessel is sufficiently powered to exceed this theoretical hull speed, it will create a bigger bow wave, which will cause the bow to rise and force its stern to sink deeper into its own wake. A vessel will continue to operate in this fashion until it reaches a speed in knots equal to at least twice the square root of its LWL, at which point it will overcome the resistance of its bow wave and begin to plane on top of the water rather than plow through it.

This principle clearly affects the basic hull design and propulsion packages of the three types of pleasure-yacht hulls discussed in the text: displacement-hull yachts are designed to operate below their theoretical hull speed; planing-hull yachts are designed to operate in excess of it; and semidisplacement hull boats are designed to operate on both sides of the "hump."

Understanding the principle of S/L ratios is a key to analyzing the hull form of any cruising vessel you might consider, regardless of its type.

In analyzing semidisplacement or planing hulls designed to operate in excess of their hull speed, flat sections aft are a plus. In the critical speed range between 1.34 and twice the square root of their LWL, they help resist the stern's tendency to sink as the bow rises to overcome the bow wave, which assists the boat to come up on plane faster. Boats with excessive (over about 16 degrees) dead rise aft cut into the water rather than providing this countering resistance, which is why it takes them longer to come up on plane.

In analyzing a displacement vessel designed solely for cruising below its hull speed, smooth, well-rounded sections aft ease the flow of water past the hull. This contributes to the vessel's operating ef-ficiency, but also gives it a more exaggerated fore-and-aft pitching motion in a head sea. As the bow rises on a wave, the rounded sections aft create lit-tle countering resistance and can cause the vessel to "hobby horse." Well-rounded stern sections also do nothing to help resist that type hull's tendency to roll. A displacement-hull vessel with relatively flat sections in the aft fourth of its hull will roll consid-erably less while giving up only a minimal amount of efficiency. In a head sea, those flat sections aft provide some resistance to the bow's attempt to rise to a wave and result in less pitching.

Appendix 2
Marine Diesel Engines

ENGINE DESIGNATIONS

The designations of marine diesel engines manufactured by Detroit Diesel Corporation (formerly a division of General Motors but now part of DaimlerChrysler) such as 4-53 or 8V-71TI describe several of the engine's key characteristics. The first number describes the number of cylinders. If that number is followed by the letter V, the cylinders are inclined alternately at a V-angle; if not, they are in line. The number after the dash indicates the displacement of each of the engine's cylinders in cubic inches. If that number is followed by the letter T, the engine is turbocharged. If the T is followed by the letter I, it is intercooled; if by the letter A, it is aftercooled. The letter N or the absence of a letter indicates the engine is naturally aspirated. All Detroit Diesel engines designated in this fashion are two-cycle and are available in both left-hand (the flywheel, viewed from forward of the engine, rotates counterclockwise) and right-hand rotations.

Detroit Diesel more recently has introduced the 6.2 L (162 shaft horsepower, or shp) and 8.2 T (211 shp) engines for pleasure marine use. Both are eight-cylinder, four-cycle diesels. The numbers in their designation refer to the (approximate) total displacement of all eight cylinders in liters. The 6.2 is naturally aspirated, and the L indicates it is available in both left-hand and right-hand rotations.

The designations of Ford-Lehman marine diesels, which are four-cycle engines, describe their brake horsepower rating.

The designations of the four-cycle marine diesels made by Caterpillar, Perkins, Cummins, and Volvo are essentially model numbers and tell you little if anything about their basic characteristics.

HORSEPOWER RATINGS

As you compare the horsepower ratings of marine diesel engines, make sure you know which horsepower you are considering. Engine manufacturers and boat builders normally rate an engine in terms of its brake horsepower (bhp), the minimum horsepower it develops with no load applied. For cruising applications, it's more realistic to compare shaft horsepower, which is the maximum horsepower an engine actually delivers to a vessel's shaft and propeller after allowing for the loss of power in its marine transmission. In some engine specification sheets, shaft horsepower also reflects the loss of power needed to drive the engine's raw-water pump and its generator or alternator. The difference between an engine's brake and shaft horsepower normally is around 3 percent.

Shaft horsepower is further reduced by propeller load, the horsepower consumed by the engine's associated shaft and prop. At low engine rpm, where torque is high, propeller load can consume 75 percent of the engine's shaft horsepower. As engine rpm are increased, propeller torque (and its load) gradually is reduced to the point of being negligible at the engine's maximum rpm.

The horsepower ratings of marine diesels are

further defined by the type of service in which the engine is employed.

The marine continuous rating refers to the net horsepower available at the transmission when the engine is operated at 90 percent or more of its maximum rpm for more than 1,000 hours a year. That rating normally is applied to engines installed in commercial workboats and is a level of operation few operators of pleasure vessels would attain.

The marine intermittent rating refers to the net horsepower available at the marine transmission when the engine normally is operated at not more than 90 percent of its maximum rpm and is operated at its maximum rpm, for not more than 10 percent of its total operating hours. This rating usually is applied to engines installed in privately owned long-distance cruising vessels which are operated for not more than 1,000 hours a year.

The marine maximum rating typically is defined the same way as the marine intermittent rating, but total engine hours normally are limited to 500 hours per year. This rating usually is applied to engines installed in privately owned high-performance boats where speed is a primary consideration and overall load factors are low.

Engine Specification Sheets

By studying a specification sheet's performance curve for a particular engine at the rating appropriate to the way you intend to use the engine, you can determine a great deal about the actual horsepower you will have to work with at different rpm settings and the amount of fuel it will consume per hour. In studying performance curves, realize that the figures assume essentially "laboratory conditions"—the engine is installed in an efficient hull with a clean bottom that is carrying about half the weight of water, fuel, and stores it is designed to carry and is operating under ideal weather conditions. A particularly inefficient hull, a fouled bottom, excessive weight, or heavy seas can reduce all the power ratings and increase the fuel consumption figures by 25 percent or more.

As an example, let's study the performance curve of a Detroit Diesel 6V-71TA marine diesel (see illustration next page). Note first that (1), all the figures given allow for the power consumed by the engine's marine gear, raw-water pump, and a 75-amp generator. At 2,300 rpm, the maximum speed at which the engine is designed to operate, it will develop 375 bhp and 365 shp (2). The cruising speed of a diesel engine normally will be 200 rpm below its maximum speed. At 2,100 rpm, as the top curve on the spec. sheet shows, the engine will develop a shade over 350 shp (3). The lower curve indicates that at its maximum speed it will consume 20 gallons of fuel per hour (gph) (4). But after allowing for propeller load, at 2,100 rpm it actually will deliver only 280 shp (5) and consume about 15.5 gph (6).

One gallon of fuel per hour develops 18 shp. Therefore, a quick way to figure fuel consumption in gallons per hour for a marine diesel is to divide the shaft horsepower it develops at a particular rpm by 18. In the case of the 6V-71-TA engine above, at 1,900 rpm, after allowing for propeller loads, it will develop about 208 shp (7) and consume right at 11.5 gph (8).

Marine Transmissions

Virtually all marine diesel engines are fitted with transmissions that reduce the number of rpm they actually transmit to their associated shaft and propeller. A diesel engine operating at 2,200 rpm through a 2:1 transmission (also called a *reduction gear*) would actually transmit 1,100 rpm to its associated shaft and prop.

Marine Propellers

Marine propellers normally are described by the number of blades they have and by two additional numbers, the first of which refers to their overall outside diameter and the second of which refers to the pitch at which the blades are positioned relative to the propeller's hub. Thus a "four-blade 24 by 32 propeller" would have four blades, an outside diameter of 24 inches, and 32 inches of pitch.

Pitch, theoretically, is the distance the propeller would advance if rotated one revolution through a

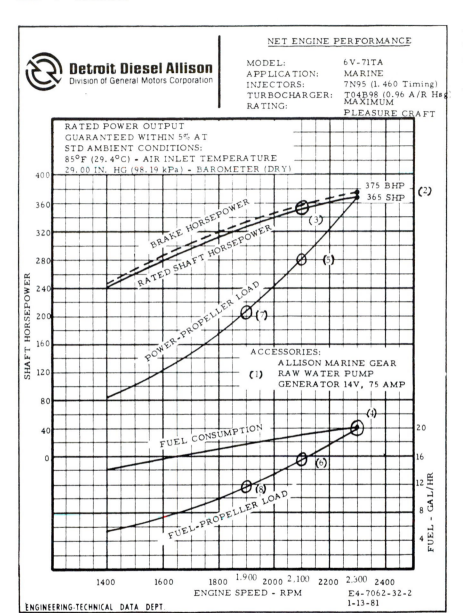

Sample performance curve, here for the Detroit Diesel 6V-71TA marine diesel. (Detroit Diesel Corporation)

solid substance. The greater a propeller's pitch, the more thrust it will provide. But pitch must be held to within reasonable limits to keep from imposing too much torque load on the engine that drives it.

Most modern marine propellers have progressive pitch, which means the degree of pitch is least at the hub and gradually increases toward the tips.

Planing-hull boats normally have four-blade

propellers; semidisplacement and full-displacement boats normally are fitted with three-blade propellers.

Diameter normally is the primary factor in selecting the props for a particular vessel. Pitch is selected for fine-tuning the boat's operation.

Rake is the vertical angle at which the aft edge of the propeller is positioned relative to the centerline of the hub. Props with minimum rake (where the angle between the centerline of the hub and the aft edge of the blade is closest to 90 degrees) tend to raise a vessel's stern. Props with rearward rake tend to raise the vessel's bow. The props on planing-hull cruisers typically have 3 to 5 degrees of aft rake, where props on semidisplacement and full displacement hulls typically have little if any rake.

Marine propellers come in right-hand and left-hand versions. A right-hand propeller, viewed from the stern of the vessel to which it is attached, rotates clockwise. (Thus, a right-hand engine must be fitted with a left-hand propeller.)

On twin-screw vessels, the top of each propeller rotates toward the outboard side.

Appendix 3
Recommended Medical Supplies

FIRST-AID KIT

Alcohol, 2 bottles, 16 oz. ea.

Ammonia inhalants, 12

Analgesic ointment, 4 tubes, 2 oz. ea.

Analgesics, 600 tablets/capsules

Antacid, 2 bottles, 16 oz. ea.

Antibiotic ointment, 4 tubes, 1 oz. ea.

Antidiarrhea compound, 2 bottles, 16 oz. ea.

Antiemetic compound, 2 bottles, 16 oz. ea.

Bandages, adhesive, 2 large boxes of assorted sizes

Bandages, elastic, 4, 4 in. by 4 ft. ea.

Bandage scissors, 1 pair

Bee-sting kit, 1

Benadryl, 50 tablets, 25 mg ea.

Benzocaine toothache gel, 4 tubes, ⅓ oz. ea.

Betadine scrub brushes, 24

Betadine solution, 2 bottles, 4 oz. ea.

Bronchodilators, 2

Cake decorating gel, 4 tubes, 16 oz. ea.

Charcoal, liquid activated, 2 bottles, 16 oz. ea.

Chemical heat packs, 24

Chemical ice packs, 24

Chlorine bleach, 2 bottles, 16 oz. ea.

Ear drops, nonprescription, 2 bottles, 1 oz. ea.

Ear syringe, 1

Eye drops, nonprescription, 4 bottles, 1 oz. ea.

Gauze pads, 1 box of 100, 4 by 4 in. ea.

Ipecac, 2 bottles, 16 oz. ea.

Lip balm, medicated with sunscreen, 10 tubes, 1.5 oz. ea.

Meat tenderizer, 2 bottles, 4 oz. ea.

Mineral oil, 1 bottle, 16 oz.

Needle-nose tweezers, 1 pair

Nosebleed packs, 6

Oral thermometers, 2

Penlight, 1 (with extra batteries)

Safety pins, 24 in assorted sizes

Scopolamine patches, 1 box of 50

Snakebite kit, 1

Sunscreen lotion containing PABA, 4 bottles in assorted strengths

Sunburn lotion, 6 bottles, 8 oz. ea.

Throat lozenges, 100

Tape, waterproof adhesive, 100 ft.

Vinyl gloves, 1 box of 50 ea.

TRAUMA KIT

The following recommendations are intended as a general guide to the equipment that would be required aboard a vessel intended for offshore cruising to allow an appropriately trained crew member to provide basic trauma life support for at least 24 hours until the victim can be transported to professional medical assistance. Specific items should be employed only after appropriate training in their use has been completed and, if at all possible, only under the direction of a qualified physician. Purchases of the recommended equipment should be made through a competent surgical supply house that can ensure that necessary equipment and systems are compatible and complete. The recommendations cover only adults. If small children will be aboard, sizes and dosages must be altered appropriately.

General Supplies

Alcohol wipes, 1 box of 200
Bandages, elastic, 4, 4 in. by 6 ft. ea.
Bandages, elastic, self-adhering pressure, 4
Bandages, roller, 12
Bandages, triangular, 4
Betadine brushes, 25
Blanket, disposable emergency, 2
Blood pressure cuff, 1
Burn sheet, 2
Dressings, multitrauma sterile, 24
Eye irrigation kit, 1
Eye patches, 2
Food wrap, plastic, 2 boxes
Gloves, sterile, 2 pair
Lubricant, water-soluble, 1 tube
Ointment, antiseptic, 4 tubes, 2 oz. ea.
Pads, compression, 4
Pads, gauze, 1 box of 50, 4 by 4 in.
Pads, gauze, 1 box of 50, 8 by 8 in.
Pads, petroleum gauze, 1 box of 50
Scissors, 1 pair
Stethoscope, 1
Tape, waterproof adhesive, 2 in., 100 ft.
Tape, waterproof adhesive, 4 in., 100 ft.
Tongue depressors, 1 box of 100
Tourniquets, 2

Airway Kit

Oxygen (see sidebar), 1 D cylinder with integral
 pressure regulator and tubing
Bag-valve-mask device, 1
Pocket mask with oxygen inlet, 1
Oxygen mask, 1
Oxygen cannula, 1
Oxygen tubing, 2 sets
Portable suction unit and tubing, 1
Oral airways, 1 set with 7 sizes
McGill forceps, 1 pair

Fracture-, Neck-, and Spinal-Injury Kit

Ladder or air splints, 1 kit of assorted types and
 sizes
Cervical collars, 1 kit with 3 sizes
Sandbags, 2 of 3 lb. ea.
Long spine-board or scoop stretcher, 1

Oxygen

Oxygen, one of the most effective substances available for sustaining life in a trauma situation, legally is a drug and must be prescribed by a physician. One E cylinder containing 22 cu. feet of oxygen at 2,000 psi will provide a typical 5 L/min. flow for approximately two hours. With a regulator to reduce its pressure to 50 psi, it will weigh approximately 12 pounds. (To compute the usage rate in minutes of an oxygen cylinder: multiply its capacity in cubic feet by 28.32 [L/cu. ft.], subtract 50 to account for pressure-regulator consumption, then divide the result by the liters per minute of flow.) Oxygen must be stored away from excess heat and clearly marked with a warning sign prohibiting smoking, open flames, or electrical sparks.

Severe Bleeding/Circulation Kit

Scissors, surgical, 1 pair
Steri-Strips, 2 boxes in assorted sizes
4/0 nylon and needles, 4 kits
Curved forceps, 1 pair
Hemostats, 2 pair
Xylocaine, topical, 2 aerosol cans
Military Antishock Trousers (MAST), 1 pair

Body-Fluid Replacement Kit

Arm board, 1
Large-bore IV catheter with large-bore tubing, 4
 sets in various sizes

MEDICATIONS KIT

Codeine, oral, 50 tablets, 30 mg ea.
Codeine, injectable, 10 prefilled syringes, 60 mg ea.
Demerol, oral, 50 tablets, 25 mg ea.
Demerol, injectable, 10 prefilled syringes, 100 mg
 ea.
Dextrose, 50 percent solution, 6 bags, 1000 cc ea.
Epinephrine (1.1000 type), injectable, 10 prefilled
 syringes, 0.5 mg ea.

Morphine, injectable, 10 prefilled syringes, 10 mg ea.

Narcan (IV push), 4 prefilled syringes, 0.4 mg ea.

Nitroglycerine, 50 tablets, 0.4 mg ea.

Oxygen (see sidebar), 12 E cylinders, 22 cu. ft. ea.

Penicillin, oral, 50 tablets, 500 mg ea.

Penicillin, injectible, 10 prefilled syringes, 1.2 million units ea.

Plasmanate, 6 bags, 250 cc ea.

Ringer's lactate, 6 bags, 1000 cc ea.

Tetanus toxoid, 5 prefilled syringes, 0.5 mg ea.

Note: Never use medications past their expiration date, as their chemical composition may have altered.

For further reading on emergency medical procedures and supplies, see John Campbell's *Basic Trauma Life Support for the EMT-B and First Responder* (see resources appendix).

Appendix 4
The Cruising Tool Kit

For coastal cruising in areas where you are likely to have access to shoreside experts and facilities to handle major problems aboard your vessel, you should carry a good tool kit that includes the following.

BASIC HAND TOOLS AND SUPPLIES

Socket wrench set
  ½-inch drive
  ³⁄₁₆-inch to 1-inch sockets
  12-inch rotating extender arm
Open-end wrench set, ¼- to 1-inch
Crescent wrenches
  10 in.
  16 in.
Allen wrench set, ¹⁄₁₆- to ¼-inch
Standard pliers
Channel-lock pliers
  10 in.
  16 in.
Vise-Grip pliers
Needle-nose pliers
Screwdriver kit, straight and Phillips, 4 to 16 in.
Hand or cordless electric drill

High-carbon drill bit set, ¹⁄₁₆- to ½-inch
Retractable metal tape measure, 25 ft.
Carpenter's hammer
Ball-peen hammer
Rubber mallet
Hand saw
Hacksaw
Trouble light

Angled mirror on extendable handle
Utility knife
Funnel
Oil can spout
Assorted-grit sandpaper
Assorted metal files
Assorted screws, nuts, bolts, and washers
Wire brush
Epoxy glue

ELECTRICAL TOOLS AND SUPPLIES

Solder iron or gun
Rosin-core solder
Volt-ohm meter
Snap-on ammeter
Polarity tester
Test light
Assorted test leads with alligator clips each end
Battery cables
Electrician's cutter–stripper–crimper tool
Assorted electrical terminals
Assorted electrical wire
Electrician's tape
Duct tape
Spray can of moisture inhibitor

SPECIAL TOOLS AND SUPPLIES

Injector timing tool
Injector nut wrench
Manual air pump, pressure gauge, and needle
Inflatable patch kit
Syntho-glass
Assorted wooden through-hull plugs

For offshore voyaging where you are likely to have to attend to virtually all repairs yourself with the tools you have on board, in addition to the items above you should also consider carrying the following.

Wheel puller, $\frac{1}{16}$- to $\frac{1}{2}$-inch
Torque wrench, 100-pound capacity
Copper pipe and joints
Pipe solder
Butane torch
PVC pipe and joints
Pipe adhesive
Manual or electric oil-transfer pump

Fiberglass repair kit
Feeler gauge set
Installed workbench vise
Small crowbar

Maintenance Supplies

Polyurethane varnish
Urethane or epoxy paint
Assorted nylon-bristle paint brushes
Paint solvent
Chrome polish
Brass polish
Vinyl cleaner-protector
Boat polish-wax

Appendix 5
Spare Parts and Supplies

As you assemble your spare-parts inventory for either coastal or offshore cruising, here is a list of replacement items and supplies you should at least consider having on board.

ENGINE

Alternator or generator
Drive belts
Starter motor
Starter switch
Starter solenoid
Raw-water pump
Fuel pump
Thermostat and gasket
Injectors
Valve cover gasket
Mechanical gauges and sensors
   RPM
   Oil or fluid
   Coolant temperature
   Oil pressure
Fuel filters
   primary
   secondary
Fuel biocide
Oil
Oil filters
Fuel-line hose and fittings
Oil-line hose and fittings

TRANSMISSION

Oil or fluid
Mechanical drive oil temperature gauge

UNDERWATER GEAR

Shaft
Strut and bearings
Propeller
Rudder
Appropriate nuts, bolts, washers, shaft keys, lubricants, and sealants
Shaft zincs
Rudder zincs

HYDRAULIC SYSTEM

Hydraulic line and fittings
Hydraulic valve
Hydraulic pump
Hydraulic fluid

AC ELECTRICAL SYSTEM

Generator relay
Generator circuit board
Generator starter switch
Generator starter solenoid
Circuit breakers
   120 volt of appropriate amperage ratings
   240 volt of appropriate amperage ratings
Air conditioning–heating unit relay
Refrigeration compressor relay
Incandescent lightbulbs
Fluorescent light tubes
120-volt light switch
120-volt receptacle

DC ELECTRICAL SYSTEM

Circuit breakers of appropriate amperage ratings
Fuses appropriate to all onboard DC equipment
Electronic compass sensor
Light switch
Pump switch
Marine head switch
Windlass switch
Depth-sounder transducer

WATER/WASTE SYSTEM

Marine-head seal kits
Marine-head supply pump
Watermaker supply pump
Bilge pump
Water pump

Impellers appropriate to all onboard water pumps
Water heater element
Water hoses, fittings, and clamps
Water pipes and fittings
Water purification tablets
Assorted plumbing washers

TENDER OR OUTBOARD

Outboard spark plug
Outboard ignition kit
    Coil
    Condenser
Outboard motor oil
Outboard fuel supply line
Steering cable, clamps, and pulleys

Appendix 6
Resources

ORGANIZATIONS

American Radio Relay League
225 Main St.
Newington CT 06111
860-594-0219
www.arrl.org

BoatU.S.
800 S. Pickett St.
Alexandria VA 22304
703-370-4202
www.boatus.com

Centers for Disease Control and Prevention
Foreign Travel Division
877-FYI-TRIP (877-394-8747)
www.cdc.gov/travel/index.htm

Coastal Harbor High Seas Station WLO
7700 Rinla Ave.
Mobile AL 36619
251-666-5110
www.wloradio.com

Divers Alert Network (DAN)
P.O. Box 3823
Duke University Medical Center
Durham NC 27710
Information: 800-446-2771, 919-684-2948
Hotline: 919-684-8111, 919-684-4326 (collect)
DAN Australia: 61-8-373-5312
DAN Europe: 41-1-1414
DAN Japan: 81-3-3812-4999
www.diversalertnetwork.org

Federal Communications Commission
1270 Fairfield Rd.
P.O. Box 1040
Gettysburg PA 17325-7245
www.fcc.gov/wtb/marine

Maritime Safety Information Center
National Imagery and Mapping Agency
http://pollux.nss.nima.mil/index/
For reports of pirate activity, check the Anti-Shipping Activity Messages section by geographic area.

Medical Advisory Systems Inc. (MAS)
8050 Southern Maryland Blvd.
Owings MD 20787
301-855-8070
www.mas1.com

Naval Atlantic Meteorology and Oceanography Center
https://www.nlmoc.navy.mil

Practical Trauma
644 Strander Blvd.
Seattle WA 98188
800-587-2331
www.practicaltrauma.com

Seven Seas Cruising Association (SSCA)
1525 S.Andrews Ave., Ste. 217
Ft. Lauderdale FL 33316
www.ssca.org

Superintendent of Documents
U.S. Government Printing Office
Washington D.C. 20402
202-512-0000

Survival Technologies Group
1803 Madrid Ave.
Lake Worth FL 33461
http://survival-technologies.com

BOATING CATALOGS

Consumer Marine Electronics
www.consumersmarine.com

Landfall Navigation
www.landfallnav.com

West Marine
www.westmarine.com

BOOKS AND OTHER PUBLICATIONS

Auerbach, Paul S., M.D. *A Medical Guide to Hazardous Marine Life.* 3rd ed. Flagstaff: Best, 1997.

Bishop, Joseph M. *A Mariner's Guide to Radiofacsimile Weather Charts.* Westborough MA: Alden Electronics, 1988.

BUC International. *BUC Used Boat Price Guides.* 3 vols. published semiannually. Ft. Lauderdale: BUC International.

Calder, Nigel. *Boatowner's Mechanical and Electrical Manual: How to Maintain, Repair, and Improve Your Boat's Essential Systems.* 2nd ed. Camden ME: International Marine, 1996.

Campbell, John E., et al., eds. *Basic Trauma Life Support for the EMT-B and First Responder.* Englewood: Prentice-Hall, 2000.

Canadian Hydrographic Service. *Charts of Canadian Coastal Waters and the Great Lakes.* Available from the Canadian Hydrographic Service, Department of Fisheries and Oceans, Institute of Ocean Sciences, 615 Booth St., Ottawa ON K1A 0E6, Canada, 613-995-4413.

Chapman Piloting: Seamanship and Boat Handling. 62nd ed. Ed. Elbert S. Maloney. New York: Hearst Marine Books, 1999.

Cunningham, Patricia, and Paul Goetz. *Pisces Guide to Venomous and Toxic Marine Life of the World.* Houston: Pisces Books, 1996.

Graves, Fredrick. *Mariner's Guide to Single Sideband.* 2nd ed. Mountlake Terrace WA: Stephens Engineering, 1985.

Miller, Conrad, and E. S. Maloney. *Your Boat's Electrical System.* 2nd rev. ed. New York: Hearst Books, 1988.

National Automobile Dealers Association. *N.A.D.A. Consumer Marine Appraisal Guide.* Annual publication. Costa Mesa CA: National Appraisal Guides.

National Imagery and Mapping Agency. *Charts of Foreign Waters.* These charts cover virtually all the waters outside those of the United States and are available from FAA Distribution Division, AVN-530, National Aeronautical Charting Office, 6501 Lafayette Ave., Riverdale MD 20737-1199. If you charge to Visa or MasterCard, you can order NOS publications by phone (800-638-8972), fax (301-436-6829), or e-mail (distribution@noaa.gov).

National Oceanic and Atmospheric Administration. *Chart No. 1.* Published jointly by the National Oceanic and Atmospheric Administration (NOAA) and the National Imagery and Mapping Agency (NIMA), it's really not a chart at all but a 100-page book that fully explains all the symbols and abbreviations used on the nautical charts produced in the United States. It's required reading for any cruiser. Spending a couple of hours browsing through its storehouse of information and keeping it aboard for frequent reference will give you a far better understanding of the information your charts provide and make them far more valuable.

National Oceanic and Atmospheric Administration. *Coast Pilots.* The nine volumes of NOAA's U.S. Coast Pilot offer a far greater wealth of information about America's coastal waters and the Great Lakes than can ever be crammed onto charts. You should definitely have aboard the volume or volumes that cover the areas you plan to cruise. The areas covered by the various volumes are as follows:

Vols. 1–5. Atlantic Coast: vol. 1, Eastport to Cape Cod; vol. 2, Cape Cod to Sandy

Hook; vol. 3, Sandy Hook to Cape Henry; vol. 4, Cape Henry to Key West; vol. 5, Gulf of Mexico, Puerto Rico, and U.S. Virgin Islands

Vol. 6. Great Lakes and Connecting Waterways

Vols. 7–9. Pacific Coast: vol. 7, California, Oregon, Washington, and Hawaii; vol. 8, Alaska—Dixon Entrance to Cape Spencer; vol. 9, Alaska—Cape Spencer to Beaufort Sea National Oceanic and Atmospheric Administration.

NOAA Chart Catalogs 1–4. These four catalogs list all the charts published by NOAA's National Ocean Service (NOS). The scale to which charts are drawn (e.g., 1:50,000, in which 1 in. on the chart equals 50,000 in. on the earth) is important. The smaller the second number, the larger the scale of the chart and the greater the detail it shows. (A chart with a scale of 1:12,500 will show much more detail than a chart drawn to a scale of 1:50,000.) In general, the larger the scale of a chart the better. The primary NOAA charts you'll be interested in are

1. Conventional nautical charts, which come in four varieties.
   - Harbor charts, which are drawn to a scale of 1:50,000 or larger and provide the detail you need to navigate in harbors and small waterways. I recommend you purchase charts for any major harbors your itinerary calls for you to pass through. The smaller scale charts you need for cruising major stretches will show major harbors, but not in the detail you need to navigate through them safely.
   - Coast charts, which are to scales from 1:50,000 to 1:150,000 and are designed for navigation inside offshore reefs and in large harbors and some inland waterways. These are the basic charts you'll need for cruising large bodies of water like Long Island and Puget Sound.
   - General charts, which are to scales from 1: 150,000 to 1:600,000 and are intended for offshore navigation but provide suffi-

cient detail for fixing your position through visual contact with aids to navigation or by depth soundings. These are the charts you need if your cruising plans call for you to do considerable offshore running along the U.S. coast and enter and leave ports along the way frequently.
   - Sailing charts, which are to scales of 1:600,000 and smaller and are used as plotting charts for offshore navigation beyond the areas where visual position fixes are possible. These charts are of interest primarily to offshore cruisers and don't show sufficient detail to be of value in inland cruising.

2. Small Craft Charts, which are drawn to scales from 1:10,000 to 1:80,000 and published in folded formats that make them ideal for use on smaller vessels. These are the route charts you need for cruising the ICW and the book format charts you'll want for cruising the Great Lakes, but in many cases you may want to supplement them with larger-scale charts of major harbors and large open bodies of water.

3. Marine facility charts, which are conventional charts overprinted with locations of marine facilities and other information of interest to recreational boat owners. These charts duplicate much of the information found in cruising guides.

4. Marine Weather Services charts, published by NOAA's National Weather Service (NWS), are a series of fifteen charts that show radio stations and broadcasting areas for all U.S. coastal waters and Puerto Rico. The primary benefit of these charts is to give you the location of visual storm warnings and the frequencies and weather broadcast schedules of FM commercial radio stations in particular areas. If you are within the broadcast area of an NWS VHF FM radio station, your VHF radio will pick up its signals

automatically on its WX 1–WX4 channels, so it's not necessary for you to know the frequency. (You also can buy bound groupings of reproductions of NOAA charts covering specific geographic areas, the pros and cons of which are discussed below under Chart Kits.)

National Oceanic and Atmospheric Administration. *Tidal Current Tables.* NOAA provides the data annually to publishers, which print and distribute the volumes. The annual editions of the *Tidal Current Tables* list the predicted time of daily maximum and minimum tidal currents and slack water, current velocities and the directions of ebb and flow at 54 reference stations and more than 2,400 subordinate stations. Separate volumes cover the Atlantic coast of North America and the Pacific coast of North America and Asia. They are invaluable in planning voyages through passages of high current flow. (NOAA also issues annual *Tidal Current Charts*, which depict the hourly velocity and direction of tidal ebb and flow at 11 selected major U.S. harbors, and *Tidal Current Diagrams* covering Long Island and Block Island sounds and Boston Harbor. The information is of interest to commercial fishermen and the masters of large commercial vessels, but is not really required aboard recreational vessels.)

NOAA charts and publications are available from a network of authorized sales agents whose addresses are listed in *Chart Catalogs 1–4.* See also contact information on page 432 under NIMA, *Charts of Foreign Waters.*

National Oceanic and Atmospheric Administration. *Tide Tables.* NOAA provides the data annually to publishers, which print and distribute the volumes. The annual editions of the *Tide Tables* allow you to predict high and low tides at any point along the U.S. coast from the tip of Maine all the way to the Aleutians and provide useful information on sunrise and sunset, moonrise and moonset, the phases of the moon, and reduction of local mean time to standard zone time.

Four volumes are available covering: east coast of North and South America (including Greenland); west coast of North and South America (including Alaska and Hawaiian Islands); Europe and west coast of Africa (including Mediterranean Sea); and central and western Pacific Ocean and Indian Ocean.

Tennessee Valley Authority. *Charts of the Tennessee TVA Reservoirs and the Tennessee River and Its Tributaries.* Available from the Tennessee Valley Authority, 1101 Market St., Chattanooga TN 37402-2801, 800-MAPS-TVA (800-627-7882), mapstore@tva.gov.

U.S. Coast Guard. *Light Lists.* The *Light Lists* give far more detailed descriptions of aids to navigation than can be printed on nautical charts. In a confusing situation, they can provide valuable information in helping to identify a specific aid. They are available in seven volumes:

Vol. 1. Atlantic Coast (St. Croix River, Maine, to Toms River, New Jersey)

Vol. 2. Atlantic Coast (Tom's River, New Jersey, to Little River, South Carolina)

Vol. 3. Atlantic and Gulf Coasts (Little River, South Carolina, to Ecofina River, Florida; Puerto Rico and U.S. Virgin Islands)

Vol. 4. Gulf Coast (Ecofina River, Florida, to Rio Grande, Texas)

Vol. 5. Mississippi River System

Vol. 6. Pacific Coast and Pacific Islands

Vol. 7. Great Lakes

U.S. Coast Guard publications are available from the contacts given on page 432 under NIMA, *Charts of Foreign Waters.*

U.S. Coast Guard. *Navigation Rules, International–Inland.* This publication gives the Rules of the Road for operating in both inland and international waters and delineates where each applies. A copy of the *Navigation Rules* is required to be aboard all self-propelled vessels greater than 39.4 feet (12 m) in length.

U.S. Corps of Engineers. *Charts and Maps of the Lower Mississippi River.* Available from the Corps' Vicksburg District, P.O. Box 60, Vicksburg MS 39180.

U.S. Corps of Engineers. *Charts of the Black Warrior, Alabama, Tombigee, Apalachicola, and Pearl Rivers.* Available from the Corps' Mobile District, P.O. Box 2288, Mobile AL 36628.

U.S. Corps of Engineers. *Charts of the Missouri River.* Available from the Corps' Omaha District, 6014 U.S. Post Office and Courthouse, Omaha NE 68102.

U.S. Corps of Engineers. *Charts of the Ohio River.* Available from the Corps' Ohio River Division, P.O. Box 1159, Cincinnati OH 45201.

U.S. Corps of Engineers. *Charts of the Tennessee and Cumberland Rivers.* Available from the Corps' Nashville District Office, P.O. Box 1070, Nashville TN 37202-1070, 615-736-7864, formsrm@irnoz.usarmy.mil.

U.S. Corps of Engineers. *Charts of the Upper Mississippi River and Illinois Waterway.* Available from the Corps' Mississippi River Visitors Center, P.O. Box 2004, Rock Island IL 61204-2004, 309-794-5338.

U.S. Public Health Service. Public Health Foundation. *Health Information for International Travel.* Can be downloaded free from the Web (www.cdc.gov/travel/reference.htm).

World Health Organization. *International Medical Guide for Ships: Including the Ship's Medical Chest.* 2nd ed. Geneva: World Health Organization, 1988.

Chart Kits and Cruising Guides

In addition to these official publications, a wide range of chart kits and cruising guides available at retail outlets, through marine book clubs and catalogs, or direct from the publisher provide valuable information of which anyone cruising the areas they cover should take advantage:

Chartbooks and chart kits are bound groupings of color reproductions of NOAA charts covering specific geographic areas and often contain supplemental information. They typically contain 80 to 100 or more charts and retail for about $60 to $100. Since conventional and small-craft NOAA charts are now priced at $13.25 each, there is no question that buying chartbooks and chart kits is cheaper than buying a full set of charts for each area you cruise. But in some cases the size reduction of the NOAA charts required to fit a chartbook or chart kit's format may make some important details unreadable. Among the better chartbooks and chart kits for the U.S. east and west coasts are the ChartKits produced by Maptech, which are sold through marine catalogs and book stores. For the Hudson River, Erie Canal, and the Great Lakes, among the best are the Richardson's Chartbooks, available through marine book stores.

Cruising guides are general guides that offer a great deal of useful information on popular cruising areas. Among the best of them are the four volumes of the *Waterway Guide*s (Waterway Guide Inc.) covering the Atlantic and Gulf Intracoastal Waterways; the *Yachtsmans Guide*s (Tropic Isle Publishers Inc., P.O. Box 611141, North Miami FL 33161), which cover the Bahamas, the Virgin Islands, and Puerto Rico; and the *Street's Guides to the Eastern Caribbean.*

Index